The
Rolling Stone
FILM READER

W9-BNN-249

For orders other than by individual consumers, Pocket Books grants a discount on the purchase of **10 or more** copies of single titles for special markets or premium use. For further details, please write to the Vice-President of Special Markets, Pocket Books, 1633 Broadway, New York, NY 10019-6785, 8th Floor.

For information on how individual consumers can place orders, please write to Mail Order Department, Simon & Schuster Inc., 200 Old Tappan Road, Old Tappan, NJ 07675.

The

RollingStone

FILM READER

The Best Film Writing From ROLLING STONE Magazine

EDITED BY

Peter Travers

POCKET BOOKS

New York   London   Toronto   Sydney   Tokyo   Singapore

To Robyn and Alex with love

The sale of this book without its cover is unauthorized. If you purchased this book without a cover, you should be aware that it was reported to the publisher as "unsold and destroyed." Neither the author nor the publisher has received payment for the sale of this "stripped book."

An *Original* Publication of POCKET BOOKS

POCKET BOOKS, a division of Simon & Schuster Inc.
1230 Avenue of the Americas, New York, NY 10020

Copyright © 1996 by Rolling Stone Press, a division of Straight Arrow Publishers Company, L.P.

All rights reserved, including the right to reproduce this book or portions thereof in any form whatsoever. For information address Pocket Books, 1230 Avenue of the Americas, New York, NY 10020

The Rolling stone film reader : the best film writing from Rolling
   stone magazine / edited by Peter Travers.
      p. cm.
   ISBN: 0-671-50111-9
   1. Motion picture actors and actresses—United States—Biography.
   2. Motion picture producers and directors—United States—Biography.
   3. Motion pictures—United States.   I. Travers, Peter.   II. Rolling
stone (San Francisco, Calif.)
PN2285.R57   1996
791.43'092'273—dc20
[B]   96-29232
                                                                CIP

First Pocket Books trade paperback printing November 1996

10 9 8 7 6 5 4 3 2 1

POCKET and colophon are registered trademarks of
Simon & Schuster Inc.

Text design by Stanley S. Drate/Folio Graphics Co. Inc.

Cover design by Lee W. Bearson; front cover photos, top to bottom:
Peggy Sirota, Mark Seliger, Mary Ellen Mark; back cover photos, top to bottom:
Albert Watson, Mark Seliger

Printed in the U.S.A.

ACKNOWLEDGMENTS

Thank you hardly suffices to honor the tireless energy and talent shown by the staff of Rolling Stone Press: Editor Holly George-Warren, Associate Editor Shawn Dahl, Editorial Assistant Greg Emmanuel and their many interns. Gratitude is heartily extended to ROLLING STONE's Jann S. Wenner, Kent Brownridge, John Lagana, Fred Woodward and Lee Bearson. Ditto literary agent Sarah Lazin and our Pocket Books editor Tom Miller. Others who are owed countless debts include Nancy Bilyeau, Marianne Burke, John McCormick and Amy Kaplan Lamb. Thanks, also, to the photographers who have so beautifully captured the subjects of this book. Most of all, let's hear it for the writers whose work appears in these pages—even the ones who called to thank me for my "fine edit" on their pieces and then pleaded and threatened to restore a few more of their precious words. That's the spirit I'll remember best about these movie-mad wretches. Rock on.

PETER TRAVERS

CONTENTS

SMELLS LIKE TEAM SPIRIT

ON THE SCENE

THE MARCH OF THE ICONS

THE NEW REBELS

THE WIZARDS BEHIND THE CURTAIN

THE REVIEWS

ROLLING STONE

NOVEMBER 9, 1967
VOL. I, NO. 1

OUR PRICE
TWENTY-FIVE CENTS

MFF

Recognize Private Gripeweed? He's actually John Lennon in Richard Lester's new film, How I Won the War. An illustrated special preview of the movie begins on page 16.

Tom Rounds Quits KFRC

Tom Rounds, KFRC Program Director, has resigned. No immediate date has been set for his departure from the station. Rounds quit to assume the direction of Charlatan Productions, an L.A. based film company experimenting in the contemporary pop film.

Rounds spent seven years as Program Director of KPOI in Hawaii before coming to San Francisco in 1966. He successfully effected the tight format which made KFRC the number one station in San Francisco.

Les Turpin, former program director of KGB in San Diego, will replace Tom Rounds at KFRC. Turpin has spent the last year as a consultant in the Drake-Chenault programming service.

The new appointment could mean a tightening up of programming policies. Rounds liberalization of KFRC's play-list may well become more restricted.

THE HIGH COST OF MUSIC AND LOVE: WHERE'S THE MONEY FROM MONTEREY?

BY MICHAEL LYDON

A weekend of "music, love, and flowers" can be done for a song (plus cost) or can be done at a cost (plus songs). The Monterey International Pop Festival, a non-profit, charity event, was, despite its own protestations, of the second sort: a damn extravagant three days.

The Festival's net profit at the end of August, the last date of accounting, was $211,451. The costs of the weekend were $290,233. Had it not been for the profit from the sale of television rights to ABC-TV of $288,843, the whole operation would have ended up a neat $77,392 in the red.

The Festival planned to have all the artists, while in Monterey, submit ideas for use of the proceeds.

In the confusion the plan miscarried and the decision on where the profits should go has still not been finally made.

So far only $50,000 has definitely been allocated to anyone to a unit of the New York City Youth Board which will set up classes for many ghetto children to learn music on guitars donated by Fender. Paul Simon, a Festival governor, will personally over see the program.

Plans to give more money to the Negro College Fund for college scholarship is now being discussed; another idea is a sum between ten and twenty thousand for the Monterey Symphony.

However worthy these plans, they are considerably less daring and innovative than the projects mentioned in the spring the Diggers, pop conferences, and any project which would "tend to further national interest in and knowledge and enjoyment of popular music." The present plans suggest that the Board of Governors, unable or unwilling to make their grandiose schemes reality, fell back on traditional charity.

The Board of Governors did decide that the money would be given out in a small number of large sums. This has meant, for instance, that the John Edwards Memorial Foundation, a folk music archive at the University of California at Los Angeles, had its small request overlooked.

In ironic fact, what happened at the Festival and its financial affairs looks in many ways like the traditional Charity Ball in hippie drag.

The overhead was high and the net was low. "For every dollar spent, there was a reason," says Derek Taylor, the Festival's PR man and one of its original officers.

Yet many of the Festival's expenses, however reasonable to Taylor, seem out of keeping with its announced spirit. The Festival management, with amateurish good will, lavished generosity on their friends.

• Producer Lou Adler was able to find a spot in the show for his own property, Johnny Rivers; Paul Simon for his friend, English folk singer Beverly, John Phillips for the Group Without A Name and Scott MacKenzie. None of them had the musical

Airplane high, but no new LP release

Jefferson Airplane has been taking more than a month to record their new album for RCA Victor. In a recording period of five weeks only five sides have been completed. No definite release date has been set.

Their usual recording schedule in Los Angeles begins at 11:00 p.m. in the evening and extends through six or seven in the morning. When they're not in the studios, they stay at a fabulous pink mansion which rents for $5,000 a month. The Beatles stayed at the house on their last American tour.

The house has two swimming pools and a variety of recreational facilities. It's a small small little paradise in the hills above Hollywood. Maybe suntans and guitars don't make it together.

status for an international pop music festival.

It is ironic that the Rivers and the rest appeared "free," but the money it cost the Festival to get them to Monterey and back, feed them, put them up (Beverly *—Continued on Page 7*

John Lennon in *How I Won the War,* ROLLING STONE, issue 1, November 9, 1967.

Introduction

As film critic and senior features editor for ROLLING STONE since 1989, I have had the best seat in the house—though sometimes it feels more like the mosh pit—to observe the contentious yet committed relationship between this magazine and the movies. The book in your hands isn't simply a collection of lively interviews, profiles, on-the-set pieces and reviews, it's a legacy of rebel film, from Peter Fonda and Dennis Hopper's *Easy Rider* in the sixties to Quentin Tarantino's *Pulp Fiction* in the nineties. Back in the first issue, dated November 9, 1967, editor Jann S. Wenner pulled a Citizen Kane and issued a declaration of principle. His publication would cover not only music but also "the things and attitudes that the music embraces." For a generation raised on rock, rebel movies have the same juice: youth, defiance, danger, fun and the promise of rule-busting experimentation that might just point the way ahead.

The first cover story on a movie didn't take long to materialize. It was volume one, number one, and carried Jann Wenner's byline. The subject was John Lennon; not Lennon the Beatle, Lennon the actor. He had taken a dramatic role in Richard Lester's *How I Won the War* and appeared on the cover in uniform wearing wire-frame glasses that couldn't hide the witty dare in his squint. "I feel I want to be them all—painter, writer, actor, singer, player, musician," Lennon said. "I want to see which one turns me on and what I'll be like when I've done it." Lennon typified the maverick urgency of rock. So did his movie, an antiwar satire out to kick Establishment ass in the name of disenfranchised youth. ROLLING STONE was out to kick ass, too, in the same way as the music—bang on, truthful, no apologies.

ROLLING STONE emerged just as Hollywood awoke from a long, dull sleep of high-priced epics (*Cleopatra, How the West Was Won*) and glossy, Oscar-winning musicals (*My Fair Lady, The Sound of Music*). In the late sixties, a generation found its voice in such films as *Bonnie and Clyde, The Graduate, 2001: A Space Odyssey, Weekend* and a low-budget chunk of guerrilla cinema called *Easy Rider* that changed the way films were made, seen and discussed. It was a rebel's game, and ROLLING STONE was there to keep score. A selection of the magazine's movie covers reproduced in this book will give you an idea of film's impact on ROLLING STONE.

In compiling *The ROLLING STONE Film Reader*, the trickiest problem came in choosing which pieces to include from such a fertile field. Many of the key players in film have been profiled several times over the years. A decision was made to catch a subject, whenever possible, at the point of a breakthrough—professional, personal or both. John Travolta was only twenty-three when he embodied the sexual heat of the disco era with *Saturday Night Fever,* while Clint Eastwood was sixty-two when his work as actor and director reached full, flinty vigor with *Unforgiven.* In the case of Jack Nicholson, grilled five different times over two decades, we have meshed these sessions into the ultimate ROLLING STONE interview, tracing smiling Jack's career from young scrapper to lion in winter.

The book begins with Chris Hodenfield's memorable meeting with Marlon Brando, the rebel king of the fifties who passed the torch to the next generation. Brando didn't grant many interviews; he still doesn't. But as Hodenfield says, "Being from ROLLING STONE got you inside." It got Hodenfield inside Brando's van, the office of Alfred Hitchcock, the set of Robert Altman's *Nashville* and the corridors of power in Washington, D.C., and Hollywood that resulted in the film of *All the President's Men.* Each of those stories is included here, abridged out of necessity but with their wit and nerve intact.

Hodenfield was among a group of pioneer ROLLING STONE writers, including Grover Lewis, Jonathan Cott, Robert Greenfield, Tim Cahill, Ben Fong-Torres, Timothy White, Elizabeth Campbell, Tom Burke, David Rosenthal, David Felton, Mikal Gilmore, Jon Landau and Cameron Crowe, who let the movies take them to the same place the music did—the truth. Jann's mandate has always been to cut through the myth and nonsense. The no-bull approach left some scorched earth—no one got off easily. Just recently, at an off-Broadway theater, Robert Redford sat next to me and recalled a 1971

ROLLING STONE interview he gave to the late Grover Lewis, who died in 1995. As if the Texas writer were still next to him in a Chevy truck roaring through Utah, Redford remembered "ol' Grover firing penetrating looks through thick glasses that seemed like bottoms of soda bottles. He was a wild man. Great writer, though—Grover could nail you with a phrase."

More recent ROLLING STONE contributors, including Fred Schruers, Bill Zehme, David Breskin, Gerri Hirshey, Anthony DeCurtis, Lynn Hirschberg, Hillary de Vries, David Wild, Jeff Giles, Rich Cohen and Chris Mundy, have continued cutting through the hype and hypocrisy in high style. A celeb du jour, a pompous director or an Oscar-bloated epic are all considered fair game for skewering.

The pieces in this book run the generational gamut from Paul Newman to Brad Pitt, Meryl Streep to Jodie Foster, Jean-Luc Godard to Spike Lee, Brat Packers to Gen-Xers. The canvas extends from Federico Fellini's *dolce vita* in Rome to Cameron Crowe's grunge haven for singles in Seattle. Brando had his method; Daniel Day-Lewis has his. You can compare both. You can listen to Francis Ford Coppola track the highs and tragic lows of his life through three *Godfather* epics and Woody Allen and Diane Keaton supply candid details about how *Annie Hall* reflected their own relationship. And speaking of great teams, how about Martin Scorsese and Robert De Niro, Paul Newman and Robert Redford, Oliver Stone and the sixties? You can share triumphant advances with Tom Hanks, Winona Ryder, Kevin Costner and Michelle Pfeiffer, or massive defeats with the cast and crew of *Heaven's Gate.* You can discover the intricacies of marketing—underground *(The Crying Game)* and mainstream *(Star Wars)*—and study the star-making machinery that produces a Tom Cruise or a Julia Roberts. You can hear

Schwarzenegger talk terminating, Richard Pryor talk comedy, and Warren Beatty and Sharon Stone talk sex. You can get inside complex heads: Dustin Hoffman as he plays Lenny Bruce, Denzel Washington as he embodies Malcolm X, Jonathan Demme as he directs *Philadelphia*—the first mainstream movie on AIDS—and Quentin Tarantino as he redefines pulp for the new millennium. The defining irony of *Easy Rider* is that there is no easy ride. For the best filmmakers, sex, drugs and rock & roll doesn't mean dodging knotty issues of censorship, racism, homophobia and violence.

The ROLLING STONE *Film Reader* also stands as a time capsule, with all the fun and games that entails. Jane Fonda's current status as workout queen puts Tim Findley's 1972 article on "Hanoi Jane" in sharp relief. During the Vietnam era, Fonda used her work to rage against the military machine. Her words, no matter how strident, sound shockingly immediate. It is that daring which this book aims to capture. In the final section, I offer a compendium of fifty essential movies of the era, followed by fifty more to get you thinking. Are these the greatest movies? Not always. But they are the movies that tried to shake us up. Watching them now on video, you can get the same feeling that is distilled on these pages: of the dust being blown off film history, leaving us with a living portrait of a rebel generation. This book is a tribute to the mavericks who make the movies and the mavericks who write about them in the pages of ROLLING STONE.

Peter Travers
ROLLING STONE
July 1996

REBEL ROYALTY

SM14170   MAY 20th, 1976/ISSUE NO. 213   85¢UK30p

THE HUGHES-NIXON-LANSKY CONNECTION:
THE SECRET ALLIANCES OF THE CIA FROM
WWII TO WATERGATE. BY HOWARD KOHN

ROLLING STONE

BRANDO
The Method
of His Madness
A Portrait By
Chris Hodenfield

BRAVE NEW WEED
Three Spaced-Age Tales of Dope Utopia • By Theodore Sturgeon,
Michael Rogers and Thomas M. Disch

GAMBLE AND HUFF
Their Solid Gold Gospel

Marlon Brando, ROLLING STONE, issue 213, May 20, 1976.
Photograph by Mary Ellen Mark

Marlon Brando:
The Godfather Roars

By Chris Hodenfield
MAY 20, 1976

Marlon Brando's body was going through the motions, awaiting the return of his personality. It was miles away. He was reeling it in like a dancing sailfish.

His van was parked by the trees in a grassy field. Inside it was quiet. The air conditioner diced the air. Minutes had passed since our introduction, but he just sat on the edge of the bed, hands in a drawer fumbling aimlessly with a hank of wires. He picked up a screwdriver and turned it over carefully.

Here was a hero whose vanity had surrendered. Beneath those wide oak-stump shoulders was a vast rippling cargo hold, 240 pounds on a five-foot-ten frame. It was neat enough in here, a small, brown space piled high with books on solar energy and Indian history, and his two congas. Cupboards were stacked with fresh T-shirts and clean towels, and the icebox was filled with Tab.

When at last he found what he was looking for—a cassette tape of Caribbean drum music—he eased across the bed and rested his head against the curtained window. The silvery blond hair rolled over his ears.

That face. He looks an old medicine man. He appears as unmovable as the city planetar-ium. The concentration level is so high that when his distant manner suddenly evaporates and he has questions about your mother, ah, the arena gets hot.

He is, indeed, a presence. On the cowboy movie set of *The Missouri Breaks,* shot on the hot, dry plains of Montana, people seemed to be no more deferential to the actor than they'd be to any pharaoh about to exact tribute.

Which is not the normal attitude for a hard-boiled movie crew. They'd see him walking in their direction, with that head balled up like a clenched fist, that forehead all knotted and complicated. People were embalmed with awe. Beethoven must have had the same air. The costar here, Jack Nicholson, had to laugh: "The man does scorch the earth, right? I mean, for two hundred miles in any direction. Not much leavin's."

Not for many moons has Jack Nicholson been second bill in a picture. I guess a guy will do some funny things for a million dollars. When Nicholson was a high school kid in Neptune, New Jersey, his very last hero was Brando. Now they are next-door neighbors in Beverly

Hills. Still, Nicholson will stare . . . at his neighbor.

"It's a big problem," Nicholson said, all glassy lizard grins. "I suddenly felt myself feeling an old symptom while working with Marlon, which is that he's so powerful, you fall so in love with what he's doing, that you want to do it yourself. I studied him *then* and I find myself now, even when I'm working with him, wanting to emulate him."

Jack is an earnest character. He was suited in a sorry cowboy costume. We stood on the broken farmlands of Montana.

"In other words, when I first came to L.A., there were ten or twelve James Dean types, *innumerable* Marlon Brando types. No telling how many people were trying to emulate his timing, his style. I made a very conscious choice not to do that, even though I might feel in my heart that Marlon and I were true soul brothers . . . it's a well-beaten path, do you know what I mean?"

Yes. Writers do the same.

Nicholson grinned. "I think there's a well-known contest in the acting profession to see who can say the best stuff about Marlon."

He was one of thousands of jaw-flexing young dogs who fell into the arms of the Method, nursing visions of *On the Waterfront* and *A Streetcar Named Desire.* Elia Kazan, director of those two, turned out a couple more wonder-boys, James Dean in *East of Eden* and Warren Beatty in *Splendor in the Grass.* They joined the ranks of Actors Studio toughs who were labeled Road Company Brandos. Paul Newman. Vic Morrow. Harvey Keitel and Robert De Niro are continuing the line.

Norman Mailer recently called Brando our noblest actor and our national lout. (Who would know better?)

Now Brando is fifty-two. His step is heavy

with reputation. He has dried out in the air of scandal. A walking collection of headlines: a front-page banner on the L.A. *Herald-Examiner:* NIGHTIE RAMPAGE JAILS BRANDO'S EX; the *Saturday Evening Post,* 1962, after *Mutiny on the Bounty* (an ill-prepared folly with a constantly shuffled script, three directors and an $18.5-million price tag): MARLON BRANDO: HOW HE WASTED $6 MILLION BY SULKING ON THE SET; *Time* magazine, 1954, over a cover painting of Brando as Napoleon for *Desiree:* TOO BIG FOR HIS BLUE JEANS?

So we arrive at *Last Tango in Paris,* where the girl, Jeanne (Maria Schneider), looks at his character and says: "I shall have to invent a name for you." Paul (Brando) looks away: "Oh, God, I've been called by a million names all my life. I'm better off with a grunt or a groan for a name."

Anyone knew that Paul was really Brando. His audience rapport has, to that effect, almost worked against him. Here, even the biographical details were the same. Grew up on a farm, dug ditches, milked cows, boxed, went to Tahiti, played the congas. (As a high school drummer, his band was called Brando and His Kegliners.)

Paul is going through the last debauch of a man crowding fifty. He remembers. . . .

Bad memories, I guess. My father was a drunk, whore-fucker, bar-fighter, supermasculine. My mother was very poetic, and also a drunk. My memories of being a kid are of her being arrested nude. We lived in a small town, a farmer community. We lived on a farm and I'd come home after school . . . she'd be gone . . . in jail, or something.

We all dig good acting, but this is going too far. He is brutal but relies on a long repertoire of little-boy mannerisms to charm his way out of the consequences.

Then he rapes the girl, *per anum,* forcing her to repeat his litany: *Go on, say it. Holy Family . . .*

Church of Good Citizens . . . The children are tortured until they tell their first lie . . . And the world is broken with repression . . . Freedom is a sin. . . .

The prayer of the alone and absurd. And what could be more absurd than being a bankable man again. A one-human corporation who has had twenty-six years of the audience's karma invested in him. It's enough to make anyone suspicious of success. Brando is. The executive producer of *Missouri Breaks,* Elliott Kastner, employed everything but extortion to nail down his contract.

Rarely found in Beverly Hills, Brando is forever on the road, attending to his five children, taking them to Tetiaroa, his cluster of atolls near Tahiti, where a grunt or a groan is enough for a name. He builds windmills, methane gas converters; he saves the turtles. He has funded a scientific study to raise cold-water Maine lobsters in Tahiti! He is as proud as a Republican farmer.

Reporters who ask for interviews find themselves presented with conditions. To talk about solar energy, or the American Indian, because Brando has received some undesirable dividends on his public image. Like the time he sat with some respected Indian leaders in a restaurant at a time when tensions were running high over the Wounded Knee trial and suddenly there appeared a woman with a plate of butter in her hand requesting a *Last Tango* performance. The actor crumpled. "Please, lady."

Arthur Penn thought a lot about this amount of romance projected toward Brando. It intimidated Penn when they first worked together in 1965 on *The Chase.* He heard, in the five weeks preceding Brando's arrival, rumors of an unstable mass about to explode.

Think of what a longtime friend said: "Unconsciously, Marlon takes on the part he's play-ing. For *The Godfather* he was very nice, very caring, always giving people little gifts. But during *Last Tango,* he was a shit."

While Penn would disagree with that appraisal, he did know that his eighteen-year-old son idolized the actor; maybe John Q. Public would not like Brando playing this hired killer. When Penn consulted the actor, he found how heavily Brando deals in images. He wanted Penn's image of the character. "I dunno," Penn said, "I see this as kind of a hermit crab. He goes into an area and inhabits someone's shell for a while, consumes everything around there and then moves on to another shell."

Brando consumed the image, and then one day he arrived on the set. He got out of the car. He walked up to an electrician and introduced himself. He shook hands with the whole gang. "Just beguiled the hell out of everybody," Penn said.

The bounty-hunter character evolved into a charming old crazy who gets to know the horse thieves one by one, each time in a different disguise, *just beguiling the hell out of everybody,* before he kills them. But this is not to suggest that Brando unloosed his screws. He didn't bother anyone. He just parked himself by the riverbank every night while the crew returned to their Ramada Inn. He stayed alone. Kicked out the awning and thought it over. He does swell imitations, you know. One night, stoned to the teeth, he pretended he was an usher in a Las Vegas nightclub. He showed people to their seats for three hours, telling the fat lady to please sit here, aren't the ribs just wonderful tonight, oh, ho, breaking himself up over and over again.

I wasn't in that van five minutes and I was playing catch-up ball. He does not take up a point and extrapolate to the far measures. He *starts* on a virgin asteroid and winds his way back to earth, free-versing and free-associating, leaving behind his poetic blur of images about the Russian troops hovering at the Mongolian border and what starvation does to a baby's brain.

He sat absolutely still, his shoulders parked on the pillow like a grand piano. The sad, brooding eyes drank in all the details. And as for the relationship between his body and the space around him, Bernardo Bertolucci's observation was very true. "We are usually dominated *by* space," the *Last Tango* director told ROLLING STONE writer Jonathan Cott, "but Brando strangely *dominates* space. Even if Brando is absolutely still, say, sitting on a chair . . . Brando has already taken for himself that privileged space. And Brando's attitude toward life is different from that of other people because of this fact."

Any mention of moviedom would be sidestepped very neatly. Finally I asked if he loathed the subject. "No," he said, shaking his head with no great commitment. The eyes darted and the great train pulled into a distant station.

"Kazan is a performer's director," he said suddenly. "The best director I ever worked with. Because most actors . . . it's very lonely out there. Most actors don't get any help from directors. Emotional help, if you're playing an emotional part. Kazan is the only one I know who really gives you help.

"Most of the time you just come like a journeyman plumber and you gotta have your own bag of stuff, ready to go. But the people who perceive most delicately are Bertolucci and Gillo Pontecorvo *[Burn!]*. I never worked with, ah . . . the guy that did *Mean Streets*. Yeah, Scorsese, he's the best American director there is. He's a remarkable talent. He uses the actors very well, his intuitions allow him. . . ."

He arrested his thought and glanced at my hands. I was twirling my sunglasses.

"What you're doing now, playing with your glasses and looking at me. Shaking your head in moments you don't plan on."

I stopped playing with my glasses, blinked and smiled.

"And blinking and smiling, moving your head. You see, all those are unplanned things. You don't know what you're going to do in sequence. And Bertolucci and Scorsese would allow you to do that. They put you in the psychological circumstances so that you would *do* all that stuff and that is . . . that's the essence of reality.

"Now the mere fact that I mentioned it set off a whole bunch of movements on your face. Because in some small measure you were frightened by it. Everybody has a very low threshold of fear, and they carry it around and they don't know it. They don't know that they're being afraid if they do something like that. You talk to some people and they'll hang on your eyes for maybe a twelve-count and they'll just *have* to get away. They can't stand eye contact. They'll look everywhere . . . and once in a while they'll give you a little flick just to make it look real.

"But they can't stand it. They're the only ones who know it, unless you're aware of patterns of gestures.

"Shakespeare said something that was remarkable. You don't hear it very often. He said, 'There is no art that finds the mind's construction on the face.' Meaning that there is the art of poetry, music or dancing, architecture or painting, whatever. But to find people's minds by their face, especially their face, is an art and it's not recognized as an art.

"Bertolucci has that and so does Gillo Pontecorvo. Gadge [Kazan] also knows when things are in and when they're out. Has a good feeling.

He works viscerally and on instinct. Bertolucci is extraordinary in his ability to perceive . . . he's a poet. Some directors are difficult to work for. Gillo is very difficult to work for, very highly disciplined. But Bertolucci is easy to work for."

Different intuitions? Different manipulations?

"Definitely. Gillo has a very stringent and disciplined technique. Kazan would say, 'Go out and rehearse this scene and bring me something back.' He'll take about eight points out of twelve or eleven, and you argue with him. He'll give you points and there's no ego involved. He's a guy that works without ego.

"There might be a difference of interpretation. But he's got the last word on that. That's the director's privilege. And they'll always beat you to the tape in the cutting room. You might say 'yeah' quick. But if you thought about it and said, '. . . . . Yeeeeah.' Maybe he thought that was too goddamn long a take, so in the cutting room he dropped out thirty-eight frames and it comes out, '. . . Yeah.' Which alters the meaning. But if you're tight with the director, you know what they're after."

You're in the business of storing up memories.

"Well, we're just big computers is all. You inevitably store stuff up, and for no reason at all; right in the middle of a conversation, you'll start thinking of a short-handled hoe. It won't be related to anything, except something in your dreams has to do with a rubber telephone. 'Why was I thinking about a rubber telephone?'" He shrugged it off.

I had the impression that you were dredging up your own memories for *Last Tango*. Were they painful?

"No, because after a while it becomes a technical thing. I was putting things in my eyes to make tears in my eyes. I was making the right noises, the sounds of sobs. But, ah, I used to do that stuff straight. But it's too taxing."

He emphasizes such a point with a pincerlike grab at his chest. "For instance, now I don't even learn the lines. I don't learn them for a very specific reason, but . . ." He groped for a reason, and his eyes rested on me. "You see, you didn't know you were gonna look down just then."

I interrupted myself in midglance.

"You didn't plan on it, you just did it. And if you know your lines, very often, most of the time it sounds like 'Mary-had-a-little-lamb-its-fleece-was-white-as-snow.' And people intuit, they unconsciously *know* that you have planned that speech. And they know, for instance, that when you get up to leave, and walk a certain, say, five steps to the doorway and then stop"—he pulled himself up and stopped at the bathroom door, suddenly a punk, and slouching—"they *know* that you're gonna turn around and say, 'Why don't you ask Edith, then you'll find it in the shoe box.' And then walk out the door."

Brando disappeared into the bathroom. The theatrical voltage arrives at such a leisurely pace that it successfully dismantles your defenses.

He bounced back out of the bathroom. "But they already beat you to the fucking scene! So that doesn't keep them outta the popcorn. You always have to be ahead of the audience, or the audience is always ahead of you."

Still, I said, *Last Tango* seemed like more than mere technique.

He waved it off. "No, when you . . ." Suddenly, his face clenched and turned away.

Jesus, I thought, maybe I hit a sore spot. He was definitely disturbed. His lips taut, his eyes torn. A sob gurgled in his throat, and his shoulders shook. For an instant I was paralyzed. I stared at him.

Abruptly, his grief collapsed into a smile.

"You just do that, you know. It just sounds like a bunch of tears. You make your face to go happy or to get mad. It's too costly to crank up. It's just too costly. If you can get by with a technical performance, nobody knows the diff. They can't tell."

I guess not, I said, wiping my palms on the bedspread. The key to his emotions seems to be in his upper lip. He has a very expressive upper lip. It lifts with a challenge, purses down when the irony of this earth gets serious. He cushions himself with irony.

I asked him if the *Last Tango* details were autobiographical.

"Oh, well he [Bertolucci] had some cockamamie notion. What he wanted to do was sort of meld the image of the actor, the performer, with the part. So he got a few extraneous details. Played the drums, I don't know . . . Tahiti . . . so that the man is really telling the story of his life. I don't know what the hell it's supposed to mean. He said, 'Give me some reminiscences about your youth.' That made me think about milking a cow, my mother's getting drunk, one thing and another. He went, 'Wonderful, wonderful.' "

Brando grinned at the thought, leaned back and joined his hands behind his head. I said that several of my friends were upset because the elements were too outrageous. They couldn't take Brando in the role. It was too close.

"Not as far as I'm concerned. I would never, I'd never . . . there's a certain line you draw . . . I mean, in the days when I used to have to crank up emotionally, I would think of things that were very personal, but I would never exploit those in a film. For some goddamn check that came in at the end of the week. Or a director. He wanted to give that impression, so . . ."

His voice trailed, as it did so often when he tired of the tack. He switched.

"It wasn't an easy film. Playing it in another language was hard, and in a way it was easy because I just made up any goddamn thing. Not anything, just sorta he wanted this theme or that theme. No matter what you did, within a given context, he leaves you alone."

He ruminated on a distant cloud. His jaw flexed.

"I don't think Bertolucci knew what the film was about. And *I* didn't know what it was about. He went around telling everybody it was about his prick!"

The laugh sounded like an asthma attack. "He looks at me one day and he says, you know . . . something like, 'You are the embodiment, or reincarnation . . . you are the . . . symbol of my prick.' I mean, what the fuck does that mean? He has some conflicts that he's quite open about. . . .

"I have no idea what that picture was about. I mean, most pictures are the extensions of people's fantasies. You learn more about the reviewer when they review. A good reviewer anyway, like Pauline Kael. I think she overwrote the picture because she was overwhelmed by some personal experience she had."

What did you see in the movie?

"I saw the picture about two years later. No, it was three years later, and I thought it was funny. I didn't know what it was about." He gazed emptily at the ceiling. "It was about a man desperately trying to find some meaning in life, full of odd symbols. He dies in a self-conscious way, in a fetal position. The woman shoots him at the end, and this whole thing was to have taken place over a three-day period. Impossible to have those transitions. It's a mythological tale; it doesn't happen in life."

His eyes unfocused. "It was fascinating, that tango scene . . . in contrast to those strange men and movements and people. Iconoclastic. But you do something . . . the idea that he simply wanted to revert to his nature, he wanted to find out what was the common denominator in his misery, what his nature is . . . and then he found that his nature is not what he thought it was. And as soon as he reverted to a more natural way, meaning a more bourgeois concept, then she finally became more savage and primitive on an unconscious level. Finally killed him. He was sort of threatening her. Maybe it's . . ."

He realized what a mouthful had passed, considering that he didn't know what the film was about. His gaze shifted out the window with a certain amount of disgust. "I don't know."

Did you catch Ingmar Bergman's remark?

"No, what he say?"

He saw Jeanne as a boy, that Bertolucci didn't have the nerve to cast a boy in Maria Schneider's role.

"Oh. Well, he came as close to it as he can get. I mean, she's a professed . . . homosexual."

There were a lot of rugged stories around that movie, that it was an emotional pounding, that you'd never do anything like that again, that it took some recovery time.

"Naaah. As soon as they let go of your leg, then it's out to Tahiti or the desert."

The taped Caribbean drum music gave way to the crying jag of Carlos Santana. When you're around Brando for a while, you think not only of his comedic timing, but that he'd probably be a perceptive director. He's only directed once, a Western called *One-Eyed Jacks,* after Stanley Kubrick was fired from preproduction.

Do you have any more taste for the job?

"I did it once," he said, shaking his head. "It was ass-breaker. You work yourself to death. You're the first one up in the morning . . . I mean, we shot that thing on the run, you know.

You make up the dialogue the scene before, improvising, and your brain is going crazy."

You wrote the script, I take it.

"Yes. But it's better if you make it up, of course. Unless you're doing Eugene O'Neill. You can't wing that." He pulled up a dimply grin. "You can't do it to Tennessee Williams, somebody that can write something. But you get in a picture with six guys like that, it's like an old whore in a lumber camp who's been fucked till she can't see straight."

The question is, how deep do you go with your improvisation?

"Well, it depends on what you're doing. If you're doing a hit-the-roof scene, you have to gas up, sorta. You don't have to kill yourself. When I first started, it was in a movie called, ah . . . *The Men.* And I got there at something like six-thirty in the morning, and by nine-thirty, when they were ready to shoot, I had shot my wad."

You were that psyched up?

"In the dressing room, yeah. I was all set to go. I had music"—he waved and snapped his fingers—"and I had poetry, everything to transport me into another realm. So I came out dry as a bone.

"If you do a scene any number of times, you just go dry. Unless you crank up very slowly to it. And then snap out of it at take thirteen. It all depends on the director; if he's fiddling around with this technical issue, there's no sense in cranking up. Because you know he's not going to print anything until the seventh take, he's just rehearsing himself.

"The trouble is, when you're playing one part, the director is playing another, and the writer is playing another part. Everybody's got a different idea. That's why it's better to get the signals straight up front. A lot of directors want to know *everything.* Some directors don't want to know anything. Some directors wait for you to bring everything to them."

John Huston, who did *Reflections in a Golden Eye,* he was supposed to be a free-swinging guy.

"Ah, well. Yeah. He gives you about twenty-five feet. He's out in the background. He listens. Some guys listen, some guys are auditory; some guys are visual. Some guys are both. He's an auditory guy and he can tell by the tone of your voice whether you're cracking or not. But he leaves you alone pretty good.

"It's the no-talent assholes who get on your back, who all think they're Young Eisenstein Misunderstood, or Orson Welles, or somebody like that. And you know fucking well when they say, 'Print,' that it's just thumbs-up-the-ass place. Those are the guys that are tough to work with. Chaplin you got to go with. [Charles Chaplin directed him in *A Countess from Hong Kong.*]

"Chaplin is a man whose talents is such that you have to gamble. First off, comedy is his backyard. He's a genius, a cinematic genius. A comedic talent without peer. You don't know that he's senile. Personally, he's a dreadful person. I didn't care much for him. Nasty and sadistic and mean . . ."

His voice trailed off. *"Oh, God.* He's like aaallll . . . You got to stop them because they'll get on you. You got to stop them dead. But nevertheless you have to separate that personal life from that artistic life. One has *nothing* to do with the other. It's like writers, or anything else.

"You can't think that understanding people, or perceptive and sensitive people, are going to be perceptive and sensitive in other areas of human relationships. It just doesn't hold true. Talent has nothing to do with it, that's all.

"There are shits who are very understanding and extremely talented, and there are shits who

are without a shred of talent. There's good guys on both sides."

The door blew open, and the event that transpired was a spiffy lesson on maneuvering this weary lion. It was his secretary, Alice Marchak, an elegant woman with exotic cheekbones. She was something of an older sister and bail bondsman to the actor, and was blunt with the news that he was not getting any day off. "They need you as soon as possible," she said. "Should I tell them you're ready?"

Brando, suddenly a kid, turned with a stage whisper. "That's a good lesson. When they tell you to go, *go!"*

And he began to hoist himself up to get dressed, when an underassistant elbowed her way past Alice to confront the man. She had a flighty airline-stewardess charm and wore pink lipstick. She sighed helplessly. Brando leaned back.

"Do you want to hear my sad, sad story?" she said to him, trying to laugh. "As you know, I am now a liar in your eyes. We got into a whole thing with this stunt that's going to take us far longer than we could take tonight. I'm *sorry.* What can I say?"

Genuinely mortified, she hurried out. He propped himself on an elbow to ponder the scene. Alice Marchak fussed with his overcoat.

"That's all such a painful collection of dog shit," he sighed, waving at the door. His voice was a low complaint. "There's no way she can just come in and say, 'Marlon, we need a shot of you coming in out of the woods, will you please get ready as quick as you can, please.' She's got to come in with the full Vaseline number first off. 'We're *terribly* sorry.' She doesn't give a shit about me. She only gives a shit about what she thinks my position is. And she relates to that.

"Whereas, if I was driving the camera truck,

it would be something like, 'Hey, lissen, asshole, get your buns over here because you got work to do, I got news for ya.' So you feel . . . utterly alienated from your society." He clawed the air with pinched fingers.

"One of the things I hate about working is that they won't let you be some overweight . . . middle-aged . . . fart who's walking down the street, who happens to be in the lumber business. They *insist* that you be somebody." His face aged with agony, then relaxed.

He stood up to peel down for the costume change.

Another day, another twenty grand. That's the way Jack Nicholson looked at it, picking up a million and a percentage for ten weeks' work. Brando got $1,250,000 for five weeks, plus a percentage. *The Missouri Breaks* was not a movie, it was a business proposition.

Arthur Penn, short and wiry, a bundle of New York nerves, his lips chapped into Brillo pads, had an eight-million-dollar baby on his hands and he wasn't going to take chances. He shot dozens of takes in hundreds of ways while 125 crew members wilted in the Montana sun.

Those 125 burnt and crinkly noses pretended not to notice when Brando moved their way, up the river's edge. He picked his way over the white moonstones, grumbling, "There's no walking with any dignity over these rocks."

Brando lowered himself down on the shoreline and let the water lap at his heels. Nobody was about to interrupt him, except the photographers. They had to ask permission before a shot. He could have been praying on the Ganges, except he had a Morse code handbook in one hand and a pocket tape recorder in the other, bleeping signals into his ear. Morse code. On a movie set.

Out in the swift water, Michael Butler and his camera crew were slogging the Panavision cameras on deck. The reclining actor was enjoying spiritual communion with the wet pink rocks. He began dropping them into his pocket. A propman saw this and fetched a red plastic bucket for the mounting collection. Soon Brando was out squatting in the shallows. The giant shoulders were wrapped in an overcoat. A flat coolie hat hid his head. He looked like Winston Churchill. "Take a shot, Marlon?" the photographers asked. For once, he said, no, please.

Arthur Penn stood behind him, sniffing out a moment's conference. He held the red bucket of rocks.

Ill winds raced in off the prairie that week, tearing off the windows and swallowing the city in a sheet of sand. Nerves got dragged on a razor strop. Dogs ran free. Idle persons turned to occult practices. Two FBI agents blew into town and they had questions.

They were a pair. Casual knit suits and sensible black oxfords. They met Brando outside his mobile home, flipped their badges at him and stepped inside.

The movie crew was parked outside a postal warehouse. Inside, a nighttime campfire scene was set up in a bunch of phony shrubs. But no horse opera would operate while the leading man was held hostage by lawmen.

They had found the actor's fingerprints on all sorts of dangerous notions. Decades ago he had worked for the Jewish terrorist group, the Irgun Tzva'i Leumi. When Caryl Chessman was headed for the Green Room, Brando joined in a vigil outside San Quentin. He spoke at Bobby Hutton's funeral. And finally, he has joined hands with a gang of un-Americans, the Indians. In 1964, he was arrested with the Puyallup Indians while staging a fish-in for their river rights. Last year, when the Menominee Warrior Society took over a monks abbey in Gresham, Wisconsin, Brando dodged the law and joined them inside. Three sleepless nights later they walked out winners.

And it was no secret that he'd housed members of the American Indian Movement, given them money and land. (The celebrated forty acres he gave to the Indians, which turned up with a $318,000 mortgage due, was settled recently. He saw to the note, and the Survival of American Indians Association took the land.)

Brando's plan to make a movie of the 1973 Wounded Knee uprising is certain not to paint a flattering, patriotic picture of our embattled FBI. And while the projected movie has been up-and-down hill, with the Indians sifting through directors and the investors waffling the money (Columbia Pictures dropped it from their schedule), the actor was still up for scrutiny. He would certainly know the whereabouts of Dennis Banks, who was at that time on the lam. (Banks was arrested January 24, 1976.)

So the agents wanted to know if Brando would give shelter to any fugitive he might know. Brando, in turn, wanted to know if the agents would turn in another agent who illegally killed someone.

They had a nice long talk.

That night Brando was anxious to scram.

Get out of town, wash off the makeup, pull on the T-shirt, get this van moving. He knew there was a good place to camp out by the next day's location, an isolated ravine.

The blue shadows of scrub prairie pines grew in the long light of evening. We swung onto the interstate. Mike, a young, weary-looking driver hired to assist Brando on this picture, gunned ahead in the Jeep. Marlon didn't try to keep up but steered the lumbering van in his own way. Slow and confident.

I asked about the financing of his Wounded Knee movie.

"Oh, it's coming along. I thought about taking this to the movie companies, saying, 'Look, you people have done more damage to the livelihood of the American Indian's cause than any other group, outside the United States government, and you ought to kick in and do something about it, you know, keep your skirts clean.'

"The whole idea of the motion picture industry is don't offend anybody. Or you can't make money. So I'm scraping my ass to get financing for this film. People don't wanna spend eight million dollars for this. They're not gonna spend for something they think they're not gonna get back. And I don't know why not, because the truth is more dramatic than anything they could make up.

"They give you a nice runaround because they want to see you coming in next time with something that's palatable. They don't want to make an enemy out of you. As long as you're hot."

That sounds familiar. As long as you're hot.

"Yah," he said, leaning on the steering wheel. "I couldn't get arrested before."

Before *The Godfather?*

"Yeah, just about then. I mean, I could get arrested, but . . . it's a variable. When you been in about four stinkers in a row—" He drew back. "When you say stinkers, they could be artistically successful, but they don't turn into bucks—it starts to wobble.

"But films . . . it's funny. People buy a ticket. That ticket is their transport to a fantasy which you create for them. Fantasyland, that's all, and you make their fantasies live. Fantasies of love or hatred or whatever it is. People want their fantasies over and over. People who masturbate usually masturbate with, at the most, four or five fantasies. By and large.

"Most people like the same food and they like the same kind of music, they like the same kind of sexual fantasy for a period of time, then maybe it changes. As it is in children. Who is it?" He drummed the dashboard. "Bruce Lee. That's the hero. Then you grow up and grow out of your Bruce Lee period, or your Picasso Blue Period, and go into another period.

"But with kids, because they outpower us, because they have no representation, because they are so dependent, all they think about is power. Dinosaurs or the Million Dollar Man, because they feel so helpless, because they have no way out of it, except fantasy. Because they are only that tall.

"And that's all films are." He had a concerned knit to his voice, like a preacher talking about his poverty. "Just an extension of childhood, where everybody wants to be freer, everybody wants to be powerful, everybody wants to be so *overwhelmingly* attractive that there's just no doing anything about it. Or everybody wants to have comradeship and to be understood.

"They become lullabies. They're 'tell-me-again-Daddy' stories. That's all television is: 'Tell me again, Daddy, about the good guy and the bad guy and the strong guy and Kung Fu and Flash Gordon.'"

His voice grew soft. "People love to hear the stories, they love to hear the lullabies.

"Tastes change, but the function doesn't. I might as well be Jimmy Cagney in *White Heat*. The same story, the positive and the negative, the yin and the yang, the antihero.

"There's no fooling. People are sheep. They'll just do any fucking thing. Anything. I mean, the sum total of everything I believe is the sum total of everything I've read, seen. I'm not told how to do it, it's just . . . something's influenced me. James Joyce or Schopenhauer or my aunt Minnie.

"But everybody's looking for the man on the white horse, everybody's looking for the one who will tell the Truth. So you read Lao-tzu, you read Konrad Lorenz, I don't know who else, Melville, Kenneth Patchen, somebody you think is not a bullshitter. Somebody who has the eyes of a saint and the perceptions of a ghost.

"They're gonna tell us the way, they're gonna show us. They never really do, and we run around being cheap imitations of all those influences."

He shrugged in a resigned way. "But there isn't much of another way."

Spending a week around the guy, it was easy to stew about this massive acting talent going to waste. All those years he was making dog movies, and now he's got offers for every role going. When I asked about his present work ethic, he expelled a large, grudging sigh.

"I built a little house in Tahiti," he said at last. "Out of sticks and grass and palm trees, droppings. That gave me an enormous sense of satisfaction. Whenever I can physically achieve some simpler way of doing something.

"Work ethics are funny things. The Tahitians couldn't give three-ninths of two pieces of lizard shit about working."

The road gave way to rutted farm tracks. The tension seemed to be easing away from his shoulders. "I mean, where do you find hope?

"On the island, there's an ample opportunity to demonstrate that it can be done . . . to put these technologies together . . . with wind and methane and solar energy. I want to build it in my own house and then just make a little flick about that.

"I've got a little community developing down there, for an experimental hotel. I dropped a considerable amount of money in research and development. I invented a windmill, but to actually produce wind is quite a trick. My wife and kids are there."

We pulled up on a rise. Somewhere on these yellow fields was the campsite. Marlon settled in his seat.

I got the binoculars. "Do you have 'journalist' on your passport?" he asked, scanning the plains. My passport doesn't say anything, I said.

"It must say something. I got so sick of writing 'actor' down on my passport that I wrote 'shepherd.' And it didn't make any difference. Except one dry English immigration officer."

He struck a Commander Schweppes pose. " 'Haws your flawk, Mr. Brando?' I said, 'Doing very well.' 'I'm delighted to hear it.' Didn't smile at all."

He dropped back into gear and shoved off.

Brando had only a few days of moviemaking left. His fifteen-year-old son, Miko, was to join him for a slow drive back to Los Angeles. They had plans together for the desert, the woods and the rivers. Father was just about finished building a river raft out of inner tubes and two-by-fours.

That night, while he camped alone, the thunderheads rolled over. He sat in the dark with a pocket computer, counting and estimating the proximity of the lightning strikes. It travels 1,100 feet per second. Enough, he said, to make him feel religious.

The Fighting Fondas

Peter Fonda and the Making of *Easy Rider*

By Elizabeth Campbell

SEPTEMBER 6, 1969

"When I did *Tammy and the Schmuckface*, I got a lot of fan mail. Thousands of letters a week, asking me for my autograph and my picture. When I did *The Wild Angels*, I didn't get much fan mail. When I did *The Trip*, and now that I've done *Easy Rider*, I get letters from people saying, 'What do I do?' 'How do I talk to my father?' 'How do I stop trying to kill myself? How do I learn something, how can I live?' Nobody's asking me for my picture and my autograph anymore. So the movie I'm making means nothing. The life I'm making obviously means something to these people."

In his twenty-nine years, Peter Fonda has acted in a lot of bad movies, been busted for grass, been blasted by the press for being plastic and by his relatives for being outrageous. All that's over now, since *Easy Rider*. He recalls stopping his car during the cross-country filming and looking back at all the trucks and cars and camera equipment and people getting out and waving traffic on, and thinking: "Far out! That's all my company. That's all there because I wanted to ride a motorcycle and I needed money to build it."

"It's the wrong way to go about it. I was taking pleasure in it rather than enjoying it. When I was just doing it, I had a better time. But there were moments when I did stop and look back and reflect. I'd say: 'Jesus. That's my company! But I'm supposed to be a failure!'"

Fonda had not only been telling himself that, it was what he'd been told. "Weren't you ever told that? Or did you kill your parents when you were young?" "You're not what we wanted," Fonda remembers, was the message passed down the dining room table. "That goes for me, and everybody I know, and everybody I don't know and their parents and their police, and their government and their church. . . ."

In the old days, before he discovered cannabis, Fonda carried a loaded gun. And he was a crack shot. "Then I met this chick in New York, and she saw a strung-out, paranoid Pisces. And she said: 'Here. Smoke a little of this instead.' And I did. And I got ripped. And I stopped wearing a gun. And I stopped drinking, and I got less and less violent."

Fonda and his costar Dennis Hopper actually turn on in *Easy Rider*, but that, he said, isn't a measure of the film's truth and honesty. "It's just a publicity gig, to talk about it. We just turned on because that's the way we wanted to do it. It was also fun."

Renegade Peter Fonda cruises across America in *Easy Rider*.
Courtesy of Columbia Pictures, copyright © 1969 Columbia Pictures
Industries, Inc. All rights reserved.

Fonda considers *Easy Rider* "cinema verité" in allegory terms, but the film is really a lecture-demonstration on the conclusions Peter Fonda has come to regarding the United States of America in 1969. It has been very successful at the box office and almost as fortunate with the critics. Most of them praise the film's integrity and its portrayal of American hypocrisy and discrimination but many critics complained about Fonda and Hopper. "We couldn't identify with them," they said.

Perhaps their protests are directed toward a certain feeling of betrayal: "If these guys represent the younger generation, why won't they let us understand them?"

The basic assumption is that the characters played by Fonda and Hopper *are* Fonda and Hopper, or at least speak for them. The irony of it all is that the lesson as prescribed by Fonda is understood exactly the way he intended it to be understood. Critics come away saying, 'Those guys aren't free! They aren't even very happy." Fonda says they weren't supposed to be.

"I play a character called Captain America," he says. "I'm Peter Fonda, I'm *not* Captain America, so I'm playing somebody else. I am representing everybody who feels that freedom can be bought, who feels that you can find freedom through other things, like riding motorcycles through the air or smoking grass. In this country, we've all been programmed to retire. We get our thing together, no matter who goes down.

"My movie is about the *lack* of freedom, not about freedom. My heroes are not right, they're wrong. The only thing I can end up doing is killing my character. I end up committing suicide; that's what I'm saying that America is doing. People do go in and they think, 'Look at those terrible rednecks, they killed those two

free souls, who needed to love, blah, blah, blah.' That's something we have to put up with.

"We don't give out any information through dialogue. We have a very loose plot; nothing you can follow. You can't predict what's going to happen, and that puts everybody off. People want it predicted for them, and they want violence to happen when they expect it to happen, so they can deal with it; they want sex to be a certain way and drugs to be a certain way and death to be a certain way. And it ain't. Neither is freedom. *Easy Rider* is a Southern term for a whore's old man, not a pimp, but the dude who lives with a chick. Because he's got the easy ride. Well, that's what's happened to America, man. Liberty's become a whore, and we're all taking an easy ride."

Easy Rider was produced by Fonda, directed by Hopper. They wrote the script, and Terry Southern came up with the title. Fonda says that the film is exactly the way they wanted it, with one exception. They had wanted to use "It's Alright, Ma (I'm Only Bleeding)" for the ending. Bob Dylan saw the film, as did the other artists whose music Fonda and Hopper wanted to use. The idea was to have the music that accompanies the cross-country cycling scenes reflect current times. All the groups approved the film and okayed the use of their music. The members of the Band walked out after the performance without saying anything, then called Fonda at 3:00 A.M. to say that their song ("The Weight") was the only good one in the film, and could they write all the music? They were convinced that there wasn't enough time.

"If there are mistakes in the film, they're my mistakes and Dennis' mistakes," Fonda says. "Nobody foisted anything on us—it's exactly the way we wanted it, with the exception of Mr. Zimmerman.

"I give no hope to the audience at the end

of the film, and Mr. Zimmerman says, 'That's wrong, you've got to give them hope!'

"I said, 'Okay, Bob, what do you have in mind?'

"He said, 'Well, reshoot the ending and have Fonda run his bike into the truck and blow up the truck.'

"I said, 'No, give me your song, Bob.'

"He said, 'How about you don't use the song and we make another movie.'

"I said, 'No, no, how about we don't make another movie and we use the song.'

"He said, 'The song's pretentious.'

"I said, 'He not busy being born is busy dying.'

"He said, 'Never mind that, man, have you heard my new album? It's a whole new number. We've got to give them *love*.'

"I said, 'I understand that. You have to love them, but you cannot give them love.'

"I kept thinking, Dylan sounds right. A lot of people are saying: 'Fonda, Dylan's right. You can't give them hopeless negative vibes.' I thought, you can't give them love either. Krishnamurti pointed that out. You can't give them a thing. They've got to take it; otherwise there's nothing happening. Freedom can't be secondhand information.

"Dylan's one of my biggies. I'm my only hero, but he's one of my biggies. Him and John Lennon. I can't understand how he can say how he made 'It's Alright, Ma' to fill out the side of an album.

"So he feels embarrassed about protesting. The truth of the matter is 'He not busy being born is busy dying.' That's the truth of the matter. And 'A question in your nerves is lit, and yet there is no answer fit to satisfy/insure you not to quit to keep it in your mind and not forget/that it is not he or she or them or it that you belong to.'

"That was the end of our movie. Dylan made us take that off and end the movie. He looked at it, and all he could hear was his bad voice and his lousy harmonica. His bad voice! . . . Oh, my God! . . . His lousy harmonica! I don't understand that. Come on, get it straight, Mr. Zimmerman!

"My name's Fonda, and it's been Fonda for years. And I won't renounce *Tammy and the Doctor*. I call it *Tammy and the Schmuckface* because it's a bullshit movie, but it plays on the tube, and I don't try to buy the negative back and not have anybody see it.

"You can't forget the past, you can't effectively do a frontal lobotomy."

Fonda was questioned closely about other decisions made in *Easy Rider* when he was in San Francisco. The questions were those that might be asked of a friend who made a movie: "Why did you shoot the commune sequence that way?" "What kind of treatment did you get from the people you ran into?"

Answers: He thinks the commune sequence is the weakest in the movie; the line he wishes weren't there is "They're gonna make it."

It was not easy to get the money to make *Easy Rider*. Fonda says he ultimately succeeded because he asked the right question at the right time. "I didn't ask for too much bread, and the way I laid it out, it embarrassed people into making the picture," he says.

Fonda took no money for producing the film or writing it; the money he had to be paid as a union actor he returned to the company after deducting taxes. Dennis Hopper, broke at the time, was paid a minimal $150 a week. Now, it won't be long—*Easy Rider* is going to be fantastically financially successful.

And that, says Fonda, is the one real Hollywood requirement. "They reject me until my film makes money at the box office, then I'm their darling. But they still hold me in contempt on the one hand and in awe on the other. In contempt because I've shown them a mirror of their own greed, and in awe because I was able to do something they can't do, which was simply to make a motion picture honestly."

The options now open to those concerned in the success of *Easy Rider* are almost limitless. Jack Nicholson, who is everybody's favorite in the movie, put it this way: "It's hard to make a movie. It really is hard to make a movie. So people who can actually do something are in tremendous demand."

After a success, Nicholson says, "your problem is to keep from going insane over all the alternatives you have."

Nicholson, Hopper and Fonda are dealing with the problem of success in a somewhat less than traditional Hollywood fashion. Nicholson, who wrote *The Trip* and *Head,* is going to direct a movie. He made that decision before the release of *Easy Rider.* "I had the ability to look at the part and say: 'Oh, people are gonna like that. I'm gonna get hot.' I've always known the movie was gonna be a big success. . . . I'd better set a couple of things, because though I've never been successful in the popular kind of way, I've seen it. And I know that I'm not the most constant person in the world . . . I like to change my mind a lot. So I wanted to set a couple of things before I got swept away."

Hopper has gone back to working on the first script he ever wrote, an interwoven Western, called *The Last Movie.* And Fonda is still trying to do something he's wanted to do for some time—a film on the American Revolution called *Conceived in Liberty.* "People always say, 'The American Revolution, which one?' I say, 'You mean you've separated yourself from the one that went down two hundred years ago? You think it stopped? And we've gotten into something new? Well, it ain't new, and we haven't finished it, we haven't implemented the Bill of Rights.'"

Fonda has not as yet been successful in financing the film. But he is confident he will be. He keeps going back, always wanting the same thing, only now, he says, "each time I hit them I've made more money in the box office with *Easy Rider.*

"So now they're calling me and saying, 'Well, what do you want to do now?'

"I say, *'Conceived in Liberty.'*

" 'Well, yeah, we've talked about that. Maybe if you get a package together.'

"I say, 'No, no, no. That's not right. That's not what you have to say. What you have to say is, *"Great!* How much do you want?" And then you have to say *"Great!* Of course you want to direct it, too, don't you? *Great!* Are you going to star in it? We'd like you to, if you will." ' "

Even though nobody has had that conversation with him yet, Fonda says it will happen. "They'll give it to me, because they think that it's hip to give it to me and that they'll make money with me, because I'm 'the hottest young actor in the business.' It's not true . . . I just happen . . . I grew up inside that industry, so I know what makes it tick."

Fonda and his wife and two children live in Beverly Hills. Their next-door neighbor is Alfonso Bell, a black conservative Republican congressman. Bell drives a Continental; Fonda drives a Volkswagen. "But I used to have Continentals. One time I had seven cars in my driveway: I couldn't decide which to drive in the morning. It's all gone. I don't have anything to say about that anymore, to anybody. I came back on two hundred and fifty gammas and saw these seven cars sitting in my driveway, and they were rusting, and they were just machinery, grinding to a halt right in front of my eyes."

He doesn't take acid anymore but feels he learned a lot from it. "Acid," Fonda says, "is to mental disorder what penicillin is to bacterial disorder." He had some bad trips, but says that "I was hip that the reason I was having bad acid trips was that I had a lot of hang-ups."

"I have two children . . . I have two hostages to fortune. When I first heard that phrase from Jack Kennedy, I thought, 'What does he mean? "He who has children gives hostages to fortune?" What's he trying to do, be Chairman Mao?' Well, then I had two kids. Hostages to fortune. I put away the gun."

Bridget, five, is an Aquarius, and Justin, three, is a Cancer. Fonda says that when his mind is "clear and quiet," Bridget can read his thoughts. He tells about times when she has known where he was taking her, before he told her . . . and when she knew he was supposed to do something when he hadn't mentioned it. (Judging from a picture of her that he carries with him, she is capable of that and more.) He says getting married was "something we did for Them."

"We don't relate to it at all. There's danger in that type of action. . . . It's a false goal."

Fonda thinks heroin—and, in fact, anything—is better than speed. He says he's tried to talk friends out of shooting speed, but it doesn't work . . . they don't believe him, either. "They're exposed to a lie, and they assume that all things therefore have been lied about, and all things will be lied about. And there's no way

you can convince them. You'd think that I would be one of the few people who could come up and say, 'Hey, man, don't do speed.' And the cat would say, 'He said it. King Drug said it.'

"But it doesn't work. Not when their mothers are taking amphetamines, and everybody's taking bennies to do an exam . . . of course it can't work."

He believes you can't tell people things. They have to be shown. "If I were to stand up like I'm talking to you now in the motion picture, and say, 'I'm dealing in fear, ladies and gentlemen, and fear is what's screwing you up. Fear's fucking you right out of your seats,' they're gonna turn it off and put their fingers in their ears. They're gonna turn away and say, 'I didn't hear that, what is he to tell me that?' "

By keeping his mouth shut, he believes he can involve the audience on a much stronger level. And on that level, it is impossible to deny that *Easy Rider* is a success. Whatever people think of the movie, or of Fonda as an actor, they all walk out of the theater talking and arguing about where America is at, and where youth is at. And without even knowing that anybody wanted them to think about these things.

Fonda is sensitive to criticism; he knows that much of it is based on a misunderstanding of the goals of the movie, but the misunderstanding still hurts. "Those are *my* balls up there, on the screen."

But Fonda says he refuses to give a performance. "The only performance I'm going to give is my life."

Hanoi Jane Fonda

By Tim Findley

MAY 25, 1972

"I did not want to be on the cover of ROLLING STONE because I feel that it's opportunistic. I don't want to sell the magazine, and I don't want people to buy the magazine because of me, and I don't think I'm the only one who should be interviewed. I think it's much more important to interview soldiers, the people who fought the war, because I think a lot of people say, 'Well, what does she know? She's just a movie star.' And why not? I mean, sure, of course they say that."

Jane Fonda slaps the table for emphasis. She is by the official decree of the Motion Picture Academy the Best Actress of 1971 for *Klute*. But she is a person whose energies are devoted to ending American imperialism, a word she avoids because it sounds like rhetoric.

We sit outside, hunched over a picnic table in the small, bricked-in patio behind her Los Angeles house while her three-year-old daughter, Vanessa, romps nearby. The one-story house looks too modest for a movie star. The living-room furniture is old. Not antique, old; Goodwill kind of old. A picture of Ho Chi Minh and a painted plate showing scenes of Vietnamese women sit on the mantel. There's no Oscar in sight.

"For the vast majority of the world, North America has been written off as enemy," Jane Fonda said. "It's enemy territory, and this is something I don't think enough of us realize."

She seems at times to be at war with herself, struggling to prove her sincerity, fighting to examine the contradictions of her life. She is important because she is a celebrity and unimportant because she is a celebrity. She is a revolutionary who happens to be an actress and a movie star who happens to be a revolutionary.

"Movie stars are a very unimportant segment of society," she says. "One time we were in Idaho doing a show at Mountain Home Air Base, and a steelworker from Salt Lake City came all the way up there to get my autograph, which opened up a conversation about why would a signature of somebody who makes movies be so important. We were talking about the fact that you could remove every movie actor and actress and film director in the country and nothing would change, but if all the steelworkers decided to sit down, history would change. Those are the people who have to start talking, and those are the people who really have something to say."

Jane Fonda is one of many of us. She has

25

grown up with the Vietnam War, and it has absorbed her life in a manner not very different from the way it has absorbed the life of a Salt Lake City steelworker. Yet it has brought some painful paradoxes to her life, because even Jane Fonda recognizes that it is not incidental to the antiwar movement that she is a famous actress.

"We're at a moment in history where there are splits among people who are normally part of the ruling class," she says. "Because the war has shown us who have privileged lives the lies—the lies that have been told us. I was brought up the way most middle-class people were, to be a certain kind of way, and I always felt uncomfortable, I always felt outcast, ill at ease. I felt stupid and I felt dumb and I felt ugly and I felt boring and I felt all those things because I didn't know how to live life the way they wanted me to. I never thought of myself as sexy; I never knew how to talk to people at cocktail parties. I never liked to date. I couldn't stand the men I was supposed to go out with, so I always thought, 'I'm really weird; I'm really fucked up.' And so I got married, and then I discovered that was even worse, and so I split after seven years of trying to be the perfect wife. At that point it was a time when you simply couldn't avoid the war. You could not avoid the lie. Once you make the step of saying, 'I'm lied to,' then I think, for me anyway, it leads to a lot of other things."

I'd assume, though, that you still wanted to be an actress.

"Oh, God, yeah. God knows there's enough sectarianism on the left that says I should stop being an actress and should split. But there are very few people in my position who feel the way I do, and there should be a lot more. The friends whom I met, the Vietnamese and the people from Latin America and the people from the Philippines, made me understand that it's

very important to be what we're best at and at the same time to maintain our ties with the masses of people.

"In that sense it was very important that I won an Oscar. It was very important that I accepted it the way I did, and it was very important that I didn't alienate people. It is important for all of us who are rebelling to be the best that we possibly can be at what we can do."

Yet criticism comes down on you from people who say you should have done what George C. Scott did.

"So what has he done?"

He didn't take the Oscar, I guess.

"Yeah, I know, but what has he done? George C. Scott's never done anything. He's never helped out. What does it really mean to refuse the Oscar? That's what I thought a year ago, and a woman who was a lot wiser than I said to me, 'You're a frigging subjective individual, an elite individual, it's really typical of the bourgeois middle-class-family girl to want to refuse the Oscar.' The Oscar is what working people relate to when they think of people in movies. That's what the kinds of people in America who think I'm a freak, and who think that people who support the Panthers and speak out against the war are all some kind of monsters, relate to. It's important for those of us who speak out for social change to get that kind of acclaim. It means that we're legitimized in the eyes of the working people—those people we have to reach and make understand that our cause is legitimate, too."

There is a point at which Jane Fonda the revolutionary clashes with Jane Fonda the actress. They are not two different people as much as they are two sets of circumstances looking for a medium in which they might both be comfortable. It lies somewhere in the difficult mode where art is politics and politics art.

"To do a bad film that's political is nowhere," she says with a grimace. "I want to make movies that people will see but that don't lie. Obviously, right now I get scripts. I read a lot of scripts from a lot of important people. I mean, scripts that will be made and they'll be the big movies of this year and of next year and so on. And they lie. They lie about women, they lie about third-world people; they make women look silly or black people look silly. Or the scripts look like they're going to make people feel bad because they don't look like the people in the movie or they don't have what people on the screen have or they just lie about American life. I don't want to make movies that lie anymore.

"It's very hard to define what a revolutionary movie is, but I asked people in Latin America what they thought a revolutionary movie should be. They told me that any movie that exposes the reality of American life is revolutionary in the context of Latin America, because they're battling thirty years, forty years of brainwashing. You know, the movies that show the big American crew-cut hero and the sexy, svelte American woman who's everything the Latin American women aren't and want to be. The blond, blue-eyed monsters and the comfortable life in America.

"Well, that ain't the way it is, you know. I want to make movies that aren't going to bore people. I don't want to bludgeon people over the head with some political message; there are other groups that do that. But I want to make movies that just tell the truth, hopefully in a way that's funny."

An honest, funny revolutionary movie.

She raced on, following a nonexistent script that might fit.

"When I drove across the country a while ago, I was astounded at the number of people who live in trailer camps, in mobile homes. It's a whole culture that's sprung up that people don't talk about. People spend their lives putting down payments on these mobile homes, and they can't afford the tires to make them mobile. They don't move. I would love to do a comedy, a black comedy, about that."

There are other, more serious areas in which Jane Fonda would like to make a new film.

"I would love to make a movie about Los Angeles, the part of Los Angeles that nobody ever talks about, which is East Los Angeles, the barrio. Nobody ever hears about that. A third of the population of Los Angeles are brown people—Chicano and Chicana people who are living in terrible conditions. Nobody ever talks about the Asian people in this country. All of those kind of things."

Perhaps a film that only exposes a simple element of how Jane feels the mass media in general have "brainwashed" America.

"You always see, for example, couples in the movies where the man is older than the woman," she says. "It's not like that in real life all the time, but it's like that in the movies. Sometime, without saying anything about it, I would like to take a situation in a movie in which I'm married and have me be ten years older than my husband—without saying anything about it. It would help a lot of women who find it hard in this society to be married to much younger men without making a big shtick about it. Or, another example, women who are friends. You never have movies where women are friends; you always have women in relation to men, either they're going after a man, or they've been rejected by a man, or they're having trouble with a man or whatever. And there's usually one woman in the movie who's really groovy and the other women are kind of uglier, according to the standards of society. Women should be shown in relation to each other as friends. That, I think, would be very important to do. I mean, there's so much to do."

I wonder if that isn't the real revolution— people who are trying to be honest in whatever they're doing, trying to overcome the corruption. Does it require an alternative film group?

"The problem is the writers. It's finding the people who know how to write movies like that and can write them so they will be popular, not boring, not proselytizing. I'm no different than anybody else; if I went into a movie theater and I saw a message coming from me a mile away, I'd get up and run."

That's got to be a hard problem for an actress to deal with. You ask a lot.

"I'm not complaining."

But it gets complicated. You are an actress and you want to act. You still could act in things that are not valid, right?

"It's not very complicated. It's just that I've run out of money, and I have to go to work now so I just have to find something that I won't be ashamed to do, and in the meantime, try to find the right scripts, the right people, the right movie. It's a matter of all of us who feel that way getting together and pooling our talents and resources. It will take time."

Spike Lee:
Do the Right Thing

By David Handelman

JULY 13, 1989

"I don't need this shit!" says *USA Today* gossip columnist Jeannie Williams. She has just seen the May 19 breakfast press screening of *Do the Right Thing* at the Cannes Film Festival, where it is competing for the coveted Palm d'Or prize. The press-conference room is abuzz with a few hundred international journalists and photographers waiting for the arrival of the film's director, Spike Lee.

"I live in New York," Williams says, her eyes flashing. "I don't need this movie in New York this summer. I don't know what they're thinking!" The ghetto in the movie is "too clean," Williams complains to a colleague, its inhabitants are "too nice," and there's too much violence.

Williams' diatribe is interrupted by Roger Ebert, the *Chicago Sun-Times* critic and TV personality, who sweeps into the room and declares, "It's a great film, a great film. If this doesn't win the grand prize, I'm not coming back next year." (In the back of the room is Tom Pollock, the head of Universal Pictures, which is releasing *Do the Right Thing* on June 30; Pollock later says Ebert's threat may hurt the film's chances of winning.)

Williams, who clearly values Ebert's upward thumb, is horrified. "How can you say that? What's going to happen when they *release* this?"

Ebert smiles and says, "How long has it been since you saw a film you thought would cause people to do *anything?*"

Without even entering the room, Lee has rocked it. *Do the Right Thing* portrays a block in Brooklyn's predominantly black Bedford-Stuyvesant neighborhood during the hottest day of the summer. The day starts peacefully and ends in a racial brawl, the murder of a black youth by a white cop and an ensuing riot. Lee's impressive, upsetting movie is inspired by—and pointedly dedicated to—black victims of white violence in New York City, like Eleanor Bumpurs, an elderly woman who was killed by police after she wielded a knife; Michael Griffith, who was chased onto a highway by white youths in Howard Beach, Queens, and killed by a car; and graffiti artist Michael Stewart, who was killed while in police custody. As complex and insistent as its title, the film is designed to spark controversy from its opening song—Public Enemy's discordant, militant rap "Fight the Power"—to the quotes that scroll before its end credits: Martin Luther King Jr. decrying violence, then Malcolm X claiming that violence used in self-defense is "intelligence."

When the wiry, poker-faced Lee, thirty-two, enters the press-conference room, he is wearing a T-shirt that says MALCOLM X: NO SELLOUT. He sits at a table with cast members and announces that today would have been Malcolm X's sixty-fourth birthday.

This leads a journalist to ask Lee about the movie's two end quotes. "The quotes complete the thread of Malcolm and Martin that has been woven throughout the film," Lee says patiently. "In certain times, both philosophies can be appropriate, but in this day and age, the year of our Lord 1989, I'm leaning more toward the philosophies of Malcolm X. . . . Nonviolence and all that stuff had its time, and there are times when it's still appropriate, but when you're being hit upside the head with a brick, I don't think young black America is just going to turn the other cheek and say, 'Thank you, Jesus.' "

Someone asks why drugs are never mentioned in the film. "This film is not about drugs," says Lee. "It's about people and racism. Drugs are at every level of society today in America. How many of you went and saw *Working Girl* or *Rain Man* and asked, 'Where are the drugs?' Nobody. But the minute we have a black film that takes place in the ghetto, people want to know where the drugs are . . . because that's the way you think of black people. I mean, let's be honest."

Another journalist says, "It's my sense that it's all going to come down this summer [in New York]. A lot of people are going to get hurt. . . . What is your impression?"

Lee smiles and says, "I see Mr. Pollock getting fidgety back there. . . . If anything happens, it'll be because the cops killed somebody else with no reason, but it won't be because of *Do the Right Thing*."

"This film," another journalist says, "takes a very despairing view of the possibility of an amicable relationship between the races."

"I think there's some hope at the end, a shaky truce," says Lee. "But on the other hand, I think it'd be very dishonest to have a kind of Steven Spielberg ending where we all hold hands and sing 'We Are the World.' "

In many ways, the same could be said about Spike Lee's relationship with Hollywood.

The question that really gets Spike Lee going is "What do you think of *Mississippi Burning?*" The Academy Award–nominated film—which recast the civil-rights movement as the triumph of a white FBI agent—came up during many of the constant interviews at Cannes, being one of the few recent Hollywood films that is even about blacks, and it symbolizes everything Lee thinks is wrong with Hollywood today. Like *Cry Freedom* and *The Cotton Club,* Lee says and says again, *Mississippi Burning* distorted history, exploiting blacks to turn whites into heroes. "*Hated* it," Lee says. "They should have had the guts to have at least one central black character."

Lee speaks in measured tones, every now and then unleashing a wild "Ha!" or a quieter "Ch-ch-ch-ch" laugh. But he mostly goes about the tedious business of answering for his movies with a deadly seriousness. Lee calls his production company Forty Acres and a Mule Filmworks (after the never-realized proposal following the Civil War to give land and a mule to each freed slave); he's published a book about the making of each of his films. In the one about *Do the Right Thing*, he writes: "I've been blessed with the opportunity to express the views of black people who otherwise don't have access to power and the media. I have to take advantage of this while I'm still bankable."

Spike Lee sees himself as a man with a mission: to shake down the creeping resurgence of racism in post-Reagan America, to inform, entertain and motivate—all the while operating in an industry entirely controlled by whites. It is a tall order for a man who stands five feet six in Air Jordans.

His path to Hollywood, Lee says, has been pitted with racist potholes. After growing up in various racially mixed Brooklyn neighborhoods and graduating from all-black Morehouse College in 1979, he went to New York University's film school and found himself in a "hostile situation."

"I had to prove whether I belonged," Lee says, "or was just another quota." When NYU professors criticized his first student film, *The Answer*, he attributed it to "cultural arrogance," because his film took D.W. Griffith's classic *The Birth of a Nation* to task for its condescending portrayal of blacks.

Lee's 1982 senior class thesis, *Joe's Bed-Stuy Barbershop: We Cut Heads*, was shot by Ernest Dickerson, the only other black to complete NYU's three-year program while Lee was there. (Dickerson has gone on to shoot all of Lee's films.) The movie won the student Academy Award. Two years later, Lee got a grant to start filming a script called *Messenger*, but the Screen Actors Guild refused to grant him a low-budget waiver of its union wages, Lee says, on the grounds that his script was "too commercial." According to Lee, white directors with larger budgets are regularly granted the waiver. "It was a definite case of racism," he says.

Lee quickly wrote the serious and saucy comedy *She's Gotta Have It*, which takes place mostly in a woman's bed, and filmed it for $175,000 in the summer of 1985. (His hilarious performance as bike messenger Mars Blackmon stole the film.) In order to keep *She's Gotta Have It* from getting an X rating, he had to shorten one of the film's sex scenes; he insists that white sex scenes in films like the R-rated *9 1/2 Weeks* were much more deserving of an X rating than what he had to cut.

She's Gotta Have It won the Prix de la Jeunesse at Cannes in 1986 for Best New Director, was released by Island Pictures and earned $8 million. This enabled Lee to get Columbia to finance his second feature, *School Daze*, a $6-million musical about activism and intraracial divisions at a black college. *School Daze* also did well at the box office, grossing $18 million despite no advertising support. It was ambitious, if problematic—suffering from overlong dance numbers, wandering plot lines and an insider tone. Lee didn't take the criticism well, particularly the pan from *New York Times* critic Janet Maslin, who questioned Lee's technical abilities. Believing her comments "dangerous, like the same Al Campanis shit that black people don't have the capabilities to be baseball managers," Lee wrote a petulant letter to the *Times*, demanding that Maslin never review his films again and ending with the line "I bet she can't even dance, does she have rhythm?"

Is this reaction racist? "I don't think blacks can be racist," Lee says. "Racism is where you put laws into effect, structures that affect you socially. What can black people do to harm Jewish people as a people? Set up laws in Congress, stop them from voting? That's what racism is.

"We still have people in America who say that racism ended when Lyndon Johnson signed the Civil Rights Act and black people were allowed to vote," he continues. "And because Michael Jackson's the number one rock star, Eddie Murphy's the biggest box-office draw in the world, Bill Cosby is the number one TV star, Mike Tyson is the world heavyweight champion, Michael Jordan is the greatest basketball player in the world, that black people have arrived, and everything is all right. But the black underclass in America now is larger than it's ever been. So you can't be lulled to sleep just because Eddie Murphy's huge."

In fact, Lee has been an outspoken critic of celebrities like Murphy and Whoopi Goldberg, who he feels have not asserted their black identities and have not flexed their money muscle to get blacks hired.

According to the *Los Angeles Times,* while 12 percent of Americans are black and blacks make up 25 percent of the moviegoing audience, minority membership in the Writers Guild is a paltry 1.6 percent. Furthermore, there are no black film executives with the power to approve a movie, and although Lee has helped open the door for black directors like Robert Townsend and Keenen Ivory Wayans, blacks directed fewer than 1 percent of Hollywood's releases last year.

Against these odds, Lee has gotten his movies made, adopting Malcolm X's credo "By any means necessary." He works without an agent, a manager, a publicist or membership in the Writers and Directors Guilds, supervising every aspect of his films down to the logos, soundtracks and videos. He's scraped around for studio "pickup deal" financing that guarantees him the final cut. Both onscreen and off, he has tried to employ as many blacks as possible, founding a minority-student scholarship at the NYU film school and a film-training program at Long Island University. He has also been able to make some pocket money from being an ad clotheshorse for both the Gap and Barneys and from directing Nike commercials starring Michael Jordan.

But the necessary means were hard to come by for *Do the Right Thing,* even though its final budget was $6.5 million, one-third that of the average Hollywood film. The first studio Lee approached, Paramount, balked at the ending,

and Disney also passed. When Universal approved the script, the executives there hadn't yet experienced the uproar over the studio's release of Martin Scorsese's *Last Temptation of Christ.* And when Lee's finished film seemed harsher than the script, there were nervous murmurs that it could be a second coming of *Christ.*

Lee hopes the controversy doesn't dampen the receipts, because his license seems shortterm. "Hollywood will overlook subject matter in my case," he says, "because my films [so far] make money. Universal did not make this movie because they're in love with me."

D*o the Right Thing* was stirring things up even before it got to film. Lee showed up at its first cast read-through with T-shirts emblazoned with the film's title and flags of Africa, America, Italy and Puerto Rico, and he distributed them to the cast he had assembled from wildly varied backgrounds. Yale School of Drama graduate John Turturro mumbled his scripted slurs, thinking, "God, what have I got myself into?"

The turning point in the movie is a fight between pizzeria owner Sal (Danny Aiello) and a neighborhood agitator named Buggin' Out (Giancarlo Esposito). And while the scene was being shot, the improvisation that Lee encourages on his sets tapped something deep. Esposito's real-life mother is black and his father is Italian; off-camera, he had gotten chummy with Aiello, and the two talked in Italian. But when the cameras rolled, Aiello, ad-libbing, suddenly called Buggin' Out "nigger," and Esposito went wild, flinging back epithets like "guinea bastard."

"When Danny said, 'Nigger,' I freaked," says Esposito. It finally came up for him. I knew that at some point in his life, he'd called somebody a nigger, and I went crazy because he was someone I liked. Danny was upset with himself, I was really upset with myself, and Spike was gleaming, because he'd gotten the scene."

"**C**an I get a dessert?" Spike Lee asks the Carlton waiter.

"Non," the waiter replies, "only drinks on ze terrace."

Lee, a near teetotaler, disappears a few seconds later, then returns in his slightly pigeon-toed, speedy gait, carrying a fruit-and-cream confection. "That guy didn't know what he was talking about," he says, and digs in.

Asked to name his influences, Lee says, "I would say my parents more than any filmmaker." Bill, a jazz musician who has scored all of Spike's films, and Jacquelyn, a teacher (she died in 1977), took Spike and his four younger siblings to dance and jazz performances and Broadway shows. "I think that's what everything's about, exposure."

The first films Lee recalls going to are *Bye Bye Birdie* at Radio City Music Hall and a double feature of *Dr. No* and *A Hard Day's Night*. But his favorites are searing cinema verité like *Pixote* and *Mean Streets* and fantasies like *The Wizard of Oz* and *West Side Story*.

As a kid, Shelton Jackson Lee (his mother nicknamed him Spike as a baby) was more of a sports fan, fighting to watch Knicks games on TV when his sister wanted to watch *The Brady Bunch*. Today, his main reading is the daily sports pages; he has Knicks season tickets, he says, "but not as good as Woody Allen's."

At Morehouse, Lee got involved with writing, directing and producing the gown-and-float homecoming coronation, a spectacle on the order of an MGM musical, which served as the inspiration for *School Daze*. He began to dabble in eight-millimeter movies, and after graduating in 1979 he went to NYU film school. "I went knowing that I wasn't going to learn anything

from the faculty," he says. "I just wanted the equipment to make films, because I knew that's how I'd become a filmmaker."

When rookie Spike Lee was in Cannes in 1986 touting *She's Gotta Have It,* he was one of eight people sharing a cramped apartment. This year, his photo is up on a billboard on the palm-tree-lined main drag and he has a two-room suite at the Carlton.

Spike Lee walks around the hotel in sneakers, athletic socks, a T-shirt, stone-washed jeans, a leather-thong Public Enemy medallion, a baseball cap and a Knicks windbreaker. He spends much of his time giving interviews, which often puts him in the dicey position of being the spokesman for Black America. He is quick to remind reporters that the movie applies not just to New York or America but to racism everywhere.

Certain questions pop up in nearly every interview:

What's "the right thing"?

"I don't know. I know what the wrong thing is: racism."

What can be done about racism?

"People cannot expect me to have answers. That is not my goal or agenda. What I have to do as a filmmaker is present the problem so that discussion can start. If America was thinking about racism, *Do the Right Thing* wouldn't be the first film about it."

Lee has few illusions about the impact of his movies. "The only time I've seen a film take real effect was *The Thin Blue Line*—that got a guy out of jail. Something like that only happens once in a blue moon. I don't think I'm gonna be able to walk through Bensonhurst or Howard Beach because of *Do the Right Thing*: 'Let's not crack him on the head with a bat because we saw his movie and we're all brothers and sisters.'"

When the Cannes Film Festival awards were announced, the Palm d'Or went to *sex, lies and videotape*. Many films wons prizes, but *Do the Right Thing* was shut out. "We got robbed," Lee says back in Brooklyn. "I guess they really wanted to stick the knife. [Cannes jury president and film director] Wim Wenders was quoted as saying, '*Sex, lies and videotape* shows there's a future for cinema,' so I guess we're not the future."

That same week, an unemployed construction worker named Richard Luke, twenty-five and black, died in a New York City jail after a struggle with city-housing police. The Reverend Al Sharpton held another demonstration. The medical examiner ruled the death was drug related. A grand jury said it would investigate.

And the summer hadn't even begun.

Jack Nicholson:
Quotations from Chairman Jack

Jack Nicholson doesn't have a lot of competition as *the* modern movie star for America's everyman, a man who does his work spectacularly well largely without indulging in the pomposities and fits of temperament associated with other great movie actors. Often seen as a hard-partying, no-bullshit street guy from Jersey, he nonetheless maintains the seigniorial distance we expect of pop royalty. When the paparazzi catch him, he shrugs it off and lets the flashbulbs glint off his shades, telling us what he wants to with the set of his notoriously expressive mouth.

As the writer Derek Sylvester described him, Nicholson, "unlike the rising young stars who followed him . . . bestrode two distinct generations of acting styles. He possessed the pugnacity of a Cagney, the virility of a Garfield, the diabolic charm of a Gable. He could be as suavely droll as Cary Grant, as gee-shucks and gangling as James Stewart, as moody and introspective as Paul Muni . . . in other words, the most *indispensable* actor of modern American cinema."

He is also heir to the alienated brooding of Brando and James Dean, but having incorporated their inarticulate (if brilliant) posturing in his craft, he has gone on to stand up onscreen in service of the great *line,* from "You know, this used to be a hell of a good country," in *Easy Rider,* to "Heeeeere's Johnny!"—a marrow-chilling and hilarious ad-lib—in *The Shining.* In between, there's been plenty of time for other unforgettable outbursts, like his rebuke to the waitress with the problematic chicken salad in *Five Easy Pieces* ("Yeah, I want you to hold it between your knees"), or his abrupt attack on a nasty bartender in *The Last Detail* ("I *am* the motherfucking shore patrol, motherfucker!").

His Oscars for Best Actor in *One Flew Over the Cuckoo's Nest* and Best Supporting Actor in *Terms of Endearment* as well as his six other nominations are official Hollywood's tributes to a maverick who has never pandered to it. *Mars Attacks,* from director Tim Burton, is the latest in Jack's rogue's gallery. In excerpts from the following interviews, conducted over two decades, a remarkable portrait emerges.

Q&A Excerpts from Alan Rinzler

APRIL 29, 1971

Jack Nicholson talks with a kind of pan-American drawl, an all-purpose transconti-

35

nental drawl, a no-shit professional drawl—on occasion sounding not unlike Norman Mailer. Which isn't so surprising since Mailer hails from Asbury Park in New Jersey, and Jack grew up in nearby Manasquan. Jack remembers the fight-song routines, the DA haircuts, Brando and Jimmy Dean. Jack always was smart-ass.

"I left New Jersey in 1954. Seventeen years old. Just took off for California, no particular reason, and got a job in the MGM cartoon department. I guess I wanted to see how films were made and get close to some real movie stars."

Seventeen years later, and he's won an Oscar nomination and the New York Film Critics Award as best supporting actor for That Performance in *Easy Rider*. This year, it's *Five Easy Pieces*. How about that, stargazers. Old smart-ass Jack Nicholson from Manasquan.

Jack's not only arrived, as they shout in the trades, but he's hotter than a Saturday-night special fired seven times in a row. Everybody flashes on his name these days, but how many people caught the early horror films and bike extravaganzas he did with Richard Rush back at American International? The Westerns with Monte Hellman? The corny dogs he cranked out with Roger Corman? How many people have seen him in *Hells Angels on Wheels* or *Back Door to Hell*, *Flight to Fury*, *The Terror* or *Psych-Out*.

"I always played psychos or the boy-next-door, you know. There were a lot of juvenile-delinquent pictures in those days. I was usually some crumby, cruddy person."

Nicholson can look pretty mean, he's reminded. "Yeah, I know it. But none of it's true. Or maybe somewhere back in there, it's maybe all true." Violent, too? "Violent, I'm not. Totally nonviolent. I think it'd be great if everybody thought I was violent and bad and all that, but I'm not. I'd *love* to say I was, though. Or

I'd love to be able to say I've balled everybody, indulged in every kind of shit in existence, gone everywhere, although I haven't. I wish all that could be a real part of my number."

Jack does numbers. Most actors do numbers. One spring night in 1969, *Easy Rider* had just opened after weeks of special screenings that established it as an instant hip-fetish event, and he's ambling around a posh East Side penthouse with a Columbia Pictures limo idling in the street below. Doing a number, as usual.

"Well, I love making movies in the country. Every scene I was in was shot either in Taos or on the road between Taos, northern Texas and Louisiana. It's too bad you can't see what that place where we filmed the smoking scene actually looked like. We shot it stoned one night in this fantastic swamp. Listen, it's the luckiest thing that's ever happened to me, and a good film, no question about it. But maybe its greatest impact has been on the business itself—the whole idea of spending on films, the kinds of things to make for this particular audience they've been trying to define. It's been a kind of explosion, a little revolution. Almost any sort of revolution is ephemeral, but there are an awful lot more job opportunities for a lot more people that I personally know."

After all the *Easy Rider* flak died (mercifully) down, Jack went back to work on a new film with some old friends called *Five Easy Pieces*. Carole Eastman wrote the script, and rumor has it she did so specifically with Jack in mind.

"Yeah, Carole and I've known each other for thirteen, fourteen years," he says. "A lot of pieces are taken from scenes she's seen or heard me go through. Working on many, many levels at once, the picture's very critical of the traditional family structure. I have a lot of antifamily feelings. I think a lot of the things that people are fucked up about at this moment can be traced back to family structures. I don't want to be the person who blows up families as a way of living in the world, but it's one message that I've thought of letting out of the bag once in a while just to stir people up."

Tim Cahill
APRIL 16, 1981

It seems to me that you are passionate about five things: art, movies, basketball, skiing and books. Is there some connection, a common denominator among them?

There's a poetry in all those things. When I look at a painting, I get involved. There is a moment of truth somewhere. And basketball: When you miss a play, it's a matter of microseconds. Like moments of truth. A game of the immediate. Skiing is like that: It's all little moments of truth and extending the limits of control.

I was talking to Michelangelo Antonioni, and he had just done *Red Desert,* which is about technology encroaching on man. Antonioni was firmly on the side of nature, of a more natural existence. And every day while he was doing the film, he drove to work along the Adriatic. On one side were the mountains: unspoiled, beautiful. The other side was encrusted with factories, all rust and corrosion. Antonioni said that he couldn't help it, he found himself looking at the factories rather than the mountains. Because that is where man was. Maybe that's how all those things tie together: They are the efforts of human beings to step out into the ether.

It's as if you've decided on doing the Seven Dwarfs of perversity. You were Dopey in "The Fortune," Sleazy in "Goin' South" and Crazy in "The Shining."

Well, I wanted a long career. I've played against the traditional standard of beauty. I designed my career to be in the European model. Europeans tend to look more at an actor's body of work, and there will be peaks and valleys in that. Americans view art as an ever upward process. The next thing you do always has to be bigger and better. With a body of work behind you—good work—you can afford to take on a project that entertains you, one that challenges you, but which may not be bigger and better in the American sense.

Nancy Collins
MARCH 20, 1984

You genuinely like women, don't you?

Yeah, I genuinely do. I prefer the company of women, and I have deep respect for them. I'm buzzed by the female mystique. I always tell young men there are three rules: They hate us, we hate them; they're stronger, they're smarter; and, most important, they don't play fair.

What attracts you to a woman? You once said you like women who are alluring but unobtainable.

It's not categorizable. The heaviest prejudice to deal with is the beautiful woman. I'd like to say, "No, it doesn't matter whether somebody's beautiful or not," but whatever I find beautiful is what I'm attracted to. As for the other, I'd like to have all the women I'm attracted to *still* with me. I don't want them unattainable. I don't even want them unavailable!

You once said about acting, "You have to determine, what is your sexuality in this scene? Everything else comes from that." The sexual part of acting is very important to you, isn't it?

It's the key. The total key. Actually, sex is my favorite subject. But it's scary for me to talk about because of Anjelica. It's like she says: "How would you feel if I were sitting down with some interviewer, telling him all I felt about sex and fucking. You know you'd flip out." And a certain part of me says, "You're absolutely right, I would." But that's the dichotomy. I yearn for honesty in life. As an artist, I yearn for the clear moment. I would tell anybody any living thing about me, and there's a lot of stuff that ain't great.

Given your sexual theory of acting, what did "Postman" mean to you?

I did *Postman* because I hadn't come down the middle with the fastball about sex in a movie. The whole reason for that movie is sex, and that's why I wanted to do it. See, Americans don't like sexual movies, they like sexy movies. If you actually start feeling warm in your groin in a movie, it becomes like a dream . . . a little too real.

The obligatory scene in *Postman* happens when the two kill her husband and she gets so hot she has to fuck right then. Now, that's those two people, not everyone. But the fact that no one who'd ever made that material had ever even attempted to do that scene was amazing, because that's what James Cain's entire book is about.

I kept saying, "Don't try to make me be the boy next door in this movie." This guy has solved every problem in his life with violence, which is why I was heavy in the movie—not as heavy as I am now, but I didn't go for the Henry Fonda gaunt look, like every other Depression picture, because a guy who's solved every problem in his life with violence doesn't go hungry.

But then, what is erotic acting, anyway? For instance, I like the idea there is not a speck of nudity in *Postman*—another stylistic thing we

did. I also liked the idea of an obvious, fresher image. There was a shot I wanted to do when he first makes love to her, when he backs her off the chopping block—a reverse angle with my clothes on, but I wanted to have a full stinger, because they'd never seen that in movies. I just knew this odd image would be a stunner. Well, I went upstairs and worked on it for forty-five minutes, but I couldn't get anything going because I knew everyone was waiting down there to see this thing. Somebody else might have said I was a pervert, but in my terms, this would've been extremely artful. Do you get turned on doing a scene like that? I don't go through many hours of the day that I *don't* get turned on, although it doesn't mean I'm going to wind up in some sexual expression of it. I particularly make a point not to be actual with actresses with whom I work.

You realize you have a reputation as a man who indulges in a slew of drugs. Is that true?

A slew of drugs? No. And never have. Do I relate to drugs? Yes, I do. But, for instance, though I've said—forever—that I smoke marijuana, I've never told anyone that I actually do cocaine. I've never said that to anyone.

Then why do you think people believe you do cocaine?

I think it's the normal assumption to make, particularly about someone who's been candid about his privacy. I can only blame myself. I'm not so sure I should've been this candid. I thought it was a very good thing to do because, first of all, I'm for legalization, and because I know what the costs are. The costs are lying."

How would you describe your drug use?

Convivial.

What does that mean?

It means I have a good time. I don't drink, although the last couple years, I've started to drink a little alcohol—a glass of wine, maybe two brandies at night after coffee.

Do you still smoke marijuana?

Why talk about it? I'm not helping anybody. I've no desire to conceal what I do, but I've tried not concealing it, and it has the opposite effect. People love to have a reason to level you. They don't have to deal with me as directly because they have this disqualifying clause in their perception of me. It's hard for me to think I live in a world where it's not good for you to be candid about something that, in your heart, there's nothing wrong with.

Would you be willing to say you don't use cocaine?

Would I say? I really have decided I have nothing further to say about this that's of any use to me or anyone else.

Some people seem to be more worried about your health than your morals, in terms of your alleged drug use.

Doctor, cure yourself. I feel that most of the time I know what I'm doing. I missed no acting classes during the twelve years I was in class, and I haven't missed a day's work from illness in thirty years. I'll put my medical charts, my sanity charts, up against anybody's. I'm not doing anything wrong. I'm not doing anything but trying to do everything right. I know what's true, who I am. I would like to say I don't care what people think, but I do. Everyone who knows me may think I'm . . . a tad boyishly fun-loving, but I don't think anybody thinks I have any negative momentum, corrupting philosophies or overly radical moral opinions. As a workman, I'm known as a model of professionalism. I have to put up with being falsely described because it's unhip to bridle at it. Besides, it's just like womanizing. I'm not so sure it ain't good for business.

You were close with Roman Polanski, whose new autobiography mentions you and details his arrest for allegedly raping a thirteen-year-old girl at your home in Los Angeles. He, of course, fled the country before his trial. Do you think he'll ever return?

It's hard to say. Roman's been the recipient of Western justice—that is, "Here's a very complicated moral issue, so, we heat you up until you get out of town," which he did. Having been the object of that and being strongly self-sufficient, I imagine Roman's point of view is, "Hey, I left. My life didn't miss a stroke. I'm not an American. I'm living in Paris, the culture capital of Europe. I've won the acting prize; my book is out; I directed a movie. I haven't missed a day's work. I don't need America." The tragedy is that I was watching Roman fall in love with America after some difficult times here. His situation is a very interesting case of what notoriety can do to you. I always felt Roman was exiled because his wife had the bad taste to be murdered in the papers.

When the police searched your house for evidence against Roman, they wound up arresting Anjelica after finding some cocaine in her purse. [It was reported at the time that the cocaine charges against Anjelica Huston would be dropped in exchange for her testimony against Roman Polanski. The charges eventually were dropped.] What really happened?

I was in Aspen. And when I heard about [Polanski's arrest], I was told, "Don't talk about it. Don't find out anything, don't become involved, since you aren't at all." And since I never knew what might happen as a result of its being at my residence, I was advised to not communicate for the good of all concerned. So I know very little about it. Anjelica was actually moving out of my house at that moment.

You were splitting up?

Yeah. And to this day, I don't really know much about this particular thing because I'm that way.

Surely you talked to Anjelica about it?

I spoke with her about it. She's been very wronged. The district attorney sent Anjelica a letter saying they'd been unethical, because in reality, Anjelica could not say anything because she simply didn't know that much about it. But it was implied in the papers that she had said something and was building a case. She reacted strongly to being mislabeled, and the DA's office wrote her a letter of apology.

Jack Nicholson and Warren Beatty. What attracts you to him as a friend?

He's very smart, very free of bullshit and emotionally undemanding. We also rarely like the same girls, which is one of the reasons we get along.

Really? You both, at different times—you first, and he second—lived with Michelle Phillips. And rumor has it that during the filming of "Reds," you developed, shall we say, a mighty crush on Diane Keaton.

Michelle and Warren's relationship had nothing to do with me. I was going with Anjelica Huston when they got together. It's just an attractive story for the press. Warren's high-school-principal parents would've been proud of the way it was handled. Michelle, being the lady she is, took the trouble to call and ask if I had any feelings about them, which I did: I thought it was fabulous, because I like them both very much. Michelle's a real stand-up woman. You can't *get* her to do a dishonorable thing. And . . . can she move it!

As for Miss Keaton, I don't want to hide behind this, but during the production [of *Reds*], that's the way it began to feel. . . . Nothing happened as a result, but there is something actor-ish about thinking, "My God, I've got a real crush and, holy fuck, this is my best friend and his girlfriend." But that's also what the movie was about—my character was attracted to Keaton's character. And I'm focused on my job all the time. In fact, during the work, I would allow myself to get overinflamed about it with Warren right there—just to see what would happen. Absolutely nothing happened between Diane and me. I'm not an asshole.

I've changed a lot. If you told me twenty years ago that some woman could go off and fuck one of my best friends [Huston briefly left Nicholson for Ryan O'Neal], and I'd end up reading about it in the newspapers, and that four years later I wouldn't even give a shit, I'd say, "You're talking to the wrong guy here. That's not the way I am. I might want to be that guy, but I'm not." [*Claps hands*] Now, I am.

Are you a self-confident man? What things don't you like about yourself?

I don't like it if I'm not creatively free-flowing—it worries me and I wonder, is this the end? Is the well empty now? I worry about the lack of self-confidence of someone who, at times, has to get himself up or hype himself. I wonder why I think I have to do it. Sometimes I'm not able to take in the positive communication that's directed at me because I'm not sure I deserve it. The difference now is, I let all these symptoms of lack of self-confidence just be. I don't let them define me. In other words, I'm more comfortable with my lack of self-confidence, so, in a way, it's more self-confidence.

Were you always sure of your talent?

I was at times surer than I am now. After *Reds*, I took two years off because I had worked every day for three years prior to that. Even the president of the United States doesn't do that. And I mean really took off. I didn't even talk about movies for a couple of years. Those two years proved to me that I don't have to act. I'm now confident that I'm not an applause junkie. But then, I've been on bonus time since I was twenty-eight. I had a great life for anybody who ever lived up until then, so past that, it's been a *big* bonus.

Fred Schruers

AUGUST 14, 1986

*D*on't you see your job as simply making quality movies about people's real emotional lives?

I still make movies I want to make. I'm just talking about—where's the soil for them? Where's the informed intelligence? I'm doing fine. I have respect for myself and my collaborators, like Mike [Nichols] and Meryl [Streep]. You know, you don't want to see this as so huge that you begin to dysfunction. But I have to whip up a foam in my spirit, or I'll just stop seeing where it's at, too.

Social graces don't come—they're not innate. You learn them, develop them. Once you're past the high-school prom, what you do on your own is what gives your life quality. *You* have to learn how to dance. *You* have to learn how to read a book. *You* have to learn how to appreciate music, to enrich your mind in order to have a conversation.

To reiterate your situation so we've got things straight: You never met your natural father. Your real mother—June—was the woman you believed to be your sister. The woman you call Mrs. Nicholson—Ethel May, whom you called Mud—was in fact your grandmother, and her husband, presented as your father, was this hard-drinking guy who was never around. The third woman in the triumvirate that raised you was June's sister, Lorraine. Plenty of company, but no real father. . . .

Well, I had Shorty. I had Smith around. He was married to Lorraine. That, believe me, is as good a father as anybody's ever going to get or need. I can be as hard on my family or friends as anybody—I'm fairly objective—but there's nobody much that's impressed me as much as Shorty. Simple guy, but many is the poem I've

written in my mind to the higher feelings he promoted in me—which he would have no ability whatsoever to articulate.

Now, Shorty's not what a civics class would pick out as a role model. He was a featherbedded railroad brakeman, you know, who went to gin mills and drank and sat around all day with his shirt off and bullshitted. Everybody did love Shorty. He was the first all-state football player from the region, and he stayed right there in Neptune. He wasn't a hidden man. It's not sentiment, this guy was advanced. Shorty just had a grasp—innate, not a conscious ability—about life. I hope I've got it.

Your natural father was someone you never met and didn't even know about till around 1975.

Both grandmother and mother were deceased before this particular group of facts came to my attention. I was very impressed by their ability to keep the secret, if nothing else. It's done great things for me. I mean, I don't have to question the abortion issue in my mind. It's an open-and-shut case where I'm concerned. As an illegitimate child born in 1937, during the Depression, to a broken lower-middle-class family, you are a candidate for—you're an automatic abortion with most people today. So it's very easy for me. I don't have to get into the debate of when does the thing come alive. And I'm very pleased to be out of it, 'cause it's not an easy issue.

They sound like a formidable group of women.

These were strong women—made their own way in a period of time when it just wasn't done that much. They did it without connections.

My basic model for women is an independent woman. There was no grandeur in that for me, because it was that way from the beginning. You know, here was Mud, and she carried everybody on her back like a tiny little elephant, and it didn't seem to faze her. She marched right through it.

They all had a great lot of style, and a lot of fun. The neighborhood idolized all of them.

You could talk out problems with them?

Had to, got to. They want to know. I'd get kept in sometimes, but . . . very Irish, very rational, nothing's-gonna-blow-anybody-out kind of environment to grow up in.

Once you moved on to Neptune City, what was the scene like there?

I started high school in 1950. Cool was invented in this period. Rock & roll did not start with Elvis Presley. In fact, to that age group, Elvis Presley was a secondary figure to Ray Charles. And, you know, Johnnie Ray. This is when all that stuff really got rolling. It wasn't as explosively widespread, but this is the seminal period of it. And peer group was everything. There was not a lot of visible rebellion, aside from the DA haircut and stuff. . . . We did everything—my friends, we'd go to New York on weekends, get drunk, see ball games, bang around . . . school was out, we just went to the beach all summer. And had fun, got drunk every night. It was the age of the put-on. Cool was everything. Collars were up, eyelids were drooped. You never let on what bothered you.

How did you dress?

I used to like to go to school in a pair of navy-blue cuffed pegged pants, a black or navy-blue turtleneck sweater, maybe a gray coat over it and a black porkpie hat that I'd gotten from the freeway in a motor accident that involved a priest. So it had a lot of juju on it. I wore it flat out like a rimmer. That was one way.

Now, when we had the dances and everything, you just got the greatest suit you could get ahold of. Always pegged, pleats, blue suedes, thinnest tie, shoulders, one button in front.

Anything like Jake Gittes in "Chinatown"?

Well, Jake Gittes' getup . . . my grandfather-father [Ethel May's wayward spouse], before he had his problems in life, used to win the Asbury Park Easter Parade a lot, as one of the best-dressed men. So he was a blade, and Gittes' style, which is the thirties, rather more than the forties or fifties, is sort of after that man, who was very natty. You know, the hair combed. I've used him a lot actually—for a man I didn't see much. The glasses in *Easy Rider* were his glasses.

I got in *Easy Rider* because I had done all these other nonunion or underground movies. I knew the movie was going to be huge. It was a progression in the genre, like *Stagecoach* was to the Western—kicked it up one more notch.

That's putting it quite humbly; people at the time thought it defined the cold war between "straight" and "counter" culture.

Yes, my character was a bridging character.

For most of your career there's been a dichotomy—your name is one of the synonyms for "box office," but you're seen as a maverick who seeks out offbeat films.

I always have to find a valid ethical reason for doing what I do. It's best if you agree totally with the ethical principles of a piece, but sometimes you're simply editorializing on where the ethics of it could lie. I mean, I played *The Postman Always Rings Twice*, let's say in a much less romantically attractive way than it had ever been done before. I mean, this *is* a murder. That's why in the first scene, I steal cigarettes from the guy who's giving me a free meal, without even thinking about it.

Lynn Hirschberg

DECEMBER 10, 1987

*P*eople lately are very nostalgic for the sixties. *Do you feel that way?*

No. I don't feel like it's the past. It doesn't

seem a distance removed or a big change. We're only one time up and down with hair in twenty years. And that's about the depth of it. I always feel public perceptions are a little distorted anyway. I didn't like the nostalgia that they had in the sixties for the thirties and forties. I'm not a nostalgic kind of person, although I'm very sentimental.

So there's nothing you're nostalgic about?

I'm nostalgic for my former weight.

You must see some differences between the sixties and the eighties. Do you think the issues have changed significantly in the last twenty years?

I think the biggest thing in terms of youth culture is AIDS. I think AIDS is a real issue. I think the Persian Gulf versus solar electricity and the environment is a *real* issue. I think lying to yourself about substance control and creating a criminal class that corrupts the legal system is a *real* issue.

Whether a Democrat, which I am, or a Republican, which I am *not,* is elected, I don't think it's as critical as any one of those things. I think conglomeration is a real quality-of-life issue. If you know what America looks like today, you know conglomeration is altering the quality of American life. And it's just as illegal as selling guns to Iran. And *nobody* seems to *give a shit.* And *that's* why I wonder if I'm ever gonna work again.

Really? But you're a great actor.

Yeah, but I need my collaborators. I *need* for someone other than a corporation to be deciding what is germane about a movie and what is not. I *need* this in order for me to function. And it ain't goin' that way.

Which way is it going?

Demographics. It's annihilating. And there's no resisting it. My livelihood is being eaten alive by demographics.

By that do you mean television versus movies?

I say it about sports, I say it about life. It's a demographic principle: Don't bet against it if it's good for television. That's what America's become, I think.

So your biggest problem with American culture is TV?

Well, I've written it in my work. In *Drive, He Said,* the radical is watching the astronaut parade on television, and he's taken a lot of drugs to beat the draft, and he stands up, pulls a sword off the wall, holds it over the television and says, *"This* is the *instrument* of the *death* of our *times."* Then he hits it with the sword and throws it out the window.

And this is very satisfying for you.

Yeah. This is how I feel. I'm an anachronism. I feel like an old fart in the theater that comes out and says, "Ooh, are these talking pictures? This is a tragedy." Do you know what I mean? But you know, television is not going to go away, so my point of view is kind of hopeless. I mean, I know I'm not gonna *win.* People become *inured.* They don't believe anything happened if they don't see it on television. It just doesn't exist.

Do you think people find their time, or does their time find them? For instance, your big break was in "Easy Rider," which certainly reflected its time.

The part in *Easy Rider* changed my life. I certainly lucked in and got picked up in a period. This doesn't happen that much, contrary to what people think. The last time before me might have been James Dean.

Was there any sense when you were making the movie that it was this testament to the sixties, this blowout statement of what this time means?

Yes, I think that was definitely the vision of the film that Dennis [Hopper] and Peter [Fonda] had. But then, so did a lot of other people about a lot of other movies. This one actually hit the mark, I guess.

Then you have "Five Easy Pieces," which has the same sort of antihero. Do you have a favorite?

Not really, because I'm one of those people who likes films that I've been in. I'm not always perfectly satisfied with what I did, as very few people are, but I take a certain pride in who I worked with and what they've done with the opportunity. I have a good record in that area.

You seem enormously happy. Are you a very happy person?

No. I think of myself as a very fortunate person, about which I'm happy. But I'm deeply moody. It's been a long time since I went through a day that I just thought was splendid and I didn't have some deep self-loathing or depression or fear.

How was turning fifty?

No fucking good. I didn't like it.

Do you have any sense of being a national treasure?

No, I do not. I can't work if people don't wanna see what I do, so they don't go see people they hate. In that way maybe I am a national treasure. I mean, I can be egotistical enough to say, "I'm not gonna work for two years, and you'll see: they're not gonna make any good movies anywhere, because I'm not there." I mean, this was just strictly a provocateur's statement, but I also felt there was an ounce of truth in it.

Are you frequently recognized on the street?

Yeah, but people don't always scream, yell and hurl some piece of their wardrobe into the atmosphere. I think it's pretty steady with me. If I go somewhere and I have to stand still, I collect your average celebrity crowd. But I try to keep moving, which I'm very, very good at. I go fast.

SEX, DRUGS
AND
ROCK & ROLL

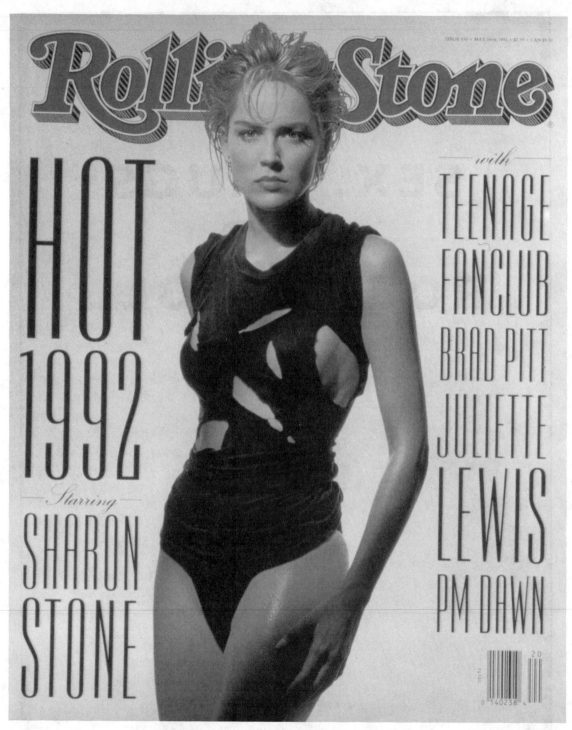

Sharon Stone, ROLLING STONE, issue 630, May 14, 1992.
Photograph by Albert Watson

Warren Beatty and Sharon Stone

Warren Beatty

By Bill Zehme

MAY 31, 1990

He is a ghost. He is human ectoplasm. He is here, and then he is gone, and then you aren't sure he was ever here to begin with. He has had sex with everyone, or at least tried. He has had sex with someone you know or someone who knows someone you know or someone you wish you knew, or at least tried. He is famous for sex, he is famous for having sex with the famous, he is famous. He makes mostly good films when he makes films, which is mostly not often. He has had sex with most of his leading ladies. He befriends all women and many politicians and whispers advice to them on the telephone in the dead of night. Or else he does not speak at all to anyone ever, except to those who know him best, if anyone can really know him. He is an adamant enigma, elusive for the sake of elusiveness, which makes him desirable, although for what, no one completely understands. He is much smarter than you think but perhaps not as smart as he thinks, if only because he thinks too much about being smart. He admits to none of this. He admits to nothing much. He denies little. And so his legend grows.

You hear Warren Beatty stories. They get around as he gets around. What you hear is carnal lore, possibly embellished, certainly superfluous. Warren Beatty, you hear, is gentle and respectful and never pushy, but he would not mind having sex right now, right this very microsecond. He loves women profoundly. Unsolicited, women tell me this and men corroborate. When Warren first meets a woman, he says (befuddled), "Now, I forget your name." Or (bedazzled), "You're the most beautiful woman I've met who's not an actress or model." Or (beholden), "Your grandmother—she was one of the sexiest women I ever knew." (One of his old opening lines—"What's new, pussycat?"—later became a movie written by Woody Allen, who once said he wished to be reincarnated as Warren Beatty's fingertips.)

Warren says many things, always chivalrously; he gives books to women as gifts; he offers to carry their camera equipment if they are film students. One very famous director remembers having a conversation with him during which Warren, the director says, "had his hand up a woman! She didn't seem to mind, and he

47

acted as though it seemed a perfectly natural thing to do." Another scenario: Warren calls an actress late on a Saturday night. Her husband answers the phone. She gets on the line, and Warren invites her up to his house right away to read for a movie role widely reported as already cast. She puts him off but takes his home number anyway. Next to the number, her husband notices, she mistakenly writes, "Warren Beauty." Many notepads have likely known this error.

Madonna has his number. She may have his number like others have not. He told someone at lunch last year, "Sometimes I look at myself in the mirror and say, *'I'm with Madonna!'* " He is reborn in love, restored to public persona. For we only see Warren when he loves deeply (we only *hear* about him when he prowls). From the sixties onward, we saw him most clearly (but never too well) with Joan Collins, Natalie Wood, Leslie Caron, Michelle Phillips, Julie Christie, Diane Keaton, Isabelle Adjani. Madonna is more famous than any of them; she is more famous than he is; she is more famous than everyone, more or less. By loving him, she makes him more famous than he was before. Theirs is a sort of vampire love: She needs his credibility; he needs her youth. He is fifty-three, and she is thirty-one, and they are evenly matched legends; hers is louder, his is longer. It works out.

When I first see him, I see him with her. They have come, the satyr and the siren, some forty minutes late to a screening room in Burbank to preview someone else's movie. When it is over, she curls onto his lap, as is her wont, while Warren discourses on directorial minutiae, as is his wont.

They are cozy together in a prickly sort of way. Their pet names for each other are Old Man and Buzzbomb. It is a comic-strip romance. She is, in this regard, Breathless Mahoney, the torchy moll who leads his Dick Tracy into temptation in *Dick Tracy,* the new Warren Beatty film—his first directing job since *Reds* nine years ago. (In between, he appeared only in the loopy $40-million stinker epic *Ishtar,* which he co-starred in with Dustin Hoffman and produced.) *Dick Tracy* will be his resurrection, his last best hope, his first Disney picture. It is a florid cartoon of a movie (to be released in tandem with a new Roger Rabbit short), blazing with gats and gunsels and deformed villains with names like Pruneface, Flattop and Itchy. Dustin Hoffman is Mumbles. Al Pacino is Big Boy. Bad guys have gooey faces. Madonna wears red and sings Sondheim. Beatty, as Tracy, wears yellow and fights evil. Often he talks to his wristwatch. Whereas *Batman* brooded, *Dick Tracy* sparkles—a $26-million thirties-era thrill ride done in seven Sunday-funny colors. It is nothing like the other Warren Beatty movies, which tend to be bittersweet melancholies about vain bandits *(Bonnie and Clyde),* oversexed hairdressers *(Shampoo),* reincarnated quarterbacks *(Heaven Can Wait)* and dead Communists *(Reds).* Not that the incongruity of *Dick Tracy* counts for much; most of the younger, hard-core moviegoers have no idea who Warren Beatty is anyway.

Warren Beatty is paranoid. He is an occluded Hollywood god, one who shuts up and off and imagines himself invisible. Afraid of being misunderstood, he says nothing and is more misunderstood. He likes it that way. Unlike, say, Brando's silence, Beatty's silence is showy. Puckish and smooth, he phones up journalists to inform them *at length* and with sly humor that he doesn't cooperate with the media. He would rather eat worms. In a dozen years, he has said nothing. Maybe a few hollow words in behalf of *Ishtar.* Maybe a futile endorsement now and again for his crony—the presidential infidel Gary Hart. It was Warren who nudged him back into the election, post–Donna Rice. Otherwise, Warren has been so mum, he has all but evaporated. *Reds* did limp business, theory goes, because Warren gave no interviews. If *Dick Tracy* dies, so, too, might his career. Posturing has its limitations.

And so he has talked. And talked. For days, I have listened to him talk. I have listened to him listen to himself talk. I have probed and pelted and listened some more. For days. He speaks slowly, fearfully, cautiously, editing every syllable, slicing off personal color and spontaneous wit, steering away from opinion, introspection, humanness. He is mostly evasive. His pauses are elephantine. Broadway musicals could be mounted during his pauses. He *works* at this. Ultimately, he renders himself blank. In *Dick Tracy*, he battles a mysterious foe called the Blank. In life, he is the Blank doing battle with himself. It is a fascinating showdown, exhilarating to behold.

To interview Warren Beatty is to want to kill him.

It is also to become fond of him. He seduces anything that is not mineral. He is impossible, but charming. Jack Nicholson, his neighbor on altitudinal Mulholland Drive, calls him the Pro. Meaning Warren knows what he is doing: I am invited one Friday night to watch him score. *(See Beatty score! Not unlike seeing Picasso draw, Astaire twirl, DiMaggio swing!)* Alas, there are musicians present; he is supervising *Tracy*'s musical score on an old MGM orchestra stage in Culver City. "I told you never to meet me here," Warren says, meeting me for the first time. (An opening line.) He looks tousled, untucked, an aging boy barely aging, with drooped shirttails and sweet comportment. He is at once good and bad and will do anything to make up for it. He fusses— dithers, really—eager to get me a chair, to get me liquids and solids, to get me. He settles onto

a milk crate—"It makes me feel puritanical and worthy," he says—and chitchats. He appraises his young publicist in her long skirt and says approvingly, "You look like . . . *the president of Vassar.*" He feigns horror to hear Vassar is now coed. *"No!"* he says, stricken. The orchestra has been laying music behind a scene in which Mahoney puts the make on Tracy; on a screen high above us, she glimmers in freeze-frame, propped on all fours, crawling across his desk. Warren studies this contortion for a moment. "I think I knew someone who had a coffee table that looked like that," he says. "The only thing missing is the glass on top."

One week later, on the night of his fifty-third birthday, the interrogations begin. Feeling celebratory, he orders in Big Macs and El Pollo Loco chicken ("Hang the expense!"). There is much for him to avoid discussing. We hole up for the first session in a Hollywood sound-mixing studio, where he's been toiling on *Tracy.* Further conversations take place in his home, that bestilled sanctuary on his private Olympus, and on the phone, his instrument of choice. Because what he doesn't say is often more revealing than what he does, this interview will frequently pause (as will Warren), so that necessary detail, commentary and homicidal impulses can be noted.

Okay, you and Madonna—the truth!
Art is truth.
That's all? You want to go with that?
[*Grins*] Okay by me.
Describe the qualities she possesses that convinced you to cast her as the sexpot temptress Breathless Mahoney in "Dick Tracy." How does she qualify?
Madonna is [*twenty-one-second pause*] simultaneously touching and more fun than a barrel of monkeys. [*Eleven seconds*] She's funny, and she's [*twenty-one seconds*] gifted in so many areas and

has the kind of energy as a performer that can't help but make you engaged.

You mean sexual energy?

[*Forty-seven-second pause*] Um, she has it all.

What's the sexiest thing she does onscreen?

She's funny. She's a wonderful comedienne. Is that sexy? Oh, I dunno. Everybody has their own criteria.

You two sing a duet, "I'm Following You," on her new album. How did you avoid upstaging her?

Upstaging her? I do as I'm told.

Warren, I would learn, has a habit of going off the record, and when he is off the record, he is almost like a person. At these times, one gets a greater sense of his playfulness. The lines blur occasionally. At one point, when we are neither on nor off the record, just sort of pacing around, he suggests that we depants his publicist, the Vassar president. He thinks it might ease tension.

What's the most ridiculous rumor you've read about you?

Really an adroit question, because if I repeat a ridiculous rumor here, it gives 50 percent credence to the rumor, whatever it is. [*Ponders, fifty-seven-second pause*] If I tell you I saw an item that said I was actually born on Pluto, 50 percent of the people will say, "*I wonder . . .*" It's a sin, you know, starting a rumor. You'll notice I picked a really outlandish one. I had to think for a minute.

All things considered, it could be true.

[*Smiles*] You know I wasn't born on Pluto. I'd get much more attention had I been.

Why do you think there are so many rumors about you?

I could say something self-serving here, so I won't.

"Fuck and suck" is Beatty's pet term for scurrilous articles written about his sexual profile. He asks me if I know about any such pieces that may currently be in the works. The prospect seems to neither disgust nor please him. He is resigned to his reputation. His sister, reincarnated actress Shirley MacLaine, says she wishes she could do a love scene with Warren. "Then," she states, "I could see what all the shouting was about."

Your friend Jack Nicholson always looks like he enjoys fame. I wonder if you do.

[*Thirty-four seconds*] Well, I can't speak for other people. I don't know whether they do or they don't. Dustin used to say that I've been famous longer than I've been a person. His theory being you're a person in the years when you're not famous. Because I got lucky with the first picture I made [*Splendor in the Grass*, in 1961], I had something like a ten-year jump on Jack and Dustin. So I haven't really dealt with being well-known as if I had an alternative to it. Although I guess there is. I could go someplace where nobody knew me at all.

Do you think you're eccentric?

Anybody who becomes a movie star when they're twenty-one, or whatever I was, is going to be eccentric. It's an eccentric situation. You become rich and famous out of proportion to that which is anticipated. Quite a candy store there.

Anything you want, within reason.

More without reason. Within reason, you're just another guy. The task is to stay within reason. I've tried. If I've been able to save myself, it has to do with my interest in art and politics, not in wealth.

You make movies slowly. You speak slowly. What do you do fast?

Prevaricate. [Note: defined by Webster's as "to evade the truth . . . to lie."]

What else?

I can dial a telephone number faster than anybody you know. [*He demonstrates—his hand falls onto a Touch-Tone panel, his fingers perform instant symphony, he passes me the receiver, an operator answers at the Beverly Wilshire hotel, where he kept a suite for many years. Dialing time: exactly one second.*] Want me to do it again? Want to see it again? [*He dials once more, full of swagger.*] That was quick, wasn't it?

That was breathtaking.

Thank you.

The telephone, of course, is Warren's second most legendary appendage. Rarely is he phoneless. It is said that he will make and take calls even while engaged in animal rapture. His mind swirls with phone numbers, memorized for the ages. His phone voice is a mellifluous purr, instantly conspiratorial. He is at home in the ear. He has been inside all the best ears. On Easter, I call and ask, among other things, if he has been hunting eggs. "Just laying them," he replies a bit luridly.

What's wrong with the film industry?

Nothing. It's making a lot of money. However, our attention span has become progressively curtailed. I like jokes that I get fast. But I like other things, too. We've placed too many restrictions on ourselves: A movie has to have a happy ending and be two hours or less in length. You've got to understand the premise from the top, so it's too often obvious. And that's too bad. Movies must be quickly understood and quickly assimilated. So that when you make a three-and-a-half-hour movie, as I did with *Reds*, some people tell you that it's *long*. "It's long," they say. "Yes," you say, "it *is* long. Three and a half hours long, yes. *Long.*"

In the spirit of speed, how would you pitch "Reds" as a high concept, in one sentence?

It would have been a pretty low high concept: a three-and-a-half-hour movie about a Communist who dies at the end, not having been happy.

After he wormed his way through the script, Charlie Bluhdorn, who ran Paramount [which bankrolled *Reds*] said, "I don't understand why you're doing this." Then he said, "Do me a favor. Take twenty-five million dollars. Go to Mexico, go to Peru. Spend one million on a movie. Keep twenty-four million for yourself. *Just don't make this movie!*" I said, "Well, I'm sorry, Charlie. I really am gonna have to do this. It's worthwhile." There was something very moving in the idealism of the American left from 1915 to 1920—particularly poignant in the life of John Reed [the journalist in the forefront]. Plus I don't believe anybody ever made an American movie with a Communist hero before.

Can you hear the word "Ishtar" without feeling physically ill?

Well, sure. *Ishtar* is kind of a funny little movie. But it cost too much. It was an ironic situation, because when Dustin and I realized what it was going to cost [$40 million], we went to the studio and suggested that we not take any money, that we'd take it on the other end. Columbia refused, based on a cable deal. We said, "Well, this is an inappropriate price for this film, and when people seem so obsessed with the cost of the thing, it'll make it hard to laugh." They said they'd be sure to keep the cost very quiet. Then they were replaced by new management, who seemed to want to make an example of *Ishtar*'s high cost. Just in a business sense, it didn't seem the most fiscally responsible way for them to behave.

You've said that every movie you make feels like a comeback. What takes so long?

I've never seen the point of just dishing it out there. I don't know that I take such a long time to *make* movies. I take a long time to *decide* to do one. I take much too long. And I think that's self-indulgent on my part, and I ought to try to get over it. Sometimes I think that I put off making movies just long enough so that I can't put it off any longer, for various reasons. Then I go make the movie.

Maybe you just don't like making movies.

No, I actually like making movies. I just don't like to make them all the time. There's so much inertia to overcome to make a really good movie. I felt that if I made a lot of movies, I wouldn't make the ones that were really tough, like *Shampoo* or *Reds*. Others are different from me.

Robert Towne, with whom you wrote "Shampoo," says you "are a man who is deeply embarrassed by acting." True?

[*Puzzled*] He said that about me? I'm very embarrassed by my own *bad* acting.

Didn't Ronald Reagan tell you that he wished "Reds" had a happier ending after you showed him the film at the White House?

[*Startled*] Where did you hear that? I wouldn't want to . . . um, well, you know he has a great sense of humor. He's a funny guy. [*Pauses twenty-one seconds*] I guess I have a lot of feelings about Reagan that I am not articulating. He is an actor and a very, very likable man. But I guess you know I'm not a conservative Republican.

How old do you feel?

Eleven.

How so?

I guess I'm not fond of schedules, and I don't see any point in keeping to some fictitious schedule of [life].

Have you had a midlife crisis yet?

Many, I'm sure. They started when I was about eighteen. Ultimately, I learned that the secret to overcoming them is to not see them as crises.

What does your mother want for you? Marriage?

Well, not just for the sake of being married. Marriage is a worthy thing to aspire to.

Do you aspire to marriage?

I have never bristled at the notion.

Would you have limitations as a husband?

No. I haven't been in a bubble. I've had very close relationships with people that have lasted longer than my friends' marriages that existed at the same time.

What's the most important thing to know about women?

[*Pauses twenty-one seconds*] That they're not very different from men.

What do you mean?

That's eight pages.

Eight classic pages. What do you mean?

[*Pauses fourteen seconds*] Well, I'm lucky that I grew up in an atmosphere in which I was taught to treat women as respectfully as I would treat men. I don't differentiate. Sometimes people don't treat themselves very seriously, but that might happen more often when this business of sexual attraction rears its head and we all get a little giddy.

Are you a better friend to women than you are to men?

I hope not. I'm probably guilty of giving more women the benefit of the doubt than men. And I think there are probably more women that give me the benefit of the doubt than men do. But I'm not even sure of that.

Describe what love feels like to you.

Do unto others.

Romantic love.

Well, as soon as you use the word *romantic*, then the word *fiction* begins to peep around the corner, or the word *bullshit* begins to lurk in the shadow. But if you say *sexual love,* which I think is not bullshit and not fictitious, that's something else. But I think there's a certain amount of do unto others even in that.

How do you know you're in love? What incites your love?

I don't know if you ever figure that out. If you're smart, you don't figure it out. Of course, you always try to figure it out. But if you're smart, you know you can't. I take great pride in my stupidity in this area. I have no clear way of being able to define at what point [*twenty-one seconds*] passion for loyalty has overcome me.

Has your heart been broken?

Sure.

How many times?

[*Laughs richly, then seventeen-second pause*] I'm sure I've reached my quota.

How do you mend yours? Give advice.

To the lovelorn? There is no away. Nobody goes away. Except the Big Away, and there's nothing you can do about it. If you really love someone [*seventeen seconds*] and they're healthy and happy . . . you ought to be able to live with that.

Can you always be that philosophical?

[*Twenty-four seconds*] Pretty close.

Do you think you're shy?

Shyness is really a form of vanity.

Here's something Robert Downey Jr. said about you: "Beatty is really knowledgeable in a lot of areas, especially fucking." Did you have any idea people talk about you in this manner?

[*Smiles*] Yes.

How do you feel about that?

Irrelevant.

How do you characterize yourself?

As someone who would prefer not to characterize himself.

A musical question. As per legend: "You're So Vain"—did you think the song was about you?

[*Laughs, fifteen-second pause*] Who wrote that?

Sharon Stone

By Bill Zehme

MAY 14, 1992

"**W**hy can't we fly to Vegas for this?" she asks. That is her request. Because you are dealing with a Sex Babe who could possibly be the Devil, it would be wise to begin where it is safe. It would be wise to begin where she cannot distract you and weaken your judgment. Because she will try. "Maybe if we just go to Vegas . . . ," she says. And you see her point, of course. You see her point always. She always *has* a point, in addition to much else. As she has said, "If you have a vagina and a point of view, that's a deadly combination." This is how she talks, by the way. But then, she is famous for her lack of inhibition. Shame wastes her time, which nothing ever should. "If there's anything I have particularly in common with the character I play in *Basic Instinct,* it's that I don't have a lot of guilt," she says. "I think I oughta do what I wanna do." For instance, she once went to Vegas and met a man whom she agreed to marry ten days later, because it was what she wanted to do. Vegas has this sort of effect on her, which is important to understand if you are going to end up in Vegas with her. "Maybe we should just go to Vegas and gamble and talk while we're playing blackjack," she says. "Let's do that."

You do gamble, but not in Vegas; not because it is unsafe there, but because she never mentions it again. She drops the idea of Vegas as if it were an unworthy suitor. Like that. As with most Sex Babes, she is mercurial this way. She is like a dice roll, with better and more dangerous possibilities. Thus, whenever you are with her, you are gambling a little. "Pick one," she says, as if to demonstrate, cupping her hands over a pastel pile of candy Tiny Conversation Hearts. You have given her your Hearts, and now she is playing with them, on the table of a swell Los Angeles restaurant where Steve Martin is having lunch right over there. She hides the Hearts from view, and you take turns blindly plucking them out and brandishing their tarty epigrams. (She is the kind of woman who turns candy into a roulette game.) Her first Heart says, COAX ME, and she thrusts it in your face, smiling coyly. (Pitifully, you parry with NICE GIRL.) Before long she issues forth with DIG ME, BE GOOD, BE MINE, SAY YES, SMILE, WILD ("That's mine for sure!"), HOT MAMA and KISS ME. She extends her hand. "Now, this time you have to pick what you wish for," she says at last, and so she picks LUV YA. "Luv ya," she sings sweetly, pushing all of the Hearts away, without having eaten a single one.

Actresses are given to confounding men's hearts. Men who know actresses know this to be true. They tell other men, and eventually most men know that actresses are given to confounding men's hearts. (Of course, this does not stop men from falling prey.) Actresses—especially those of the Sex Babe variety—are born with wiles that are always at work, beguiling and bedeviling. It is a natural phenomenon, probably rooted deep in the psyche, over which the actress has little control. Nevertheless, such women are not unaware of their impact. They watch themselves being watched by others; they watch themselves drive men to despair. They see everything they do, often without feeling a part of it. "Sometimes it's like watching your life at a drive-in movie," she says.

I have watched Sharon Stone, America's Premier Sex Babe, watch herself being watched on-screen. In *Basic Instinct*—itself the very reason why Sharon Stone has come to our attention—the world was permitted to look up her dress. (The vista, which stares out between her shifting thighs during a police investigation, quietly upstaged all other erotic histrionics in the movie.) "You can see right through to *Nebraaaaaaaaska!*" she says a bit unhappily, as though duped by her director. "Fuck! I wanna have the *indication* of *that*, but I don't wanna *see that!*" But that is exactly what the world saw, and as a result, she now owns the world. "That was Malcolm X's Theory of Pussy Power, wasn't it?" she says, seizing all the power anyway, because it is what she wants to do.

If she is the devil, Hell has improved. Without question, she possesses many of the requisite qualities. "I'm a *great* deal maker," she says, citing just one, to be helpful. "I think I'd be a great agent." For certain, she has at least *played* the Devil, if we are to believe the one who wrote *Basic Instinct*. In a deal Mephistopheles would have envied, Joe Eszterhas was paid $3 million for his improbable screenplay about a blond, frequently nude, bisexual ice-pick enthusiast and the detective who loves her. "Eszterhas' original concept was that she is the Devil," says the film's Dutch director, Paul Verhoeven, adding that the script initially called for "Sympathy for the Devil" by the Rolling Stones to play over the final scene. "If the Devil looks this good," he says, "that's why you have the sympathy, right?" (To becalm the angry homosexuals who have taken his film's dark vision personally, the director says: "The Devil, like God, is probably bisexual, or should be, if he wants to love everybody. I see Satan in the same position as God.")

Though it is not difficult to do, Verhoeven can plainly see the Devil in Sharon Stone. "I surely do," he says, having first spotted It while directing her as Arnold Schwarzenegger's evil wife in *Total Recall*, her other Big Movie. "She's very seducing. She does a lot of flirting. One of the most threatening things about her is that she can change in a split second, so that in her eyes there's either a loving person or the Devil. I have hated her with all my heart, and I have loved her, too. She can be so goddamned mean. She can be very clever with words and hit you [with them], right in front of the whole crew. And if you're not careful, she can be the victor.

"I think you would have to be a really strong guy if you wanted to marry her," he continues significantly. "Otherwise, she'll blow you away. Like Odysseus, when he was sleeping with the witch Circe, he always had the sword between him and her. I think that's the way to handle Sharon. Have the knife ready." ("He cannot abide that he adores me," she says gleefully, upon hearing this. "It drives him fucking crazy! Oh, he *adores* me, the fool!")

Sharon Stone is the kind of woman who always keeps a tube of Krazy Glue in her backpack, and you find yourself worrying about what she might do with it. She is that kind of woman. "I have it in case I fall apart," she explains, but clearly that is not ever going to happen. She is, after all, a woman of great resilience, having withstood for a decade a blighted career of Bad Moves and Worse Movies. Largely, her oeuvre swims in the bowels of cable, where she can be seen as the Blonde in such works as *Action Jackson, Police Academy 4, King Solomon's Mines* and *Allan Quatermain and the Lost City of Gold* (both with the great Richard Chamberlain), *Above the Law, Scissors* and *He Said, She Said.* "When I came here," she says of Hollywood, "I looked like an inflatable Barbie doll, and nobody wanted me to play anything too edgy. Then it started to become apparent that, you know, I was *good* at that. . . ." To this end, she adds, "I never thought that I looked on the outside like I was on the inside. On the inside I feel like a dark Semitic girl with curly hair. I have never felt blond."

Here, then, is the kind of woman she is: First of all, she is no Lady; she is a Broad. "I am for sure a Broad," she says. "My friends tell me, 'You're a great Broad.' Nobody ever says I'm a Lady." She keeps a large punching bag in her garage and regularly beats the hell out of it. In life, she fends for herself. "I've hit a few people, yes," she says. "I've knocked a couple guys across the room." Because she needs a lot of room, she recently knocked down all the walls inside her house in the Hollywood Hills. "I took the sledgehammer and started smashing stuff," she says. "It was very freeing." She is the sort of woman who in one moment will say, "Isn't Tourette syndrome great?" and in the next speak of being moved by a Chet Baker trumpet solo. She is a fight fan and a Lakers fan and

aspires to act the way Magic Johnson passes, meaning, "you know, the No-Look Pass," she says. "Almost a Zen-like sensibility about everything going on around you." She owns two double-barreled, pump-action shotguns she will not hesitate to use and has known no greater joy than squeezing off ammunition rounds on an Uzi. "Oh, it's *wonderful!*" she says. "You put it under your arm and hold it close to your body, and you feel the heat of the bullets as they pass out by your back!" She lists among her rules to live by: "Never play cards with a guy named Doc. Never eat at a place called Mom's. And never fuck anybody who has more problems than you do." She grins and says, "It's Broad wisdom."

Her nails fork Michael Douglas' bare back all over town: on billboards and bus-stop signs and such. Well before *Basic Instinct* opened, her Devil eyes were already ubiquitous, peering over her leading man's shoulder in poster art everywhere. It is the day after her thirty-fourth birthday, and she has never seen so much of herself. She steers her black BMW beneath her enormous billboard gaze on Sunset and turns into the Saint James's Club driveway, listening all the while to job offers on the car phone. It is a vaporous Hollywood moment, now captured forever. "Can you imagine being Julia Roberts when this happened to her?" she says, once she has settled poolside in her capri pants, white blouse, sneakers and shades. "How old was she? Twenty-one, twenty-two? She's a kid, you know, she's a child! Do you remember when you were twenty-one? I couldn't make my bed! You don't know what you're supposed to do. You could think, 'Well, this is just how it goes!' I mean, this is my eighteenth movie, so I'm sure this is *not* how it goes."

Here in fact is how it goes, if you are Sharon Stone: You are born humbly, to a dye maker and his bookkeeper wife in Meadville, Pennsylvania, a town the size of a shoe. You have three siblings, and you are brighter than you look, since you look extraordinary (but feel homely, anyway). Your IQ measures out as Einstein's superior, so basically you are brighter than *everyone* looks. You are skipped ahead in school, where you are still mostly bored. You attend local Edinboro State College on a writing scholarship but soon drop out to become a fabulous international model, living in Paris, Milan and New York, where Woody Allen casts you as a fabulous doomed reveler aboard a train in the opening sequence of *Stardust Memories*. In *Irreconcilable Differences* you are officially introduced as a Home-Wrecking Starlet who sings badly, which you do very well. Everything you do next, however, is mostly futile or forgettable or both, until you seize the opportunity feared by all the Name actresses, which is to play the Devil and feign great quantities of graphic film sex with Michael Douglas, which you do very well.

"I've spent some quality time with her, yes," Douglas acknowledges, sounding tired still. "To create the illusion of the Fuck of the Century for ten or eleven hours a day, over four or five days [of shooting]—I mean, you're *exhausted*." To conserve energy, great sacrifices were made, the most prominent of which was Stone's now legendary decision to work without her Crotch Patch. Boldly, selflessly, she and Douglas agreed to expose their genitals to each other for their craft, with nothing between them but molecules! Thus, she would forgo the arduous task of strapping herself into a specially contoured, netted, moleskin G-string pubic shield—the Crotch Patch—for the following reason: "Every time you have to pee," she says, "you have to unglue and reglue it, which is quite painful. Besides, Michael's a real professional, and obviously there wasn't gonna be anything untoward,

so I felt very safe. And of course, there isn't anything sexy about doing sex scenes." She shows no mercy, in fact, on those who might imagine otherwise. "Oh, it's incredibly realistic!" she scoffs. "It's clearly some male sex fantasy that the woman's gonna, like, jump down in the bed and have three orgasms in four minutes. You know, that's how it goes at my house. I think they should have cut to Michael at the end of the sex scene, and he should have been smoking an entire pack of cigarettes, like twenty of them all around his mouth."

On a whim, she decides we must go to her favorite secret place, where we will see insects fornicate. She drives. "I wonder if I should drive like I drive when you're not in the car," she says, meaning she wonders if she should drive recklessly, which is what she does, anyway. She weaves through red lights and makes wild U-turns and puts *Getz Au Go Go* on the CD player and sings in a soft samba, "I feel so gay, in a melancholy way, that it might as well be spring . . . ," and pedestrians flee for their lives. As we plunge into the Santa Monica Mountains toward our obscure destination, she speaks of passion and how it smells. "You know how you can kind of smell passion?" Stone says, sniffing orange-blossom breeze. "I have this sensation that it's near. It doesn't happen to me that much. But when I am passionate, I am a person who is just completely, totally absorbed and involved and gone." She sighs and says, "It's been years."

It's true, though perhaps unthinkable: "I don't have a fella," she tells me resolutely, even though she seemed to have had one when we last met a few weeks earlier. "But I have my *eye* on someone," she says, giggling. "You know, I'm a girl who really likes boys. . . ." Indeed, she has been as unlucky in love as the next Sex Babe.

The death of her three-year marriage to producer Michael Greenburg haunts her still, for he was the man she met in Vegas and about whom she says, "I would lay awake at night and watch him sleep." She laments, "I wonder how many heartbreaks a heart can hold. Mine's like a tightly closed little clamshell." But now there is a smell.

"Oh, look! They're fucking!" she says brightly. We have just hiked halfway up one side of Franklin Canyon, where here is a little-known national preserve that is her favorite secret place. It is here that she hides when she needs to hide, amid the rattlesnakes and the bee farms and the audible skittering of unseen paws. "I like to commune with nature," she says. At the moment, we are in fact hunched over a spruce sapling on whose top branch she has spied—from five paces away—a pair of ladybugs actually copulating, one astride the other's back. (Such is the power of her sex radar!) "They *are* fucking!" she says, thrilling to the wee spectacle. I've never seen that before! They're on their high-rise honeymoon. That's what we really call lucky ladybugs!" Thusly inspired, she will soon after skip like a schoolgirl down most of the mountain trail, her hair swinging around her neck, the picture of happy liberation.

Lenny Bruce and Richard Pryor—Lives on Film

Lenny

By Tim Cahill

DECEMBER 5, 1974

In April the ugliness was beginning to sprout like warts on a cover girl's nose. At two-thirty in the morning, after sixteen straight hours of work, Dustin Hoffman loses his temper. Out on a wet, chilly Brooklyn street, he finds himself shouting at the associate producer. Where the hell is the food? Who works for sixteen hours without food? The crew and equipment are due at Brown's Hotel in the Catskills that evening and nothing is packed, nothing is ready to go.

Hoffman is working on *Lenny*, a film about the life of Lenny Bruce. He started in late fall of 1973 with eight weeks of rehearsal. Filming began January 21. Now it is the last week in April, and the shooting is more than a week behind schedule. For Hoffman, playing the part of Lenny Bruce is the most difficult thing he has ever done. It rips at him and tears at him and eats up the bulk of his humor, leaving him edgy and obsessive about his work. There are moments when he looks a decade older than his thirty-six years. Sometimes the cameras have to be halted—entire seconds when he drifts out of Lenny and into Dustin, when his eyes go wild with confusion and fatigue and bitterness.

The first filming in Miami was pleasant enough. There were high spirits then: a lot of dirty-mouth antics and the practice of mooning over Miami. Pull down the slacks and bend over. Gotcha, ha ha.

Valerie Perrine, the actress playing Lenny's wife in the film, Honey Harlowe, realizing she was going to have to shave for the stripper scenes in which she would wear a G-string, sculpted out a neat little pubic heart and told director Bob Fosse it was his Valentine's Day card.

The movie kept dropping behind schedule, and the crew worked six and seven days a week, ten to sixteen hours a day. The antics and high spirits gave way to an unceasing general depression. Lesser members of the crew focused their resentment on Robert Fosse's demands, on his persistent coldness. "He'll do twenty-five takes," one crew member says, "then walk over and move a glass on the table—move it half an inch—and do it all over again." At first the *Lenny* people didn't mind the double time and triple time, but now it is wearing on them. A general below-the-surface Fosse Bitch has developed. In outline, the Bitch goes like this:

59

Lenny is the first film Fosse has done since 1973, the year he swept America's most prestigious directors' awards for film, television and stage: an Oscar for *Cabaret,* an Emmy for *Liza With a "Z"* and a Tony for *Pippin.* "The guy is overrated and he knows it," one disgruntled crew member is saying in April. "He knows the critics will be gunning for him, so he's trying to cover his ass. And he's hard on the actors and the people behind the camera. It's like he's always saying, 'I don't think you have it. I think you're shit. Show me what you can do, but I don't expect much.'"

Between 1959 and 1964, Lenny Bruce was one of the funniest men in America and certainly its most controversial comic. It was, some thought, sinful to challenge folks' attitudes on race and social inequity and drugs and language and law and chicken-fucking. The fact that there was a nearly rabbinical lucidity in some of Bruce's best bits only made matters worse. Lenny was labeled "sick." First of the sick comedians. He said words like *fuck* or *cocksucker* onstage.

But there is here a larger point to be made. Lenny Bruce was a man who chose his own battles. Because he knew his words had meaning and merit—and that they were funny as well—he always assumed that he would win. That knowledge gave him a patented brass-balls approach to his act, and that approach attracted customers, which in turn attracted more and more offers from club owners.

The approach also attracted police. The busts and notoriety fed on themselves. Marvin Worth, Lenny's onetime manager and producer of the film, thinks that it got to be chic to bust Lenny. "I mean," he says, "I talked with some of the same guys who busted him back then and they all say, 'Oh, no, we wouldn't do it today,' and they start talking about the prevailing social climate or some such shit. And then they tell you how they had a job to do but they thought Lenny was great this and terrific that. I always have this urge to ask them, 'Well, if you felt that way, why didn't you just give him a fucking medal and be done with it?'"

After the first busts—September 29 for narcotics in Philadelphia and October 4 for obscenity in San Francisco, both in 1961—any police department that didn't harass Lenny when he was in town apparently assumed they weren't doing their job. He was eventually banned from entering both Australia and England and arrested five more times: twice for narcotics and three times for obscenity. By 1964 any club owner anywhere who hired Lenny Bruce could expect financially crippling attention from the local authorities. Suddenly bathrooms that had always been adequate needed more toilets. The last fire inspector had overcalculated the club's maximum capacity by 150 persons. Things like that.

Lenny was effectively frozen out of most of the major clubs in America. He had earlier established a precedent and had some success with his one-man concerts in large halls. He again played some concerts as well as the few smaller clubs where he was still welcome, but he was obsessed with his legal battles and the bills he couldn't pay. And the sad fact is, toward the end, Lenny Bruce was no longer all that funny.

In San Francisco in October of 1965, Lenny Bruce was declared legally bankrupt. On August 3, 1966, he died of an overdose of morphine. The Los Angeles Sheriff's Office took the last photos of America's sickest comic. The photos look a bit overexposed, possibly because Lenny's skin was so white against his bathroom floor. He was forty years old, forty pounds overweight, naked and dead.

After the Brooklyn scenes, Dustin Hoffman

rides up to the Catskills in a limo, arriving at Brown's resort in a cold, gray, false dawn. His room faces the resort pool, and a couple of hours after he gets to bed, the pool's public-address system begins pumping out calls for Mr. and Mrs. Bloom, for Dr. Swartz, for Mr. Levine. At eleven it is the maids. Unaware that the movie people got in at dawn, and anxious to finish their work, they take up gestapo tactics.

Bam, bam, bam, on the doors. The key in the lock.

"He still sleepin'?"

With contempt: "Maybe he daid."

"No, I seen him move. He still . . . *sleepin'*."

Hoffman is up at noon for six hours of interior shooting, then has dinner in the mammoth dining room. He orders "garden fresh sautéed vegetables." What he gets are ugly wet little cubes fresh from a can.

Enter a cheerful elderly widow from an adjoining table. She's got the rhinestone cat's eyeglasses and the white shawl opened down the front but buttoned at the neck. "Mr. Hoffman, may I have your autograph?" She's holding out a soggy napkin and a ballpoint pen. "It's not for me, it's for my daughter."

Hoffman doesn't look up. "Can't you see I'm eating?" The woman thrusts the napkin in his face. Hoffman picks up the vegetables in both hands and stuffs them into his empty water glass. Next he pours his wine into that glass, then dumps it all on his plate.

"I'm eating," he shouts, and several people at other tables turn to watch the little drama.

"Oh, I see," the woman says, smiling uncertainly, "you're *acting* for me."

Hoffman splashes his right palm into the mess on his plate. "I'm eating. Can't you see I want to be left in peace?"

"Well," she says, "I'll come to see your movie anyway." Exit the old woman, limping slightly.

There is a leaden silence at the table, then the tired, sad truth from Hoffman's own lips. "She'll never see any movie I ever make."

The next night there is an outdoor rain scene to be shot. Hoffman sits in his trailer between takes. It starts with jokes—the thermal underwear makes it hard for him to use the toilet. Somehow the conversation gets serious. "The pollution," Hoffman mutters. "I think we've got ten years to clean up or the human race just isn't going to make it."

I had been with the *Lenny* crew since Brooklyn—long enough to fall into the general malaise of exhaustion and edginess. Somehow Hoffman's prediction of ecological disaster strikes me as both inane and galling. I mention that the Lenny death scenes were shot not long ago and that there may be a bit of psychic dead weight from that work contributing to Dustin's sudden sense of apocalypse.

"That's not it," Hoffman says with what I take to be false conviction. "I think we've got about ten more years unless we clean up our act."

"I don't believe you," I say more sharply than I intended. "I don't believe you really mean what you're saying."

Hoffman terminates the conversation by turning his back on me. He appears to be controlling his temper.

Later, while the rest of the crew eat at Brown's again, Hoffman is a few miles down the road at a Chinese-American-food truck stop. There is a bit of standard interview talk before the food arrives. Hoffman was born in Los Angeles, studied piano at the L.A. Conservatory of Music before taking up acting at the Pasadena Playhouse. He moved to New York and shared an apartment with Gene Hackman. He supported himself with odd jobs: He waited on tables, checked coats, sold soft drinks, demonstrated toys at Macy's and worked for six months as an attendant at the New York Psychiatric Institute. He also acted.

There were small parts, larger parts, then, suddenly, rave reviews and recognition for an astounding variety of stage roles: for the hunchbacked Nazi homosexual in *Harry, Noon and Night;* for the pinched-face Russian clerk in *Journey of the Fifth Horse;* for the Cockney plumber in *Eh?*

Director Mike Nichols was impressed and invited Hoffman to try out for *The Graduate.* The story goes that just before his ten-minute reading with Katharine Ross, Hoffman gave her an empathetic pat on the butt. A warm-up gesture. Ross whirled on him and gritted, "Don't you ever touch me." Dustin blew most of his lines and left the audition in defeat. Nichols, however, loved the test. Hoffman projected just the sense of confused earnestness he wanted. Dustin began work on *The Graduate* in his twenty-ninth year. By the middle of his thirtieth year he was a film star.

Hoffman waited another year before accepting his next part: the sleazy, tubercular Bronx hustler Ratso Rizzo in *Midnight Cowboy.* It was a calculated decision. He wanted to prove that he was more than a one-role actor. *Cowboy* was the perfect vehicle to prove his versatility, and it remains one of Hoffman's favorite films.

Lenny will be Hoffman's ninth film. It is, he keeps saying, his most difficult role: the most demanding in terms of his craft, the most shattering in terms of emotional outlay. "I never played anyone who lived before. Someone who died only eight years ago."

The theory goes that any stand-up comic a decade ago who didn't stick to inoffensive material had to be self-destructive. That's the essence of the night shot the *Lenny* crew is shooting at Brown's Hotel. What happens is this:

Lenny says a nasty onstage.

Jack Goldstein, a fictional club owner played by Guy Rennie, is upset. Lenny agrees to work clean. Onstage the next night, to Jack's great delight, Lenny apologizes with a flourish and humility. Having bowed through a big round of applause, he utters a calculated, vindictive and terminal nasty. Cut to night scene, rain. Lenny and wife Honey getting into a car in a contemporary exit-from-paradise scene. Club owner Jack Goldstein as avenging angel.

Goldstein: "Believe me—everybody is going to be warned about you. You'll never work another resort—club—room—anything! You're finished, believe me, in show business."

Oh, it's a satisfying scene. Anyone who ever worked for anyone else can identify with it. A calculated resignation, yes, but a resignation that leaves the bastard who signs the paycheck spluttering for words. A resignation with the force of a heavyweight contender's right cross.

It is two o'clock on a dull, gray Catskills afternoon. Upstairs, somewhere in a rat maze of corridors, Dustin Hoffman is sleeping fitfully. The *Lenny* crew quit work on the night scene about five-thirty this morning. They quit work because the sun was coming up. The sun rose to a shower of curses.

Some of the early risers on the crew are up, rubbing sleep from their eyes and mumbling around the lobby. A few of them have stumbled into the large room just off the lobby. They are instantly transfixed by the bizarre scene before them.

A couple of hundred hotel guests, mostly women in their middle years, are sitting in a pewlike arrangement of folding chairs. Bobbing, weaving, whirling and gesturing before them is a fast-talking Kissinger-haired fellow of about forty. The man is dressed like a crude parody of a used-car dealer. He's got the soft shoes and the double-knit slacks and clashing sports jacket. Trailing behind like an electronic tail is about twenty feet of cord for a microphone, which he handles like a tent evangelist.

The man says that he is selling "ott."

He is selling paintings of crying clowns. He is selling paintings of laughing clowns and of juggling clowns, and of serious, noble-looking clowns. He is selling paintings of balloon vendors and of children with big sad eyes. And he is selling them at a tremendous discount.

The only member of the *Lenny* crew with any taste for the high-pressure ott is director of photography Bruce Surtees. He enjoys the auction—in part because he makes a great pretense of not giving a rat's ass for art. Words like *chiaroscuro* annoy him and he prefers the title "cameraman" to "cinematographer."

Lenny is being shot in black and white. Surtees, on the first go-around, is likely to say that "what I'm striving for here . . . is proper focus." Later, if he's decided you aren't going to invite him for some kind of film seminar at Harvard, he'll open up a little more. "With black and white we'll get very sharp focus and sharp light. Hardly any gray tones. You should be able to count the hairs on the actors' eyebrows.

"This film requires a lot of reality, and reality isn't always that grainy, documentary effect." Surtees settles back in his folding chair. "Oh, Jesus," he says, "just listen to this guy."

The auctioneer is making a lot of sincere eye contact. "You don't buy a genuine Chagall lithograph and get it for under eight hundred dollars."

The point is taken: Poor and slavish copies of genius go for cheap. This truth lies at the heart of Dustin Hoffman's struggle with the role of Lenny. He knows that he is not a particularly good mime and his gift is not impersonation.

His Lenny is a characterization—an effort, he might say, to tell the same truth by making it his own.

Hoffman spent three months listening to the records, watching the films and reading the books. He interviewed more than fifty people who had known Lenny well. What he wanted was some small seed from Lenny that he could relate to his own life. It was a method that had served him well in *The Graduate*. The seed there was simple and personal. He spent hours furiously remembering—forcing himself to relive—the first time he ever tried to buy a pack of rubbers in a drugstore.

The seed for Lenny was both more complex and more immediately personal. "What I was told several times," he says, "by his mother and his daughter and his ex-wife and some of his friends, was that there were certain aspects of me that reminded them of him. They might say, 'Jeez, he's a lot like Lenny.' I would ask them what they meant, and I would try to zero in on those things. They said he was circumspect, a listener. That he wanted to figure people out.

"His mother and I talked a lot in Los Angeles. She said that there was a certain spontaneous side to him, strange things he might do in public. In the middle of a meal in a restaurant he might get up and go into the kitchen and talk to the guy washing dishes. I tried to close in on those things in me that they said were reminiscent of Lenny."

Hoffman has his own unique overview of the Lenny story, but even on the set, there are different interpretations of what the movie will say. The script was written by Julian Barry, who also wrote the 1971 hit play *Lenny*, in which Cliff Gorman played the title role. "In the play," Barry says, "I mythologized Lenny Bruce. I felt that the last thing people knew about him was that he died like a junkie on the bathroom floor.

So my personal feeling was to do it larger than life. American folklore. John Henry and his fucking hammer. Lenny and his fucking mouth.

"The film is different. Maybe if I had never done the play, I would feel different about not canonizing Lenny in the film. Bob Fosse worked with me on the script and our approach was that . . . it was a race between Lenny being destroyed by himself and being destroyed by the police. The point is that the punishment so outweighed the crime—whatever that was—that a cold, objective approach to Lenny makes his case even better. He never wanted to be canonized. The whole beauty of Lenny, everything political notwithstanding, is his message: We're all the same schmuck. That's what he was saying."

Producer Marvin Worth, Lenny's longtime friend, finds it a more personal story: "I think it's a study of hypocrisy, including his own. Lenny always said 'we' in everything he did. But I also think it's about Honey and Lenny, the two of them. They're like F. Scott and Zelda, only this time it's junk instead of booze. It's a love story in its way. Two kids, wild-eyed, setting out to grab the world and being destroyed like that. And destroying one another."

Dustin Hoffman has his own queer, sharp, artist's perception of the Lenny myth. At issue here is the importance of creative work: "It's a key thing that Lenny didn't use drugs to flake out, to get wasted. The drugs were usually uppers, amphetamines, from what I understand. They were used, if anything, to keep him going for four days. He'd do a tremendous amount of work, writing, taping. It kicked him into his work. The obsession with his work is a central thing.

"I know from my own experience that I'm most happy when I'm deep into my own work. Working was very, very important to Lenny. And that's why when the work was taken away

after all the busts, he began to fall apart. He couldn't get on the stage and it really hung him up. That's when the whole weight-gaining thing started.

"The proof of it is to look at the body of work from the time he started to hit until the busts crippled him. That's only about five or six years, but it is the fruit of his work. There's a tremendous amount of records and appearances and tapes and books that came out of that time. Which solidifies the idea that there were twenty-four-hour workdays that had to go into that production. After that, all that energy went into his various legal battles but the real work was gone."

The *Lenny* crew wraps up the shooting two weeks after I leave. It is to be an intricately edited film, and the final mix takes six months to complete. In late October I fly to New York to see the prepremier screening.

The film itself is a surprise, because there are laughs in it and there is tenderness. The stark lighting and Surtees' cinematography are brilliantly evocative. Bob Fosse's perfectionism—which had been irritating, then almost unbearable to those on the set—translates into a thorough-going intelligence on film. Levels of meaning—emotional, social and legal—emerge in quick cut and somehow manage to illuminate the tired cliché that comedy grows out of pain.

Valerie Perrine is stunning. That is the talk one hears after the screening. Hoffman makes for a curious Lenny—a shade too thoughtful, perhaps. The effect may be calculated: It lends weight and inevitability to the final scenes in which Dustin's demoralized Lenny is an intensely disturbing experience.

Disturbing enough, in fact, to keep me up much of that night recalling another evening six months earlier—that last weary night in the

Catskills. The small truth that eluded me becomes self-evident as I reread what I have transcribed from my tape recorder from that bus ride back to New York:

Something is going on at the Jerry Lewis Theater at Brown's Hotel. There's a comic up there under the lights and he's working his heart out for these people.

"And now, ladies and gentlemen, your favorite movie stars, singers: I will try to impersonate them. You tell me what you want to hear and I will attempt to indulge you.

"Ladies and gentlemen, I came here tonight as a comic and an impressionist and a singer. As you know by now . . . I hope I came here as a friend. Thank you. Thank you very much . . . for liking me. God bless you."

Blessed and happy, the crowd files out of the Jerry Lewis Theater and onto the paved walkway to the hotel. There are lights on the hill above, but few seem to notice.

What they miss is only another weary take, this time a close angle on Guy Rennie, as he rasps that Dustin/Lenny will never work another club, room, anything.

"Hit the rain."

"Speed."

"Camera."

"Action."

Guy Rennie: "Believe me. Everybody is gonna be warned about you . . ."

"Guy, wait a minute please," Fosse says. "Where's your cigar? You're supposed to have a cigar."

"I . . . I must have put it down. It must be in the trailer."

"Cut. Will somebody please go find Guy's cigar?"

"Kill the rain."

A man at the rain tower has missed the command. The downpour continues for several seconds. It's getting late. The sun will be up in a few hours and no one wants to stand around shivering through the same damn scene tomorrow night. The next shout is very loud, very angry.

"Will someone kill the goddamn rain?"

Pryor

By David Felton

OCTOBER 10, 1974 • MAY 3, 1979

AN ATTACK OF THE HEART

PEORIA, ILL. (UPI)—Black comic Richard Pryor, whose violent temper and obscenity-laced spoofs of black society kept him at loggerheads with television censors and the law, died here today after being admitted to Methodist Medical Center for what doctors termed "exhaustion and poor color."

Pryor, a former Peoria native, reportedly collapsed while attending a birthday party for his grandmother, Mrs. Marie Bryant, also black.

"We deeply regret the passing of a promising young talent," said an NBC executive who refused to be identified. "Richard Pryor had a bright mind. Had he solved some of his personal problems, he might have been another Carlin or Newhart, using humor as a tool to fight social ills." He added that although he'd never met Pryor personally, he had heard the comedian was known to use narcotics while engaging in interracial sex . . .

Well, thank God we've never had to read *that* kind of bullshit. But I'd fully prepared myself for it on the afternoon of November 10, 1977, after a local radio station reported the news of

Pryor's death. The day before, Pryor had been rushed to the Peoria hospital and placed in a coronary unit. Naturally, the rumor took hold that he'd suffered a heart attack, and since he was only thirty-six, with a turbulent history of self-abuse, indulgence and destruction, there were other rumors as well.

It's not good for a nation to lose its funniest people, I pontificated that evening to some fellow moody brooders. We'd already had our fill of comic martyrs—Lenny Bruce, Lord Buckley, Freddie Prinze and Ernie Kovacs—and to me Pryor was way beyond those guys, an authentic American humorist on the order of Mark Twain, with a vision of truth and human beauty that bordered on the spiritual.

And even when we learned that the broadcast was wrong, that Pryor was alive (a hospital spokesman reported that "when he came in, he was a very sick man," complaining of chest pains), my fears did not subside. I often suspected the poor bastard might pull a Lenny, making the Big Exit before most people—due to the canned morality of network television—would have a chance to catch his act in its pure form.

This is no longer a problem, thanks to his

new film, *Richard Pryor Live in Concert*, an uncensored documentary of a stage performance last December at the Terrace Theatre in Long Beach, California. It's more than a movie, really, it's an event. Millions of people for the first time are viewing the essential Pryor. As he himself put it, they "get to see what I do."

Those familiar with Pryor's previous stage work are also surprised by the film. His material—all seventy-eight minutes of it—is brand-new, conceived and assembled in the previous five months. And his performance is more unified and more personal, the best example yet of his ability to see and convey the humor in pain.

The difference is that, in the past, much of his material was inspired by the pain around him—the pimps, drunks, cons and junkies of the street, members of his family and his circle of friends. In *Richard Pryor Live in Concert,* the pain seems pretty much his own, particularly the pain of this last year. Maybe that's how he survived it.

Even by his standards, 1977 was a rough year for Pryor. He appeared in two movies, *Greased Lightning* and *Silver Streak,* and was working on three others, *Which Way Is Up?, Blue Collar* and *The Wiz.* In May, Pryor turned to the battleground of television, starring in his own prime-time special for NBC. He created a number of new and imaginative characters, and the show was a critical success.

In late summer, he made a deal with NBC to do a weekly series of four one-hour shows. The network, desperate for ratings, scheduled him opposite ABC's *Happy Days.* From the start there were nasty censorship hassles. Pryor planned to open the first show with the ludicrous announcement that the network had allowed him to be himself. The camera would pull back and show Pryor stark naked . . . without genitals! The bit was taped and shown to a studio audience, who laughed hysterically. NBC killed it.

Pryor retaliated with a maneuver that should earn him a place in the *Guinness Book of Poetic Justice.* He gave NBC four hours that were so bizarre and puzzling that the network had no way of censoring them, because no one knew what the fuck was going on. In one segment Pryor played the lead singer in a Kiss-style band, chanting an atonal song called "Black Death" to a 'luded-out group of rock & rollers. The song ended with the band spraying the kids with pills, heroin, machine-gun bullets and poisoned gas—leaving no survivors.

The series bombed. Some of the more nervous affiliates refused to carry it. NBC fired the last salvo by covering its ass. Even though the contract was for only four shows, the network announced the series was canceled due to poor ratings.

Pryor was starting to get bad press, and it only got worse. In September, he was placed at the top of the gay shit list after appearing for fifteen minutes at a gay-rights benefit in the Hollywood Bowl. Initially, he was warmly received. His account of the time he sucked a man's dick got a lot of laughs. But somewhere along the way, he apparently misjudged the delicate sensibilities of his audience. It may have been his frequent use of the word *faggot.* When people started booing, Pryor mumbled to himself, "Shit . . . what the fuck . . . this is really weird."

Finally Pryor exploded: "This is an evening about human rights, and I am a human being. I just wanted to see where you was *really* at, and I wanted to test you to your motherfucking *soul.* I'm doing this shit for *nuthin'.* But I wanted to come here and tell you to kiss my ass . . . with your bullshit. You understand? When the niggers was burnin' down Watts, you mother-fuckers was doin' what you wanted to do on Hollywood Boulevard . . . didn't give a shit about it." And then he walked off the stage, yelling to thousands of jeering homosexuals, "Kiss my happy, *rich* black ass!"

It was this sort of thing that made it appear, as 1977 drew to a close, that Pryor was heading for the edge. And on the first day of the next year, he went over it. Even today he refuses to discuss the incident. "Don't even ask me about it," he says. "Check the court records."

A few months earlier, Pryor had married his fourth wife, Deboragh McGuire. He'd told friends this was it, she was the love of his life; marriage was wonderful.

As it turned out, he was mistaken in this. At dawn, after celebrating New Year's Eve, Pryor got into a huge blowout with his wife and her friends and threw the friends out of his Spanish mansion in Northridge, California. As they started to drive off in their Buick, he rammed it with his Mercedes. They ran away on foot; he ran into the house, got his magnum and emptied it into the Buick, causing about $5,000 damage. Later, police arrested Pryor on two felony counts of assault with a deadly weapon and a misdemeanor charge of property damage. Deboragh moved out.

That's when I figured Pryor had lost it—a newlywed fires point-blank into a car just because his wife's friends had been sitting in it, he's probably under some pressure, right?

I didn't realize the guy was gathering material.

"I would say this has been one of the hardest years I've had, and one of the most productive. To be cliché, it's like, you can't keep a good man down. Like I reclaimed my life."

Richard spoke softly and thoughtfully, some-times halting to pare down an idea to its most useful parts. He seemed cheerful and relaxed, possibly because he was vacationing in Hawaii at the time, in Hana on Maui. He'd spent the day fishing. Caught two. Now, he sat back in his hotel room and lit a cigarette.

"I just am happier than I've ever been."

Quite a contrast from a year ago, I thought. How had he made it from there to here? What happened after his marriage broke up?

Richard mulled the question over for a moment. He cleared his throat. "You know, I felt it was over . . . I was splintered . . . in many pieces, right? And it was just all—actually, I felt *relieved.*" He started to laugh. "To tell the truth, now that I think about it, I felt relieved. And then my life was my own again. I had a chance to do what I really love."

"How come the marriage failed?"

"It happened," he said, "maybe because I was immature, or maybe because it wasn't right. You write your own script, you know what I'm sayin'? Create your own drama. You have to, some-day—you ever do this?" Pryor's voice grew airy, like he was telling a bedtime story. "My uncle taught me this. He said, 'The thing to do is, you go and take some time for yourself, and you review your whole life. You look at everything that you've ever done, or ever thought. And you don't deny no thoughts, and you don't deny no actions you ever committed. And you see who you are.'

"The good, the bad, the horrifying and all that shit—you look at it, square in the face. It's kinda like purging yourself—cleaning out, fac-ing them demons and wiping 'em out."

By June the process had apparently worked.

"One night I was driving in Beverly Hills," said Richard. "I was comin' from dinner with some friends, and I just turned the car around and went to the Comedy Store [an L.A. improv club]. And I got onstage and started working.

"Had you been thinking about it for a while?"

"No, I hadn't. I really hadn't. I just had to go up and work, that's all I know, and get in contact with my people again. And like the stuff, it just came out, man, right? I just emptied my head out, see. Like you go up there, and if you only got five minutes, just do that five minutes, but go *ahead*—keep your head open and see what new comes in. And it came outta that. I worked there till August, then went on the road."

It seemed so incredibly fast. Hadn't Lenny Bruce once compared putting together a new hour's material to writing a novel?

Pryor shrugged. "I don't know. I like to do that, though, 'cause I figure if you pay new money, you should see a new show."

"**D**on't breathe."

The voice is deep and mean. Richard Pryor's right fist attacks his chest and burrows in, his right arm swinging up and snapping his whole upper body to the left.

Bewildered, Pryor looks nervously left and right. "Huh?"

The fist and now his face have become his heart—an angry, talking heart that tightens its lips and twists and shouts again: "You heard me, motherfucker, I said don't *breathe*."

Pryor winces in pain. His mouth drops open, and he pleads in a panicked, cascading falsetto, "Okay-I-won't-breathe-I-won't-breathe-I-won't-breathe."

"Then shut the fuck"—attack!—"*up*, then."

Pryor's heart continues its assault. "You know black people got high blood *pressure* anyway, don'tcha."

The word *pressure* knocks Pryor over on his left side, facing the audience. "Yeah-I-know-it-I-know-it."

"Then watch yo' *diet!*"

"I-will-I-will." Pryor's voice drops to a gasping whisper. "Don't-kill-me-don't-kill-me-don't-kill-me-don't-kill-me." He sits up, resumes his natural expression and faces the audience.

"You be thinkin' about shit like that when you think you gonna die," he says, laughing.

The heart attack is a perfect metaphor for the show. It's as if in seventy-eight minutes his life passes before him. And us. He shows it to us with such accuracy and honesty that we laugh. It's weird, watching a whole audience laughing at a man dying onstage, and maybe it's a weird kind of laughter, something that comes from a little deeper inside; but the evidence is right there on film. They laugh.

Pryor shows us his childhood, getting whipped, going to a funeral, fighting with his father and grandmother, hunting deer in the forest, fighting in the ring. He doesn't just tell us about the stuff, like most comedians, telling jokes. He brings it to life and exposes its soul.

Richard grew up in Peoria, Illinois, having been born there in 1940. "I was born in St. Francis Hospital—I was meant to be a Catholic, you know," he recalled. "That was pretty hip to be born in St. Francis, 'cause not many niggers was born in a hospital, in Peoria. Most cats was born at home, in the kitchen. We were very *affluent*—had the largest whorehouse in the neighborhood."

"Really?" I asked. "Your mother and father . . . ?"

"My grandmother. She was the madam. We had three on one block—313, 317 and 324 North Washington. My grandmother was the rule, the power base, a very strong woman. Still is."

Richard was pretty evasive about his parents,

saying only that they "did the best they could" and that his mother, a Catholic, died five years ago and his father, a gentleman, a year later. "He died fucking a twenty-two-year-old chick," he said. "She was a junkie, he was helping her get off dope."

From 1967 through at least 1970, he underwent what might be called his Super Nigger period, a time when, perhaps, financial success went to his head, or more specifically, to his nose. Richard admitted that he was then heavily into cocaine—"Aw, man, like I bought Peru, you know?"—and booze; and that in general he "wasn't taking care of business."

But more details were recently made public when Pryor was indicted for failing to file his federal income tax during those four years, in which he earned a total of $250,000. After plea bargaining, he pleaded guilty to one of four counts—1967—and on May 13 was fined $2,500 and sentenced to ten days in jail, beginning June 4.

Later I phoned federal probation officer Marcus Woodard, who elaborated on Pryor's syndrome of irresponsibility. According to Woodard, the comedian's first legal hassle was in April 1967, when he was busted at the San Diego border for bringing in less than an ounce of marijuana. He was convicted of possession and placed on probation.

Woodard, after emphasizing that "personally I have nothing but admiration for Richard Pryor the entertainer," said the following:

"In discussing the matter with me, he told me that during those years he did not take care of his tax obligations, that he was involved, rather heavily involved, in alcohol and narcotics. He said that he just simply wasn't taking care of business, period. He said about the only person who got taken care of by him was his dope man." (A writer who interviewed him three years ago for *Ebony* magazine recalled that Richard was so coked-up at the time, he was unintelligible; the tapes had to be thrown away. He said Richard was then snorting up $100 to $200 a day.)

In 1970, Richard moved to Berkeley, where he holed up for two years, keeping pretty much to himself except when performing. He performed in clubs, wrote scripts and acted in films—the most public medium he was least likely to be censored in. Eventually Richard's interest in acting made him dissatisfied with his act, and he again quit the stage, moving to Hollywood and devoting the next two years exclusively to films and writing.

"To be free and rich and as emotionally abandoned as Richard is, you have to give up certain safeguards; you risk banana-land, and he risks it every day. He gives himself to each moment in life, totally, without a governor, without a super-ego clocking every moment. The one thing that Richard is devoid of is vanity—he is the least vain man I know."

Well, those are certainly some nice things for Mel Brooks to say about Richard Pryor. Still, Brooks seemed at times to be praising with faint damns; his choice of words occasionally raised bothersome questions.

"We know that once he settles down and he shakes off a couple of, you know, anxious, uh, *emotional traits,* he's just gonna be one of the great ballplayers of all time," Brooks said.

Anxious emotional traits? We'd heard this rumor—that Richard Pryor had at one time been considered for the lead role in *Blazing Saddles,* Brooks' last film, but that he blew it while working as a writer on that film by indulging excessively in coke and booze. (The role—a slick, Gucci-tailored black sheriff in a town of shabby white bigots—went to Cleavon Little.)

Brooks emphatically denied that this was the

case. "I heard of that reputation," he said of Pryor's past drug history, "and it proved to be wrong when I was working with him. He was always in and working on our job, and there was no audience waiting to love him—it was just fucking hard work, you know, and he was there."

However, Brooks also denied that Pryor had ever been seriously considered for the part. "That's a studio choice. Very simply, they're afraid to go with an unknown, unknown as far as they are concerned, vis-à-vis dollars and the public."

Yet Pryor, somewhat bitter that he didn't get the role, had told me that Brooks had wanted him to have it. Brooks started hedging. "Oh, yeah, when we were *writing* it," he said, "before I even, you know, *thought* of anybody. When we were writing it, it was so natural; I mean he was just acting out so many things so beautifully. But it was just simply out of the question. They weren't gonna risk all that money on an unknown."

So what "anxious emotional traits" was Brooks referring to? I mentioned the rumor about Pryor's coke habit and another report about his failing to show up last year for a scheduled seminar on comedy at the Sherwood Oaks Experimental College in Hollywood. Richard shrugged and said nothing.

"What, you don't want to talk about that?" I asked.

"No, man," he said sourly, "I don't want to talk about it."

I explained I was bringing the matter up because there was this riddle I couldn't understand. Here he was, one of the most innovative comedians around, and he obviously knew it. I mentioned that during our interview he had indirectly compared himself to Miles Davis, that he had said, "I think I've had a lot of influence

on the scene. I see a lot of comics working different, in dealing with themselves. After a comic comes and sees me, I don't think he could do anything less. It's like a young trumpet player go watches Miles, you know, and he either goes to drums or he practices." And yet, for some reason, Richard wasn't getting the full recognition he deserved.

For several moments Richard was silent, his face silhouetted by the harsh, late-afternoon sun streaming in through the coffee shop window. Finally he leaned forward over the table, his forehead furrowed all crazy, and said haltingly, "Frustration . . . is the worst thing, you know?" He lowered his head, studying the table, his mouth open and grasping for words. When he looked up, his eyes were filled with tears.

"Sometimes . . ." Richard's voice broke off, and now the tears began to flow like rivers down both sides of his nose. ". . . it seems there just ain't no way. . . ." But the words stopped coming. He wiped his eyes slowly with a paper napkin, held the napkin out in front of him, looked at it and for some reason let out a quick, hysterical laugh. Then he lowered his head again and continued crying, silently, for another minute.

It may be that Richard Pryor, in his ability to laugh at a paper napkin stained with tears, has discovered a secret to survival in these jive times. So far he seems to be surviving well, but his problems could continue for some while. And, because of the bold artistic route he has chosen, they are problems he must handle pretty much alone.

Just before Richard was to enter prison, probation officer Marcus Woodard said this about him:

"Interestingly, he told me he visits his grandmother in Peoria, Illinois, occasionally. I asked him if, when he goes back, the town sort of throws the welcome mat out for him, since he is a success. He told me that there is no such treatment for him, that many of the people that he knew, that he grew up with, are no longer living. Either they have been killed by police during the commission of crimes, or some of them have overdosed and are no longer living.

"He seems to feel that the people back there who *are* living, that he grew up with, just don't care for him, that they're a little offended by the fact that he got away from there and made a success."

Singles Journal

By Cameron Crowe

OCTOBER 1, 1992

"**A**ndy's dead," the voice said flatly. It sounded so unlike my old friend Kelly, this dispassionate monotone on the answering machine. Kelly was one of the most excitable guys I knew. In recent years he'd become a rock manager, guiding the career of a fledgling Seattle band named Mother Love Bone. Its lead singer and frontman, Andy Wood, had successfully been battling a nagging heroin problem. But the night before Wood was to meet his boyhood idols Paul Stanley and Gene Simmons of Kiss, he'd scored some deadly heroin on the street. They found him comatose in his apartment, his favorite T-shirt mysteriously ripped to pieces in the washer. After several days on a life-support machine, Andy Wood slipped away. "I'm still at the hospital," Kelly said with a sad sigh. "I'll be home later."

My wife and I stared at the answering machine. Within a few minutes, we'd psychoanalyzed Kelly's voice. He was in trouble. No, worse, he was a ticking time bomb. He needed help. He needed friendship. We got in the car and drove to his house—immediately.

Rounding the corner to Kelly's place, it was obvious that his other friends had the same idea. Cars lined the streets. Inside the small house were Andy Wood's friends, his band mates, members of other bands from throughout the city. The same odd look on all their faces—*I've never had a close friend die before*. And still they kept arriving, these dazed Seattle musicians—a breed all their own, the inspired children of pro basketball and Cheap Trick and Led Zeppelin and Black Flag and Kiss.

I was thirty-two at the time and felt a part of something. Somewhere around midnight, warming over a barbecue pit, I felt rocked by the whole experience. I'd been working pretty steadily since I was fifteen, and looking back, most of my friends were made through work. They were *acquaintances* more than friends. And here were these disconnected single people, many from broken homes, many meeting each other for the first time, forming their own family. In the coming years, many of the musicians in that room would see success far beyond their early dreams, beyond even the arena dreams of Andy Wood. But that night it was mostly about staying warm, pulling together. It was almost instinctual. And I thought about Los Angeles, where musicians would already have slipped audition tapes into Kelly's pocket.

I was rewriting an old script of mine at the

Bridget Fonda and Matt Dillon play just one of several screwed-up couples in the Seattle-grunge homage, *Singles*. Copyright © 1992 Warner Bros., a division of Time Warner Entertainment Company, L.P.

time. It was called *Singles,* and that night it took a different course. I wanted to write something that captured the feeling in that room. Not Andy's story but the story of how people instinctively need to be *together.* Is anybody truly single? I knew I'd soon be rewriting the rewrite of my script, and I knew I had to direct it, too.

Three years later, *Singles* is a movie in the can. It's the story of six Seattle urbanites, their lives in and around the apartment complex where they reside. A lot of the music was provided by local musicians and bands, but contrary to some advance reports, it's not a movie about the birth of the now-hot Seattle scene or even the story of how Mother Love Bone gained a new singer (Eddie Vedder) and became Pearl Jam. It's the story of disconnected single people making their way, forming their own unspoken family. Everything about the movie screamed obsession. Making it in Seattle became an obsession. Getting it perfect became an obsession. And early on, I started obsessively keeping a journal.

Looking at the stacks of pages of diaries, I feel like the guy on *The Outer Limits* who revisits the home he lived in three hundred years earlier. Printed journals often have a self-serving sheen over them. Like bad date talk, they're often a laundered version of reality. I wanted this to be different. Some of my earliest reading pleasures were Pete Townshend's 1970–71 essays in ROLLING STONE about his work with the Who. His writing gave me the feeling that he was sending a letter to a friend, and in that spirit, I wanted to keep a running account of *Singles.*

Some nights making the movie, I'd write for an hour, other times only a few minutes. (One entry reads only: "Aaaaaaaaagh!") These raw, nocturnal entries were more like a cleansing ritual than a guide to intelligent filmmaking. To anyone offended, please know that I intend to offend myself as well. So for whatever reasons, perhaps in the spirit of preventing *you at home* from developing a need to write and direct a collagelike movie with eighty-seven speaking parts, I present this to you now.

10-15-90: Campbell Scott will play the part of Steve Dunne, the traffic engineer at the center of *Singles.* Everything is exploding at once for Campbell. Today he got the part opposite Julia Roberts in *Dying Young.* He's playing a leukemia victim who falls in love with his nurse. A problem surfaces—in *Dying Young* he loses his hair. Many nervous calls are traded between our movie and *Dying Young.* Toward the end of the day, it's resolved. *Dying Young* will not actually cut his hair; he'll wear a bald cap with a wig over it. Whew.

2-24-91: Campbell has arrived in Seattle. We meet for dinner. His hair is very, very short. He is pale. He looks like a leukemia victim. Sitting in a dark restaurant, my early fears slip away. We'll do something about his hair. Campbell is psyched to play the part of Steve. We're in sync. I raise a toast. "Don't jinx it," he says.

2-25-91: First day of rehearsal goes smoothly. We blast through the scenes. Kyra Sedgwick and Campbell Scott have a nice chemistry together. Around lunchtime, we step out into the daylight. I see problems. Campbell still looks like a leukemia victim. We still have two weeks. What kind of vitamins make hair grow?

Today, Bridget Fonda and Matt Dillon arrive in town. Matt, who will play a Seattle musician named Cliff Poncier, has already spent time in New York with Mother Love Bone's Jeff Ament, Stone Gossard and their intensely shy new lead singer, Eddie Vedder. Their new band is called Mookie Blaylock, after the New Jersey Nets basketball player. [Later they're renamed Pearl

Jam.] In the movie, they will play Cliff's fictional band, Citizen Dick. Matt has already got a lead singer's walk down—all attitude, chest puffed slightly out. I wanted rehearsals to begin weeks early so the cast could soak up the local atmosphere and the music.

Tonight we go to see Mookie Blaylock and Alice in Chains performing at the Off Ramp. The cast meets for the first time in the lobby of our hotel. For a few minutes, nobody says much. ("I hope this isn't a yuppie movie," Matt announces, picking an odd conversation opener.) We go to the club. It's sweaty and packed, and the cast slowly makes friends as we sit in a corner booth.

2-27-91: We read through the script today, and it sounds good. Afterward, the cast hangs around in my office, with downtown Seattle as a backdrop. They've become friends. Six months of casting is paying off. It's still mind-bending, though, to see the characters you've written sitting around and talking *in character*.

3-1-91: Campbell's hair is shaped. It's like shortening the legs of a table. In the process, more is mistakenly cut.

3-9-91: Campbell's hair is becoming a flash point. I sense he's picking up on it. Rehearsals fall apart.

3-10-91: Nancy [my wife] tells me I talked continuously in my sleep. "Sick hair," I said, over and over.

3-11-91: Kyra is in the first scene, and she's like clockwork; she's excellent. We have a celebratory lunch with the cast—except for Campbell, who has disappeared.

3-12-91: Campbell shows up this morning to report that he married his longtime girlfriend Anne over the weekend. What a way to start a movie called *Singles*.

3-13-91: No sleep. Warner Bros. sees the dailies. "Campbell Scott looks sick," they say.

3-14-91: I'm keeping the studio's panic from Campbell, but he senses something is wrong. He's starting to make odd cracks and barbed jokes; they fire in every direction. It's getting under my skin. I take him aside and ask him what the problem is. He is instantly apologetic. "It's my sense of humor," he says. Later in the day, a WB executive calls and suggests replacing him. I stand by Campbell and hope for sun and speedy hair growth.

3-17-91: I call Campbell and suggest a wig. He takes it well, but just beneath the surface I feel his angst. I admire actors; it can't be easy approximating real life with a huge, glowing camera in your face.

3-18-91: Jim True, the celebrated stage actor from Chicago, is loose and funny as the maître d' and amateur Francophile named David Bailey. True has had tough luck in movies. His performances in smaller parts were trimmed from *The Accidental Tourist* and *Fat Man and Little Boy*. It will not happen in this movie.

Campbell says there is a wig he wore for a photo in *Dying Young*. It looked very realistic. Calls go out: *Get that wig*. In the meantime, he finds a strange long-haired wig on the set and casually strolls around wearing it. His self-effacing move defuses the pressure. He wins everybody over. What a roller coaster.

3-22-91: The *Dying Young* wig arrives. Campbell and I work on his look in the hair-and-makeup trailer. Nobody is allowed to see him. Finally, when the wig is right, we test it out. Seattle actor Johnny "Sugarbear" Willis arrives for a small role and, knowing nothing of the hair crisis, tromps into the trailer. He chats with us for five minutes about crab fishing. We seem to be getting away with it. Then Johnny leans forward, eyeing Campbell carefully. "That's not your hair, man," he says.

I meet Campbell out in the hallway and tell him we're going to go with his real hair, shortness be damned. Back to the trailer we go. In the three days we've taken to find his wig, Campbell's hair has grown *just* enough to work.

3-27-91: I'm starting to sound like Matt Dillon. It's infectious, his New York jukebox accent. For all his tough-guy parts gone by, he is a loved actor on the street. Strangers tell him they're "chillin' like Matt Dillon." He takes it all in with a bemused grin. He was slow to commit to the part of Cliff Poncier, but now he's here, and it feels right. Walking around the set in his GREEN RIVER T-shirt, he looks perfect. A dedicated music fan, his trailer blasts with Tyrone Davis, the Replacements and the Clash. He's brimming with ideas.

"I love Bridget," Matt says several times today. "I'm in love with her." I think he means it. He's anxious to play a reversal on the usual romantic male lead. In this movie, he will pursue the girl. ("And I don't want to smoke; I see my old movies, and I'm always smoking.") He's almost always dead-on with his first take, and if he isn't somewhere around take five he might disappear around a corner. Then you might hear the sound of someone slugging a wall with his fist. Returning with laserlike concentration, Dillon's next take is usually perfect. His knuckles are bulky reminders that he's been acting almost nonstop since he was fourteen. "Sometimes I'm hard on myself," he says. "No big deal."

3-31-91: Easter, a day off. I look out the window at the water, and the sky goes blue. Two things about Seattle: One, this whole town is jacked on coffee, and two, on the right day it looks like the cover of *Houses of the Holy.*

4-1-91: The Bridget Fonda phase of filming is kicking in. She plays Janet Livermore, the architecture student killing time in an espresso job. Janet is in love with love, and I wrote the part for Bridget. For months, in person or on the telephone, we've discussed every aspect of *Singles.* Like a dry young Barbara Stanwyck, she nailed down every small detail of Janet's life. Seeing her finally do the part, I realize she's deceptively low-ball. From three feet away, it appears like she's not even acting. Seeing the same thing on film the next day, she explodes.

4-4-91: Tonight the studio calls to say the movie is getting serious. This is probably not a compliment.

4-8-91: "Kyra is in tears," says the production assistant. In her trailer, Kyra confesses that she's not sure how she's doing playing Linda. Haven't I been telling her all along? "Yes," she says, "but you're so enthusiastic that when you get quiet, I get worried." She's right, of course. I have been quiet. My working relationship with Campbell is deteriorating daily. The air is thick with the unspoken. I know it's not easy for him. Steve Dunne is the hardest part in the movie. All around him are characters with odd and interesting quirks. His is the Curse of the Normal Guy.

4-9-91: The day ends with the last scene of the movie—Matt and Bridget alone in the elevator. It's a romantic scene, and it has some intricate timing. We film it fourteen times. Between takes, Bridget pluckily explains that kissing scenes are much easier when she actually likes the guy. "He's a sweetheart," she says of Matt.

4-10-91: Finally, the confrontation with Campbell. The hostile humor is creeping into his performance. "And who are you?" he says, when I try to talk with him. I am mystified again by human behavior, even as I stand here trying to direct a movie about the mysteries of human behavior. A few minutes later, while the camera is rolling, Campbell cavalierly flips off the camera assistant Shawn Hise as he snaps the slate. (Shawn looks wounded; he's a Campbell fan.) That's it. I take him aside and tell him again to knock off the endless sarcasm. Campbell goes off, his voice booming. He's pissed off at the way actors are treated. He wants me to understand him. He wants actors *everywhere* to be understood. The sheer volume of his voice is astounding. And then it sort of sinks in. . . . *He's yelling at me.* I cut loose myself. I start yelling at him. It's freeing, and he backs down. In fact, he seems grateful. Now we just want to make friends again, like two guys who just had a fender bender and, their hearts racing, have to bond over the crisis. He tells me he respects me, he thinks I'm a great writer. Pointedly, as thirty waiting crew members pretend they're not listening, he doesn't add the occupation I'm currently pursuing—*directing.* Maybe I'll just be a writer. This part of it, when blood is in the water, is not my favorite.

4-11-91: Mark Arm from Mudhoney brings Sonic Youth to the set. They arrive on an important day. Today is the French Club scene. It has been the target of countless assassination attempts in story meetings at the studio. ("Take it out. It'll never end up in the movie.") The scene survives because they are wrong. Proudly, I collar [Sonic Youth guitarist] Thurston Moore. For some reason, I feel the need to explain the French Club scene to him in great detail. He nods courteously. His eyes glaze. Thurston invites us all to their big concert tonight with Neil Young. Can't wait for this show.

4-12-91: Passed out in the hotel and missed the show.

4-19-91: This movie is a freight train. Eric Stoltz has joined us for a few days. During *Fast Times at Ridgemont High,* Stoltz once promised to be in "everything you ever write." In *Singles* he plays a Bitter Mime. Typically, he is twisted and savagely funny in the part. Stoltz and Bridget are a couple in real life, they're good together, their relationship seems destined for a life outside of news photos.

It's a loose and goofy night, and we finish a ton of work. By 4:00 A.M., Campbell, Eric Stoltz and I are doing Michael Bolton impressions. Bolton sings Zeppelin. Bolton sings Guns n' Roses. We are all so tired that just the word— *Bolton*—sends us into hysterics.

4-22-91: The studio calls and floats a (lead) balloon. Isn't the title *Singles* "dated"? Isn't there a popular song that would be better? I hope this issue goes away. Jeff Ament comes to the set at lunchtime with the first rehearsal tape of potential songs for the movie. Mookie Blaylock is now Pearl Jam. The first song, "State of Love and Trust," is ferocious. It's about battling with your instincts in love (". . . help me from myself \ . ."). Somehow it matches the movie-in-progress. The tape contains four other new Pearl Jam songs. A little over a year after losing Andy Wood, Ament walks with quiet pride. Like maybe lightning is striking twice.

4-28-91: We film Alice in Chains playing live at the underground club Desoto. It's a boost. I can't tell you much about the precise filmic style of John Ford's Westerns, but I can tell you about the pure emotional perfection of Todd Rundgren's *Hermit of Mink Hollow* or the Replacements' *Tim,* Mother Love Bone's "Crown of Thorns" or even the Beach Boys' *Pet Sounds.* To get that feeling watching *Singles,* that would be something.

4-30-91: The Car Crash scene goes well. Today I overhear two grips having a conversation about me on the radio-mike headset. I hear that I look especially happy today, that I must have gotten laid last night and that after all the talky scenes it was great to get out there today and "T-bone that fuckin' car."

5-24-91: Tonight is the wrap party. Extras are starting to get drunk now, telling me how this has been the best time of their lives. Where was I? I feel like I blinked and the whole thing was over. I am proud to have made a movie in which Bridget Fonda shares a scene with the legendary Sub Pop thrash rocker Tad. But now our de facto family is breaking up. Movie-crew people are nomads. They'll go on to three or four more movies, and I'll still be with the child—*Singles*.

7-23-91: Today is the day we look at the first cut of the movie. It's two hours and forty-five minutes long. Parts are thrilling; parts make me squirm. Back in the editing room with Richard [Chew, our editor] and Art [Linson, executive producer], we attack the problems. Nothing is as funny as we'd hoped. Everything feels long. Oddly enough, I don't feel panicked.

9-9-91: I'm starting to panic. Perspective is slipping away. I'm lucky to have Richard, a careful editor, a protector of characters. Forty minutes have been taken out of the movie. I hope it's the right forty minutes. I know this—the French Club scene is staying in.

10-4-91: I have reached tunnel vision. It's a strange syndrome. All I do is watch *Singles*. The only people I see are crew people who watch *Singles*. I want to go out with my wife, maybe to see *The Fisher King*, but I can't. It's too dangerous. I might feel bad about *Singles*. I am Bubble Man. All I can see are bona fide classics from another era—which don't count—or very bad contemporary movies. I stay home and watch Elvis in *Live a Little, Love a Little,* and all is right with the world again.

10-30-91: Whatever cockiness that surfaced, and was deliciously enjoyed, a few months ago is disappearing fast. Every conversation with the studio lately is about the Cards. The future course of this movie will be set by four hundred Glendale [California] moviegoers between the ages of seventeen and thirty-four, recruited mostly at malls. They will fill out . . . the Cards. The Cards are then tallied, and the result is what WB is truly after . . . the Numbers.

11-6-91: Today is the first preview. I get a speeding ticket. I'm a mess. I inch toward the preview, feeling very nervous. The movie begins on time; the audience seems to really pay attention. Then, a restlessness sets in. I die with every walkout. I study the way they walk. Are they going to the bathroom? Will they come back? *Come back!* (Most do.)

The Numbers are average. There is an immediate and powerful desire to point fingers. Typically, I think I've run from the raw emotions in the movie. I went for the jokes. I'm reminded of words I've heard from close friends my whole life: "I don't know when you're kidding and when you're being serious." Tonight, I think it's true of *Singles*.

12-19-91: I agree to take the French Club scene out for one screening.

1-1-92: Soundgarden's Chris Cornell sends in a rich collection of incidental music. This movie takes music like a sponge. For me, Cornell is the very soul of Seattle music and its endearing darkness. I remember him the night Andy Wood died. He put a hand on Jeff Ament's shoulder. "I'm gonna call you tomorrow," Cornell said, angry at the world. "We're gonna ride bikes and fucking smoke cigarettes." It's an odd moment to remember so clearly. Something about it just nailed this city.

1-24-92: WB has offered new title suggestions: *In the Midnight Hour, Love in Seattle, Leave Me a Message* and a grim selection of others. It's all done politely, of course, but the pressure is unmistakable. Now, with the success of Nirvana, they've come up with yet another title: *Come As You Are.* I am powerless to stop them.

2-7-92: There is confusion about how to sell

a realistic movie about love in a *Lethal Weapon* world. I tell the marketing executives that *Singles* is a movie for college-age audiences. They don't believe me. Their research says the movie appeals to Young Girls. We have lost our April release date. *Singles* is adrift.

I have to put all this out of my mind. We have looping to do with Campbell Scott. Our past scrimmages still hang in the air. He asks about this journal. I tell him if it ever gets published, it shouldn't be a fluff piece. "Write about us fighting and everything," he says.

2-10-92: My stealthlike attempt to return the French Club scene to the movie is thwarted by Richard Chew.

2-13-92: L.A. is in the midst of an intense thunderstorm. Our third preview goes well nonetheless. The Numbers inch upward. [Tonight, the rating goes up with Young Males and down with Young Females. A new corporate panic sets in.) I'm happy, although I feel that there is still something missing at the end.

I read the Cards for an answer. I get the creepy feeling that the same four hundred people are shaping this movie . . . and every movie. To read their comments, they seem drunk with power . . . or maybe just drunk. "More wicked tit," says a fourteen-year-old, who also adds that he's married. A nineteen-year-old who checked the boxes "Male" and "Female" ("I'm bi") as well as "Black" and "White" ("Nabisco Oreo") writes in large, looping letters: "I love the sexual activity and the hooters. I love the Anal Fury. The music was awesome, bra." This one goes on my refrigerator. It's hard to read this stuff. It's like hearing people talk behind your back. I've got to remember the goal . . . a personal movie about relationships, a collage of lives and emotions. "It's honest," says another girl. I want to kiss her. I've got to sleep a little, wipe the stress off my face. What is Anal Fury?

2-16-92: Sleep comes in small bursts, as I dream of an intricate movie version of *Hawaii Five-O.* Even my dreams are trying to be more commercial. . . . The studio is not impressed with the Numbers. They are full of suggestions on how to make the movie more palatable. I have made the right movie for the wrong studio.

This is the biggest crime of test marketing. It hits directors at their most vulnerable time. You start out proud and alone, defending your vision. By the end, you're wobbling on two rubbery legs, obsessed on how to reach Young Males. It's a trap. Suddenly, all poetry is replaced by equation. All you want is to survive, to get those Numbers up. To get your movie released.

4-1-92: The last marketing preview will help determine our release. The screening goes well. A flash of perspective hits me. The movie needs to be set in context. Privately, I vow to restore the original ending, a voice montage of people all over the city, everywhere, obsessing about love. *Singles* is not just about six characters; it's about a world of people needing to make that *connection.* That's the last piece in the puzzle.

5-22-92: We're in New York for three screenings, the first time the completed movie has been shown outside of Los Angeles. It is the first time we'll show it to a (mostly) college-age crowd. There is loud, heartfelt applause. Hearing it now, in New York City, is a real high. Jokingly, I later tell Richard Chew that I want to put back the French Club scene. "No," he says. A good-humored man, I have rendered him humorless on this subject. I will say this about the French Club scene, and then I will let it go. There's always laser disc.

5-23-92: When will filmmakers fight back against the damning effect of market research? Why is *Singles* still adrift? We continue to fight the currents. First, the Numbers . . . then the

Cards . . . then the Release Schedule. Maybe *this* is Anal Fury.

6-2-92: "Congratulations," says the smooth voice on the telephone. "You have a release date."

I'm packing my desk to move out of our office. We've been in postproduction for over a year. There are stray artifacts from the filming—Steve and Linda's pregnancy test, Cliff's guitar picks and then a strange-looking white hatbox. I reach inside.

It's Campbell's wig. I pick it up. Except I don't see a *wig,* I see the making of this movie. I see every expectation, dashed hope, every exciting and exhausting aspect of filmmaking. How fragile the whole process is. The movie is finished, and I'm proud of it. Soon it will have a life of its own. I pack the wig in the back of my car. Like any great obsession, *Singles* dies hard.

Tonight, I'll sleep.

SMELLS LIKE TEAM SPIRIT

Madonna and Rosanna Arquette, ROLLING STONE, issue 447, May 9, 1985.
Photograph by Herb Ritts

Woody Allen and Diane Keaton on Love and *Annie Hall*

By Ben Fong-Torres

JUNE 30, 1977

Annie Hall (Diane Keaton) is getting ready to engage Alvy Singer (Woody Allen) in their first conversation. They'd just met for a doubles match at this tennis club in Manhattan, and now they're back in street clothes, which means for Annie a white men's shirt and baggy, wrinkled tan slacks, a black vest and a white polka-dot black tie that falls out over her belt buckle. Her hair is mostly swept up under a black fedora, and she enters laughing and waving . . . "Hi, hi."

Alvy Singer returns the greeting. Hall stands there, swaying a little, cups her hands together and smiles big. "Well," she says with another wave, "bye!"

As she turns to go, Singer speaks up: "You play very well." She pounces, "Oh, *yeah?* So do you!" and is immediately stricken. "Oh, God, ooh, what a dumb thing to say, right?" Nervous giggle. "You say, 'You play well,' then right away I have to say, '*You* play well.'" Her hands go to her hips, in reprimanding position. She shakes her head, looks down, all contrite, lets her left hand drop. "Oh, God, Annie . . . well, oh, well—" Her scolding is over, and she is bright again—"La-di-da," she singsongs. "La-di-da."

It is only thirty seconds into the scene, but the movie audience is already in love. They applaud Keaton's "La-di-da."

A romance begins.

And I become, like Alvy Singer, a man for whom love is too weak a word. I *lurve* her, I *luff* her, I *loave* her.

Jeez, what a way to be talking. I mean, I'm supposed to go and *interview* Diane Keaton.

Her doorbell makes a loud, jarring sound. Seconds later, she opens the door, fast, and backs up, welcoming me in. "Hi, hi," she says, extending her hand. She is dressed in men's clothing: a white shirt, an old vest, oversize suit pants with subdued striping and rolled-her-own cuffs. I hand her a small bouquet of apricot roses—an old New Journalism ploy—and she goes into a spasm: "Oh, wow," she says in her singing, soprano voice. "Wow . . . jeez, you didn't have to do this."

Well. So this is Diane Keaton, Woody Allen's leading lady in *Play It Again, Sam; Sleeper; Love and Death* and, last and most of all, *Annie Hall.*

At age thirty-one, Keaton is the closest she's been to emerging from behind Woody Allen's diminutive shadow. Through her title role in

Annie Hall she has become *the* comer among actresses. A dramatic lead role in the film version of Judith Rossner's *Looking for Mr. Goodbar,* due out this fall, is expected to nudge her even higher.

Today, though, she is straight out of *Annie Hall.* There are her clear, excitable blue eyes, her high, round cheekbones, her long, straw-brown hair and those large, fluttery, wayward hands. I expect a flustered Keaton, speaking sentences the way my father drives, as if she knows she's headed for an accident and must make all these sudden stops, backup moves and surprising little turns.

She does not disappoint. At her kitchen table, we talk about being Capricorns and being pigeonholed in all the astrology books as humorless. I note that Keaton doesn't seem to mind a laugh now and then. "Just occasionally, you know," she says, "not very often. I have a severe life."

Her kitchen is very white—walls, doors, floors, white appliances, Braun coffee grinder and Osterizer, white salt and pepper shakers, spice rack and watering can, Keri lotion in a white container on the white kitchen shelf. And a white wall telephone.

"White," she says, "is very cleansing for me. Also, I like a lot of room. It opens things up to me. I don't like it closing in."

And yet, her outfits are mostly dark and layered, so that most of her body is constantly covered up. "I feel most comfortable that way, relaxed," she says. "I'm very self-conscious about my body." Her clothes, she says, date back to her childhood in Santa Ana, a suburb of Los Angeles, and going through thrift shops with her mom for fun—and for actual clothes, which Diane would design and Mom would sew. "Stores were a way of expressing ourselves," she says, "since there were not a lot of *museums* in Santa Ana." She studies her pants, which look like they belong in a museum. "It's beautiful fabric, isn't it?" she asks gently. "I love patterns and stripes." She says she thinks she found today's outfit in a men's store. And, yes, that ensemble she had on in the tennis club scene in *Annie Hall* was out of her own closet. "Mainly, I like that kind of clothing," she says. "I don't have a lot of gowns." A laugh begins to build. "And I don't have *any* tiaras!"

The rest of the apartment is sparse and contemporary. Her bed, which is a yard off the ground on a wooden platform, also serves as a dresser. It is tightly made, a white cotton spread shrink-wrapped around her mattress.

Diane's apartment is in the Upper Sixties; Woody Allen's penthouse is a few blocks north. Like Keaton's place, it is clean and open, but it is filled with color, the tasteful, dark colors of rugs and wing chairs and chests and canisters and shelves full of chinaware and books. Allen has lived here some eight years, including the year he and Keaton lived together, 1971. And guess who helped him decorate?

Allen, himself decorated in tan slacks and blue work shirt over a T-shirt just beginning to tatter, says Keaton accounted for "tons of stuff all through the house. In recent years, she's gotten more and more interested in a kind of gallery, spare, white look. But she's crazy about it here. Our tastes have coincided an enormous amount, which I found very surprising, considering that I came from an urban New York Jewish background and hers was totally different."

Well, now, you're what Grammy Hall would call a "real Jew." She hates Jews. She thinks they just make money, but let me tell you, she's the one, is she ever.
—Annie Hall to Alvy Singer

Keaton and Allen are best friends. Allen wrote

Annie Hall (with Marshall Brickman, also his co-writer on *Love and Death*) for Keaton (whose last name is actually Hall; Keaton is her mother's maiden name). Although it is not exactly their story, there is an understandable tendency to take what is on the screen to be what happened in real life. For example, that quality of Keaton's, that comic nervousness and self-deprecation that makes her so lovable, so easy to want to reassure. Allen knows it well.

"I think it's something that she grew up with, and she probably learned at an infant's age that that kind of thing is very endearing to people," he says. "But it's not at all calculated. Tony Roberts [costar in first the stage, then the film version of *Play It Again, Sam*] used to feel that she was the type that would wake up in the morning and *immediately* start apologizing. She's one of those people who is forever putting herself down—and always coming through."

When something counts, says Allen, Keaton gets all jittery. And she does not eat. So at the Caffe Tartufo, while I lunch, she orders a Perrier water and tosses a carefully rolled stick of Doublemint into her mouth. "I love gum," she says. "It's very pleasing for me to crack it."

She talks about how she met Woody. She had been in *Hair* on Broadway in 1968 and heard about auditions for this new Woody Allen play called *Play It Again, Sam.* Allen had written a vehicle for his own acting debut; he would portray a recently separated film critic with a Bogart fixation and an apparent problem finding dames. (Allen himself was going through a divorce from Louise Lasser at the time.) The female role was a small one: Woody's best friend's wife, with whom Woody falls in love.

Keaton had impressed Allen and the play's director, Joe Hardy, right away, but they had to go through some fifty other actresses. Finally,

she was called back as a finalist. "And he had to come up and audition with me," says Keaton, "and he was as scared as I was. And I thought he was great—I'd seen him on television before and I thought he was real cute—you know? He looked good to me. I liked him. Mainly, he was as scared as me, which I found real appealing."

Woody, indeed, remembers being nervous. "I was scared because—first of all, I had never acted in my life. I was strictly a nightclub comic. And then, when we called her back, we were worried that she'd be too tall, you know, and we didn't want the joke of the play to be that I was in love with a, you know, superlooking woman. And so we got onstage together, and *both* of us were nervous—I felt, 'Oh, this is a real actress, she was in *Hair,* and I'm just going to waste her time' . . . and we measured back to back, and it was like being in the third grade." Allen, who usually maintains a sober, jokeless air during interviews, laughs at the memory. "And we were just about the same height, and so that was it."

Keaton had an immediate crush on Allen, and Woody was also openly smitten. Something in the way she dressed:

"She'd come in every day with an absolutely spectacularly imaginative combination of clothes. They were just great." Asked for an example, Allen himself gets imaginative: "Oh, she would—she was the type that would come in with, you know, a football jersey and a skirt . . . and combat boots and, you know"—he is cracking up again—"you know, *oven mittens* . . .

"And I thought she was very charming to be around, and of course you always get the impulse with Diane to protect her. And she was so bright and so quick. She's also a real easy laugher, which is very seductive, and we kind of drifted together is what happened."

"**T**he first time I called for Diane in California, I picked her up in Santa Ana, and she . . ."

Allen looks out one of his floor-to-ceiling windows, as if measuring distance. "From here to across the street was a supermarket—and we wanted to get some gum, 'cause she always had, like, a chaw of gum in her mouth, like a baseball player, and she said, 'Well, let's get in the car and go.' And I said, 'You're going to get in the car and go?' And she said, 'Yeah!' Her whole life, she had been getting in the car and driving four hundred feet to the supermarket. She said, 'You're not going to walk, are you?' And I said, 'Well, yeah, of course, I mean, I walk *thirty times* that length without thinking to get the newspapers,' and she couldn't believe it. And I walked with her, and she said, 'You know, hey, I guess you *can* walk.' I mean, it was *so shattering.*"

Woody and Diane acted together in *Play It Again, Sam* for a year—"A long haul," says Keaton—and every night, Woody would lose—or give—Diane back to her husband, the way Bogie gave Bergman back to Henreid. But in real life, it was the beginning of a beautiful friendship.

Keaton got a small part, "about six minutes," in 1970, in a comedy called *Lovers and Other Strangers*. Then it was Woody Allen almost all the way, beginning in 1972 with the film version of *Play It Again, Sam,* for which Allen expanded her role, and followed by *Sleeper* and *Love and Death*. With Allen, Keaton matured into a comic actress able to help shape her own character and able to move into drama, in the *Godfather*. While Keaton is most often referred to as "Oh, yes, Woody Allen's girlfriend," she has done more than hang on to his coattails with her oven mittens.

Faced with the suggestion that Allen has been her crutch, Keaton's voice becomes cold steel. Even her gum is quiet. "I don't believe that at all," she says. "I feel that everybody has a career based on somebody and we're influenced by somebody and I have to feel that I have the talent to back it up. And I feel I've worked hard. I don't agree with that. Otherwise I'd kill myself."

Woody: "I have not been a crutch for her at all. It's been absolutely aboveboard. You could reverse that and think that she's been a crutch to me in many ways; I mean, she's been an enormously supportive person to *me* on projects."

Keaton, he says, is "the best person in the world to let read a script, because she's totally ingenuous. She's not trying to be impressive, she doesn't care if it was written by Chekhov. She's perfectly willing to pick it up, read it and say, 'I think it's boring' or 'I think it's wonderful.' I feel secure working with her. If she tells me something is creepy, I reexamine it."

In her vocabulary, Keaton alternates "wonderful" and "neat" to indicate her highest approval.

ALVY *(picking up a book): Sylvia Plath. An interesting poetess whose tragic suicide was misinterpreted as romantic by the college-girl mentality.*
ANNIE: *Oh, yeah, right. I don't know, some of her poems seemed neat to me.*
ALVY: *"Neat?" I hate to tell you this, but it's 1975. "Neat" went out about the turn of the century.*
　　　　　　　—Alvy and Annie in their first talk

'You'd never know it from just a quick meeting with her—or the quality she projects—but Keaton is a genuine intellectual," says Woody. "When you meet her, she is a gangly, sometimes awkward, sweet kind of actress, and you tend to think of the other actresses you meet who are obsessed with the part and agents and parties, and she's not that way at all. She is very responsive to books and ideas. If she reads Camus or Dostoevsky, it doesn't just wash over her. She gets very, very involved with ideas and knows what they're saying and how it affects her life, and life in general. Her personality belies that completely, and that's the most curious thing about her."

Woody was not exactly Keaton's Henry Higgins. "When I first met her," he says, "all the equipment was there, but she had come from Santa Ana, California, and had not been exposed to any kind of cerebration at all. And she gradually got more and more exposed to theater, literature, poetry, art and photography. She just took to it naturally."

That's precisely what Keaton is to Allen: a natural, in her humor, which he agrees is more attitudinal than verbal (or even visual); in her intellectual growth, and, most of all, in her acting. "She *wishes* she could work on parts the way other actors and actresses do it"—in fact, Keaton points to Robert De Niro and Katharine Hepburn as two of her favorites, for their enthusiasm and "gung-ho attitude" toward the craft of acting—"but she's a natural."

Woody Allen, of course, is a little biased. But he absolutely swears that being madly in love with Keaton had nothing to do with his instincts. "It was in*ev*itable," he says, "it was just apparent the minute I was acting with her in *Play It Again, Sam* that she was a major comic talent. And it was confirmed for me by people who would come to the show. I remember Jack Benny came one night and said, 'That girl is going to be gigantic.'"

Allen enthusiastically joins the critics who have taken to calling Keaton "the consummate actress of our generation" *(Hollywood Reporter)* and "one of the most dazzlingly and beguilingly funny girls in movies in years" *(New Yorker).* And people close to her—her mother, for one—are saying she'll be the next Hepburn.

"That is *exactly* what's happening to her,"

says Woody. "I've always thought she was born to be a movie star. She's got a real *American* quality."

ALVY: *I love what you're wearing.*
ANNIE: *Oh, you do, well this tie was a present from Grammy Hall.*
ALVY: *Who? Grammy, Grammy Hall? What'd you do, grow up in a Norman Rockwell painting?*

Diane and I sit, side by side, in her two canvasback living room chairs, like fellow passengers on an airplane. She is a touchy talker; her hands are constantly busy, going through her hair, or to my elbow or hand. She does not talk a cappella; there is always accompaniment, whether by her eyes, hands, a crack of a stick of gum or, most often, by an easy, open laugh.

I ask about her mother. "My mom, Dorothy?" she wants to know. "Um, let's see. We were a very tight family, and I really liked my mother an awful lot. She's a crafty person. She did rock collages, and she became a photographer, too. She's a very emotional, sensitive woman, a journal keeper, a letter writer." But, no, she never wrote professionally. "She doesn't think she's good enough."

Her father, Jack Hall, fifty-five, is a civil engineer who worked for the city of Santa Ana, then built a business of his own. "He was the one who in my career was really, really, he really, you know, was supportive, in a real emotional sense."

Diane was the first of four children (she has a brother, Randy, who is a draftsman and a poet; Dorrie, who graduated college with a degree in art; and Robin, a nurse who sings well but "doesn't have the confidence to get out there," according to Mom).

From the beginning, Diane was a two-sided person—shy and private, with a flip side that longed to be special, to attract attention and approval. For example, her parents (who still live in Southern California) remember how, at age five or so, Diane put on productions in the living room, in front of the fireplace, "singing and dancing, just ad-libbing. She was always entertainment-oriented, but she was shy about it. She entertained *us.*"

At age six, she faced her first real audience, for a recital in Sunday school. She forgot her lines. "I just burst into tears and broke down sobbing, and they had to take me off the stage." But she soon became a regular in the church choir.

As a teenager, Diane had no boyfriends. To gain attention in junior high, she tried out for the talent shows—unsuccessfully. When she was rejected, she would organize and star in her own neighborhood productions. But she also kept trying at school. "It took a couple of years," she says, good sport in her voice, "before they saw the wonderfulness of my talent, that it should be seen and shared by all."

"High school," she says, "was a big popularity contest, at least it was for me. Being popular, and that's too bad. I just wish I had a little more sophistication and a better education."

The telephone in the kitchen rings, and she tells "Max" that she is having an interview and gets off the phone. "Max," it turns out, is Woody Allen. During the Broadway run of *Play It Again, Sam,* Keaton and Tony Roberts got to calling Allen "Max" because "he didn't like to be recognized on the street." In *Annie Hall,* Roberts and Allen call each other "Max." (Allen, by the way, calls Keaton "Keaton.")

In junior college Keaton studied drama, and at age nineteen she took off for New York and acting school. While attending acting school, she joined a friend, Guy Gilette, and his brother Pip in a rock & roll band, the Roadrunners.

"I played tambourine and danced. I sang a couple of Aretha Franklin songs and 'In the Midnight Hour'—let me tell you, that was real bad. I was not, needless to say, a very good rock & roll singer. But I loved it. We'd play around, but not in the city. We'd get ten dollars a gig."

From there, with only a couple of stops in summer stock, Keaton went on to Broadway, and to *Hair,* "the American tribal love-rock musical."

She started out in the chorus (on the Broadway cast album, you can hear her singing her part of Black Boys—"Black boys are so delicious . . .") and then took over the part of Sheila. Sheila? Keaton sings lightly: "How can people be so heartless?" then switches over, still singing, into "Good morning starshine . . ." That was a featured role, I remark. "Yeah," she says. "La-di-da."

Keaton became known, over the years, as the one cast member in *Hair* who wouldn't remove her clothes at the finale. "I didn't think it meant anything." (Also, she was, is, self-conscious about her body.)

Diane had breezed through adult life with hardly a political thought in her head, and then, at age twenty-three, in *Hair,* she became only more removed. "I was strongly suspect of things. *Hair* had a lot of 'peace and love' as what it was saying, and then being a member of it, and knowing all the political things that went on inside, and how important it was for people to get more attention for themselves and who got more publicity. There was a lot of inner rivalry. So I have a tendency not to be political in an outgoing way. I would like to deal with my own—get myself straightened out before I go around sounding off ideas."

Being in *Hair,* Keaton could not help but be influenced in some way by what went on around her. "Drugs were around," she says. "Personally . . . I smoked dope, but I didn't like it. I wasn't naive. I knew about homosexuals, drugs, masochism. . . ." In *Hair?*

"In life!"

In *your* life?

"No!" She makes a gum-popping sound. "That wouldn't be good. I don't need that. That would *really* make me crazy!"

References to her "getting better" pop up regularly in our talks. I ask if, over the last couple of years, she doesn't feel more, as they say, "together"?

She is uncertain. "I don't know if I want to say I've gotten better." I venture that she has.

Her eyes widen. She is all hope. "You think so?" she asks.

Annie and I broke up and I still can't get my mind around that, you know, I keep sifting the pieces of the relationship through my mind and examining my life and trying to figure out where the screwup came . . .
—Woody Allen as Alvy Singer

It would seem that these kids had everything going for them: a shared sense of humor, a mutual trust, even dependence, in their film careers, a common interest in the arts and letters. They are both, as Keaton says, "sort of isolated." And finally, there is that remarkable similarity in their heights.

Woody Allen has gotten to where he can laugh about it. "People tell me all the time that *Annie Hall* is autobiographical, and I keep telling them that it's *not* really very autobiographical, but nobody wants to hear that. And one review—one out-of-town review that I had gotten said that in order to really enjoy the picture you had to know a lot about Diane's and my private life together—and of course, this is completely untrue, because I would say eighty percent of

the film is totally fabricated." (Which reminds me of Keaton's mother discussing Allen's relationship with her daughter. "Woody's had a very positive influence on her," she said, "very much like *Annie Hall.*" To which Jack Hall added, "It's eighty-five percent true—even to Dorothy and my mother!")

The debate gives me a way to ask about the breakup. In *Annie Hall,* it was sudden and straightforward, Annie turning to Alvy and saying, "Let's face it. I don't think our relationship is working." I ask Allen how it was off the screen.

"It was nothing like that," he replies. "She was not involved with anybody else and she wasn't running away to California. She lived here, and at one point we talked about the idea that we had been living so closely for years and it might be nice, we thought, to try it with her *not* living here. This was a mutual decision. And if we didn't like that, we'd move back in together again. And she took an apartment, and I helped her move in and all that, and we were very friendly and still seeing each other. I mean, we were still lovers intermittently after that for a while. Gradually, we sort of cooled down and drifted apart more. But it was *nothing* like in the movie."

Keaton says she is still uncertain just why she and Allen broke up. "I don't know," she says. "It's very hard to say." But she points out another difference between Annie and Diane: "The point of the movie was that [Alvy Singer] was too isolated and not able to like life, which is what my character says: 'You're like an island, all to yourself. I want to go out a little more.'" Which, she says, is not exactly her. She laughs: "I mean, lookit my life!"

Diane Keaton does not care to see her own films, but she saw *Annie Hall* at a theater in her neighborhood. "I thought it worked emotionally," she says. "I was surprised that in the end, I felt something when we said good-bye."

How did Keaton allow herself to do *Annie Hall*, to lay herself (albeit fictionally) on the line?

"I think," she says, "that being an actor in any case, you lay yourself on the line. Now, this seems more personal, but everything is personal. I'm for it, and I also have my conflicts about it.

"I'm very involved in expressing myself; hopefully I'm not a fool for doing it; hopefully there's some merit in it; even if it's just amusing, that's okay. It's a balance, you see, you have to watch it. I don't think you ever work out that conflict. So I visit my analyst and we talk about it." She laughs. "I save it for her; she can hear all the horrors. She's a brave soul."

Keaton started seeing her analyst four years ago—shortly after her split with Woody Allen. He encouraged her. "It's an interesting experience," says Allen, who's had twenty-one years of it. "And certainly one that can't hurt."

Keaton began with three sessions a week, then increased to five. "Time is very important. It takes a long time. I don't believe in any of these quick, weekend things. It's complete idiocy. It's too much of a jerk-off idea, to me, it's too easy, it's easily taking care of things for the moment. It's like—'Oh, yes!'—like *acting*, in a certain sense, getting it all out: 'I feel much better, now my life is' . . . and of course it isn't, because you really have to examine it."

Keaton finds herself too concerned and wasting too much time worrying over "the negative aspects of life. Life is nothing but a series of conflicts, in a way, surmounting one and coming to the next." But she *is* getting better. She knows all about her self-deprecatory act. "Sure, and that's manipulative on my part, to get that response, that you're okay, 'It's all right, nice

Di.' Absolutely. Lots of times people apologize for something just to make sure they've hit the bottom line and they can do nothing but go up. That's real obvious and it gets real boring. However, in my past I've done an awful lot of apologizing. I always liked to say I'm sorry before anything happened, but I don't do that as much anymore."

Still, Keaton is by no means ready to dump analysis. In fact, she says, if she couldn't afford her shrink, she'd go to a pay-what-you-can clinic, the way Woody Allen did in his leaner years. Keaton—can you believe this?—has had problems with men.

Back in junior high Diane was constantly fantasizing about sex. "But I must've had a lot of guilt feelings about it because I was very frightened of the whole idea—but I was also very, very caught up with it, too." When she finally got around to making out, she didn't make out so well. "I was scared." And her sex life, early on, was a series of fits, starts and stops. "I was always getting in relationships where it was 'If he likes me, I'm not interested, and if I like him, he's not interested.'" She both feared men (because she feared sex) and distrusted them (because she feared being dumped). "So in the past, I would say good-bye first."

Aside from her time with Woody Allen, Keaton was in a rut. "I was disgusted with the idea of male-and-female relationships because I had not had anything that I considered really wonderful, so I thought that one way to deal with it would be to not be involved at all, as if that was the way to live, which is of course pathetic."

In *Play It Again, Sam*, Diane Keaton turns to Woody Allen the morning after their first night together and asks, "What were you thinking about while we were doing it?"

"Willy Mays," says Woody.

"Do you always think about baseball players when you're making love?"

"Keeps me going."

"*Yeah,*" says Diane, "I couldn't figure out why you kept yelling, 'Slide!' "

In *Annie Hall*, Woody Allen looks gratefully at Diane Keaton moments after the first time they do it and says, "That was the most fun I've had without laughing."

I ask Diane Keaton, "In real life, was Woody actually funny in bed?"

"Oh," she says, "I'd rather not talk about it." But, she adds, she generally approves of "amusing things" happening in one's sexual relations. "I don't want to have anything to do with someone who can't make fun of it once in a while."

The Secret Code Between Robert De Niro and Martin Scorsese

By Chris Hodenfield

JUNE 16, 1977

Martin Scorsese was in a cold-blooded fury one day last summer because the newspapers kept describing him as a short, sensitive asthmatic. He had a towering, insensitive fit. For laughs. The movie director, age thirty-four, spirals, ratchets, thrusts his chin like Mussolini. Director-friend Ken Dixon watched him rocket around the stage for his movie, *New York, New York,* and the friend was riveted: "Inside, he's John Wayne. There's just this part of him that's seven feet tall, big as a house, and wants to rifle-butt everybody around. 'He knows better than they do what's good for them.' "

Martin Scorsese hasn't minded putting his demons in the public stockade, but he and his star, Robert De Niro, just wanted to have a good time with this film. His movie sets are usually windstorms on Mars, bared teeth and conspiracies behind locked doors. *Mean Streets* was filmed literally on the run, hiding from Teamsters, whose union rates would have killed the movie. While they staged murder scenes for *Taxi Driver,* real human bodies were getting riddled just around the corner, and Scorsese didn't

know if all these cops were in costume, or on a case, and by that time he couldn't care. The scum on the streets, the blood on the walls . . .

No, this would be about his old New York home, all shot "in Hollywood, U.S.A. . . . with costumes . . . music . . . could be fun," he said. Nothing more violent than two ambitious people on the make, a saxophonist (De Niro) and a singer (Liza Minnelli). He gets into hard bop; she gets into the movies. They have a baby, have a fight, make up and break up. Movie ends with a whoopee production number, "Happy Endings." Scorsese hung two *Variety* headlines on his office wall: WATCH GUTTER LANGUAGE, BOYS and YOU DON'T HAVE TO BE VIOLENT TO BE A BOX OFFICE SMASH.

Scorsese had to face a vast, humid set packed with jitterbugging soldiers and their dames, and he raced around as if his life were parked in a towaway zone. He traded grins and shot out imaginary punch lines to unsaid jokes. He paused. "This is a combination of all those places from movies of the forties and fifties. The color, the deco. We called in one hundred extras, but it wasn't enough, so now we've got five

Napoleonic director Martin Scorsese studies his longtime star
Robert De Niro. *Copyright © 1976 Columbia Pictures*

hundred. We're getting familiar with the geography." He pointed to the camera boom, big as hinged telephone poles, on which he established God's point of view. "All these shots are moving, so each time we punch into the band, the camera is moving. Like in *Woodstock*."

He saw me staring.

"Well, not like *Woodstock* . . ."

Scorsese gives the impression that all hell could break loose any second. The wallet strapped around his neck looked like a shoulder holster. His alter ego in this picture is, as usual, Robert De Niro. They are a perfect pair, like Dietrich and von Sternberg, Brando and Kazan. Both have had couch-time in analysis, both go through obsessive examinations of character. Directors often play up an alter-ego character. In 1973, in *Mean Streets*, writer Mardik Martin agreed that De Niro and Harvey Keitel could have represented both sides of the Scorsese coin: "One, Keitel, is the guilt-ridden nice guy who's basically a coward. The other, De Niro, is a crazy doer who doesn't care how he destroys himself."

It was eventually seen in *New York, New York* that De Niro borrowed very heavily on Scorsese's personality to shape the character Jimmy Doyle. The crazy side of Scorsese, the comedian. Doyle, when frustrated, throws tables around the dance hall. Scorsese's been known to throw telephones around the room. He keeps a couple of breakaway chairs, the kind stuntmen smash over heads, to splatter against his office wall.

When De Niro walked onto the stage, a cloud of tension moved up. His eyes darting like a pair of forked tongues, he slithered into view. Suddenly he was there. Quietlike. He had the bearing of the blood-splattered guy sitting across from you in a subway car, too late at night, half-looking at you, a tilted nonstare.

Here, with Vaselined hair and a semidignified zoot suit, he carried his tenor saxophone to the corner of the soundstage holding the Harlem Club scene. In the dim-bulb darkness, a tall tape machine honked into his face a mad sax solo that he was to mimic in the upcoming jam scene. De Niro flubbed along and finally asked the soundman for a rematch.

All around him the recruitment of Hollywood's black extras studied him. Ermines and pearls on everyone. De Niro appeared bandy-legged, uncomfortable, distracted. Just what's the big deal? To use an old Howard Hawks expression, the camera loves him. He had a simple scene one day, just standing by the bar and talking into a pay phone, looking at the bandstand. His words weren't even being recorded. He was just reacting. As the scene was filmed, it looked like a wall full of nothing.

Watching the scene in the next day's rushes, I saw on his forehead millions of flickering people. The eyebrows, the asides, a scene loaded with stealthy mannerisms.

His work is total immersion, and the fetish for privacy continues on the soundstage. When filming, he'll clear out whoever's in his line of sight, or else have a friend stand there. As he practiced in the gloom, one man was watching him who was very impressed that the actor actually learned to play a saxophone. He was Sonny Olvera, the musical coordinator, a spindly, white-haired fellow behind Mr. Peepers glasses who in his thirty-five years of musicals played drums behind Judy Garland, rode the cranes with Busby Berkeley. Never before had Olvera seen the leading man's hands being filmed at an instrument.

It was nothing at all like, say, John Garfield in *Humoresque*, the violinist triumphant at Carnegie Hall, you remember, while Joan Crawford, listening to all that soaring Wagner on the radio, hurls her glass into the fireplace and commits suicide . . . all this intercut with Garfield weaving and lamenting upon the violin. . . .

Actually, Garfield's hands were tied behind his back. One man's arms came out of the darkness to pull the bow, another man hunched behind him and fretted the strings. Garfield just wore a sensitive face.

This shadow play was not necessary here because De Niro went through the migraines of learning a bop solo finger by finger, and Sonny Olvera didn't mind saying that this was a hell of a note.

Robert De Niro seems to be a Dr. Jekyll who shifts into an endless number of Mr. Hydes. He doesn't imitate people, he stages an Inquisition. Already famous is his work method for *The Godfather, Part II*, re-creating Brando's role in the younger version: He constantly replayed a videotape of Brando's Don Corleone; went to the same dentist for a cheek-stuffing dental plate; went to Corleone, Sicily, and had people read aloud script passages into a tape recorder. With less than a page of English dialogue, he took an Oscar.

Before, as the Italian bike racer in *The Gang That Couldn't Shoot Straight* ("My first big-deal movie," he said), he blew all his bit-part pay on a trip to Italy, getting the clothes, the accent. He did it so well, everyone thought he *was* just off the boat and didn't know English. Didn't help keep him in gainful employ.

These stories were reprised on *New York, New York* as he stalked the sidelines during the first two weeks. That was all Liza's time, for "Happy Endings." De Niro was holed up in Greta Garbo's dressing room, practicing. He leaned over Scorsese for advice, endless advice. He was

quiet, nervous, forbidding. An assassin. Then one day he breezed through the soundstage in a loud Times Square novelty shirt, chewing gum, hair slicked back, cracking wise. His agent saw him and recognized that De Niro had just "locked in." Turning to a bystander, he said, "There he goes. He's off. A metamorphosis right in front of us."

The same guy who coaxed script readings out of Sicilian barflies (who in turn demanded to know why *The Godfather* wasn't filmed in their town) wilts when asked questions about his own life.

Scorsese acknowledged De Niro's self-protective superstitions. "His whole thing is concentration. There could be a *war* going on, you know, he could be in the middle of the DMZ, and he'll be like this—in a trance. 'Are you ready?' 'Huh? Yeah, I'm ready.' 'I mean, go, now you go first.' 'No, no, after you.' 'You sure?' 'No, I'm fine.'

"Bobby. It's incredible, we have a shorthand. We have a longhand, too. We talk a great deal. Very often we talk about the same thing over and over."

When Scorsese stops for a moment's gab, he gives full attention. It might be gone after a few moments' automatic fire, but at least he's there. De Niro seems the opposite. In this hothouse of Official Circumstance, anyway. It's onscreen he has the concentrated eye juice. It keeps your attention riveted with that same distraction in Greta Garbo's eyes when she turned away after one mad kiss because this love cannot be. In person, De Niro just looks shifty-eyed.

De Niro was raised on Fourteenth Street, and he was vaguely aware of Scorsese and his crowd. (They met officially Christmas Day, 1970.) He was the son of an abstract painter, Robert De Niro Sr. (once described by art critic Thomas B. Hess as "tall, saturnine, given to black trench coats, his face as sharp as a switch-blade—with a temperament to match. . . . The theme of Greta Garbo in *Anna Christie* has run through his oeuvre for decades, in images based on movie stills . . .").

An indifferent student, De Niro the younger dropped out of high school at sixteen and spent three years in Stella Adler's acting workshop. This was followed by Brian De Palma's first feature, *The Wedding Party*.

"And there were many years of not doing anything," he once said. "You know, going out on auditions. All that. After that, I didn't want to act for a while, because . . . I was afraid that I would get wrapped up in it so much that I wouldn't have time to do what I wanted, like travel. Travel around Europe, which I did. So I spent a few years doing that, hitchhiking around Europe. Lived in Paris for a while. And then when I came back, I didn't do anything for a year or two. And then when I was around twenty-four or twenty-five, I committed, started to look for stuff. Go out on auditions, sent out résumés, the whole thing."

He kept to the East Coast actor's life, playing off-Broadway and dinner theaters, avoiding Hollywood because that meant television. Still, in Manhattan, he slipped into *Search for Tomorrow*.

One night after filming had finished, he finally agreed to talk. We agreed we would get to know each other before committing our intelligence to anything. His studio dressing room was spare, trimmed only with a clock mounted on petrified wood, a record player, a few swing-band albums and a radio playing the news. He wore brown corduroy jeans and a sport shirt. Indicating the couch, he explained that he liked his room simple and didn't want any posters to get in the way of his concentration. He apolo-gized for all the delays. I said there was always lots to do around the lot.

"Yeah, it's like high school," De Niro said, nodding. That's what I think of . . . the cafeteria, seeing people that you know. I've been doing this for some time. Look, do you want a Coke, some coffee? I don't know how good this coffee is. It's old. I've only got Cremora."

He had an uncertainty in his manner. He would give a little, then retreat. His neck muscles and face seemed to be flushed, and I realized that he'd just been working out in the gym in preparation for the next picture, in which he'd be prizefighter Jake LaMotta. So I said: You've been working out?

He caught this and weaved a little. Headlines flashed before his eyes. "I don't even want to talk about that," he complained. "I mean, like, 'He had just come from the gym . . .' I just don't want to get into that."

He looked over his coffee cup, nodded toward the door. "We spent a lot of time on this movie, got a lot of material, which I like, because I had a lot to deal with. It was more frenetic. . . .

"I made two movies, *The Godfather* and the Bertolucci movie [*1900*], where I was on it like eight months or so, and there was a lot of time spent outdoors, waiting for the weather, with a lot of time to think. But this, it just depended on . . . it wasn't waiting on the weather, it just depended on *us*. If *we* were ready."

Bertolucci has a lot of camera work.

"Yeah." He gave it deep reflection. "Lot of camera work. Not so much . . . well, he's all right. Not so much set shots, but dollying in and out, in and around, so you had to do it just right, you had to be right there."

The Conformist is a favorite.

"Yeah, it's one of mine, too. I like it a lot. Bertolucci is good, he's good with actors. Like,

Kazan is *very* good with actors—he was an actor at one time. And a lot of young directors really don't understand actors, how to work with them. They're into techniques, effects. But Kazan really knows. He's schooled. He's—as far as I'm concerned—the *best* schooling."

We were slumped in our chairs, feet on the coffee table, and the small talk was easing into the technical. Seemed a good time to ask about pulling out a tape recorder. But he froze. "No, let's, ah, get to . . . let's not. I don't want to make your job difficult for you. And I don't want to be conspicuous by my absence. Like, I'm the only one you didn't talk to."

We made all kinds of promises. He was good at making promises.

Scorsese is of a generation of moviemakers whose history seems to be composed of the movies they've watched. They celebrate other filmmakers' memories. Especially that old New York crowd. Maybe New Yorkers were the original archivists of filmdom; they live with history in their streets. This was Scorsese's first chance to use the old film language of photography, editing and the forgotten "Technicolor" shades. No dirty words, no close-ups except for love scenes, and no handheld camera. This is the first time he had the money to do it.

Scorsese credits the inspiration of John Cassavetes, who in 1960 finished directing a three-year ordeal called *Shadows*. The show could have been subtitled "We'll Show Them." Said Scorsese, "This was the first picture we saw that proved that you could make a film . . . and keep making film. First, get a camera, and move it."

That New York film crowd included Brian De Palma, Paul Morrissey, Robert Downey and James McBride. In time, Scorsese would handle lights for the Maysles Brothers; then he'd be camera assistant for John Avildsen; then he'd

teach film at New York University, which provided a financial base for his first feature, *Who's That Knocking at My Door?* which was photographed by Mike Wadleigh, who in turn became the director of *Woodstock,* which was part-edited by Martin Scorsese.

He lived on Elizabeth Street, in the insular Italian neighborhood just south of Greenwich Village. His mother will point out her window to her birthplace across the street. Here is the son's influence, the silver-haired woman's voice that rises with ringing drama, all trumpets and fanfare. She makes regular cameo appearances in Marty's movies.

Charles Scorsese was a clothes presser with lots of spare afternoons to take his son to the Loew's Commodore theater. At age six, Martin saw *Duel in the Sun*. Before each of numberless doctor's visits for asthma, he got a *Classics* comic book. Still has them today, wrapped in plastic. They would go to the Paramount and the Strand to see the likes of Benny Goodman and Paul Whiteman. He stepped over the Bowery drunks on the way to Saint Patrick's school. Later he took a few steps toward the priesthood, but was given the boot. His hoodlum past. A student at NYU in the Village, he was halfway to becoming an English teacher when the Movie Jones took hold. He and Mardik Martin stayed their ambitions by teaching film there. Scorsese, married and living in Jersey, cooling his heels for two years, doing "Johnny Carson monologues" for his film students. He plotted the plots with Mardik Martin while both the wives were up in arms.

They were so hungry, so ambitious, so crazy with failed film projects that they considered titling a picture *This Film Could Save Your Marriage*. Instead, Scorsese spent three years filming *Who's That Knocking at My Door?*—which was his own diary, and a sketchbook for *Mean Streets* as well. It starred Harvey Keitel as the repressed Scorsese figure who's fascinated by a worldly blonde but is then smashed to find she's not a virgin. It was The Neighborhood.

While the film now gets art-house screenings, in 1969 he couldn't sell it to save his soul. Now he knows why. Now he can laugh: "At that time it was all 'open sexual expression.' *We* were talking about repression—we didn't know what we were saying, aside from expressing personal feelings."

So well had he chronicled The Neighborhood that maybe now you'll hear of "Scorsese's old gang." Only he was always the guy who arrived after the dust cleared. "It wasn't my gang. I wasn't even in the gang. They used to fight the East Side Italians, or the West Side Italians, or whatever. Some guys had ridiculous reasons for actions. One guy always *wanted* to fly through plate-glass windows. You know"—he clasped his hands like a lawyer—"I just decided that wasn't in my line of work."

But he got off on portraying it. When he saw *The Wild Bunch* in 1969, the slow-motion death finale put him in shock, and he told friends that he fell with each of the 250 federales. He'd already done slow-motion terror in *Who's That Knocking*, a guy with a gun scaring people at a party, no shots fired, but faces all frozen: "It gets slower and slower, it goes to one hundred and twenty frames a second. It gets very violent, and the violence is in slow motion. There's no dialogue in the scene, it's only a Ray Barretto song, 'Watusi,' which is a very dangerous song. Which is a song I love.

"I get a lot of ideas listening to music. The scene, the idea, is based on something that's real, but the progression of it came from an old Jan and Dean record."

Said Mardik Martin, "Marty told me many times that he's trying to exorcise his conflicts

onscreen, visually. Most of his work deals with that, especially *Who's That Knocking*, which was like the purest Scorsese. He's a very logical, straight person, but every once in a while he dreams in nightmares."

Scorsese made commercials in Europe, edited CBS News film and found a temporary home cutting such rock movies as *Woodstock* and, later, *Elvis on Tour*. Brought out to Hollywood to rescue the acid-twisted hulk of *Medicine Ball Caravan*, he tacked on his wall a movie poster that he thought sounded appropriate: *Two Weeks in Another Town*. But then fate stepped in and messed up the scheme.

He made a quickie potboiler for Roger Corman called *Boxcar Bertha*, starring David Carradine and Barbara Hershey. The usual Corman stuff: rudely fast. Scorsese rationalized that he *liked* exploitation pictures.

He was all set to make *I Escaped from Devil's Island*, just to keep the ball rolling, when he screened *Boxcar* for his old pal and mentor John Cassavetes. He got a sound three-hour Talking To and was told to reach for the heart. Scorsese dusted off an old script called *Season of the Witch* and turned it into *Mean Streets*.

He crammed in everything he'd ever left out of the other plays. "*Mean Streets* comes from feelings, from myself, my own life in a sense. People are always talking right on the edge of their emotions, always yelling. It's a way of life. The idea was never to build up to it. Suddenly there's a fight in the background, there'll be an explosion between two people, immediately. That's the way the characters live. That's the way I am. Somebody'll throw a pizza slice across the wall. . . ."

While it is an anthem to New York street life, only six frenzied days were filmed there, helped by the neighborhood guys like their safecracker pal Larry the Box. Before hauling back to Hollywood, Scorsese filmed all the streets and hallways he was able: "The best I could do was put the people in the middle of the buildings and let the buildings do all the talking."

It was not until later, when filming *Alice Doesn't Live Here Anymore* with Ellen Burstyn, that Scorsese had the illumination thrown on his path. Came from Marlon Brando, who saw *Mean Streets* and figured (as Burstyn had with *Alice*) that Scorsese would be the director for his Wounded Knee movie. Brando flew to Tucson and found Scorsese working.

Big stuff. Age eleven, Scorsese had seen *The Wild One* and stepped into an identical black leather jacket. He had also listened continually to the soundtrack of Brando's *Julius Caesar*.

Brando wanted to talk about *Mean Streets*.

Scorsese: "It was the highest compliment: He understood it, he understood the picture. I told him I was shooting a picture [called *Italianamerican*] on my parents. He looked at me and said, 'You realize what you're doing?' I said yeah. I thought he meant, 'Do I realize I'm making a picture of my parents?' Later on I realized he meant something else entirely. He meant looking for an identity, you know, the Italian American. Okay, which is not as crucial as the blacks, or the American Indian, but it's still yourself. You die alone."

Italianamerican, a long, beautiful dinner-table revelation, received a standing ovation at the 1974 New York Film Festival, and Mother was there to blow kisses to the crowd. Martin's been a good son, named his first daughter after her, and called her up at 5:00 A.M. from France to tell her he won the Cannes Grand Prix for *Taxi Driver*. When she visits her boy in Beverly Hills, she doesn't have to cook for the whole film crew anymore; but see here, Bernardo Bertolucci was visiting as she served up her best lasagna. "He

said it was delicious," Kate said, beaming. "But he liked my linguini better."

And there on the edge of the *New York, New York* set were the short, nervous parents, ready for their cameo appearance. They'd been to the wardrobe department. Charlie Scorsese got one of Edward G. Robinson's old suits.

Yes, *New York, New York* was supposed to be a lot of good, clean fun. Then one day fate stepped in and put the finger on them. While making a movie about an ambitious couple breaking apart over the birth of a baby, Scorsese and De Niro entertained pregnant wives. "We call it Pick-a-Reality," said wife Julia Cameron Scorsese, who gave waddling lessons to Liza Minnelli. A reporter and a playwright, she also rewrote vast sections of the script and finally had to acknowledge that Liza's character, Francine Evans, was composed of many parts Julia.

De Niro's real-life wife, meanwhile, actress Diahnne Abbott, had her pregnancy concealed when she put the torch to "Honeysuckle Rose" in the Harlem Club scene.

The Pirandello reality kept shifting as they all hammered Earl Mac Rauch's script and replaced the wisecracks with some very personal material.

"It's a story about people thrown together at a certain period of life; very talented and *can't* get together," Scorsese said one worried day in his office. "Because their careers, their drive and ambition is so strong. The career drive is so strong that it just destroys . . . what's there. The reality destroys . . . the baby and the whole thing. It's a very straight story. It reflects something we've all gone through. Very often you go through it all the time. I mean, I have to live at the studio. And that's difficult because I'm directing the same things!"

Scorsese had a condemned man's last laugh.

"It's more personal than I thought it would be. Maybe it's just me trying to figure out something about the past, I dunno. Figure out something about the first marriage. Or parents. What was that all about? It's a hard thing to do, it's like being on the road and if the wife is doing something else, she'll disappear for five or six weeks at a time.

"How does that relationship survive? That's with established people. Imagine with unestablished people who are trying to make it? We're trying . . . we're trying . . . to analyze it."

He picked up the intercom and begged the secretary for tissues.

"The movie was a matter of recapturing in my mind a certain thing about the past, my memories of my uncles in uniform. I was born in November of '42, so I don't remember any of that. I do remember the music. . . ."

His face screwed up. "Tissues. Just a minute." He clawed the intercom again. "There's tissues out there, aren't there? Really got to have them, it's getting embarrassing." The door crashed open and the secretary, Jamie, handed him a box. He took it and looked at her. "He asked me a few questions and I'm crying." Loud honk of the nose. "She knows I get hysterical at times."

Of course, he was nowhere near crying, but the drama livened up the scene. He sat down and tried on a reasonable look. "Really, it's about . . . you could take that love story and put it against the background of any time. Any period."

Music has always been a factor to the flow of images in his movies. The first viewings of *New York, New York* footage were breathless affairs; here was a director who *listens* to music. Maybe it's the first movie to see the historical progression of this music and tell what happened the day the big-band music died and got taken uptown to have the seams let out. The original screenplay even had De Niro end up an R&B record producer in 1953, but that was deemed illogical for "the guy who lived only for his horn."

Scorsese has always edited film to music, and *Mean Streets* was not only shaped along a beautiful rock score, but, he said, the incidents were strung together "in an operatic structure, like a piece of music, the same scenes repeating but more intense each time." Life in the old neighborhood was best expressed by the Ronettes singing "Be My Baby." He once remembered: "We used to hear that late at night . . . echoing in the streets. The music was very important because you can go by and hear the march from *Aida,* and as you walk by another room, you can hear 'Handy Man,' and then in another place you can hear Eric Clapton, and then in another place you hear old Italian folk songs, and you keep going and there's Chinese music. Especially in the summertime. It was incredible."

He had not only the spectrum of music to play with this time (besides the Kander and Ebb originals, even "The Man I Love" gets a shot) but also the subculture of musicians, as he called it. The all-time advice giver on that was Georgie Auld, a graying, finger-popping hipster with a carnival barker's voice. Once a big-tone tenor saxophonist behind Basie and Goodman bands, he put De Niro into training, brought him a horn, taught him the scales and a novice version of "Tenderly." Soon, De Niro had him stick around to orate the finer turns of bop lingo. And, very likely, to be a fine demonstration of the tried-and-true egomaniac musician that fit the Jimmy Doyle description. Auld ended up portraying the bandleader Frankie Hart.

Another saxophonist was Clarence Clemons, the intimidating-looking player from Bruce

Springsteen's band. He shaved his beard, trimmed his Afro and put on a bulky tan suit that hung on his shoulders like an airplane hangar. They handed him a trumpet, put a gold tooth in his smile. He did not look so intimidating. Had he ever acted before? "Every day of my life," he said, grinning.

Scorsese likes the Springsteen band very much. Once, taking time off from shooting *Taxi Driver,* he and De Niro went to New York's Bottom Line to catch the group and watched enthralled as Bruce Springsteen answered the tumultuous encore applause by coming out alone and doing, *"You talkin' to me?"*

Sometimes when Liza Minnelli's prerecorded voice boomed over the soundstage, people swore that certain low notes carried deep silhouettes of Judy.

The royal dressing room was sprayed with red roses and hung with portraits of Liza joined with well-remembered faces. Everybody wore a high-buff smile. These hallowed walls. Liza had a cheerful greeting, with a warm, moist hand and a girlish, rubbery voice. She was breathless. I got the idea that she wakes up in the morning all out of breath. She had just been rehearsing. Which I figured had all been finished months ago.

"No," she said. "Because, what happens, you see, is it changes on you. Suddenly something you thought of before you started working together . . . is not in character anymore. We only got to rehearse like that two hours a day, and *then* we decided that wasn't going to do at all. So we went into these six-, seven-hour sessions."

That could be intense.

"It is, but with the two of them it's terribly exciting. Marty does rehearsals on tape, and he takes all the videotape home."

All seven hours of tape?

"Yeah. So it's all on tape, the different scenes we've rehearsed, and we usually spend up to two or three hours on one scene. You know, because we go crazy, we take it every possible way we can take it. From those tapes he takes the very best moments. And builds the scene."

That's a hell of a way to write a script.

"Umm. The most natural, the best, the gems that he considers, like, the inside of a diamond. And from five hours, it's suddenly like two pages. But it's all there, all the beats are there.

"Marty's incredible, isn't he? And Bobby is *so* dedicated. Bobby is just . . . just fabulous. I think he's addicted to film itself. In rehearsals, man, he opens up and he's terribly funny. People think that he's introverted. Whereas, in fact, he's quiet. He's intense, and he's very shy. Introverted always somehow means a flaw in one's character. When somebody's introverted, that usually means something is wrong with them. I don't think there's anything wrong with Bobby."

His portrayals of uncontrollable thugs were real enough, so that when De Niro addressed the Sherwood Oaks Experimental College one evening in April, the film students *had* to know about the violence of it all.

De Niro sat on a high chair and fielded questions. Questions about gore. How, he was asked, did he detune from all that violence? Were you afraid while shooting *Taxi Driver?* When you got shot in the neck in *Mean Streets,* how did your energy keep up? Do you feel Travis Bickle should have taken at least one shot at the candidate? Didja get nervous in the gun scene?

These questions were deflected, but fledgling actors—the more serious ones—stood in the aisles and asked other questions. They wanted to crawl inside De Niro's head. How, for instance, did he show paternal feelings in *Godfather II*? With his eyes?

"I dunno . . . I just think it. The main thing in acting is not to show, not indicate, because people don't indicate. Like, I know I run into people who had tragic things happen in their life. Their wife was raped and murdered and so on. And they tell me the story, they tell it flat, no drama, no retching, no nothing. You see the scene on television and right away the tears start coming. And that's not the way it is."

The lights were doused for two *Taxi Driver* excerpts. The first showed Travis Bickle practicing his fast draw in the mirror. Scorsese once explained that he always liked characters who talked into mirrors. When he told De Niro to do this, the director, on the floor wearing earphones, couldn't hear and kept asking for repeats. De Niro, thinking Scorsese wanted something different, did variants on "You talkin' to me? You talking to *me?*"

What was his reaction upon first seeing *Taxi Driver?*

"Well, it's revulsion, usually. No . . . I think of all the terrible things that I did. It's hard. I'm so used to seeing myself that now when I watch rushes, I cringe at things. But I sit through it, and just because I know I have to sit through it, I'll learn something. When I saw it the first time, I felt terrible. First of all, leave the screening room right away."

He was asked if he ever thought that he would be a superstar.

"That's odd, because there's a part of me that can never believe it can happen; and there's another part of me that says it's—and I don't want to sound like an egomaniac—but that's the way it should be. It's like, it's the reality you accept. But I could easily accept the other reality. I don't know. I'm happy the way it should be. I don't know but what you know."

One persistent fellow, already snubbed once with his question, made his way to the microphone. He wanted to know about the Scorsese character in *Taxi Driver,* did he actually kill his wife?

"I . . . I . . ." De Niro faltered. "That's obviously never resolved. But I think that's part of the coloring he wanted to show of New York City, the craziness of the city. It didn't necessarily have to be resolved, I guess. A guy gets out of the cab, and that's the end of it. Unless you read about it in the *Daily News.*"

"It all hit me," Scorsese said months later, over salad in his office. "Were we going to be able to keep up the energy, keep up the level, not to be scared? Will you settle for things instead of pushing further? When you start pushing further, then you start pushing into each other's egos, personalities. . . ."

His worried grimace faded into a grin. *"That's* when things start to spark, and *then* things come out. That's what had to be kept going. That's what scared me."

At this stretch, Scorsese was living at the studio, going home on weekends. He was trying to make sense of three pictures shot in 1976. Two weekends were spent on a documentary that his wife, Julia, scripted. Then he took his crew to San Francisco to direct a movie of the Band's final concert/all-star jam, *The Last Waltz,* which promises finally to be a visual recording of rock to match the sound recording. He did this one "just for my own regeneration, to get things back moving."

It also meant enough moving pictures flying through his head to paralyze any six eyeballs, as all three movies were being cut at once. His editing periods always seem to be at once rejuvenating and traumatic. His editor, Irving Lerner, died of a heart attack on Christmas Eve, 1976.

He was sixty-seven. The occasion drove home memories of Bernard Herrmann, the legendary film composer who finished recording the score for *Taxi Driver* and returned to his hotel room and died on Christmas Eve, 1975.

Scorsese sat in his office hung with movie posters.

"You wake up, it's like being in prison. Kind of a nice prison. The couch is nice and soft, the rooms are painted nicely now. You wake up, have some sort of breakfast, you go wash, shower and shave. They tell you when they're ready for you. Because my best hours for working are usually from nine o'clock until three in the morning. For me. So that just means that you're *here*. It's just one long day, from Monday till Friday, there's no driving back home. At five o'clock, six o'clock A.M., you just stumble over the dressing room and fall asleep."

He looked down at his desk. "You'll have to excuse these salads. I've been living on these salads. They're disgusting."

The Jake LaMotta prizefight movie with De Niro was next, and De Niro had already built up neck muscles the size of goiters . . . and Jesus, he'd like to do a movie about a real Catholic saint; or the final chapter of the *Mean Streets* trilogy; and he wants to do a Biblical movie, but he can't think of the music. It's the key. Once he hears the music, he'll see the picture.

Redford and Newman:
Two Views of Butch and Sundance

Robert Redford

By Grover Lewis

APRIL 15, 1971

SOMEWHERE IN UTAH—Robert Redford is one of those freak-of-nature golden boys who has, ness pah, Everything. Hurricane star status in films; a fetching, interesting (Mormon) wife and three strapping kids; a great ruddy snow-tan from slamming hell-for-leather around the slopes of Sundance, his recently opened spa for ski ascetics looking for a wholesome place to break their legs in Utah's Wasatch Mountains; a cathedral-aerie of a house on an adjacent peak and a co-op apartment in Manhattan; even a bristling red muff of a beard grown for his title role in *The Saga of Jeremiah Johnson,* all that wiry rasp of hair encircling a brace of blinding-white teeth intently chomping away on a slab of Bazooka bubble gum.

Well ... almost Everything. What he doesn't have, specifically, is a driver's license valid for the State of Utah. Or valid for any other state, for that matter, the good and simple reason being that Redford drives like a crazed grunt dodging incoming mail. Nevertheless, license or not, the *Jeremiah* location is shifting from the area around Provo, three hundred miles downstate to St. George, and jumping off on the trip south. Redford stomps a mud-crusted cowboy boot down on the accelerator of his power-pak Chevy Cheyenne and lets it hang there, dead close to the floor, glancing nervously over his shoulder now and again at the matched pair of Yamaha trail bikes lashed upright in the rear of the truck. "Is that fuzz trailing us? Goddamn, I hope not. Those assholes have given me a hard enough time as it is. Even threw me in jail a couple times."

Assured that no red dome lights are in sight, Redford cracks open a couple of cans of Coors beer, draining off a long swallow around his wad of Bazooka. Soon, the snow and the mountains drop behind, and the truck is hurtling through that kind of sawtooth terrain where if you happen to skid over the lip of one of those drops, you just keep bouncing until you're in Nevada. Chevy Cheyennes have no brake pedals on the passenger side.

Beer can snugged between his knees, Redford seesaws up and down excitedly, pointing a gloved hand at something beyond the frost-rimmed windshield. Up ahead, hanging over a humpbacked mesa to the west, an enormous nimbus cloud catches the last spill of the sun, glowing like a fire just over the rim of the earth.

106

"Holy Christ, look at that *cloud*," he says. "Things like that work on me. And look at that *road*. Beautiful, I love it. I'd made twenty-seven trips across the U.S. by the time I was twenty, you know—bummin' around, hitchin'. I always had that urge, that drive to move through space. . . . For that reason, Kerouac hit me hard. Henry Miller, too. *Hard* is hardly the word.

"Listen, I've just got to tell you about ol' Henry and me. I first read *Tropic of Cancer* in '57. I was in Paris, trying to be a painter. Hell, I thought the book was about *me*—I was broke, down-and-out, no friends, horny. So I had this great admiration for him. I could listen to people telling stories for days, if they know how to do it—to me, that's a good index to character—and I just knew Miller had to be one of the greatest storytellers ever.

"Well, later, I was back in the States, still just a kid, and I hitched up to Henry's house at Big Sur. Got to within a hundred yards of his door, hung around all afternoon and never went in, never knocked. I decided it was—*dumb*, didn't make any sense. What could I say—'I read your book, and I think you're great'? Bullshit. So I gave up on the idea of meeting him.

"Then, still later, after I was making films, I was driving along Sunset Boulevard one day near a place called the Hot Dog Show—great, great place—and school let out. Kids were making a lot of racket, havin' a good time, cruisin' in their cars. Traffic was clogged up at a signal there, and the kids started yelling at this funny-lookin' old guy walking a bicycle across the intersection.

"Well, I took one look and realized it was Henry. He had a tweed cap on, knickers, a moth-eaten, old European-cut jacket, shades. There it was—this was my shot after all those years. I was right next to him, and my head just about *exploded* with the possibilities of what to say. And all these kids were yelling at him— 'C'mon, old man, move it or dump it,' all those jive-ass things. So as he tottered past, I poked my head out the window and sang out, 'Take your time, Henry.' And drove off." Redford explodes with laughter, pummeling the wheel with his fleece-lined gloves. The truck bucks and lunges in the twilight slipstream of the highway, the nimbus apparition still hanging in the west.

"Around that same time I went up to visit Miller, I used to hitch up to North Beach in San Francisco a lot, hang around the Bagel Shop, the coffeehouses. I guess I felt comfortable there. I first got interested in writing then, first really learned to *read* then, and I still like a lot of writers. Nowadays, I like, lessee, Raymond Mungo . . . Umn, I *liked* Kesey, but I don't know what he's up to now. I've got a lot of admiration for Mailer because—well, shit, he's hung it all out to dry where people can see it. He allows whatever's happenin' inside him to be on public display, and as a result, you can see how far he's grown. He's *chasin'* something—"

Scrubbing a hand through his beard, Redford bites off the idea and falls silent for a few miles. Small towns glide by in the smoky dusk—Springville, Eureka, Lynndyl, Delta— and a neon sign above an abandoned-looking motel blinks: STA HERE AND SAVE $. When Redford speaks again, there's a metallic edge in his voice.

"Critics. I used to be indifferent to them, but I'm getting increasingly intolerant of the breed. Since they're capable of the same failings I'm capable of, and I know what *I'm* capable of, it scares the shit out of me what they can do to someone who's devoted a lot of his time and life to writing something, making something— whatever. You see what the book critics did to Jim Jones' latest novel? The poor asshole must be goin' out of his mind. I have the *least* amount of tolerance for critics who dismiss things, who skewer people. It's not right. It's a pretty damaging thing to do to a man. It's rough enough just getting up in the morning, let alone *making* something.

"It's different with acting. You get yourself into the spot you're supposed to be in, then you just do the best you can. Then when it's over, it's really over. One of the things that helps me on that score is that I don't believe in working very often. It's been a year and a half since I made *Little Fauss and Big Halsey.* You catch that one? A fucked movie. Good intentions on everybody's part, but they got fucked somewhere along the way. A lot of the pictures I've been in have been like that—*This Property Is Condemned, The Chase, Willie Boy*—I ask you, whoever heard of an Indian maiden with baby-blue goddamn eyes? *Butch Cassidy* was fun, sure. What the hell, you're doing all the things you did in make-believe as a kid, and you're getting paid for it, right? But of all the pictures I've made, the only one that came close to making it for me was *Downhill Racer.* Maybe that's because I helped *generate* the film, all the way from the plotting-scheming stage to execution.

"I *respect* writers, for Christ's sake. To even a greater extent than the director, the writer makes or breaks a given picture—certainly not some smooth-faced, empty-headed actor, strutting and preening. Writers often get blocks, and I'm sympathetic to that, too. The same thing used to happen to me as a painter."

"One of the truly pain-in-the-ass things about being an actor," he says in a brooding tone later on, the truck still straining toward St. George, "is having people make a big-deal fuss about you all the time. Snap us a couple more Coors, would you? But then . . . I guess acting has worse drawbacks, come to think of it. For instance, I've never liked anything I've done, not

really. It's sad, but I can't get genuine enjoyment out of my own work because—I can't *see* it. I don't like seeing myself on the screen—I don't *feel* anything. I'm never made to laugh, never made to be even interested. Just as often as not, I disagree with critics who give me good notices. If they're 'right,' they often seem right for the wrong reasons. It's sad.

"All you have to go on is how you feel when you're really doing something. The 'end result' is shit, anyway. I don't believe in the end result—that's for other people. If I'm acting and I'm enjoying myself, that's good enough. Same thing for skiing, biking, making love, you name it. Listen, I once drove to L.A. from Salt Lake City in just under nine hours—165 mph, a lot of it. In a 904 Porsche . . . Man, they had to pry me out of there when I finally stopped—it was like I'd been welded in the car. I doubt that I'd be able to do that again—that kind of tension can burn you out. . . .

"But acting—there're times when I enjoy it. There're times when it's a very, very private affair, and it can be fucking terrific then. In the theater, and less so in films, everything necessarily gets *quiet,* and if you just concentrate on what you're doing, you have all this . . . luxury . . . of silence to operate in. It's a fantastic incentive to *do* something."

Redford does something right now, something altogether startling: He flips off the headlights and guides the truck through the luxury of Utah's vast nighttime silence with only the stars to point the way. After a couple of miles, he switches the lights back on, and with a probing, measuring glance, asks politely for a cigarette.

"I like to smoke when I travel," he explains, grinning. "Smoking, drinking, grass—it's all okay, I guess, in perspective. I mean, part of my own orientation is as an athlete—make that a guy who's athletically inclined—and I guess otherwise most of my values came from my grandfather in Texas, the values I have today. I like ... rituals, you know? For instance, I believe strongly in shaking hands with people—that kind of contact—even if I've seen them only a few days before. In Texas, to have a cup of coffee with somebody and talk in the kitchen, that's a big thing. ...

"Some of that reality of things will be in *Jeremiah,* hopefully, although it's a much crueler reality. I'd like to think about it as being ... an informative film. It's about what happened to a man, a real person in our history, who went about trying to establish a life for himself in the mountains. It's about a mountain man, and face it, most of the mountain men who helped settle the West were crazy. In fact, most of the people who pushed beyond the frontiers in this country were absolute freaked-out whackos—not capable of functioning around other people—they just couldn't, no way. So, like Huck Finn, they lit out for 'the territory.'"

At the outskirts of the town of Beaver, Redford wheels off the interstate and pulls up at the Ponderosa Cafe, where he tucks away a twelve-ounce steak and the trimmings. During the meal, he chouses good-naturedly with the waitress, but again nobody recognizes him. Back on the road once more, he yawns hugely, stretches, lolls his head back, and snorts a long "Ah-h-h-h"

at the recollection of a particularly punk joke told to him by New York mayor John Lindsay.

"Lindsay and I are strictly sports enthusiasts together—we never talk politics, and I don't have the vaguest idea what he plans to do in '72. Hell, for that matter, I don't know what *I* plan to do in '72 in terms of politics. I've never voted—since I've been of voting age, I have not voted. I'm not sure why. ...

"But it galls me, all those fools and assholes calling it 'the government of the people,' while in actuality, most politicians are just running their private games on people. Look, I'm an American, whatever else I may be, but it makes me ashamed, what's going on in the country. Nixon, Agnew—goddamn them to hell for bringing such a blight on the young people—on us all. I can resent them for many things, but that's outright criminal to me. Demeaning—insulting to intelligence.

"I remember passing Nixon in the Bel Air Hotel once, back when he was out of office. Man, he was so wooden, so lifeless, it was like passing a cigar-store Indian. Or maybe the highest art of the mortician. Goddamn him. Goddamn them all, and the horses they rode in on."

Redford brakes the truck to an angry stop, lunges out triggerishly onto the gravel shoulder for a few blind strides, then returns to poke his head through the window with a lopsided grin. "You want another Coors? There's plenty more in the back." It's still a hundred whistling miles through the dark to St. George.

Paul Newman

By Grover Lewis

JULY 5, 1973

April in Chicago—this year anyway—is the cruelest month. On a dreary Monday morning, coming down just after the frenetic early-hour commuter boogie in the Loop, a pall of ice-water rain, laced with stinging shards of birdshot sleet, is freezing the streets in a muddy glaze. Despite the vile weather, however, a crowd of about a thousand spectators is milling about in the high-vaulted waiting room at Union Station. All these men, women and children—with the emphasis distinctly on women—are waiting to catch a glimpse of their fantasies fleshed out: to watch Paul Newman and Robert Redford enact a brief location scene for a film about Depression-era con men called *The Sting.*

By now, George Roy Hill, the director who worked with Newman and Redford on *Butch Cassidy and the Sundance Kid* in 1969, is taking an experimental ride on a dolly to calculate whether the setup he has in mind will work.

A hush falls over the station as Newman, trailed by Redford, strolls down the center aisle toward the newsstand. Newman and Redford are both decked out in three-piece, worsted suits and soft-crushed fedoras.

The eerie suspension of noise in the vast ter-minal sustains itself until Newman surveys the crowd with a jolting blue glance and flashes a dazzling smile to one and all. Then a pandemonium of cheers and applause breaks loose—quite literally, it's a standing ovation. A little sheepishly, Newman acknowledges the crowd's worshipful tribute by raising his hands like a champ in the ring, then cuts a beeline for the newsstand, where he helps himself to a double handful of popcorn and listens, head bent intently, snapping, electric eyes alert in concentration, to George Roy Hill's instructions about the upcoming scene. Redford gestures self-effacingly—it's one of his most appealing mannerisms—and glances fondly in Newman's direction. "It's Paul's day, I guess," he says, and shrugs.

Later, walking with Redford and this writer to the Teamster-driven limo that will drive us to the Ambassador Hotel, Newman waves gaily to the people behind the rope barricades who are calling out to him and mutters out of his mouth, "I'm always just faintly embarrassed by all this, if that makes any sense."

In the car, Redford, scowling, complains at length about film critics and writers. "Ah, nobody reads that shit," Newman scoffs.

"Well, I think the end of us is going to be Pauline Kael," Redford mutters darkly as the limo swings into the auto portal at the hotel. "She claimed that in the end of *Jeremiah Johnson*, I was giving the Indian the finger. The *finger*, for Christ's sake."

Newman laughs and stretches forth his hand. "In the last scene? When you were going like this?"

"Yeah, I just reached my hand out. That, she claimed, was the final blow, the final insult. When I read that, I realized that she was so out of line, she was so bent that she's probably a woman who ought to be locked up somewhere, you know. When you get that balled up, it's bye-bye time."

Redford goes his separate way for lunch, and upstairs in the corridor outside his suite on the hotel's ninth floor, Newman fumbles through the various pockets of his suit, searching for his room key. "I've got a memory like a sieve," he says with a rueful smile. "Maybe I didn't even bring it. No, here it is, here we go."

Inside the suite, Newman sails his fedora onto the couch, gestures for the writer to make himself comfortable, dashes cold water on his face in the bathroom, fetches two icy Heineken beers from the minifridge in the bedroom and makes two brief phone calls to business associates. Then he plops down in a wingback chair facing the couch and takes a long, satisfying tap of his beer.

The writer asks Newman if he's bored with his charismatic superstar status.

"No . . . I'm not bored by it. You can't be bored by it. You can be plenty embarrassed by it, though, because what they're applauding has nothing to do with me. They're applauding *Harper, Hombre, Hud*—all those celluloid manifestations of what I'm supposed to be like. But

those characters were created by writers. That's why it's embarrassing, because people don't seem to be willing to separate the allure of the character and the actor who plays him.

"It's funny, because I never knew what to make out of all that. I mean, I suppose you could say there's been one constant in my life, and that, of course, has been the theater. It annoyed me, actually, because it was the only thing I had any talent for, even as a kid. I would've loved to have been a professional athlete of one kind or another, but I had no talent for it at all. So from the time when I was just a little kid, I was always in something—school plays in Shaker Heights, repertory theater in Cleveland, one thing or another.

"Then I gave it up for six or seven years. My family was very upper class, half-Catholic, half-Jewish. Oddly enough, I was raised as a Christian Scientist, but that didn't really take on me. My boyhood was cloistered, I suppose. My father owned a sporting-goods store in Cleveland—one of the greatest sporting-goods stores in the country. It's no longer in the family. After my father died, my brother ran it for a while, but then the family sold it, and my brother became a film-production engineer.

"I mean, it's so funny to trace these things," Newman reflects, tugging at his neatly clipped mustache. "It always seems to me that most things are accidental. There's so much accident in getting places. You know—being in the right place at the right time, falling into a certain kind of vacuum. It's all an incredible sham.

"After high school I enrolled in Kenyon College, but just about then World War II broke out and I enlisted in the navy. I served three years as a radioman-gunner. The combat situation was . . . well, we got a few submarine patrols and so forth when we were flying torpedo planes out of Okinawa and Guam.

"After the war, I went back to Kenyon, on the GI Bill. That's where I got heavily involved in the whole thing of theater again. That came about because I got thrown off the football team and also thrown in the clink. What happened was, we were six guys on the football team, and we got into a brawl with some locals, and we all got thrown in the clink. Three of the guys were thrown out of school, and two of us were left on probation. All the guys who were thrown out graduated Phi Beta Kappa from some other university. Hah!

"Oh, God, it was really funny. It was a funny night. Brawls were fun in those days, you know. Like I got a black eye or a busted nose or something, but what the hell? There was a kind of gallantry about it.

"Anyway, the cops rousted us, and the next thing I knew it was morning and I woke up in the clink. I remember that the *Cleveland Plain Dealer,* which of course, is the big newspaper where I come from, had a story on the lower two columns of the front page: KENYON COLLEGE IN TROUBLE AGAIN. Christ, I mean, we lost our quarterback, tackle, halfback, you name it.

"In my case, it was no great loss. I was one of the *worst* football players in the history of Kenyon. I was a defensive linebacker, and I weighed 152 pounds. *Crunch*—oh, man, I used to get *hit.*"

Grinning, Newman broken-field sprints into the bedroom and returns with two more frosty bottles of beer.

"Well, that was an accident, see what I mean? Getting thrown in the jug, that was accidental. Because I had given up the theater—I was an economics major at the time. So, I mean, because of that quirky little thing of getting bounced off the team, I had nothing to do with my free time, so I just went down and read for a play. That started it, really. That was at the beginning of my junior year, and I did ten plays

between then and graduation, including lighting, directing and starring in a musical.

"All of that was an accident. Then you go to the point where my mother died, which left me with no further obligation to continue the family business. That left me free to go to the Yale Drama School. After I left Yale, I walked into a major part in *Picnic,* a play that won the Pulitzer Prize and ran for fourteen months. That was luck. If that play hadn't been successful—I was married to my first wife by then and had two children—I don't know if I could've stayed in the theater. I mean, a play that would last fourteen months to study by myself at the Actors Studio—that's absolute luck.

"And the Actors Studio was fabulous in those days. Lee Strasburg and Elia Kazan were still teaching there in those days. Jimmy Dean was there, Geraldine Page, Kim Stanley, Eli Wallach, Annie Jackson. It was exciting. I learned more in those fourteen months of studying there than in the twenty-five years that preceded it. *Easy.* Because you see, when I came to New York, I was really collegiate. Also, I'd just gone through a terrible bomb of a movie. Luckily, I was already in the play before it was released. That was the clinker called *The Silver Chalice,* my first picture. That was the only one I took an ad out in the trades warning people not to watch on TV in L.A. Except that move backfired, and *everybody* watched it to see what I was talking about."

Newman takes a hit of his beer and squirms around uneasily in his chair.

"Listen," he blurts, "am I boring you? I mean, I wish I could come up with some reflections about all this. Repeating the history of my career, you know, almost bores me, so I always have the feeling that I must be boring the shit out of the other guy. No? You sure? Okay.

"Well, I mean, I try not to have too much of

a fat head about myself. Actually, the advantage that Redford and I have had is that it's a very, very slow process making it up the ladder. I first appeared professionally as an actor in 1950, and this is twenty-three years later. And you can't get a fat head from that kind of thing, because it happens very, very slowly. The people I feel sorry for are the instant celebrities, the guys like Mark Spitz. I figure those guys have got a very, very tough time of it.

"Oh, sure, it's flattering to your ego to have droves of women flocking after you. At first, anyway—but then I'm happily married and have been for a long time. I remember first noticing that beginning to happen to me when we were filming *Hud* down in Texas. I mean, women were literally trying to climb through the transoms at the motel.

"God, I remember this one broad was banging on my door at three o'clock in the morning for about fifteen minutes." Newman grins lopsidedly. "Finally, I had to let her out, I felt so old."

The writer asks Newman, who used to be touted by studio flacks as the "new Brando," his opinion of the actor.

"I've got to tell you, I had fun with that comparison thing between Brando and me. When I first went out to Hollywood and everybody was referring to me as the 'road company Brando' and things like that, I found it was kind of interesting, 'cause that's what I consider lazy journalism. I liked to nail those guys, and it's very simple to do. You ask them, 'What is Marlon's basic quality? What does he carry within himself?' Well, they're absolutely stumped, and they flop around a lot, and I ask, 'Well, what do you think my basic quality is?' And they wouldn't know that, either. They didn't have the vaguest idea of what Marlon's focus is, which is eruptability. Eruptability is always in the poten-

tial of the masses-type hero. And the quality that I carry is Ivy League—Shaker Heights and like that.

"I certainly don't disagree with Marlon's sympathy for the Indians. My own political views are pretty well known, I guess. I campaigned extensively for McCarthy in '68. I've also been involved in the civil rights thing, and—hah!—Zero Population Growth. I laugh because it's difficult to do that for a guy who's got six children."

Newman gestures wearily.

"What's happened to me in a political sense is that I've gotten tired. Actually, I think, say, Jane Fonda is probably a little more radical than I am, although not all that much. I suppose the main thing she and I have in common is that we are both fighters for certain causes, but at a particular point I got tired, and it'll be interesting to find out if she does, too. It'll be interesting to see how long her fire lasts. The main distinction between Jane and me, I think, is that she enjoys it—she enjoys all that hassle. Me, I never enjoyed the hassle. Making speeches, shaking hands, dealing with the press—it's all a pain in the ass.

"Which is why I wouldn't ever get into politics. It would drive me *wild*. It would blow my marriage and drive me crazy. If Joanne suddenly found herself in a position where she had to throw one of those fancy Washington bashes, she would—well, that'd be the end of the relationship. She'd say, 'Well, you're on your own, kid.'"

Newman tosses off the last of his beer, stands, yawns, stretches and rubs his stomach: "What time's it gettin' to be? Must be two o'clock. Whyn't we head downstairs and grab some turkey?"

Newman leads the way to the Pump Room, a dimly lit, overpriced bistro whose rococo pretentiousness could only be done justice by a graphic artist with a consummately decadent eye. The restaurant is filled to near-capacity with aging businessmen, sitting beside sleekly coiffed young hotdogs and talking in imperious tones into plug-in telephones. A majordomo in an absurd plumed helmet stands at a rigid parade-rest position near the entrance.

Seated, Newman props his chin on his elbows and gazes curiously around the room. "I can remember eating dinner here thirty-eight years ago with my family," he muses. "I must've been about five. This was *the* place then, one of the legends."

A waiter appears, pencil and pad at the poise. Both Newman and the writer order medium-rare cheeseburgers and beer. "I'd like a paper-thin slice of onion with that," Newman adds. "And have you got any dill pickles back there?"

"Oh, yes, sir," the waiter assures him before hurrying off.

"Jeez," Newman sighs, "things're starting to look up. I'm starving. You know, I've always felt there should be a great ritual about eating. I always try to do it that way. It's interesting . . . I'm turning slowly into a vegetarian. Joanne's a vegetarian now, and so are two of my daughters. And I think the whole family will be vegetarians inside of a few years. The younger kids are too young to make choices like that."

The waiter serves the beer.

"Ah, great!" Newman beams. "God, at this rate, we'll go *lurching* out of here."

The writer asks Newman how he and his wife get along when they're working in a professional capacity.

"It's very simple," Newman says, nodding emphatically. "We respect each other."

Newman points to a klatch of a dozen or so elegantly dressed young women who're assembling under a spotlight in the center of the room. Up on the dais, the pianist strikes a series of peppy arpeggios, and an overripe chalupa steps up to the mike:

"Good afternoon, welcome to Pump Room Fashions. I'm Lucia Berriault. We have a very lovely show for you today. But I think the real show is right in this room."

"Oh, no," Newman mutters, ducking his head. "I think she's going to—"

"And at the front, the superstar who directed his wife, Joanne Woodward, in *Rachel, Rachel* and his current *The Effect of Gamma Rays on Man-in-the-Moon Marigolds*. He's in Chicago for about ten days filming a new picture, *The Sting*—Mr. Paul Newman!"

Smiling sheepishly, Newman rises for his round of applause, then hastily sits back down and takes a gulp of beer. The fashion show continues on the dais, and the models begin to parade around among the tables for closer inspection.

One of the models stops at the table and, catching Newman's eye, pirouettes gracefully to show off the scarlet chiffon maxi she's wearing. "Smashing!" Newman cries. "And you're smashing yourself!" As the woman smiles and strolls away, she's silhouetted from behind by a bank of bright gel lights, and Newman does a double take. "My God, did you see *that?*" he whispers. "You could see right through that dress, and that ravishing creature didn't have a stitch on underneath! Where's my telescope? Should we tell somebody? No, they'd turn off those lights. Let's just quietly watch the parade and think dirty thoughts."

The waiter brings the food, and Newman attacks his cheeseburger with gusto: "My *God, incredible*—this is going to be a seven-napkin sandwich, at the least." Chewing hungrily, Newman peers at the writer's plate. "If you're going to eat that with a fork, you're going to be a real shit. If you'll cut that in half, it'll stay together better. I'm very knowledgeable about beer, popcorn and hamburgers.

"To tell you the truth, I think if I could afford to give up acting, I'd never act in another film. That's right—I've just gotten to the point where I feel I'm repeating myself, and also the whole sense of making films is changing. You get a sense that you don't have it, really. There are some actors, I guess, who have . . . *Lord,* this is a glossy lunch, isn't it? I don't eat very many glossy lunches."

Across the room, the fashion show concludes and the pianist segues into "The Very Thought of You."

"The thing is," Newman says, talking with his mouth full, "after a while, when you find yourself developing all the successful mannerisms, that's the time to get out of it. The directing and producing end of films—I don't know if I want to get into that all the way or not. I think I'd like to open a restaurant—or a popcorn stand."

Newman chuckles and takes a deep swig of beer. "I figure if you make one good film out of four or five, you've done very well. See, I don't usually tend to rate myself. There are too many imponderables. I mean, was *The Outrage* a better performance in my own eyes because I crawled out of my own skin, or does *The Hustler,* which was the most difficult script to start working with, hold up better? Is *Harper* the best performance because the character wasn't anywhere near as clearly defined as in *Hud?* One is easy for the actor, and one is difficult for the actor."

The waiter pushes a pastry cart close to the table and asks Newman if he cares for dessert. Newman mock-groans, but orders a twisted chocolate chip and a cup of Sanka. A plump matron in a violet pantsuit takes advantage of the lull in the conversation to lean in close and

ask Newman for his autograph. Newman expels a mournful sigh: "I love you, dear, but I don't give them. What're your children's names?" Flustered, the woman stammers, "Why, P-Paul and Monica." Newman clasps the woman's hand warmly: "Well, tell Paul and Monica I love them, too, will you?"

When the woman, smiling radiantly, departs and the waiter serves Newman his pastry, the writer brings up the subject of *Pocket Money,* explaining that Lee Marvin, Newman's costar in the film, had expressed the feeling a few months before that Newman had "finessed" him out of the picture.

Fork arrested in midair, Newman stares in surprise: "*I* finessed him? I never even *looked* at the picture. Well, no, now I made some recommendations about the ending—two voice-overs that the two of us have—but that was the only comment I made. Did he really say that?"

"Well, it's just absolutely not true. I mean, Redford and I have got operational egos, but you never see that in terms of performance. *Pocket Money* didn't make it, for sure, but I was delighted to play that character, that adolescent. I think the picture was too repetitious in terms of the humor, and it didn't really know where it was going. It was fey and artificial.

"Joanne and I once did a film together at Paramount that wasn't very good, either. It was called *A New Kind of Love.* Joanne read the script, and she said, 'Gee, this is kind of fun. Why don't you read it?' So I read it, and I told her, 'Well, I don't think it's fun—I don't think it's *anything.*' She said, 'I was thinking we might do it together.' I said, 'No, *you* do it, and I'll watch and clap soundlessly from the wings.' She said, 'You sonofabitch! Here I've made my career subservient to yours—I've raised your family, and not only my children and your children, but your children from another marriage,' and blah-blah-blah, and I said, 'Say no more, love. I'm really anxious to do it, I'm really chafing at the bit.' And that's how *that* project got off the ground. The family wash."

Newman laughs wryly and takes a final bite of pastry.

"A plus about making pictures is that you learn something new on every one, whether it's a good one or a stinker. If nothing else, you meet new people. I didn't want to do *Exodus,* for example. I thought it was too cold and expository, and actually I tried to get out of it. But I did get to know [Otto] Preminger.

"He's got the reputation of being such a fascist asshole, and he is on the set. I mean, he can pick out the most vulnerable person and then walk all over him, you know. He could walk down a line of two hundred people at a fast pace and pick somebody out and make lunch out of him. Off the set, though, I found him articulate, informed, funny, absolutely lovable.

"Hitchcock, hmm . . . We just didn't have a good script for *Torn Curtain.* And that always colors things, you know. Good scripts are damn scarce. I recall I wanted to do *The Hustler* with Bob Rossen from the word go. That picture was something special for Rossen, who was already terminally ill, because he was familiar with the world of pool and that whole hustler era, and he just pulled himself together to do the film, and he was incredible. I blame the blacklist in part for Rossen's death. I think the second he succumbed to that, he hurt his pride to a fatal extent.

"There was one scene in *The Hustler,* though, that I always had a big quarrel with—the scene on the hillside where Eddie tells the girl what it's like to play pool, right? Well, the way it was originally written, I thought it was a nothing scene—it just wasn't there, it had no sense of specialness. So I told Rossen he ought to somehow liken what Eddie does to what anybody who's performing something sensational is doing—a ballplayer, say, or some guy who laid 477 bricks in one day.

"Well, we were shooting on Fifty-fifth Street in New York, and Bob listened to what I said, and we walked into his office, and it couldn't have been six minutes later that he came out with the four-page scene that was in the film. He was that type of artist. He did the whole goddamn thing."

Across the room, Redford enters and semaphores his arms, motioning to Newman that it's time to return to the set. Grinning, Newman asks the waiter for the check and strolls over to the cashier's stand. "I hope you got all those girls cleared out of your room, buddy boy," Newman says teasingly to Redford. "This is a class joint." Redford puts on a long face and lets his shoulders slump dejectedly. "All gone," he clucks. "They all went back to Decatur on the Greyhound."

The following morning, a predicted six-inch snowfall fails to materialize, but it's snapping cold as the film troupe sets up shop in a vacant lot adjacent to the el station at Forty-third and Calumet. The morning's location site lies in the heart of the tough South Side ghetto, and the crew members tread cautiously as a predominantly black crowd of onlookers assembles. "Hey, there's the Sundance Kid!" a skinny kid with a bushy red Afro cries, pointing at Redford, who's walking toward his dressing-room trailer carrying a dog-eared copy of David Halberstam's *Best and the Brightest.* "Wonder where at ol' Butch Cassidy is? He the one I wanna see."

Stationary jogging to keep warm, the kid with the Afro, who answers to the name of Nickel Bag, has started up a flirty shuck-and-jive conversation with a spindly-legged girl wearing a T-shirt bearing the stenciled motto: I AM SAGITTARIUS—I'M CRABBY. "You seen any movie stars yet?" she asks him. "Naw. Oh, yeah—seen the Sundance Kid. Ol' Butch Cassidy, though, he ain't showed up yet. He the main one I wanna see. He a stone righteous dude, man."

One of the technicians overhears the kid and tells him that Newman isn't scheduled for any of the day's scenes.

The kid looks outraged. "What kinda shit is that, man? Sheeit, I done hooked school today to see that dude, man." Dejected, the kid reflects for a minute, then has an inspiration. He slaps the girl's palm.

"Looka yere, girl, you got any main man?"

"Naw, uh-huh," the girl titters.

"Well, you got one now, sugar. And I'ma tell you what—if you got any bread, I'ma take you to see *The Mack.*"

And with stern authority, Nickel Bag takes her arm and steers her toward the stairs to the street.

The Force Behind George Lucas

By Paul Scanlon

AUGUST 25, 1977

One sunny spring afternoon last year, an old friend and fellow movie buff drove me to an inconspicuous two-story warehouse in Van Nuys, California. The building was headquarters for Industrial Light and Magic, an organization of young technicians charged with creating special visual effects for *Star Wars*, writer/director George Lucas' $9.5-million space fantasy.

Lucas and the principal unit had just started shooting in Tunisia, but the activity around IL&M that day was so intense you'd have thought the film was opening in a month or two. Modelmakers were hard at work putting the finishing touches on miniature spacecraft (chiefly by cannibalizing store-bought model kits); a team of animators was hard at work on prototype effects; the explosives people were worrying about upcoming tests and everyone was fussing over the camera that John Dykstra and his technicians had constructed—from scratch—to shoot the space sequences.

Dykstra, the film's special photographic effects supervisor, who had worked previously with Douglas Trumbull *(2001: A Space Odyssey)*, led a bunch of us upstairs to a makeshift screening room littered with chairs and a couple of old overstuffed sofas. One of the young animators had just completed a series of laser blasts for Dykstra's approval. The room went dark and we watched the "lasers" light up the screen. The better ones were greeted with applause; the most spectacular ones got cries of "Wowie!" "Whoopie!" and "Far out!"

Later, I was peering at some storyboards—sequential pen-and-ink illustrations—of a planned space battle scene. Several shots featured a hairy creature with enormous teeth apparently at the controls of a spacecraft. "What's that?" I asked a passing technician. "A Wookie, of course," she replied, and continued walking without further explanation.

Even back then it was pretty easy to see that this young and gifted crew was fired up by George Lucas' peculiar vision and exceptional imagination. He says that all of his films are characterized by "a sort of effervescent giddiness." Whatever you want to call it, it's a quality that seems to affect the people who work for him and audiences alike. His first feature film, *THX 1138*, was technically brilliant but no crowd-pleaser. Still, it has attained cultish status and has consistently done well through campus rentals over the past few years. Then came *Amer-*

ican Graffiti, George's paean to the class of '62, cruising and rock & roll. Made for $750,000 with a small crew and a twenty-eight-day shooting schedule, it has become the eleventh-largest grosser. And in case you've been asleep for the past couple of months, or on Mars, George Lucas' third feature, *Star Wars,* may well become the biggest grosser ever. Not bad for a film that almost never got off the ground in the first place and was an unknown quantity almost right up to the release date.

When I visited the set in London later that spring, there was a notable lack of effervescent giddiness. It was certainly impressive enough— all eight of the EMI Elstree Studios' sound stages were in use for *Star Wars*—and everything seemed to be on schedule, but George Lucas was worried. Some of the actors were questioning their dialogue. The robots didn't look right. A whole sequence with Peter Cushing had to be reshot because *it* didn't look right. There were script revisions. The Alec Guinness character was going to be killed off two-thirds into the film, and the studio didn't know it yet. The English crews worked a strict eight-hour day, and had two obligatory tea breaks. . . .

At his home in San Anselmo later that summer, George and producer Gary Kurtz were looking more worried. The studio was demanding a rough cut, and the special effects were barely one-third complete. The robots were looking even worse. The score wasn't ready. There were lighting problems, sound problems. . . .

Somehow—basically through around-the-clock efforts—it all came together. A week before opening there was still no answer print. George and the sound people were looping sound effects into the seventy-millimeter version right up until the last minute. The only question remaining was, would it fly? It did.

It's not a difficult movie to synopsize. In fact, *Star Wars* is straight out of *Buck Rogers* and *Flash Gordon* by way of Tolkien, *Prince Valiant, The Wizard of Oz, Boy's Life* and about every great Western movie ever made. Our hero, Luke Skywalker (Mark Hamill) is a farmboy from an arid desert planet called Tatooine who suddenly finds himself—through a series of unlikely events—smack in the middle of a galactic civil war. His allies include Han Solo (Harrison Ford), a daredevil space-pilot-for-hire; Ben Obi-Wan Kenobi (Alec Guinness), a mystical old gent who is the last of a group called the Jedi knights, and who knew Luke's father when; Princess Leia Organa (Carrie Fisher), who is one of the chief rebels opposing the Empire; Chewbacca, the Wookie, an eight-foot-tall, intelligent and ferocious anthropoid; and two wise-cracking robots named R2D2 and C3PO (the former speaks android, the latter English) who practically steal the film.

The chief bad guys are Darth Vader (David Prowse) and Grand Moff Tarkin (Peter Cushing), aided by a horde of flunkies and storm troopers. They operate out of the Death Star, an enormous satellite designed specifically to go around the galaxy zapping recalcitrant planets unwilling to side with the Empire. It is clear, early in the film, that confrontations are inevitable. It's also clear who's going to win.

What sets *Star Wars* apart from its predecessors are the special effects (some 365 separate shots) and the extraordinary richness of Lucas' imagination. There's the Cantina sequence, for instance, where the heroes stumble into a bar whose patrons are the scum of a dozen galaxies. And there are ancillary creatures such as the Jawas, tiny, chattering beings who hustle used robots for a living. As for the opticals and miniatures, Lucas and Dykstra have come up with a new standard against which all future space-fiction films must be judged. Before *Star Wars* was released, Dykstra told an interviewer that the final battle sequence would be every bit as exciting as *The French Connection* car chase. He was right.

So here sits George Lucas, thirty-three, in a hotel suite overlooking New York's Central Park. He's in town to see the premiere of his friend Martin Scorsese's film, *New York, New York,* which was edited by his wife, Marcia (who also cut much of *Star Wars*). Somewhere out there, folks are queuing up for the next showing of his movie, and George Lucas, fresh from Hawaii, is smiling.

So how does it feel; did you really expect that "Star Wars" was going to take off like this?

No way. Right after *American Graffiti*, I was getting this fan mail from kids that said the film changed their life, and something inside me said, do a children's film. And everybody said, "Do a *children's film?* What are you talking about? You're crazy."

You know, I had done *Graffiti* as a challenge. All I had ever done to that point was crazy, avant-garde, abstract movies. Francis Ford Coppola really challenged me on that. "Do something warm," he said, "everyone thinks you're a cold fish; all you do is science fiction." So I said, "Okay, I'll do something warm." I did *Graffiti* and then I wanted to go back and do this other stuff, I thought I had more of a chance of getting *Star Wars* off the ground. Because *Graffiti* pointed out that kids forgot what being a teenager was, which is being dumb and chasing girls, doing things—you know, at least I did when I was a kid. I saw that kids today don't have any fantasy life the way we had—they don't have Westerns, they don't have pirate movies, they don't have that stupid serial fantasy life that we used to believe in.

So you do a "Star Wars."

I was a real fan of *Flash Gordon* and that kind of stuff, a very strong advocate of the exploration of outer space, and I said, this is something, this is a natural. One, it will give kids a fantasy life, and two, maybe it will make someone a young Einstein and people will say, "Why?" What we really need to do is to colonize the next galaxy, get away from the hard facts of *2001* and get on the romantic side of it. Nobody is going to colonize Mars because of the technology, they are going to go because they think maybe they will be able . . . well, it is romantic, it is the romantic aspect of it that needs to be looked at for a second, which nobody had ever looked at before. I mean, everybody had looked at the hardware end of it.

You firmly establish that at the beginning of "Star Wars" with the words: "A long, long time ago in a galaxy far, far away . . ."

Well, I had a real problem because I was afraid that science-fiction buffs and everybody would say things like, "You know there's no sound in outer space." I just wanted to forget science. That would take care of itself. Stanley Kubrick made the ultimate science-fiction movie and it is going to be very hard for somebody to come along and make a better movie, as far as I'm concerned. I didn't want to make a *2001,* I wanted to make a space fantasy that was more in the genre of Edgar Rice Burroughs; that whole other end of space fantasy that was there before science fiction took it over in the fifties. Once the atomic bomb came, everybody got into monsters and science and what would happen with this and what would happen with that. I think speculative fiction is very valid, but they forgot the fairy tales and the dragons and Tolkien and all the *real* heroes.

So that was the mainspring of your decision to make "Star Wars."

Right, and that is really the reason I did it. I had done sociological research on what makes hit films—it is part of the sociological bent in me; I can't help it.

And yet you encountered a lot of resistance on this project?

Yes. When I went to one studio, United Artists, I said, this is what I'm going to do, it's *Flash Gordon,* it's adventure, it's exciting, sort of James Bond and all this kind of stuff, and they said, no, we don't see it. So I went to Universal and got the same thing.

I think I got $20,000 to write and direct *Graffiti* and they wanted me to do *Star Wars* for $25,000. I was asking half of what my friends were asking, and the studio thought I was asking for twice as much as I would get, and they said, no, no. It is too much money and we don't really think it is for us, so they threw it out the window. And then I finally talked Fox into doing it, partially because they sort of understood, they had done the *Planet of the Apes* movies. They said, I think it's got potential, so they went with it, but *nobody* thought it was going to be a big hit. I kept doing more research and writing scripts. The problem in something like this is you are creating a whole genre that has never been created before.

How do you explain a Wookie to a board of directors?

You can't, and how do you explain a Wookie to an audience, and how do you get the tone of the film right, so it's not a silly child's film, so it's not playing down to people, but it is still an entertaining movie and doesn't have a lot of violence and sex and hip new stuff? So it still has a vision to it, a sort of wholesome, honest vision about the way you want the world to be. I was also working on themes that I worked with in *THX* and *Graffiti,* of accepting responsibility for your actions and that kind of stuff. So it

took me a long time to get the thing done. About the time we finished the preproduction, we did a budget on it. The first budget actually came out to $16 million, so I threw out a lot of designing new equipment and said, okay, we'll cut corners and do a lot of fast filmmaking, which is where I really come from. *Graffiti* and *THX* were nothing, both under-a-million dollar pictures. So we started applying some of our budget techniques and we got it down by $8.5 million, which was really about as cheap as that script could possibly ever be made by any human being.

When I first met you in London, you were complaining that you could make a $2-million movie for $1 million but you couldn't make a $14-million movie for $8 million.

It was terribly difficult but we made it. We set the budget for $8 million; they said, no, make it seven. When we finally got the budget down to $7 million, we knew it couldn't be done, and we told Fox it couldn't be done. They said make it $7 million anyway. I was practically working for free and my only hope was that if the film paid off, and if it cost $8 million, that would mean it would break even at $20 million.

What was your actual salary for directing?

I think in the end my actual salary was $100,000, which again was still like half of what everybody else was making.

Do you have percentage points in the film?

Everybody has points, but the key is to make them pay off. I figured I was never going to see any money on my points, so what the heck. I also had a chance to give away a lot of my points, which I had done with *Graffiti.* Part of the success is the fault of the actors, composer and crew, and they should share in the rewards as well, so I got my points carved down much less than what my contemporaries have. But I never expected *Star Wars* to . . . I expected to break even on it, I still can't understand it.

Why?

I struggled through this movie. I had a terrible time; it was very unpleasant. *American Graffiti* was unpleasant because of the fact that there was no money, no time and I was compromising myself to death. But I could rationalize it because of the fact that, well, it is just a $700,000 picture—it's Roger Corman—and what do you expect, you can't expect everything to be right for making a little cheesy, low-budget movie. But this was a big expensive movie and the money was getting wasted and things weren't coming out right. I was running the corporation. I wasn't making movies like I'm used to doing. *American Graffiti* had like forty people on the payroll; that counts everybody but the cast. I think *THX* had about the same. You can control a situation like that. On *Star Wars* we had over 950 people working for us and I would tell a department head and he would tell another assistant department head, he'd tell some guy, and by the time it got down the line it was not there. I spent all my time yelling and screaming at people, and I have never had to do that before.

I got rid of some people here and there, but it is a frustrating and an unhappy experience doing that. I realized why directors are such horrible people—in a way—because you want things to be right, and people will just not listen to you, and there is no time to be nice to people, no time to be delicate.

This was something else you said in London: "I'm tired of being a director, I want to go back to being a filmmaker."

Well, that's true, that is really what I want to do. I've done this thing now. I've directed my large corporation and I made the movie that I wanted to make. It is not as good by a long shot as it should have been. I take half the responsibility myself and the other half is some of the unfortunate decisions I made in hiring people, but I could have written a better script, I could have done a lot of things; I could have directed it better.

Back in California last summer you were again upset. You said the robots didn't look right. R2 looked like a vacuum cleaner. You could see fifty-seven separate flaws in C3PO, you didn't like the lighting, everything seemed like it wasn't coming together. Was it coming together?

Well, for one thing, by the time we got back to California I wasn't happy with the lighting on the picture. I'm a cameraman, and I like a slightly more extreme, eccentric style than I got in the movie. It was all right, it was a very difficult movie, there were big sets to light, it was a very big problem. The robots never worked. We faked the whole thing and a lot of it was done editorially.

How?

Every time the remote-control R2 worked, it turned and ran into a wall, and when Kenny Baker, the midget, was in it, the thing was so heavy he could barely move it, and he would sort of take a step and a half and be totally exhausted. I could never get him to walk across the room, so we would cut to him there and cut to a close-up, and cut back so that he would be over here. It is all really movie magic more than it was anything else.

That's why it's amazing because when I finally saw the film, I was surprised. I couldn't see any seams. So I went to see it again and maybe saw a couple of seams, but that was it.

I can see nothing but seams. A film is sort of binary—it either works or it doesn't work. It has nothing to do with how good a job you do. If you bring it up to an adequate level where the audience goes with the movie, then it works, that is all. It is a fusion thing, and then every-thing else, all of the mistakes, don't count any-more.

Well, the "Star Wars" audience has no trouble sus-pending disbelief.

Right. If a film does *not* work, then you can do an impeccable job with making the movie. People still see the mistakes, and they get bored and it just doesn't work. And so, what can you say? *THX* was about 70 percent of what I wanted it to be. I don't think you ever get to the point where it is 100 percent. *Graffiti* was about 50 percent of what I wanted it to be, but I real-ized that the other 50 percent would have been there, if I just had a little more time and a little more money. *Star Wars* is about 25 percent of what I wanted it to be. It's really down there quite a bit. It's still a good movie, but it fell so short of what I wanted it to be. And everyone said, "Well, Jesus, George, you wanted the moon for chrissake, or you wanted to land on Pluto and you landed on Mars." I think the se-quels will be much, much better. What I want to do is direct the last sequel. I could do the first one and the last one and let everyone else do the ones in between.

It wouldn't bother you to have someone else do the ones in between?

No, it would be interesting. I would want to try and get some good directors, and see what their interpretation of the theme is. I think it will be interesting; it is like taking a theme in film school, say, okay, everybody do their inter-pretation of this theme. It's an interesting idea to see how people interpret the genre. It is a fun genre to play with. All the prototype stuff is done now. Nobody has to worry about what a Wookie is and what it does and how it reacts. Wookies are there, the people are there, the en-vironment is there, the empire is there . . . every-thing is there. And now people will start

building on it. I've put up the concrete slab of the walls and now everybody can have fun draw-ing the pictures and putting on the little gar-goyles and doing all the really fun stuff. And it's a competition. I'm hoping if I get friends of mine, they will want to do a much better film, like, "I'll show George that I can do a film twice that good," and I think they can, but then I want to do the last one, so I can do one twice as good as everybody else. [*Laughs*]

Did you create Jawas and Wookies out of your readings in anthropology?

They didn't really have any basis. The Jawas really came from *THX*. They were the shell dwellers, the little people that lived under-ground in the shells. And in a way, part of *Star Wars* came out of me wanting to do a sequel to *THX*. Wookies came out of *THX*, too. One of the actors who was doing some voice-over for radio talk, Terry McGovern, came up with the word *Wookie*.

Didn't I hear his voice in "Star Wars"?

They're the San Francisco/San Anselmo/ George Lucas players, a bunch of disc jockeys, Scott Beach, Terry McGovern. Terry was the teacher in *American Graffiti*—they've been in all my movies—we were riding along in the car one day and he said, "I think I ran over a Wookie back there," and this really cracked me up and I said, "What is a Wookie?" and he said, "I don't know, I just made it up." And I said, "That is great, I love that word." I just wrote it down and said I'm going to use that.

There are lots of great pseudolanguages in the film—the Wookie, the Jawas, R2 and Greedo, the hit creature of the Cantina sequence, to name a few. Were these elaborately constructed?

Yes. Right when the film started, we hired two people—one was an artist, Ralph McQuar-rie, and the other was the soundman, Ben Burtt. I just went to one of my old instructors at USC and I asked, who is the best guy you've got, in terms of working on sound? And so Ben spent two years developing sound effects—he did all the ray guns, spaceships exploding, and toward the end he worked for like three or four months to come in with R2. I said I wanted to have beeps and boops and that. Well, it is easy to say that, it's another to take those beeps, boops and sounds and actually make a personality. He spent a long time coming up with sounds. And I would listen to it and I would say, no, no, we need something with a little more sensitivity, he needs to be sadder here, he needs to be happier there. We need to know he's angry here. And he would go back and he would work on the Arp and the Moog, he would talk into the mike and he would run it fast and he would run it slow and he would combine all these things, and he finally came up with it. It didn't sound all the same, like a Touch-Tone telephone. To some people I guess he still sounds like a Touch-Tone telephone.

R2 has a very distinct personality.

Yeah. Ben had to write out the dialogue I never wrote. I just wrote, 3PO says, "Did you hear that?" and the little robot goes, "Beep-a-da-boop," and Ben had to sit there and say, "Hmm, well, of course I heard that, you idiot." So then he had to take that and he had to translate it. He did the same thing with the Wookie, a combination of a walrus and bear and about five or six other animal sound effects that are all put together in a very sophisticated manner electronically to create one voice.

I was fascinated by the relationship between robots and humans. Droids seem to be second-class citizens, as 3PO is quick to point out from time to time. But on the other hand, there is a very warm bond between droids and humans.

Well, the droids were there to serve. Obviously droids are servants of man. They do as they are commanded and all that kind of stuff, but at the same time I love droids, they're my favorite people. I didn't want them to be cold robots. Even the robots in *THX* are very friendly. They're not malevolent. In *Star Wars* I really wanted to get into the robots and their problems in life; a little equal time for robots, who have taken a lot of shit over the years and have never really had a chance to prove themselves.

3PO has obvious affection for R2.

Right. They were designed as a sort of Laurel and Hardy team. They were the comic aspects of the film, the real comic aspects, the ones who were supposed to tell the jokes. I didn't want the whole thing to be a comedy, but I wanted to have a lot of fun. I didn't want the human characters to crack jokes all the time so I let the robots do it, because I wanted to see if I could make robots be like humans.

Whose voice belongs to Darth Vader?

That's James Earl Jones. He was the best actor I could possibly find. He has a deep, commanding voice.

Was the other Darth Vader angry that his voice was knocked out?

No, he sort of knew when we hired him. He is an actor, David Prowse, and he has a very strong brogue. He played the weight lifter in *A Clockwork Orange*. He owns a chain of weight-lifting gyms, is very rich and does movies for fun.

Why does Darth Vader breathe so heavily?

I had wanted to do that and tie it in with the dialogue.

It was a nice touch, because it adds to the bogeyman quality of the character.

Ben had a lot of work in that, too. He did about eighteen different kinds of breathing, through Aqua-Lungs and through tubes, trying to find the one that had the right sort of mechanical sound, and then decide whether it would be totally rhythmical and like an iron lung. That's the idea. It was a whole part of the plot that essentially got cut out. It may be in one of the sequels.

What's the story?

It's about Ben and Luke's father and Vader when they are young Jedi knights. But Vader kills Luke's father, then Ben and Vader have a confrontation, just like they have in *Star Wars,* and Ben almost kills Vader. As a matter of fact, he falls into a volcanic pit and gets fried and is one destroyed being. That's why he has to wear a suit with a mask, because it's a breathing mask. It's like a walking iron lung. His face is all horrible inside. I was going to shoot a close-up of Vader where you could see the inside of his face, but then we said, no, no, it would destroy the mystique of the whole thing.

I was quite happy to see Vader spinning off into deep space at the end, but not dying. The only thing missing was a title on the screen saying, "To be continued soon at a theater near you."

Right, the idea was doing the film on a practical level and leaving room for sequels. When I did *THX* I realized that I put in an enormous amount of effort that I will never be able to use again. I know the world of *THX.* I could make movies about *THX* forever, but it took me so much time and so much energy to develop all that stuff, and then it got touched upon in one movie. Normally in a movie it's maybe a book or a piece of history or a piece of my life. I sat down and wrote *Graffiti* in three weeks, it was easy. With something like *Star Wars,* you have to invent *everything.* You have to think of the cultures and what kind of coffee cups they are going to have, and where is the realm between technology and mankind and where does ESP play a part of this. . . . And you go and sort of find the levels that you want to deal with. How far out do you want to go? Will the people relate to that?

Do the inevitable comparisons between "Star Wars" and "2001" bother you?

No, I expected actually a lot more than it got. In fact, I am fairly pleased that they haven't compared it that much to *2001.* Actually it is being compared more to Westerns than *2001,* which is really what it should be. On a technical level it can be compared, but personally I think that *2001* is far superior. You know it had ten times more money and time and obviously it came out better. In special effects one of the key elements is time and money. Most of those special effects in *Star Wars* were first-time special effects—we shot them, we composited them and they're in the movie. We had to go back and reshoot some, but in order to get special effects right, you really should shoot them two or three times before you figure out exactly how it should work, which is why it costs so much money. But most of our stuff we had to do as a one-shot deal. We did a lot of work, but there is nothing that I would like to do more than go back and redo all the special effects, have a little more time.

Which takes us back to this period of the last few months before release. The editorial thing that you were mentioning earlier, pulling things together by sleight of hand. What was it like leading up to the actual opening night? I heard that you were looping and cutting up to the last minute.

The whole picture was very difficult because it was made on a very short schedule—about seventy days on the sets and locations. In England we couldn't shoot past five-thirty, so we worked eight-hour days. Whereas I visited Steve [Spielberg] and Marty [Scorsese] after I finished shooting, and they were filming twelve to fourteen hours a day. So they were actually getting another day's work every day. They would have, like, a 120-day schedule, but if you counted the hours, they really had two hundred days to shoot. While I had seventy real days to shoot, and it was very short for something that was that complex. It was the same in the finishing. The studio wanted to finish it for the summer, I wanted to finish it for the summer, and so we were up against the wall. When I came back from England, we were supposed to have half of the special effects done, and actually they had about three shots finished and they were not up to what I felt were the standards of the film. Industrial Light and Magic had spent most of the early part of that year and a million dollars—which was about the whole budget in the whole time they had to shoot—building cameras and developing electronic computer systems and stuff. They didn't really concentrate that much on actually making shots.

Were the cameras that shot the miniatures built from scratch?

Yes, everything was built from scratch. We built optical cameras, Moviolas, a whole system based on VistaVision. John Dykstra built it and he really is a very talented guy who worked as a cameraman for Doug Trumbull. He is very, very knowledgeable in building sophisticated camera-motion systems. He developed systems along with several of the people who worked with him in electronic and mechanical designs. It was quite extraordinary; we built a whole operation.

But you and Dykstra were at odds a lot, weren't you?

Well, we weren't so much at odds as much as I was more interested in the shots. I didn't care how we got the shots, I just wanted the composition and the lighting to be good, and I wanted them to get it done on time. On a real production you have no time and you are doing the impossible every day, at a very hectic, acceler-

ated pace. Special-effects people have a tendency to think that if they get one shot a day, they are really quite pleased. They don't work on the same pace that the regular production unit works. I believe that you can do special effects with the same intensity and in the same schedule that you shoot a regular movie, so there was a little bit of conflict there. And at the same time, I wanted the shots to look a certain way and be designed a certain way and we had difficulty with what was actually technically possible with the time laid out to accomplish it. It was purely a working problem, and being at odds with John was no greater than being at odds with everybody else. I had just as many problems with the robots and the special-effects people in England as with the special-effects people in California.

Was that one of your key administrative problems then, the wedding of the location footage with special-effects footage?

No, I was just trying to get the special effects up to a quality that I wanted. I was happy with a lot of the special effects toward the end. The operation got very good. In the beginning the cameraman was still learning how to fly the airplanes, because it was a very complex animation thing, where you're moving cameras and rolling, doing little motor things. When you watch it happen, you are not working in real time; it is very difficult to plot out the way one of those planes move in non-real time, using tilting cameras and motors. It's easy to take your hand and say, I want the plane to go this way, and it is very difficult to actually translate that onto paper and then film so that you actually get the ship to do that, and it took a long time just to figure out how to fly. There are problems that have never really been coped with before. In *2001*, the ships run a straight line; they just go away from you or they cross the screen, they never turn or dive.

What about the final battle sequence, the dogfight?

The dogfight sequence was extremely hard to cut and edit. We had storyboards that we had taken from old movies, and we used the black-and-white footage of old World War II movies intercut with pilots talking and stuff, so you could edit the whole sequence in real time. My wife, Marcia, can normally cut a whole reel—all ten minutes of the film—in one week. I think it took her eight weeks to cut that battle. It was extremely complex and we had forty thousand feet of dialogue footage of pilots saying this and that. And she had to cull through all that and put in all the fighting as well. Nobody really has ever tried to interweave an actual plot story into a dogfight, and we were trying to do that, however successful or unsuccessful we were.

How about the John Williams score? Pretty stirring stuff.

I was very, very pleased with the score. We wanted a very sort of Max Steiner–type, old-fashioned, romantic movie score.

It's very much like a serial—like, of course, "Flash Gordon"—you hear it throughout the film.

There are ninety minutes of music in a one-hundred-ten-minute film. I wanted to use some of Liszt, Dvořák, some of the *Flash Gordon* stuff, and Johnny said no. He wanted to make some strong theme, fairly reminiscent in a few places but at the same time very original. The whole thing was really designed like *Peter and the Wolf*. We did it so that each character has their own theme and whenever that character is on the screen that theme is played.

A space opera.

Well, they used to do it all the time, writing music for movies was closer to writing for opera or symphony. One interesting thing about the music—which is sort of like the movie itself—is

that I really expected to get devastated in terms of people saying, "Oh, my God, what a stupid, old-fashioned thing and how corny can you get?" I am amazed that people just said, "Gee, that's fine." I really expected to get trounced very badly about the whole thing. And Johnny did, too, a little bit. A lot of lines in the movie are sort of . . . I wince every time I hear them.

You mean you expected to get trounced on everything? I thought we were just talking about the score.

I expected to get trounced on everything. Especially in the end when it came down to the score, which was romantic and dramatic. Not only a slightly corny dialogue here and a very simplistic, sort of corny plot . . .

Some of Mark Hamill's lines are pretty corny.

There is some very strong stuff in there. In the end, when you know better, it sort of takes a lot of guts to do it because it's the same thing with the whole movie—doing a children's film. I didn't want to play it down and make it a camp movie, I wanted to make it a very good movie. And it wasn't camp, it was not making fun of itself. I wanted it to be real.

Even though Harrison Ford's character, Han Solo, is right up to the edge of camp, very John Wayne–ish.

He goes as far as I let anybody go.

"I been from one end of this galaxy to the other, kid." But he did pull it off.

[*Laughs*] It fits in his character. Harrison is an extremely intelligent actor, and we balanced on a lot of thin threads when we went through this movie. And when you're doing it, you never know when you are going to jump off the other side, which is one of the things like with the score. There were a lot of little discussions about if this or that would make it go too far, would it be too much. I decided just to do it all the way down the line, one end to the other, complete. Everything is on that same level, which is sort of old-fashioned and fun but going for the most dramatic and emotional elements that I can get.

The Peter Cushing character, Grand Moff Tarkin, certainly applies to that formula. He got off some great lines. Especially right near the end, "Abandon the station, now at the hour of my greatest triumph?"

The stuff in that is very strong. Peter Cushing, like Alec Guinness, is a very good actor. He got an image that is in a way quite beneath him, but he's also idolized and adored by young people and people who go to see a certain kind of movie. I think he will be remembered fondly for the next 350 years at least. And so you say, is that worth anything? Maybe it's not Shakespeare but certainly equally as important in the world. Good actors really bring you something, and that is especially true with Alec Guinness, who I thought was a good actor like everyone else, but after working with him I was staggered that he was such a creative and disciplined person. In the original script Ben Kenobi doesn't get killed in the fight with Vader. About halfway through production, I took Alec aside and said I was going to kill him off halfway through the picture. It is quite a shock to an actor when you say, "I know you have a big part and you are going to the end and be a hero and everything and all of a sudden I have decided to kill you," but he took it very well and he began to build on it and helped and developed the character accordingly.

Was the studio upset when you told them Kenobi would die?

Everybody was upset. I was struggling with the problem that I had this sort of climactic scene that had no climax about two-thirds of the way through the film. I had another problem in the fact that there was no real threat in the Death Star. The villains were like tenpins; you get into a gunfight with them and they just get knocked over. As I originally wrote it, Ben Ken-

obi and Vader had a sword fight and Ben hits a door and the door slams closed and they all run away and Vader is left standing there with egg on his face. This was dumb; they run into the Death Star and they sort of take over everything and they run back. It totally diminished any impact the Death Star had.

It was like the old Bob Steele Westerns where they all had about fifty shots in their six-shooters.

Right, but those kind of things dissipate without having a lot of real cruel torture scenes and real unpleasant scenes with the bad guys in order to create them as being bad or make them a threat. I was walking that thin line between making something that I thought was vaguely a nonviolent kind of movie but at the same time I was having all the fun of people getting shot. And I was very careful that most of the people that are shot in the film were the monsters or those storm troopers in armored suits. Anyway, I was rewriting, I was struggling with that plot problem when my wife suggested that I kill off Ben, which she thought was a pretty outrageous idea, and I said, "Well, that is an interesting idea, and I had been thinking about it." Her first idea was to have 3PO get shot, and I said impossible because I wanted to start and end the film with the robots, I wanted the film to really be about the robots and have them be the framework for the rest of the movie. But then the more I thought about Ben getting killed the more I liked the idea because, one, it made the threat of Vader greater and that tied in with The Force and the fact that he could use the dark side. Both Alec Guinness and I came up with the thing of having Ben go on afterward as part of The Force. There was a thematic idea that was even stronger about The Force in one of the earliest scripts. It was really all about The Force, a Castaneda *Tales of Power* thing.

Well, then, theoretically there could be a sequel

about *The Force*, there could be a sequel about the *Wookies*, about *Han*, about *Luke* . . .

Yes, it was one of the original ideas of doing a sequel that if I put enough people in it and it was designed carefully enough, I could make a sequel about *anything*. Or if any of the actors gave me a lot of trouble or didn't want to do it, or didn't want to be in the sequel, I could always make a sequel without one.

Do you have agreements with the principal characters?

Yes. All the actors except Alec Guinness. We may use his voice as The Force—I don't know. One of the sequels we are thinking of is the young days of Ben Kenobi. It would probably be all different actors.

The film's success should guarantee some success in the merchandising program you've launched.

One of my motivating factors for doing the film, along with all the other ones, was that I love toys and games. And so I figured, gee, I could start a kind of a store that sold comic art, and sold 78 records, or old rock & roll records that I like, and antique toys and a lot of things that I am really into; stuff that you can't buy in regular stores. I also like to create games and things, so that was part of the movie, to be able to generate toys and things. Also, I figured the merchandising along with the sequels would give me enough income over a period of time so that I could retire from professional filmmaking and go into making my own kind of movies, my own sort of abstract, weird, experimental stuff.

When does "Star Wars" open overseas?

It opens in Europe in October. And then I think it will open next July in Japan. I like Japan. I was going to shoot *THX* there and I spent some time over there. My wife says I am a reincarnated shogun, or at least a warlord. I'll be fascinated to see what happens over there; *Star Wars* is slightly designed for Japan.

It's not a Toho production; a Godzilla movie.

No, science fiction has reached this very crummy level in Japan. They love it but it is still very crummy. It's been exploited just like they did in this country. The wrong people have been doing science fiction. Science fiction—speculative fiction—is a very important genre that has not been taken very seriously, including the literature.

And there are important ideas there.

Yeah. Why do space suits look the way they do? Why, when we went to the moon, did the astronauts look just like men who went to the moon in *Destination Moon*?

Which was made in 1950.

Because the art director designed those space suits based on what he thought they would look like in terms of scientific input. But when you get down to it, a bunch of art directors from a bunch of old movies and speculative pulp fiction drew space suits and stuff way back when, and I have a feeling that they had a lot of influence on the way things look today, and the way things are, because the engineers and designers and all those people grew up.

Also, just on a theoretical/philosophical level the ultimate search is still the most fascinating search, what is it all about—why are we here and how big is it and where does it go, what is the system, what is the answer, what is God and all that. Most civilizations, whole cultures and religions were built on the "science fiction" of their day. It is just that. Now we call it science fiction. Before, they called it religion or myths or whatever they wanted to call it.

The epic and heroic tradition.

Yes. It has always been the same thing and it is the most significant kind of fiction as far as I am concerned. It's too bad that it has gotten that sleazy comic-book reputation, which I think we outgrew a long time ago. I think science fiction still has a tendency to react against that image and try to make itself so pious and serious, which is what I tried to knock out in making *Star Wars*. Buck Rogers is just as valid as Arthur C. Clarke in his own way; I mean, they are both sides of the same thing. Kubrick did the strongest thing in film in terms of the rational side of things, and I've tried to do the most in the irrational side of things because I think we need it. Again we are going to go with Stanley's ships, but hopefully we are going to be carrying my laser sword and have the Wookie at our side.

So now you have made your bid.

So I made my bid to try to make everything a little more romantic. Jesus, I'm hoping that if the film accomplishes anything, it takes some ten-year-old kid and turns him on *so much* to outer space and the possibilities of romance and adventure. Not so much an influence that would create more Wernher von Brauns or Einsteins, but just infusing them into serious exploration of outer space and convincing them that it's important. Not for any rational reason, but a totally irrational and romantic reason.

I would feel very good if someday they colonize Mars when I am ninety-three years old or whatever, and the leader of the first colony says, "I really did it because I was hoping there would be a Wookie up here."

Madonna and Rosanna Arquette Get Desperate

By Fred Schruers

MAY 9, 1985

Rosanna Arquette opens a leather wallet as big and thick as a hotel Bible and shuffles through credit cards, vital jottings and snapshots to pluck out a blurry Polaroid taken during the last few days of shooting on *Desperately Seeking Susan*. She holds it up: "We're really tight." There they stand, Rosanna and Madonna, all sassy grins and Harpo-and-Chico goofball camaraderie, two full-figured and comely young women whose only real-life money problem is where to spend and store it. They wear identical hats, just-bought porkpie jobs in black leather. "I never met anyone who has such a focus," Rosanna says of her costar. "She goes right for it, and she gets what she wants. I admire that a lot. But I think behind all that is a little tiny girl inside."

Our ostensible subject is *Desperately Seeking Susan*, the bargain-budgeted ($5 million) little film, directed by Susan Seidelman, that went from being an oddball artistes' showcase to big box office. Though the picture breaks many rules, both artistic and commercial, the result is one of the fresher entertainments to make it through the Hollywood bottleneck in these formulaic times.

Part screwball comedy, part satire, part set designer's equivalent to "out" jazz, *Susan* turns on mistaken identity. Arquette's bored housewife, Roberta, follows the trail of Madonna's gutter-ball schemer, Susan, into a slapdash murder mystery that scrambles suburbanites and hipsters into something between farce and dreamy fable. Early on, Roberta gets a knock on the head that gives her amnesia, and the two undergo an identity switch, setting up a skein of sardonic jokes that bounce off the wall at unexpected angles.

Madonna owned a platinum LP when she signed on to the project and has since earned a second one. The consensus, even among industry skeptics, is that the singer has the goods onscreen, too. What clearly has Arquette cutting conversational wheelies, though, is Orion's promotion of the film, in which she seems to play background to Madonna's phosphorescent pop icon.

"Can you blame them?" Arquette says. "A studio sees a hot commodity, and they immediately capitalize on it. It's a little misleading, because it's not a teen movie. I know the preview has been playing before *The Purple Rose of Cairo*, and it's been booed. The audience was people who love Susan Seidelman and who would go to see me, and that's sad."

Precious few young actresses can give Rosanna a power outage, onscreen or off. From a speck on the horizon, hitchhiking cross-country and arriving in Los Angeles at age seventeen, she's built a career mostly on the kind of quicksilver expressiveness she showed in *Baby, It's You* and in TV's *The Executioner's Song;* at twenty-five, she's in the front rank of actresses arriving at stardom. Today she drove in to Hollywood from her new house an hour up in the Topanga Canyon hills, leaving a coating of ocher dust behind the back tires of her otherwise gleaming Saab Turbo. Her silky, silvery dress is a bit of a war whoop among all the cut glass and linen of this Beverly Boulevard restaurant's cool, mirrored spaces, yet there's something more fundamental out of place. It's as if her heart were thudding audibly, even visibly, while she charges forward and back in a virtual self-interview.

"I've never been like this. I'm a wreck. I get hurt very easily. I don't have a tough shell. That's why I'm so freaked out. I'm so insecure. It's pretty stupid of me to be in this business, isn't it?"

Rosanna pauses, then gives a little tadpole wriggle with her right hand to signal that she's not really waiting for an answer. She glances once more at the Polaroid and tucks it away. She can't stifle these complaints, yet she can't stand voicing them. "We're great friends," she concludes in her trigger-burst style. "All these things I said to her. I think her performance is really good. All I'm saying is, 'Let her be an actress.'"

"'I had a few scenes where I was really shittin' bricks," say the twenty-six-year-old refugee from Pontiac, Michigan. "A few times I was so nervous I opened my mouth and nothing came out." Madonna is anything but mute tonight, as she takes a break from the Los Angeles rehearsal sessions for her first tour, and though she pauses occasionally to punctuate a phrase with a Mae West–ian secret smile, she lets you into the conversation only edgewise. "I think I surprised everybody, though, by being one of the calmest people on the set at all times. I think that had to do with the fact that I was in total wonderment: I was gonna soak everything up."

One keeps waiting for the brittle bitch, the self-absorbed bombshell who's supposed to lurk under her winking, vamping, wriggling electronic image, but the Madonna who sits talking over coffee comes on disarmingly humble.

Rosanna has expressed resentment over the insertion into the movie of a Madonna song backing a quickly written scene in which the Susan character gyrates around a New York club. A video clip using the unreleased tune "Into the Groove" spotlights Madonna. "It does take things out of context a bit," says Madonna, "kinda calls attention to another facet, but . . ." What that "but" means is, it sells tickets, chump. Still, it's become an issue. . . .

"Yeah, really?" says Madonna. "Who's it become an issue with—besides Rosanna?" Her laugh is quick and not unkind. Insiders say the song found its way into the film on its own virtues. "Susan Seidelman was not out to make a pandering rock & roll movie," says executive producer Michael Peyser, thirty-one, who worked on *Susan* after serving as associate producer on *The Purple Rose of Cairo*. One of the music coordinators, Danny Goldberg, had no time to compile a soundtrack LP when the film's release date was pushed up, but in talks with MTV execs, he paved the way for "Into the Groove" to air, even though the song might never show up on vinyl.

Madonna is not naive about the studio's gambit: "I have a big audience of kids for my music, and you know how they use soundtracks to push movies—I think they're using me in the same way, and it's really a drag, because I'm trying to establish myself as an actress, not as a singer making movies. But I'll be happy if it becomes a commercial success, simply because it's a different kind of movie than most of what's out now. There are a few formulas people have been using the past five years, with *Flashdance* and *Breakin'* and all that stuff; this movie is like a return to those simple, straightforward caper comedies Claudette Colbert and Carole Lombard made in the thirties. They give you a taste of real life, some poignance, and leave you feeling up at the end—none of that adolescent-fantasy bullshit."

If Madonna is a fan of screwball comedy, Susan Seidelman is more intent on spray-painting her own signature on the canvas of the blank generation she grew up with. "I think I'm a little bit of a satirist," she says. "I grew up in the epitome of sixties suburbia. You know, Dunkin' Donuts shops, TV dinners. We had canned vegetables at home because we thought it was more modern than having fresh vegetables. So that pop—Andy Warhol—whatever aesthetic is something I took for granted.

"Inside that, I wanted to make a fable about identity and appearances. But this film isn't an essay. I dislike movies in which the theme becomes the plot, where everything is like an essay on Loneliness or Frustrated Housewives or Sexual Whatever. If you look at movies like *Some Like It Hot* or *Tootsie*, you could probably write a lot about sexual roles, but the films don't get bogged down in their message. To be able to show something rather than tell it is much more interesting, and the best devices are the ones that work most invisibly. I mean, if Rosanna's character is torn between her husband and an-

other guy, and we see her in a magician's box being sawed in half—that works great if you think about it, but it's gotta work on an immediate level, too. To me, a script is a skeleton that I liked enough to—well, hang my skin on."

The skeleton of *Desperately Seeking Susan* had been rattling around Hollywood for five years before finding its skin, and it would be there still were it not for a coming together of inspired amateurs who—not incidentally in this male-run industry—are mostly women. The script was the debut effort for Leora Barish, thirty-six, who had quit life as a sometime saxophonist in Manhattan's East Village and moved to California seven years ago. She brought it to a close friend, Sarah Pillsbury (who indeed is from the Minnesota cake-mix clan her name evokes), who went from Yale to producing documentaries, including a 1979 Oscar winner. Teamed with friend Midge Sanford, savvy in the Byzantine ways of Hollywood development deals, Pillsbury optioned Barish's script as their first project. It floated through studio limbo, gathering praise from many women and indifference from most men, but it refused to die. "We reconceived it as a lower-budget, up-and-coming-star kind of movie, as opposed to using the older, established actresses we'd been talking about," says Sanford, and finally Orion took up the option. Sanford and Pillsbury sent Arquette's agent the script, and a week later, in June of last year, she signed up. The producers had been fans of independent filmmaker Susan Seidelman's critically lauded debut film, *Smithereens,* and they tapped the director for *Susan* early on.

Seidelman, thirty-two, had come out of the split-level Philadelphia suburb of Abington, studied fashion design at Drexel University and clerked for a few months at a local TV station before applying to film schools; New York University "shocked" her with an acceptance. She moved to the Lower East Side in 1974, when Saint Mark's Place was a strip of shuttered hippie boutiques. She gravitated toward directing in the three-year course and began piling up awards with her twenty-eight-minute debut, "And You Act Like One, Too," about a too-married woman. *Smithereens,* begun in 1980 with $10,000 from her grandmother's will, became the surprise hit of the 1982 Cannes Film Festival. ("I think they wanted to make a statement about mainstream American films," she says diffidently.) In it, young actress Susan Berman played Wren, a sort of punk-rock groupie living by her wits against the harsh and indifferent backdrop of the Lower East Side and its punk raja, Richard Hell.

So messy and wheedling are her heroines that Seidelman's films seem to have at least one foot in the genre pundits are calling "slob comedies." Madonna's Susan is an empress of trash, a libidinous but untouchable she-wolf who washes down cheese puffs with vintage wine, cadges triple tequila sunrises and steals other people's goods and services with an amiable, Pigpen-ish air.

Madonna admits that when she arrived in New York in 1978, she, like Susan, "relied on the kindness of strangers." When Seidelman heard of the singer's interest in the part, she invited her over: "She was nervous and vulnerable and not at all arrogant—sweet, but intelligent and verbal, with a sense of humor. I just started seeing her as Susan." The chiefs at Orion were skeptical—some two hundred actresses had read or been videotaped for the part—so Madonna was given a screen test. "She had this presence you couldn't get rid of," says Sanford. "No matter how good the other people were, we kept going back to that screen test."

"Susan is conniving, an opportunist," says Madonna, "but she really did care about [Ro-

berta's husband] Gary Glass and her boyfriend, Jim, and all these people." Part of her cockeyed charm is a warmth underlying her aloof facade: "Anybody who goes around acting like nobody matters obviously is protecting themselves and hiding what they really feel. So I always wanted to have that little bit underneath there."

What's underneath may be the "little tiny girl" Arquette is sure she sees in Madonna—perhaps the girl whose mother died when she was six. "I knew I had to be extraspecial super-charming to get what I wanted, 'cause I grew up with a lot of brothers and sisters [she was the third of eight children], and we had to share everything. I did all I could to really stand out, and that nurtured a lot of confidence and drive and ambition."

Poet Edward Field wrote that Mae West "comes on drenched in a perfume called Self-Satisfaction," and it's a knack Madonna shares. She and Seidelman had a decent rapport, but conflicts between the young director and three precocious pros—Arquette, Laurie Metcalf (as Roberta's vituperative sister-in-law) and Aidan Quinn (as Roberta's love interest)—were frequent. Production veteran Michael Peyser often picked up the pieces. "Susan has a wonderful quality; she's guileless, totally honest," he says, but he pegs her as a Hitchcock-style director: "She comes from *filmmaking,* as opposed to directing. She was working with some excellent people, like Laurie and Aidan, who are and will be major stage actors of their generation; they're used to a little more stroking."

"I really do like actors," says Seidelman. "I'm not manipulative, at which Hitchcock prided himself. I'm not good at hiding what I feel. I can't say, 'Oh, brilliant'; when I'm unhappy, it's written on my forehead."

Amid the production's turmoil, Madonna took consolation from Mark Blum (so likably obtuse onscreen as Roberta's husband, Gary). "If I'd get upset, he'd take me aside and tell me a joke or make an analogy about the situation, chill me out."

Rosanna, fresh from her dream collaboration with director Martin Scorsese on his forthcoming *After Hours,* was not to be chilled out. She and Seidelman staged tense debates over the degree of Roberta's amnesia, and during one twenty-hour day, an angry Rosanna burst into tears. Stalled and frustrated, Seidelman cried, too. "You could say it was cathartic," says Seidelman. "You scream, cry, get it out and go on."

"Our whole souls were in it," says Rosanna now, "but any film I've ever made was hard. By the second month, she would look at me and I would know what she wanted. It's just that I had never worked with a director who needed complete control of me."

Arquette had few problems making Lawrence Kasdan's film *Silverado* and the recent disaster *The Aviator.* Rosanna's onetime boyfriend, Toto drummer Steve Porcaro, had been so upset at the love scenes in *The Executioner's Song* that she says she made *The Aviator* partly because "it didn't have any nudity, it was safe—one of those all-American kind of movies." Her eventual breakup with Porcaro spurred her recent spate of work.

"I don't want to talk about my relationship with Steve Porcaro anymore," she says with some heat. "We're very good friends. But everybody's gotta ask me, 'Well, you're the Rosanna in the song,' and blah-blah. Isn't it boring? Say this: 'I am *so bored* talking about my relationship with Steve Porcaro.'"

She made another change around the time of the breakup. "I had gone to a drug program with a friend. That was another thing [reported in the media], that I was the one with a drug problem. I did take drugs. I smoked a lot of pot. I don't think I was an addict." (These days, Rosanna will not touch drink or drugs, and her choice for lunch is a spinach-and-avocado salad and mineral water.)

"Life is wonderful. Why do you guys have to look for the shit? 'Cause it's bad karma for you to do that, do you know that? It's not proper journalism."

It has become clear that Rosanna just had a crash course in this subject: "I did nine interviews yesterday." The actress and her publicists seem determined to blow back the Madonna promo machine by filibuster. The problem is that the quick-draw dramatics that are a blessing in front of the camera make her emotional dynamometer shudder ominously during what should be a simple talk.

"I grew up pretty fast," she says of her gypsy-like upbringing on the artsy-hippie circuit traveled by her actor father and writer mother. "I think I was nineteen when I was fifteen. And now I'm fifteen. Madonna taught me a good lesson, because she just laughs off the bad press. They think they're hurting her, and she just laughs: 'Ah, that's bullshit.' But I still get hurt."

Rosanna abruptly jumps up and reaches into her coat pocket, fetching a plastic bag of sizable vitamins in assorted colors. She counts out a handful, recounts and downs them with water: "Stress depletes your body of vitamins B and C." As an afterthought, she pops one more. The ritual seems to take the pedal off the floor, and she looks across the table apologetically, coat over her arm. "This is who I am, just hyper and emotional. I always have been. My emotions have always been right there."

Demi Moore and Other Brat Packers in Crisis

By Elizabeth Kaye

SEPTEMBER 26, 1986

The average age of Judd Nelson, Ally Sheedy, Andrew McCarthy, Demi Moore and Rob Lowe is twenty-two. They are among those actors who have benefited most from the fact that the majority of moviegoers are fourteen to twenty-five years old and that Hollywood producers are catering to that age group.

But these five actors are not only successful, they are also testimony to the age-old truth that success is not quite what it's cracked up to be.

They have what everybody seems to want: rewarding work, money, praise, fame. Once you have these things, you live with the dread of losing them. Then again, not losing them poses other problems.

Rob Lowe is driving. He drives the way he walks: quick, cool and assured. His pale blue eyes, which make the young girls weak, are obscured by sunglasses with pink-and-black frames, one of the ten pairs he currently owns. He is dressed in a white T-shirt, black short shorts, the white high-top sneakers he always wears unless he is wearing cowboy boots. He and his dog, Wolfie, are headed for the beach. *Born in the U.S.A.* is on the tape deck. Rob speaks

of Bruce Springsteen with the same fervid passion with which the young girls speak of *him*.

It's a beautiful summer day, the kind that helps Rob forget the pressures that make him feel there is a weight bearing down on him, but today, the sun cannot soothe him. Last night, in a restaurant, he had a protracted fight with Melissa Gilbert, his girlfriend. They met when he was struggling to be an actor and she was starring in a television series. That was three years ago, and things have changed. Rob stops his Mustang at a pay phone and goes to send Melissa flowers. He sighs and shakes his head. "It's scary when love gets undignified," he says.

At twenty-one, Rob Lowe is unusually at ease with himself. On the one hand, he is a California boy who uses words like *radical, happening* and *gnarly* and attends screenings and Hollywood parties with such panache that his friends call him Shecky Showbiz and the Warren Beatty of the eighties. On the other hand, he is an articulate young man who delights in making fun of "the business" and loves quoting his own and other people's bad reviews, laughing as he recalls that the *Washington Post* once said he had "the charisma of a doorknob."

At the beach, Wolfie darts along the sand

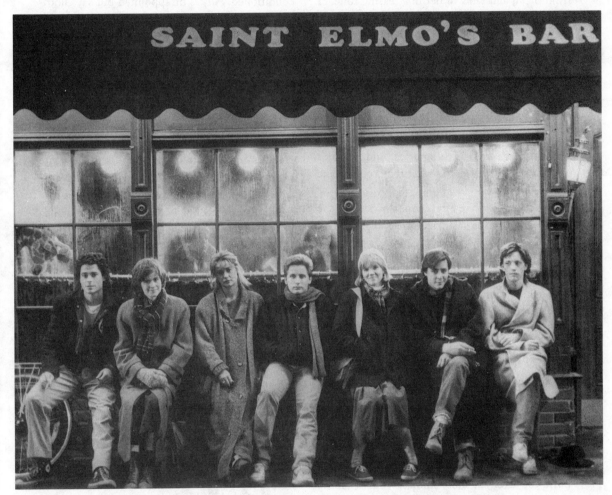

Rob Lowe, Ally Sheedy, Demi Moore, Emilio Estevez, Mare Winningham,
Judd Nelson and Andrew McCarthy precipitously hang together in
*St. Elmo's Fire. Courtesy of Columbia Pictures, copyright © 1985 Columbia
Pictures Industries, Inc. All rights reserved.*

and is beset by three male dogs with amorous intentions. Rob runs to her, coaxes her away from them, and talks to her in a teasing tone. "I guess that to other dogs, Wolfie, you probably have a great body and great eyes," he says. "I guess in the dog world, Wolfie, you're a really sexy lady."

He looks around at the nubile girls whose bikini bottoms resemble G-strings. "California girls," he says, "are a different breed, because so many great-looking people came to California hoping to make it in the movies, and couldn't make it in the movies, but what they could make was beautiful kids."

For the rest of the afternoon, Rob sits on the sand, talking to his best friend from high school, Jeff Abrams. They haven't seen each other for six months because Rob has been making movies or publicizing them. At this beach, many people have known Rob for years, but their sidelong glances, and outright stares, say they no longer feel he is one of them.

Ally Sheedy is driving. Her dark brown eyes, set deep in her pale, fine-featured face, are fixed intently on the road ahead. She wears a white T-shirt, white moccasins and a soft, full pink skirt. For all her cuteness, there is nothing coy about her. She is utterly direct and self-contained, qualities reminiscent of Katharine Hepburn, the actor she most admires. It is a manner that makes her seem tranquil and older than twenty-three.

Nonetheless, she drives her big black jeep with a zeal just verging on the maniacal, and wherever she goes, her Sony tape player is beside her, and Eurythmics or Tina Turner or Van Halen is blaring.

On this particular day, she is going to a photo session for Italian *Vogue*. She does not like posing for fashion layouts. It's 103 degrees, and she is looking forward to an air-conditioned photographer's studio. The studio is not air-conditioned. Ally is disappointed but says nothing, getting on with the business at hand with the determined briskness that helps explain why coworkers call her One-Take Sheedy.

Her hair is greased into punkish spikes, and thick makeup is applied to her face and eyes, while she sits absolutely erect, a posture she developed when she was six and dancing with the American Ballet Theater in New York City. She changes into a pair of jeans and a large white satin shirt, then follows the photographer outside, where he poses her against a tree. The tree trunk sticks into her back. It hurts. She smiles as the photographer snaps away.

She wants to say, *I hate these poses, I hate the heat, I need to have music playing, I hate the clothes.* Instead, she thinks about Katharine Hepburn. *Katharine Hepburn wouldn't complain about the heat, Katharine Hepburn would remember these people are here to do their work, not for the pleasure of taking my picture, Katharine Hepburn would never complain.* She poses for two hours, outwardly at ease, inwardly repeating the words about Hepburn, again and again, like a mantra.

Andrew McCarthy is walking. He ambles down a Greenwich Village street with easy, long-legged grace. He is dressed in baggy khaki pants, a faded T-shirt, a baggy seersucker jacket. His mobile, expressive face is dominated by his eyes, which can be clouded with caution one moment, alive in a crinkle-faced smile the next. There's a slice of pizza in his right hand, a large bag of laundry over his left shoulder. He goes into a deli to buy a pack of Camel Lights. He began smoking for his role as a writer in *St. Elmo's Fire* and hasn't been able to stop. "How you doin', sport," he says to the man at the counter. "Sport" is his customary greeting to men. He greets women with "Hi, doll."

Andrew watches a little girl perched high on a park bench, swinging her legs. "I love the way she's sitting," he says. Then he ambles on, searching for new sights to take in, managing to seem, as always, simultaneously laconic and intense.

He enters the small two-room apartment he shares with a cat. Before he moved here, he lived for two years at a New York University dorm; before that, he lived in New Jersey with his three brothers, his mother and his father, who is a stock analyst. In the living room, there is a faded Oriental rug, piles of shirts on the floor, a lamp with two hats on the shade, a desk littered with papers and parking tickets, and a mantelpiece covered by a lace cloth. On the mantelpiece is the Bible that Andrew read for his part as a Catholic student in *Heaven Help Us;* beside it are *The Great Gatsby* and *Tender Is the Night,* which he read for *St. Elmo's Fire,* having decided that Fitzgerald would be his character's favorite writer. His own favorites are represented by a huge Springsteen poster and a framed cover of a 1948 *Life* magazine, featuring a photograph of Montgomery Clift.

Andrew goes into the small bedroom and turns on his black-and-white TV, which is connected to a VCR. He puts in a tape of *Indiscretion of an American Wife,* one of his favorite Clift films. He watches the scene in which Clift walks dejectedly through a railroad station. He has seen it dozens of times, but still he rocks back and forth with excitement. As he talks, he keeps raking one long, slender hand through his thick brown hair.

"See how he drops the trench coat?" he says. "What a great moment, what making something out of nothing! The first time I saw this, I bought a trench coat. I carried it around for

days. I must have dropped it a hundred times. I could never get it right."

He watches the scene again, then looks at the clock. It is time to leave for the off-Broadway theater where he is appearing in two one-act plays, an engagement that will end the next evening when he leaves for Los Angeles to begin his fourth movie. He goes to the kitchen to feed his cats. On the refrigerator door is an advertising flyer. It reads VERNA SAYS: MEN AND WOMEN, 17–62, TRAIN TO BECOME A CASHIER. Andrew looks at it and grins. "Whenever I start getting cocky," he says, "I think of Verna."

Judd Nelson is driving. An Adidas T-shirt is draped over the back of the driver's seat. The top of the jeep is down, and the doors are off. On the floor, there's a golf ball, empty gum wrappers, an empty pack of Anacin and one of those joke headbands that make it look like a knife is going through your head. It was given to him by Ally, and Rob suggested he wear it while reading his reviews. On the backseat, a basketball rolls back and forth. Judd plays basketball for hours at a time; at his publicist's office, secretaries know he's arriving when they hear dribbling down the hall.

Judd, who is twenty-five, always seems tense, perpetually pulled in opposite directions. He dresses either in flannel shirts he bought years ago at L.L. Bean, when he was growing up in Maine, or in the newest Japanese clothes, selected by him and his girlfriend at New York and Los Angeles boutiques. He can read for hours, sitting virtually motionless, or talk incessantly, stalking back and forth with a restlessness that once caused him to try climbing a fifty-foot Marlboro sign.

He disdains the trappings of Hollywood, yet the woman he lives with, Loree Rodkin, is also his manager and gives lavish parties that Cher and Streisand attend, and is, at thirty-two, the embodiment of a certain kind of self-conscious Hollywood glamour. Through her, Judd leads a stylish life without ever having to make the choice to do so.

Judd's parents, both lawyers, still live in Maine, where his mother is in the state legislature. His father is the one person he wholly admires. "My father is honest," Judd says, "he works hard, he always strives to find a balance between work and personal life. And he's positive-reinforcement-oriented: If you fall down when you're ice-skating, he'll say, 'It's okay, you were up for a few seconds.' He lives such a good life that if he died tomorrow, it would be okay."

Judd drives to B. Dalton at the Beverly Center, where he shops for books at least once every two weeks, buying four to seven at a time. For years, he thought he wanted to be a writer, and in high school he worked summers to make money to live in Paris, where he planned to write a novel. "I found out I didn't want to write a novel," he says. "I found out I wanted to be Hemingway in the twenties."

After shopping, he goes upstairs to a restaurant and gets a turkey-and-sprouts sandwich on whole-wheat bread. While he's eating, a man in a business suit, about thirty years old, approaches him.

"Aren't you Judd Nelson?" he asks.

Judd hesitates, then nods.

"I want to give you a card," says the man. "I do medical disability. I put together a proposal for Debra Winger. A man in your position needs insurance. You could be playing basketball and break your leg."

Judd grins. "Hey, take that back."

"I just want you to know," the man tells him, "that we don't work with the average person."

Judd watches the man walk away. He shakes his head. "People treat you like you're not nor-

mal. Like, I'm no better looking than anyone else. I don't deserve more attention from women than anyone else. If someone is a good mason and they build a wall, you say, 'Good wall.' You don't say, 'Good wall, can I come over to your house?'"

Demi Moore is driving. Sometimes she rides a black Kawasaki motorcycle, but today she is in her gray Honda Accord, in which a bear-shaped cat deodorant dangles from the radio dial and a picture of Emilio Estevez, her boyfriend, is clipped to the sun visor. She wears small diamond earrings and an antique diamond ring, all given to her by Emilio. Usually, she describes the ring as "a gift from a secret admirer," words spoken in a voice as warm and luscious as melting brown sugar. She is wearing a purple-and-yellow dress, yellow socks, a purple headband and no makeup. The bright, scrubbed face and little-girl clothes, combined with the husky voice, suggest a spirit that is as gently vulnerable as it is womanly and exuberant.

Demi's black daily planner is in her lap. In it, she draws pictures to indicate her appointments. A picture of an airplane symbolizes the plane she took from New York last night. In the back of this book, pressed in plastic, is another picture of Emilio, an E-Z-Floss, her MCI number, an emergency quarter and a slip of paper from a fortune cookie that reads FOLLOW YOUR TRUE BELIEFS AND STAY STRONG.

This morning she drew lots of little pictures in her book. She is keeping busy today, just two days before the release of *St. Elmo's Fire,* a time when she is, as she puts it, "waiting for the verdict to come in."

She was also busy in New York, publicizing the film. "When we go on these trips," she says, "the studio takes care of everything. They take care of our room, our room service, our telephone calls, the transportation, and once you get treated like that, with *the* best limos and *the* best hotels, you know, you don't want to lose perspective, but you do. On this trip I just had, the limos *weren't* as nice as on the trip before, and it *wasn't* as great a hotel. It was still wonderful, but . . . it's very easy to get spoiled on these little excursions.

"It all goes along with the fear that your career could be fleeting. Because you can get so used to how good they *can* treat you and how good things *can* be, you know when there's something wrong." Demi lifts her long, heavy hair and twists it into a bun. "And you can see," she says softly, "how easily it could all disappear."

Andrew is having his hair fixed in the makeup trailer on the set of *Pretty in Pink,* a movie in which he costars with Molly Ringwald. "Can I have some shampoo?" he asks the hairdresser. "I washed my hair with Ivory soap for the second day in a row."

"This guy," the hairdresser announces loudly, "makes upwards of $10,000 a week, and he can't buy a bottle of shampoo which retails for $1.29."

Andrew gives him a look. Then he looks in the mirror at his hair, which has been smoothed and coiffed and sprayed. "Do I not look like David Cassidy with this hairdo?" he says in a voice even louder than the hairdresser's. "It's a fucking David Cassidy hairdo."

The hairdresser laughs. "Dismissed," he says.

On the set, there are problems interpreting a scene, and everyone is on edge. Andrew and Molly wait to make their entrance. Andrew laughs out loud as he recalls a story about a director who gave an actor the worst direction he'd ever heard. Now, to break the tension, he repeats that direction to Molly. He turns to her and smiles. "Tense up," he says.

Later, in his trailer, Andrew puts Dylan's *Empire Burlesque* on the tape deck and lies down. The power in the trailer goes off. The music is silenced, the lights flicker and die, the air conditioner goes dead. Andrew smiles. "I bet the power doesn't go off in Molly's trailer," he says. The electricity comes back on, then goes off again. Andrew angrily stubs out a cigarette. "This is like my life," he says, "this power situation."

He opens the door of the trailer and looks out, thoroughly disgruntled. A male voice instantly calls, "What's wrong?"

"No power," says Andrew.

"You got plenty of power."

"Would *I* lie to *you?*"

The man comes into the trailer. He appears to be about forty-five years old, and Andrew, who is twenty-two, becomes aware, as he often does, that many people in a subservient position to him are twice his age. He stares at the man. "I'm sorry," he says softly.

"I should be saying that to you," the man says, not understanding what Andrew meant.

Rob, his twelve-year-old brother, Micha, and Rob's friend Jeff are at a Dodgers game. Rob drinks three beers and eats a hot dog and a box of Cracker Jacks. "Nothing," he says, "to dispel my all-American image."

The girls in the stands notice Rob, nudge each other and stay away from him. But in the sixth inning, with time running out, they draw near, clutching pencils and scraps of paper. They have names like Buffy, Stacey and Joy, and they stare at him with the awed, hopeful look that Rob himself may have worn when he was eleven and asked Loretta Swit for her autograph at *Battle of the Network Stars.* In those days, he was a stagestruck kid just come to Los Angeles from Dayton, Ohio. Now he has trouble comprehending that he is famous (*"Elizabeth Taylor* is famous," he says). Still, at a recent party in Manhattan, one of the reigning sirens of rock & roll said, "I want to lick his balls," an indisputable index of fame, circa 1985.

Now Rob tries to watch the game, but the line of girls is unrelenting. Again and again, he signs small scraps of paper, "Love, Rob." "I always wonder," he will say later, "how much do I owe people because of what I do, and how do you draw the line between that and what you have to keep to yourself? I've never been able to fully get a handle on that one.

"What's even stranger is when I get the feeling that people don't want any personal contact with me. That they just want an autograph, something physical that they can take away with them. That's spooky in itself."

Rob and Jeff go to get another beer. Eager girls trail after them. Rob comes back a few minutes later, laughing. "This guy asked for an autograph for his daughter," Rob tells his little brother, "so I gave it to him. Then the guy looks at me and says, 'Okay. Now who *are* you?'"

Andrew hears a knock on his hotel-room door. It is Rob, who was visiting someone else and decided to stop by. The two do not socialize much but have known each other since 1983, when they worked together in *Class,* a film that starred Jacqueline Bisset and did not do well at the box office.

Andrew told Rob recently, "I see you as part of the great Hollywood tradition of Bobs: Bob De Niro, Bob Redford, Bob Culp, Bob Denver and Bob Lowe." Now, when Rob enters the hotel room, Andrew says, "Hi there, Bob," his voice thickened with the sarcasm he employs

sometimes for his own amusement, sometimes as a defense.

"Marty Ransohoff called me," Rob says. "He says he wants to make a sequel to *Class."*

Andrew laughs. "Called *Second Class,"* he says.

"Yeah, it'd be like me doing a sequel to *Oxford Blues."*

"No need to do that, Bob," says Andrew. "Just rerelease it. Nobody saw it the first time."

Demi is at home in the small house she owns, a salmon-colored dwelling that reminds her of New Mexico, where she lived until she and her family moved to Los Angeles, when she was sixteen. Her father, who sold advertising for the Scripps-Howard newspaper chain, died three years ago. Last year, when Demi was twenty-one, she bought this place, with money she made during the two years she appeared on *General Hospital.* In those days, she was constantly recognized by people who thought of her as the character she played. Now she has made three movies, and she is being recognized as herself, an unsettling experience that can make her feel strangely, suddenly shy.

Demi sits cross-legged on the floor of her bedroom, where there is flowered wallpaper and a white iron bed, covered with a delicate antique quilt. She is listening to messages on her answering machine. Some of the messages pertain to work. Demi has not worked since *St. Elmo's* wrapped. She carefully takes down the names and phone numbers that have been called in, then hears a familiar voice: Emilio's. "It's me," his voice says. "It's twelve forty-five. I love you. I love you. I want to put a smile on your face, so smile, beautiful lady." She does smile, and then she listens to another message from him. "It's me," his voice says. "It's quarter to three. You're still not home. You don't love me. There's no smile on my face. But I love you."

In a few days, Emilio will leave for North Carolina, where he is going to star in a film. But tonight, they are meeting at his place in Malibu, as they do most nights. Demi feeds her two cats and three kittens, then opens the big black leather bag she carries when she stays at the beach. She packs some herb tea, her jogging clothes, the notepad in which she writes her nightly journal, paperback copies of *A Tale of Two Cities* and *The Color Purple,* a tape she bought as a joke, *The Best of Doris Day,* a white lace blouse, an antique flowered skirt, a red vest with gold buttons, a package of rice cakes and her Q-Tips. ("I love Q-Tips. I put them in my ears and my eyes start rolling. I call it eargasms. I must have the cleanest ears of anyone I know.")

Demi opens the back door, on which there is a handwritten sign that reads MACHINE ON? GO BACK AND TURN IT ON, DILDO. She slings her bag over her shoulder and picks up her dog, Henry, a two-and-a-half-pound miniature terrier. She grabs a huge container of garbage and drags it down to the street. She grins. "This is the glamorous life," she says.

Andrew is in his hotel room, eating dinner: two Fatburgers, an order of fries and his favorite drink, Stoli on the rocks. He's been staying here for two months while filming *Pretty in Pink* and has re-created the astonishing clutter of his New York apartment in this orange-and-peach-toned suite.

MTV is on, as it almost always is in his room, and the "Raspberry Beret" video has just begun. Andrew watches Prince take the stage, amidst a bevy of adoring fans. Andrew smiles when Prince coughs just before he starts singing. "What a great touch," he says. "It's like he's saying, 'I'm here, I'm doing it, but it's taking its toll.'"

Since *St. Elmo's Fire* opened, Andrew's own celebrity has been established, and he has received many requests to be interviewed. Interviews make him uncomfortable for several reasons, among them something he realized while watching *Donahue.* "Judd and Ally and Rob were on it," he says, "and they were very good and they were very charming and intelligent and funny and stuff. They were great. But it kept gnawing at the back of my head: *What the fuck do we have to say?* We're twenty-two-year-old kids. There's people in fucking Beirut that are getting killed, and we're talking about how we're suffering or we're out there or we're happy or we're sad. I mean, our lives are very dramatic and real to us, and we feel all the pains and whatever that anybody does at any age. But they're only important to us.

"It's interesting that people want to hear it. I guess it's the whole American fascination with bigger than life. With something you don't have. But I just think it's amazing. We don't have a fucking thing to say." Andrew laughs. His laugh is a short, sharp burst. "Am I wrong?" he says.

Ally, Rob, Andrew, Demi and Judd have appeared in a total of fourteen movies. These movies cost $100 million to make and have been seen in theaters by one hundred million people.

For each of these young actors, it is the ordinary things in their lives that center them and enliven their work. They want to act in movies. They need to be ordinary people.

It isn't going to be easy.

Surviving *Heaven's Gate*

By Jean Vallely

FEBRUARY 5, 1981

"This is it," thought Michael Cimino as he took a deep breath, packed up the last reel of *Heaven's Gate,* rushed into the waiting limousine and sped off to catch the red-eye to New York. Since September 16, 1978, *Heaven's Gate* had consumed Cimino's life. He was obsessed, and not simply with making a movie. He wanted to make a masterpiece. His obsession had taken him and hundreds of others to the wilds of Montana for six months of location shooting and then back to L.A. for sixteen-hour days in the editing room, seven days a week. And his obsession also cost United Artists an estimated $40 million. No one but Cimino, producer Joann Carelli and the editors had seen *Heaven's Gate.*

Kris Kristofferson, the star of *Heaven's Gate,* had arrived in New York the day before and was settled in his suite at the Carlyle Hotel. He knew *Heaven's Gate* was his best work, but he could not shake his uneasiness. Impulsively, he grabbed his jacket and headed for an afternoon showing of *Raging Bull.*

Isabelle Huppert lit a cigarette. She had lost count of how many she had smoked since leaving Paris for the opening of *Heaven's Gate.* Though she was well-known in Europe, this was her big chance to break in in the States.

Jeff Bridges was also on his way to New York. Bridges had worked with Cimino in his directorial debut, *Thunderbolt and Lightfoot,* and he'd given up star billing for the chance to work with him again. In New York, Bridges was anxious. While making *Heaven's Gate,* he'd sensed he was a part of something great.

In the early-morning hours, Cimino's plane hit the runway at JFK. He raced directly to Cinema One, where, in less than six hours, *Heaven's Gate* would have its first press screening. The machines were threaded, the sound tested. Cimino felt he still needed more time. But time had run out, finally. It was 2:30 P.M., and the lights were going down. An hour later, Cimino, standing way in the back of the theater, knew his film was not working.

Early the next morning, Cimino was on the phone. He wanted to reach Kristofferson before he saw Vincent Canby's review in the *New York Times.* After listening to a demolished Cimino, Kristofferson called room service for a paper. He figured Cimino was overreacting, but he was wrong: Canby had blasted Cimino out of the water. Out of the universe. *"Heaven's Gate* fails so completely," he wrote, "that you might sus-

144

pect Mr. Cimino sold his soul to the Devil to obtain the success of *The Deer Hunter,* and the Devil has just come around to collect. . . . Mr. Cimino has written his own screenplay, whose awfulness has been considerably inflated by the director's wholly unwarranted respect for it. . . . You thought the wedding feast that opened *The Deer Hunter* went on too long? Wait till you see *Heaven's Gate.*"

As news of Canby's devastating review hit Hollywood, cackles of glee could be heard in executive suites all over town. The corridors of United Artists were very, very quiet, however.

It was meant to be festive, but the first-class section of American Airlines' noon flight to Toronto the next day looked more like a funeral train. Kristofferson and Huppert sat together and tried to talk—about the weather and about what they'd been doing since last seeing each other. Their hearts weren't in it, though, and eventually they went back to reading and gazing out the window. Jeff Bridges buried his nose in *Time.* David Mansfield, who both acted in and composed the music for *Heaven's Gate,* tried to teach himself to play Go on a magnetic board. Producer Joann Carelli made notes. Cimino looked like a zombie. "I thought the critics might go after me, the story, my direction," he said quietly, "but I thought they would love Kris and the others. And Vilmos' photography. And the music." Cimino looked off into the distance. "Could I have been so wrong?" He looked back at the actors. "They all trusted me."

In Toronto, the waiting limos and the hotel suites, decked out for a celebration, somehow seemed, well, *off.* Kristofferson, Huppert, Bridges and the others went to their suites to get ready for *Heaven's Gate*'s public premiere. Carelli called Gene Goodman, a UA senior vice president of sales management, and told him

that she and Cimino wanted to pull the picture and reedit it. Goodman said he would get back to her.

In his hotel suite, Kristofferson, a Blake scholar at Oxford some twenty years ago, smiled and said, "I told Michael that they never gave Blake a good review. They didn't even publish his poems until after he was dead. He was never famous, always broke. But he never lost faith in himself and in his vision, which was totally original. People still think he was insane because he said he talked to angels." Kristofferson rolled his eyes. "If Blake says he talked to angels, by God, I believe him."

It was most unusual and could cost UA as much as an additional $10 million, but they would stand firm behind Cimino and the decision to pull the film. That was the word from Gene Goodman when he got back to Carelli. Cimino sat down at the desk in his suite and composed a letter to UA president Andy Albeck. The letter would run a few days later in the trade papers:

"It is painfully obvious to me that the pressures of this schedule and the missing crucial step of public previews clouded my perception of the film. . . . So much energy, time and money have gone into the making of *Heaven's Gate* that I am asking you to withdraw the film from distribution temporarily to allow me to present to the public a film finished with the same care and thoughtfulness with which we began it. . . ."

"At Michael Cimino's request United Artists is canceling the screening of *Heaven's Gate* . . . ," read the telegram that was sent to twelve hundred people the day before the L.A. premiere. When word that *Heaven's Gate* had been pulled reached the Polo Lounge, the room erupted in cheers.

Not even the chilly Canadian air could energize the reluctant stars for the Toronto premiere. Nor could the splash of flashbulbs, lights, television cameras and girls screaming for Kristofferson's autograph. As the houselights went down, Kristofferson and Bridges focused intently on the screen. Huppert perched on the edge of her seat. The actors studied their performances. Could they have been so wrong? Halfway through, Kristofferson whispered, "Vincent Canby drinks his own bathwater."

At intermission, Huppert jumped up and ran to Cimino. "I was confused seeing it for the first time yesterday and then reading the review, but it is good. I am proud."

At the end of the film, the audience—no press this time—applauded. Cimino looked pleasantly confused. Maybe his decision to pull the film had been premature? No, Carelli replied. She had checked with her sources in New York and the rest of the reviews would be bad.

The successful screening in Toronto had lifted everyone's spirits, and the mood on the flight to L.A. was a good deal more cheerful.

Carelli, who had had very little sleep in the last twenty-four hours, took off her headphones and yawned. What had gone wrong? She shrugged her shoulders. "It was a combination of things. Michael was a little crazy up there in Montana. He won those two Academy Awards and really believed they meant something. He was definitely out of control." She paused. "You know, that can happen to all of us, but the thing is, you have to know who your people are and you have to be prepared to listen to them. Michael was not. That's the sad part, because there were people there to help him. They didn't desert him. He deserted them. He was given everything.

"After the first month of shooting, UA kept calling and asking, 'How can we stop this?'" Carelli continued. "I told them I would show

them exactly how, but they would have to back me up." Carelli shook her head. "We should have said, 'No, Michael, no. You cannot build the town larger than you said you would. No, Michael, no. You cannot have one thousand extras when you said one hundred. I would say no, and UA would not back me up. Everyone was afraid to say no to Michael. It was an impossible situation.

"I would have done things differently," said Carelli. "A producer walks a thin line. I shouldn't side with either the studio or the director. I am working for the good of the film. I should have said to Mike, 'Do what I say or I quit,' and I should have walked off." She paused. "But for whatever reasons, Michael just started to expand this film and there were no controls. He is a perfectionist, and it just got bigger and bigger. Mike is a secretive guy, and he didn't want to show them anything. He would ask me, 'Why do they want to see the rushes?' And I would say, 'It's simple. It's their money.' He would ask, 'Why are they making me shoot all these pages so quickly?' And I would say, 'Any other studio would have fired you by now or moved up here, into the room next to yours.' Mike just didn't understand."

In retrospect, Cimino admitted that he should have listened to Carelli. "Sometimes the most rational voice is the one you don't hear."

"It looks like a conspiracy," said Huppert as she studied the newspaper reports. Canby's review was just the beginning, and it set the tone. The *New York Daily News* torpedoed the film, as did *Time, Newsweek* and the *Village Voice.*

The reviews were followed by news stories, which were followed by analytical pieces. There was no letup. Claudia Cohen, gossipmonger at the *Daily News,* hammered away, day after day: "Here it is, gang, the beginning, and blessed end, of Michael Cimino's brief advertising (if not directing) career."

On the West Coast, the *Los Angeles Herald Examiner's* Jeff Silverman ran the "First Annual *Heaven's Gate* Contest," which challenged readers to guess the running time (in minutes) of the reedited version of *Heaven's Gate*. First prize, four tickets to the reedited film; second prize (of course), six tickets.

Heaven's Gate played for six more days at Cinema One before it was officially pulled.

"What do they want?" asked Cimino. "For me never to work again?"

"I haven't seen the film," said producer Frank Yablans, former Paramount Studios head, "but I seriously doubt that it is as bad as they are saying it is. They are reviewing the budget and the indulgence. Cimino had the misfortune to come out at the wrong time with the wrong budget. If *Heaven's Gate* had come out in the summer, there wouldn't have been any of this trouble. The fact that these big-budget films—*Star Trek* [$40 million], *Blues Brothers* [$36 million], *1941* [$32 million], *Raise the Titanic* [$40 million]—all got by by the skin of their teeth last summer created an atmosphere that made Cimino's film seem even more reprehensible. The industry was looking for a scapegoat, and Cimino was perfect: his excesses, combined with the fact that he is an outsider."

"He has complete disregard for everyone but himself," carped a filmmaker. It was an opinion held by most of the people I talked to, none of whom would go on record. "His film kept going further and further over budget, and all of us who had deals at UA suffered. Some projects were actually canceled because of Cimino's indulgence. Imagine! He kept all the crew and the extras on call all the time, even over weekends. He wanted everyone there just in case he woke up in the middle of the night with an idea. He did this for six months. Most of us who make movies try so hard to be responsible and stay on schedule and on budget. Cimino was totally irresponsible. And a total egomaniac."

"You reap what you sow," said an agent. "Cimino is arrogant, cold and behaved like an asshole."

"Cimino is the most disliked man in Hollywood," added a producer. Stories about Cimino abound. He's quick to claim credit when he doesn't deserve it. He's doctored his past. He blew up a horse on the set of *Heaven's Gate*. He deliberately ran over extras with buggies—for effect. He threw a champagne party when he surpassed the amount of film shot for *Apocalypse Now*. He was responsible for the paralysis of a still photographer. It goes on and on.

"That's just absurd," sighed Cimino.

"If he did all these things," Carelli wanted to know, "how come he's not in jail?"

All this talk about arrogance and ego. I, for one, have never met a humble director. And I wonder how Cimino's arrogance is any different from, say, John Landis' or Steven Spielberg's. Or Stanley Kubrick—he spent almost $20 million of Warner Brothers' money on *The Shining* and would not allow any of the executives to see it until the day before its official press screening—too late for them to do anything about it if they didn't like it. To top it all off, Kubrick took his film back after the press screenings and made extensive reedits.

What about Warren Beatty, for that matter? Word in the industry is that his film, *Reds,* is already over $40 million and still is not finished. I am willing to wager that if *Reds* is a disaster, Beatty will not be strung up the way Cimino has been. "Beatty earned his right," snapped a studio executive.

"To get final cut takes a dramatic track record," observed a director with just such a track record. "Michael earned his right to call the shots on *Heaven's Gate* because of the overall critical and financial success of *The Deer Hunter.*"

Aaaah. *The Deer Hunter.* The amount of revisionism at work regarding *The Deer Hunter* would make any good Stalinist proud. The critics seem to have used *Heaven's Gate* as a way to rereview *The Deer Hunter,* and to point out that they never really liked it.

Lest we forget, *The Deer Hunter* won five Academy Awards, including Best Picture and Best Director.

A few days after *Heaven's Gate* closed, studio exec Steven Bach sat in his office at United Artists and lit a cigarette. "I keep reading things like, 'How did it happen? How did they let it happen?' This notion that we were all inexperienced and cowed by Michael is just not true. Cimino had an established relationship with UA at the time *Heaven's Gate* was submitted. We had concluded a two-picture deal with him to direct *Dogs of War* and to write the script for *The Fountainhead.*"

Bach paused and went back to the beginning. "We had a pay-or-play deal for *Heaven's Gate,* for $7.5 million. The original budget came in at $7.8 million. By the time the picture was ready to go forward, the budget had risen to $11.6 million. Beyond that, we expected the movie to go to $15 million."

So how did it get blown up to $40 million? Bach took another drag on his cigarette. This has not been an easy time for him; rumors are his head might roll if Cimino cannot pull *Heaven's Gate* out of the bag. "What happened," Bach resumed, "was that once Michael got up there in Montana and saw what he could do, he lost perspective. He'd use the fifty extras we

knew about, and the scene would look skimpy, or the mountains in the background would look too grand, and he'd say, 'I need two hundred extras.' That, of course, affected the hairdressing, the makeup, the costumes.

"The thing I have learned is that I will never again allow myself to be maneuvered, to publicly display a movie about which I have as many reservations as I had with *Heaven's Gate.* I think that was possibly our biggest mistake.

"The thing that was out of our control and I didn't know what to do about it was Michael's perfectionism," Bach concluded. "Perfectionists are to be greatly valued and to be wary of, at least in a business as expensive as this one. We believed in Michael and the film and his vision. The movie simply got away from him. We believed him when he said it was going to be shorter and that his perceptions were not clouded. If we did anything wrong, it was an error of faith."

Said Cimino, "They either call you a perfectionist or a hack."

"I feel so bad for Michael," said Kris Kristofferson. "We all put in a lot of time, but Michael, well, it was his vision. After the Oscars, I think Michael sensed that he was in a position to move, and he took the ball and ran with it. I just wish he'd get credit for going for something with quality. They keep calling it an ego trip. That must be the newest easy way to attack people. They did that with Streisand. They even did it with Carl Sagan. Did you see all the letters to the editor in *Time?* When someone gets that high, they really come gunning for you. He was just the next target."

"I have a feeling," Huppert said, "that in America it's okay to spend $40 million for this concept of entertainment, but if you spend such an amount for a personal film, one that forces you to think, then people get suspicious. In all the reviews and negative things I have read about *Heaven's Gate,* there has not been the least attempt to understand what is in the film. They say it is too long, too expensive, but the critics don't try to analyze. I can't imagine the European critics not trying to understand. . . ."

''I feel oddly full of energy," said Cimino. "I am trying to keep working, to keep it together, but it's hard with all the stuff going on. From what I've heard, it's past the point of criticism. It's slander."

Oliver Stone and the Sixties

By Fred Schruers

JANUARY 29, 1987

In June 1965, a big-shouldered Yale dropout of eighteen named Oliver Stone arrived in Saigon. It was the year American forces in Vietnam would grow from 23,300 to eight times that number, and Stone's arrival coincided roughly with that of the army's First Infantry Division and precisely—the night he arrived—with the Mekong restaurant being blown out of the water.

He'd been hired by a church group to teach school to Chinese kids in the suburb of Cho Lon, a job he would stick at for six months while playing tennis at the Cercle Sportif with rich French planters, various CIA men and even Gen. William Westmoreland. Just then, Stone says, it all seemed rather grand: "The streets started to look like Dodge City, soldiers carrying weapons, a lot of whoring, and one felt oneself on the verge of a great new experiment, like 'We're gonna beat the Vietcong.'" Two years and three months later he would be back in the country as a grunt with a rifle. Two wounds, several decorations and fifteen months after that, he would have the brutal education from which he and this country are still recovering.

Today his autobiographical account of that time under fire in the Vietnamese jungle, *Pla-*

toon, is the subject of a critical love feast and a multiplying popular reception. Film critic David Denby wrote that in *Platoon* "the realistic details, soberly gathered, culminate in the explosion of surreal horror that Francis Coppola labored for in *Apocalypse Now.* . . . With this movie, Oliver Stone completes his amazing transformation from bum to hero."

Yes, Stone did do time as the critics' bum—not just for his half-baked big-budget directorial debut, *The Hand,* but for his scripts (including the Oscar-winning one for *Midnight Express*), which some saw as so much violence and rightwing heavy breathing. But before and even during that artistic transformation, he fought a private battle with the almost spectral presence of his father, who also figured him for a bum. The weight of his father's judgment helped send him into the recruiting office in 1967, where, he says, "I asked for Vietnam, I asked for Eleven Bravo, which is infantry, and they gave it to me—and I felt, like the kid in the movie says, that maybe from down here in the mud I can start up again and be something I can be proud of, without having to fake it, see something I don't yet see, learn something I don't yet know."

Oliver Stone's sizable, twenties-vintage house

150

sits on a large lot on one of the patrician, northerly streets in Santa Monica. Up close, Stone, wearing khakis and a blue, button-down shirt, evokes his touchstone since college days, Joseph Conrad's Lord Jim: "He advanced straight at you with a slight stoop of the shoulders, head forward, and a fixed from-under stare which made you think of a charging bull. . . . His manner displayed a dogged self-assertion which had nothing aggressive in it." In his characteristically hushed tone—he speaks at a good clip and laughs easily—he offers greetings and introduces his mother, Jacqueline—a warm, energetic sort with a Gallic half smile. "She took me to movies when I was a kid," he says later, "used to make me play hooky from school and slip me a note to the school doctor saying I'd been sick. She was very optimistic, affirmative . . . the complete opposite of my father."

Oliver was born in New York City on September 15, 1946. His father, Lou, was a stockbroker who'd met his French Catholic wife while serving as a GI in Paris. Oliver spent summers in France with a grandfather wounded in the First World War, and back home he went first to the snooty Trinity School, across the park from their East Eighties apartment, then to the Hill School, in Pennsylvania. Lou Stone published a well-known investors' newsletter, had a strict conservative's hatred for Roosevelt, wrote plays and poems on the side and, his son says, "always felt it was unseemly to express yourself or show emotion."

Stuck in steel country at an all-boys prep school, Oliver found he'd traded the mood at home—"like the Dreiser books, that mood of repression"—for the sexless Catcher in the Rye ambience at Hill. He first learned that his parents' marriage had gone awry when the headmaster told him of their impending divorce. At

sixteen, he says, "the happy boyhood came to an abrupt end."

Oliver eventually enrolled at Yale (Lou's alma mater), where he lasted a year, hating "the sameness," before dropping out for the job in Saigon. When he grew restless in Vietnam, he shipped out as a wiper in the merchant marine, making a nightmarish forty-day crossing of the wintry north Pacific to Oregon. Upon landing, he took off for Mexico, stayed in Guadalajara long enough to write a novel titled A Child's Night Dreams, about his Asian adventures, then returned to Yale to await its publication.

The book was rejected, and Oliver was making straight zeros. "I was upset," he says, "and soon thereafter volunteered for the draft, partly with the idea of being anonymous. The novel had brought out the ego part of me, the showing-off part, as my father would say, and I wanted to bury that once and for all." He took basic and advanced infantry training at Fort Jackson, South Carolina, and on September 14, 1967, took off from Oakland in a transport. He set down, age twenty-one, to become part of an invasion force that had swelled to nearly five hundred thousand strong.

If the next fifteen months became his Iliad, the stuff of Platoon, his return stateside constituted a nerve-racking, decade-long odyssey. Soon after hitting the West Coast, he managed to get busted crossing the Mexican border with Vietnamese pot. He was tossed in an overcrowded San Diego jail, where the public defenders were slow to turn up. It took a call to his father, who greased the legal machinery with $2,500, to spring Oliver.

Back in New York, he enrolled at NYU and had the good luck to study film under Martin Scorsese. Never a popcorn-movie man, Oliver made student films that emulated Godard, Buñuel and Resnais. (His student epic was called *Last Year in Vietnam.*) "I should have moved right from NYU to Los Angeles in 1971," he says. "It's more democratic here. In New York it took me seven years of struggle. I drove a cab, I was a Xerox boy—I wrote eleven scripts in six years and didn't even have an agent at the end of it. I thought, 'This is not meant to be, I should quit,' and I almost did a few times."

He took quantities of drugs, remaining "so stoned" that he didn't mind living in a broken-down tenement on Houston Street, a place where the snow would drift into his bedroom. He married a Lebanese woman, Najwa Sarkis, whose job at the Moroccan mission to the UN helped support them. He got precious little encouragement until 1975, when a friend passed one of his screenplays on to producer Fernando Ghia, who passed it on to Robert Bolt—"known to me at the time," Stone says, "as the best screenwriter in the world." Bolt liked it and helped him rework it. "I suddenly felt I could get somewhere."

Still, his marriage had broken up, and Oliver had little to show for his postwar years. As the tall ships rode in the harbor on July 4, 1976, he says, "I came out of this spin I'd been in" and began writing *Platoon.* "I thought, I've forgotten a lot in eight years. If I don't do it now, I'm gonna forget. It's a pocket of our history nobody understands—what it was like over there, how the everyday American, wild, crazy boys from little towns in Ohio, who grew up by the 7-Eleven store with the souped-up cars and the girls on Friday night, turn into these little monster killers."

Apparently, 1976 was not yet the time to show America just how that process had occurred. The *Platoon* script was rejected throughout the industry; Columbia Pictures, though, was impressed enough to assign him the script for *Midnight Express.* Stone took the true story

of young Billy Hayes, who was jailed in Turkey for smuggling hash, and made it a searing, rage-laden prison drama. The abrupt success that came when he received an Academy Award in 1979 was more than he could handle. "It was like being on a magic carpet. In a two-year period, I lived intensely all the fantasies I'd had of Hollywood. I had the Oscar and a bachelor apartment in West Hollywood, so I was living pretty wild, lots of parties and wild escapades, a new girl every night—I was trying to be Warren Beatty—and everybody knew I was sorta crazy, either alienated from cocaine or tripping on acid or ecstasy. I remember mushrooms were very popular, and mixing stuff, ups and downs."

Stone's next project, directing his own script of *The Hand* for producer Ed Pressman, in 1981, found him, not surprisingly, "in a very dark frame of mind; it was a film about the disintegration of an individual." *The Hand,* which featured a significant cameo by a frighteningly grungy Stone as a bum, was an unsuccessful hybrid of horror film and psychological thriller. "As a result," he says, "I was sort of unemployable for four years as a director."

Stone wrote a script for *Conan the Barbarian* (later much changed by director John Milius), and even in his drugged-out state he looked to be a good man to write Brian De Palma's *Scarface.* After researching the film via trips to South America and Miami and via liberal substance abuse at home, he woke up. "I could feel a staleness in all my thought processes, I knew I was in trouble, and I cut it in 1981," says Stone. "In order to break the habit, you have to break away from the people you know." Stone went to Paris with Elizabeth, his new wife. "It was cold, the heating was poor, the food was good, and I had a whole set of friends who were all drug free."

He wrote the *Scarface* script there "as a farewell to drugs, really," and by the time the movie came out, he had moved back to New York. He cowrote *Year of the Dragon* with Michael Cimino and *Eight Million Ways to Die* with David Lee Henry. All of the films were met with critical hoots and disappointing box-office results, capping Stone's "bum" phase in the business.

Despairing and a bit desperate, Stone focused on *Salvador,* a project that took off from the experiences of his friend Richard Boyle, a gonzo combat photographer and documentary filmmaker he'd met in the late seventies while writing the script to Ron Kovic's Vietnam book, *Born on the Fourth of July.* He wanted to direct the movie on the run and on the cheap in its actual Salvadoran settings, but official cooperation froze up after Stone and Boyle's contact in the government was shot to death on an El Salvador tennis court in March 1985.

Increasingly radicalized by his research on the project, Stone shopped his script around till feisty, liberal Hemdale Film Corporation agreed to produce it in Mexico. The picture came in under $5 million, and although it came limping out due to distribution slip-ups, *Salvador* had a great impact on the critics, the studios and a still-growing audience. Stone dedicated the movie to his father, who had died the year before and would likely have been appalled by its politics.

Stone credits Hemdale with his comeback: "They really went out on a limb for me." The company gave him $6 million to film his long-dormant script for *Platoon,* and Stone set about meeting the strict nine-week shooting schedule with martial efficiency. He hired retired Marine captain and Nam vet Dale Dye to drill and torment his cast until they acquired a grunt's-eye view of combat and airlifted his twenty-five actors to the Philippines, where the jungles, bugs and heat could stand in for Vietnam. They arrived around the time of Corazon Aquino's bloodless revolution, which meant cutting new deals with the military men who would supply hardware, choppers and battalions of extras.

To know the script is to know Stone's own Vietnam story, that of a college-boy rich kid arriving by his own, nearly absurd choice in a hell populated mostly by poor white trash and their black urban counterparts, a cherry who has no clue about war and woodsmanship and every chance of getting hurt. He did get hurt, within two weeks, in a firefight on a night-ambush mission when he froze up at the sight of the enemy. That flesh wound and some shrapnel he caught months later in the butt and legs were emblems of the war's escalating violence, within which he veered between the angry killer and the sensitive onlooker. In hamlets near the Cambodian border, he glimpsed the bloodthirsty rage that heat, no sleep and the threat of death could invoke in him.

Stone shares with his fictional hero, Chris Taylor, an apocalyptic New Year's night, 1968. The perimeter of Stone's battalion was overrun by the North Vietnamese—it was just before the launch of the monthlong Tet Offensive—after which, says Stone, "it was evident we weren't going to win." Stone and Taylor also share a moment of glory, a do-or-die lobbing of a grenade into an enemy foxhole during a bloody ambush. "Something went crazy in my head," Stone says. "I charged the hole and threw a grenade right in it. If I'd missed, I would have killed a few Americans." It was a feat that won Stone a Bronze Star, but when he recounts it from the couch in his Santa Monica den, which overlooks a pool and semitropical garden, he almost shrugs it off: "I was pissed off, 'cause I knew the guys that had been killed, and I had been smoking a little dope that morning."

Oliver Stone seems to like walking the tightrope between bum and hero, to like living as a gambler in the Dostoyevskian sense, placing his own happiness at stake. Maybe that's why he's burrowing into a complex tale of contemporary Wall Street. It goes without saying he's got a few demons to exorcise down there. "It's a radical shift for me," says this master of blood, mud and gunpowder, straight-facedly. "It's much harder to shoot indoors."

While we talk, Charlie Sheen arrives. As Chris Taylor, the Stone character in *Platoon,* Sheen is poised between Tom Berenger's savage Sergeant Barnes and Willem Dafoe's gentler Sergeant Elias. "I was always satisfied that Charlie had the right spacey quality, which is what I had at the time. He looks like he's sort

of floating, and early on, he has a completely lost look. Then week by week as we shot, another layer of hardness would come on."

Our first look at Sheen in *Platoon* is as he leaves the transport plane. A fresh-faced, almost dewy recruit in a peaked fatigue hat, he is caught in the yellow haze of an airstrip—amid body bags and malarial, hollow-eyed combat vets—brushing grit from his eye. It's also the last shot we see in the film's reprise, as the principal actors roll by in still shots.

"What prompted you to give me the last card, Oliver?" asks Sheen. The director, coming out of one of his characteristic spacey pauses, turns to squint at him. "I just thought that said it all," he replies, "like saying, 'Remember, that's the way he was.'"

ON THE SCENE

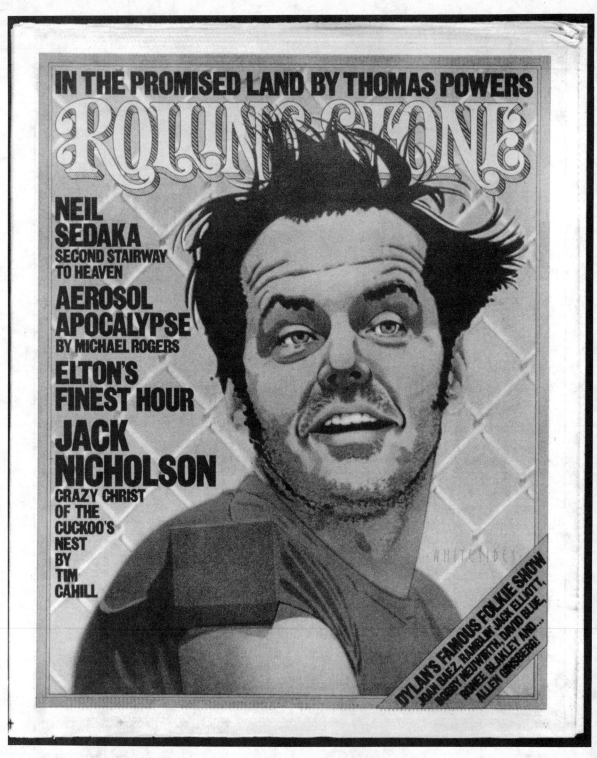

Jack Nicholson, ROLLING STONE, issue 201, December 4, 1975.
Illustration by Kim Whitesides

Bogdanovich's *Last Picture Show*

By Grover Lewis

SEPTEMBER 2, 1971

Flying west, through Texas, you leave Dallas–Fort Worth behind and look out suddenly onto a rolling, bare-boned, November country that stretches away to the horizon on every side—a vast, landlocked Sargasso Sea of mesquite-dotted emptiness. There are more cattle down there ranging those hazy, distance-colored expanses than people, and in turn, more people than timber topping out at five feet, for this is cowdom's fabled domain, the short-grass country—*yipi-ti-yi-yo, little pardners*—the Land of the Chicken-Fried Steak, where, if your gravity fails you among the shit-kickers, chili-dippers and pistoleros, negativity emphatically won't pull you through.

Somewhere down there, too, slightly more to the west, in a decaying little ranching hamlet called Archer City, a protean-talented young Hollywood writer/director named Peter Bogdanovich is filming Larry McMurtry's novel *The Last Picture Show,* in its true-to-life setting. McMurtry—Archer City's only illustrious son—previously wrote *Horseman, Pass By,* from which the film *Hud* was made. *Picture Show* is to star Ben Johnson, Clu Gulager, Cloris Leachman, Ellen Burstyn, Jeff Bridges and a couple of promising young unknowns, Timothy Bot-

toms and Cybill Shepherd. And, save us all, I'm to be in it, too, playing a small supporting part.

The Ramada Inn on the Red River Expressway, where the sixty-odd members of the *Picture Show* troupe are quartered, is big, seedy and expensive, a quadrant of fake-fronted colonial barracks overlooking a dead swimming pool and a windswept compound full of sawgrass and cockleburs. "Hah yew today?" the desk clerk, a platinum-streaked grandmother in a miniskirt, trills cheerily as I check in at midafternoon.

My room—at least a city block from the lobby as the crow flies—is *de rigueur* institutional ugly. In sluggish slow motion, I stretch out across the bed to doze and await instructions from somebody in Archer City, forty miles to the southwest, where the day's shooting has been under way since early morning. When the phone jangles a few minutes later, I snap alert, sweating, disoriented. Waking up in Whiskeytaw Falls storms my mind; less than twenty-four hours ago, I was bombed-and-strafed in the no-name bar in Sausalito.

Through a crackling connection and a babble of background din, the film's production manager is shouting to ask what my clothing sizes

Peter Bogdanovich directs Timothy Bottoms in his first feature role in *The Last Picture Show*. Copyright © 1971 Columbia Pictures

are. "Peter wants you out here on the set as soon as possible," he commands, barking out staccato directions on how I'm to connect with a driver who'll fetch me to the location site.

Feeling wary and depressed, I wander downstairs and wait in the lobby. Christ, I haven't done any acting I'd admit to since college, when I was typecast as the psycho killer in *Detective Story*. Now, I'm supposed to play "Mr. Crawford"—the village junkie-geek of Archer City circa the Korean War era, a character maybe twenty years my senior. More typecasting, I figure sourly.

The driver, a large, loose-limbed black man named James, lifts my spirits on sight. "Fuck them long cuts, ain't I right, Grovah? I'ma take a short cut and git you to the church *on time*," he announces, pumping my hand like a handle and grinning through dazzling silver teeth. On the way out of town in a Hertz station wagon, we pass the M-B Corral, a notorious hillbilly dive where fourteen or fifteen years ago, Larry McMurtry and I stood among a circle of spectators in the parking lot one drizzly winter night and watched a nameless oil-field roughneck batter and kick Elvis Presley half to death in what was delicately alluded to afterward as a difference of opinion about the availability of the roughneck's girlfriend. McMurtry and I were wild-headed young runners-and-seekers back then, looking, I think, for a country of men; what we found, though, together and apart, were wraithlike city women in blowing taffeta dresses. And the shards and traceries of our forebears, of course, trapped in the stop-time aspic of old hillbilly records.

The Spur Hotel, a rattletrap cattlemen's hostel commandeered by the film troupe as production headquarters, hasn't seen as much elbow-to-ass commotion since the great trail drives to Kansas in the eighties. Throngs of stand-ins, crew technicians, bit players and certified Grade A stupor-stars course in and out of the makeshift office like flocks of unhinged cockatoos. Phones ring incessantly; nobody moves to answer them. The location manager mutters into a walkie-talkie, and the agile-fingered men's wardrobe master deals out seedy-looking Western outfits to a queue of leathery-faced extras like soiled cards from the bottom of the deck.

Making faces into the mouthpiece, the location manager does a fast fade on the field phone, pours a couple of cups of coffee and brokenfields across the crowded room to say hello: "You play Mr. Crawford, right? Far out, good to meet you. . . . Don't let this spooky dump spook you, hear? Looks like a rummage sale in a toilet, don't it? Well, that's show biz. . . . As of this minute, anno Domini, the production is—well, we're behind schedule. Which means that Bert Schneider, the producer—you won't meet him, he only feels safe back in Lotus Land—Bert's begun to act very producer-like and chop out scenes. Peter just had to red-pencil the episode where the gang of town boys screws the heifer, and I hated like hell to see it go. That sort of material is disgusting to a lot of people, but, shitfire, man, it's true to life. These hot-peckered kids around here still do that kind of thing as a daily routine. You've read McMurtry's book, haven't you? Why, Christ, to me, that's what it's all about—fertility rites among the unwashed." Grinning amiably, he lifts his cup in a sardonic toasting gesture: "Well, here's to darkness and utter chaos, ol' buddy."

Polly Platt materializes out of the crush, her hands in her jeans pockets, Bette Davis–style. A poised, fine-boned blonde with sometimes complicated hazel eyes, she is the production designer as well as Bogdanovich's wife. After an intense discussion with the wardrobe master about what constitutes a village geek, she coordinates my spiffy Crawford ensemble—baggy, faded dungarees, a shirt of a gray mucus color and a tattered old purple sweater that hangs halfway to my knees.

Humming off-key, Polly waits while I change into my new splendor between the costume racks, and then the two of us stroll across the deserted courthouse square toward the American Legion Hall. She laughs with girlish delight as we pass the long-shuttered Royal Theater—the last picture show in both fact and fantasy—and chats fondly about Ben Johnson, who's already completed his part in the film and departed:

"He's the real thing, Ben is—an old-fashioned country gentleman from his hat to his boots. Why, he didn't even want to say 'clap' when it came up in dialogue. Peter and I were both flabbergasted. Later, I asked Ben about the nude bathing scene in *The Wild Bunch*. It turns out Sam Peckinpah had to get him and Warren Oates both knee-walking drunk to get the shot, which wasn't in the original script. . . . But Ben and Peter ended up working beautifully together. Wait'll you see his rushes"—she gives a low whistle of admiration—"Academy stuff all the way, as they oompah in the trades."

Inside the ramshackle Legion Hall—a confusion of packed bodies, snarled cables, huge Panavision cameras and tangled mike booms and lighting baffles—Polly leads the way to a quiet corner and begins tinting my hair gray with a makeup solvent recommended to Bogdanovich by Orson Welles. In the crowd milling around the center of the hall, I single out Cloris Leachman, whom I've just seen in *WUSA;* Bogdanovich, head bent in intent conversation with cinematographer Bob Surtees, whom I recognize from a press book promoting *The Graduate;* Clu Gulager, foppish-perfect-pretty in

Nudie's finest ranch drag and manly footwear; and several teasingly familiar faces I can't quite fit names to. Glancing our way, Bogdanovich smiles and waves to indicate that he'll drop over to chat when he's free.

"Orson may turn up down here, you know," Polly muses as she dabs at my temples with a cotton swab. "The old rogue's making a picture about a Hollywood director—*Jake Hanniford*—and as usual he wants to steal scenes from somebody else's setup, if he can. Orson thinks Peter's some kind of nutty intellectual, so he's written him into the script in that sort of burlesque part. Peter says *Hanniford*'s going to be the dirtiest movie ever made. . . . Whew, you sure get to know people fast, having to fool with their hair. Let's see what you look like. Oh, fantastic, great! I like your face—it's so *ravaged.* With the hair jobbie and those grungy old clothes, you look lunchier than Dennis Weaver in *Touch of Evil.*" Typecasting, I mumble under my breath.

Bogdanovich, a slight, grave-faced young man wearing horn-rims and rust-colored leather bell-bottoms, shakes hands in greeting, eyes my scruffy getup narrowly and nods agreement; yes, he likes my ravaged face, too. "Just don't wander out on the streets without a keeper," he murmurs, deadpan. "I don't want you getting arrested." Motioning for me to follow, he strides briskly across the dense-packed room toward the camera setup, stopping along the way to introduce me to Cloris, Gulager, Surtees, Cybill Shepherd and because she's standing nearby, a pale, pretty young bit player from Dallas named Pam Keller. Finally, I make my shy hellos with Tim Bottoms, the tousle-haired, James Dean-ish actor who's to play my estranged teenaged son in the upcoming scene: "Hi, son." " 'Lo, dad."

Oblivious to the racketing noise and movement around him, Bogdanovich blocks out our paces and patiently coaches Tim and me on our lines. It's a muted conversation scene the two of us are involved in, a long, Wellesian dolly shot set against the backdrop of a country & western dance. Tim and I rehearse our moves until Surtees signals Bogdanovich that he's ready to roll; Peter, in turn, motions for Leon Miller's string band, arrayed on a platform at the head of the dance floor, to strike up "Over the Waves." The cameras whir; we go through the motions of the complicated shot twice. The second time around, it feels good. *"Cut,"* Bogdanovich calls. "Print both takes. Good work, everyone. *Stellar!"*

"Academy," a disembodied voice bawls from behind a bank of glaring klieg lights.

Feeling washed-out and blank, I settle in a folding chair on the sidelines next to Pam Keller, who is "almost twenty" and who plays the part of Jackie Lee French—"Clu's dancing partner," she explains with a wry laugh, "which makes her a kind of semipro floozy, I guess." As if on cue, Gulager wanders by with chat-up on his mind; playfully, he makes a feint at Pam's ribs and bottom. "Oh, don't be such a wimp," she protests, frowning. Gulager, who speaks in a deep glottal rattle like Jimmy Stewart, gives her a pained look: "What was that you said, little lady?" "I don't stutter, buster," Pam snaps icily.

Dismissing him with a stare, Pam turns to ask what I do besides playing village junkie-geeks. Polly, who's stood by watching the exchange, grins and flashes Pam the V sign as Gulager stalks disgustedly away: "Way to go, sweetheart. He's a real Hollywood showboat, that yo-yo."

The interminable delays between takes stretch into hours that glide past like greased dreams.

Around midnight, the tedium shades off into stuporous exhaustion, and abruptly seven or eight of us are headed back to the Ramada Inn in an overstuffed Buick sedan.

The conversation rises and falls desultorily. "Do we work tomorrow?" Gulager asks Cloris edgily. "Maybe we don't work, huh? That'd be nice. I'd like to spend the day limbering up at the Y."

Cloris doesn't know, shrugs fatalistically. "God, I've just been thinking about that gross asshole who plays my husband . . . This is the saddest picture," she reflects with a wilting sigh.

The next day begins and ends with the ritual viewing of the dailies in the hotel's cavernous banquet room. Sitting with Bogdanovich, who seems tense and distracted, and Bob Surtees, who is always medium cool, I watch enough footage to confirm Polly's estimate of Ben Johnson's performance as Sam the Lion, the dying proprietor of the last picture show—he's magnificent. Academy all the way. Then I hurry off to board the charter bus headed for Archer City.

On the hour-long ride to the set, I share a seat with Bill Thurman, who plays Coach Popper, Cloris Leachman's husband in the film. Thurman, whose meaty, middle-aged face is a perfect relief map of burnt-out lust and last night's booze, is kibitzing across the aisle with Mike Hosford, Buddy Wood and Loyd Catlett—*Picture Show*'s resident *vitelloni*. The term springs automatically to mind to describe the three randy young studs because, in essence, they're playing themselves; onscreen and off, they're the high-strutting young calves of this short-grass country, always on the prod for excitement, and maybe a little strange to boot. Loyd, who is seventeen and something of a self-winding motormouth, is plunking dolefully on a guitar and munching a jawful of Brown Mule.

"Terbacker puts fuel in mah airplane," he explains expansively. "Say, look-a-here, Thurman, you seen our scene the other night—you thank we was any good?"

Thurman puts on a mock scowl and snarls, "Shit naw, kid, I thought y'all sucked—buncha little piss-aint punks." "Hmph," Loyd snorts, "that's what that dollar whiskey'll do to your brains, Ah guess." Under his breath, he hisses, "Kiss mah root, you boogerin' ol' fart." Without preamble, he breaks into the Beatles song about doing it in the road, and the other boys join in the singing with gusto, if no clear command of harmony.

"Me and Cloris are gettin' along real good together in our scenes," Thurman remarks, looking as if he'd give a princely sum to believe it. "I guess the production's been a little bit disorganized up to now, but all things considered, I b'lieve we got a real grabber on our hands here, don't you agree?"

On the set, which is being busily readied for another take in the dance sequence, the wardrobe master sits slumped on a camp stool, firmly clutching the prop purse that Cloris Leachman will need in the upcoming scene.

"We need a huge container of water, Lou," Bogdanovich calls out to the second propman. "Waterloo!" the first assistant director crows. "That's what this whole deal is about, right?" "We hired Rube for his wit, not his talent," Bogdanovich murmurs as he peers through a viewfinder.

The hall is chill and drafty; the first raw gusts of a blue norther are rattling the windowpanes and doors. I find a chair near a gas heater and sit down to scribble some notes, idly thumbing through the pages of a paperback copy of the novel version of *Picture Show* (Dell, seventy-five cents, out of print). Set in a grim, mythical backwater called Thalia in 1951–52 (and "lovingly dedicated" to Larry McMurtry's hometown), the story focuses on a loose-knit clique of teenagers who have ultimately nowhere to go except to bed with each other, and to war in Korea.

The adults who alternately guide and misguide their young—even Sam the Lion, the salty old patriarch who rules over the town's lone movie theater—are no less disaffected by the numbing mise-en-scène of Thalia; in Dorothy Parker's phrase, they are all trapped like a trap in a trap.

The tenor of life in Thalia is described this way by a wayward mother to her soon-to-be-wayward daughter:

"The only really important thing I [wanted] to tell you was that life here is very monotonous. Things happen the same way over and over again. I think it's more monotonous in this part of the country than it is in other places, but I don't really know that—it may be monotonous everywhere. I'm sick of it, myself."

As far removed from grace or salvation as the Deity is reputed to be distant from sin, the town boys haunt the picture show, where they're permitted a few hours of "above the waist" passion with their girls on Saturday nights. Inexorably, boys and girls together careen into out-of-control adulthood in the Age of the Cold Warrior. But as they do, the symbols and landmarks of their childhood become lost to them, and in the end, even the picture show is gone.

Weighing the book in my hand, I try to weigh it in my mind as well—objectively, if possible. The narrative is sometimes crude, more often tasteless, and always bitter as distilled gall. But it is true—true to the bone-and-gristle life in this stricken, sepia-colored tag end of nowhere. So it goes in the short-grass country. It's hardly a thought to warm your hands over, but it occurs to me that I've been in Archer City only a scant few hours, and like that daughter's mother in Thalia, I'm already a little sick of it, my own self.

Maneuvering around to catch a glimpse of my notes, Pam puts on an impish smile and cajoles in an orphan-of-the-storm falsetto, "Oh, make me famous, will you, please? Are you famous by any chance? Clu Gulager is famous, you bet. He's famous-er than anybody, in fact. Just ask the rat bastard."

Near one of the too-few heaters scattered around the hall, Bob Glenn, who plays a nouveau-dumb oil baron in the film, is remarking that he appreciates the unstructured makeup of the location company—"No snotty star types, all the lead actors mingling with everybody else." Fred Jackson bobs his head in agreement; one of the stand-ins, he's a tall drink of water from over Throckmorton way who looks uncannily like Buck Owens. "Hail yes, Bawb," he says. "So far, ever'body high and low's just acted like we'us all in this thang together, you know what I mean? Dju meet ol' Ben Johnson while he'us down here? Shit, he's just *folks,* that ol' boy. He's sposed to come back one a these times and go huntin' with me."

Over an electric bullhorn, the first assistant director booms out, "All right, everybody be of good cheer. All together now, let's have some *smiles!*" "Let's have some liquor," somebody groans in reply. Scowling distractedly, Bogdanovich kicks at a thick hummock of recording cable. "Let's have some lunch," he sighs quietly.

With manic zest, Gulager titillates the townspeople dining at the Golden Rooster, Archer City's lone indoor eatery, by pasting pats of butter on his cheeks and forehead. "It wouldn't melt in your mouth, honey," Cloris observes ac-

idly. Cybill Shepherd, who plays Jacy, the film's teenaged sexpot, looks pained at the buzzing commotion Gulager is causing among the diners; wordlessly, she picks up her book—Thomas Mann's *The Magic Mountain*—and leaves before the meal is served. It's an interesting reaction; I determine to try to talk to her if a chance arises.

A local filling-station owner approaches the table and shyly asks Gulager for his autograph; the big, sunburned man pretends not to notice the trickle of butter oozing down the actor's jaw. Not to be overlooked in the crowd, Cloris launches into a rambling singsong recitative about George Hamilton taking a sleeping-pill suppository during a cab ride in Paris. She projects the maybe-apocryphal story just like an actress, but she breaks just like a little girl when nobody but Jeff Bridges laughs at the punch line. Gratefully, she tousles his hair: "Give my love to your daddy, Jeff-boy. Is he still all water-puckered from *Sea Hunt?*" Jeff grins bashfully and mumbles something into his plate.

Gulager, milking the butter shtick to the last drip, scrapes the runny yellow goo off his face and spreads it on a slice of bread, then wolfs it down with extravagant gusto.

Pam, who's sat rigid with distaste throughout the meal, looks pensive during the two-block walk back to the Legion Hall. "Clu Gulager," she announces at last in a tiny, constricted voice, "is just another pretty face. All smeary with butter, at that. *Blechh!*" Like Loyd, in his way, she reminds me of everybody decent I ever knew in this empty, perishing, hardscrabble country.

Back on the set, the crew members are beginning to trundle the monstro Panavision equipment out into the parking lot where the night's shooting is to take place. By this time, it's six-thirty, dark as the grave and biting cold. The chief camera operator is telling a spectacular-breasted teen queen from the neighboring town of Electra about working on *Drive, He Said.* "Well, it was a weird experience, I tell you that, sugar. Jack Nicholson's what they call far-out, you know? Dope and rebellion, all that shit. Me, I'm more or less a law-and-order person myself, so I told him after we saw the rough cut, 'Jack, it's a cute picture, but it's not anything I'd want to take my wife and kids to see.' Listen, uh . . . Dottie . . . I'll probably have to work here until pretty late, but, uh . . . what're you going to be up to around midnight?"

Loyd Catlett rushes in with the news that the generator truck has caught on fire. "The *lost* picture show," Mae Woods, Bogdanovich's secretary, groans, dashing outside to take a look. On a rump-sprung sofa near a fireplace that doesn't work, Cybill Shepherd and Jeff Bridges try to remember the words to "Back in the Saddle." A rash of domino games breaks out around the fires.

Outside, towering floodlights illumine the '52-vintage cars ringing the entrance to the hall. The minor generator blaze has already been dispatched by the Archer City Volunteer Fire Department, some of whose members remain behind, striking stalwart poses. As usual, the shot Bogdanovich plans is diabolically complicated:

(1) Cybill, as Jacy, is to park her '48 Ford convertible near the hall's entrance, get out of the car and be greeted by Randy Quaid, who plays Lester, a goofy-looking idle-rich suitor. They're to exchange a page or so of dialogue before (2) Jeff and Tim Bottoms, as Duane and Sonny, respectively, barrel into the parking lot in a battered Dodge pickup against a moving frieze of extras shown in deep focus getting out of cars, walking across the lot toward the hall's side entrance, etc. Tim exits from the truck toward that rear door while Jeff advances to em-

brace Cybill. During the clinch and subsequent dialogue, the camera pans around to show (3) Clu Gulager, as Abilene, escorting Pam Keller—Jackie Lee French—through the front door.

"All of that in one so-called fluid take," the dolly operator groans piteously. "Hell, Peter, it's not only difficult, it's impossible." "With patience and saliva," an electrician pronounces sagely, "the elephant balleth the ant."

"Peter, can we shoot this shit?" the boom man screams out from overhead. "Or not?" "Strictly speaking, Dean," Bogdanovich mumbles, squinting at the setup, "possibly." He motions toward the first assistant director: "Meester Rubin! I theenk it iss time ve vill take a live vun." "Damn, Peter," the second assistant director snorts, "you're getting to sound just like Otto. That prick." "Ready when you are, C.B.," shouts the first assistant director.

In a sudden hush, the cameras begin to roll, but Cybill blows the take by missing her mark parking the convertible. When she stammers out an apology, the sound mixer stage-whispers gruffly, "Sympathy can be found in the dictionary between *shit* and *syphillis,* sister."

After the eighth consecutive take has gone down the tube—this time because Jeff has rammed the pickup into the side of the building—Bogdanovich murmurs through blue lips, "Well, back to the old drawing board." "We're as shit out of luck tonight as a barber in Berkeley," the key grip grumbles. Polly Platt wanders around looking worried-in-general. "Our l-left foot doesn't seem to know what our other left f-foot is d-doing tonight," Polly complains through chattering teeth.

It's a wrap at last on what must be the eleventh or twelfth take. The actors and crew look numb and gray-faced with exhaustion; Pam looks distressed, as well. Her face is wind-chapped, she has a big red bump swelling on her forehead, and she's worried sick that she may lose her receptionist's day job at the Royal Coach Inn in Dallas because Bogdanovich says he needs her for an additional day's shooting. "I didn't count on this movie changing my *whole darn life!*"

During the postmidnight screening of some late-arriving rushes in the hotel's banquet room, Bogdanovich, Polly, Bob Surtees and six or seven other production aides drowse through some routine interior establishing shots, then snap alert at a brace of electrifying takes showing Gulager, as Abilene, seducing Jacy—Cybill Shepherd—in a deserted pool hall. Even in its unedited form, the scene has a raw and awesome power; at one point, Gulager's right eye, slightly cocked, gleams out of the eerily lit frame like a malevolent laser beam. *"Academy,"* the first assistant director murmurs reverently in Surtees' direction. "Wow—Clu looks positively *ogreish,*" the second assistant director crows in delight. A brittle female voice pipes out of the dark at the back of the room, "Nothing that mental and spiritual plastic surgery couldn't cure, honey."

In the morning on the set in Archer City, the cast assembles and waits fretfully for the final hours of shooting on the dance sequence to begin. Polly Platt, renewing the tint job on my hair, is saying from behind her enormous blue oval shades, "I was a Boston deb—can you believe it?—so I had a different notion about dances when I first got here. . . . Now, I'm miserable and deliriously happy at the same time. I miss my baby girls to the point of pain—they're with Peter's family out in Phoenix—but I'm elated about the way the movie's coming along. . . . Of course, part of the agony is that Peter is no longer my friend or lover or companion;

Peter is making a movie. . . . He has a terrific nostalgia for his teenage years in the fifties—Holden Caulfield ice-skating at Rockefeller Plaza with wholesome young girls in knee socks, like that. . . . Somehow, he's managed to transfer those feelings about his own adolescence to the totally different experience of the kids in the film. . . . Have you noticed? He's very—tender with the young actors. . . . So, I ended up 'doing' Cybill—her overall appearance as Jacy—to lock into those longing fantasies of Peter's. In reality, I created a rival for myself, I guess. . . . Well, anything for art, huh? There, now—you look properly geekish again. Get out there and wow 'em, kid. Win this one for the Gipper."

I stroll around for a while among the extras. Most of the men are unsmiling, stiff-starched, gleaming with brilliantine. The women, as a hard rule, are pinch-faced, mean-spirited cunts who make me wonder how I managed to couple with their spitting images so long without turning raving queer.

Over by the bandstand, where Leon Miller and his boys sit slumped like zombies after having played "Put Your Little Foot" for approximately the 527th time, Loyd is dogging the heels of the casting director. "Ah heard they gonna aw-dition three nekkid girls from Dallas today," he whispers to me with a wink, "so Ah'm ona see if ol' Chason'll let me sneak a little peek."

It's a moment of truth for Pam, who's just had a long, nerve-rattling talk on the phone with her boss in Dallas. While Bogdanovich blocks out the paces of her final scene with Gulager, Thurman moseys by, notices her woebegone expression, and asks, not unkindly: "Whatsa matter, sugar? You look like somebody cut yore piggen strang." Pam makes a fetchingly grotesque face at him, but doesn't answer. "Yeah, Pam, what's up?" Bogdanovich prods with fond amusement. "You gonna get fired or what?" "I don't *know!*" she bursts out, an oyster's tear away from real tears. "A fat lot you care, anyway, Mr. Bigtime Director—you're making a *movie*, right? The show must go on, right?" "Right," Bogdanovich says unevenly, turning away. Polly, who's been following the conversation, bites her lip but says nothing.

Out on the dance floor, Bogdanovich has a setup at last. When the actors are all in position, he sings out: "This is a take, folks. Movies are better than ever! Roll 'em!"

"Mark it," the sound mixer growls.

"Five-nine-charlie-apple—take one," a grip intones, clapping a slapstick.

"And . . . *dancing!*" the first assistant director booms out.

It's a wrap in one so-called fluid take, and the crew lustily yodels its approval: "Way to go, Pam baby!" *"Academy!"* "Nice work, Clu."

Over on the sidelines, a blue-haired matron of fifty-odd in a psychedelic-splotched pantsuit interrupts to ask Pam: "Listen, can I git your autograph, dumplin'? You do play Jacy, don't you?" "No, ma'am, I play Jackie Lee French—" "Aw, well," the woman sniffs, "that's about as good, I gay-ess." Looking stricken, Pam signs a paper napkin, then quickly scratches off her home phone number on a sliver of envelope and hands it to me. "If you happen to see the rushes I'm in," she blurts, "call and let me know what you think, would you? I'm not sure I ever want to be in any more movies, but I'd like to know if I did good or not in this one." Hugging Polly good-bye, she hurries off after a driver who'll take her the first leg of the way back to Dallas.

Loyd watches Pam leave, then turns to Polly: "She say she don't wanna be in no more movies? Is that what she said? Sheeit, boy, Ah do! Ah'd lahk to be in about a million of 'em—"

"Hush, Loyd," Polly says in an absent tone.

Feeling twitchy and fogged-out, I cash in my costume early and hitch a ride back to the Ramada Inn in Bill Thurman's blue Lincoln. Bob Glenn takes the wheel next to Gulager, while Thurman stretches out over most of the backseat, drinking what he calls "toddy for the body"—Old Taylor out of the bottle. Pause for a deep swallow. "Course now, Mr. Bogdanovich . . . you know, Peter . . . he's somethin' else altogether, cain't you agree, Clu?"

Gulager, slumped in the front passenger's seat, doesn't deign to answer at once. Thurman goes on: "I mean, to me, I thank he's got the makin's of, uh, well . . . a great artist, maybe." "Mebbe," Gulager concedes, sounding unconvinced. "Personally, I don't like the script cuts he's making, but I guess he doesn't have much choice about it. But shit, look, Thurman, that's the only reason I took my role—which is a fat zero of a nothing part—because there was a lot of other good stuff in the script. It read good to me, it read *honest*. As to whether Mr. Bogdanovich makes it or not, that pretty much depends on how this picture comes out. Both of you guys work mainly out of Dallas, right? Well, I make my living in Hollywood, and they write you off quick if you fail in my city." The cutting edge of finality in his voice is chilling.

I drift off to the hotel bar to belt back a few healing brandies. Later, on my way to bed, there's a phone message for me at the desk from the Yankee Lady out in California: *Sleep warm.* After a bit, I do just that, dreaming at some surreal point that I'm Dennis Weaver in *Touch of Evil*, only *Touch of Evil* has somehow become a Saturday-afternoon Western playing at the Last Picture Show in Archer City—the old shuttered Royal Theater—and my grandfather and I are sitting in the hushed dark alongside— who're those two ol' boys in the seats next to us?—Larry McMurtry and Elvis?—yes—and suddenly my own ravaged face swims into focus on the silvery screen, bigger than life, and the camera pulls back to show me tap-dancing on a sofa in a driving rain while Bill Thurman, Bob Glenn and Clu Gulager ping away at my feet with six-shooters. My grandfather leans forward as the scene unreels, lifts one liver-speckled old man's hand as if to greet his own surprise, and says with an expiring sigh: *"Academy, boy. Academy all the way."*

The next day's call sheet lists the setting to be used as EXT GRAVEYARD, and summons all the principals of the cast and crew. The assembled caravan will converge on the Archer City Community Cemetery, where the funeral of Sam the Lion is to be shot.

As the actors file off the bus and mill curiously about a freshly dug grave to be used in the scene, the first assistant director unslings his ever-present bullhorn and intones solemnly: "Let us now praise famous men, ladies and gents. Welcome to Lenny Bruce's cafeteria."

Bogdanovich sets up the master shot of the funeral scene with uncommon speed, but close-ups and dialogue fakes last well into the morning.

Jeff, who's by now as hooked on dominoes as Bogdanovich's secretary, starts up a game a few paces away from Larry McMurtry's family burial plot. The markers for McMurtry's paternal grandparents read:

Louisa F.	William J.
and	
1859–1946	1858–1940

The sight of the stones sets up an aching urge in me to be away from the place; I've been to too many of these country boneyards for real.

Over by the wind machine, Bill Thurman is sounding off to Bob Glenn about how loaded he's gotten the night before: "I was so pissed outa mah mind, boy, I couldn't have drove mah dick in a can of lard. You orta been there."

A grizzled old extra in a string tie and Mexican-tooled boots squints disapprovingly at Tim Bottoms, who's lying facedown on a grassy slope beyond the last row of gravestones. "Wouldn't know a gol-danged rattler if one taken a gol-danged bite out of him," he sneers.

"Texas is almost all depleted now," Gulager says with a brooding scowl. "It's twenty million square acres of fucked-up land, that's it."

After a while, when the cameras move elsewhere, I go look into the open grave wherein Ben Johnson—Sam the Lion—is supposed to be laid. The brand name on the casket-lowering device says FRIGID, and you'd better believe it, little pardners.

My part in the picture is finished by now—so I'm essentially hanging out the next day when the shooting commences with a brief picnic sequence in Hamilton Park—the Beverly Hills of Wichita Falls, kind of—then shifts to the Cactus Motel on Old Iowa Park Road for the exteriors of a tryst scene involving Cybill and Tim.

As the troupe disgorges from the bus, the sun beats down, fleets of semi trucks roar by on the highway and a gaggle of townspeople gather to gawk and shyly shake hands with the actors they recognize. *"It's so inneresting,"* a rabbit-toothed woman in pedal pushers exclaims. "Look," somebody hisses softly, pointing at Jeff, who's hunkering down alongside Loyd on a plot of dead grass beside the generator truck, "there's Beau Bridges." "Who?" "Lloyd Bridges' kid." "Oh."

While the prop men are dressing the scene, Bogdanovich lounges against the hood of a car, doing a fair-to-middling imitation of Peter Lorre. As all good secretaries do on such occasions, Mae Woods registers 100 on the laugh-meter. Cybill sits off to one side, intently squinting into the pica-choked pages of *Crime and Punishment.*

Meanwhile, on their tiny plot of dead grass, Jeff and Loyd are embarked on an extraordinary exchange of their own. Jeff is saying in a casual, offhand way that he knows Loyd doesn't do much reading, but anyway, he's got this spare copy of a book called *Steppenwolf* in his room at the hotel, and he wants to lay it on him . . . you know, whatever . . . just in case Loyd ever gets the urge to read something in an off minute.

"Steppenwolf. Is that that rock group?" Loyd asks. "Shit, boy, Ah lahk rock—it puts fuel in mah airplane."

No, Jeff explains—still ever so offhandedly, casually—the rock group in all likelihood took its name from the book, which is about—well, about this dude named Steppenwolf, Loyd'll just have to read about it for himself to understand. . . . But if there's an overall *message* to the book . . . you know . . . well, maybe it's something like—*keep moving.* . . . Or, whatever . . . It's only a book after all, but still and all, Loyd might get something out of it that might . . . you know . . . change his way of thinking, his values, stuff like that—

"Ah ain't good at books—Ah don't have to tell you that—but Ah lahk that message, whatever you call it," Loyd says, worrying at his teeth with a stem of grass. " '*Keep movin*' '—shit, that's mah meat, awright. Listen, Jeff—you reckon Ah'd make a fair Western star? Ah'm savin' mah money so's Ah can go out to California when this outfit's done shootin' here, but what happens then? How do Ah go about gettin' in the union, do you know? The Screen Actors Guild? Mr. Surtees said he wants to do some stills of me if Ah ever make it out to Hollywood. And John Hellerman—you know, he's an awful fahn little man—he gimme a mixed drank last night

up in his room at the ho-tel and tole me Ah could bunk at his place when Ah git out there. Well, shit fahr and save matches, maybe ever' thang's gonna turn out awright, you thank so?"

Jeff, no longer offhand or casual, hunches his shoulders forward intensely and gestures in an agitated circle: "I don't *know,* Loyd. Nobody knows anything for sure, so nobody can tell you anything for sure. If some dude says he can, then he's bullshitting you. That's why it's important to *keep moving*—keep tryin' to understand yourself better in the world, the *real* world of true recognitions."

Unused to such talk, Loyd passes a troubled hand across his face, then blurts impassionedly: "Gawddamn it to hell, Jeff, it's hard for me to keep thoughts lahk that in mah head, but Ah'll try, and you got mah word on it, buddeh! Hell, Ah wanna know about all that stuff you mean— values and thankin' and all that shit. You just way out ahead a me, is all, and it's hard as hell to catch up. Ah guess just bein' in this movie, gettin' to know a guy like you and all—that's changin' mah lahf, ain't it? . . .

"Ah was thankin' the other night at the house—you know, just settin' around thankin', lahk a guy'll do—and all of a sudden, Ah was on the subject of God. *Jesus Christ,* Ah says to mahself, what's goin' on here? Ah never did figger it all out to suit me, but anyways, what Ah was thankin' was—you limit yourself to God, but He don't limit Hisself to you, does He? Ah mean God can be whatever he takes a notion to be—a tree or a rock or whatever the fuck . . . But a guy cain't be nothin' but a human man, see what Ah'm gittin' at? And you know what? Alla that made me feel—lonesome, somehow. Ah don't know how to explain it, but Ah guess you cain't hep but feel lonesome sometimes, can ye?"

Later, leaving to go back to the hotel, I draw Loyd to one side and thank him for being in my movie. He looks surprised for a minute, then gives me a gentle poke on the arm. "You're kiddin' me, ain't ye, doctor," he says pleasantly.

The next afternoon, under a lowering sky, Cybill puts aside her books and sets out for a meandering stroll to the Wichita Cattle Company auction barn, located about a mile from the hotel across the kind of middle-class black ghetto that would have been unthinkable anywhere in Texas a decade ago. Along the way, she languidly waves at children playing in the scrupulously clipped yards and ticks off the key events of her *vita brevis* with the heatless detachment of a NASA lifer selecting trinkets for inclusion in a time capsule:

A wealthy "philistine" upbringing in Memphis . . . growing up absurd, all that . . . winning a "Model of the Year" contest . . . moving to Barrow Street in the Village . . . meeting an "older man," a Manhattan restaurateur, who introduced her to the Truly Important Things—music, the theater, abstract expressionism, the European literary heavies . . . "I never learned how to make friends," she reflects moodily, peering down into the dung-pungent shadows of the deserted auction arena. "But . . . I learned early how to fill needs."

Prowling around the barn's maze of tunnels and chutes, she wanders out on a raised plank walkway overlooking pens of cattle being fattened for sale. "What do cows do mostly?" she asks abruptly. The usual things animals do, she is told. "Eat, you mean? Sleep? Make love? I think I might like to be a cow."

On the way back to the Ramada, she chews on a piece of straw and confides that the illusionary business of making a movie is troubling her. "It's like living in a hall of mirrors," she says, smiling a fragile, very private smile. "It's like being dumb but reading Kafka, anyway."

The *Picture Show* cast begins to scatter in all directions like M.B. Garrett's limber-lock geese; by now, Bob Glenn has returned to the sci-fi mother ship in Dallas, Cloris Leachman and Clu Gulager have departed on separate flights back to L.A., and I'm scheduled on a San Francisco flight out early the next morning. While I'm packing, it occurs to me that I've missed seeing Pam Keller's rushes. Debating whether or not to call her, anyway, and try to bluff it through—*Terrific, Pam baby. Academy all the way*—I head down to the hotel restaurant and join Eileen Brennan for coffee.

Eileen, who plays a salty-tongued barmaid in the film, has just boosted a pair of eighty-nine-cent sewing scissors from a five-and-dime store, and she crows about her petty thievery elatedly as she knits and purls on something gruesome and fuzzy spilling out of her lap.

Late that night, there's a small birthday gathering for me in Jeff's room; from Mae Woods or somebody, word has gotten around that my ravaged face is a year older. Cybill Shepherd shows up, and so do Eileen Brennan and Loyd, Tim Bottoms and the location manager. Soon, some imported Mexican hors d'oeuvres are making the rounds, and Jagger is bleating "Sympathy for the Devil" on a tinny cassette machine.

Loyd, his hat shoved back at an angle on his dark hair, is sitting in the middle of the floor, taking the first toke of his life in the real world of true recognitions. He sputters and coughs and grins lopsidedly: "Sheeit, that stuff makes ye feel boneless, don't it?" Before the Stones have given way to Elton John, he's sprawled out full-length, asleep. The music and the Mexican imports burn on. Sure, you can go home again, I hear myself telling someone much later, if you're making a movie.

Fellini's *Roma*

By Robert Greenfield

NOVEMBER 11, 1971

"*Bellissimo!*" As the owner of the Fiat tries to make himself understood to the owner of the Volkswagen, who can't speak a word of Italian. The Fiat owner flings his hands in the air and balls his fists. He paces around his car to restrain himself. The veins in his head throb and the fury mounts until he can stand it no longer, and . . .

Whram, whram, whram, goes his head, three times, hard into the hood of his car.

"*Bellissimo!*" the crowd murmurs.

Existential. More than two thousand years of civilization, and all the Romans have left is the grand gesture, the finger-biting scream, the palm smashed against the forehead in anger, the gesture so grand it really has no meaning.

"More than twenty centuries, man," Carl says, strolling past the accident, totally uninvolved, "of bad karma. They fed Christians to the lions in the Coliseum . . . and got off on it. Are you kidding?" Carl, our guide to the wonders of the Eternal City, is an actor from California. He speaks English. "They never beat the first riff here," he says. "Mama's cooking and the womb. They stay boys until they die. The whole peninsula will fall into the sea before anything changes."

For nothing ever *does* change in the Eternal City. It just keeps on happening illegally, with more money being paid to those in power to let it continue. *Playboy* is banned but can be bought under the counter everywhere. The Vatican speaks out against divorce, and Roman pimps still take their meal-ticket ladies out to the side of the highways and leave them there to service truck drivers.

Fellini's *Roma*, Europe's great whore madonna city, is Federico Fellini's next film.

"Who do you want to know about—Fred?" Carl asks. "Everybody's got a different figure on him. They worked for him, they like him, they hate him. He's a closet queen, an egomaniac, a clown . . .

"All I know is he called a friend of mine the other day to say he was finally ready to take some LSD with him on Sunday."

Inside a concrete-cube building on a movie lot that looks like a junior college in Los Angeles, Fellini is at work. The lot, Cinecitta, was built by Mussolini in the late thirties to become the new Hollywood and churn out costume epics about the glory of the Roman Empire, epics that

170

would inspire the Italians to help Il Duce create a new one.

The back lots are dusty and unused, old Western towns one wall thick. Four hundred yards of highway have been built for *Roma*, meant to look like the Raccordo Annulare, the road that circles Rome. The great stone head from *Fellini Satyricon* sits by the highway, now just an unused prop. In Theater Five, workmen bang nails into a life-size reconstruction of a Roman street. The "stone" crumbles easily. It is made of Styrofoam, and if needed, the particles can be used as snowflakes.

Push through a door into Theater Two and the sun vanishes. You're somewhere back in the early forties inside Iovinelli, Rome's premier vaudeville house.

Ladies in long dresses fan themselves with rolled pieces of paper. Men in short-sleeve shirts rolled over the biceps spit and talk and smoke, creasing and bending yellow straw hats nervously with their hands. A four-hundred-pound man with the face of a boy sits sweating placidly through his T-shirt in the last row of seats.

"Silenzio," the man in the brown linen suit commands. *"A posto. A posto. Motore."* Fellini on the set, in the center of his own universe, created with the aid of makeup men, script ladies, one hundred fifty extras and a bullhorn. "Silence," Fellini commands. "Places. Action."

Three hobo clowns in tails and starched white shirts, spats and droopy pants come walking up the aisle. With their faces chalky white and their eyebrows outlined in pencil, they look like ambassadors from a world where Charlie Chaplin's little tramp is president and all meetings of state are held in the center ring under canvas.

They bounce up the aisle, dignified, absurd, as the band in the pit vamps away. They reach the front of the house and open their mouths to sing. A long, wet fart rings out from the audience. People snigger. One of the clowns rolls his eyes in fear and bobs his Adam's apple up and down.

"Stop!" Fellini says, coming out from behind the camera, displeased with something, mopping away the perspiration with the white handkerchief he keeps knotted around his neck.

"Mau-rizio," he calls out, in the special tone he reserves for summoning people he needs, breaking their name into two syllables like a mother hanging out a tenement window yelling, "Lou-ee, come to dinner. Your father, he's waitin' on you."

"Fume, fume, Maurizio, why aren't they smoking?" Fellini asks, exasperated. He eyes the heavens. Why has God sent Fellini people who cannot follow directions? *"Fume, fume,"* the order is repeated by assistants, and more packs of cigarettes are distributed. People suck deeply and exhale. The propmen fan fuming cans of frankincense with pieces of cardboard. Perfumed smoke billows across the set and shrouds everything, like the steam that hangs around Guido and the Cardinal in *8½.*

The great iron doors at the sides of the building are bolted shut to keep out the light. The temperature rises.

Second take. "Stop!" Third take. "Stop! Walk like this, lower with the hands," Fellini directs one of the clowns, gesturing. Fourth take. Fifth take. A makeup man comes to tissue the sweat off the faces of the clowns. Sixth take.

The clowns come up the aisle in time; the fart rings out on time (someone's lips against the back of their hand). A little boy runs up the aisle to stare at the clowns and is called back by his father and slapped.

Fellini beams as it unfolds, perfectly. He stands smiling like a little boy. He calls out, *"E questa."* "Print it."

Then he turns and shouts, *"Mau-rizio."* It begins all over again.

*R*oma will be Federico Fellini's eleventh feature film in this, his twenty-second year of directing movies. It is the only film currently being made at Cinecitta, where the movie industry is not in much better shape than it is in Hollywood. Something to do with the people who make the films all over the world being mostly so much older than the people who are going to see them in America.

Fellini finds himself one of the few directors that established money trusts to make a film that kids will go see, an honor won with his *Satyricon.*

Production costs for *Roma* have been estimated to run as high as $5 million. The director himself laughs at this and says, "After the producers lie to the distributors and the distributors lie to the exhibitors . . . United Artists gave me $1.75 million, no more. It costs the same as *Satyricon.*"

Forty minutes of the film are already edited, and the shooting will continue through September ("October," one friend of the director says. "December," another assures).

As for its plot, its coauthor, Bernardi Zappone, who also coauthored *Satyricon* and *The Clowns,* says, "There is no story for this one, no protagonist. The character is Fellini himself when he first came to Rome, but in the film he has no name. He is not even in the sequence they are shooting now. He is an image. It is Federico's most abstract film."

*I*f you believe studio biographies, he was born on January 20, 1920, in Rimini, a small town on the Adriatic coast of Italy that has since become a fashionable resort. His father was a salesman, and his parents lived modestly but well. At the age of eighteen he left home. He went first to Florence and then Rome, where he worked as a cartoonist for a popular newspaper. His status as journalist earned him exemption from service in Mussolini's army.

Fellini wrote his first film script in 1943. He was "found" by director Roberto Rossellini, working in a shop where Allied servicemen could have quick caricatures of themselves drawn. The two collaborated on the script for *Open City,* one of the landmark films of postwar neorealism.

Fellini was thirty-four when he made *La Strada,* starring his wife, Giulietta Masina, Anthony Quinn and Richard Basehart. Here, neorealism is combined with Fellini's sense of the mystic and the metaphysical. *La Strada* is a soft, fragile film, delicate and circular. Only Anthony Quinn's character can be said to be totally real in the conventional sense. Both Masina, who rides with him on his motorcycle trailer, giving shows in provincial town squares, and Basehart, a high-wire walker, seem visitors from another, gentler sphere.

La Strada won an Academy Award and made Fellini world famous. It was not until *La Dolce Vita* in 1960 that he himself began to attract as much attention as his actors.

La Dolce Vita was a scandal in the making, with rumors sweeping Rome of the affairs between the stars and/or the director that had paparazzi climbing the wall to get into Anita Ekberg's back garden. Whispers of impending censorship by the Church and hysteria about who exactly the "beautiful people" in the film were in real life kept the city busy with gossip of the highest (or lowest) order.

Fellini's next film was $8\frac{1}{2}$. This time, everyone knew what to expect. Fellini, they said, had no script. He was making up the film at night and shooting by day. He was bankrupt. He was using aristocrats to play servants and old women to play priests (he was—he also used boys to play nuns in *Juliet of the Spirits*).

The hero of the film was obviously Fellini himself, and the theme the emptiness of his own life now that he had made it to the top. It was even more painfully obvious to all that *Juliet of the Spirits* was the story of the breakup of his marriage. If everything they attributed to Fellini's life from his films were true, he would need to be either a committee or behind the walls of an asylum.

His next film was *Satyricon*. Fellini called it "a trip in the dark, a descent by submarine, a science fiction, a psychedelic picture . . . that the young ones grasp without asking, 'What does it mean?'"

Fellini the acid filmmaker? More rumors. None of *Satyricon*'s actors spoke the same language, but they were still able to carry on unspeakable set practices, both on and off screen.

About *Roma*, they have less to say. All the gossip has been used, at least once before. Fellini as a subject is almost beyond discussion now. He is becoming an institution.

"You know in the beginning," the director's press agent confides, "he did not like this film very much. Now he is beginning to love it. Have you been on the set? It is a circus, no?

"Whenever Federico works," he says, laughing, "it is a ship . . . about to sink."

The *Roma* set looks like a full-color reproduction of the last thoughts you have before you go to sleep at night, peopled with more than one hundred extras, few of them actors. For them, the movie continues when the shooting stops. The boys playing young soldiers are just boys . . . they stare with obvious hunger at the incredible kewpie-doll mamas who play the dancers. The mamas are total tomatoes with

henna-rinse curls and painted faces. In spangled sailor's suits, they cross their legs and keep on chewing gum. Onstage a girl comes out of a sliding door in a battleship and is carried in Busby Berkeley circles by slim-hipped male dancers.

Fellini. Talking through a megaphone, peering through the camera, laughing with friends who come to visit, he is indomitable. He always knows exactly what he wants and usually gets it.

In one scene, the audience indicates its feelings by throwing peanut shells at the band. The maestro of the band has to turn, show displeasure and throw a glass of orange soda back at the audience. A simple thing. He can't do it.

"Take the glass with the left, pass it to the right, throw it," Fellini instructs, "with the left."

Two takes, nothing. Three takes. Fellini has asked for the sack of peanut shells and is burning them in from about eight feet away, zinging them off the maestro's balding head and thudding them into the sheet music.

The maestro blows it. "With the left, the left," Fellini says. The maestro panics, knocks the glass of soda off the piano, the soda hits a light, the light explodes.

Fellini ignores the explosion totally, pops a peanut in his mouth and says, "With the left." He scores a few more direct hits on the maestro's balding head with the shells, and after five takes, they get it right.

"Tell me," the lady journalist from Italy's great daily newspaper asked one day at lunch, "what do the young people in America think of Federico? Do they feel he is on their side?"

Across the table Fellini continued eating. Conversations about his life and work often go on in front of him.

The lady journalist chattered on, telling Fellini about her editors in Milan who refuse to print the truth about him when she writes it.

"Only they want to hear about the scandals and the affairs."

"They tell people what they pretend they want to hear," Fellini said. "That movie people are free and easy and happy . . . it is always the same thing. Did I not work for a fascist newspaper myself."

"All newspapers are fascist," someone grumbled.

"No," Fellini said. "Information is fascist. To give someone information is to gain power for yourself."

"There will be hippies in this film," he says, "in scenes to be shot on the Spanish steps. They are just a pretext for a speech about the hero's sexual initiation in a whorehouse. As a contrast for the freedom now and the ignorance then. Some of the young ones are incredulous; they cannot believe such things are possible. And others are quite delighted to learn of such a place. 'Where is it?' they ask.

"Although things seem dark and confused to many now, it is only because the storm is now. What comes after, we will see.

"I have confidence."

By five-thirty that afternoon everyone on the set is exhausted, sapped by humidity that Rome in June shares only with New York on special days in August. People are looking for a place to sit thinking about how nice it would be to take off their shoes and go home for a bath.

Fellini is playing. His three clowns are back. They stand in front of the audience, singing, ghostly old men that Fellini is obviously in love with. It occurs to him . . . maybe. He puts in a little bit of business. A young worker-tough comes out of the audience while the clowns sing and lights a cigarette off the candle that one holds.

The actor does what Fellini tells him to. Fel-lini says no. He changes the change, resetting the camera so that the actor has to half-face the lens while lowering the cigarette in his mouth toward the flame. Still no good.

Finally, Fellini moves out in front of the camera to show how he wants it done. He bends his head to the flame, lights the cigarette and then turns to the audience and flashes a beautiful, derisive smile to his buddies in the house. The smile is so perfect as to be obscene. A small gemlike gesture, as particularly Italian as it is universal.

"Please," Fellini says one day, "you are editor, producer, director, everything of ROLLING STONE, no? Ask me questions about what we do on the set. Interrupt me."

"The business yesterday with the cigarette and the candle, was that in the shooting script?"

"Ah, no. It comes from the atmosphere, of the set. Once that is there, all else follows. It is like before you make love, do you not know what movements, what positions you are going to use, or do you?"

"Sometimes not even after."

"Ah. There, you see. Good."

"Sometimes on the set, it seems you have become a corporation rather than filmmaker. So many depend on you for their living."

"This may be true, but for me it is still the first picture. I do not know. Once they are made, I never see them again. I remember the crews, some moments on the set but . . . all of it for me is realizing images, like a painter. We shoot a scene with cardinals in a church, we shoot in a whorehouse, for me they are the same. Images."

"And the responsibility . . . ?"

"It is a contradiction, no? I have made a world where I am faced with choices every moment, a light, the camera, a movement. And it is a sufferance for me. I like everything. Do you understand? Everything."

"Yes . . ."

"Excuse me, I must go shoot."

"Fellini speaks to you, eh," a friend of the director says after he is gone. "He gives you interviews, tells you answers. He is very charming. He has been doing it so long. Of course, he always says the same things to everyone."

Another lunchtime, in the director's office at Cinecitta. Today, there are seven places set around a round white table. Bernardi Zappone is present, as is Fiona Florence, an actress who has completed her part in the film. Zappone is a slight, pleasant man who seems perpetually ill at ease, a feeling that sometimes comes with the turf when you're a writer. Fiona has a classical face. Her black hair is drawn back into a bun, and she wears a black velvet choker around her neck. Fellini refers to her exclusively as *"la bella Fiona."*

"I ask you to look at this lady's complexion," Fellini says. "Is it not a masterpiece of nature?" Fiona blushes.

The telephones are ordered turned off. Fellini hears them no matter how softly they ring, and his lunch hour is not to be disturbed. Between the slices of prosciutto and the slightly moist hunks of white mozzarella cheese, the talk turns to politics.

Fellini shakes his head sadly and says, "You know here in Italy, the fascists made great advances in the last election. Mama and papa . . . it is a condition of humanity that they keep wanting to be children. To hear only what they have heard and see only what they have seen and have proven only what they already know. It is Man. He does not want to be free. It is too hard to live, to make choices."

But no one can be somber for long. The food is too good. Soon the talk is about published reports of the affair Fellini and Fiona are supposed to be having. Fellini laughs and holds the hand of his script lady. She has the same kind of joyous warmth in her face that shines from Fellini whenever he jokes with someone.

Round and round the discussion of the affair goes in rapid-fire Italian. Eyes crinkling, mouths puckering, a montage of smiles, winks, choked laughter.

"We are discussing whether or not it does not help to make love three or four times a day," Fellini explains helpfully. "What is your viewpoint?

"A lady of your beauty, Fiona," Fellini intones, "with all your natural endowments . . ."

"Wine?" Zappone asks, and Fiona and her glass take on the same color.

"You know," Fellini says, "this is funny. In the first part of the film we are in a whorehouse, and Fiona she plays a prostitute. Yet I cannot convince her." And off he plunges into Italian to explain to Fiona that art and life must come to resemble each other.

Through it all, Fiona is becoming more and more embarrassed, a blush spreading up her neck into her face. Fellini finally ends it by leaning over and patting her on the hand like a jovial European uncle, assuring her that is has all been a joke, as foolish as their rumored affair.

"La bella Fiona," Fellini says after lunch, on his way back to the studio. "She is fantastic, no? The way she maintains her integrity too." He moves off.

After he is gone, a friend says, "You know, of course, that she plays a whore. The prostitute who was Fellini's first love when he came to Rome. It is his image of her he is in love with."

At six o'clock, the heat starts to drop, shadows stretch from the trees that shade Cinecitta streets. Fellini emerges from the smoky studio into bright sunlight to find a horseshoe line of people with expectant looks on their faces.

A shape up, with Fellini going down the line looking for faces. Workers, fat ladies, hugely fat ladies, young children . . . all Italy on parade for the maestro to choose from. He passes them up, walking quickly, peering, two small blond girls (he nods), an old lady, a lady with a baby.

He completes the circle and says thank you, then climbs quickly into his car and is driven away.

The lucky ones have their names taken and report to work as extras at 18,000 lire a day ($30).

Agency men, paid by the studio to find the extras, move among the people, jotting down the names of the chosen ones.

"Fellini, he sees so many faces maybe he for- gets who he choose," a bystander says, "so they slip one or two in on him. Now the agency men make the people give ten percent of the salary back to them. A kickback. They get paid twice, once by the studio, once by the extras.

"It is no right, eh? Yes, but it is very Italian."

"Today," Fellini told a writer for another mag- azine, "we are finished with the Christian myth. And we await a new one. Maybe the myth is LSD. And the new Christ comes to us in that form." Boldly, he then invited the writer to take some LSD today.

"Hey," Carl, the actor from Rome, told me the last time we spoke. "You know that friend of mine who Fellini was going to take acid with? Yeah, well, he called Fellini all day long the Sunday they were supposed to do it."

"And what happened?" I asked.

"No one answered the phone."

Making Altman's *Nashville*

By Chris Hodenfield

JULY 17, 1975

He was misbehaving in the manner of a street-corner hobo. Rocking back and forth, snapping his fingers. Satan's own grin. He pretended to pop out his eyeball, put it into his mouth and then polish it on his shirt. From the baton-waving motions, you'd of thought he was orchestrating an orgy.

Robert Altman was directing a movie.

We were in a dark nightclub. He stood off to the side of the Panavision camera, elevated, a bearish hulk in tan jeans, old shirt, white beard and fading crinkle of hair. The movie, *Nashville*, was a sprawling *Grand Hotel* epic about Music City, Tennessee, five days in the life of twenty-four deep-fried souls.

And this club, the Exit Inn, was where the local bohemians watched. We all watched. Altman watched with the smooth confidence of a man dangling marionettes.

He watched Geraldine Chaplin at a table, portraying a pompous reporter and a hifalutin groupie wrangling an interview out of two surly singers, Allan Nicholls and Cristina Raines. David Arkin was the chauffeur, Norman, who nursed dreams of fame. Their lines arrived on a wing and a prayer.

The situation looked too casual to be a movie set. The camera was buried in the corner. No boom mikes swung through, because the actors were wired for sound. You couldn't tell the score without an earphone. There stood Altman like an overweight Toscanini. He got an idea. He shouted out: "Drink, Norman!" Arkin, not missing a beat, grew nasty and poured a stiff jolt. The dialogue twisted down side streets. When it ended, Geraldine Chaplin's slender hand flew to her mouth: "That took me com*pletely* by surprise."

Your bystander could see all this clearly. Introduced to Altman just an hour before, I was directed to an empty chair there, just behind the action. My sleeve was in camera range. It grew tense. This is the moment, as George Segal once explained, when Altman asks you: "*How do you like my friends so far?*"

Altman had a few more ideas, which he did not shrink from shouting aloud. In the corner, strangers exchanged glances.

Upon Altman's shoulders rested a heavy "pressure to perform." I was advised that he was volatile, huge and that I should get the interview out of the way fast. He entertained the pressure of twenty-four uncertain actors in a hot Southern town, juggling at least sixteen different plots. That's not counting the off-camera intrigue.

They seemed to be working at the pace of lunar changes. The actors would get maybe two days before the camera, then kill another week of time back in their motel rooms. In all, a splendid opportunity to develop their vices.

It seemed like an encounter group meeting during the last days of Pompeii. I was off the plane a half hour when David Arkin informed me that the last reporter around here got busted in the chops. (The dirty so-and-so called David Arkin "Alan.") David Arkin further said I better appreciate what Altman was trying to do.

All right. We wouldn't want Altman to end up in that trackless purgatory of the "cult director." He is an insider's favorite, an actor's director, a *bankable* director, no matter how lousy he reads the market. Take note. While the market is crying out for dramas concerning forty famous people drowning in an elevator, he makes a movie about Nashville, forty people drowning in . . . their own passions, I don't know. He doesn't know.

Last season, when gambling and buddy-buddy movies were the ticket, he made *California Split*, but quirky and unpretty. It confounded even the executive producers by making money. But he was not yet assured of that in Nashville.

He had only this cult, you see, a label that could pertain to his floating repertory group of actors or the uncertain box-office receipts. His last commercial success was *M*A*S*H* and that was 1970. One of the all-time biggies, it earned $40 million. The running joke goes, however, that it financed his next seven pictures. Even with the exultant reviews and growing attention in all the correct circles, only *McCabe & Mrs. Miller* broke even.

Brewster McCloud, Images, The Long Goodbye, Thieves Like Us—all took a licking. He's also done a few rounds with the big company brass, who get cranky when they don't know how to push the product. They are just noticing that Altman is Noticeable. In a new kind of movie that is more episodic, nonlinear; it's an exploded storytelling sense that goes against the classic grain. Obscure eloquence. The plot thins. He has made all of chaos his province. (This movie-making doesn't have a name yet—and I hate to think of the tag some critic will eventually hang on it. Like, "neosurrealism.")

Movies that jump to mind are *Fat City, Five Easy Pieces, Scarecrow, Payday, Alice Doesn't Live Here Anymore,* the Cassavetes movies. You could go back to *Last Tango in Paris* or *Performance,* and not a dot does Altman mind if you compare *Nashville* to Fellini's *Amarcord.*

"This is written like a piece of music," said *Nashville* scripter Joan Tewkesbury, "where things go out and recur."

Nashville is a sentimental postcard of a town, razzed with gaudy images, string ties and housewife slippers, the earmarks of a distinct culture. Distinct language. Faces. Hollywood is here creating it over again. "Because we're dealing with the country," Altman told his people, "we're dealing with country & western music, we're dealing with a success. It's a place where people get off the bus, like Hollywood was many years ago. The money is generated and there's a crudeness to the culture."

This is the Athens of the South, the town fathers say. Oh, how the town reveres its stars. Stored in the Country Music Museum is the wig that Patsy Cline may have worn during that fatal plane crash. There is a man walking around Nashville who claims to have Hank Williams' last needle locked in Lucite.

Among the people who got off the bus for this movie were Lily Tomlin, Henry Gibson,

Karen Black, Keenan Wynn, Barbara Harris, Keith Carradine, Ned Beatty. Some of the featured roles are the erotic doughnut waitress, the dirt farmer looking for his runaway wife who wants to sing, the groupie in platform shoes, the phantom on the motorcycle, the boardinghouse landlord, the womanizing heel who orchestrates his seduction scenes with his own records, and the black country singer who's *not supposed* to look like Charley Pride, the country queens who *don't* resemble Loretta Lynn and Tammy Wynette, the patriot big daddy *unintentionally* in the Hank Snow drift. Plus the nameless multitudes. Ransacking the entire movie is the ominous third-party presidential campaign of a populist claghorn named Hay Phillip Walker, arousing the political statement and the shock finale. We'd need Tolstoy to outline half the plots, so forget it. It was twenty-four characters in search of a movie.

Conclusive evidence was gathered at the dailies—rush prints of the scenes shot the day before. Very holy atmosphere in this party. Altman shows them each night and it becomes group therapy; nerves-on-edge city. The cast and crew sprawled on folding chairs in a motel banquet room. Faces were aghast and anxious, a row of overcooked cauliflowers.

It was evening. Summer lightning storms dirtied an ashtray sky. Lily Tomlin, making her acting debut, was purposely about to miss seeing one of her scenes.

"Every night you go to the rushes," she said, weary, knowing. "A fraction of it will ever be in the film. But you go to the rushes every night, and then you've got to face them all when the lights go on. Sometimes you're wrong, you think you didn't do too bad and you lose perspective. Or sometimes you watch and you get involved in it and you think *aaaah*."

Lily has an elastic face, a disarming grin that is at once wicked, prankish and conspiratorial. "You're just here with your little ego and your little life," she said. Inside the banquet room, Altman stood in back by the projectors. The lights were doused. The images began.

THE SCENE: The dimly lit Exit Inn. Lily is the small-town preacher's daughter on the periphery of Music City. She sits back against the wooden wall, alone. Up comes Robert Doqui, the black ex-con lately working as a busboy. Sits down next to her. The camera zooms in slowly. One long shot.

Two takes of the scene passed, with nearly the same dialogue, but they were as different as night and day.

Doqui pulls on a beer, says he's been doing time, just been on death row for two years. First-degree murder. It doesn't faze her. She knits her fingers, then quite suddenly jumps off the script and remembers that her mother once owned a matching billfold set that was made by a prisoner. He gets drunker. Says his mother was the only one who loved him. Died last year, but they didn't tell him because they couldn't find him. "What do you mean you couldn't find me, man? I was on death row!"

The first take, that line was very funny. Everyone laughed. Next take, there was a catch in his voice. It had you reaching for your hanky. There was a light rain of clapping hands.

"It's like jazz."

Altman was clearly the grandee, the lodestar of their lives. "He has his image and his legend," said his assistant director, Alan Rudolph, "and some people just don't get beyond that."

It was time to get down to cases. I waited in Altman's trailer for an audience. We were parked on a quiet suburban street one afternoon. Keenan Wynn sat there, too, clawing his stomach, looking like everyone's uncle who ever did time in a pawnshop. "I never drink while I'm working, you know that. Bob gave me this." He rattled the ice in his whiskey glass. "A little hair of the dog, to steady my nerves."

Altman's legend includes tattooing dogs, piloting a B-24 over Borneo and eight years of industrial films in hometown Kansas City. A quickie potboiler script in 1957, called *The Delinquents,* led to a necromentary he both wrote and directed, *The James Dean Story.* Alfred Hitchcock was impressed by that and gave him a shot directing TV mysteries.

He did six years of that, learning "guerrilla warfare," working as fast as bad taste allowed. Two and a half days per show, two shows per week, *Roaring Twenties, Bonanza, Bus Stop, Kraft Theatre, Whirlybirds,* and he never read the scripts. Each show was his version of a classic— say, duplicating *Foreign Correspondent.* Television is where he learned to fight dirty, and he remembers making a blatantly erotic episode of *The Millionaire.*

He made a million; he spent two.

For his below-decks ways, he got fired with regularity. Jack Warner sacked him after his feature *Countdown,* in 1968, because of overlapping dialogue. The critics still call him on his densely packed soundtracks; everybody speaking at once. Like people do.

He's getting the last word. He's been using an eight-track recording unit to squeeze in even *more* dialogue. With all the Nashville characters and music, he had it beefed to sixteen tracks.

Altman climbed aboard the trailer with a tray of catered food. He jostled around to his cramped table, and through mouthfuls of burrito he fielded questions:

"It's like jazz. You're not planning any of this that you film. You're capturing. You can't even hope to see it; you just turn on the camera and hope to capture it. There's a structure, but you

do what you do . . . you give the actors the basis to work around and they fill it in."

He has a flat Kansas voice that promises blarney. The jovial head looms like a capitol dome, flickering cheeks and long hands. Doctor's hands. Aquamarine eyes.

"It's almost like painting. You start out with a set idea of what you want; there's an empty space there on your canvas. Then you fill it in and it all changes. Painting, you start out being very specific and then one day you're set free. You get lucky.

"Sometimes I look at a scene afterwards and see that I missed entirely what I wanted, but that I got something much better instead. And people talk about scenes in my films that aren't even there. Which is fine, you know. Penelope Gilliatt [*New Yorker* critic] saw *Split* twice and then asked to see the script. In the script she read a scene that was cut out of the movie, but she was so sure she saw that particular scene in the movie. Well, that's great, because it was that real for her." He tore into his salad.

What about this quote of yours that a "great film has never been made"?

"By that I mean in terms of potential. I don't think we've found a format for movies yet. I think we're still imitating literature and theater. I don't believe film should be limited to photographing people talking. Or walking from a car into a building, the kind of stuff we do. It can be much more abstract, impressionistic, less linear. What we were talking about before, about painting. Music changes form all the time. I think if you just establish a *mood* with a film, it might have more impact than anything we've done, just a *mood.* . . ."

When did you recognize the patterns?

"I don't think it will go recognized at first. Like any other achievement. I don't think I ever articulated it. That's why I'm not doing it. One of the drawbacks of film is that it's linear."

Movies are linear?

"Sure, it's always two hours, twelve minutes long, however."

But it can be a long or short two hours.

"Well, that's your salvation. That's why you're always changing time for people, with flashbacks and so forth. So does a book, too, I guess. *M*A*S*H* had no plot, really. And *Split* was just a mood thing on gambling. And this movie doesn't have any scenes as such; we just set up situations and let people pass through them."

A documentary?

"Right. Just a feeling. It's as if we're setting events and filming them in a documentary fashion, but most of the dialogue . . . well, I don't even listen to it. Sometimes I'll listen in the headsets to see if the sound level is right, but as I get confident in what the actors are doing, I don't even listen to it. I find that actors know more about the characters they're playing than I do. When you're shooting this kind of material, what difference does it make what anybody says?"

I replied that a lot of people can't hear what's said in some of his movies. His eyes jerked up like fishhooks.

"Who said that?"

It's around.

"Yeah, but for every person that says that, there's three people who just flip over the sound. That's always going to happen, that's just education of the audience.

"I'll say I heard that more during *McCabe & Mrs. Miller,* the not being able to understand the soundtrack. Part of the reason for getting the sixteen-track sound unit was to solve that sound problem. But I'm not going to change my technique because three people said, 'Oh, shit, I couldn't hear every word.' Because it's not designed to hear every word."

From a capsule around his neck he extracted a gold toothpick and stuck it in his teeth.

"I think the worst thing you can say about a film is, 'Oh, I've seen it.' That's what the old American movie was, you've seen it once and that's it. We try to distill it, so that I see things later that I didn't see at first. Things I didn't know the actors were doing. . . .

"Actors? Well, I like most actors. I'm just in awe of Geraldine Chaplin now; I can't wait to find a good vehicle for her. What she does, it's what a comedian does, isn't it?"

I recollected a stoned, obnoxious interview months ago with his three-time star, Elliott Gould.

"Listen, if you've been treated by the press the way he's been treated, you might be obnoxious, too. I get along with him famously, I find. I think he's trying foolishly to be a totally honest person, and he'll be destroyed by it, if he ever achieves it. I think as a performer he is extraordinary. His sense of himself and what he can do . . . and I know he makes a lot of people nervous. He's hard to understand because he doesn't go through all the usual bullshit we all go through with one another. He cuts through and consequently that's threatening to people."

Robert Blake once said you have to approach Gould as if he's the first person you've ever met. . . .

"Well, Robert Blake is a prick, and I find him totally obnoxious. I don't like him at all. Blake is the kind of actor I don't like. I think he's arrogant, selfish. I don't like his work. I don't like George C. Scott, either. I think he's a lousy actor. He's just a caricature of himself. He's skillful and all, but I don't believe all that."

Didn't you once write magazine articles?

"I have . . . and some short stories that were

never published. I once wrote continuity for a radio recipe program. I'd look up a recipe and write out a script for, uh, Dick Smith and Mary Marbles, somebody. 'What have you got for the folks today, Mary?' 'Well, Dick, I was thinking about meat loaf.' 'Oh, that's my favorite because I love meat-loaf sandwiches.' "

When the laughter stopped, he winked and stuck his gold toothpick back in the case.

He really is a general. He's got his lieutenants out there and why pull punches? He's a general. He has to be.
—George Segal, another place

He's no general. Oh, he looks like one, but inside he's just a baby. Like the Wizard of Oz.
—Elliott Gould, another time

Perhaps the real reason behind Altman's popularity among actors is that he trusts them with their brains. Because the actor lives for the all-powerful, all-transcendent Moment . . . *Call off your dogs, warden!*

"What I'm looking for, instead of actors," he said, "is behaviors, somebody who will bring me more."

Given the freedom to develop their own characters, some actors go conservative, some blossom into cartoons, some wear their hearts on their sleeves.

It's said that director Mark Rydell *(Cinderella Liberty)* played a part in Altman's *The Long Goodbye* just to discover Altman's technique. I mean, how exactly could Altman persuade twenty-four actors to work out here for the measly $1,000 a week, or less. (Chicken feed, sir, when you consider the costs of managers, agents, accountants, lawyers, L.A. rentals and long-distance calls to Poopsie.)

The director/actor relationship has been likened to the shrink/patient bond. Olivia de Havilland once called the director/actress link "the most intimate kind of collaboration . . . sexual without being physiological." In Nashville, Barbara Harris compared Altman to a porno book she bought for him the other day: *Doctor on Roller Skates.*

Out here, the principals not only write up their own characters but their own songs as well. Which is most unusual, considering that some hadn't even sung in the shower before this movie. So what if Lily Tomlin has the vocal timbre of a pencil sharpener? It was a Moment.

Screen playwright Joan Tewkesbury originally plotted the movie on a wall-sized chart. They had ninety-four characters. The staff locked themselves in a room one night and battered these back into twenty-four solid pieces that fit together with the precision of a cloud formation.

The prospect of twenty-four actors/writers would normally be grounds for the scriptwriter's suicide, but Tewkesbury was something of a mother adviser here. (Much laughed about is the case of Ring Lardner Jr., who reviled Altman bitterly over the butchering of his *M*A*S*H* script. Then he won the Oscar for Best Screenplay.)

Altman's big dream is a movie of *La Belle Epoque,* all the characters living in their costumes, packed off together in a big country house. . . . *Nashville* was close enough, and spending one week among these people was like swimming in a river of Moments.

• Allan Nicholls portrays a singer whose wife is cheating on him. A jovial guy, he never gave the betrayal much thought outside of their scenes together. Then one night at the dailies, he saw the scene of his movie wife, Cristina Raines, in bed with the movie Don Juan, Keith Carradine. Right there on the screen. "I been shit on!" he nearly screamed. He couldn't get it out of his mind for three days, unable to speak.

• Karen Black . . . well, you can shake hands with Karen Black or you can sink your fist in a bowl of warm tapioca. What's the diff? She has the eyes of a mystic and a fine, pillowy smile. "I flew into Nashville and Richard Baskin [musical director] met me at the airport. And as we drove back to the motel, he said I was to sing the next day for five thousand people." Karen smiled graciously.

"At the Grand Ole Opry." Karen buried her head in the pillow. "So you go out to Bob's place and everybody's smoking dope. Even though I don't smoke, I thought it was amusing. Like, they'd be in a restaurant and the black waiter would shut the door and smoke. I thought it was funny.

"Bob is . . . well, I have this routine which I call A Chicken Vomiting. Now you ask anybody, 'Do you want to see a chicken vomiting?' and they'll say, 'Sure, kid.' But Bob said, 'Okay, let me see it.' Just calm and normal. He really wanted to see it.

"So you're in Bob's room and everybody's wrecked, and Bob's cooking for everybody. Then he decided we should sing, so we did. And this incredible guitarist came up with all these blues chords and we just sang every blues song that was ever written. All night long." A dreamy look stole upon her face.

• Ronee Blakley was found as a last-minute replacement for Susan Anspach to play the country Camille. Already an established folk/blues singer, her last acting job was long ago in a high school play. And she damn near finished off the movie, a fragile country queen seized onstage by inner demons, trembling like the underside of a leaf in a windstorm. The script called for her to faint. Altman said, "Well, you've fainted once already, this time just go catatonic."

But she had other ideas and wrote up a monologue for a crack-up. Days after the scene was shot, she was still visibly upset. "That speech," her brother Steve laughed and revealed, "I could tell you stories about that speech. And where it all came from." Ronee pushed him gently and turned away with an embarrassed smile.

HOW TO WRITE A SCRIPT

The Scene: Bill and Mary are slowly killing each other. It is the morning after, here in the King of the Road Hotel. The room looks like any hotel room destroyed by musicians. As it happens, they are married and two-thirds of a singing trio. She's unfaithful, he's competitive.

Pan back from the twelfth-floor view. . . . She is buried asleep. He is in the next bed, idly stitching his guitar, his cigarette jammed into the tuning knobs. "C'mon wake up, will ya?" She sleeps. "You wanna talk about it now?" He sees the balloon hanging there, swings his guitar neck so the glowing butt pops the balloon. She wheels out of the covers, spits, "Fucker," at him, clomps over his bed, splashing his breakfast tray.

"Terrific!" says Altman. Zooming back, there stood Altman waltzing by the Panavision, watching Raines and Nicholls. "That balloon thing was terrific." It was new on him. "Are there more balloons so we can do another take on that?" No. Messengers were dispatched. "And get some blue ones."

Waiting for the balloons, he prepared the twosome for their fight scene. "Now, the situation is this. Tina, why don't you go into the bathroom and, Allan, you're banging on the door. You know: 'Get the hell outta there!' And then Tina, you come out here and take your things out of the drawer. Does that drawer come all the way out?"

Altman yanked the drawer out of the chest. "Yeah, good. Why don't you dump all the clothes on the floor there. And here, then hand him his turtle."

Privately he warned her not to call Nicholls a "fucker," because he was looking for a PG rating here. For once.

The zoom lens is his voyeur's trick. "The zoom is a great help when dealing with actors," he has said. "You can't lie to them or even fool them; that's why I let them watch the rushes. But with a zoom, no one was quite sure what was happening. I could get a tight close-up from one hundred feet away."

"He shoots film like he sees life," Alan Rudolph would rapture, "tucked away in the corner, seeing everything, picking up all the intimate details. Karen Black said she's never worked with a camera like this before, when she didn't know what was being picked up. Usually the camera is the star of the set."

Altman retired to work on a crossword puzzle. His aides collaborated as intensely as if it were the next script. In the next room, Michael Murphy paced the floor, repeating his lines on silent lips. You see, he rewrote all his lines the night before. Now he was memorizing them . . . *in case all else fails.*

That afternoon I had coffee with Keith Carradine, whose T-shirt front reads SON OF CARRADINE, whose back says BROTHER OF KUNG-FU. He said: "This has been a little disconcerting to me some of the time. It's strange, in that working with the typical director in the normal way, when you get near the end of the scene, you realize if you've forgotten any lines. You know exactly what you've done. But in improvisation, you get near the end of a scene and you can't remember anything you've done. It's like life, you don't remember exactly. It's like sitting in a restaurant with somebody." He toasted his coffee cup toward the bystander, who remembered it all exactly.

Nashville ends in an assassination. The bystander began to think of this tragicomedy as *M*A*S*Hville.* Frankly, the presenting of the climactic in-concert murder seemed hugely immoral. Some of the actors who'd spent their lives on stages, they had their private misgivings.

These dark thoughts were stewing in my mind one night while watching the evening news, motel-room edition. Some solace. There was South Korean president Park and his wife getting ambushed by assassins. The news cameras recorded the event in chaos.

The next morning, riding to the set in his van, Altman was very chipper. He wore a fine smile. He asked his group of aides: "Did you see Park's wife on the news last night? Hm? I know just how I'm going to shoot that final scene now, I know just how to do it. Park was speaking at a podium when the shots went off. He ducked and she got hit. Yeah, oh, they carried her out with her feet up, the whole thing. But the guys filming it, they zoomed in . . . and then back, and pointed here and there and all over. 'There's a shooting!' 'Where?' The whole place was in absolute pandemonium. That's just how to shoot a scene."

He beamed. "That makes three live-on-film assassinations that I know of."

We talked about televised death until we arrived at the set. A cemetery.

CODA

The movie was structured like an artichoke. An eight-hour artichoke, because Altman took that much movie back to Los Angeles, back to the editing tables in his colonial office spread, Lion's Gate Films. There, all the king's men spent their days hacking, stuffing, dicing, marinating the eight hours of film until it was in rough continuity.

When he had an hour's worth that looked presentable, he'd call his fellow travelers over for a look-see. He'd say: "This will be the greatest hour of film you will ever have seen in your life."

And why not? Nothing has been normal up to now, why not communal editing? The actors and pals dropped by and got ripped and deeply spiritual and they watched the movie. When Altman sensed a restlessness in the crowd, he cut. As Tewkesbury said, it's a shame when egos get stepped on.

It made Altman feel good. He was not so thin-skinned. He'd even lost weight. He had deals cooking. For the upcoming *Buffalo Bill and the Indians,* with Paul Newman, everyone had their noses in an Indian-lore book. Some critics who had despised him were suddenly wise. Money that wasn't there suddenly was. And people wheeled through the doors all day with scripts under their arms, looking for Uncle Bob's advice, and upstairs two ex–Hell's Angels labored as carpenters and the Lord said that it was good.

It made Altman feel good. *California Split,* which he once called "just a mood thing on gambling," was suddenly "just practice for *Nashville.*" The $4 million at the box office was just gravy.

The month went by, the parties continued, the movie divided into *Nashville-Red* and *Nashville-Blue,* and then into one movie. Maybe some egos were by that time boiled in oil. Several good movies lay on the cutting-room floor.

The last time I saw Altman he was wearing a navy blue suit, at a Washington, D.C., premiere where he shook hands with George McGovern, Sargent Shriver, Ron Nesson, the rest.

In front of me sat a young guy with the overbite of famous royalty. Michael Kennedy, son of RFK, his face hidden with a curtain of hair, he kept still through the movie's mention of "the Kennedy boys."

But came the death, the following queasiness, the personal resolution in horror—Kennedy's face was damp, bleached white. He left quickly.

George and Eleanor McGovern walked into the night. He'd had a rugged day and the picture moved him to desolation.

"I can't say it left me in high spirits. It had that combination of tragedy and comedy which characterizes both good drama and the poignant condition of our lives in the seventies."

He thought about it. "It looked into the soul of the country and it ended without any answers."

Inside the *Cuckoo's Nest*

By Tim Cahill

DECEMBER 4, 1975

Jack Nicholson was thinking about very special chickens—specifically those deadly flying hens, reeking with venom: the kind that will bury their beaks in your belly as you sleep, the ones that cackle in dark closets and lurk like vultures just beyond the transom. More properly, Jack Nicholson was thinking about people who are obsessively concerned with such chickens. "People who see chickens," he concluded, "don't belong in places like this."

It was just before Christmas of 1974, and Nicholson was in his second week of researching his role of Randle Patrick McMurphy for the upcoming filming of Ken Kesey's classic *One Flew Over the Cuckoo's Nest*. It was 6:00 A.M.—an hour to go until dawn—and Nicholson, a nurse, a doctor and a technician were tiptoeing down a long, drab hallway on the third floor of the Oregon State Hospital. The technician was pushing a small machine that rolled silently on four rubber wheels. A long electric cord was coiled on top of the machine.

Every few feet there was another barred door and, above, a heavily wired transom. The four were as quiet as possible. Behind the doors slept the most certifiable deranged individuals in the state. No reason to wake them unnecessarily,

perhaps stir them to anger at the sight of the machine.

Nicholson considered himself a reasonably conversant parlor psychiatrist. He had read Frances Farmer's *Will There Really Be a Morning*, a horrifying account of one actress's battle with insanity, had dipped into Freud and Jung, occasionally paged through an issue of *Psychology Today*. A decade ago he had read *One Flew Over the Cuckoo's Nest*, never dreaming that he would one day play the lead in the movie version of that book, never dreaming he would see what he was queasily about to see.

Prior to his research in Oregon, Nicholson had been convinced that the term *insanity* was archaic. He associated it with people who saw chickens. But the patients he met in the OSH wards seldom saw chickens, and their behavior seemed to Nicholson no more loony than that of an average weekday shopper in Salem's Pay Less department store. The problem was that a few of these people had been involved in crimes of extreme violence and cruelty. One friendly fellow had inflicted twenty stab wounds on a person he had never met before. A gentle, dignified, older man had committed rape twice, and the rapes involved mutilation and maiming. One spindly, prematurely gray man discussed bombs in the same leering, lustful tone that another man might use to describe a sexual conquest.

This last broke Nicholson. He was living in a rented house in Salem, getting up before dawn every morning and plodding off to the hospital in a dank fog. After twelve to fourteen hours of talking with patients and doctors and aides, he plodded back home in what seemed to him to be arctic desolation. Winter in Salem, Oregon, can add several hundred pounds of bad psychic baggage to the soul of a Southern Californian like Jack Nicholson. There is a constant chill fog, and the sun, at high noon, could possibly be that faint glimmer behind the brightest cloud bank. It is like living inside an Edgar Allan Poe poem, minus twenty degrees centigrade.

Further, something about Salem failed to lend itself to after-dark socializing. By state law, all Oregon institutions must be located in Marion County—which in practice means Salem, which is also the state capital. The town is overladen with cons and ex-cons, with social workers and therapists and hardship cases, with psychiatrists and mental patients and ex–mental patients and politicians. The cliché, of course, is that it is impossible to tell one from the other.

There are a number of bars in Salem, but Nicholson is not much of a drinker. He imagines that he is amusing after four or five stiff ones. After that, he says, he is likely to wake up in his garage with half his entrails on his chest, the taste of soiled sweat socks in his mouth and two tiny men playing bass drums just behind either eyeball. Nicholson much prefers to light up, mellow back and listen to music. Compatible company—of either sex—for Nicholson was not to be found.

So he went home alone, to an empty house, and brooded about what he was learning. The gray and gawky young man who loved bombs

had constructed, of discarded electronics parts, a cigar-box electroshock machine. One morning before dawn he had strolled through his ward, shocking his fellow patients into a sudden, startled wakefulness. It seemed perfectly obvious to Nicholson that a man capable of building such a machine would also be capable of building one of his beloved bombs. This young man was slated for release very soon: some kind of state law. Nicholson, despite himself, didn't think the young man was ready; he imagined him back within a month, likely leaving destruction and possibly death behind him.

The truly mad and violent ones they ought to keep locked up forever, Nicholson found himself thinking. He did not much admire himself for these thoughts, and the first level of depression settled in like a bitter winter fog. Wasn't he the man who made his fortune playing alienated losers? Shouldn't his most natural sympathy lie with the patients? Nicholson is deeply concerned with justice: He will tell you that Charlie Manson was railroaded and that the total evidence against him was one fingerprint and the testimony of someone involved who got total immunity. He will also tell you that he slept with a hammer under his pillow for weeks after the Tate-LaBianca slayings—that he would be bullshitting himself to pretend he didn't fear that kind of murderous irrationality.

Nicholson worried about what he identified as a personal twinge of self-righteous injustice. If you could deny due process to the gray and gawky man who saw bombs instead of chickens, or possibly to Charlie Manson, wasn't it possible that you could be the kind of man who would one day find himself in some howling lynch mob?

The first depression had to do with fundamental values and induced a kind of migraine circular reasoning. The second depression was philosophical, emotional. It had to do with the machine and the long electric cord.

On the bleak February morning when I first visited the *Cuckoo's Nest* set, I noticed a certain coiling of the intestines as we approached the hospital.

There was an early-morning fog swirling about the three-story, solid-brick structure; all the surrounding trees were gnarled and bare. Thunderheads were massing for another storm. The place would have looked just fine with lightning bolts churning madly on all sides and with huge bats spewing out of nonexistent turrets.

Driving the car was a jovial publicity man who described how coproducers Michael Douglas and Saul Zaentz held a New Year's Eve party for the inmates when these supposedly hard-eyed movie folks could have been out swiving starlets, or whatever it is they do on their off time.

The publicist allowed that a running joke had started among cast and crew that they weren't going to be released after the filming had been completed. We approached the back door to the hospital, where the fog was scuttling among the overstuffed garbage cans.

As it happened, no one was at the door, and presently we were walking down a long hallway, fifteen feet wide, institutional-green hallways on either side—some unhealthy bursts of déjà vu here—our footsteps echoing off the aged linoleum floor. I am not ordinarily given to phrases like *bad vibes,* but I tell you, in those hallways, one can feel the palpable presence.

We passed through a door into a bleak game room where strange men shot pool in their pajamas. Intent as loons, they were, on thumping the little balls into holes only slightly larger. An old man with an unruly shock of white hair watched dully, and a tall man with no hair or fingernails wandered about aimlessly. An attendant in a starched white coat kept a wary eye on the game. These men, as it turned out, were not patients at all but actors enjoying themselves during a break in the filming. The attendant was a patient in costume; he plays an attendant in the film.

The publicist hustled me off to a room that had been converted into an office and introduced me to Michael Douglas, the son of Kirk Douglas, costar of the highly rated TV series *Streets of San Francisco* and coproducer of the *Cuckoo's Nest* film. Casually dressed in jeans and light jacket, Douglas seemed young and vulnerable, not at all your basic cigar-chomping producer. Over coffee, he recounted *Cuckoo's Nest*'s snafu-plagued thirteen-year history as a property.

Kirk Douglas had purchased stage and screen rights in 1962, when the book was still in galleys. He hired playwright Dale Wasserman to adapt it for the stage. The play ran on Broadway in the fall of 1963. Kirk Douglas himself played McMurphy. Reviews were mixed, and the play ran only about six months. The play became a "property" at one major studio, then another. The wrong people kept being fired or demoted at those studios, and a film never developed. Meanwhile, Dale Wasserman sued the elder Douglas over rights to the screenplay and lost. A subsequent appeal, which failed, kept *Cuckoo's Nest* in legal limbo until 1966.

Douglas again tried to launch a movie version of the book and again failed. "By 1970," said Michael Douglas, "he was getting discouraged and thinking of selling the screen rights. The book was showing up on college reading lists and the play was being revived on both coasts with great success. He got some serious offers.

"I had read the book several times, and I loved it. I said to my father, 'Why don't you let me take it over, and I promise that I'll at least make your original investment back for you.' That was in 1970.

"C'mon, let me show you the set." Off we went, down another long hallway, our footsteps echoing off the walls like *Last Year at Marienbad*, except that it was all in living color and the fluorescent light, glaring off of the drab greenness, gave our faces a sickly complected cast the color of rotting limes. The set was a reconstructed ward, circa 1962, but the walls had been painted a warm off-white, and the ceiling had been lowered and covered over with an acoustic tile that killed the omnipresent echo. It was by far the most pleasant place in the hospital.

"We could have left it that awful stark green," Douglas said, "but I think it would have hurt. There are some scenes of high comedy in the film. Christ, I remember spending years trying to raise the money for this. I was talking to people who had never read the book and trying to describe how funny it was, and when I finished, they'd ask me, 'So how come you want to make another *Snake Pit?*'"

(In defense of movie producers everywhere, let it be said they are extremely busy people who must often get up quite early in the morning, make dozens of phone calls a day and be prepared to fly off to the French Riviera at a moment's notice. They don't have time to read books. They read "treatments," which are at best a few pages long. Writers Joan Didion and John Gregory Dunne came up with a classic money-raising—albeit tongue-in-cheek—single-sentence treatment for *The Panic in Needle Park:* Romeo and Juliet on junk.)

In 1971, Michael Douglas connected with Saul Zaentz, chairman of Fantasy Records, which by then was taking a serious interest in films. After watching an unreleased two-and-a-half-hour cut of *The Last Detail,* the coproducers settled on Jack Nicholson as their McMurphy. Czechoslovakian-born Milos Forman was the odd, inspired choice for director. His films out of Prague in the sixties—*Black Peter, Loves of a Blonde, The Fireman's Ball*—were lovely, funny, unstructured tales about ordinary people. Although most of the actors in those films were nonprofessionals, many of the scenes were totally improvised. His American debut, *Taking Off,* an amusing but slightly off-the-mark film about the generation gap, followed the same pattern.

"We wanted Forman," Douglas said, "because he is a realistic and a funny director. We knew we needed someone who could handle the comedy. He has a very delicate eye: a great ability to go from humor to pathos, sometimes in the same frame. He's been living in the States long enough to understand the peculiarly American aspects of the book, but he still has that profound Central European sensibility." Douglas and I tried to define exactly what that sensibility was, deciding finally that it had something to do with a fear of institutions so minutely refined that the fear itself becomes an object of the blackest humor.

Casting, says Milos Forman, is 50 percent of a film. He and Michael Douglas scrutinized more than nine hundred actors for sixteen roles, excluding McMurphy and Chief Broom. The actors were narrowed down into a series of what amounted to therapy groups and were asked to improvise against someone reading Nurse Ratched's lines. They did not always pick the best actors; they think they picked the right actors. Forman was greatly encouraged in this belief when a flustered geriatrics nurse tried to quickly process four of the older choices so they wouldn't be standing around aimlessly when the professional actors arrived.

After casting, Forman spent six weeks living at the hospital, working on the final script and doing research. "The research is important. We have funny ideas about how people in mental institutions act. We think of drooling and people going booga-booga and climbing the wall. These are exceptional cases. It's like playing alcoholics. Only naive actors play drunkenness with—blah—big sloppy gestures. Real alcoholics are desperately trying to act sober. It is the same with mentally disturbed people. They are basically normal except for one thing, which may not show up for weeks or may be so subtle you can hardly notice it."

Forman, according to Jack Nitzche, who will be doing the music for the film, even stumbled onto a "perfect McMurphy" during his research. The patient was young, contemptuous of authority and full of life. He wore a black leather jacket on the wards and had one of those macho-jocky senses of humor. Forman watched him with interest.

One morning, in one of the upstairs wards, an aide came upon a grisly sight. Lying on a bed in one of those barred rooms was the corpse of a feeble old man. He had been murdered and the blood on the wall attested to the brutality of the slaying. It was said that the killer was Forman's "perfect McMurphy." He explained that the old man was in pain and wanted to die.

Records at OSH show that the story cannot be true. The last murder of one patient by another occurred over five years ago. The fact that the story was widely repeated among the crew probably has more to do with the vertiginous effect of the institution on the minds of sane folks than with behavior of the patients. "It sounds assholish, I know," said William Redfield, who plays the patient Harding in the film,

"but you become used to these constant tragic stories. You know what bothers me most? It's the echo in the game room. Your voice gets lost in the rumbling babble and you keep catching disjointed comments and phrases that don't seem to make any sense. You get disoriented and start thinking that there are men two floors above you playing the same games, probably talking about the same things. You wonder about yourself.

"Forman," said Redfield, "is very good with improvisation. I'd guess that 20 to 30 percent of what you eventually see on the screen will be pure improvisation. He knows the magic thing—which is achieving the effect that it is really happening to you, happening for the first time.

"Surprise is probably the most difficult emotion to play. I remember at one point McMurphy has hidden his medication in his mouth. I tell him he can get in trouble for that, and he spits it right in my face. Well, that's in the script. I know it. Jack knows it. And it has to happen on cue. Luckily we've both been around long enough to know we're in trouble here. So he did everything possible to fool me: not only where he spat it, but when and how. Out of the seven takes there was one time he got me. I was totally surprised. And that was it, the magic moment."

The least improvisatory role is that of Nurse Ratched, played by Louise Fletcher, last seen in *Thieves Like Us*. Ratched is the straight woman, and she has been played as a bitter, intractable tyrant in most of the stage versions. "I play her differently," Fletcher said. "She smiles and greets the patients and really believes her methods are good ones." Forman has cursed her with a 1945 hairdo for a film set in 1962. He says this is because she is a woman who stopped relating to people in the mid-forties.

"In thinking out this role of Nurse Ratched," Fletcher said, "I have drawn on a very rich background. That's a pun, because there is a specific person in my past—not my mother—who, in my childhood, used to give me and my brother and my sister an enema every Saturday night. It hurt, a lot. But she told us it was for our own good, and we accepted it as something everybody did. It wasn't until I was seven or eight—old enough to compare notes with my friends—that I realized everybody didn't get an enema on Saturday night. She was so sure of herself, you see, that she convinced us that this painful, humiliating thing was perfectly normal. She was a lovely woman, and we kids thought the world of her. But I've always remembered that: the indignity of it and the well-meaning, distorted thinking that went into it."

When I talked to Forman on the *Cuckoo's Nest* set in February, I noticed an anthology of Kafka novels on his table. "In Czechoslovakia," Forman said, "we consider Kafka a very funny man. A humorist. I first realized that Americans think differently when I saw Orson Welles' *The Trial.* I think one of the reasons it didn't come across is that he made it a deadly serious film. And if you read the book, it is very, very funny. There is nothing you can do with such awful absurdity but laugh.

"You ask me, is McMurphy crazy? I don't want to know this. Is he a hero? I don't know this either. A modern hero is very ambiguous. I went through some very rough times in Czechoslovakia—the occupation by the Germans at the end of the war. We had people going against their tanks with brooms. Are they nuts or are they heroes? Because when you see it, you say, 'This man is insane.' When it's over, you yourself—who wouldn't go—you call him a hero."

Have I yet suggested that the effect of a winter's day in Salem can best be experienced by wrapping oneself in thirty pounds of wet blankets and standing inside of a meat locker for twenty-four hours? Even on the outside set—the scene of a basketball game between the *Cuckoo* patients and aides—the crew has set up enough lights and reflectors for standard twilight shooting. This at high noon. Rain threatened.

The master shots of the game are in the can. Today the actors playing "chronics" will be shot reacting to the contest. During the bulk of the shooting these men have been asked to act bored—no great task—wander around aimlessly, or stare at the wall in an interesting manner. This is their improvisatory day before the camera, and there is a feeling of pleased anticipation under glowering skies.

A young man in orange slacks and a lime-colored sweater, his arm in a sling, hovered about on the periphery of the set. He smiled easily but his eyes were set in a contradictory and fearful frown. It was his first day downstairs since the unfortunate incident on eighty-three, the men's medium-security ward. The crew had been filming some scenes on that third-floor ward and had strung the needed electric cables through an unlatched window. A technician blames himself for what happened. Joking with the patients—nice guys, stable fellows, don't belong here, the technician thought—he had said something like, "Boy, if I was nuts, I'd go right out that window."

Moments later there was some shouting, a powerful thud and a groan of pain. The leaper had gone out the window and was making his run for freedom, listing a bit to one side. Two of the patients working with the crew ran him down and took him off to the hospital medical facility. He had broken his collarbone.

"Hey, how are you," Michael Douglas said to the leaper. "Welcome back."

"Are you mad with me?" the leaper asked.

"Shit no. I thought you might be mad at us."

The leaper seemed not to have considered this possibility. "You know, you made the papers," Douglas said. The headline read ONE FLEW OUT OF THE CUCKOO'S NEST.

The leaper raised his right fist to his temple in a gesture of pained amusement. "I didn't fly. Who can fly? I tried to slide down the cable, but I couldn't hold on."

"I know," Douglas said. "But why did you slide down the cable in the first place? I mean, you had ground privileges. Why didn't you just walk down the stairs?"

"Well . . ." The leaper looked to the Lord for an appropriate answer. "I wanted to go home," he said. Time passed while the leaper seemed to meditate his own answer. Suddenly he shrugged and broke into a bright, helpless grin. "I was emotionally disturbed," he said.

Incidents like those of the leaper—especially in the state capital—might easily have ended the film then and there. A pious state assemblyman, for instance, might take the time to read the book, then make an issue out of "dirty words being filmed in our state institutions."

Cuckoo's Nest, as a screen property, has been buffeted by controversy. Ken Kesey wrote the first screenplay for the production. Rumors about Fantasy Records had it that Kesey—true to the book—had kept Chief Broom as narrator. The producers, along with Forman and later Nicholson, felt that the Indian's introspective interior monologues in voice-over would weigh the film down and interfere with the objective reality of what was happening. Lawrence Hauben and Bo Goldman collaborated on the final script, and the Kesey effort was rejected. At press time, Kesey, claiming that his creative efforts were being exploited without proper remuneration, was threatening a boycott-*Cuckoo* movement. In reply, Saul Zaentz said that Kesey was paid $10,000 plus expenses for the rejected screenplay and that Kesey would receive 2.5 percent of the net on the film.

"You know," Michael Douglas told me on the outside set in February, "we cast the crew as carefully as the actors. We knew we were going to be cooped up here for a long time, and we wanted to be sure everyone got along with everyone else." There was, however, one major conflict. Within the first month of filming, it became apparent that director Forman and cinematographer Haskell Wexler differed significantly on a number of major points. Talk on the set had it that Wexler was pushing for a more organized approach, for a more moody feel with greater emphasis on framing the shots. Forman preferred to flow more loosely, to trust more to improvisation and inspiration. Whatever the reasons, Douglas and Zaentz were forced to fire Wexler. Bill Butler took over the cinematography, as he did on *The Conversation* when Wexler was fired from that film.

"Firing Haskell," said Douglas, "was one of the most difficult things I've ever done. He's a strong, intelligent man who has directed before. It wasn't a reflection on his talent, nor even his concept. It just wasn't our concept. We had to go with Milos. He has the eye we wanted."

An assistant director called for quiet on the set, and Forman took a position behind the cameras. Behind him, two stand-ins played a full-court, one-on-one basketball game. Dwight Marfield, the first of the chronics, danced a delightful jig of anticipation, his eyes following the ball downcourt, upcourt and . . . two points for the patients. Marfield, a mime, fluttered about in helpless ecstasy. The entire set erupted into spontaneous applause, and they were joined by patients at the windows of wards eighty-three and eighty-four.

The mood, suddenly, was one of wondrous good cheer. After each of the chronics' performances—Peter Brocco in his wheelchair raving on about my bully boys taking the fort—there was more laughter and applause. Forman once or twice literally doubled over with laughter. For the first time that day, my intestines stopped tying themselves into knots. Someone even claimed to have seen the sun.

December 1974. The new man on ward eighty-four noticed that his hands were shaking ever so slightly as he stood at the urinal. A dozen other men, some still woozy from yesterday's medication, padded about the communal bathroom, relieving bladders and bowels, preparatory to another gray day in the hospital's "penitentiary standard" ward. No one spoke to the new fish, which was just fine with Jack Nicholson.

His immediate plan was to zip up quickly and get back out by the main door where two sleepy attendants would be able to pull him out of the middle of any unexpected outbreak of violent lunacy. Ward eighty-four, with its double-barred doors and barred and wired windows, housed the most dangerous mentally ill men in the state of Oregon.

Nicholson considered the muscular black fellow at the next urinal. For all he knew, the man could be a convicted ax murderer—they have their share in the rural areas of Oregon—at OSH for a few years of therapy before serving a life term of straight time. On the other hand, the guy could be in for dining and dashing, then being seriously goofy at the point of arrest. Nicholson threaded his way out of the bathroom—careful not to accidentally bump someone—and made his way to the bench opposite the attendants. Letting himself get surrounded

in that bathroom, out of sight of the attendants, had not been one of the very brightest moves of his life.

Watching ward eighty-four gather out in the sitting room, Nicholson was struck once again by a curious anomaly: These supposedly dangerous men seem considerably less confused than some of the really loopy people in the minimum-security wards, especially geriatrics. There was something peculiarly unsettling about that observation.

More unsettling had been the effect of the electroshock machine on the fat man two hours earlier. The patient had been asleep, loose-lidded, Nicholson concluded, from yesterday's medication. As the nurse brought him conscious, the doctor poked about in the suet with his needle. He missed once, twice, then found the vein. The powerful muscle relaxant hit in about ten seconds: The fat man jellied visibly. Nicholson watched as they fitted him with a device that looked like an aviator's headphone, except that one part came up under the jaw and another fitted over the areas near the temple.

The doctor nodded, and the technician readied the machine for the single prescribed jolt. Nicholson tensed. A week earlier he had asked the administration if he could see a lobotomy patient, but they had none to show him. At the time, he had assumed that the same would be true of electroshock—that it was a punishment more than a treatment and that it had gone the way of other bedlamite relics.

Not so, he had learned. By Oregon law, electroshock may not be administered unless the patient gives his "express and informed consent." This right may be denied by the director of the hospital after consultation with and approval of an independent examining physician. Electroshock, though used sparingly, is considered "a good therapeutic modality" at OSH.

This is where Nicholson sank into the second level of depression. Before his research, he had been willing to consider electroshock one of the great manifestations of psychic evil. A film that depicted such treatments, he assumed, could conceivably be guilty of a kind of celluloid yellow journalism. And yet he could see with his own eyes that there were some people so violent or depressed they simply couldn't be contacted for meaningful therapy without shock treatment. These people, the administrators claimed, would have to be strapped up for years—a condition that violated the officially stated major goal of the hospital, which is "to help [the patient] return to the community as soon as possible."

The technician loosed a single measured jolt. The fat man winced, as if he had heard an unexpected and extremely loud noise, very close. He lay in a special hospital bed—it looked like a crib—and was held at the shoulders as the convulsions started. The fat man made an *uh-uh-uh* grunting sound as the convulsions rippled down his torso in irregular waves. It was, Nicholson thought, as if the patient was in the throes of some delirious orgasm, trying vainly to control the thrust and angle of his dick.

Nicholson saw then the reason for the muscle relaxant. A strong man, in the midst of such convulsions, could literally crack the vertebrae in his own back. The facial contortions—and these Nicholson noted with a mixture of professionalism and pain—were unimaginably grotesque. The fat man's face contracted as if it had been placed in a vise just at the moment of some terrible pain. The eyes clamped tightly shut, like the eyes of a man about to burst into tears.

Within an hour and a half, the fat man was up and walking about. He seemed childlike in his docileness and complained only about the fact that he couldn't seem to recall where he was

or who anybody was or what had happened in the past few days. Other electroshock patients told Nicholson that the machine was a horror to them, but the administrators cited statistics that showed electroshock to be beneficial in a majority of cases. They introduced him to articulate patients who considered the treatment the equivalent of going to the dentist: It isn't pleasant and it hurts, but one emerges from the session a healthier individual.

So, sitting on the bench in ward eighty-four, Jack Nicholson dealt with his depression. There are some issues you can think through for so long that nothing seems to make sense. To the left of Nicholson, there was a heavy hanging bag that a patient may punch at will without saying that he is striking doctor or hospital or woman or life. A big man with huge hands and greasy black hair began to pound away methodically at the bag. Nicholson watched for a while and he thought, the only conclusion you can reach is that you can't make a conclusion—not until it happens to a relative or a loved one or you yourself.

Breakfast was served on eighty-four: pancakes, a favorite. Nicholson took his place in line, waited, then ordered a single flapjack. No use putting on extra pounds during research. But why were people looking at him like that? Ward eighty-four regarded Jack Nicholson in silent freeze-frame as he moved away from the table in slow motion. Is this all because I only ordered one pancake? Nicholson wondered. Look at them looking. Ultimately I am the sanest man in this room, he thought, and it is strange that I have managed to do the craziest thing any of them have seen so far this morning.

Jack Nicholson likes to tell the story of Freddy the Banker, because it was guys like Freddy who helped lift him out of his depressions. Freddy's the fellow who robbed the same bank twice on the same day. On a whim he had written a note that said his friend had a shotgun. The friend was a fantasy. When Freddy showed the note to a teller, she had handed over a whole drawerful of money. Freddy spent the remainder of the morning sampling intoxicants. Presently he found himself in front of a bank that seemed remotely familiar. The bank was full of police officers and FBI men, one of whom clamped the cuffs on Freddy. The judge gave Freddy to believe that while the criminal often returns to the scene of the crime, his case was something special. "Ward eighty-four for you, Freddy," the judge said.

By the time the *Cuckoo* cast had arrived, Freddy had worked his way down to the minimum-security wards. He was given a job with the crew. Nicholson liked Freddy straight off: he even gave him his nickname, the Banker. A cautious friendship ensued. Midway into the filming, Freddy was released from the hospital. Nicholson saw it happen with increasing frequency: The most likable of the patients did, in fact, "return to the community." Many people—he could see it with his own eyes—genuinely got better at OSH.

And that, the final uplifting note, is the spirit of the completed film. Building slowly, Forman has crafted a brilliantly understated movie about the human spirit, an anthem really, which has more to do with men like Freddy than with confinement and confusion.

"It's an Easter pageant," Nicholson said in Oregon. "That's as broad a stroke as you can take at it."

Filming a Cover-up:
All the President's Men

By Chris Hodenfield

APRIL 8, 1976

Bob Woodward remembers well the Friday when the phone rang and the voice said: "We've got to talk. Tonight." Woodward said, Fine, come by at nine. A taxi dropped the man off at the curb. Woodward answered the door to greet the rumpled figure—broken, footsore and full of questions. "There it was," Woodward recalled, "the exhausted reporter." Robert Redford.

Woodward took him into the kitchen and fixed a plate of cold ham and frijoles. Redford said, Boy, this is really good. Woodward stared uneasily at the frijoles. Redford was there to ask him how he and Carl Bernstein wrote that book *All the President's Men.* How do you break a case? Redford was going to portray Woodward in the movie.

Woodward wished he had some beer in the house. He relaxed. "You're going to get a feeling," he said, "about what it's like to be exhausted and go for that nine-o'clock interview and you don't know whether it's gonna pay off."

They went upstairs to the library. "I got out a lot of Watergate notes," Woodward said, much later, "and it was really the first time we had to sit down and talk for hours. And I could see that he was ready to go to sleep. But he just kept on going because his curiosity was going.

"There was something about seeing the exhaustion, that I realized a lot of information reporters get is because the people, the subjects see what the reporter is going through. The agony, the uncertainty: 'What are all these names?' 'What does all this mean?' People will look at the reporter over there and they'll start getting things out they wouldn't normally get out."

Woodward saw straightaway that Redford was not only on his last legs but on the level, and so he got out the long, involved story. He drove the actor all over Washington, showing the inside tips.

Woodward was known as the office galley slave, a quick but clumsy writer who was on the paper nine months before the break-in case. He had page-one stories all the time.

His wife calls him the Rock. Formerly of Yale, Woodward caused his father, an Illinois judge, much bereavement when he skipped law school for the journalism racket. His shoulders are bunched up in his tailored suits, and with his impassive eyes and slow, careful speech, it is an honest shock when he blurts out the word *fuck.*

Redford was very impressed with Woodward,

196

a guy who would just cut you off when you ceased to interest him. "When I first met Woodward, I was struck by his impatience, his politeness," Redford said. *"Patronizing* is not the word . . . it was like he was taught to respect elders, to be respectful of people. But in truth, underneath, there was no patience for all that. He was going through the motions.

"He always appeared to be politely enduring what you had to say, because he had something else on his mind. That was my first impression. His eyes were moving around a great deal. His eyes seemed to be categorizing props in the room as he talked to you. He'd—"

Here, he mimicked a man whose wandering attention was seized by a houseplant.

"I became fascinated with what he was seeing around me. He appears to be moving in slow motion, but in truth he's moving like a house afire. He's deceptively fast.

"He was almost abnormally decent. He said, 'Look, the trust is there. If it's broken, it's broken. Up to the point it's broken, I'm trusting you.'"

Redford thought both reporters looked nervous, scared. The stories were just breaking, and they were different people then.

"Very different," Redford said. "That's a story in itself. The effects of success, some of it predictable, some of it not. I thought we had a lot to share from that standpoint—I was going through a strange time. I was getting a certain amount of success, some of it surprising, some of it confusing. And a lot of it abusing. I was having troubles dealing with it. They seemed yet to go through it."

This would be after *The Sting* and *The Way We Were.*

"It was like a lot of sudden fanfare. I was eager to share that with somebody. This is

something you shadowbox. You spar with it; you don't embrace it.

"And Woodward is so locked into a style of his own, in terms of being a workaholic." Redford's face gloomed up. "And I don't know about being a workaholic. Everybody keeps applying that word to him. He's obsessed with work, but a lot of it is curiosity. It's an easy toss-off to say workaholic, because Washington is a town filled with workaholics, it's like a receptacle for workaholics."

Redford watched a very serious man, a man who didn't make the cocktail-party circuit, didn't really know what was on the end of his fork other than his present assignment. He had a moral code so clear that it was established in one declarative sentence that there would be no talk about the identity of Deep Throat. "He stopped me from even wanting to pursue it," Redford said.

The decisive moment for Redford happened one miserable night in an airport cafe when Woodward reached over Redford's arm and grabbed the check. Redford protested, don't be silly, this can go on the production. But Woodward said, no, he'd like to do it. Then later, after coffee, Woodward said sincerely, frankly, *"Thank* you for letting me pay for this."

Redford, who pays attention to the rituals of man, was moved.

They were an improbable pair, Bernstein and Woodward, an odd couple, wildly opposite in dress, manner and politics, thrown together on June 17, 1972, to look into a burglary at the Watergate complex. It was a local job.

Robert Redford joined many other observers in wondering about these two gumshoes. He has had a heavier impact on their first book than is widely known.

He first approached the reporters during

their roughest time, when their names hadn't been entirely cleared and the administration was sliding on the brass knuckles. Courts all across the country were getting shitty with the idea of a reporter's "secret sources." And Nixon said, on September 15, 1972, which was recorded on his tapes, "The main thing is the *Post* is going to have some damnable, damnable problems out of this one. The game has to be played awfully rough." Woodward and Bernstein's sources told the two men they were being bugged and tailed.

When Woodward got Redford's call, he thought it an impossible dream and went on about the nation's business. It took a month before he got around to telling Bernstein.

They had by October 1972 traced the sabotage ring right into the White House, and despite the election, the story wasn't making much of a dent. The book they then contracted to write was to be a definitive study of John Mitchell and Gordon Liddy, a Nixon study going back to 1970. A sort of *Best and the Brightest* affair, with the working title *The Worst and the Dumbest.*

But the events they helped set in motion were moving too fast, and by March 1973 the story was out of hand, their book a shambles. Then Redford waltzed into town with his vision of a movie: the real story would be their actual detective work. A whodunit, if you will, even if everybody knows whodunit.

Woodward found himself cornered by Redford and his pal William Goldman, the novelist and scenarist. "They had it all figured out how to end the movie, in fact," Woodward recalled. "The ending would be a scene in which Carl and I go to a party [a White House dinner] and we meet somebody who had been a source on the telephone, for the first time. And there's a flash of recognition: 'I know you and you know me, but we both have to pretend we don't know each other.'"

The reporters fought a couple rounds over that concept of a book, each claiming it would be self-serving, narcissistic. But their deadline was a month away. Woodward sat down and knocked out a first chapter. By their usual practice, Bernstein the stylist took it, rewrote it, changed it to third person. It worked. Had an air.

They moved down to a small Florida town and in five weeks raced through a first draft. The idea of a movie was still some laughable notion that was so funny they forgot to laugh.

Carl Bernstein: "Interesting, I think the same kind of relationship developed between Bob and Dustin Hoffman as developed between Woodward and myself. Dustin wasn't about to let Redford run away with the movie, and Redford wasn't about to let Dustin run away. And they're always yelling about each other's judgment on one thing or another. But with real respect."

The competition between Hoffman and Redford goes back before the contracts were signed, in fact. Dustin first heard about the book from his brother Ronald, an economist who lives in Washington and makes the cocktail circuit. Ronald got the manuscript from a friend at the *Post,* passed it to Dustin, who immediately tried to buy the movie rights. When he found out that Redford had already staked off the property, Hoffman refused to call him—said he didn't want to hustle anyone.

He turned to directing a play—*All Over Town*—and noticed daily in the trade papers that every actor in town with dark hair seemed to be up for the role of Bernstein: De Niro, Benjamin, Arkin, Pacino. Hoffman gave up with a shrug.

At that time, Redford was having a devil of a time finding a director. When British director

John Schlesinger got wind of it, he reportedly said, "No, it is the province of an American." Even Costa-Gavras was considered.

Finally, still without a director, Redford dropped by Hoffman's rehearsal hall and popped the question. Hoffman's reply: "What took you so long?"

Dustin Hoffman is a fiend for research, a desperate man, throwing himself into it as if he were to be parachuted behind enemy lines. He has to research. Immediately after securing the role of Carl Bernstein, he got hold of every book on the business of reporting. The two that sank in deepest were Timothy Crouse's *Boys on the Bus* and *Post* editor Barry Sussman's *Great Coverup*. Hoffman is a short man of ferocious energy. He sleeps little, is a mimic and an observer and loves to capture vignettes of the sidewalk and then replay them.

For the first time he was able to interrupt shooting in progress, go to his dressing room, phone up his role model and find out just what happened. He remembered: "I'd phone and say, 'Carl, I'm going to do this scene now. You got the book? You got the page?'

"One time he was sleeping—he gets very tired, he'd work twenty-four hours straight and then sack out. I'd be doing the bylines, and I'd say, 'Now does this say, "Woodward-dash-Bernstein"? Did you use capitals? I want to be specific, how did you guys do it?' And he says, 'Ah cain't, ahm kinda tired, call me Wednesday.' 'Carl, I know you're tired, but I can't, just give me this one question, just answer this one.'

"And then he answered it. I said, 'Okay, thanks, can you just tell me the answer to this one?'"

Hoffman grinned delightedly. "And suddenly there was this pause and he said, 'You fucker, you're finally learning.' And I thought

that was terrific. He says, 'You're acting like a journalist.' Because I wouldn't let him go back to bed."

For Hoffman, that seemed to beat any Oscar.

The first goods Hoffman dug up about Bernstein was that the guy had a legend. "There were stories going back to the time he was a copy aide. In terms of his borrowing money, never paying his bills, buying fifty suits from fifty places that he owes it to, all this colorful stuff about him. Falling asleep on the bench at the Virginia legislature, where he was caught when he was supposed to be reporting. None of that stuff is in the movie. The movie isn't called *Carl*."

Almost to Hoffman's regret. He would much have preferred to do a psychological study. And Bernstein would have been a weighty casebook. Bernstein was the office Lothario, a brash and stylish character with a battered face and a searching, hunted look to his eyes. With strands of gray weaving into his dark seaweed, he looks older and wiser than thirty-one. Too many migraines in his youth, too many emotional entanglements . . . all of which, friends say, have subsided with his new security.

"Carl is not so pushy," said an office poet. "The worm of ambition does not coil so around his soul."

Yes, but there was a time. He likes to say he grew up in the newsroom, starting as a copyboy at age sixteen, dropping out of college at nineteen to go reporter full-time.

The actor and the reporter hit it off grandly. Of course, they had to. As they first circled each other, Dustin thought: "I can't alienate him, because I'm doing him and want to be able to hang around him. He can't alienate me because I'm doing him onscreen and I'll make him look like an asshole."

They roamed around town and dropped in

on the famous and the knowledgeable. They drank beer and fought back sloppy sentiments. They got high together.

"He struck me right off the bat as a guy who presented a facade and watched you from behind it," Dustin said. "He's a guy who'll, 'How *wah* ya, how ya doin', how the *fuck* are ya?' Like that, that Washington-not-Southern-but-homespun kind of thing. But behind it, he's watching you, *bam-bam-bam,* like that.

"I got a street feeling from him, as opposed to Woodward. Which was interesting in terms of Redford and me. Something about Bernstein was *street,* like he was probably one of the first persons to have long hair on that paper."

One habit they share, Hoffman and Bernstein, is their emphasizing points with loud, crisp fingerpops.

"The word out on Carl was that, while Woodward was very [*pop-pop-pop*] A-B-C-D-F-and-G-leads-to-H, Carl would be A-B . . . L . . . *P!* And could make jumps, in terms of the story. That kind of deductive logic. He gets hunches, smells. And I felt that was similar to me."

They spent Passover together with Bernstein's family out in Silver Spring. Hoffman was bowled over by the activist, Peoples Unite atmosphere. Of course, the actor was a big hit. Uncle Itzel and Aunt Rose were there, and Aunt Rose mentioned they had been married for sixty years. Dustin looked at her and said, "Sixty years. Did you ever fool around?"

Mrs. Bernstein was a very strong lady, too proud to offer advice. But she was still a Jewish mother.

"One day she came on the set when we were shooting," Dustin remembered. "She looked at the way I was dressed, cigarette ashes all over, coffee stains, she looks at me and says, 'That's Carl.'"

"'I realized my second week in it that this was the most fun I ever had researching," Hoffman recalled. "This wasn't hanging around Forty-second Street for *Midnight Cowboy,* or searching around the country for people who knew Lenny Bruce to tell me stories and they'd wind up crying.

"This was going to a newsroom, staying at the fucking Madison Hotel, staying in a nice suite overlooking D.C., going to the newsroom every morning at nine o'clock. I got a kick out of putting on a tie and going to work. I hadn't done that since I was a temporary typist. It was nice to feel that. Get up, get dressed, wear a tie because Harry Rosenfeld [assistant managing editor, portrayed by Jack Warden in the movie] wanted me to wear a tie. Go to the newsroom every morning at nine o'clock, getting the coffee, 'Good morning, good morning,' the kind of success I always dreamed about when I was a kid. Sit at a desk, use the phone, go and talk with the editors, I loved it. Three and a half months, on and off."

He was mainlining printer's ink. In the newsroom up on the fifth floor, he stationed himself next to Fred Barbash, a reporter who was then investigating some political-corruption scandals in Maryland. The mouthpiece was removed from the next phone and Hoffman listened in.

"I could hear people lying, that wonderful thing of how they lie . . . it got to the point where I was starting to drive him crazy. I was saying, 'Did you ask him this, and did you ask him *this?!*' And suddenly I realized I was in it."

Woodward was different. "He was like Marciano," said Hoffman. "Always pushing, pushing, pushing."

"It was the classic ant-and-the-grasshopper story," remembered Jay Mathews, a roving reporter whose desk was next to Woodward's during the dark season. "Bob was the ant, very diligent, always pushing. But the beauty of the duo was the way they worked. They fit. Carl's temperament was such that he would work when he got a little shove. Carl is a great writer and stylist, creative but lazy. And Bob was the tireless worker. Not a great writer, but getting better. You'd usually see Bob yelling at Carl to get a move on."

They all still laugh about the time Carl came running into the office, late from New York, claiming his plane had been stacked up. Woodward immediately dialed Eastern Airlines to find out how the flights were running. They were all on time, and the hot words flew.

"Woodward is such a mother hen," friends murmured.

Every reporter in town must have reached for his Maalox when he heard that Woodward and Bernstein sold their stories to screenland. That is tantamount to a pact with the devil, as anyone raised on John Garfield movies and Walter Winchell columns can testify.

The Washington press corps was up in arms, according to Woodward's wife, Francie Barnard, also a reporter. "Because reporters don't write stories about *how* they write or what goes on in the background," she said in her El Paso lilt. "They wait years and years and then write a novel about a middle-aged, tired reporter, male, who has an affair with a Commerce assistant's secretary."

There was heavy shaking of heads in all the press galleries, because here were a couple of under-thirty cityside reporters who hadn't risen through the ranks, hadn't trod the prestige beats and therefore couldn't have developed the important sources inside the cloistered cells of government.

Francie Barnard: "Everyone in the press gal-leries was asking, 'Why aren't they asleep on the leather couches up here with the rest of us?'"

Reporters have an idea of the shadow that falls between the perception and the act of typing. A movie would only add to the kudos, the money, the notoriety, said their chief, Benjamin Bradlee (who is played by Jason Robards). All those losers out there will be waiting to cut them a new asshole. That's the way Bradlee talks. He called Woodward into the office one day and said, "Woodward, you realize that no matter what you or I or any of us do for the rest of our lives, as we are portrayed in this movie, we will forever be known."

"I thought, my God," said Woodward, "maybe he's right. Now I'm convinced he's wrong."

The editors bared their souls in a manner that Redford found disarming. "I walked into the fifth floor—I was taken there by Woodward and Bernstein—and I was very nervous about going there. I felt extremely intimidated. I was sensitive to people thinking, 'What the hell is he doing here?'

"I tried as much as possible to blend in with the woodwork, but I found out very quickly that it wasn't necessary, because they were so busy opening up to you, saying, how are you, this is my desk, this is how I keep my papers, have you seen the Teletype, let me take you over there. It was like, open arms.

"The editors were fantastic. In fact, you couldn't stop them from talking. They were all concerned with how they were to be portrayed. I felt that one of the reasons they were all coming on so strong and being so cooperative is that they wanted it done right."

"Suddenly, we were doing them," remembered Hoffman, "and there was a silence, a fear. There was talk of, 'Who's going to play me? How are they going to do us?' They were looking at us very, very closely. Wondering what kind of minds we have, where our thinking was."

Hoffman slapped his chest. "The way I am when I'm being interviewed. The way I observe an interviewer. You do so many interviews and read them, you begin to understand the interviewer as a person. You see where you're misquoted, or where you're framed."

Director Alan Pakula is another fiend for researching. Yes, Pakula knows all about fear, said Redford, and his movies *(Klute, Parallax View)* show it. He is a tall, bearded and very pale man of forty-seven. His only coloration seems to be a hint of orange on his fingertips. Attentive, full of questions and theories, he was accepted by all the editors as a brother. Pakula is a listener. His eyes do not project; they receive. He set up shop in the Madison Hotel and began filling up dozens of notebooks.

"It was a wonderful adventure for me," said Pakula months later, interrupting the editing of the picture. "Journalism is an area I could easily fantasize myself in at some point. There are great similarities. Bob Woodward will say that one of the things about being a reporter is that you're coming into people's lives when they're at their most exciting, their most intense and emotional. And you'll leave them when they start to go dry.

"That has a little to do with making films as well, the whole voyeur thing, the fascination with people's lives."

He thought of himself as a minister without portfolio, just listening, the Invisible Man.

Woodward and Bernstein began taking their lunch breaks over in Pakula's hotel room. A tape record would usually be running. Woodward began claiming that Pakula should've been a reporter, and if not that, then a goddamn

shrink. The newsroom boys began calling Pakula the Resident Analyst.

In fact, at Yale, Pakula was headed in that direction, only a few inches away from going premed when he found his true calling directing a one-act Chekhov. It made him feel like some character out of *Look Homeward, Angel.*

For Woodward and Bernstein, the hours of interviews dredged up a lot of memories, and later Woodward fessed up that it would have been a much better book had they written it after these confessions.

When Pakula first read the book, he couldn't understand why all the reliable sources, the underlings, would spill the information. During the interviews with Woodward and Bernstein at the *Post,* he found out.

"Everybody wants to be important, everybody wants to have some sense of contributing in some way.

"First of all, if you're genuinely interested in somebody and what they have to say . . . it's very rare, no matter how successful you are, that anyone is interested in what you have to say. Just that somebody is *that interested* is, I think, very hypnotic. Carl Bernstein said everybody wants basically to tell the truth, to be thought of as a 'truthsayer.' "

The movie people soon found that they weren't the only actors in town. Sadly, the movie that will never be seen is how the actors and reporters switched identities. When the actors talked about breaking the Watergate case, they sometimes referred to "they," the reporters, or "we," the reporters. But Redford came to be grieved by a town whose heart seemed to pump gossip and rumor, part of it being the tendency of the press to "be so paranoid and obsessed with its own image."

It's unanimous, said Hollywood; both worlds seem to exist on talk. Of course, it's only a cocktail-party illusion trick, and after a few of these parties, Dustin Hoffman found himself thinking that "everyone was kind of a facade, as if they were relaxing their senses . . . but underneath, it's like you're one of the Quiz Kids. The kind of fencing you read about when language was king."

"Gossip about political power," said Pakula, "is much more interesting than gossip about The Business."

The grisly idea of Hollywood-on-the-Potomac started years ago, lately blossoming into the notion, the New Mediacracy.

"Washington is the center of the mediacracy," said *Washingtonian* magazine, "because Washington is now the capital of the media, more the creator of myths than Hollywood in the thirties."

Besides, Hollywood myths won't make the trains run on time.

"Government and show-biz," said former Kennedy aide Letitia Baldrige, "so disparate and so publicized. They couldn't be further apart. One is based on sex and one on power. They're symbols of things each would like to get close to, but they never could."

The old newspaper slogan goes that today's scandal is tomorrow's fishwrap. In this case, the fishwrap started as a $6-million picture and finally went out the door costing $8 million.

And in addition to money problems, the moviemakers had to deal with a sketchy hold on reality. Richard Nixon and his men would be playing themselves, of course, when seen on television. That had Pakula very worried. Pakula was born to worry. "There's a very fine line in this," he said, "in getting your kicks the wrong way. You have to be very careful you're not exploiting it for its wowie value. If you wanted to, you could have one goddamned irony after another with these television appearances."

Jason Robards wasn't worried when he looked at those old television-news reruns. "I got so mad I wanted to kick the set in," he said. "Those sonsabitches are on there. What's-his-name? Spiral Igloo."

Any intimidation that Redford might have felt in the *Washington Post*'s office was nothing compared to the sock on the jaw that awaited the reporters when they visited Hollywood.

They should've been prepared, because they saw production designer George Jenkins measure every inch of the *Post* newsroom, take more than a thousand photographs of every desk in the joint, confiscate boxloads of trash and clutter. Jenkins, who also claims an ability to forge signatures, said he was going to duplicate the *Post,* every desk in it, but no one really imagined the nightmare detail.

Bradlee was one of the first. He arrived at the Los Angeles airport, drove out to Warner Bros. soundstage number five in Burbank and walked into . . . his office. His knees buckled and his hand went to his forehead. He walked over to "his" office and found the same pictures, the same mementos, the same books in the library. But instead of having a fifth-floor view of Fifteenth Street, out the window was a cinderblock wall.

It was right out of the Twilight Zone, a time warp where 1972 phone books and newspapers were scattered on desks, and pinned to the entranceway was, for the actors' benefit, the day's *Washington Post* that they were to be working on. TODAY IS MONDAY, JUNE 19TH, 1972, 7 P.M.

People would uneasily walk over to the elevator, forgetting that it was a dummy. Harry Rosenfeld got dizzy. "It was confusing time and place, somehow. It was unnerving to be there, in a sense euphoric."

The difference was that here the "reporters" sat around reading *Variety*.

Pakula was glad to be out on his turf, three thousand miles from the pressures of Washington, away from the ghostly shadow of the *real* Carl and Bob. "There's that doppelgänger, whatever you want to call it. The real person and not the road company Bob Woodward or the fake Carl Bernstein, when the real one calls up and says, 'Hi, how are ya doing?' . . . Such an absurd sense of déjà vu.

"In Hollywood, we were in *our* newsroom, Ben Bradlee was a visitor in *our Washington Post* newsroom. You have to give the actors that, you have to say, 'This is my world; I'm not a visitor there.'"

Suddenly, in this great hall of mirrors, the tables are turned again. The research completed, the minor actors chosen, the serious dramatics begun, the actor/reporters were besieged by every investigative scandalmonger on the West Coast.

Pakula writhed at the possibility of a bunch of rubbernecks overseeing his dramatic alchemy. He told the unit publicist to bar reporters from the set.

You leave people when they start to go dry. While the actors were still faithful and adoring clones to their role models, the romance with the real *Post* had withered on the Hollywood and Vine. Each faction did what it does best: after several months of researching in the *Post*'s office, the people from Tinseltown had worn out their welcome, and the *Post*, naturally, printed a story about the "havoc," a story that left many a hard-boiled reporter soft-scrambled with alleged misquotes.

Dustin Hoffman grumbled to Bernstein, boy, people worrying about Hollywood being unfair . . . that story was about as unfair to Hollywood as it gets.

"Looking back," said Redford months later, near the finish, "I was shocked to see that the *Post* did one of the worst reporting jobs I have ever seen in my life." He readily admitted that the hordes of movie people had an impact on the city room; great story idea, in fact. Annoyance had curdled his flat voice. Shocking to hear him so touchy.

"I was really naive at first. I learned a lot of their reactions to my being there by the story the *Post* printed.

"It was stunning to me to find out what people were really thinking in the newsroom. This great hypocrisy: you'd hear a lot of side things going on. Redford thought he was a movie star, Redford thought he was a superstar."

People reacted to him and he didn't catch it. Which was surprising, because he loves to talk about people, watch them from cafe windows. He carries a briefcase, lobbies Congress for environmental causes, builds an empire in Utah, appears organized and on the move, but he's still a fogbound romantic, easily slipping into memories of foreign ports, inky harbors, the diaries of his youth, in which he was just another Edgar Allan Poe.

So you didn't read these people right, I said.

"No, I didn't. I took them at face value, because it was new to me. I had nothing to offer. If they wanted to know what's so-and-so like, or that last movie you made, I was quite prepared to do that. But they didn't ask. They seemed to conspicuously avoid being interested. I first met Harry Rosenfeld, and the first line out of his mouth was, 'Gee, you don't look like Woody Allen.'

"I didn't really think about it. I guess I was selfish. Everybody being so cool and blasé that you don't realize they're maybe starstruck, impressed or snowed, or whatever. And it all comes out in the way they react behind your back.

"It's the same old gripe. . . . I've seldom heard somebody liking something that was written about them. I guess it's because we see ourselves differently. But that one was really inexcusable, completely irresponsible.

"I worry about the newspaper business, you know. That the proportion of hard news and soft news is getting out of whack.

"For people who are supposed to be in the perception business, I found that newspaper people are among the most unperceptive I've every come across. In my experience. Occasionally you meet someone who has a perception. . . . Actors are better, painters are better at drawing portraits of people."

Redford started out as a painter before acting. And now? Now he's writing a story for *National Geographic* magazine on the Outlaw Trail.

It was two very relieved reporters who, at different times, flew out to the Coast to see the rough cut of their biographical movie. Bernstein was already prepared. A week before, he heard it was already a Coming Attraction at a Washington theater. The movie playing was some softcore-porn epic, but he and his best friend, Richard Cohen, plopped down the seven bucks just to see the two-and-a-half-minute preview.

It was a mind-numbing jolt.

"I can only remember impressions of the trailer, because it was so shocking. I just remember Dustin being like that on the phone"—he hung an imaginary receiver over his ear—"saying, 'This is Carl Bernstein.' It sort of threw me. But then, having seen that, when I went to see the movie, I was much better prepared to watch it. I was able to watch the movie very detached."

Woodward, the Rock, also caught the preview in a neighborhood movie house, and while his wife, Francie, was terrified that everyone would break out in hysterics, Woodward just sat there immobile.

Whereas Bernstein might be ready to have his sensibilities blown, Woodward remains the Trappist monk. Whereas Bernstein has lately been writing a feature for the *New Yorker,* promising to return to the *Post* by June, "maybe even earlier," Woodward has been back since January, now on the national staff, digging some good stories that are blessed by a singular byline. Asked whether they'll work together again, Woodward says, maybe someday, probably not. They've had some ugly fights these last years. "Difficult, strained, but the collaboration works. But I'm not sure either of us wants to go through the agony of it again. Carl and I have different points of view on things, we always have. He never said, 'I want to work with Woodward.' And I never said, 'Gee, if I work with anybody at the *Washington Post,* I want it to be Bernstein.' It's almost too much collaborating with the different phases of one's own personality."

So when I asked him about the reality of this movie, he was quick to cut me off: "I don't think there is a reality to it. I feel very distant from it. Don't you think?"

Look, I said, you have to retain something of your anonymity.

Francie, who was with us at the Trader Vic's bar, shook her head. "But theirs was gone before the movie."

This was all too much for the Rock. "It's not gone," he said patiently, firmly. "That's a joke. Today—I noticed today because we were supposed to be talking—I spent the whole day on the phone and I had to spell my name four times to people. No sense of 'loss of persona' or, 'Oh, my God, Robert Redford on the phone.' It's just not."

All right. The movie wasn't due out for another month. We raised a glass to all our anonymity.

Kevin Costner Dances With Wolves

By Fred Schruers

NOVEMBER 29, 1990

On a November day north of Rapid City, South Dakota, on the winding Spearfish Canyon Road in the midst of a forest, Kevin Costner is organizing a troop movement along a stream that snakes through snowy ground. It's a pivotal scene for *Dances With Wolves*, the three-hour epic Western in which Costner not only stars as a renegade Union officer living among a tribe of Sioux Indians but also makes his debut as a director. Some 150 bluecoat Union soldiers are saddling up in the early-morning mist. "Okay, let's smoke it up," says Costner, and the mist is noisily augmented by smoke blown down the road from a massive wind machine.

The shot starts low, on a pair of boots kicking snow into a fire, then pulls wide as the camera is levered on a long crane to see the cavalry file. Even as he gives instructions to an assistant, Costner nips forward, grabs a long-handled shovel and rearranges some burning scraps of log for the shot. "The man mounting is your pacesetter," he tells cinematographer Dean Semler. Buggy about detail, Costner doesn't waste a second on the set—his body-language cues to the camera crew are constantly alternating with his meticulous set dressing and prop

arranging and his sotto voce directions to the actors. Now he ducks out hurriedly—the smoke is curling subtly across the stream the way he likes it—hops up a muddy bank and hollers the familiar call for action.

The bluecoats Costner's camera is tracking today are definite villains in his piece—not just because they're chasing down Lt. John Dunbar, the character he plays, but because their seeming goal is the destruction of the Lakota Sioux tribe that the audience will come to know intimately along with Dunbar. George Custer's comeuppance about two hundred miles west, at the Little Bighorn in 1876, is one subtext of this film, but a more pertinent reference point for today's fictional scenario is the army's massacre of 146 Sioux men, women and children at Wounded Knee Creek in 1890. Not even such seventies message films as *Little Big Man* and *Soldier Blue* dealt as empathetically with Native Americans. "The Indians were just not ready to fight," says Costner once he's got his shot. "They had all their war games in the summer."

Costner, who will be inducted into the Lakota Sioux the day of his film's Washington, D.C., premiere, insists that telling the story accurately is a practical move. "It's a chapter we know so well, but nobody wants to put the label *genocide* on it," says Costner. "We won't acknowledge how many Indian cultures we destroyed. But that's our Brazilian rain forest, right there. When you look at this part of the country, you realize there was a lot of bloodshed over ownership of the land, like we had to have this. But if you fly over this land now, nobody's here, not really. There's Denver and Kansas City, and Rapid City over here. But the reality is—we didn't have to have it."

The lecture, even one this cogent and heartfelt, is not Costner's style, and he pauses a beat. "I felt that economically, it was too big a risk to make a movie about Indians and not treat them right," he says. "I thought a movie like that would get creamed. That's not a highbrow approach. It's just easier to go with the truth."

If he doesn't think he's taking a risk here, one wants to ask Costner why his is the first major feature to approach the Native American history without patronizing clichés and the first to use an authentic Indian tongue with subtitles. But he's already half-jogging up the road, boots scraping the pebbles, to set up his next shot.

Rodney Grant is a young and relatively inexperienced Indian actor whose sculpted face Costner and casting director Elisabeth Leustig could not resist. She had glimpsed him in last year's little-seen film *War Party*. "Rodney in a stern mood looks like he'll kill you," says Leustig, "but when he smiles, he's like a three-year-old." As the warrior Wind in His Hair, Grant at first challenges Costner's Dunbar, who is singlehandedly manning an army outpost in Sioux territory. Later the two men learn to understand each other. Grant's mutable face has served him well, and today is his sign-off scene.

It's no close-up. In fact, a long lens is pointed skyward at Grant as he sits astride a pony perched on a rock outcrop that you or I wouldn't step on for money or glory. (True, he's waist-roped to a stake, so at the worst, he'll only go mumblety-pegging a few yards into the granite face.) The crew members indulge in some covert snowball action; that is, until Grant delivers his impassioned farewell line—English in the subtitles, Lakota as he almost sings it. Sound and movement stop as every head swivels. Grant repeats the line, modulates it to his own drummer as the sound bounces around this narrow cul-de-sac in Spearfish Canyon. Costner's job is to ride through the shot emotionless, but on his way back for take two, he has a private smile.

Grant had almost blown this whole gig. He's an Omaha, from the tribe that lived on the Missouri's banks and lent the city its name. Omahas are gentle, Grant says, not warriors. He came to the picture with a notable eloquence in English and thought he'd pick up the Lakota easily. But he was so hopeless in rehearsals, for which Costner set aside a month of language lessons, that the director sent him away for more practice. "I don't want to have another rehearsal till you get the lines down," Costner told him. Leustig took over. "My ass was on the line," she says. "I promised Kevin these people could function." Leustig drilled him until Grant said, "Too much." Then she blew up, giving him a dose of the French-accented wrath that she'd hidden under her ebullience. "I don't have to do this," she told him, mindful that Costner might demote him to an extra. Grant sulked awhile, thought about it and approached her the next morning. "I'm sorry," he said. "I'm gonna make you proud of me."

A few more takes, Grant's call coming down on the wind; everyone standing by is clearly moved. "Okay, we're out of here," says Costner.

He hollers up the hill: "That was beautiful, Rodney. That was magic."

In the film, Dunbar goes to the frontier at his own request, after his suicidal solo charge across a Confederate line of fire in the movie's eye-opening initial sequence turns him inadvertently into a hero. We have that context for Dunbar's slightly mysterious loneliness, and his noble-fool aspect makes us believe that he's open to partnership not just with his buckskin mount, Cisco, but with a wolf named Two Socks and even with an Indian tribe that's beginning to learn that white men are murderous. After facing the hot-blooded mistrust of Wind in His Hair, Dunbar next encounters Kicking Bird, played by Graham Greene (an Oneida from Canada), a holy man who has already raised the captured white woman Stands With a Fist (played by Mary McDonnell). Kicking Bird wants to question the white man about who else may be coming.

The leisurely pace of the film allows Costner to contrast the white and Indian cultures. Costner takes over three hours to tell his tale, but the time is well spent. The Indians call Dunbar, amusingly, Loo Ten Tant and, finally, after spying on his antics with the wolf Two Socks, Dances With Wolves. But there's no condescension in the joke. When Dunbar thumps about in a busy charade to depict a buffalo, we laugh with the Indians as they bemusedly note, "His mind is gone."

Costner says it was scenes like this that drew him to directing the picture. "You've got to want to do it because you believe in your story," he says. "People don't go into directing for power. They go in for the completion of something they want to see. *Dances* needed a tone. Somebody else might not have done subtitles. I wanted to see it in the Native American language. Somebody else might have made it shorter, because they don't think people can sit with this movie. I think they can."

Costner's insistence on retaining final cut of his own picture meant that he and coproducer Jim Wilson had to look for their first investors overseas. They got a goodly percentage of what they needed, then came back to the States seeking an independent company to go on their adventure with. They simply assumed that no major studio—not even Orion, for whom Costner has been consistently boffo box office—would want to plunge into such an imposingly risky project. "I knew I was going to experiment," says Costner. "Some things were not going to work out right, and I didn't want to pay the price of talking all night long to some junior executive who said things didn't look right. I know when it doesn't look right. I know that. And I'm going to fix it. I'm not doing things I don't think I can do."

In the end, Orion—on the strength of its belief in Costner—agreed to stay hands-off yet distribute the film. Orion did, however, assign a zealous completion-bond company to eavesdrop and kibitz on the film's making. Sure enough, some weeks into shooting, Costner's expanding vision started to play havoc with his planned limits of time and money. Wilson held an early-morning meeting with his director, who offered a financial safety valve: Costner would defer something over $2 million worth of his own $5-million acting salary, and the production could use that money to meet the needs it would have near the expanded schedule's end.

The plan worked, and the picture finished more or less on time, for some $18 million, a relative bargain in an age of $60-million-plus budgets. But Costner will not soon forgive the hectoring bond company. "I offered to buy them out a week into the movie," he says. "I told them, 'I'll pay your salary, just get the fuck out of my life.' That shocked the shit out of them. They are necessary for people who do runaway things. But to people who are fiscally responsible, they're a giant pain in the ass. They endanger a project that's trying to run the line. They start telling you you can't do things. I ended up doing everything I wanted."

By the time Costner came to shoot an almost unprecedentedly dangerous buffalo-hunt scene in *Dances*—riding and mock-shooting among a surging sea of 3,500 buffaloes—producer Wilson and stunt coordinator Norman Howell were hovering nearby in the hope that their star would decide not to ride. "I was really nervous," recalls Cindy Costner. "I was making myself physically ill. I couldn't tell him what to do when he was directing *Dances*. At night I could chew on him a little bit, but he was gonna go out there the next day and do what he wanted to do."

Michael Blake, the screenwriter of *Dances*, vividly recalls the shooting of the buffalo hunt. "Kevin took one of the most hellacious falls I've ever seen in my life," says Blake. "I'm going to get it on tape, because it's one of the worst falls from a horse you'll ever see. Here's what happened: Kevin's horse is going along straight, then the Indian rider comes sideways and loses control of his horse, just like a car accident. Bam! Kevin goes straight up in the air, somehow twists and is coming down facing backwards while his horse is at full speed. Kevin hits the ground, bounces about two feet straight up in the air and rolls over like a big sack of flour."

A documentary crew accompanying the shoot got the accident on tape. Almost more remarkable than the fall was the dazed Costner's immediate rise to his feet. By the time he shoved his army pants back into his boot tops, he had decided to remount—which he did by taking the reins of a horse that his stunt double, Norman Howell, was ready to ride into the ongoing shot in his stead. "Norman said, 'What do you want to do?' and I said, 'I want to ride,' " Costner says. "He knew I wasn't playing a game."

Insurance risk or no, at the box office Costner has begun to resemble a sure thing. The film has borne out Costner's confidence that he knew what he was about—*Dances With Wolves* is a *tour de force* directorial debut done with sparks of wit and evident heart, both sweeping and authentic in its finest particulars on Native American themes. He did it with the help of two friends, Michael Blake and Jim Wilson, and the hoot for the trio is that this boldest Costner move is the one that's worked best of all.

There were small jobs along the way for Costner, and one, which can now occasionally be seen in the video stores as *Stacy's Knights,* is acutely significant. It began as a script called *Double Down,* commissioned by young Jim Wilson from Michael Blake. Those two had met at what Blake calls "a sleazy little operation" called the Berkeley Film Institute.

Blake, a rangy, strawberry-haired man with a sly, infectious grin, flashes back to their casting sessions. "It was an open call, and we'd seen all these people who construed 'a local guy from Reno whose father used to be a gambler' as a guy with a cowboy hat, toothpick in his mouth and probably a mustache," says Blake. "So I see this skinny, kind of tall guy walking back and forth, totally concentrated on this piece of paper—looks like a chicken on a piece of seed. And I said to myself, 'I hope that guy reads.' It was Kevin. As soon as he read, we knew that he could play our man. He's a really fine actor who can instinctively figure out what a character's mantle is."

Once cast, Blake says, "Kevin was extremely

excited. I went up to Reno about two weeks after shooting had started, knocked on his motel-room door, he opens it, and he's grinning from ear to ear. He went and sat down on the bed, there was some money spread around—like a five, a ten, a twenty, probably some one-dollar bills—and he just lay back on the bed and said, 'This is so incredible. I'm doing exactly what I want, and I'm getting paid five hundred dollars a week.'"

The better part of the decade would pass before the three again collaborated. Wilson prospered mildly, continuing to direct and produce a variety of projects, including how-to videos, and gradually, as Costner ascended, being brought into Tig Productions as a producing partner. Blake, meanwhile, continued in his maverick ways and launched a number of unsold screenplays. He often lived by the grace of friends, sometimes alternating between Costner's and Wilson's homes. One night, at Kevin's, Blake talked out the story idea for *Dances With Wolves*, an idea that excited Costner so much he advised him not to put it in another screenplay. "My friends felt bad for me because I had probably written ten screenplays, only one had been produced, and I still didn't have a pot to piss in," says Blake. "Kevin told me to 'write a book'—I thought he was gonna grab me and shake me: 'Write a book.'"

That Blake did, living from March through December out of his Chrysler as he migrated between their houses, often reading sections to Wilson and his wife as they sat in bed. The finished book was "a doorstop" to the busy Costner, but Wilson insisted it would make a fine screenplay. When Costner finally dug in, he called the book "the clearest idea for a movie I'd ever read."

Blake, meanwhile, had moved dispiritedly to Bisbee, Arizona ("I felt a deep sense of failure in my life"), and become a dishwasher in a Chinese restaurant. He'd been getting care packages—food, a sleeping bag, necessities—by mail from Costner. A couple of days after he'd been fired from his dishwasher job for insisting on a new pair of rubber gloves, the call came. "Kevin said, 'Look, we think we want to do this, and we've got some money, will you come back?'" Blake says. "A few days after that, I was on my way back to Hollywood, straight to his house. Perfect timing."

Given this sudden change in circumstance, one has to give Blake credit for his gumption in almost immediately informing Costner that the actor wasn't quite right for the role of Lieutenant Dunbar. "From the beginning, I thought Kevin would be a great director," says Blake. "But I wanted another guy, Viggo Mortensen [seen as Molly Ringwald's menacing husband in *Fresh Horses* and now acting in Sean Penn's *Indian Runner*], to play the part. I said, 'Kev, I don't know if anybody's going to really believe in you [in this part] after seeing your other movies.' And he said, 'Don't worry about it.' One thing I've learned about Kevin is that you do not bet against him, no matter what he's going to do. As it turns out, I think he's done some of his best acting work in this movie."

Michael Blake is on to something about his friend. It's best to talk to Costner about directing first. The famous thing, the sexy thing, tends to produce consternation. "I don't think fame is a cultural achievement," says Costner. "I mean, acting has a place, but celebrity as an achievement?" Costner lets a leg flop half off the couch, as if this dull idea of fame has put it to sleep. "I've had my share—more exposure than anybody has a right to have," he says. "Enough at this point for the rest of my life, as far as I'm concerned."

"I don't think people have a clue how I approach my work," he says. "They think, 'Leading actor, good times, good life,' and they don't realize that probably the most fun for me is being in my office and writing. I mean, I'm like the Corleone family. I put the mattresses against the wall, like in a war, have a big bowl of pasta going and get a tremendous joy out of that. I like getting dirty with film and that is my life—the movies and how they work."

THE MARCH OF THE ICONS

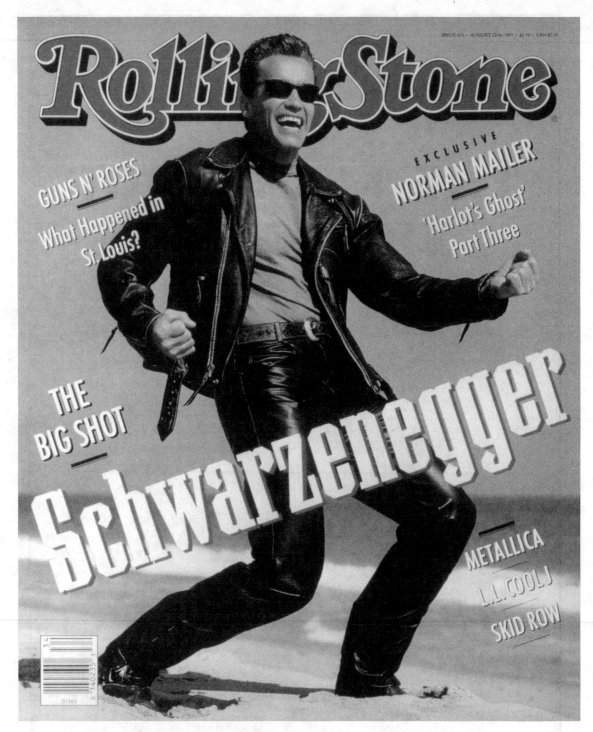

Arnold Schwarzenegger, ROLLING STONE, issue 611, August 22, 1991.
Photograph by Herb Ritts

Cowboy Clint Eastwood

By David Breskin

SEPTEMBER 17, 1992

At Euro Disney, outside Paris, four high-profile architects have built five hotels celebrating various aspects of the American landscape: the Hotel New York, the Sequoia Lodge, the Cheyenne, the Newport Bay Club and the Hotel Santa Fe. This last inn, a Southwestern tongue-in-chic extravaganza, is punctuated with rusting vintage cars, a saguaro cactus in a glass cage and a parking lot that evokes a drive-in movie theater—the guests have to walk under the screen to enter the hotel. The architect, Antoine Predock, wanted to leave this giant movie screen provocatively blank. (The Europeans would simply raid their memories for images to project.) But Disney said no. A blank screen would not do. Well, then what do you paint permanently onto a movie screen outside Paris to conjure the myth of the West?

Clint Eastwood—of course. "There is no one more American than he," Norman Mailer said, hitting the nail on the hard head, steely gaze, tight jaw. There is always a bullet in his gun, pain in his heart and a cold, gray rain of rage in his eyes. For years the biggest international movie star on the planet—turf that he ceded in the last half of the eighties to actors with bigger biceps (in Hollywood) and bigger guns (in

Washington)—Eastwood has metamorphosed not into the dusty legend we might expect but rather into an ambitious filmmaker.

Eastwood, who first came to prominence in a trilogy of Westerns for Sergio Leone, has added to the lore with *Unforgiven,* his sixteenth feature as director and thirty-sixth as star. *High Plains Drifter* (1973), *The Outlaw Josey Wales* (1976) and *Pale Rider* (1985) are Eastwood's grand triptych of Westerns; *Unforgiven* is the frame that changes how we view them. A polished piece of rawhide revisionism, it's antiromantic, antiheroic and antiviolent. It's Eastwood's first dance with myth where the music's not cartoonish: It's mature, and now, at sixty-two, so is he. If *Unforgiven* is not his last Western, it should be; if it's not recognized right away as a classic, it will be.

I met Eastwood at Mission Ranch, a hotel he owns near his home in Carmel, California. Cordial but distant at first, he was quite friendly by the end of the night, though he keeps self-analysis a stranger in town.

What's the most vital thing to you about the work you do?

At this point in my career, it's the constant reaching, the constant stretching for new ideas

215

or even, in the current project, variations on a theme. It's very hard to find things that haven't been done. But I'm always looking for that excitement. *Unforgiven* I read as a sample of [writer] David Webb Peoples' work, figuring it wasn't available. Francis Coppola had it at the time, and he couldn't get it going. So I called up to ask about the writer's availability for something else, and he told me it was available. That was a surprise. It seemed to me very timely.

How long have you owned it?

Since 1983. When I look back, I've kind of spun off of instinct and *luck*. *The Outlaw Josey Wales* came to me as a blind submission. I read it and liked it.

Let's talk about the Eastwood hero. I'm sure there are a hundred different things to say about this character and as many exceptions as rules, but one thing that does strike me is that the Eastwood hero is a deeply damaged guy who has been profoundly hurt and is acting out of that hurt.

I think so. I think the heroes all have something that is nagging at them. Dating back to *A Fistful of Dollars* and those stylized things. Most of the heroes I've played have definitely had something in their background that's painful. Up through *Unforgiven*, where he's really got damage. Through some pain, through some trial and error, through some suffering in life, you come to what you are. And guys of great strength who get things done—whether escapist heroes or not—have to have something in their lives to bring them to that point. They couldn't be guys who just had a normal life—a normal job—and this fell into place. It just can't happen that way.

Would you say that you're one of those sorts of guys?

Are you looking for a parallel in my life? [*Long pause*] I don't know. I don't get into a self-analytical position very often, and I try to avoid it. I could say that I have the ability to take the things in my life—the hurts and disappointments, whatever—and channel them into moving forward, channel them into a positive force.

Did you feel your roles were tapping into something that was not a stretch for you? Obviously, you didn't grow up as a gunslinger, but you were a lumberjack and a gas pumper and a—

I beat around. I had my beat-around years and my years of being lost. Lost in that I didn't know what I wanted to do or what I thought I could do. But I've never sat and analyzed how they fit in. I think it's strictly an imaginative thing. Just as you can imagine something positive in someone's life—a force going forward—so can you imagine a background that's slightly damaged. It's just the imagination of the actor. You have to give yourself that obstacle to make the character interesting, to give it some depth. It can be somebody who has really had some *pain* in his life, like the outlaw Josey Wales or William Munny in *Unforgiven*.

The wounds those characters carry are profound.

It just takes a little imagination to do that. They are all suffering through a lot more than I've suffered in life.

Another aspect of the Eastwood hero is his fundamental and overriding decency to others—but when riled, a sort of termination with extreme prejudice.

Yeah. Yeah, that's true.

They are not characters that bend. They snap. Is the fascination for you in what makes him snap?

What makes him snap is always interesting. What was so fun in playing this current character is that he's sort of forced by lack of prosperity into doing the only thing he really knows how to do well. And he has bad feelings about that, and he keeps bringing up his own demons—people he has killed. There's a morality. It's not like doing penance for the mayhem

I've created on the screen over the prior years, but in *Unforgiven*, it's the first time I've read it in a way, have been able to interpret it in a way that death is not a fun thing. Somebody is in deep pain afterward, even the person who perpetrates it.

There are consequences to the violence.

There are consequences all the way down the line.

Now, one of the things you've been slammed with over the years is that your pictures don't show the consequences of violence. They show the bottled rage, the explosion—which is very cinematic—but they are weak on the consequences of violence, emotionally and otherwise. This picture changes that formula.

Yeah, it does. And I think that was the big appeal to me when I bought it in '83. I sort of nurtured it. I put it away, like a little, tiny gem that you put on the shelf and go look at it and polish it and think: "I'll do this. Age is good for the character, so I'll mature a little bit." Three years ago I decided I've got to do this. And today a lot of the stuff that has gone on this last year and a half, where a *decision* is made that is maybe not the right decision—where force was used to the extreme, like the Rodney King incident—is like, Gene Hackman in *Unforgiven*.

Why do the repercussions of violence matter to you now when they didn't matter to you so much before?

I think just generally changing in life. Hopefully, we're gaining more knowledge as the years go by. I'm not smart enough to have written it down, so all of a sudden I say, "That's it, that's the element that's been missing for me, that I haven't been able to deal with properly." Maybe skirt here and there but not really explore it.

The world of "Unforgiven" is a complicated world. It's an adult world: It's a world where violence doesn't solve any problems, it just changes the problems. That's a sea change for you.

Exactly. And that was very appealing to play and to explore. We're talking about people purging themselves and changing attitudes—I remember when I first spoke to Gene Hackman about playing this role, he said, "Well, I don't want to do anything with any violence in it." I said, "Really?" He's had his share of violent films, too. I said, "Gene, I know exactly where you're coming from. I've been involved in a lot of violent films, but I would love to have you look at this because I think there's a spin on this that's different. I don't think this is a tribute to violence, and if we do it right, it's not exploiting it; in fact, it's kind of stating that it doesn't solve anything." So when he read it, he could see where it was headed, and he decided to do it.

Did you relish demythologizing your persona?

Yeah. It was nice. It was fun. And you've got to be uncompromising there, too; there's nothing glamorous about it. He's a guy who's pretty much on the bottom.

What about demythologizing the West, the "Wild West"?

I didn't mind that either. Because it's been demythologized along the way. It's great to do it because I didn't have to work at it; it was there as part of the nature of the story. It was in the structure and the honesty of it. It was odd to start out with a guy who's quite inept. He's having trouble getting on his horse [*laughs*], he's rusty. It's different than the characters I've played, where of course they couldn't miss with the gun.

And I don't think there's ever been a Western where the fear of death is discussed so openly. William Munny sees the maggots at the door, so to speak. Tell me about your attraction to this idea.

The first philosophizing about death is when he's reminiscing about killing the guy whose teeth he shot through the back of his head; he's haunted by the memory of this guy who didn't do anything to deserve to get shot. And then when he has fever, he starts hallucinating, and he sees a guy with maggots crawling out of his head. He's constantly pursued by the visual image of what he's done in the past. Or images he's seen. Like for a guy who's been to war. Like for a guy who's seen the Lieutenant Calley [My Lai] massacre.

Like for the guy who's made violent movies and carries around a lot of visual images from those movies in his head?

[*Smiling*] Well, I don't know if that's analogous. . . . It could be that the guy has all those violent images portrayed on the screen, and along comes a piece of material that allows him to do something that he's never been able to do in the past—which is to show where it all leads to. To philosophize about, what is the value of it all?

Did the Rodney King tape get to you?

[*Pause*] Yeah. First time you see it, you're overwhelmed. You're overwhelmed—boy, seems like a little much to me. Course, you don't hear anything or see the prelude to it all. But anyway, under any circumstances, that seemed excessive. But then I got tired of it, and I got mad at the media for running it—'cause I think they are exploiting it. The exact same people that are critical of the exploitation of the violence are in there exploiting it every time they can, running it again and again. The media has gotten so callous. It's all one-upmanship for ratings, so that's annoying. But without knowing it, there are certainly parallels to what goes on in *Unforgiven.*

In this film, the punishment never fits the crime. It's never about justice but about vengeance meets commerce, which I guess is what a bounty really is.

Justice never becomes part of it.

Justice is never even on the horizon.

Yeah, justice doesn't have anything to do

with it. It's about conscience more than justice. [*Long silence.*]

When you were finished filming the shoot-out in the saloon, were you conscious of the fact that that may be the last time you'll do something like that?

Uh-huh [*pause*].

How did that feel?

It felt good. I was even conscious throughout the film that this might be my last Western. This was the perfect story to be my last Western. I also thought this might be the last time I do both jobs—acting and directing. Maybe it's time to do one or the other. It's funny, you're the first person who's picked up on that, but I did have a feeling when I was doing that sequence that it would probably be the last time I'd be doing that.

Earlier you said, unprovoked by me I might add, that you are "not doing penance" for all the other characters you've played. Obviously, that concept is on your mind.

I said that unprovoked, but I said that in such a way that maybe *it is.* I'm not *consciously* doing penance for the mayhem I have created on the screen in the past, but in a way it fits in. Because he is a man that is haunted by this experience. I think it's not a conscious thing to do penance—if I hadn't done those other pictures, nobody would even think about it. But like you were mentioning, a lot of those people had things in their backgrounds that were kind of painful. This is the first one where you know all about it. He's been involved with some pretty bad mayhem in his day.

Leaving this movie, I couldn't imagine you playing a comic-strip action character again.

Yeah, I probably *can't.* I think the days of me doing what I have done in the past are gone. This is the present for me. To be saying smart lines and wiping out tons of people—I'll leave that for the newer guys on the scene. And that's just part of my growing process. I wouldn't know what to do with such a thing now; I'd have a hard time concentrating on it. At one point, I could throw myself into that; now I need more of a demand. I don't know how to equivocate it: It's like you need more foreplay or something [*laughs*]. You need something better.

Disco John Travolta

By Tom Burke

JUNE 15, 1978

It's clear the instant John Travolta lopes into the Imperial Gardens on Sunset Strip—clearer even than during his stunning opening *Saturday Night Fever* walk—he will be revered forever, in the manner of Elvis, James Dean and Marilyn Monroe, and for the same reasons. No one ever really felt they would know Elvis, Marilyn, Dean or that they *should:* Certain personalities seem born for the remoteness of the movie screen, not the vulgar, ersatz intimacy of television. Actually having such mythical creatures in one's living room would destroy the lush, intricate fantasies they permit you in the dark of the movie house.

Travolta's personal impact has nothing to do with what he says, sitting next to me in the restaurant, which is "Hi." He barely needs to speak: The grin does, as do the eyes, which glow perpetually in otherworldly blue. Neither is his real-life walk especially remarkable. Currently, journalists assert that he always walks as he did in *Fever*'s opening, his weight in his hips, shifting them like gears, but that's ludicrous. That was acting. Actually, he lopes, hunching a bit, vaguely simian, as are his features. But his force is physical, not-quite-accessibly sexual; he burns a hotter temperature than the human mean, as animals do.

This, more than anything else, explains his swift TV-to-cinema progression. Television could not contain him. Those who enter the republic's rumpus rooms via the Chromacolor window on the world aren't really supposed to burn hotter temperatures than the middle-American-norm. The medium was *meant* to embrace, say, Mary Tyler Moore, but consider the *men* who've done more than moonlight a picture and then, if lucky, fade back into regular TV pay: the fate of Henry Winkler, who, sadly, just doesn't burn hotter.

Not that you're supposed to bring up these matters with Travolta. Waiting in the expensive, crowded Imperial Gardens 'with his publicist, Michele—his *Welcome Back, Kotter* taping has run overtime again, he'll be late for dinner—I suggest that it will be interesting to know what John observed about the rather opulent sexuality of *Saturday Night Fever*'s actual Brooklyn discophiles; and Michele, more efficient than foxy, expresses alarm in her proper British accent.

"Um, you're not really going to ask John that?" Michele gasps courteously. "I don't know. I think that would . . . embarrass John."

Possibly Michele is right. In addition to, and working in tandem with, his sexuality is a

The King of Disco Cool, John Travolta, seduces the camera in *Saturday Night Fever.* Copyright © 1977 Paramount Pictures

marked ingenuousness, an almost callow vulner-ability. If I were kinder, I would call this a genu-ine sweetness, a less-than-casual interest in pleasing others. Michele exits as soon as John enters, and I find myself aiding him, conversa-tionally: Though eager to ingratiate, he seems unsure how, or of what to say. First, he simply smiles.

The oriental waitress executes a mini No play, "What's Your Order?" John requests tem-pura and a Coke and politely awaits a question. Why is it so inviting to mistrust him? Because he looks too good and made it too big too fast? Because he must know full well how seductive his presence is? Ask him about that, and he grins and blushes; he is probably not yet accom-plished enough as an artist to blush on cue. He is rising to the occasion. *Why* has he talked so little to the press? I don't ask that now, however, for he's suddenly discussing *Grease.*

". . . It was fun, on one level. Nowhere near as complicated as *Saturday Night Fever,* but it still wasn't easy because I'd never had to play a *fifties* dude on the screen before."

Travolta does not have that much to say about *Grease,* which is not surprising. As early as last January, word was out that the movie version of *Grease* was less than stupendous, but no one around Paramount or RSO was wearing Scotch tape, at night, between the eyebrows, to erase worry furrows. *Grease,* after all, has The Man.

"That's what they called me when I went to the 2001 Odyssey disco in Brooklyn to start working on *Fever*—The Man." John grins at that; it pleases him in an uncomplicated way. As he eats tempura, he wipes his fingers methodi-cally between each bite. "They said that because of Barbarino, naturally." It's important to note that during *Welcome Back, Kotter*'s genesis, Tra-volta was in no way meant to be the show's star.

"Reading the *Kotter* scripts, I saw right away that Vinnie Barbarino was written as a dumb punk. I knew I'd have to work all the time to give him humanity. I saw him as really a naive kid, you know?"

Actually, in all his roles so far, Travolta has had to work with considerable imagination to flesh out the characters, from the cretinous punk in *Kotter* to the sadistic punk in *Carrie* to the chauvinistic punk in *Fever* to the libidinous punk in *Grease.* It's John who says yea or nay to everything, right down to which of his publicity stills are used and where and when he makes personal appearances. The interviews he does are dispensed like pieces of the True Cross. He is not being aloof, only selective; he cares.

But back to *Saturday Night Fever.* First he read the magazine article on which the scenario was based, *Tribal Rites of the New Saturday Night;* he signed for the role before a script was ready. "Now, Danny Zuko in *Grease,* no matter what else he may or may not be, he's not difficult to grasp, you can see immediately how to act him. But Tony Manero—I was in the middle of the TV show. I was too close to Barbarino, and all Tony looked like to me was an extension of him, okay?"

For months, flacks have warned that John Travolta just doesn't discuss the late Diana Hy-land, and yet he just brings her up. When he says her name, his eyes become even more lumi-nescent, as they did when she won last year's best-TV-performance Emmy posthumously, and John accepted it for her, shouting, "Here's to you, Diana, wherever you are!" They met in 1976, when Hyland, a Broadway and TV vet-eran, was cast in John's made-for-TV-movie ve-hicle *The Boy in the Plastic Bubble,* about a young man born without natural immunities to disease and forced to live sealed in a germ-free artificial environment, as he watched other teenagers from his window, cavorting, sexually and otherwise. Diana Hyland played his mother.

Diana Hyland was forty, Travolta was twenty-two. He had never been involved with any woman as deeply as he became involved with her, and the magnitude of their affair stunned him daily. Last spring, when she died in his arms of cancer, friends doubted he'd recover.

"You *knew* her?" He's ecstatic. I explained that Diana was a casual friend in her New York theater days. "Then you know how ... unbelievable she was! Diana gave me the confidence."

Abruptly, John looks as Kris Kristofferson did when one asked him about Janis Joplin. Kris had murmured, "I don't like talkin' 'bout Janis now, it's like grave robbin'." John doesn't say that, but as he's spoken of his dead lady, another presence has, curiously, overtaken and possessed his own. His voice has coarsened with the inflections of South Brooklyn or North Philadelphia, and his heavy jaw, hard, inverted parenthesis of a mouth and his nose, subtly humped at the bridge, have arranged themselves into a sort of defensive arrogance. The young Brando had these features and would arrange them thus when he wished pain not to show (when he did, it did, sharply).

John Travolta, however, seems almost to catch himself doing that, and he smiles in a publicly pleasant way again. A weary furrow appears between his brows, as if someone had pressed a dull knife there, and he wants to leave. His Mercedes 450 SL coupe is brought up to the door. Though Travolta drives it with concentration and professional care, once, at a corner of Sunset Strip, he executes a fast, rakish turn, as though it had occurred to him that he was being taciturn and unglamorous and wished to interject a colorful moment. Perhaps he worries that he bores people. I ask him that, and he grins and nods.

"Besides this, I drive a 1955 Thunderbird," he offers, "a collector's item, a classic. Okay? When I come to the auto shop now, they triple the bill. Had the T-Bird in there for months, the bill was unbelievable, way beyond what it would have been if ... They aren't even subtle about it anymore."

And why should they be? It's common knowledge that following *Fever*, John can ask $1 million a movie. "Well, but I'm no millionaire, man." That he almost snaps, and he stresses it again.

"It sounds like I make a lot," Travolta insists quietly, "but I'm in the 50 percent tax bracket. Everyone seems to get a piece of the action. You might be surprised as how little cash I actually have, okay?"

Oh, come off it. Ultimately, he'll be loaded. "Well, I don't like talking about money. Or thinking about it. I never thought I would get *Kotter*. It was *never* a sure thing. I was *sure* they'd say, like they do in TV, 'You could *act* the part, but there's this other guy who *is* the part.' Mostly, they cast that way, but this time they went for the acting, which I really respect." Grin. "Naturally. Okay, so I got it. Yeah, more than $750 a week. And I thought, 'John, you now *deserve* to buy yourself something.'"

So he bought a DC-3. "That was the first true airliner," he explains. "I, uh, bought one of these. A real one. Actually, I have another plane now, too, a single-engine Air Coupe, really a *little* plane. As a kid in New Jersey, I'd lie awake nights listening to planes flying in and out of La Guardia Airport, heading west, and I'd have dreams about the people in them, who were going places. It was a very romantic vision to me, okay?"

It had to be. Englewood, New Jersey, where he grew up, though green and affluent, was, in John's words, "hardly any place at all." His father, an ex–star athlete, ran the Travolta Tire Exchange there. John does not attempt to portray his childhood as drab or deprived. His parents were the town's "hot" couple: His mother was an actress who coached acting, and his three sisters and two brothers all made stabs at show business. When I ask John to recall his growing up, the memories seem to begin at age twelve, when Actors Studio, the New York thespians' school attended by, among others, Brando, Al Pacino and Robert De Niro, held workshops in Englewood. "My mother got me in as an observer, but she didn't have to urge me. Man, nobody pushed me into show business, I was aching for it! And those rehearsals knocked me *out!*

"The first time I visited class, I came in when some of the Studio people, the advanced students from New York, were in the middle of doing a scene. After a couple of minutes they, like, broke character to ask the director a question, and I was *stunned.* I mean, I didn't know they'd been *acting*—that's how believable they were!"

Of course he joined the group, but he didn't go on studying acting at any length. "I could sort of duplicate what I saw those people do in class as soon as I saw it. I don't mean imitate them—I mean I always did have this ability to observe people, watch them awhile and very quickly absorb their . . . essence and then reproduce it. Nobody told me to do that. I just always stored things up about people, and when I had a character to create, I found I had this whole reserve of behavior and mannerisms to draw on. You remember the guys you knew who are like the guy you're playing, you build a character that way. The last thing you do is you add your own emotions to the script. That part's the most important of all; it's like, inside a character's fa-

cade, *I* live. I really come alive when I'm doing that."

It's late now, Travolta has to get up in the morning for *Kotter,* he would like to shut up and crash, but he stifles yawns, because he has assigned himself this talking. "I took the chance on going west because, sure, I really wanted the Barbarino role. I knew what a TV series could do for an actor . . . and I saw that Vinnie could be a 'hot' role, one I could really *flash* in. Okay?" If John is honest about his ambition, he's also careful to emphasize what he's done for art's sake.

The next morning is inexplicably cold, the L.A. sun is metallic. At ABC, Travolta is figuratively imprisoned. Here on the *Kotter* lot, he ceaselessly paces his dressing room, which is not grand, sparsely furnished and temporal; it is a space he could vacate rapidly, without looking back.

Actually, John hasn't much wanted to talk again today; he guards his press encounters closely, and one must battle and bargain for every minute spent with him.

There is this possibility: That although he is anything but dumb, he genuinely fears being thought so. Like a lot of high school dropouts, he's reached the age at which he's apprehensive about his lack of book learning. You sense, by now, that he is not so much callow as unformed; that Diana Hyland's death jarred him profoundly and began the shaping of his character; that, given time, he'll touch depths within himself that will dazzle movie cameras, provided he goes on finding directors and cinematographers as respectful, and loving, as *Saturday Night Fever*'s.

Oddly, it's the mention of Hyland's name that restores his good mood now. "I got the *Fever* script, I read it that night, frowning all through it. I wondered if I could give it enough dimension. Diana took it into the other room, and in about an hour she burst back in. 'Baby,' she shouted, 'you are going to be *great* in this! This Tony, he's got *all* the colors! First, he's angry *about* something; he hates the trap that Brooklyn and his dumb job are! There's a whole glamorous world out there waiting which he feels only when he dances. And he grows, he gets *out* of Brooklyn!' She went on like that a long time. 'He's *miles* from what you've played, and what isn't in the script, you're going to *put* there!' I said, 'He's also king of the disco. I'm not that good a dancer.' Diana said, 'Baby, you're going to *learn!*'"

John started dance practice the next day with a member of the Dancing Machine, a top disco group, and he began physical workouts with the trainer Sylvester Stallone used for *Rocky*. "I ran miles and miles, dropped twenty pounds, got a whole new body out of it." Still, he was dubious. In New York, he began his sorties to the 2001 Odyssey disco in Bay Ridge, Brooklyn, with *Fever*'s scenarist Norman Wexler, to observe the tribal rites. "The first time, I tried . . . disguises, you know? A hat, dark glasses." This seems to embarrass him. "Well, it didn't work, and it's not the right way for me, anyway. I had to do my observing as *myself,* see how they'd react to *me.*" The Odyssey's manager would admit him through a side door, he'd sit in the back, in the shadows. "It would be an hour before anyone saw me, and during that time I concentrated on every detail of their behavior I could. Their whole way of dancing, moving, conversing, relating to their girls, was ritualistic. It had its set rules."

When he was spotted, he claims, no one yelled, "It's Barbarino!" In her review of the movie, critic Pauline Kael wrote of the Odyssey patrons: "These boys are part of the post-Watergate, working-class generation with no he-

roes *except* in TV-showbiz lands; they have a historical span of twenty-three weeks, with repeats at Christmas." Yet John asserts that when they recognized him, they'd say, "Hey, man! Hey, it's fuckin' Travolta!" without any marked surprise that he was present. After all, every Thursday night, he entered their living rooms.

"A couple of guys would be talking to me, their girlfriends would come up, they'd say, 'Hey, stay away from him, don't bug Travolta. Don't bother me, I'm talking to The Man!' And they'd actually push the girls away: Tony Manero's whole male-chauvinist thing. I got it from watching those guys in the disco."

When filming in the Odyssey began, director John Badham decided to use some of the Brooklyn kids as extras; several asked Travolta home for dinner to meet their families, "and a lotta the stuff in the scenes at home, at the dinner table, and the ones with my brother in the picture, who's leaving the priesthood—I got the feel of those moments from those Brooklyn dinners. Yeah, I was raised Catholic, but it never had the huge importance in our house that it has in those Italian families in Bay Ridge."

When he talks of the Bay Ridge boys, he unconsciously begins imitating them, or rather, them imitating him imitating them, as he did performing Tony Manero. The inflection coarsens again, but it's not Vinnie Barbarino's this time. Here you recall what happened in *Saturday Night Fever:* Obviously director John Badham, shooting more or less in sequence, rehearsed extensively but did few retakes of scenes, allowing John to grow in his performance as the story progressed, and the character of Tony Manero to grow with him.

"Right, that *did* happen. I never really find a lot of things about a character when I'm reading a script, and that was doubly true with Tony. Even after Diana talked to me, I still saw the negatives in him; he read flat to me, and not sympathetic, the way he treats women, and so on. I had to find his vulnerability, so you cared about him, so that *I* cared about him." No, he did not ask for script changes. "I felt it was up to me, to incorporate in him some line of integrity: his caring about the girl's dream to get to Manhattan, even though she's bitchy to him."

So rehearsals were vital, not just dance rehearsals, to allow John Badham to accomplish his very long, unbroken takes of the disco dances. "I *can't* create a lot until I'm actually rehearsing with the actors I'm going to be working with—I don't know what *they're* going to do in a scene, or what I'll get from them to react to. My response to what another actor gives me may be a million times better than a choice I've made four months before we start working together." And though his character's pretty much set, before shooting starts. "I like to leave at least half of my creating until the camera's rolling. That way, the work doesn't have a set, 'acted' look, it's spontaneous, it . . . flows. In *Fever*, I'd suddenly add things, during takes, then ask John Badham if he liked that, and especially Norman Wexler, because he wrote it. I mean, to me, the writer of a script is *source*. . . ."

It's a word Scientologists use a lot, and disciples of L. Ron Hubbard will drop it into a conversation in order to proselytize. Not Travolta. He has to be asked about it. "Yeah, I discovered Scientology a few years ago. I'd get very depressed, for no reason. Psychoanalysis wasn't for me, but Scientology made sense to me right away because it seemed like a means of *self*-help. A meter shows you when you're responding to a bad experience in your past, you find the source of pain, acknowledge it, deal with it. That seemed to me very logical, and I was right. I get answers, that way. Okay?"

Definitely okay; more than enough said. He's restless now, because he's talked a lot again, or because in a moment, he'll have to go back to the set and be Barbarino, or both. Bring up Bay Ridge's curious sexuality, and he doesn't blush, but he doesn't grin. "Oh, yeah. That. Well, I mean, it was in the script. The guys having the girls . . . blow them, instead of the usual. No, I didn't, um, research that. You think I *should* have? Maybe that's a lack in me. Also, it could be simple birth control, *very* important. Remember, the girl who wants to make out with Tony. She says, 'I don't have any protection.' Tony says something like, 'Forget it, I'm not gonna have you get me to get you pregnant, you're not going to stick me with *that* problem.' See what I'm saying? Tony's only intention in that scene was . . . to get his rocks off."

John is not trying to be funny; he doesn't smile. Clearly he wishes he hadn't said it. "I remember one thing about those kids more than anything. The guys who'd gather around me—I don't know how many of them said to me, very respectfully, 'Wow, man, *I wish I was you.*' I've thought a lot about that."

So Pauline Kael was right? John's assistant had given me her review to read. "I think so. I guess there *are* no more heroes, except what TV and movies provide. I don't mean I'm *playing* heroes, I'm not, I don't want to. I mean *I'm* a hero to them, which is weird to me. Maybe a whole generation is . . . materialistic, and not much else. They were so awed by fame. Money. They thought it was the best possible world, to be in my position. That seems sad to me, you know? I'm *not* saying to you, it isn't good, that I don't enjoy it or appreciate it. I'm glad every day for it. That Oscar nomination, I was high on that for weeks, the recognition of work that it is—just the nomination. But when you start thinking this is *all* there is, then you're just swallowed up in a lot of bad values. Star time, you know? It's why I've *got* to get away weekends, get into the sky alone. Those Brooklyn kids, they were so *excited* by their *idea* of being me, I didn't want to lay the reality on them. That it is very hard work, very uncertain, to get big in this business very quickly. Why spoil it for them, talking about the *choices* you've got to make—that they are *very* tough, and if you make the wrong ones, you blow it all, and you've got to make them by *yourself.* You got to think 'work' *all* the time."

When he walks away, to work, he's hunched again; from the rear, he appears slightly weary and unwilling. Why do I regret seeing him go? He's been informative, but not enthralling; pleasant, but hardly intimate. There's been no suggestion that we're going to be friends, yet that's what I wanted. Which is, again, what stars do: if only you *knew* him. His charisma is, finally, like a good movie. You don't want it to end.

Nice Guy Tom Hanks

By Bill Zehme

JUNE 30, 1988

Tom Hanks is still a single man when I meet him. Within two weeks, he will pledge his connubial troth, and that will be that. For the moment, however, freedom prevails. Possibility is at hand. There is still time to indulge whims, to tempt fate, to fly in the face of responsibility. He suggests we play golf. "Wanna go tap the Titleist, whack the Wilson, spank the Spalding?" he asks, but it is all for naught, since rain douses the City of Angels even as we deliberate. I propose that we do what he normally does, but what he normally does is drink coffee, read newspapers and yammer on the phone (as he is inordinately fond of pointing out). He mentions something about going to the car wash, but, damn, the rain again. We decide at last to see a movie. On a lark, I suggest we take in a switch flick, one of those yarns wherein a gawky adolescent mysteriously finds himself trapped in the body of Dudley Moore or Judge Reinhold or George Burns. Hanks contorts his face at the notion.

In *Big*, the latest Tom Hanks film, a gawky adolescent wishes he were bigger, older, more formidable—and he wakes up the next morning as Tom Hanks. ("Maybe this has happened all over America," Reinhold says in *Vice Versa*. "In-

vasion of the body switchers!") It is the quixotic allegory for our fast times: a wistful fable about fleeting innocence, about growing up too quickly, about the inalienable right to act geeky. I ask Hanks what he would call the genre. "Planet of the apes," he says. "Well, that's what *I* heard."

Hanks' performance in *Big* transcends the film's premise. This is a controlled, sustained, sensitive, sweet piece of business. He is vulnerable. He is uncoordinated. He plays puberty as though his body hair sprouted yesterday. It is his finest work to date. And never once in the film can he be accused of being a smart-ass, his trademark attitude. "I was a little worried about that," says Penny Marshall, who directed *Big*. "His fans like him to be irreverent onscreen; most of his parts have been very sarcastic. But this is an actor's part, and he's an actor."

He is certainly no wisenheimer, this Hanks. I expect arrogance, smugness, glibness. I expect rapier retorts and high-voltage banter. Instead he is courteous and sincere. His liquid eyes, with their almost Asian set, are even a bit melancholy. They are never quite mirthful. Yes, he's funny, but almost never frenetically so. His laugh is an old guy's laugh, a slow, lumbering,

228

fogyish sort of *huh-huh-huh.* And yet at thirty-one he has a childlike enthusiasm about him. He drives a Dodge Caravan, he says, because "I like sitting up high; it's nice to see what's causing the traffic jam." Whenever he spies an accident on the road, he lurches with excitement: *"Whoa!* What happened here?" When he stumbles upon a good parking spot, he crows: "Look at this! *Beeyooteeful!"* Even weather sparks him: "This rain is *crackin' me up!"*

Hanks wants to see *Stand and Deliver,* so we head over to Westwood, a community that doubles as a multiplex Cinerama. It is early afternoon, and since he hasn't eaten anything today (he does not believe in breakfast), we first duck into one of his favorite Mexican haunts, a simple, cafeteria-style cantina. As he devours his burrito, a gangly guy in a business suit approaches tentatively.

"Tom, right?" says the suit guy, screwing up his courage. "Can I just shake your hand?"

"Sure," says Hanks, warmly offering his grip.

"Just so I can say I've shaken your hand," says the guy.

"You did," says Hanks with a tolerant grin.

"Really appreciate your movies," says the guy. Hanks graciously thanks him. The guy then says, "I saw you over here and thought, 'Wow, he looks like an old friend of mine.' "

"And," says Hanks, chuckling, "you thought, 'Who the hell *is* that guy?' "

Self-deprecation aside, Hanks has raised a salient issue here. *Just who the hell is this guy?* "I guess I come off in movies as a guy who you wouldn't mind hanging around with," he says, not exactly answering the question. Of course, in *movies* he's our old friend, the life of the party, the king of quippery. But that's entertainment. The guy sitting across the table from me just spilled his grapefruit fizz all over and didn't even joke about it. Invariably, he is portrayed by

the press as nerve-deadeningly normal, but that doesn't seem quite accurate, either. As Peter Scolari, his partner in drag in the gender-bending sitcom *Bosom Buddies,* says: "There's nothing normal about the guy. He is an imaginative, eccentric individual. He's a very quirky, very unusual young man."

According to Sally Field, Hanks' costar in the forthcoming *Punchline* (in which Hanks plays an ace stand-up comic), "It would be one thing if he was just this great, goofy guy. But that lasts for about thirty seconds, and then you want to meet somebody real. The reason he's a movie star and is going to stay one is that he's much more complicated than that.

"Yes, he's very entertaining and funny and easy to be around. But you know there's somebody else underneath, somebody dark. There's a sad side, a dark side. And that's what makes him so compelling on the screen."

Just don't try to pin him down on matters dark, sad or angry. He won't hold still long enough to allow for scrutiny. He bops and jostles through conversations and changes subjects so adroitly that hours and days pass before you realize that he has done so.

"Did you ever watch the TV show *Then Came Bronson*?" he asks in a rare wistful moment. "Michael Parks as Jim Bronson—now *that* guy I honestly wanted to emulate. I wanted to be a friendly guy on a motorcycle who gave everybody a fair shake and yet always rode out of town at the end of the hour."

We are now drinking coffee, killing time before the movie. So I ask him about regular stuff, like his impending wedding to actress Rita Wilson, who costarred with him in *Volunteers* and now shares his living quarters. Hanks blanches slightly; talk of personal details, no matter how mundane, makes him nervous. He takes privacy seriously. For this reason, he politely refuses to let reporters visit his Brentwood residence. I innocently ask whether he'll be married at home, but he stiffens and says pleasantly enough, "No, it will take place at a location whose whereabouts will remain under lock and key."

Rita Wilson will be his second wife. He entered his twenties under the freight of early wedlock and fatherhood. It's a subject fraught with peril. He has been known to turn surly in deflecting discussion of his first marriage, to actress-producer Samantha Lewes, a union that gave him a son, now ten, and a daughter, five. The divorce was finalized within the last two years; he remains devoted to his children and keeps their visits frequent and regular—"like clockwork."

He will say this much about the approaching wedding: "It's a wonderful thing to do—such a neat, optimistic, good-feeling, cleansing separation between an old life and a new life." I ask him what he values most about his relationship with Rita. "We say what's on our minds without worrying about any repercussions," he says after a moment of consideration. "Just very open communication, good news and bad news. As well as being able to laugh. We have laughed an awful lot. You need that. The person you're gonna marry is somebody you're gonna probably talk to every day for the rest of your life. You're gonna have to want to do that."

Earlier, I noticed on Hanks' dashboard a greeting card propped open just enough to reveal a message from his bride-to-be—"I love you always, Rita" and a tiny hand-drawn heart.

She seems to stir in him an almost profound sense of gallantry. Last year, Hanks took Rita to the Oscar ball. At the boisterous party, he encountered a most unsettling trespass. "Bette Davis was sitting in my fiancée's chair," he says, still incredulous. "She just came over and sat

down! Arlene Dahl, who was sitting at our table, said, 'Oh, go over and tell her to get out of your chair! Do it, she'll love it! Go tell her.' So I went over and said, 'Miss Davis, you're sitting in my girlfriend's seat, but if anyone can sit in her chair, you can.' She just looked at me and finally said, *'I can't hear a word you're saying.'*"

"**D**id I mention to you that this is a private screening?" he blusters as we step into the minitheater, which is virtually empty for the midafternoon showing of *Stand and Deliver*. "I bought out the house." He finds a seat and crumples into a comfortable slouch, then hollers, "Okay, Rocco, *roll it!*" The screen, of course, remains blank. A teenage couple straggles down the aisle. "Hey!" Hanks calls after them. "Hey! I think you folks are in the wrong theater! Hey!" The couple ignores him and plops down ahead of us. *"Damn,"* he says, grinning stupidly.

At last, a truly Hanksian display. Frankly, I had begun to worry. I had even proposed that we storm through some torpid business office where he could cast sly bons mots at hapless working stiffs, the way he did in the triumphant—and largely ad-libbed—opening moments of *Nothing in Common*. Hanks brightens at any mention of that film, a seriocomic exploration of strained father-son relations, in which Jackie Gleason portrayed his cranky old man. "It changed my desires about working in movies," he says of the experience. "Part of it was the nature of the material, what we were trying to say. But besides that, it focused on people's relationships. The story was about a guy and his father, unlike, say, *The Money Pit*, where the story is really about a guy and his house."

The remainder of Hanks' oeuvre doesn't depart too radically from this sort of formula. Take, for instance, *Splash:* a guy and his fish. *Bachelor Party:* a guy and his libido. *The Man*

With One Red Shoe: a guy and his footwear. *Volunteers:* a guy and the Peace Corps. *Dragnet:* a guy and his badge. *Every Time We Say Goodbye:* a guy and—um, has anyone actually seen or, for that matter, *heard of* this movie?

"I don't think I've ever gone back and repeated myself, though," he says. "There have been times when it was close. The guys I play all have a lot of flaws. Part of that is the confines of this face and this body. There's not a lot I can do to change it." Here he is just being cagey. As Penny Marshall says, "He has that handsomeness that isn't too beautiful. It's approachable. I think he's adorable."

Legions of women agree. They see him as a youthful avatar of romantic comedy, the rightful heir to Cary Grant. Last year a major men's magazine built an elaborate fashion spread on the concept, togging out our boy (a celebrated jeans enthusiast) in all manner of debonair pastels. *"Bad* duds," he says. "I looked like a sleazy French golf pro."

Now Hanks just looks rested, which he rarely is. *"Big* is my tenth movie," he says wearily. "That's almost too many. I made *Splash* [his first film] in '83. In five years that's a lotta work. For a while there I made movies in an absolute flurry of activity. But the opportunity was there. And I had a great desire to be working. You do get these feelings that you're never ever going to work again." Last year alone, he made three films—*Dragnet, Punchline* and *Big*—which left him so worn-out that he caught pneumonia and had to spend a month recuperating.

So far he has taken this year off and has no concrete plans for his next project. He is lying low. "There are other things that are just more important than being a hotshot-celebrity movie actor," he says, uttering those last words a tad contemptuously. "I simply want to pay attention to those other things for a while, things like life

and love and going to the bank and organizing your garage.

"When I'm on film sets, so much of life is completely put on hold. Eventually, you realize, 'When this work is done, I have to go home to a place I've had so little personal investment in that it might as well be just another hotel room.' Which is just no way to live. And that's how actors get all fucked up. People tell them they're wonderful, and then they go sit alone in a hotel room or in a very nice house, which has been decorated by somebody else, where the furniture has been placed by an *absolute stranger.* You have no connection to it!"

We visit Hanks' office the next day. Since November, his office has been located on the Disney Studios lot, in Burbank. The decor is Spartan, but there are *touches.* On the coffee table: crayons and a coloring book, plastic dancing raisins, a ball autographed by Hanks' beloved Cleveland Indians. Tacked to the bulletin board: an Indians T-shirt and a map of the United States. "I had that in my briefcase one day," he says of the map, "and decided to put it up so I can look at it and say, *'Here's our land!'* "

Because he's so intuitively childlike in *Big,* I had asked him earlier when he most feels like a kid. "I never feel like a kid," he said, "but yet I *always* feel like a kid." He is now playing with a Duncan Imperial yo-yo, so the subject resurfaces naturally enough. Childhood for Tom Hanks was a many-splintered thing. His parents divorced when he was five. He and his older sister and brother moved out with their father, while his younger brother stayed with his mother, who subsequently remarried three times. His father remarried twice and, due to a peripatetic career in the restaurant industry, continually uprooted Tom, his siblings and their step-siblings and lugged them all over California. "I moved about a million times," says Hanks sunnily. "I think we moved every six months of my life."

He steps up to his map and, jabbing his index finger at it, diagrams his youthful wanderings for me. Beginning at Concord, his birthplace, his finger thumps repeatedly at points up and down the Golden State, with a brief detour to Reno, Nevada. He taps meaningfully at Sacramento, where he attended Cal State for a year and a half, then his hand darts eastward all the way to Cleveland, where he interned for three seasons at the Great Lakes Shakespeare Festival (and discovered those Indians!). His finger flicks up to New York, where he stayed long enough to attend a cattle-call audition for a sitcom pilot called *Bosom Buddies*, and then whisks back to where it came from, landing approximately upon the spot we occupy this very moment.

But what kind of kid was he? "A geek, a spaz," he says. "I was horribly, painfully, terribly shy. At the same time, I was the guy who'd yell out funny captions during filmstrips. But I didn't get into trouble. I was always a real good kid and pretty responsible." Philosophical, too. He considers all of his early moving an excellent primer for the actor's life. "It made me flexible," he says. "It gave me confidence to think I can be in any sort of social situation and know how to gracefully get out of it."

Like when I ask for phone numbers of relatives who might give me a good quote. "They won't tell you anything that I wouldn't," he says very sweetly. "Problem is," he adds, thinking aloud, "what you need is my own self-examination, which, well, I don't do." He shrugs helplessly. I ask him whether he thinks he's easy to know. "No, probably not. A guy with whom I once worked on a movie said somewhere that people on the set felt they knew me and yet nobody really knew me. And that's pretty much

true. If I make people feel at ease, well, that's a wonderful thing. If they don't feel as though they're my best friend in the world, that's a wonderful thing, too."

He fetches a remote-control gadget off the desktop. "Want to see something amazing?" he says excitedly, leading me toward the doorway. "Stand back. Watch this." I step into the outer office, and from inside, he aims the remote at the door. It automatically swings shut in my face. The symbolism is not lost on me.

"Here they are!" Penny Marshall says. Hanks and Rita have just arrived—fifteen minutes late—at the Zanuck Theater on the Twentieth Century–Fox back lot, where five hundred people have been seated for a Sunday-night test-screening of *Big*. This will be Hanks' first viewing of the film. He and Rita, a spirited brunette in a billowy white windbreaker and leggings, race up the theater steps, where they are greeted by Marshall, producer Jim Brooks and a handful of studio people. Hanks apologizes to them, explaining that he just drove his children to the airport (to send them back to their mother) and got stuck in traffic.

In Rita Wilson's company, he seems looser, livelier, more Hanksian. Elizabeth Perkins, who costars in *Big*, says of the couple, "They both complement each other's energy. She bubbles over, she's so effusive. When the two of them are together, there's just another force at work." Tonight they josh and laugh and eventually slip into the back row of the full, darkened theater. To prevent being discovered, Hanks keeps a Chicago White Sox cap tugged down across his brow.

He is pensive as he watches himself onscreen. He never laughs at his own funny moments, although they convulse Rita and the crowd. After a half hour, the film suddenly melts in the projector, and the picture dissolves into molten goop. "Hey," says Hanks, "great effect!" This happens again twice; each time it does, the houselights come on, and Hanks leans into his future bride, hiding himself.

At one point I ask whether she knew in advance that her fiancé would be so convincingly pubescent in the role. She looks at me incredulously and guffaws. "I *live* with this man!" she howls. "This is a man who plays hockey inside the house with a bag of Milano cookies!" Hanks protests: "Oh, stop it!"

Finally, the projector is fixed, and the film winds to its lovely, bittersweet conclusion. Hanks and Rita gallop out ahead of the throng, and it isn't until they are well away from the theater that I see that both are crying. He sweeps her up in his arms, pressing his face against her neck. "It was so sad," she says with an embarrassed laugh. "It's just a movie, hon," he tells her softly. "You'll get over it." He honks his nose and adds, "What a sweet movie. I didn't expect to cry."

A stray cat slinks past them. Hanks, who seems to be gaining buoyancy, affects a mock-showbizzy mien and announces, "Ah, one of the many studio cats here tonight!" Rita joins in the conceit and says, "He's the informer cat, the one who gives away the ideas to the other studios." Hanks snaps his fingers to a Vegas beat and actually begins to sing. Loudly. "He's a stoooooooodio cat," he croons. Rita is now dancing around in the dark, meowing in accompaniment. Hanks giddily belts out another line: "He's a snotty, kooky, wacky, nutty, supah studio caaaaaaaaaattt!"

Strangely enough, it is an exhilarating spectacle, a little bit of private lunacy they will forget by morning. He slips his hand into hers, and they saunter off across the empty movie lot, howling exultantly into the night.

Studly Richard Gere

By Richard Price

SEPTEMBER 30, 1982

Richard Gere, for five years the sexual grenade of Hollywood's substar leading men,
has suddenly become America's sweetheart.
With the unexpected success of *An Officer and a
Gentleman,* he's broken through the narcissistic-
punk, *Goodbar*–*Gigolo* persona to become a heroic heartbreaker, a romantic lead who not only
gets away with literally sweeping his leading lady
off her feet in a dangerously cornball finale, but
also manages to leave everybody in the house
teary-eyed and smiling.

An Officer and a Gentleman marks the first time
Richard Gere has truly won over an audience.
Even with all the exhibitionism of the obstacle
courses, the karate and the hot-cha love scene
with Debra Winger, his role never makes him
look like he's being used to sell some kind of
high-tech bodybuilding equipment or bikini underwear for men. Everything seems to click. He
plays it from Anytown instead of *Angst*-ville. His
character's pain is right at eye level. He gets
pissed off instead of acting tortured. He
squawks and sputters instead of writhing. He
falls in love like a person. Despair is not glamor-
ized. Isolation not ennobled. He plays your
basic vulnerable kid with a chip on his shoulder.
Although it seems to be another one of his

loner-learns-to-love characters, this one doesn't
fool around. His education is so linear you feel
like you're sitting through a training film. Made
in America.

I first met Richard Gere in 1977, a few weeks
after he had landed his first starring role, the
teenage hard hat in *Bloodbrothers,* the movie
based on my novel. Gere was living in a less-
than-stylish Greenwich Village pad, a former
plumbing-supply shop on ground level, in the
shadow of the West Side Highway and flanked
by heavy-leather gay bars. Although I showed
up twenty minutes late, his girlfriend at the
time, Penny Milford, who won a best-support-
ing-actress Oscar nomination for her work in
Coming Home, had to entertain me because Gere
was napping.

When he finally emerged, Gere was wearing
his finest BVDs and smoking a cigarette that
hung from his lips in a Belmondo vertical drop.
He mumbled, "Hey," gave me a hug and
dropped on the couch as if he were suffering
from combat fatigue. Despite his casual,
gummy-eyed beefcake act, despite the fact that
he never seemed to fully wake up or raise his
voice above a lazy murmur, and despite the fact

that the dude was definitely *on* from the minute he made his entrance, the room seemed to shrink to the dimensions of a broom closet. It had nothing to do with his glamour or physicality. It was something deeper, more anxiety provoking. He projected a furtive alertness, an acute self-consciousness, with a mind that never stopped checking out the scene. There was a part of him standing across the room, not only sizing me up but sizing himself up as well.

None of this was apparent in his words, posture or eyes; all we did was have a warm, mutually flattering conversation. In fact, he seemed curious and attentive to a fault, but the air was so charged that I felt like a medium sitting in a room full of ghosts. He seemed so convinced of his own presence, so effortlessly insistent that I *watch* him, that I just happily leaned back and passed the popcorn. The opening moments of *An Officer and a Gentleman,* in which Gere's character wakes up and stumbles around in his shorts, dragging on a cigarette, were so identical to his show in the loft that I felt as if I'd already seen the movie. But I would no sooner have called Richard Gere vain on that first encounter than I would have called a kamikaze a flyboy. Vanity doesn't shrink rooms.

I felt that it was important to Gere that I liked him and was taken with him. I felt he was wooing me, offering himself. But despite the obviousness of his deciding to enter a room in his BVDs to meet a stranger, it wasn't sexual. And it was a successful woo; not because of the preening and shtick but because the preening and shtick were so humanly transparent. He seemed so self-consumed, so self-conscious, that he laid out more cards on the table than he realized. In his own ass-backward way, he was one of the most honest and open people I'd ever met. I liked him tremendously.

The only thing I remember of what he said to me that night was that earlier in the week he'd been mugged by some Chelsea teenagers who had regularly been victimizing lone men on the dark gay-bar strip near his loft. "They probably thought I was fucking gay because I had on a leather jacket and motorcycle boots. I've always worn that. I'm into motorcycles for years. Pisses me off."

Gere was born and raised in upstate New York as one of five children in a good Methodist family that was "amorphous middle class," in his adolescent estimation. "My old man's an insurance salesman," he says, "but he's not one of those huckster types. He's really great at it because he believes in it. He's like a minister; he really wants to help people, and they love him."

Gere not only learned to play trumpet, piano, guitar, banjo and sitar, but wrote the scores for several high school productions and acted in them. "I was a child prodigy," he says. "When I was fourteen, I played trumpet in a local symphony orchestra. My whole family plays something. When I go home, we all play together, then switch instruments and play something else. They're great people, my family."

He was also a good gymnast, but his grades weren't so hot. He left high school feeling "pretty confused," going through what he calls his "paranoid stage—you know, when it seems like the whole cosmos is trying to rip your balls off."

In 1967, he enrolled at the University of Massachusetts, studying philosophy before dropping out and joining the Provincetown Playhouse for a season and moving on to the Seattle Repertory Theater for another. After a period of long-haired hippiedom in Seattle, Gere headed back east. He made a brief, abortive effort at forming a rock band with old school friends in Vermont. "We called ourselves the Strangers or something," he says. "It only lasted three months. We hated each other with a passion." Eventually, he moved to a Lower East Side walk-up in New York City.

In 1972, Gere landed a part in the fast-folding, fatefully named rock opera *Soon,* but despite this inauspicious big-city debut, he began to get roles that got him noticed: Danny Zuko in the Broadway and London productions of *Grease,* some Shakespeare at Lincoln Center and an appearance on *Kojak* and in the TV movie *Strike.* The latter work brought Gere to the profound conclusion that television is a "disgusting, humiliating experience." But his growing visibility had its rewards; he was working on a regular basis. His intense performances as a pimp in *Report to the Commissioner,* a shell-shocked raider in *Baby Blue Marine* and a condemned murderer in Sam Shepard's *Killer's Head* earned him the lead in Terence Malick's beautiful bomb, *Days of Heaven.*

Then came the release of *Looking for Mr. Goodbar,* in which Gere played the menacing stud who danced around Diane Keaton's bedroom with a switchblade. It was a flashy, electrifying piece of work that had the audience sitting up straight. After the release of *Goodbar* in 1978, Gere says he had enough offers to play "Italian crazies for the next fifteen years."

To change his public image, he reluctantly decided to start playing the publicity game. This meant dealing with industry types—"leeches, vampires and hustlers"—and doing interviews, which he loathed. One reporter described his attitude toward interviews as the same "sentiments a dog has for flea baths."

Bloodbrothers was a flop, and in *Days of Heaven* he and the rest of the cast played second fiddle to the cinematography. However, he got a lot of magazine coverage: lots of full-page photos of his bedroom face and gymnast physique. Next

thing you knew, he was a star, complete with his own blowup poster.

That same year, 1978, saw a whole new crop of male sex stars: various dark, smoldering, androgynous, Italian-looking actors in their late twenties, but most notably Gere and John Travolta. Newman, Redford and Reynolds were over forty, and these young bloods were the new wave.

Some critics—confronted by the glut of young dark angels who seemed spawned more out of a photogenic "come hither" look than from any sustained, *tour de force* acting—started screaming bloody murder. If Gere had been born with blond hair and blue eyes, he might not have been able to ride the wave, but his reviews might have focused more on his art. As it was, Gere, like the others, caught it in the neck.

"Richard Gere is to Robert De Niro what *Beatlemania* is to the Beatles," smirked Pauline Kael in her review of *Bloodbrothers.* And other critics referred to him as a *movie star* as opposed to an *actor,* as if he had simply lucked out, the millionth customer to walk through the door. They never gave him any slack. They bitched about his posturing and self-involvement but rarely referred to the energy and intensity at the source. His magnetism was reduced to just so much meat.

In 1979, he appeared in *Yanks,* directed by John Schlesinger, and in Paul Schrader's *American Gigolo* (in the lead originally intended for John Travolta). *Gigolo* earned him mixed critical reaction, strengthened his sex-bomb charisma and added fuel to his detractors' claim that he was all pinup boy.

Back in 1977, I was having dinner with Gere when a nervous, smiling fan approached our table and Gere straight-armed him with an icy mutter that had the guy walking away backward. Gere was a relative unknown then, and I had a hunch that as his visibility increased, he was going to have a lot of trouble leaving the house. Two years later, it seemed that the bigger problem was his *insistence* on leaving the house.

Gere appeared to go out of his way to court the press' derision. "Richard has always been very uptight about the press and being asked stupid questions," explains Taylor Hackford, the director of *An Officer and a Gentleman*. "He's a really complex guy who values his private life. He is not an arrogant asshole."

In 1979, I bumped into Gere at a party given in the lobby of an off-Broadway theater. Photographers cruised the crowd for faces, but none of them dared approach Gere. A few shot him looks that suggested they wouldn't mind photographing his funeral. It was terrifying.

Gere tried to come off as though he were oblivious to all this tension, but the unsmiling tightness of his mouth betrayed him. I couldn't imagine he had come to the theater in anticipation of a good time. The night seemed like some blind foray into the combat zone. If Gere had exploded at that party, I don't know if he would have screamed, "I hate you!" or "Why don't you love me!" or "For Christ's sake, will you let me just go to a fucking party in peace?"

Although the directors' raves seem unanimous, the response of the ticket buyers had always been mixed before *An Officer and a Gentleman.* Young women and young gay men seemed to be turned on to Gere almost straight across the board. But when you talked to others, he ran into some trouble; they found his sexuality diluted by his inability to reach out and make them feel needed. As an actor, Gere is a plunger; his concentration is sea deep. But on the screen, it can repel as well as attract. He

can act "too hard," as one semifan said, and cut himself off.

Despite Gere's appeal as a smolderer, despite his ability to look at you and ask the time as if your Bulova were strapped to your soul, there's another, perhaps more compelling, side to his screen persona that prior to *An Officer and a Gentleman* I'd only seen once or twice: Gere as protector.

There's a scene in *Bloodbrothers* in which Gere, playing a hospital attendant, tells a roomful of eight-year-old kids a ghost story. He speaks in a playful spook-house whisper, and the kids are pop-eyed with fascination. By the end of his tale, he's turned it into an allegory about brotherhood. Despite the potential bathos of that scene, he received a spontaneous standing ovation when the film was shown at the New York Film Festival. Sweetness and earnestness might not make an audience horny, but it can warm people—it can get them on your side. Sex doesn't last, but cooking does.

The last time I saw Gere was at the home he was renting in the Hollywood Hills for the duration of his work on *Breathless,* an L.A.–Las Vegas remake of the jazz-cool Parisian classic that made Belmondo.

When he opened the door, my first reaction was that he was nude but had somehow managed to airbrush his crotch. He was wearing a pair of flesh-colored bikini underwear. Jesus Christ, not again.

The white, sunlit house, which once belonged to Cole Porter, was buttressed by a blue-tiled pool hanging over the cliff like a setup for Biblical judgment. It seemed to be a statement of triumph and stature for Gere. It was a long way from the plumbing store in the Village, and he damn well knew it. When I asked for the bathroom, he said with a straight face, "There's two.

The bigger one's on the left." When I came back, he asked me which one I'd used and seemed disappointed that I hadn't used the big one.

As we sat across from each other by the pool, Richard leaned back almost spread-eagle, centerfold style. I thought about getting into the spirit of things by squinting at him and saying, "You know, it really *is* kind of hot up here. . . ." Then, I'd take off my pants, sit back in heart-print boxer shorts, black dress socks and black shoes and turn on the tape. But I balked, not sure he'd laugh.

We talked about success, fucking up, Shakespeare, the old days, William Burroughs and about how having a house with two bathrooms was better than a house with one.

A half hour into the talk, I saw why he could finally pull off *An Officer and a Gentleman*. He seemed like a different person—softer, easier. He'd lost that look of someone who's got World War III going on inside his head. He seemed more aligned. Back in 1977, the text of his conversation wasn't nearly as compelling as the subtext, but now it felt as if he could finally reach the ends of the table.

When I asked him if there was anything in particular that accounted for his success, he answered without hesitation. "Focus. I knew people who were as talented as I was who didn't have it. I think I've always felt that it was focus and commitment and concentration that made the thing happen. When things fuck up, you just keep going. Most people give in and say,

'Fuck it, I'm not cut out for this,' and they do something else. You got to outlast all the fuck-ups and just keep going, keep going, keep going."

He chanted, slightly rocking, his eyes locked on the blue of the pool. It struck me that during all the times I had met him in the past, he was so taut, so entrenched in his *keeping going*, that I never thought he could abstract the words.

"Richard, would you say you're the happiest you've ever been in your life?"

He took a deep breath and let it out in a slow hiss. "Let's put it this way: I'm the farthest from suicide that I've ever been."

For some reason, I thought it was the funniest thing I'd ever heard, and I started to laugh so hard I had to turn off the recorder.

Gere giggled tentatively, more out of delight at my reaction than because he meant it to be a funny line. "You know, I was very lucky," he said. "Opportunities arose when I was ready for them. I didn't get things I was not ready for, so I wasn't exposed before I was ready."

A true star must possess a seamlessness, an easiness on the screen, that can warm an audience like a shot of brandy. He must be able to cultivate rapport, a winking intimacy and recognition. He must be able to laugh at himself. In the past, Richard Gere never struck me as someone who could laugh at himself. But suddenly I had the thought that if I'd actually stripped down to the boxers, he just might have cracked up. And if he had, I'd be willing to bet anything that his stock as a star was soon going to go through the roof.

Serious Meryl Streep

By David Rosenthal

OCTOBER 15, 1981

Meryl Streep gets nervous. Not all the time, mind you. But there are occasions when an eerie chill rides down her spine, introspective moments when it seems as if the walls of her well-constructed edifice could tumble down with an ignominious crash.

She'll be chatting, a concerned look crossing her lambent face, about her fears of nuclear accidents, her worries about the world's safety with the bomb at Ronald Reagan's fingertips. And somehow, though these sentiments sound sincere, there's something hollow in the presentation. Meryl insists they're anything but ersatz, practically scoffs at the suggestion, in fact, but then concedes a bit. An actress, perhaps better than anyone else, can always detect a false note.

"I'm not really self-analytical," she says slowly. "But I've been thinking that maybe a lot of my anxiety about these things may have to do with—it's a way of displacing my own anxieties about my own incredible good fortune. Maybe that's my way of dealing with it. So much happiness has come to me, and I think somewhere, somebody's got to pay."

You almost get the feeling that Meryl Streep would like to get the dues-paying over with. When you've risen to celebrity as quickly as she, when in five years you've gone from drama-school graduate to the most sought-after actress of her generation in Hollywood, when talent and beauty have combined to produce a performer capable of playing any role, something's probably got to give. Even if she doesn't fail, someone will inevitably stand up to say she did.

"I'm sure that everybody's chomping at the bit to do that," she says, calmly anticipating a pen in the back. "It's because of all the glowing, gushing things that have been said. And I'm standing in the middle of this: One pours flowers on me, the other one sees that, so now it's time to dump shit."

This is, indeed, a reasonable expectation, the ways of a world of fickle idolatry. But would-be demystifiers are in for stern competition; her self-assessments are far more scathing than anything a critic might concoct. The higher you get, the steeper the fall. Meryl Streep considers herself lucky and knows just how good she is, so she is determined to keep questioning herself to continue the ascent.

Consider *The French Lieutenant's Woman*. As Sarah, the mysterious caped heroine of John Fowles' rural Victorian Britain, Meryl must—for the first time in her career—carry the dual burdens of a starring vehicle and the screen usage of an obscure accent. Just before filming commenced, Meryl sat with an acquaintance in a London park, quivering, "I'm so frightened, I'm so frightened about something as important as this." The director, Karel Reisz, also became aware of this perturbation and was worried whether Streep could handle the difficult quirks of nineteenth-century vocal inflections so crucial to the part. "Meryl was very concerned at first," he said. "We even had it up our sleeve that we could lip sync some of those parts if it was necessary."

It wasn't, though. Meryl concentrated, focused and applied the sort of intensity that awes everyone she's worked with. She hired a voice coach and spent endless hours reading aloud from Jane Austen and George Eliot to perfect her efforts. By the time *French Lieutenant's Woman* was under way, Meryl's involvement was so acute that a close friend she called in New York didn't recognize her voice.

Now, this transformation is not unique in a fine actress. All part of the job, this stepping in and out of roles. But what makes it so odd in Streep's case is that despite her effortless skills, her uncanny way of squirreling inside any character's life and psyche, she has grave doubts about her ability to pull it off. Perhaps because she's never failed to meet a professional challenge, there's an internal pressure within her, a dynamic defensiveness, which spurs her to greatness while preventing the slightest slip into complacency.

And her approach, the one that ostensibly accounts for this angst, is simply to assume the life of whoever it is she is about to portray. To become part of the landscape, as Meryl aptly puts it, to see a character's world and simply step right in. To disappear into the warped reality of acting fiction and emerge as someone else.

To do this too well can be scary.

At age thirty-two, Meryl Streep is well-armed. Always in control, cautious to a fault. The world is perilous, and Meryl goes to great lengths to keep its vague cruelties away from her door. Acting is how. Just as it is difficult to separate the dancer from the dance, so one must reach to divine the Meryl Streep beneath the grease-paint. "It's seldom that Meryl's not involved in the acting task," says Joe Papp, head of New York's Shakespeare Festival and the producer of many of Streep's theatrical triumphs. "I don't think she gives that up, in a play or anyplace else."

Does Papp ever feel uncertain whether he's dealing with his close friend or with a strange, famous actress? "It depends on the social situation," he says. "If we're having dinner and her kid is there, and her husband is there, that's one thing. But when it's a more public situation, her antennae are out and the warning signals go out. Actually, she has a certain shyness, and a lot of that is protecting herself."

The reason for this is more pragmatic than neurotic. The cutting edge of celebrity is exposure and risk. She talks about weird people waiting outside her lower-Manhattan apartment when she comes home from the theater late at night; she, her husband, Don Gummer, a sculptor, and their infant son, Henry, are now moving to a similar loft, but one with far better security. It is a sensitive subject, one that infuriates her if breached. Her reaction to a small-town reporter who virtually printed the directions to her secluded upstate New York home—a tiny, three-room house surrounded by ninety-two acres of Christmas trees—was practically venomous: "I wrote her: 'What's going on in your mind? I don't live like the Kennedys. I don't have a compound and nine weimaraners running the grounds. You just make us sitting ducks.'"

The flags go up every time she opens her mouth. "At home, I don't have any defenses," she says. "I'm not wary. But I am very wary in this business, generally, so I'll be careful of what I say. It's a sad thing, because I used to be more opinionated—I mean, I'm still opinionated, but I used to be louder about them. Now, the size of my opinions is distorted into something important. So if I say, 'So-and-so really *stank* in that,' it really gets around, all out of proportion to the way I felt. And it's so tiring to go around and sweep up after yourself and say, 'Look, I didn't mean it that way.' You feel like a politician. Who wants to live like that?"

The solution, Meryl has found, is simply not to go out anymore. It is a trade-off she's made but abhors, a bow to a gossipy, nosy culture that's now made it hard for her to go to museums or galleries or just wander about without being recognized or annoyed. "It seems to me," she says, "when you become famous, a lot of your energy goes into maintaining what you had before you were famous, maintaining your sense of observation, being able to look at other people. If they take away your observation powers, you're lost."

For an actress, that is a harsh jolt. So why has she done a limited amount of, though enough, publicity to make her face an object of almost freak attention? Certainly to assist in the promotion of films she believes in and also to further her career at a juncture where stars either soar or turn into novae. It needs to be done, but Meryl well understands the absurdity and transience of a public persona.

There is a story told around the Public Theater in New York, for example, about the time Canadian prime minister Pierre Trudeau attended one of Meryl's performances. After the show, Trudeau came backstage to extend his best wishes and then promptly asked her out. Meryl, slightly stunned, politely demurred. When Trudeau finally left, she said to a colleague: "I don't understand it. Why do famous people only want to meet other famous people?"

The notion gets funnier. "Put yourself in this position," she says. "You're passing the newsstand at Fifty-seventh Street and Sixth Avenue, and there's your face on the cover of a magazine. And one week later, you're on the subway, and there's that cover, with your face, on the floor. Somebody's probably pissed on it. It's an immediate sense of recognition of what this is."

So it is a joke, a harrowing joke, but a joke nonetheless. To escape, the mask goes back on and Meryl is someone else. With *The French Lieutenant's Woman,* the appeal was to pretend, to let her imagination become the truth. After playing contemporary women in all her previous major films, Meryl chose to dress up by switching places with a lady one hundred years in the past. "I said to my agent, 'I've got to do something outside of Manhattan, outside of 1981, outside of my experience,'" Meryl recalls. "'Put me on the moon; I want to be someplace else. I want to be held in the boundaries of a different time and place.'"

As Karel Reisz says: "Some actors feel humiliated by costumes. Meryl feels liberated by them."

There is a tremendous temptation for a star approaching peak earning power to go for the brass ring quickly, to get his or her name above the credits in any sleazy, wealthy production and let the critics fall where they may. But Meryl Streep does not do junk; she refuses to. All of her cinematic ventures—*Julia, The Deer Hunter, Manhattan, The Seduction of Joe Tynan, Kramer vs. Kramer* and *The French Lieutenant's Woman*—have been quality products and not even necessarily the most lucrative ones. In fact, for *French Lieutenant's Woman,* Meryl received $350,000, not a grand sum by today's standards in Hollywood. It is all a by-product of enormous pride and an uncompromising nature that is more willful than stern.

Streep says she's just discriminating, patient and motivated by a need to be "engaged" by whatever she's working on, avoiding boredom by playing characters whose souls have more than a single dimension. "This is a particularly unadventurous time intellectually and artistically, even in terms of entertainment," she says. "And I feel worried, because my livelihood is threatened because I'm not interested in doing most of the films that are being made. People think you make choices based on some array of characters that are placed in front of you. Well, it isn't that way. There are so few beautifully written scripts that if there's something with any promise, you latch on. *You* pay them to do it."

This isn't as elitist or self-righteous as it sounds. Merely realistic, arrived at through a commanding stature of ability and taste and uttered with a twinge of pain. But it also stems from something else, perhaps Streep's exceptional streak of good fortune. Meryl has rarely been forced into a corner, and things have generally come easily to her. She's someone who's always strived, not struggled.

"I'm in a position where I can turn down jobs," she says. "I'm not supporting five kids all alone and trying to get a commercial on the side. I have that luxury. Sure, when you have the ability to wait between jobs, you can have all the integrity and scruples you want."

But what if she didn't have that liberty? "I don't know what would happen. I've never tested it. I haven't gone on unemployment just to see what I would do."

Yes, but if a moral dilemma did develop? "I just don't know. But I've always thought this: Never run for a bus; there'll always be another."

This unyielding temperament extends far beyond her work. When she attended Vassar, Meryl refused to join the antiwar protests because she thought the key participants were hypocritical. "It was the first year Vassar was coed, with forty-some men and sixteen hundred women. But the whole strike committee was boys; they took over and got off on it. I'm so sensitive to theater, and these boys would get up and perform. Everybody was a mini–Abbie Hoffman in front of this adoring swarm of girls. I just thought it was bullshit."

As for her private life, Meryl will only rarely discuss it, for fear of peddling the intimacies of her existence. This is especially true if the subject turns to John Cazale, the fine young actor who was Meryl's lover until his death from cancer in 1978. They had completed filming *The Deer Hunter* together, and then Meryl went off to Austria to shoot *Holocaust.* She returned in time to spend his final months at his bedside, cutting herself off from the world, focusing solely on keeping his spirits alive by her unswerving companionship. It was the one real tragedy in her otherwise porcelain life.

One thing that makes Meryl Streep so intriguing is the abject lack of an "interesting" past. Her life, her youth, seem commonplace and mundane, a comfortable setting that does little to reveal the inner secrets of the performer that she is.

The childhood was in Bernardsville, New Jersey, a suburban enclave of well-kept homes and well-to-do families. Neither of her parents had a theatrical bent (though her business-executive father sometimes composed songs), and Meryl had no early ambitions toward the stage. Until high school, in fact, she found herself barely presentable: homely, glasses, unhappy hair, the sort of girl you always avoided on the bus home from school.

But with a dramatic flair, she changed her teenage self, and it was quite a performance. Gone was the nebbish look; peroxide hit the hair, and a cheerleader, an athlete and a homecoming queen were born. "Everybody's self-conscious at that age," she says. "You want to conform, be perfect, fit in, have the right shoes. You want to make sure that you're not scaggy so that everyone doesn't throw up when they look at you."

And while blooming socially, something else was happening. Meryl had been taking voice lessons since she was twelve, and as if to round out her healthy, ultranormal teenage life, a tryout for the school play was in order: first, *The Music Man,* and then it might as well have been Broadway.

It is difficult, you see, to write intelligently about Meryl Streep's development as an actress. Because what is most remarkable about her is that her talents seem to have arrived fully formed, making her a kind of idiot savant of the stage. Meryl is the sort of consummate player whose stagecraft is so radiant, so compelling, she could only have been a natural.

"One of our directors, Clint Atkinson, asked me, 'Why don't we do *Miss Julie?*'" recalls Evert Sprinchorn, once head of Vassar's drama department. "I said no. I didn't want to see it butchered, and it has only three roles. So Atkinson said, 'Well, why don't you come to a reading tonight and see what you think.' So I went, and after about ten minutes, I saw that Meryl was just outstanding. It hit you right in the eye. I looked at Atkinson across the table and nodded yes."

What made this all the more astonishing was that Miss Julie is a notoriously difficult part, and

Meryl had neither seen that play—nor any other serious play—until her collegiate performance. Soon after entering Yale Drama School on a scholarship, she became that company's top attraction, drawing attentive audiences, New York critics and producers.

Meryl declined drama-school dean Robert Brustein's request that she stay in the theater's repertory unit after graduation, and owing Yale $4,000, she left New Haven for Manhattan. She was sick of academic pressure, tired of teachers trying to impose a variety of techniques on her style and ready and able to hit the big time. She passed her first audition, a Papp production of *Trelawny of the Wells* at Lincoln Center.

Since then, she has refused to take it easy, driving herself and her peers to theatrical highs. Meryl argues strongly with directors and cast members to get her ideas across, and although she's willing to listen to counterproposals, she generally stands firm. "Meryl doesn't wilt," says Papp. "She's a tough actress in rehearsal and in everything else. She can be kidding around and girlish, but though she plays, there are no games."

This no-nonsense attitude both frightens and draws respect from her coworkers. "Whenever she suggested something, I trusted her and at least tried it," says Jeremy Irons, her costar in *French Lieutenant's Woman.* "If ever there was a possibility for a confrontation, I tried it her way.

"When we shot the barn scene, where Meryl wakes up to me watching over her, it wasn't going well after many takes," Irons continues. "So she came over to me and physically shook me and said, 'It's hard, it's hard. You have to do it, though, it never is easy.'"

Irons says Meryl's rattling had a good effect on him, an effect generally shared by those who have encountered her devotion to doing the best. "Anything she says she can do, she can," says Robert Benton, who directed Streep in *Kramer vs. Kramer.* "She will fight in a way that's reasonable and intelligent. I've never seen a display of temper from her at all. She is a remarkably wise person. She has always been able to find in characters a resonance and humanity that I sometimes was not even aware was there."

And for Streep? Why these incessant attempts at perfection? "Because it pays off," she says. "Maybe only a few people will see the lie if you just go ahead and do it. But more people will see the truth of what you're doing. They don't always see the fakery, but when something is right, they see it. An audience says: 'That's it. My God, that happened to me.'

"But, you see, outside my area of expertise, I don't give a damn. I'm not fastidious. I'm a slob."

Meryl laughs heartily at the crack in her own veneer. "It's only when applied to my work that I really care. Because it's a boundary I understand. I can be as demanding within the boundaries of fiction as I want."

Pretty Woman Julia Roberts

By Steve Pond

SEPTEMBER 9, 1990

It was not the kind of night to be standing around in your underwear. Outside, on the South Carolina seashore, it was freezing. Inside, in this makeshift house erected by a movie company, it was no better. This was a time and place to be warm, dry and insulated.

Julia Roberts was none of these things. Instead, she was soaking wet, shivering and clad in an undershirt and panties. What's more, she wasn't going to don anything warmer in the foreseeable future. Roberts was there to shoot a movie, and this particular scene—which she had been shooting for much of the night—called for her to run around the house in her Skivvies. So she decided it was time to exercise some of her movie-star clout.

"It was absolutely freezing," Roberts says of the moment from the recently completed suspense thriller *Sleeping With the Enemy*, which costars Patrick Bergin *(Mountains of the Moon)* as her jealous, abusive husband. "I said to the crew, 'I think we need a little group support here. So *drop trou.* If you're not going to take your pants off, you can't stay in the house.'"

The command, says the film's director, Joseph Ruben *(The Stepfather)*, "made a kind of perverse sense." About half the film crew bailed out; the other, braver half stuck around and dropped their drawers. Roberts has pictures of the survivors: the lighting men who crouched in the corner in their shorts; the crew member who wasn't wearing underwear and so wrapped a towel around his waist; the mild-mannered camera assistant who shocked everybody when it turned out he was wearing fuchsia boxers emblazoned with words like *bam, whap* and *zap.*

Roberts details who was wearing what, then laughs. "It had nothing to do with acting and everything to do with just getting everybody as naked and cold as I was," she says. "And I think everybody was very silently thrilled by it." Then she grins—it's one of the biggest grins in show business, because she has one of the biggest mouths. "It was *the bonding thing*, you know?"

Roberts likes bonding things. On any movie set, she says, "I've always made a handful of really close friends." Talk to her about her movies and you'll hear about people with whom she became close: the cinematographer who wrote her a sweet note, the makeup man who went antique shopping with her, the grip who gave her his filter because she said it'd make a good necklace. This is a woman who finds bosom buddies every time she goes on location; it's no

245

wonder she's been linked with leading men ranging from Liam Neeson *(Satisfaction)* and Dylan McDermott *(Steel Magnolias)* to Richard Gere *(Pretty Woman)* and her current beau, Kiefer Sutherland *(Flatliners).*

But if Roberts has many friends and paramours, she's also made a flashy career mark. Since debuting a scant three years ago with *Blood Red,* a Western that headed straight to video, she's had a quick string of movies that have showcased her attributes—among them a restless, bright sexiness, a striking mane of unruly hair and, says director Garry Marshall, what are "possibly the longest legs since Wilt Chamberlain." Roberts quickly ascended to the $1-million-a-movie club and became perhaps the strongest young female draw in the movies. *Pretty Woman,* the modern-day Cinderella story that blew things wide open for Roberts, isn't the only fairy tale in the life of this twenty-three-year-old who left Smyrna, Georgia, five years ago, won an Academy Award nomination for her role as a self-sacrificing diabetic in *Steel Magnolias* early this year and wound up atop the box-office charts.

Roberts is hot. If her latest film, director Joel Schumacher's afterlife thriller *Flatliners,* is a hit, her box-office allure is a big reason why. Ask around about Roberts and you'll hear a litany of praise, with a few identical perceptions. She's friendly and adored by crew members. She's serious and vulnerable during emotional scenes. Otherwise, she's very fond of jokes and pranks. She's tough to get a handle on, though. Near the end of their shoot, Ruben said to her, "I still don't quite get you." Smiling, she replied, "You don't think I'd let you figure me out, do you?"

"There's this wonderful dichotomy with Julia," says Schumacher. "There's this woman, this little girl, this shitkicker, this very innocent lady. There's a *My Fair Lady* thing in there, and

I think the reason she can pull it off is that all those people are in her."

But there's another frequent perception about Roberts, and it has to do with that bonding thing. She is, agree all of her coworkers, uncommonly supportive of others; she also needs as much support in return.

"She performs well when loved," says *Pretty Woman* director Marshall. "Richard Gere and I took great pains to try and make her feel comfortable and make her feel loved and make it a pleasant experience—not because we're such nice people, but because we felt that was the best thing for the project."

Certain scenes, Marshall says, were especially difficult for Roberts. "The dramatic moments where she was going to be very vulnerable were very hard for her," he says. "You're with a guy like Richard Gere for six or seven weeks, and suddenly you do this scene where he screams in your face and yells at you. And it hurts her. He's used to that, but she was devastated in that scene. After each take she was crying, and we'd have to hold her a moment to make sure she was all right. That's her work process, and you have to understand that and be supportive. And the other area of her vulnerability was the scene where she had to talk about her father. I didn't ask her about that, but I could see she was touchy. So I just held her between takes of those scenes, and then she was fine."

In *Sleeping With the Enemy,* Roberts had many of those dramatic scenes; even in casual rehearsals, says Ruben, she'd call up moments from her life and begin crying. "It's as if she has the thinnest skin imaginable," he says. "There's a vulnerability there that knocks you out. She's got two things going. There's something that happens photographically with her, that star quality you hear about. And she's got this emotional vulnerability that lets you see and feel everything that's going on with her. And the two of them together—*bam*."

Talking about Roberts months after *Pretty Woman*, Marshall still sounds protective. "I miss her, frankly," he says. "She's a very, very good, kind girl. And I hope she will stay that way, and I hope nobody will hurt her."

"**W**hat is this association with me and horses?" asks Roberts. "Is it my *teeth?*" Sitting at a back table in a Los Angeles coffee bar, Roberts is trying to figure out why people keep using the same word to describe her. The word is *coltish*, and she's seen it in reviews, interviews, profiles. "It's the season," she says with a shrug, "for me to be coltish."

Then she laughs. "But what a great word," she says. "I mean, I love horses. So it's a wonderful word, a wonderful association. I wholeheartedly accept it. I mean, I've been called a lot worse, so I'm kinda digging *coltish*."

And as she sips her iced coffee and chainsmokes Marlboros, Roberts lives up to the adjective. She once described herself as "loud and weird," but those words seem harsh; instead, she's outgoing, fairly outspoken, a little kooky, a little larger than life. It's not that she's especially tall—she's three or four inches shy of six feet—but a lot of things about her are big: her enthusiasm, her energy, her laugh, her smiles, her legs, her hair. . . .

Well, scratch that last one. Until recently, Roberts did indeed have big hair: luxuriant, tangled hair that went from dark brown to red to blond, depending on the movie and her whims. "Mood hair," she calls it. "Every time I turn around, it's a different color." But two days earlier, she'd tired of her big hair, which had become damaged from repeated dye jobs.

"I wanted to cut my hair off a while back," Roberts says, "but everyone was like, 'Oh, no,

that will be *horrible*'—like it was gonna cut off my personality or something." But when she called Kiefer Sutherland, he said, "Aw, get a crew cut." Roberts didn't go that far, but her close-cropped style is a drastic enough change, she says with a laugh, to make writers scramble to find new ways to characterize her.

"Yesterday my girlfriend was saying, 'They'll have to come up with new adjectives now,'" she says, laughing uproariously. "It'll be 'Julia Roberts, without that big hair' or 'Julia Roberts, with her coltish charm but no longer with her big hair, still has her big lips. . . .'"

So the new, short-haired Julia Roberts, dressed in jeans and a white tuxedo shirt, sits and talks about the last few months of life with big hair. It's been nonstop work. By the time she got to *Sleeping With the Enemy*, she didn't know if she would have enough energy to make it through the scenes of physical brutality, the shots in her underwear—and worst of all, to listen to her, the months in Abbeville and Spartanburg, South Carolina.

"The people were horribly racist, and I had a really hard time," she says of the shoot. "I mean, the town had no restaurants in it. I would go home and sit in this small room with my dog and say, 'So, there's nothing to eat. . . . You wanna go to sleep?'" She grimaces. "I didn't feel like I was on location anymore. I didn't feel like I had a job. I felt like this hell was where I lived."

That scenario isn't completely far-fetched, because Roberts grew up in a small Southern town. She remembers Smyrna, Georgia, as "a nice town, with friendly people" but is nonetheless dismayed every time she returns to visit. "I got back and see that there's been no movement in time," she says. "I'm so easily enraged by the flailing ignorance, which is tossed about as if it's God's words. In Abbeville, I felt so assaulted and insulted by these people that I just didn't want to be nice anymore."

Smyrna, she says, wasn't nearly this bad—though in the sixth grade she was called names and her locker was painted when she entered a dance contest paired with a black classmate. Her family was liberal: Her parents ran an acting and writing workshop and she remembers seeing summer productions in the park. "I come from a real touchy family," she says. "A lotta hugging, a lotta kissing, a lotta love. 'You're going to the market? See you later, I love you.' And it's funny to bring that outside of the Roberts house and into the real world."

Roberts' parents were divorced when she was four. Her brother, Eric, eleven years older, moved to nearby Atlanta with their father and soon began an acting career; she and her older sister, Lisa, stayed in Smyrna with their mother. Julia took care of the family's many animals and says as a little girl she wanted to be a veterinarian—"I was very coltish then as well"—but from childhood on, acting was a strong interest. "It was just kind of there in my mind all the time," she says.

So Roberts headed to New York to live with her sister and study acting, but she never made it to many classes. Instead, she got an agent and spent a year and a half going to auditions; finally her brother lent a hand, and she was cast as his sister in *Blood Red*. The jobs started coming: *Satisfaction*, a silly musical drama in which she played bass in a band fronted by Justine Bateman, and *Baja Oklahoma*, an HBO movie in which she played Lesley Ann Warren's free-spirited daughter. And then came her breakthrough parts: the low-key sleeper *Mystic Pizza*, followed by *Steel Magnolias*, in which she shared the screen with a bevy of Hollywood veterans and came away with the only Oscar nomination. Suddenly, five years after leaving Smyrna and three and a half years after getting her first role, Roberts was a movie star.

But before *Steel Magnolias* opened and the fuss began, Roberts had taken a fancy to a downbeat script about a hooker and a ruthless corporate raider. *Three Thousand* was its title, after the hooker's price for a week of work. When the movie's original deal fell through, the producers took the project to Disney. The studio liked the idea but wanted something lighter. Disney brought in Garry Marshall and ordered a rewrite and a new title. Roberts had to decide if she even wanted to do the movie that would be known as *Pretty Woman*. Then she had to win the part all over again.

She did—and Disney's participation made it easier to tell her mother that she'd be playing a prostitute. "My mom works for the Catholic archdiocese of Atlanta," Roberts says. "I mean, my mom's boss *baptized* me. So I called her at work, and it was like, 'Hi, Mom. I got a job.' She said, 'You did? What'd you get?' And I said, 'Oh, it's a Disney movie! I gotta go, I'll talk to you later. . . .'"

During filming, Marshall kept another Disney character in mind. "We try to shoot each performer differently," he says. "And the approach for Julia, quite honestly, is that we shot her like Bambi. She moves around, Julia. She never quite stands still. You just kinda, sorta see her, and that's the way we shot her: She's there, she's beautiful—bam, she's gone. We kidded about it: 'All right, we're doing *Bambi in the Penthouse* today.'"

Marshall also tried a combination of support, frankness and pranks to make her comfortable with the movie's love scenes. The first scene that involved seminudity was one in which Roberts lounges in a bubble bath, negotiates with Richard Gere over her fee and delightedly submerges herself when a deal is struck. Before the scene was shot, Marshall says, he was blunt. "I said, 'Now you're gonna take off your clothes, and there are men here with tattoos.'" He enlisted Gere and the crew as coconspirators; when she went underwater, they all fled, and she surfaced to find the camera running but not a soul left on the set. "That was kinda fun," he says.

And while she was in South Carolina, she says, "everything kind of *tilted.*" *Pretty Woman* came out, and suddenly Roberts was famous. "This was a very emotional and topsy-turvy time for her," says Joseph Ruben. "Strangers called her name, stopped her or even grabbed her on the street, while back at the hotel she'd get calls from fans who just wanted to chat." Says Roberts of the sudden attention, "It's a very funny world we live in."

Roberts, for her part, says acting isn't even the chief priority in her future. "I mean, acting is a true love of mine," she says, "but it's not *the* true love. There are times when I get so bogged down by the politics of this business that I just have these great domestic fantasies. Being at home, and being quiet, and reading, and having a garden, and doing all that stuff. Taking care of a family. Those are the most important things. Movies will come and go, but family is a real kind of rich consistency."

She slumps down, leaning her head against the wall and hugging the back of her hard wooden chair. "It's funny, because I've spent the last year and a half making movies and giving and giving and giving," she says. "There would be nothing left, and I'd find one more thing, so I'd give that. But there comes a point where you're losing sleep, and it takes a long time to get anything back from all that giving. It's a great thing to have the opportunity to give like that—but at the same time, you know, when you have family, friends, and there's love in your life, and you give to that, you can see instant

gratification. You can see somebody smile or just pick somebody up or something. And it's easier to give that way than it is to just be giving to this . . . *black machinery.*"

Roberts remembers a particular day when she spent fourteen hours crying and flailing her way through a difficult scene, then left the set exhausted and in tears. On her way out the door, she says, one of the grips took her hand and squeezed it. "It was worth fourteen hours of what I did just for that," she says. "Because it told me that I had done something, you know?"

Finally, this kind of talk gets to Roberts. "Ick," she says, making a sour face. "I'm feeling so *grotesquely* philosophical today."

Lest she get too bogged down in talk of bonding and support and goodness, Roberts remembers one more day on the set of *Sleeping With the Enemy.* It came early in the movie, when her character is struck by her husband and falls to the floor. Ruben was shooting a close-up of Roberts as her character hits the marble floor, bursts into tears and is kicked for crying. The film crew did everything they could think of to make her comfortable: She sat on a furniture pad so the hard floor wouldn't be too awkward, and a sandbag was placed next to her leg for the actor to kick.

When Ruben called, "Action," Roberts' job was simply to pull her hands out from under her and fall to the floor. But the first time she did it, she flinched, and the whole thing looked patently phony. So they did another take—and this time, in her zeal to make it look right, she fell so hard that her head bounced off the marble floor. "I almost stopped the take," says Ruben. "I thought she had hurt herself. Instead, what it did was open up this outpouring of tears and emotion. She went all the way—to the point where everybody who was there was horrified. But she was willing to do that to get to that place where she really needed to be."

When Roberts tells the story, it sounds less like an actor's conscious decision and more like a painful mistake. "I cracked the floor so hard that I had a black eye," she says, wincing. "And what made the take really that much more exciting was I cracked my head on the floor, I'm in so much pain, and the actor that I was working with comes up to kick the sandbag, misses the sandbag and kicks me right in the leg. So I'm just a blithering idiot at this point. I cannot even see straight. When the take was over, the director said, 'I wanted to call, "Cut." ' And I said, 'If you'd have called, "Cut," I would have wrung your neck. 'Cause I'm not gonna do *that* again.' "

And then Roberts grins again and sounds a little less vulnerable than you might expect. "It's gratifying," she says, "to know that you did something that when people are gonna watch it, they're gonna go, 'Holy shit, that looked like it hurt.' "

Top Gun Tom Cruise

By Christopher Connelly

JUNE 19, 1986

He can feel it coming. Then again, maybe any twelve-year-old who's moved around as much as Thomas Cruise Mapother IV would've developed a sixth sense about these things. The little town outside Ottawa, Canada—what is it, the fourth, the fifth town he's lived in? He's always trying to fit in, trying to make friends, to explain himself to his new neighbors and classmates, and always ending up alone. Through it all, he's at least had the love and support of his family: his mom to comfort him, his dad to stick up for him when things got especially rough. But he knows that something's up.

On this day, his parents sit their four children down—Marian, Lee Anne, Tom and Cass—and tell them what Tom has suspected all along: Their marriage is breaking up. Around the room, the flow of tears is uncontrollable. It was, Tom would remember, like someone had died.

Later Tom's father takes him outside to hit a few baseballs. But how can he forget what's just taken place? Tom cries so hard that he can't even breathe. His father is leaving—this time for good—and one great fear echoes through his mind: *What's going to happen to us now? What next?*

An ashen Jerry Lee Lewis, looking like he's just back from a stop at the embalmer's, is belting a surprisingly vital "Great Balls of Fire" onstage at the Lone Star Cafe in New York—while Tom Cruise, who does his own yelping version of the tune in his new movie, *Top Gun,* bobs appreciatively to the beat in the packed balcony. Once the set's over, Cruise quickly retreats to an out-of-the-way table and nurses a diet Coke. Though he's unfailingly genial and polite, he's not much for crowds. You sense that what he mostly needs is to be *outta here,* so it's down the stairs and out on the street and . . . "Hey, Tom, willya sign this, please?"

Well, *sure,* he will.

"Thanks. My daughter really loved you dancing to that Bob Seger thing."

Right, the Bob Seger thing. Ron Reagan Jr. parodied it on *Saturday Night Live.* Campbell's soup ripped it off for a commercial. It started as one line in Paul Brickman's *Risky Business* script: "Joel dances in underwear through the house." But when Cruise's Joel Goodsen cranked up the stereo and slid out in a button-down shirt and BVDs to Bob Seger's "Old Time Rock & Roll," he kicked off a memorable one-minute sequence of sexy air-guitar strutting and mock-macho hilarity that endeared Cruise to film audiences.

251

An uncommonly stylish loss-of-virginity movie, *Risky Business* made $65 million in the theaters. It was equally popular on cable, and its witty takes on entrepreneurship and getting into Princeton made it the *Easy Rider* of the MTV generation. Cruise was that much more able to write his own ticket in the movies—at an estimated price of $1 million per picture. Instead, he disappeared in '84 and '85. What happened?

In a word: *Legend.* Director Ridley Scott's rococo fairy tale kept Cruise in London for what turned out to be more than a year, playing—*yuck*—Jack o' the Green, a long-haired agent of goodness possessing all the emotional depth of Luke Skywalker; Cruise himself characterized his role as "another color in a Ridley Scott painting." The film's considerable production difficulties were dramatically augmented midway through when its set was destroyed by fire, but it was finally given a U.S. release in April. It took a year out of Cruise's life, and eighty-nine minutes out of its audience's.

So it was clear enough, right? *Legend* was just one of those mistakes that an actor can make—"I'll never want to do another picture like that again," says Tom—and *Top Gun* was just the thing to put him on track again: a high-flying saga of elite navy fighter pilots. Cruise headed off to Miramar to study and fly with the pilots—"These guys took one look at me and they said, 'We are going to kick your *ass*'"—and spent a lot of time working on the script.

The key problem was Cruise's character: Pete "Maverick" Mitchell, a spiky-haired rogue whose antics are too reckless for his fellow flying aces. From the beginning, the role showcased Cruise's ineluctable energy and, at least occasionally, his handsome face (the fliers wear masks for much of the film). The chief worry was the asshole factor—how could Maverick be ultracompetitive and still be likable? Toward

that end, Cruise and company created scenes in which Maverick reveals his self-doubts to his flying buddy. And a subtext for Maverick's actions was established—his need to prove himself and to discover something about his father, lost mysteriously on a mission over Southeast Asia in the sixties.

A guy who's lost his father? Yes, Tom Cruise could portray that. It was hard for Cruise to explain, but the year he spent in London making *Legend* was really important to him. The isolation of the set, the disruption of his personal life, even the profound innocence of the character he played—each of these seemed to rekindle some of the pain and fear of his childhood and enabled him to develop new strength. He learned to be patient: not to worry if something didn't get done that day, or that month, or this year. He found out how to ask the same questions that he had asked when his father left—*What's going to happen to us now? What next?*—and be filled not with horror but with hope. He now had the ability to say good-bye to something precious—a romance, a career opportunity, even a parent—and come out of it stronger.

It was all a little hard to convey, you know? So maybe it wasn't time to go home after all. Maybe it was time to take a long walk uptown and talk it through.

What Tom Cruise wants right now is some ice cream, only it's not so easy to find at this late hour, even in Greenwich Village. He walks up to one stand that's just closed, waving a dollar bill at the people cleaning up inside. "Look!" he yells to them, a big smile on his face. "I have *money.*" But it's no-go.

Finally, he tracks down a Häagen-Dazs, gets a coffee-chip cone, and we start to trek toward his uptown hotel. Though it's been months since filming wrapped on *Top Gun,* he's still charged up over the experience.

What of his involvement with the structure of the film's story—specifically of the details about the family? Cruise pauses for a moment. "Well, obviously, my father wasn't a fighter pilot and he didn't die a hero, but I think a lot of the gut-level, emotional stuff—the love of the father and the conflict in that—is in there. And the love of my mother, also."

His father, Thomas Cruise Mapother III, was an electrical engineer, something of an inventor, born in Kentucky and a graduate of the University of Louisville. His mother, Mary Lee, was a vivacious, outgoing, religious woman who was a talented actress. "I was always interested in theater, but I never did anything with it," she recalls. "When I was growing up, if you went to Hollywood, that was really risqué. I would have lost my religion, my morals, all those things that young girls thought of back then."

Thomas and Mary Lee had four children: Tom, their third, was born in Syracuse, New York, on July 3, 1962. The family moved to a handful of cities, wherever Dad's job took him. Once settled in, Mary Lee would find a way to get involved with a local theater group. And according to her, young Tom showed an early theatrical aptitude. "He used to create skits and imitate Donald Duck and Woody Woodpecker and W.C. Fields when he was just a tiny tot. I guess I was his greatest audience. He had it in him then. But as he got older, he was more into sports, and it stopped completely."

For Tom, sports provided an outlet for his natural aggressiveness, gave him a good way to make friends quickly in a new town and lent him some self-esteem—esteem he didn't usually get in the classroom because of his dyslexia. He began at an early age with baseball, and when the family moved to Canada, his father noticed that, by golly, Tom could skate backward as well as those Canadian boys who'd been doing it all their lives. Here, also, Mary Lee—with a little help from Thomas III—helped to found an amateur theater group in an Ottawa neighborhood.

But their family bliss was short-lived; Mary Lee refers to the divorce today only as "a time of growing, a time of conflict." It was also a time of poverty. With precious little income, she and the children returned to Louisville and tried to start their lives again. "You know, women have dreams of having careers and being whatever," Mary Lee says. "I had a dream of raising children and enjoying them and having a good family life."

Mary Lee worked a series of jobs to keep the family afloat: hosting electrical conventions, selling appliances, anything. One Christmas there was no money to buy gifts, so the family wrote poems to one another and read them out loud.

Tom's involvement in athletics continued. He played hockey over the Kentucky border in Indiana, with kids older and bigger than he. "He was so fast they couldn't keep up with him," remembers Mary Lee. "One guy finally got so exasperated that he picked Tom up by the scruff of the neck and the seat of his pants and moved him outside the boundary. I *laughed!*"

Tom pitched in financially with his paper route—occasionally swiping Mom's car for the purpose—and helped out in other ways, too. "Every night I'd come home, bathe my feet and sit in the family room, and Tom would massage my feet for a half hour," recalls Mary Lee. "This went on for six weeks, then Easter came and went, and the Monday after Easter I came home from work expecting the same treatment. And he said, 'Hey, Mom—Lent's over.'"

"After a divorce, you feel so vulnerable," says

Tom, tossing his ice-cream cone away as he crosses Fourteenth Street. "And traveling the way I did, you're closed off a lot from people. I didn't express a lot to people where I moved. They didn't have the childhood I had, and I didn't feel like they'd understand me. I was always warming up, getting acquainted with everyone. I went through a period, after the divorce, of really wanting to be accepted, wanting love and attention from people. But I never really seemed to fit in anywhere."

School became a horror show of close-minded teachers and rigid cliques, a place to do time as painlessly as possible. "I remember walking to school one time with my sisters and saying, 'Let's just get *through* this. If we can just get through this somehow . . .'

"I look back upon high school and grade school and I would never want to go back there. Not in a million years."

Mary Lee met Jack at an electronics convention; Jack worked in plastics. They got married when Tom was sixteen. "In the beginning, I felt threatened by my stepfather," Tom remembers. "There's a part of you that's in love with your mother. But he is such a wise, smart man. He loved my mother so much that he took us all in, four young people. We'd bet on football games, and he was a terrible bettor, so I'd make lots of money."

The family settled down in Glen Ridge, New Jersey. By senior year, though, Tom was still unfocused; after graduation, he planned to travel for a few years before entertaining any thoughts of college. When a knee injury terminated his varsity wrestling career in the winter, there seemed little to look forward to.

He'd never been *great* at anything, not even athletics: he was hyperenergetic to compensate for his lack of skill and tended to flit from sport to sport. He would tell himself, "If I could just focus in and do something, I know I've got the energy and creativity to be great." Then, on the advice of his glee-club instructor, Tom decided to audition for his high school's production of the musical *Guys and Dolls* and nabbed the leading role of Nathan Detroit.

Mary Lee still remembers opening night. "I can't describe the feeling that was there. It was just an incredible experience to see what we felt was a lot of talent coming forth all of a sudden. It had been dormant for so many years—not thought of or talked about or discussed in any way. Then to see him on that stage . . ."

But the bigger surprise was yet to come. "After the show," says Mary Lee, "Tom came home and said he wanted to have a talk with my husband and me. He asked for ten years to give show business a try. Meanwhile, my husband's thinking, 'What's this gonna cost me? Ten years of *what?*'" She howls with laughter. "It's kind of a joke in the family. Sort of a joke and not a joke. At any rate, Tom said, 'Let me see. I really feel that this is what I want to do.' And we both wholeheartedly agreed, because we both felt it was a God-given talent, and he should explore it because he was so enthused about it. So to make a long story short, we gave him our blessing—and the rest is history."

Tom skipped his graduation, shortened his name and moved to New York City. Cruise tore into the struggling performer's life: busing tables by night, hustling to auditions by day, catching workshops at the Neighborhood Playhouse when time permitted.

He may have been raw, but he was handsome, and those who saw him then recall an urgency in his performing that was hard to dismiss. Within five months of moving to New York, Cruise bagged a small role in the film *End-*

less Love. Before a year had passed, Cruise had fired his manager—"She had me doing errands for her"—and had been cast in a minor part in *Taps.*

Cruise was to play a sidekick of the hotheaded military cadet David Shawn. But the actor playing Shawn wasn't hitting on all cylinders. "Cruise was so strong that the other guy didn't have a chance," remembers Sean Penn, who costarred with Timothy Hutton in the film. "Very intense, two hundred percent there. It was overpowering—and we'd all kind of laugh, because it was so sincere. Good acting, but so far in the intense direction that it was funny."

Director Harold Becker offered the role of Shawn to Cruise, who reacted with horror. "Tom told the producer, 'If this isn't all right with the other actor, I don't want to do it,'" says Penn. "To the end he was like that. He really was a total innocent. Talk to Hutton, he'll tell you the same thing." His naïveté about the film business soon cost him, in the form of *Losin' It,* a first-time-in-Tijuana teen titillater that he starred in with an equally embarrassed Shelley Long. "That's an important film for me," says Tom. "I can look at it and say, 'Thank God I've grown.' I thought *anyone* could make a great movie, all you had to do was just knock yourself out. I didn't know anything about anything."

By this time, Cruise had met agent Paula Wagner and outlined his career plans to her: to grow as an artist, to work with the best people and not to care about money. She took him on—and he went on to do *The Outsiders,* with Francis Ford Coppola at the helm.

And that's where Cruise—who had already distinguished himself by mooning the camera during *Losin' It* and sawing up lawns in a jeep during *Taps*—made a real name for himself as a prankster. He scrawled "Helter Skelter" onto Diane Lane's hotel mirror and smeared honey on her toilet seat. For which he was rewarded with a bag of guess-what on his doorknob, courtesy of Emilio Estevez.

And then came *Risky Business* . . . and then came everything else. At twenty-one, Tom Cruise was a movie star.

Penn recalls a night out with Cruise at a New York club after *Risky Business* was released. "The group of people we were with was *amazing,* you know? De Niro, Mickey Rourke, Joe Pesci. All these girls were coming over. And this *really* pretty girl came up to Tommy and started talking to him. And he realized that she wanted him for his *body.* And he screamed at her, 'I have a girlfriend I'm in *love* with!' And the girl said, 'You should have told me that five minutes ago!'"

That girlfriend was his *Risky Business* costar, Rebecca De Mornay. Despite their incendiary love scenes, they didn't start dating until after the film's release in late summer of 1983.

In the first months of their relationship, De Mornay, also twenty-one, noted that she and Cruise had a lot in common. "We have very similar backgrounds, with all the moving around and stuff, except that mine was through Europe and his was through the United States.

"He really is a pure person," she said at the time. "There's something earnest and virtuous about him that's quite rare. There's definitely something different about kids who come from broken homes. They have this sort of *searching* quality, because you're searching for love and affection, if you've been robbed of a substantial amount of time with your parents. I think that's true of Tom."

Tom's stardom—and the intrigue of his relationship with De Mornay—turned up the flame of public interest. *People* asked him and Rebecca to pose for a cover; paparazzi stalked them outside their New York hotel; Rona Barrett tracked Tom down for an interview. The public started discovering how wholesome, gracious and kind he could be. But there were still areas of his life he hadn't yet come to terms with.

The voice on the phone was hale sounding, robust with good humor, but it wasn't coming easily. It was late 1983—when *Risky Business* was a hit and *All the Right Moves* had just been released—and Thomas C. Mapother III, Tom Cruise's father, was very ill. "I've just had a cancer operation," he told me. "It was pretty serious, and I've still got cancer other places, so it is still kind of a serious problem."

At first, he was extremely reluctant to speak about his son: "Tom and I are not in contact. I can't take any credit for his success. I'm the last person who'll ever criticize him. Maybe that's one favor I've done for him."

But there was something he wanted to say. "All four of my children showed up at the hospital, and all I could do was cry. That's how bad the strain has been because of the divorce situation. It had been about four or five years—a long time, at least to me."

His voice thickened with emotion. "I couldn't believe it when he walked into the room. I was a little concerned that I wouldn't see my son, because I'd seen a lot of the pictures in the paper and the publicity shots. And that wasn't my son. He walked into the room . . . and I knew who he was." He began to weep. "What those kids did for me, I could never explain. . . ."

Tom was in Los Angeles, about to go to London for *Legend,* when the phone rang. "You know how sometimes the phone rings and— *ping!*—you just *know?*" He knew. His father was dead.

"It cleared up a lot of kind of fog that I had

about the man," says Tom of his final meetings with his father, as he walks along Fifth Avenue. "I think that he felt remorse for a lot that had happened. He was a person who did not have a huge influence on me in my teens; the values and motivation really came from my stepfather. But he was important. Really important. It's all sort of complex. There wasn't *one* thing I felt."

Cruise had decided to do *Legend* just before his father died. "After what I was going through emotionally, facing death and all of that," he says, "somehow it was important for me to try to get back to the innocence within my own soul." He sighs. "I'm just glad I had acting then. I don't know what I would have done without my work. It gave me a place to deal with all those emotions."

Of course, not every problem responds to determination and resolve. Sometimes, says Tom, you have to let go. He and Rebecca sustained their relationship through the months of *Legend*-enforced separation—only to break up for good upon his return to America to begin work on *Top Gun.*

"For a while there I felt like I had to do everything in a weekend," he says with a laugh. "Then, for the first time, someone died in my life. When someone close to you dies, it makes you face the fact that *you* are going to die one day. And then I started to realize—when I was living in London—it's okay. I can take my time, I can start trusting the fact that I'm gonna live a little longer. I've just grown a lot. I'm a little more relaxed."

The earlier part of this year finds Cruise in Chicago, filming *The Color of Money*—a sequel of sorts to *The Hustler*—with director Martin Scorsese and Paul Newman. Tom thinks he's one lucky guy. Lucky to get to do *Top Gun,* lucky to get to star opposite a truly major star. He says as much to Newman one day on the set: "Gee, I'm lucky."

"Funny you should say that," Newman replies. "I said the same thing once to George Roy Hill [director of *Butch Cassidy and the Sundance Kid*]. Know what he said to me? There's an art to being lucky.'"

On another day, Newman takes Cruise out to a nearby racetrack. After a few laps, the champion race-car driver asks Cruise if he wants to take the wheel for a high-speed spin. You bet, says Tom.

"Okay," Newman says, strapping himself into the passenger seat. "Just don't show me how brave you are, kid."

"Aw," replies Tom, "stop givin' me shit." And he floors it.

Catwoman Michelle Pfeiffer

By Gerri Hirshey

SEPTEMBER 3, 1992

As it was laid out in her fat, annotated script, Michelle Pfeiffer's first day before the camera as Catwoman looked to be an easy one. She just had to stand silhouetted in the frame and deliver one line: "Meow!"

She tottered to her mark on nosebleed-high heels. *Creak, zzzz, creak* went the bun-gripping rubber Catsuit, a corseted, peel-away number that required being powdered white as a jelly doughnut just to tug it on. *Creak, zzzz, creak.* BLAM! The lights hit.

"*Meeeeeeeow.*"

"*Cut. Print.* Again, please."

Off to the side, Michael Keaton, a.k.a. Bruce Wayne, a.k.a. Batman, was enjoying the hell out of the moment. Oh, it was tasty. Here was Ms. Two-Time Oscar Nominee, Ms. Actor's Actor, Ms. TOTAL Get-It-in-Two-Takes PROFESSIONAL, held in check by a few pounds of wet, sucking latex and a pair of pointy ears. Later, Keaton would look back on it as his favorite day on the shoot.

"There she was, working her little *heart* out," Keaton says. "The look on her face was totally committed. *But . . .*" He allows himself a Beetle-juician laugh. "Behind it was—'*How did I get myself into this?*'—the look of *total fear!*"

He felt it himself when he first clomped onto a soundstage in the 1989 *Batman* sporting his own mondo rubber appliance, that scene-stealing Batsuit.

"You're committed," he says. "You're determined to act *through this suit.* Which is nearly impossible."

He says he felt wretched back then, until he had a Bat-epiphany—one he chose to share with the freakishly zooted Jack Nicholson. He leaned over to the green-faced Joker and confided the path to box-office bliss:

You gotta WORK THE SUIT, man!

Mercifully, it didn't take Pfeiffer long to make peace with her steel-belted, Michelined new self. Soon, she and Keaton were plunged into the knottier problems of rough-and-tumble Batsex. Not that the Suit ever let up; you can still hear that creak on the film as she straddles her caped quarry and kitty-licks his face. By the operatic climax, the Suit unravels with Catwoman's nefarious plots, an effect that left deep welts after an hour's exertions. But there was no mewling for the pricey balm of some Laurel Canyon masseuse.

"She's a *gamer,*" says Keaton.

Michelle Pfeiffer is the cat's meow of *Batman Returns.*
Copyright © 1992 Warner Bros. Inc.

As an accomplished character actress, Pfeiffer has been working the Suits in major features for well over a decade, unafraid to sacrifice allure for effect. Wrap her in the pink polyester of a Hell's Kitchen hash slinger and she is Frankie the waitress opposite Al Pacino's short-order cook in *Frankie and Johnny*. Set her up in a dark wig, Lee press-on nails and a nimbus of angora and she cracks gum and one-liners as Angela de Marco, Mafia matron in Jonathan Demme's comedy *Married to the Mob*. As the virtuous Madame de Tourvel in Stephen Frears' *Dangerous Liaisons*, she loosed whalebone stays and convent mores for John Malkovich's cruel seducer. It cost Madame her life in an especially haggard deathbed scene and won Pfeiffer her first Oscar nomination.

With the exception of lounge singer Susie Diamond's slinky velvets in *The Fabulous Baker Boys*, few of Pfeiffer's chosen Suits have been flattering in your standard Hollywood way. All told, she's snapped gum more than she's sipped champagne. She seems fearless, willing to look like heaven or hell. It's the other requirements of working the Suit that make her freeze like a spooked ingenue in the headlights of an oncoming tour bus.

"This is not a natural thing for me," she's saying. It's taken, like, *fourteen years* to get to this—sitting here on this couch."

She is lying back, barefoot, staring at the ceiling. But this is not some analyst's four-figure BarcaLounger. Pfeiffer is bivouacked deep into the gray flannel of her interviewer's swaybacked sectional. Having held forth among the floral tributes and gaudy fruit pyramids of too many luxury suites, she has turned the tables and asked to come to my apartment. For three months, on and off, she's been in New York shooting Martin Scorsese's adaptation of Edith Wharton's *Age of Innocence*. With a week or two to go, she's a bit, um, restless. Nonetheless, she's on the rack here because hey, *Batman Returns* is *the* summer movie, one that will easily be the biggest grosser she's ever been in. Its record-shattering $47.7-million opening weekend was further sweetened by Pfeiffer's best-in-show reviews as Catwoman. But Pfeiffer is quick, almost obsessive in pointing out that she's never been a streaking comet atop *Variety*'s weekly b.o. column: "Someone said to me the other day, 'You're a box-office commodity now.' I said I'm not, because most of my movies haven't really made any *money*. I'm always afraid to say that, 'cause I think the studios haven't figured it out and they keep letting me work."

Pfeiffer smiles in wan acknowledgment of her own folly. Maybe *Frankie and Johnny* did "drop like a rock." But she took home an estimated $3 million for her troubles. And she knows that in fact it *was* box office and not her best work that jumped her career into overdrive. "*The Witches of Eastwick* was the one that really changed things," she says. "It made a lot of money."

With Cher and Susan Sarandon—the three-some have since become pals—she was part of Jack Nicholson's small-town harem. Through much of it she wore sensible shoes and a large cold sore, but afterward there were suddenly *choices*. "From there," she says, "I was able to do *Married to the Mob*, which shattered many people's preconceived views of me." Which were? "They thought I was either the ice queen and/or the sunny blond Californian character."

Dogged in proving herself, she went for the parts where blondness—and all its lightweight connotations—was hardly a requisite. Like Jodie Foster, a twenty-three-year veteran whose first megahit was last year's *Silence of the Lambs* (in a role Pfeiffer turned down), Pfeiffer has earned more respectful reviews than ticket sales or percentage points, but she's hip to savvy women's gambits like starting her own production company to pan for great parts.

Look closely at her work and it is held together by a pliable alloy of nineties guts and thirties glamour. Her choice of parts could well be explained by her favorite screen creation, Susie Diamond. It was in the grand, heck-of-a-dame tradition of Bacall's "Just put your lips together and blow" that Susie explained to Baker Boy Jeff Bridges why she chain-smoked Paris Opals at $3.50 a pack: "I figure if you're going to stick something in your mouth, it may as well be the best."

So why, now, a character from dime comics? Pfeiffer breaks into that nasal sixties anthem: *DAH-na-na-na BATMAN!* She says she loved that TV series. And Julie Newmar's Catwoman was irresistibly bad to the bone to someone who describes herself as "the Mafia don" of her grammar school: "She was just such a *forbidding* kind of heroine for so many little girls."

Stories abound about how that Tinseltown trickster Sean Young tried to breach director Tim Burton's office in a cat suit, campaigning for the part in *Batman Returns*. But few realize that Pfeiffer had launched her own assault long before the first *Batman* was shot. She had friends on the production. "I asked them to *beg* Tim Burton to write me one scene," she says. "I said I would do it for free."

Burton says he found her feline enough when he was ready to cast the sequel. He figured she had the moxie, but he tried to warn her how hard it would be.

To get ready, Pfeiffer crammed her days with kick boxing, bullwhip training, gymnastics and yoga. Before the cameras rolled, she could hit a target with a whip or wrap a wrist, a waist, a neck, her own body, with eight feet of whistling cowhide. "She was better than her stunt people," says Burton. "She made the whip beautiful, kind of an art form."

Pfeiffer's own assessment involves more anxieties than aesthetics. Should the going get tough, fear ratchets up the performance. "Fortunately, I have a real strong survivor instinct," she says. "I'm so terrified that I will do *whatever it takes* not to embarrass myself."

She's not one for discussing the humiliatingly bad old days except to say that they're over. She coulda been a series lifer, jouncing along on *Baywatches,* then aging into those psycho-alkie suburban-mom gigs with the Joan Van Arks and Linda Grays. Pfeiffer's Daughter of Orange County dossier did not hint at one destined for greatness: second of four children born to Dick Pfeiffer, a Midway City, California, heating and air-conditioning contractor, and his wife, Donna. Elementary-school bully, Huntington Beach surf bunny, bitchin' blonde in a cherry red '65 Mustang. Working girl. She stocked stone-washed jeans at 4:00 A.M. when the malls were at peace; put on a red cashier's smock and yes-ma'am'd coupon-waving seniors and smart-ass leathernecks at the El Toro Vons.

After a brief tussle with court stenography, she figured she'd try acting. To meet an agent who was a pageant judge, she snapped a swimsuit over her petite rump, marched into the Big Hair fray and wound up Miss Orange County. Blew the Miss Los Angeles title but landed the agent, a few lame commercials and a one-line walk-on for *Fantasy Island*. Did a very California turn in a spiritual cult that sapped her will and her bank account. Got rescued by a handsome guy, Peter Horton. Married him, this actor. They grabbed their glossies and set up house in Santa Monica with the rest of the Young and the Hopeful.

She made it from dippy deb in *Charlie Chan*

and the Curse of the Dragon Queen to major-feature bitch when Brian De Palma okayed her as Elvira in *Scarface* after a jaw-dropping reading with Pacino. She was twenty-three.

"I was terrified, so terrified," Pfeiffer says. "I couldn't say two words to him [Pacino]. We were both really shy. We'd sit in a room, and it was like pulling teeth to try and find any words at all. And the subject matter was so *dark*. There was a coldness in the [film] relationship."

Pfeiffer remembers De Palma's approach as stylistically obsessive. "I was objectified," she recalls. "If there was one hair out of place . . . I remember once I had a bruise or something on my leg, and he made me go back and take off my panty hose and have makeup put on, because he could see an imperfection."

"Basically, she's a character actress," says Pacino, who now counts her as a pal. "I think that's a strength. She's someone who will endure because she'll find characters to play. And she happens also to be a leading-lady type, which is, I guess, glamorous. She has both." He laughs, then waxes a tad mystical. "I mean, is someone doing what they *should* be doing? That's the question."

Pfeiffer does not torture herself with the Big Career Questions. It's the small voices in very distinct moments that have her ear. "I've always had pretty good instincts about character," she says. "I haven't always known consciously why I've made certain choices. But I know if it moves me or not. And I know that if I can *hear* the character as I'm reading, it's made some connection."

We decide to leave the relative comforts of the couch for lunch around the corner. Pfeiffer gathers up her slight baggage—a slouchy leather bag, sunglasses, a roll of Certs. She's dressed for the soupy rigors of a ninety-three-degree Manhattan dog day in striped trousers and a sleeveless navy vest. No makeup, no jewelry on these well-cut Soloflex arms. But even on this sleepy side street she's inflicting gawker whiplash. Though she's polite and attentive as fans zero in, she notes that it's never this bad in L.A., where they're more used to movie stars. She can't wait to get home.

She was married for seven years to Horton. She acknowledges a brief and long-past fling with Michael Keaton; there have been reports of a disastrous affair with John Malkovich that nearly cost him his marriage and left her dark eyed and tremulous for more time than she'd care to remember. Darkness doesn't scare her in her work, she says: "I *like* dark."

There is one line that cannot be crossed. She will not—cannot—share her screen women with the men in her life: "My husband used to say, 'You don't talk to me about your work; you don't let me in.'" Instead, she keeps secret diaries in the margins of her scripts.

"Michelle's very difficult to know," says Cher. "I told her this once, and I believe it: 'If you came up to me one day and said, "Cher, this is my son, he's six—I just didn't think I could trust you until now," I wouldn't be surprised.' She has to know that she can trust you, and you have to really go through a whole lot of stuff."

Pfeiffer concedes Cher's point. "I don't get close with many people," she says.

"Actressy" is what they call a star who carps when the *Today Show* invades her working day on a Moscow shoot of *The Russia House*. "Attitude" is what they murmur when she snaps at the piggyback film crews intent on getting the making of *Batman Returns*. This whole Behind-the-Scenes market makes her wild, fractures concentration, dilutes the Work. Pfeiffer could not believe, watching *Hearts of Darkness,* the documentary on the making of *Apocalypse Now,* that Francis Coppola and his wife approved the release. Eleanor Coppola shot the dark, freaky, on-the-set footage; she secretly taped her husband's midnight confessions.

"Are they still together?" Pfeiffer asks, looking amazed at the affirmative. "See, I'm not very sophisticated. I guess I'm a little old-fashioned. As Cher would say, 'That's not very Valley, is it?'"

Cher says she first used the phrase to describe a mutual lapse in Ventura Boulevard savoir faire. "We're both Valley Girls," says Cher. "And I've been through everything you can go through in this business. I mean, we think we're pretty cool. But every once in a while, I'm real naive, and so is she. And we have to say, 'That's not being very Valley—is it?'"

"Girl code," Pfeiffer explains. "A life necessity." She has to confess that what she calls "the idea of girlfriends" has been recent. "Growing up, my stronger relationships have been with men, my friendships. I think that my relationships with women have become more important the older I become."

Ask her if she keeps those old, scribbled-in scripts she uses to build her characters, and she looks horrified. "If I have a script that has a lot of personal notes in it, I end up throwing it away," she says. It's a corollary to the old always-wear-clean-underwear Rule of Life: "What if I *die* and they find it? I couldn't bear the thought of anybody reading it." She keeps no record of others' impressions, either—no reviews, no clips, no magazine covers. "I've always had this fear of living in the past, particularly in this profession. I guess you'd say this is my moment of glory."

And so her closets are only populated with today's Suits. Unlike Cher, who's been known to hold garage sales to purge last season's Vegas froufrous, she will not suffer public rummaging. And there's little private memory hoarding. The only scripts she keeps now are clean copies, no traces of Michelle. Should she *endure,* as Pacino predicts, the biographers and filmographers will bloody well starve picking over these slim remains.

Not very Valley—is it?

Terminator Ah-nuld Schwarzenegger

By Bill Zehme

AUGUST 22, 1991

Men are in crisis, whereas he is not. He does not know the meaning of *crisis*. Or perhaps he does, but he pretends otherwise. He is Austrian, after all, and some things do not translate easily between cultures. (Lederhosen, for instance.) Throughout the world he is called Arnold, but that is because there are too many letters in Schwarzenegger. By now everyone has come to know that the literal meaning of Schwarzenegger is "black plowman," and like many black plowmen before him, Arnold knows exactly what it feels like when a horse falls on top of him. There is much pain, yes, but pain means little to Arnold, especially when there are stuntmen available. Anyway, Arnold is never in crisis. For this reason, it is imperative that Arnold be Arnold so that others may learn. And, from what society tells us, there has never been a more crucial epoch in history for Arnold to be alive, which is, at the very least, pretty convenient.

It is a woeful time to be a man. It is a time when men gather to bemoan all that has become of them. Men, experts believe, went soft somewhere. Now, to correct matters, hordes of them retreat to the woods for strange rituals in which they strut about in loincloths and howl at trees,

trying desperately to find the wild man within themselves, previously lost for generations. Men, alas, have forgotten how to be men. Arnold, himself, once said, "If I am not me, then who da hell am I?" Of course, he said this in the film *Total Recall* while wearing a wet towel on his head, so who can tell whether his heart was in it? (Lest we forget, he is an actor, first and foremost.) Still, it is a good question, applicable to most men, but certainly not to any man whose name is Arnold Schwarzenegger, for he is a man who knows exactly who he is: the biggest star in the world, a strong and handsome man of forty-four possessing a Germanic accent, who likes his cigars expensive, his motorcycles purple and his dialogue sparse.

Arnold is a formidable fellow, difficult to know personally, although easy to tell apart from Erich von Stroheim. (Arnold would be the one who is not dead.) He is protective of his time, which he prefers devoting to the accumulation of untold fortunes in outside business ventures. Luckily, however, understanding Arnold takes little time and effort, which is why he's become the enormous star he is today. In fact, it is precisely this quality that earned him a reported $12 million for his work in the colossal hit film *Terminator 2: Judgment Day,* in which he gives what is perhaps his finest performance ever as a cyborg. We live in complicated times, and complicated times demand uncomplicated heroes. Among those who are uncomplicated, Arnold stands without peer. (Even the titles of all of his fifteen films are blissfully primal, a small sampling of which includes *Commando, Predator, Raw Deal, The Running Man, Stay Hungry, Conan the Barbarian* and *Conan the Destroyer.* You can almost smell blood on the italics.)

"Arnold is a kind of role model, and some might say a dark role model, in a sense," says James Cameron, who directed Arnold in both *Terminator* films. "He's never gonna play a character where he sits around in an office and wrings his hands. He is about *direct action.* He's about being decisive. He's about knowing what you want and going for it. He's very clear." John Milius, who directed Arnold in *Conan the Barbarian* and who is himself a celebrated man among men, adheres to this theory as well. "Arnold is the embodiment of the Superior Man," he says. "Arnold is the Nietzschean man. There's something wonderfully primeval about him, harking back to the real basic foundational stuff: steel and strength and will. And that's what Arnold's about."

"I don't ask for too much," Arnold says, as if to explain why he reigns in a world where failure prevails. "I don't ask for anything impossible."

Understanding Arnold the man, a selective dossier: Arnold is not aware of the fact that American men are in crisis but explains that he was recently in Japan for a week, so he is behind in his reading. When Arnold wants to pay a man a compliment, he says of the man, "He's in control." There is no higher praise than this. When Arnold is greatly amused, he is the type of man who will toss back his head, clap his hands, laugh heartily and announce to anyone present, *"I love it!"* He favors tan pants, wears them whenever appropriate, for he knows he looks good in them. "I always wear tan pants," he says. He is happiest when gazing at the color purple. He says he has no idea whether the Terminator is capable of having sex. Arnold owns guns but has never hunted. He is a leader of men, a reformed pursuer of women. (He does not protest, however, when women pinch his ass at the gym.) He fancies himself a decent dancer, but adds, "I wouldn't say that I'm going to show the kids so they could see what dancing is all about." He plays Strauss every day for his tiny daughter, Katherine, and waltzes her around in his arms. He characterizes his singing voice as "the worst" and claims to do no impressions of famous people. He can subsist on three to five hours of sleep per night. He will nod off in most any chair if he is tired enough. If he finds something extraordinary, he will invariably exclaim, "It's wild, I tell you!" Of his wife, NBC correspondent Maria Shriver, he says, "She is a jewel," pronouncing it *choo-well.* When asked if he, like Kevin Costner in *Robin Hood,* used a butt double for his *Terminator 2* nude scene, he says, "I don't know. It's for you to find out. You be the judge."

And, as with most political aspirants, he swears to have no political aspiration, although he tells friends otherwise. "He's always said he's going to be the governor of California," says Milius. "That is part of his plan, you know. He even said I could be head of the state police."

Arnold drives a humvee, which is basically a tank with wheels. It is a military vehicle, a massive war wagon, devoid of frills (gun turret is optional), painted the color of sand and recently used to great effect in the Persian Gulf. Arnold is the first civilian to own a humvee; it was specially made for him by AM General and stenciled with lettering that reads TERMINATOR. (Lesser mortals must wait a year for assembly-line models.) Arnold already has a regular Jeep but finds it offensively luxurious and streamlined. "It's beautiful," he says of the

Jeep, sneering. "But there is a tremendous demand out there for something that looks a little ballsier, something that is a statement, you know?" He saw his first humvee in a military procession while in Oregon shooting *Kindergarten Cop* and fell in love. It reminded him of his youth, when he served for a year in the Austrian army and drove tanks frequently. How he had thrilled in those days to their demonstrations of strength and power!

"Isn't it wild?" he says to his friends, showing off the humvee the morning after its delivery. He has just steered his leviathan into the parking structure of World Gym in Venice, California, where he begins most days of his life. (His parking space is demarked by a slab of terrazzo marble on which his name is emblazoned; often women leave roses there to honor him.)

Arnold shames all men. Shame, he knows, is an excellent motivational tool. It is said that his father used it on Arnold when he was young and impressionable—and look at the result! Today, Arnold goads others on to personal greatness. He shames both by example and by taunt. "What's the matter with you?" he once asked his distant relatives, musclemen Hans and Franz, on *Saturday Night Live.* "I send you over here from Austria to become real hard-core Terminators, and look at what you are! Little *termites!*" Conceded Hans, greatly humbled: "Ahnold, you could easily flick us with your littlest finger and send us flying across the room until we landed in our own baby poop."

Even now Arnold enjoys telling friends and acquaintances: "Look at the love handles! You could pull 'em over your neck and use it like a shopping bag!" At World Gym he introduces a man with long hair like so: "This is Alan—or as we call her, *Alice.* Isn't that right, Alice?" On the set of *Kindergarten Cop,* he spotted a little girl who was crying over a skinned knee. "Why are you crying?" he asked her. "Because my knee hurts," she said. "But this sounds like a little girl," he told her. "Real tough people don't cry. They fall on their knees, they look at it, maybe tears come to their eyes, but then they swallow and say, *'To hell with it!'* "

Arnold, on the other hand, can himself no longer be shamed. For instance, Patti Davis, the prodigal Reagan daughter, corners him in the gym, where she, too, works out, and says: "I'm trying to think of what your car means in terms of penis envy. Isn't it sort of phallic-gone-mad?" Arnold grins and says, "I have no problems." He then accuses her of being a media addict. "She loves journalists," he says. "Shut up, Arnold," she says, laughing. "Media addict," he says. "You are!" she says. Moments later, two writers from a muscle magazine approach him. "Talk about being a media hound?" Davis yells. Arnold smiles a beatific smile and says, "Jealous bitch."

The meaning of Arnold: John Milius, who among other acts of testosterone wrote the films *Magnum Force* and *Apocalypse Now,* tells what is perhaps the quintessential Arnold tale:

"Arnold and I were coming back from skeet shooting one day and we stopped at Tommy's Hamburgers in the Valley. We were sitting there and this motorcycle gang came up—the Hessian Motor Family or something. They surrounded the table and began chanting, *'Conan! Conan! Conan!'* It was real tense. Arnold looked up, and I don't remember what he said, but this guy called Road Pig sat down and said to him, 'Hey, man, I always wanted to arm-wrestle you, bro.' So Arnold said to this big guy, *'Look at this arm.'* Then he took his arm out of his sleeve, and it's faceted like a stone. He said: *'Have you ever seen such a beautiful arm? If I was to use this arm on you and I hurt it, how would I feel?'* And this guy, satisfied, claps him on the shoulder. Then the next guy says, 'Hey, man, would you fuck my old lady?' Arnold looked over, and the old lady was good-looking. He said, *'If I fucked her, how would she feel with you then afterwards?'* Finally, to appease them, Arnold rode a couple of their motorcycles around the block. In the end they wanted to give him their colors and make him an honorary member of the gang.

"I sat there amazed by it, because suddenly you realize that everybody owns Arnold. He is accessible to everyone. It works on every level. It works with his Kennedy in-laws, and it works with this motorcycle gang. If Stallone were there, they'd have wanted to *challenge* him, they'd want to see how tough he is. But Arnold became theirs. No, ours."

Arnold is an external man, living an external life, from which he has benefited greatly. His body, and what he has made it do, gave him his fame—he is, of course, a seven-time Mr. Olympia and five-time Mr. Universe—as well as the opportunity to appear in films with many firearms and, once, with Richard Dawson. Much is known of Arnold's physical being, a being that looks especially memorable in black leather jackets. But we know little of Arnold's interior life, largely because there doesn't seem to be much of one to know. Arnold's genius is that his brow does not often furrow. Unlike other men, he is never ambivalent. Life does not weigh upon him, and if it did, he could bench-press it easily. Who, insofar as this quality alone, would not aspire to be in his place? As he would say, as only he can, "I was very lucky so far."

Consider the calm in his face. "It's sort of Cro-Magnon or Neanderthal," says Milius appreciatively. "Arnold doesn't say a lot, but his face says everything." Meaning, it says all it needs to say. It was Milius who first urged Arnold to capitalize on this, during the making of *Conan the Barbarian.* "I said to him, 'Whenever you kill somebody, I want your face to have a Zen-like grace, always the hint of the smile.' And he's never forgotten that. He has an absolute serenity that gives a real power."

The Arnold face masks no confusion, for example, since he is never confused. "You have to understand that I'm looking at everything in a much clearer way," he says. "I see it very simple in front of me, so there are no complications. Other people look at everything in a twisted way maybe. It's very hard for me to relate to this, and that's why I'm sometimes very hard on people. When I was young, I had zero patience. As soon as someone complained about being depressed, I was outraged." Does *he* ever get depressed? "It maybe happens, but I would not even dwell on it. It's never held me back, that's for sure. I don't walk around with a sour face."

Indeed, a quick tour of Arnold's subconscious registers few bumps: He fears nothing, as far as he knows. He does not have a fanciful or dark imagination. Death does not cross his mind. "I haven't had these thoughts," he says. He recalls few dreams. "Some people train themselves to wake up and write them down," he says, incredulous. "Then what? What do you do with that information?" There is only one recurring dream he remembers: "Before I start shooting a film, I sometimes have dreams where you're out there lying totally naked in a forest, and you have no clothes, and you hear somewhere, *'In two minutes we roll.'* All of a sudden, the lights come on, and you say: 'Wait a minute, what scene are we doing now? Why am I lying out here and where's the clothes? What are the lines?' I'm caught totally off guard, like I wasn't prepared."

Might this be the effect of having huge budgets, like the purported $100 million spent on *Terminator 2,* riding squarely on his shoulders? "Consciously," he says, "I am not aware of it. I never feel the pressure at all, consciously. I never go to the set and say, *'My God, it's a lot of pressure!'* "

Some men imitate Arnold, as well they should. Arnold understands the lure. "I play the characters that they would like to be," he says. On this day, he has arrived at a *Terminator 2* convention being held at a Stouffer Hotel near Los Angeles International Airport. Here, among nearly a thousand fervid delegates with more free time than other people, several young men have come to participate in a Terminator look-alike contest. They wear much black leather and shaded eyewear and do so with great conviction, never breaking into knowing grins, even as they wander around the hotel. Arnold's appearance will close the day of festivities, when he will judge those who best emulate his character. Cash prizes will be awarded.

"Everyone would like to be a Terminator," Arnold has been known to say. "Everyone would like to be a person who can take care of the job. Whoever makes you mad, you can get even. There's a tremendous amount of frustration in human beings, and I think this is a way of fantasizing to get rid of those frustrations. To think, *'I can do this, too.'* It's a release, especially when you throw in a few cool lines of dialogue that always signal that you're not even concerned about the danger. You make fun of danger, like John Wayne. You never heard John Wayne talk hectic, even when bombs went off around him. You think, 'Wow, how can he be so cool? This guy is standing in the middle of a bombing and *he's in control.'*"

Onstage in the Stouffer ballroom, after sufficient buildup, Arnold emerges from a cloud of pink fog. He is in full Terminator dress. *Terminator* soundtrack music pounds and pulsates. Conventioneers grow hysterical. Arnold, expressionless, stalks the stage, then elects to perform the twist. Finally, he silences the mob and addresses them, somberly, as befitting a cyborg.

"In the first movie," he says, "I told you, *'Fuck you, asshole.'*" Crowd roars. "But I also told you, *'I'll be back!'*" More roaring. Arnold says, "The main man is back!" Delirium has taken hold. Love grips all. People are on their feet. Someone shouts, "Down in front!" Arnold glares, as only he can. *"Fuck you, asshole!"* he says. His legion thunders with approval. (Jim Cameron has said this of Arnold's Terminator: "What is enjoyable about him is that he's kind of the ultimate rude guy.") Arnold speaks a bit about the new film's merits, then announces: "Jim Cameron and I have just decided backstage that we're going to do another *Terminator*. The title will be *The Sperminator*. 'I'LL COME AGAIN!'" Thunder.

A moderator intercedes in an attempt to begin the look-alike proceedings. Arnold halts him. "Remember one thing," he tells the fellow. "Whenever I talk, *never interrupt!*" This, of course, is just the sort of humiliation lesser men yearn to dispense. Naturally, it receives a well-deserved ovation from the conventioneers. At last, five contestants march out to stand before the man who represents all they dream of becoming. Arnold stares them down slowly, then taps one particularly sullen finalist as his choice. He pulls the lucky youth, named Scott, away from the pack. He deposits a leaden arm across Scott's shoulders.

"Congratulations, Scott," he says slowly. *"You look cool."* Scott shuffles modestly. Arnold continues his appraisal. "I like those sexy lips of yours," he says, teasing. "It's true, Scott. They're driving me *wild*, I tell you!"

Everyone, of course, laughs. Everyone except Arnold, whose eyes dance behind his shades. He will be gone in an instant, out through the loading dock to a waiting car, taking with him yet another memory of his effect on mankind as we know it. For now he must rest. There is, after all, a world full of broken men left to fix.

THE NEW REBELS

Brad Pitt, ROLLING STONE, issue 696, December 1, 1994.
Photograph by Mark Seliger

Daniel Day-Lewis

By Hillary de Vries

FEBRUARY 8, 1990

He leans forward—the jeans requisitely shredded, the raven hair ponytailed—and, in the queen's English, jerks your chain. "Is that machine working?" he asks. The miniaturized bit of Japanese electronics is whirring away, recording his every word. "I'm panicking you," he says, recoiling with a cool smile.

Daniel Day-Lewis, the actor who can play anything—the stripe-haired punk in *My Beautiful Laundrette,* the monocled Victorian prig in *A Room With a View,* the silky Casanova surgeon in *The Unbearable Lightness of Being*—is playing the temperamental interviewee. And playing it very well.

Notorious for his hermitlike privacy, Day-Lewis is allowing his Byronic visage to grace the printed page in behalf of *My Left Foot,* a screen adaptation of the autobiography of Christy Brown, the celebrated Irish writer, painter and cerebral-palsy victim whom Day-Lewis plays with shocking, spittled verisimilitude. For eight weeks, the actor prepared for the role in a clinic near Dublin. He learned to paint and type with his left foot, since Brown's movements were restricted to that extremity. During the six-week shoot, Day-Lewis spent each day sitting twisted in a wheelchair, speaking in strangled tones, being fed and cared for by other cast members.

Even for this chameleonic actor, who added *Hamlet* to his résumé last year—at London's National Theater, no less—this is a breakthrough performance. So much so that Day-Lewis recently won the Best Actor Award from both the New York and the Los Angeles film critic associations [he went on to win the Oscared.] despite competition from *Born on the Fourth of July*'s Tom Cruise, a highly touted, homegrown actor also playing a wheelchair-bound character. But for the present, Day-Lewis is under a doctor's care for exhaustion (he withdrew from *Hamlet* in August), taking pills at regular intervals and avoiding coffee and alcohol. Gaunt enough to cause concern, lanky enough to be folded into his chair several times, the actor is stiffly *en pointe.* "Begin wherever you like," he says warily.

Considering Day-Lewis's Garboesque history, his Hamletian brooding, his doctor's excuse, I try an easy pitch, high and outside. "Where do you find your characters' realities initially?" I ask. "In the text? In the physicalization?"

There is a very long pause.

"If I were to try and answer that question, it would be a reinvention of the truth," Day-Lewis says. It's not so cold-blooded a process. It's a more chaotic, more unknowing, more innocent process."

Not that innocent. Like all Day-Lewis performances, this one is charged with subtext. There's quite a gap between the surface amiability and the you-think-I'm-going-to-tell-you-anything attitude simmering beneath. No wonder the guy wins awards. Besides, it's a fascinating real-life take on his film roles. All of Day-Lewis' characters have been boy-men hiding behind their psychological plumage. What Day-Lewis does is make that emotional remoteness immediate, give it a depth, a passion, a reasonability. He lets you know what's *not* being said.

"It's his spiritual quality," says Jim Sheridan, the Irish director and screenwriter of *My Left Foot,* who cast Day-Lewis as Brown after seeing his mute but powerful entrance in *My Beautiful Laundrette.* "Other actors have a physical presence, but Dan could play a saint. Or the opposite." Indeed, playing Brown—another boy-man struggling to overcome isolation—is less a departure from Day-Lewis' earlier roles than a logical progression.

"No, it strikes me that the roles seem like unrelated incidents," says Day-Lewis, prickling at any attempt to pigeonhole his work. "The only common denominator is that I've done them."

Take the repressed Cecil in *A Room With a View.* "He was a human being who deserves one's compassion," Day-Lewis says. "I don't recognize Cecil in myself, but he represented a kind of dimension which I occasionally occupy, when communication seems very difficult. His humanity was buried very deep. But it was there."

Well, isn't this similar to the surgeon in *Unbearable Lightness*? To Christy Brown? "No—yes," Day-Lewis says. "I know what you mean,

this thing of communication. I am much more touched by people who have difficulties with that. To varying degrees, we're all incapable of communicating. It's the thing that causes us the most distress, which forces us to confront our isolation, our aloneness, and that's inescapable. It's something we shouldn't have to be fearful of, something we should understand as inevitable. But it's something that frightens us a lot. And the less able we are to communicate in a conventional way, the more aware we are of that isolation. In my nightmares, I occupy that same dimension. Do you understand what I mean? Would you hate it if I smoked a cigarette?"

Even the actor's smoke is tightly controlled, coiling above the head of this darkly handsome boy-man, who in person looks far younger than his thirty-two years, far more boyish than any of his film roles. Never mind the chic off-duty actor's getup, the leather jacket, the scuffed boots, the insouciant sweep of black locks. Day-Lewis is the moody, brilliant schoolboy possessed of a rapierlike tongue and a devastating wit.

He is maddeningly out of reach, like his on-screen personae, and he knows it. Questions about his personal life (he is of Irish and Jewish heritage, the son of the former British poet laureate C. Day-Lewis) he scoffs at as "old news." Probes into his acting technique are met with even less tolerance. "I hate the way *Method* is used to describe some performances and not others," he says. "It's such a load of shit." Yet just when you think you've lost him, he dances close. What kind of article are you going to write? What did you think of him as Christy Brown? "Yes, let's talk about him," he says with sudden warmth.

As the story goes, the script of *My Left Foot* came in over the transom, literally dropped through the mailbox of Day-Lewis' London home last year. Although the film's financing was dicey, Day-Lewis met with Jim Sheridan, a theater director turned screenwriter and film director. The chemistry seems to have been automatic. Day-Lewis wormed a six-week hole in his schedule and signed on.

"All I knew is that I found Christy irresistibly attractive," says Day-Lewis, who carries an Irish passport. Sheridan insists that Day-Lewis' eight-week residence in Dublin's Sandymount clinic for the disabled and the intensity of his work (many of the paintings seen in the film were painted by the actor) were the actor's ideas. "Was it difficult to learn to write with my foot—was it difficult?" Day-Lewis asks with an incredulity somewhere between mock horror and actual disdain. "What do you think? You're an intelligent woman, don't demean yourself by asking those kinds of questions. I could say it was difficult or at the same time that's the easiest stuff. Anyone can learn to paint with their foot. But not everyone *has* to learn to paint with their foot."

Day-Lewis' insistence on remaining in character throughout filming, however, proved somewhat problematic. One day, the actor inadvertently met Brown's relatives on the set, an encounter during which he never broke character or rose out of the wheelchair but spoke to them as the mangled Brown. "I became grossly inconvenient," he says without elaboration. "You imagine that you're beginning to clutter up the landscape with your frail, unappealing body. And sometimes I did cause a lot of trouble. Christy gave me great license to say what I really thought. People have such firmly rooted fears of disability, of confronting something that offends our sense of order and aesthetic beauty. It's only the disabled people themselves that force us to confront that, and Christy was one of the pioneers."

Day-Lewis speaks repeatedly of "the terrible tension between the anchorage of [Brown's] body and the flight of imagination. I think he wanted desperately to normalize himself. That's the fascinating thing about Christy. In a very intense way, he lived out the things we do. He had to discover his sexuality and try and fulfill it. He fought with his father and had to come to terms with a very close relationship with his mother. In this very intense way, he had to come to terms with everything we do."

It's a description that could fit the actor's own life very well. The only son of famous parents (his mother, actress Jill Balcon, is the daughter of Sir Michael Balcon, the former head of Ealing Studios), Day-Lewis led an idyllic childhood—for a time. There was the vast Georgian house in Greenwich, the progressive socialist parents who sent their son to a ratty local school that he loved. Later it all began to unravel. His father fell ill (C. Day-Lewis would die when his son was barely fifteen years old), and Day-Lewis was packed off to the Sevenoaks boarding school. It was a time that the actor recalls with loathing. "The tremendous cruelty involved, the premature severing of the cord [to the family]," he says. "Not that I had anything against my parents—I loved them dearly—but I couldn't understand when I was so plausibly miserable why I had to keep going there."

Day-Lewis didn't. He eventually ran away and joined his sister, with whom he is still very close, at another private school. The history gets murky here, and Day-Lewis isn't about to help. "I've gone on and on about my fucking education. You don't care about that in the States. Only in England does anybody care. Hanif Kureishi [the screenwriter of *My Beautiful Laundrette*] is going to hate this article. He gives me such a hard time whenever I'm encouraged to speak about my father, which inevitably I am.

He says, 'I'm sick of hearing about your fucking father, your grandfather, your mother. What is it with you?'"

Despite his reluctance to revisit the past, Day-Lewis admits that school provided his first brush with acting. "It wasn't acting, it was just fucking about," he says. One of his first memorable roles was a minor part in a school production of *Cry, the Beloved Country*. 'I played a little black boy, and I loved the fact that I could never get all the makeup off, that it made my sheets filthy every night, that I had a license to sully the sheets." Later came his admission to the National Youth Theater. Did this please his father, the poet laureate? The answer is chilling and telling: "I think he was dead. Yes, he was dead. So I'll never know."

The youth theater's prestigious acting program did help Day-Lewis regain his equilib-rium. "It was a really diverse group of kids bedding down on floors, making some kind of theater," he says. "It was very, very exciting." To this day, the antipathy toward class structure and the need to define himself outside of society's normal strictures remain a driving force in Day-Lewis' work.

"The thing about performance, even if it's only an illusion, is that it is a celebration of the fact that we do contain within ourselves infinite possibilities," Day-Lewis says heatedly. "It's not to say that we live immorally, but principles are also very often why people do murder each other. There is something wonderfully irrespon-sible and unprincipled about performing."

Yet for Day-Lewis, acting also exacts a toll. "I can't stand the thought of displaying myself in public," he says softly, "but I need to do it, *need* to do it. Maybe I just want to be punished for the rest of my life."

Jodie Foster

By Gerri Hirshey

MARCH 21, 1991

"I really liked the autopsy scene."

Jodie Foster spears some fat, glistening cannellini beans from the antipasto plate and describes a satisfying day's work on her upcoming film.

"There's a body on the table, murdered, with grotesque mutilations," she says. "But the more my character gets into the work, she experiences a kind of—I know this sounds weird—a kind of exhilaration. She's *excited*. She wants to get inside the skull of the man who did this."

"Oil and vinegar, miss?"

Over the pretheater blare of this jammed Manhattan trattoria, Foster is assessing the grisly leavings of psycho killers. Sure, she knows that Hollywood was built on Panavision corpse counts. But Foster, the thinking actor's actor, wanted explanations about these creeps. Explorations. She wanted to see the deranged stalker analyzed, not Freddy Kruegerized on film. Couldn't somebody do it *smart?*

Which is why she ended up acting in the aforesaid autopsy scene and others equally grim in director Jonathan Demme's thriller *The Silence of the Lambs*. The film is based on the best-selling Thomas Harris novel of the same title. Foster stars as Clarice Starling, an FBI trainee specializing in behavioral science. She is engaged in trying to catch Buffalo Bill (Ted Levine), a particularly resourceful serial killer. Helping her is the lethally brilliant Dr. Hannibal "the Cannibal" Lecter (Anthony Hopkins), a jailed maniac whose culinary skills with a human pancreas are three haute stars above Sweeney Todd's meat pies. Onscreen, *Silence* is make-you-sweat scary, with an unusual literacy and what Foster describes as a "progressive, politically correct" subtext. Marketwise, that's smart indeed. "I think it has real commercial potential," says Foster as she ponders the dessert tray. "It's the first time I've done anything like that. I mean, my movies nobody ever goes to see."

"That's bullshit," says Jonathan Kaplan, who directed her in *The Accused*. "She's a much bigger star than she realizes. You can't tell her that, though." Enough Academy members saw Foster play a gang-rape victim in *The Accused*—a low-budget, politically correct film shot in Canada—to give her the 1988 Best Actress Oscar. "She has a huge following in Europe," Kaplan says. And here? "They've watched her grow up. They've known her. They feel that she's *theirs*."

275

Jodie Foster demands attention from Hannibal "the Cannibal" Lecter in
The Silence of the Lambs. Copyright © 1991 Orion Pictures

By and large, it's a benign possessiveness—with a single notable exception. Though her 1976 performance in *Taxi Driver* as the preteen prostitute Iris also earned her an Oscar nomination, it was the devotion of just one very immoderate fan of that film, John Hinckley, that put her in the headlines five years later when he tried to kill the president in her honor. The ensuing news coverage and her deposition in Washington, D.C., made for a tough double bill to follow. But Foster went back to work shortly after and has averaged about one film a year. She describes most of her recent films as non-mainstream, art-house offerings, small movies like *Stealing Home, Five Corners* and that baffling film noir *Siesta*. She is a beautiful woman, but there has been little pretty about her work. Not since she was twelve and tugged at Robert De Niro's fly, saying, "So how you wanna make it?" She doesn't make the gossip pages with ego crimes and misdemeanors. Directors, actors and producers consistently describe her as one of the most respected actresses working. The *smart* one. A Yalie and magna cum laude. Crew members call her likable and never stuck up.

Demme says he likes Foster's Clarice "more than anything she's ever done. It's the first character I can think of where Jodie didn't have to hide the intelligence she possesses as a person. I think she's always had to mask that one way or another."

Foster was cheered by the fact that Clarice is a savior, not a victim. It was a welcome change, though it's her screen casualties that she has the greatest affinity with. She has this victim thing. . . .

"Not that I want to overplay what I do in *Life* or any of that. I play disenfranchised people that are in most cases pushed out of the way or cast aside," she says. "Part of my agenda with that is out of some kind of need to save them. To be

the representative of those people." They are alienated schoolgirls and runaway teens, factory-town waitresses, carny hustlers and stouthearted Appalachian white trash—American misfits, misunderstood and rarely short on pain. When Martin Scorsese cast her in *Alice Doesn't Live Here Anymore,* it was as an achingly wise Tucson, Arizona, subteen compelled to explain her after-school wanderings. ("Mom turns tricks from three on at the Ramada Inn.") A year later, when the director asked to meet with her in Los Angeles about the *Taxi Driver* part, the girl who had also played Becky Thatcher in *Tom Sawyer* showed up in her school uniform, with pixie-short hair.

No matter. Scorsese told Brandy Foster, Jodie's mother, that he had never considered anyone else for Iris. The California Labor Board objected because of her age and ordered a psychiatric evaluation for her protection. After two hours, the board-appointed UCLA shrink emerged from his office, laughing. It was no problem. Jodie could *handle* it.

"I grew up three blocks from Hollywood Boulevard," Foster says, describing that strip where hookers in fuchsia spandex blossom at every bus stop. Hers was not an especially privileged childhood; she is familiar with these marginal people. And she says she likes putting them on the big screen "to portray their stories in fiction and have them resolved and be heroes in the end." The hardest part of *The Accused,* she says, was not in playing a victim but in being allowed to play a very imperfect heroine, a hard-working trailer-park honey who drank and smoked dope and spent her table-busing tip money on a vanity license plate that read SXY SADIE. Foster says her concentration on Sarah Tobias' K Mart aesthetic was fine with Kaplan but not so popular with Paramount executives. Playing it the way she wanted to was, she says, "a big milestone for listening to my instincts. You have to take huge risks to create anything people *want* to see. They'd rather see comedies. They don't want to see a drama unless it's going to take them someplace breathtaking and controversial. Someplace they normally wouldn't have gone. You have to take those risks or all you're ever going to be is mediocre." She makes a face at the last word. To Foster, who always got straight A's, mediocrity seems to hold more horrors than the autopsy table.

"I talk a lot," she says, "probably too much. Some of my friends do call me Miss Authoritiva, and I doubtless deserve that. But I need to talk. It's not something people tend to do where I come from."

Beginning a discussion about her childhood, Foster is quick to point out that it was *not normal.* "You can't shove Ozzie and Harriet down my throat and tell me to be happy, because it's not me," she says. For nearly two decades, Foster has had reporters dissecting her early years—particularly her relationship with her divorced mother and manager, Evelyn "Brandy" Foster.

"I get analyzed to death, and that's *okay,*" Foster says, grinning. "That's what I'm here for." Talking about her childhood, she can do serious, she can do Freudian. And she can do jokes, just like her mom did every time she'd wisecrack, "*Hey,* where's my *dad?*" "Immaculate conception" was Brandy Foster's stock answer, though Jodie knew her mother had filed for divorce before she realized she was pregnant with her, the fourth child. Born in the Bronx to a strict German family, Brandy Foster was raised in Rockford, Illinois. In the fifties, she left home for Los Angeles, where she married Lucius Foster, an air-force officer who became a real-estate executive. The marriage lasted ten years. Jodie has seen her father only a few times. She is sev-

eral years younger than her two sisters and one brother. While she watched cartoons, they went through the customary periods of rebellion. They had parties when her mom wasn't home. Her brother was a surfer. The big kids had the big fun. (It *was* the late sixties.) Jodie was good. "I was the model child," she says. "I spoke three languages and got straight A's, had no curfew, wore a uniform." In school she was obedient, did her homework ahead of time. Though she tested as gifted academically, she says her real precocity had to do with reading people.

"I was born more sensitive to events and behavior and what they mean," she says. "I paid attention to it. That's part of what makes me a good actor, I think. And my history is very different than other people as well. I mean, I wasn't raised in the nuclear-model American family." They were mainly women—her mother among them—stuck in late-sixties California with no husbands, plenty of kids and back-alimony blues. "The single-parent family obsesses me in some ways because it's all I've ever known," she says. "Everyone I grew up with was a single-parent kid. All my mom's friends were divorced women, and they would sit around and talk about that asshole and that bastard, whatever." Men might come and go, but the women were always there.

When Jodie wasn't working, Brandy picked her up from school—the French-speaking Lycée Français—and took her to movies by Truffaut, Chabrol, Blier, Fellini. And if Brandy helped expand her cultural and culinary horizons, she also taught her kids about personal boundaries. "She's an only child, and she doesn't like to be around people that much," Foster says of her mother. "When I was a kid, we had a whole area that we weren't allowed to be in. She'd go there, read her watercolor books,

books on architecture." Again, the sensor is going off. "I think that's *good*. That's cool."

Foster says she finds this need for solitude just as compelling. "One of the things that worked well with my mom was that we left each other alone," she says. "We could be alone together." Often, weekends were spent just wandering around the house with books and magazines, eating takeout, watching old movies. "We were the pajama family," she says.

There is a place where it's cool to ask for things, where it's expected that people listen, that everything be better than okay for Ms. Foster. In her twenty-five working years, she has never felt better than she did in this place, and when she talks about it, the smiles come easily and often. "My favorite set is my own set," she says. "It's dictated by my neuroses and the things that make me feel good."

Jodie's Set was a series of locations in Cincinnati, where she directed and acted in *Little Man Tate,* playing the single mother of a child prodigy (Adam Hann-Byrd). She says it was the dream exercise for a self-confessed control freak.

"You know my reputation," Foster says. "I'm not a pain in the ass. I'm bossy, but I'm not a pain. And anything I demand is always about the movie. It's not about comfort or vanity."

On Jodie's Set there are rules, unspoken but very clear to those who know her. No prima donna trips. No personality dustups. And above all, no sucking up. "I don't like people that are afraid of me," she says. "It bugs me to have people who are obsequious. If someone's humoring or manipulative, I won't have it. The truth I can handle. I can't handle *not* knowing what they're thinking or feeling." For herself, the golden rule was simple: "Never make an actor feel like shit." It's happened to her more

than once—no names, thank you. "The director who says you suck, you're ugly, and you can't do a fucking thing," she says.

"My time off is regeneration time, and I'm entirely selfish," Foster says. "Somebody calls and says come out and have lunch, and I say no, because between twelve-thirty and two-thirty, I eat in my car. That's my thing. *I eat in my car.*" Jodie's Set offscreen is something she describes as a reverse fantasy. She doesn't like to think she's rich or different. Foster talks about one final obsession: intimacy. She is not about to divulge romantic secrets. That part of her life is, and always has been, a closed set. Professor Foster is discussing intimacy as a Concept. In doing this, sometimes she cracks herself up. "I have this fascination with public personas and private people. Like a movie star eating enchiladas in a car hung with dry cleaning? She laughs and agrees that, yes, you do convey life's intimacies with the tiny details. Just like a good novelist. "Small things, rather than explosions or lava flows," she says. There are small but finely wrought things about Foster's screen misfits. Like Sarah Tobias' terrified courtroom walk in *The Accused.* And Clarice Starling's visible aversion to noise in *Silence.* They're insecurities writ large, and Foster, former Wise Child, has no compunction about dragging them out in front of company—say, several million people. "There's something about real intimacy that I need to see onscreen," she says. "That I need to do onscreen. Things that other people never see. Showing the pathetic. It's very much an actor's impulse." If she has to define her limits, it's this: "There are certain parts that I cannot play. It's not in my reservoir. True and absolute passivity. I can't do it." She can do vulnerability, will even manage a dumb blonde. "But I don't know how to cry," she says. "I don't know how to approach weak."

Denzel Washington

By Joe Wood

NOVEMBER 26, 1992

At daybreak Spike Lee was barking Arabic, and the eleven-dollar-a-day extras were shuffling on cue, and the white boys playing CIA agents were lurking behind some wide-eyed children. The medina was appropriately busy for the cameras, but afterward, at lunchtime's end, our corner of Cairo was all shadows and ancient buildings, as still as a Sunday in Georgia. We'd filled our bellies with lunch, then watched as most of the crew packed and went on to the next location. Left to ourselves under the tent, bunched at the end of a long table, we talked barbershop style about the persecution of our people and the insanity of the world today and about the things we let our hearts believe. We were Denzel Washington, novelist John Edgar Wideman, journalist Ralph Wiley and me. One actor and three writers: four Americans, four black men, four brothers, putting our knives—our thoughts, voices, eyes—on the table.

Denzel was chief barber; we had come to observe him so that we could go back home and tell the story—it was his house, and we were only scribes. Denzel the barber became Denzel the preacher and then, more subtly, Malcolm, like the man he'd played earlier in the day, Malcolm X, flexing knowledge about some of the hard rocks in the Nation of Islam.

Denzel assured us: "We talked to some of those brothers." He had studied up on Malcolm, and now he was teaching, and I listened before joining in the talk: about the Nation, the state of black America, faith. "It's spiritual warfare," he was saying. "On every level. Good and evil . . . I have faith in God and hope in man." The driver came, and Denzel offered us a ride in his yellow limousine. After we got to the hotel, someone said, "Denzel was sure weird when he got on that spirit number, boy, he's got some strange ideas." I thought: "Yeah, maybe, but so what? At least he knows he isn't the point."

At thirty-seven, Denzel Washington is Hollywood's premier serious black actor, the certified, approved, anointed African-American male lead, our Sidney Poitier for the nineties. In person he is a regular guy with ten pounds or so extra on his waist, courteous and polite and friendly almost to a fault. Denzel's charm is constant and genuine—it never stopped—but it is also an ancient form of image control, a veil to keep privacy.

Denzel's wife, Pauletta, was along for the

As Malcolm X, Denzel Washington proselytizes at the podium. *Copyright ©*
1992 Warner Bros., a division of Time Warner Entertainment Company, L.P.

trip. Pauletta is a down-to-earth woman, an earthy sister, more like Ethel Waters than like Diana Ross, real folks. She, Denzel and their children are an authentic family, and Denzel, a preacher's son, is a self-described "family man." "I may go out every now and then," he says. "But ain't no regular group of people I'm calling up, like 'Let's go do this.'"

The Washingtons live in Los Angeles but stay away, by and large, from Hollywood society. Denzel claims he doesn't actively shun the Hollywood scene—Columbia chief Mark Canton took him and John Singleton to a basketball game, he reports—but he spends nearly all of his time between projects with Pauletta and their children (the eldest of whom, John David, has a cameo in the film's climactic classroom scene featuring Nelson Mandela). He and Pauletta are concerned enough about the atmosphere that they pulled a son from his school to send him to a place where he could "be around more black people." The L.A. most movie stars enjoy doesn't afford much of that, and for Denzel and for his children, what they were seeing wasn't enough.

Denzel was reared in Mount Vernon, a middle-class, mostly black suburb of New York City. His father was the minister of a Pentecostal church ("Every time Dad came over it was like being at a church service," Denzel says, laughing); his mom a beautician. The future actor played ball with some of the brothers around my way, Baychester, a neighborhood in the Bronx just inside the county line. But much of his schooling took place outside of either neighborhood at mostly white schools, where he was one of a very few black children. "I remember in fifth grade," he says, "we were in English class, or spelling, and the word *Negro* was up on the list, and I was checking the heads, like counting the people in front of me, to see if *Negro* was going to come up for me, if I had to spell that word. I didn't know how to describe it when it was happening to me: being like an alien."

But being on the outside didn't keep Denzel from doing well enough to gain admittance to the Bronx's Fordham University. It was there that he took up acting. In 1981 he tried out for and won the role of Malcolm X in the Negro Ensemble Company's *When the Chickens Come Home to Roost,* the story of an imagined encounter between Malcolm X and Elijah Muhammad. Denzel got another major break with his award-winning performance in the ensemble's production of *A Soldier's Play,* subsequently landing a part in the film version *(A Soldier's Story)* and a regular spot on TV's *St. Elsewhere.* Such films as *The Mighty Quinn,* Spike's *Mo' Better Blues* and *Mississippi Masala* cemented his reputation as a romantic leading man. But two political roles showed more than a passing resemblance to Malcolm X—*Cry Freedom*'s Stephen Biko and *Glory*'s headstrong Trip (for which he won an Oscar as Best Supporting Actor). Denzel sees no grand scheme behind it; Malcolm was not on his mind when he began acting.

Before *Chickens,* in fact, Denzel had no idea of who Malcolm X was. "When I took that job, it was strictly $125 a week, and I needed the money," he says. "And one guy's name was Malcolm, and the other's Elijah—bet. Let's get busy. Which one am I?" He hadn't read Malcolm's autobiography, and no one in school or the hoods talked about him—Malcolm hadn't been in the air, even at home. Like Nick, the charmed, successful black man he plays in *Ricochet,* Denzel was raised a preacher's kid, a King man, not a Malcolmite. Even so, *Chickens* had captured Denzel's conscience; the first time Denzel read Malcolm, his head turned. By the time Spike stirred the dust around the issue of whether a white filmmaker (Norman Jewison was originally slated) or a black one (Spike) should direct the film, Denzel—already signed on to the project—was a believer.

Denzel began intensive preparations for his role immediately after finishing *Ricochet*. Traveling to New York to reacquaint himself with the city Malcolm X made his home, Denzel spent twelve hours a day reading speeches, reviewing films and videotape and, as the first day of shooting approached, taking "boot camp" classes with the Fruit of Islam, the Nation's security wing. "In the evening, brothers would come by and set up class," he says. "They'd set up like a mosque or temple and go through with it. We had to march, we had to learn our general orders. There would be a subject that this main speaker would speak about, or they would ask someone to come speak—all kinds of things like that. So it just gave it the right orientation, as well as an education." The actor hired an orthodox Muslim assistant to instruct him in Arabic and Islamic tradition; he even stopped drinking alcohol and limited meals to one a day, without meat, in Muslim fashion. His final night partying, he says, was the Fourth of July.

Two days after Denzel came to New York, his father died. "When that happened, I wanted to use that," says Denzel. "I'm dealing with the spirit of Malcolm, and I'm dealing with the spirit of my father, too. That's who I always thought about, those two men." The conflation fit into Spike's understanding of Malcolm as "someone always looking for a father figure" and for truth. In the movie, as in life, each of Malcolm's fathers fails him—Elijah, Baines (a composite figure who recruits Malcolm into the Nation), West Indian Archie (a hustler who takes young Malcolm under his wing) and his own dead father. In Spike's reckoning, the failures "crushed" Malcolm; while truth and growth may have set Malcolm free, it lost him fathers, too. Denzel sees it slightly differently. "Ultimately, [Malcolm] reached the ultimate father, God," he says. "Anyone's quest in life is the truth. I think that was Malcolm's quest—for understanding, for God. I interpret it as that evolution."

After breaking with the Nation, Malcolm traveled to Ghana, Nigeria, Egypt, Saudi Arabia, in pursuit of new ways to better his understanding of the world. He became a sort of perpetual pilgrim, a seeker of spiritual truth, until he was killed by members of the Nation of Islam, more than likely with assistance from the U.S. government.

Truth, true spirit, to the Christian faithful, can be seen only in glimpses. "I had a lot of strong spiritual folks around me," says Denzel. "And I had studied some of those speeches so that I could take concepts from one [and] tie ideas back in and go back to something else of his." In the Pentecostal congregation of Denzel's father, believers would speak in tongues when they felt the spirit. Malcolm's words would come out of Denzel just this way, blindingly full, and they'd have a revelatory effect on everyone listening. "You're up on the podium," Denzel says, "and then you're speaking the great truths that Malcolm spoke, and the people, the extras, are responding honestly, because what he said then makes sense now. You didn't have to work with the extras, all you had to do was do the speeches, and they'd go off." This was theater, in its ancient sense, true democratic theater and, to Denzel, church. Father becoming son, son becoming father. The spirit was overwhelming.

Winona Ryder

By David Handelman

MAY 18, 1989

Winona Ryder is doing something *totally* illegal. The sunny, dark-haired actress is blithely motoring around Los Angeles in her friend's rental car—and, at age seventeen, she's too young to drive it. It's early March, only three weeks since Ryder moved out of her parents' house in Petaluma, California, and her own car is still up there, along with her collages, her bible—*The Catcher in the Rye*—her vast collections of handbags, socks, charm bracelets, Barbie dolls, *Twilight Zone* and Monty Python tapes. Oh, and the screenplay she wrote and sold. So just by driving to the mall, she's flirting with danger.

As Ryder reaches a major intersection, the traffic light turns yellow. "Should I go? No, better not." But she's already halfway across, so with one hand clutching her head in terror, she glides through, emitting yelps: "Huh! Oh! *Uh!*"

An oncoming car screeches and honks. "Sorry! I know, I'm sorry! That guy *hates* me now. Was that my fault?"

Her L.A. driving may be tentative, but otherwise Winona Ryder brims with self-confidence. "Insecure people," she says, wrinkling her nose, "don't fry my burger." Precocious enough to hold her own with adults, she radiates the quali-

ties of a child who has always been encouraged: a chatty, optimistic disposition and an unselfconscious creativity.

"It's amazing," says her friend Robert Downey Jr. "She'll just call me up and say, 'I wrote another script,' like 'I did another load of laundry.' To me, that's like bench-pressing the Sears Tower." While most kids her age are still months away from their high school graduations, Ryder has already completed her home-study degree ("four point oh," she chirps) as well as six feature films.

From her first moments onscreen—in *Lucas*, filmed the summer after she was in the eighth grade and released in 1986—Winona Ryder has been someone to watch. In her second film, *Square Dance* (1987), she had more scenes than costars Jason Robards, Jane Alexander and Rob Lowe; in last year's *Beetlejuice*, she played the character who kept her head while everyone else was losing theirs. Her alert, expressive eyes telegraph a startling combination of intelligence, gravity and self-possession.

Driving down Wilshire Boulevard, Ryder passes a gaggle of elementary schoolers in uniform. "I can't wait until I'm grown-up and have kids," she says, rubbing her tummy. "I want little boys. Want to hear the names I'm gonna name them? I like baseball names. Vida Blue Ryder. Cool Papa Ryder. Unless I marry some guy that has a better last name than me." (She had already "bettered" her own last name, Horowitz, when the titles were being put on *Lucas*.)

Though she doesn't envision getting married until she's at *least* twenty, Ryder is perched on the precipice of adulthood, rushed there somewhat by her recent roles. As Veronica Sawyer, the ambivalent high schooler in the daring black comedy *Heathers*—which Ryder made against the advice of her parents and agents—she deftly vacillates between a vulnerable teen scribbling away in her diary and an action heroine capable of murdering her best friends, all named Heather. And in *Great Balls of Fire*, Ryder plays Myra, the child bride of Jerry Lee Lewis (played by Dennis Quaid); the movie includes a wedding-night scene in which, as Ryder guilelessly puts it, "he's devirginizing me."

Ryder's incipient womanhood, however, is not without its headaches. Guys who previously viewed her as "jailbait," she says, are now making advances, and ill-informed gossip is driving her bonkers.

"I can't believe the rumors!" she says, rolling her eyes as she parks in the Beverly Center garage. "I'm going out with Dweezil Zappa. Alec Baldwin and I are getting *married*. Meg Ryan wants to *kill* me because Dennis Quaid and I are having an affair. And what's the other one? Oh, yeah, that the *1969* cast, Kiefer Sutherland and Robert Downey and I, are having a *ménage*-and-*trois* affair!" Her active eyebrows wiggle, and she laughs a loud ha-*ha!*

"The first time I heard things about myself," she says, "I was really hurt. People say, 'Just ignore it, or laugh it off.' It's hard, because *I* hear stuff about people and believe it. 'Ooh, really? She's a slut? Hoo!' So people are going to think it's true about me. And I'm sure I'm gonna be getting a lot more of it."

Looking very junior high in a zippered sweatshirt, a white T-shirt and jeans (in contrast with the spandexed and moussed Beverly Hills mall vixens around her), Ryder rides up the escalators to Bullock's department store. "Stores like this totally scare me," she says. "They're so *colorful.*" She zips around making speedy but accurate household purchases—picture frames, towels—using crisp hundred-dollar bills, which she pulls from an envelope in her pocket. "I don't have any checks yet," she explains. "And I'm too young to have credit cards—which is probably a good thing." (She is also shopping for a house in the Hollywood Hills, which she wants to share with two of her friends and which she says will be "very sitcomish.")

She pops into a store specializing in designer party dresses, looking for something to wear to the imminent Academy Awards ceremony, her first. A saleswoman in a billowy scarf and green leather pants tells her, "Because you're *very tiny,* you need something that's not cut too big, so it won't *dwarf* you." Ryder (who says she's five feet four "when I'm not slouching") grimaces and leaves, muttering, "I hate people like that."

Throughout her mall trek, Ryder is never recognized by passersby or salespeople. This blessed anonymity, however, is probably not going to last.

"People have been telling me that things might get a little weird," she says, heading back to the rental car. "People who know me know that I would have a difficult time handling fame, because I don't think I would take the precautions, because I have no sense of 'who I am.'

"The only time I ever feel like I'm in the business is when I go somewhere public and there are photographers saying my name; I get a really weird chill. I wish I could sit and think about it, but every time I do, I get so nervous that I end up changing the subject. Sometimes I really sort of resent what I've gotten myself into."

Ryder proceeds to the massive Rose Bowl flea market in Pasadena, where she starts spending her C-notes on presents for her *Heathers* co-workers: a pocket watch for director Michael Lehmann, a silver belt for producer Denise Di Novi and antique fairy-tale books for writer Daniel Waters.

Then she spies a trapezoidal bookcase, painted a zany aqua-and-black speckle. "This is very cool," she says. "Very Tim Burton."

It's true—the bookcase is right out of Burton's demented vision of *Beetlejuice* and *Pee-wee's Big Adventure;* so, in a sense, is Ryder herself. It's no accident that Burton and Lehmann, two of the best new young Hollywood directors, cast her as the voice of reason in the midst of cartoon chaos. She's hip and wacky enough to get the joke of modern life—and savvy enough to be able to play against it.

"Noni was offered nine thousand light-comedy, feel-good, hits-of-the-summer movies," says Robert Downey Jr., "and she chose one where she kills all her friends. She's a pure-at-heart person who knows that the darkness is all around her. She brings to light that there is truth and love even in the darkest impulses."

All this is probably news to Ryder. "I don't think she's into deep self-analysis," says her friend Lisanne Falk, who plays the least bratty of the three Heathers. "She doesn't think about it, she just does it."

"I think, I *think,* that I'm a pretty natural actress," Ryder says. "I try to do things as naturally as possible. I hate rehearsing, because I always like to save everything for when I do it. I just try as much as I can to really be 'in the moment.' I know that sounds corny and everything."

Still cruising the flea market, Ryder mentions that she's planning on getting QUE SERA, SERA tattooed on her arm. "I almost got it once, then they asked me my age. It's the greatest saying ever. 'Whatever will be, will be.' I was also going to get one that said BUDDY HOLLY on my ankle. Then again, I don't know if I'm going to get a tattoo."

The song "Que Sera, Sera" is used in *Heathers,* and the movie has clearly left its mark on Ryder's personality and lingo. She read the zingy script—"one of the best pieces of literature that I've ever read; it was the closest I've been to anything since *The Catcher in the Rye,* and that book really changed my life"—and latched onto it like a barnacle. During filming, she applied herself as never before. "I matured a lot," she says. "Before, I'd sometimes try to see how lazy I could get. All my directors had been more or less father figures, and all I'd have to do was be really cute and I could get away with anything. But it didn't work with Michael."

Not to say that she doesn't still have her ways. "She's got me totally bamboozled," *Great Balls of Fire* director Jim McBride says affectionately. "She's just a kid, but she's been around the pool a couple of times, as we say out here. She's certainly not anywhere near as innocent as she seems. She was real nervous about the love scene for several days before shooting and indicated to me that she was very inexperienced in this area, and I had to sort of fill her in on things—verbally, that is. I took it all very gently and gingerly and tried to lead her there, but when we got to doing the scene, she leapt in with both feet and gave a very convincing performance. I'm not saying she's sexually experienced, I'm saying she's a good actress!"

The first time Ryder watched the finished

scene, she says, "I got really embarrassed. I realized it was going to be in the movie, that it wasn't just what happened one day on the set. No part of my body is exposed, it's just that the camera is on my face a lot, especially during the pain part. And then she starts to enjoy it, and that was the really embarrassing part. The face I chose is really revealing—I couldn't believe it was *me*. It looks really weird to me: Dennis is so big, and I'm so little, I don't look a day over thirteen, except when I take off my shirt and I have this fifties bullet bra on. I was just going by what I thought it would feel like. I watch these other people's love scenes, everybody's *so* sexy, everyone tries to be really subtle. With me, it's very different. I don't think I was very sexy."

Winona Ryder is cooking pancakes. It's a bright Sunday morning, and she's bopping around to a Buddy Holly CD in the kitchen of the cheerful, desert-toned two-bedroom apartment she shares with an aspiring actress named Kris Greenberg. Her bobbed brunette hair is up in a clip, and she's wearing a red-and-white gingham jumper, a white T-shirt and stockings and red suede cowboy boots.

"We need something more *inspiring*," she declares, replacing Holly with AC/DC's "Hells Bells." But she prefers fifties music. "It leaves more to my imagination, because I don't see the groups everywhere, plastered everywhere." Still, she does watch MTV with a passion, using videos as a sort of horoscope: "Okay," she'll say, "the next one is going to be a message to me about guys." If it turns out to be a poser group like Warrant, she gets depressed.

Though Ryder says she's going to eat only one pancake, she downs two, then grabs her waist and grimaces, saying, "I'm *soooo* full." She skips into her cluttered room and rummages

through a disarray of clothing, photos and books for some show-and-tell.

She pulls out an old class picture, dated 1977–78. "Look at that outfit!" Ryder says. "I was such a weirdo, wasn't I?" Second-grader Winona Horowitz has long, dirty-blond hair and is wearing a baggy dress over pants, a strange frilly-collared shirt—and a bemused smile.

"Noni wore the most inconsistent getups, yet on her they looked great," says her mother, Cindy Horowitz. "She had her own style, which she had no intention of altering."

Ryder's personality is the product of a sort of alternative childhood, similar to the ones enjoyed by such young celebrities as Uma Thurman, River Phoenix and Chynna Phillips. "I see Noni as one of the first members of a new generation," says her godfather, Timothy Leary. "The Kids of the Summer of Love."

Her parents, Leary says, are "hippie intellectuals and psychedelic scholars." Cindy went to San Francisco in 1965 with her first husband and participated in the first be-in, then discovered Buddhism, macrobiotics and Aldous Huxley's utopian ideals. In 1970, Cindy married Michael Horowitz, a book antiquarian who was Leary's archivist.

In October 1971, Winona was born near Winona, Minnesota. Soon after, the family returned to San Francisco, sharing a house in the Haight with Cindy's ex and his second wife. Winona toddled around the Zen preschool or hung around while her father drank coffee at the Cafe Trieste with Allen Ginsberg. During these years, her parents were editing books: *Moksha*, about the psychedelic, visionary experiences of Aldous Huxley, and *Shaman Woman, Mainline Lady*, about the spiritual discoveries of women from Cleopatra to Patti Smith.

"My parents know what it's like to, like, take

a drug and go out in public and *flip out,*" says Winona. "They always said, 'If you ever want to do anything, you just have to tell us about it, and you have to go through us.'"

As a result, Ryder seems unlikely to be a young Hollywood casualty: "Noni's never gonna end up with a cocaine habit!" says Leary. "These kids who've grown up in houses where marijuana was smoked are not going to go berserk the first time a guy in a raincoat offers 'em something in an alley."

When Winona was seven, the Horowitzes left the Haight for a three-hundred-acre Northern California enclave of seven families, which Leary terms "one of the most successful, upscale hippie communes in the country."

"It wasn't as hippie-do as it sounds," says Ryder. "A lot of people, when they hear the word *commune,* connect it with, like, everyone's on acid and running around naked. This was more like this weird suburb, if suburbs were really cool. It was just a bunch of houses on this chunk of land; we had horses and gardens. You have so much freedom, you can go roaming anywhere. We didn't have electricity, which was weird, but it was great to grow up that way. We didn't have TV, so you'd have to *do* stuff. My friends' names were Tatonka, Gulliver and Rio. We'd have hammock contests, sit around and make up stories, make up weird games. I don't know—it was a weird, weird childhood. I mean, it was great."

It was the less than idyllic aspects of her childhood that propelled Ryder into acting. Because Michael's city job and the older kids' school were too far away, in 1981 the Horowitzes went nuclear, leaving the commune for Petaluma. Winona soon discovered that her close-cropped hair, tomboyish clothes and offbeat interests (she would join Amnesty International at twelve) made her a suburban reject. On her third day at her new junior high, she was standing at her locker when she heard someone say, "Hey, faggot." She turned around and, mistaken for an effeminate boy, was beaten up. Not wanting to return to school, she was put on home study; this quickly bored her, so her parents suggested she take an acting class at San Francisco's prestigious American Conservatory Theatre.

"We weren't thinking of her being professional," says her mother. "We just wanted her to be happy, to be around more imaginative peers."

At A.C.T., says Ryder, "they'd give us these weirdo plays like *The Glass Menagerie,* and there were always these twelve-year-old girls playing these *women.* So I asked if I could find my own monologue to perform. I read from J.D. Salinger's *Franny & Zooey.* I made it like she was sitting, talking to her boyfriend. I had a connection with Salinger-speak; the way she talked made sense. It was the first time that I felt that feeling you get when you're acting—that sort of *yeah!* feeling."

Talent scout Deborah Lucchesi noticed, and she submitted a screen test of Ryder for the movie *Desert Bloom;* Triad Artists saw the videotape and signed Ryder without even meeting her. Director David Seltzer saw the tape when he was casting *Lucas;* after watching seven actresses do the same scene, he suddenly sat up and stared at the screen. "There was Winona," he recalls, "this little frail bird. She had the kind of presence I had never seen—an inner life. Whatever message was being said by her mouth was being contradicted by the eyes."

Meanwhile, Ryder had reenrolled in public school at Petaluma's other junior high. One day, she remembers, she walked home "like a hundred miles, the longest walk. And I always carried my book bag with the strap around my head. So I walk in the house—I practically had whiplash—and my sister goes, 'Oh, you got the part in that movie.' It was really cool."

It's a few weeks before *Heathers* opens (to mostly rave reviews), and Ryder and costar Christian Slater, nineteen, are about to appear at a promotional screening at a New York adult-school film class. The mostly suburban, middle-aged audience is clearly troubled by the movie's lighthearted treatment of diabolical themes, and many stalk out midway, muttering epithets like "awful" and "lousy."

Backstage, Ryder is worried—will the audience hate her, too? She gets an idea and whispers it to Slater. When the screening ends, the two actors come out from behind the curtain and sit in chairs onstage, holding hands.

"What, are you nervous?" teacher Ralph Appelbaum asks. They look at each other.

"We just got married," says Slater, grinning.

"Last week," Ryder says, "in Vegas."

Some class members applaud, others look befuddled. Slater and Ryder never drop the conceit, calling each other "honey," and their charm overpowers their critics.

A few days later Ryder is striding briskly through Central Park wearing Slater's leather biker jacket; the zipper won't zip, so her hands clasp it shut against the chilly spring breeze. She laughingly recalls the idea of marrying Slater. "We talked about how we were going to do all the Hollywood marriage things," she says, "like stage fights in restaurants, be really reclusive but then leak out everything; he'd cover my face when photographers came, like Sean and Madonna."

But after Slater went on a TV talk show and proposed to her on the air, Ryder suddenly tired of the joke. "People have been calling me about it," she says. "It doesn't sound too good. Marriage would be fun, but I don't think I'm ready for it yet."

The funny thing is, Slater *did* fall in love with Ryder. He and the actress playing the lead Heather, Kim Walker, had been dating for a couple of years when *Heathers* started shooting. "We never fooled around or anything during the movie," Ryder says. But after the filming, Slater broke up with Walker and started dating Ryder.

"It was only for a couple of weeks," Ryder says. "It was too weird. You know, when you're really good friends with somebody? It's hard when you *try* to make something work. It's bogus. It should just happen naturally."

She plays idly with a silver ring on her middle finger. She says that it's Irish, signifying love, friendship and loyalty; wearing it with its small crown pointing up means she's "taken." Currently, she's wearing the crown down. The longest relationship she's had, six months, ended because she was away on movie shoots all the time.

"I don't have a lot of time for that kind of stuff," she says, "which is a drag, but it's almost a blessing in disguise." She does note that since she finished *Heathers,* "I'm taking more of an interest in the way I look. I actually became a little more feminine. Before, I just dressed *however.* I'd go to the set in my pajamas."

Heathers had another effect. "It taught me a lot about what I want to do with my life, my career," Ryder says. "Which is never do anything I don't feel one hundred percent about. I don't have any big floor plan, but I wouldn't do a movie where I thought I'd influence anybody in a bad way.

"Having people look up to me freaks me out," she says. "It's actually motivating, because it makes me want to do a really good job. But what if I do something really stupid? That could, like, shatter somebody's image of me. So I don't have the freedom to do really stupid things." She realizes what she's saying and cackles. "Which *is* what I'm striving for!"

Ryder takes a seat on a park bench and stares out at the rowing pond. She suddenly looks tired. She's been doing *Heathers* promotions for a few weeks running.

"A lot of people ask me if I'm missing out on anything," she says. "I don't think so. Sometimes I'll be talking to Helene, this friend back in Petaluma who's still in high school, and I'll think, 'God, it would be so fun to be like Helene, being on the track team and going to the Valentine's dance and stuff like that.' But then I realize that I don't really have it in me to enjoy the social thing. I was always one of the geeks."

The shadows grow longer as the afternoon winds down, and feeling chilled, Ryder gets up from the bench to head back to her hotel. The cold air has gotten to her, and now her nose has begun to run. "Do you have a handkerchief I could borrow?" she asks. "It's okay—it's just little-girl snot."

"*L*ast night I decided," Winona Ryder says. "I'm moving. Getting *out* of L.A." Her phone voice is frazzled, but her resolve sounds firm.

It's the night of the Academy Awards, and she's in her apartment waiting for Slater to pick her up in a limo.

The source of her new vexation is, again, gossip. "Last night this friend called me on the phone and told me there were these *other* rumors about me, and I *flipped out*," she says. "I *hate* it when you can't clear something up. I must be such a wimp. I think I'm gonna find a cottage somewhere. Maybe New Orleans. Or I'm going to go to college, like, *soon*. Of course, you have to apply, don't you."

She never did find an Oscar dress, so she's ended up wearing her roommate's black, sequined miniskirt, black high heels and red lipstick. "I look very sixties," she says. "I'm wearing, like, eight pairs of stockings 'cause I don't want to get a run."

She cheers up when she remembers the review of *Heathers* in this week's *Village Voice*. "This is going to sound really obnoxious," she says. "But listen to what it says: 'Winona Ryder plays the conflicted Veronica with deeper-than-Method conviction.' That's good, isn't it?"

The limo honks outside. "Oh, wait!" she cries. "Should I bring a jacket? Ohmigod, should I bring a purse? What will I keep my lipstick in?" She hangs up midcrisis. *Que será, será.*

Jennifer Jason Leigh

By Philip Weiss

MAY 17, 1990

The actress Jennifer Jason Leigh has arranged to meet me where she walks her dog, at a dead end high in the Hollywood hills. "The famous hills," I said when we were making the date. From the dirt roads up there, you can see Errol Flynn's old estate.

"Famous nothing," Leigh said. "They're just some mountains in L.A."

As a native of Studio City, Leigh has a birthright to talk this way. But her lack of awe also reflects the fact that at the age of twenty-eight, with more than fifteen movies behind her, she has built a career outside of Hollywood expectations—a delicate blonde who hungers to play bad women, exploited women and other types that would make Demi Moore blush.

In *Miami Blues,* she portrays Susan Waggoner, a prostitute turned kept woman of a crazed criminal played by Alec Baldwin. Leigh described the role to me when we planned the dog walk.

"A lot of my character is based on my dog, Bessie," she said. "The desire for unconditional love and the willingness to go through hell to get it. When you meet Bessie, the first thing she'll do is roll over on her back with her legs up in the air, saying, 'You're the boss, you know, love me.'"

As it turns out, the little red cockapoo has no time for such appeals. When she arrives, she bounds out of Leigh's black Legend and runs up the dirt road ahead of us.

We pass a dozen other dog walkers that afternoon, but none of them seem to recognize the pretty actress wearing a vintage blue dress with a scalloped neckline. Movies like *Flesh + Blood, The Hitcher* and *The Big Picture* have not made Jennifer Jason Leigh a star. The classic Leigh film possesses all the trappings of a B movie, stays in the theaters for only a few weeks and is memorable mostly for a mesmerizing performance by Jennifer Jason Leigh. So far, the story of Leigh's career has been a string of forgettable films and publicity along the lines of a recent *Interview*-magazine blurb that was next to a big photograph of her suggestively sucking a bottle of soda. It's emblematic of her fortune that she passed on the role in *sex, lies, and videotape* that instantly made Laura San Giacomo's career.

Unlike her often ruthlessly ambitious peers, Leigh seems ambivalent about taking bigger parts in bigger movies—maybe because she grew up in Hollywood. Maybe because Hollywood (in the filming of *Twilight Zone—The Movie*) killed her father, actor Vic Morrow. Or

291

maybe because something keeps drawing her to disturbing roles.

Whether she likes it or not, though, Leigh may be about to break out. *Miami Blues* is a higher-profile project—it costars Baldwin and was coproduced by Jonathan Demme—and its release will be followed by *Last Exit to Brooklyn,* an adaptation of Hubert Selby Jr.'s harrowing novel in which she plays a fifties hooker named Tralala. Her stunning back-to-back performances in these films have already won attention inside Hollywood and could finally lead her to movies as promising as she is.

In the climactic scene of *Last Exit to Brooklyn,* Leigh as Tralala is on the floor, her skirt up, her shirt off, having invited an incredibly drawn-out and graphic gang bang. Standing offstage, watching the scene being filmed last year, Hubert Selby broke into tears.

"As a man, when you see a scene like that," Selby says, "at some level in the back of your head, you're thinking, 'Hey, take it off. Fuck her!' But you couldn't conceive of having such a reaction to Tralala—your heart just goes out. What Jennifer gets you to experience is Tralala and her suffering. The fact that she brings such humanity to such a degrading situation is an indication of her magnificence as an actress."

"That scene is what you hope for when you're acting," Leigh says as we continue our walk. "It's so clear and powerful and real. Of all the scenes in the movie, that was the easiest to act." *Last Exit* is so dark that it's unlikely to become a hit, but it's part of a shift in Leigh's career strategy. "I made a decision after *The Big Picture,*" she says, "to do movies where I liked the whole. A lot of times, I used to do a movie where I thought, 'Well, this is an interesting character, I want to get inside of someone and explore this,' and the movie ends up being a real piece of shit. Yes, playing the character a lot of times felt great. But when it's a terrible movie, that's painful."

Jennifer Jason Leigh says she wants to be a character actress, a choice that may ultimately give her a much longer and fuller career than most women have in Hollywood. "There are actresses in this town who are just little pieces of meaningless fluff," says casting director Jane Jenkins. "This business just eats them up." While others have been playing brighter characters and having no-nudity clauses written into their contracts, Leigh, says Jenkins, "has been experimenting . . . building her craft."

"Barbara Stanwyck was also off-center," says Elaine Rich, Leigh's longtime manager. "She was not a love goddess; she was not an ingenue."

After guiding her dog past a ferocious pair of boxers straining at their leashes, Leigh explains that "the roles that I did *not* pursue were generally in movies about people who are well adjusted and have good careers or are not in a profession that I find interesting. I mean, prostitutes are professionally minded, too, but it's a different category.

"Playing a prostitute is so complicated," Leigh continues. "You're getting paid to be humiliated, so you feel this amazing power that you have, but at the same time, you know you're the one crawling on your hands and knees being fucked up the ass. Susan Waggoner hates it. Her dream is that she'll get fired, and of course she won't."

But *Miami Blues* never mentions this dream. "No," Leigh says. "It's just something that I know about her."

For Leigh, "a character infiltrates your life." The need to connect with people is in fact why she became an actress. "It was a means of communication for me," she says, "a way of making friends, a way of feeling alive."

Growing up the middle of three sisters, Leigh was the good girl who cleaned her room without being asked, a bookworm who was so reclusive her mother sometimes lost her in the house. Her broad face and well-cut features resemble those of her father, whom her mother, Barbara Turner, a television actress turned screenwriter, divorced when Jennifer was two years old. It was 1964, and Vic Morrow was becoming a household name as tough-guy Sgt. Chip Saunders in the TV series *Combat*. A few years later, Turner married Reza Badiyi, a prolific director of episodes in TV series ranging from *Mission: Impossible* to *Cagney & Lacey*. Leigh grew up seeing her parents go off to the set every day, so a movie career never seemed out of reach. "Hollywood was demystified for me," she says.

She got a taste of acting at nine, when Badiyi hired his stepdaughter for a nonspeaking part in his movie *Death of a Stranger*, filmed in Germany. At Pacific Palisades High School she acted in and directed plays, and at fourteen, Leigh's listing in an actors' directory landed her a role in the Disney TV movie *The Young Runaway*. At sixteen, she got her Screen Actors Guild membership through appearing in a *Baretta* episode, and Jennifer Lee Morrow dropped the Morrow from her name ("I didn't want to be perceived as Vic Morrow's daughter"). She took the name Jason as an *hommage* to family friend Jason Robards, but in Hollywood people still made the Morrow connection, and it helped Leigh get noticed. The following year she got a big role in *Eyes of a Stranger*—as a deaf, dumb and blind girl stalked by a rapist—and she dropped out of high school just six weeks short of graduation, promising her mother she'd take the equivalency test one day. She never did.

Her early roles had a willful, use-me quality. In *Fast Times at Ridgemont High,* she played the nubile Stacey Hamilton, who searches for love and discovers sex. "I went through a very similar thing," says Leigh. "Differentiating between love and sex was hard for me. Just searching out an identity and wanting to be something."

That role became controversial after Leigh gave an interview to the *Los Angeles Herald Examiner* in August 1982. In it, she complained that her sex scene had been cut to get the film's rating down to an R, and she observed that her male counterpart had been uncomfortable being on the set naked, while she hadn't.

The timing was peculiar: Leigh agreed to grant the interview the day after the funeral for her father, who was killed early in the morning on July 23, 1982, during the filming of *Twilight Zone—The Movie*. As Vic Morrow waded across the Santa Clara River forty miles north of L.A. with two Vietnamese American children clutched in his arms and a movie village burning in the background, a helicopter crashed beside him. All three actors were killed—Morrow was decapitated by the copter's rotor. At the time, Morrow's career had been reduced to intermittent roles and was overshadowed by the work of his daughter, who in a *People*-magazine interview referred to him as a "stranger."

Following Morrow's death, Leigh went into therapy, and her acting began to grow more complex. The bimbo she had played in *Grandview, U.S.A.* in 1984 was a predictable one—gum-chewing, teetering around stupidly in heels, catering to an older man.

The whore Leigh plays in *The Men's Club* (1986) is more in control of the situation. Teensy makes herself up like a pubescent Jean Harlow, outfantasizes her johns and takes deep pleasure in having sex with a fatherly trick played by Frank Langella.

"Tell me about your wife," Teensy says to Langella in a zoned-out voice. "Was she a good fuck? . . . There was stuff she wouldn't do. . . . What was your stupid wife's name?"

Leigh seems to thrive on such salacious psychodrama. "Jennifer has a lot of introspection," says Elaine Rich. "She has gone through a very tumultuous time in her life."

In the aftermath of Vic Morrow's death, the Los Angeles DA charged *Twilight Zone* director John Landis and four others with involuntary manslaughter in the killings. The trial lasted seven months and ended in acquittal for all five defendants. Leigh and her older sister, Carrie Ann Morrow, then sued Warner Bros. The matter was settled quickly—it could hardly have been in Leigh's interest to pursue drawn-out litigation against a major studio in a case that was bitterly dividing Hollywood—and the sisters were reported to have collected more than $800,000, though neither will confirm that number, and Carrie Ann, for one, laughs at it.

Leigh says that after her father died, she called MGM and had a copy of his movie *The Blackboard Jungle* sent over to her house. "It was my favorite," she says. Anything more than that, she says, "I just don't want to talk about. That stuff I don't even talk about with my friends. I rarely even talk about it in my therapy."

Vic Morrow's will was filed for probate in the Los Angeles Superior Court. He had planned to leave $10,000 to a Cass Martin of Studio City but scratched that out. Morrow put another female friend's name on a Swiss bank account, then scratched that out, too. (This friend, however, wound up with Morrow's Screen Actors Guild insurance.) Fifty thousand went to a close friend, and as for the rest of Morrow's million-dollar estate, the will—written seven months before he died, in purple felt-tipped pen on yellow paper—reads: "To My DAUGHTER Jennifer LEE MORROW, I LEAVE 100 DOLLARS—One Hundred.

"THE REMAINDER of My ESTATE—INCLUDing . . . MACHO, My DOG WHO MUST BE TAKEN CARE OF, I LEAVE TO My DAUGHTER CARRIE Ann MORROW."

"Why he did what he did, I don't know," Carrie Ann Morrow says by phone from her home in Mount Shasta, California, where she is raising two children. "Sometimes adults act more like children than is necessary."

When all the taxes were paid, it worked out to about $600,000 for Carrie Ann Morrow.

Jennifer Jason Leigh got her inheritance in two installments. At first, anticipating the chunk the IRS would take from the bequest, the estate wrote her a check for a conservative amount: $74.97. Then in January 1987, the tax case was settled and the lawyers figured out how much was still due her. Jennifer Jason Leigh accepted that payment, too. Her signature on the form reads, "Jennifer Leigh," in a signature's typically zigzagging, unclear strokes. Then the name Morrow—her father's claim from the grave—is added neatly at the end, in printing.

That payment was for $3.21.

The day after Leigh and I go on our walk with Bessie, Leigh's publicist calls. She says Leigh feels we haven't talked enough about her two new movies. So we set up a lunch interview at Hugo's, an unpretentious industry hangout in West Hollywood. I want to ask why she even bothered to pick up the spiteful sums from her father. But just the mention of the discrepancy between her bequest and her sister's stuns the actress. She stops gesturing. A flash of anger darkens her eyes. Then her face crumples, and Leigh begins to cry. "I'm sorry," she says, covering her face. "Maybe one day I'll be able to talk about it."

Leigh's mother had agreed to meet us for coffee, and she comes into the restaurant now, while Leigh's hurt is still in the air. Barbara Turner sits down quietly. She is a gentle, observant woman with dark hair and a refined face. Leigh kisses her mother on the cheek, then excuses herself from the table.

Turner is willing to talk a little about Vic Morrow and their daughter. Asked to compare the acting styles of the two, she says, "In terms of approach, they're extremely different. Even as simply as male-female, it's different sensibilities. She's a very generous actress. She gives to other actors. She loves what they give her, and she loves giving back."

Turner stops. "He was a very guarded actor." But in the early sixties, this country wanted endless tales of savage men who struggled and performed, and Vic Morrow simply took on the job with passion. He died doing yet another heroic task, thrashing across a river with two heavy children under his arms. Back home in Ventura Canyon, he left the gun from *Combat* mounted on the wall, pearls belonging to his girlfriend and Macho (value: $0, according to the probate record).

Leigh has been out on that battle-scarred terrain herself, tracking her father's footsteps but on the psychic landscape. The women she's created are ones America would like to forget or to caricature; she's been trying to change our culture's view of its victims. Before long we'll surely know Jennifer Jason Leigh for characters of broader comic and romantic appeal. Until then, there may be more demons to play out.

Jaye Davidson

By Jeff Giles

APRIL 1, 1993

READ NO FURTHER

Or at the very least, be warned that this article will reveal a now-legendary plot twist from Neil Jordan's mind-bending thriller *The Crying Game*. The movie is about many things, but mostly it's about an Irish Republican Army man who falls for a woman who is not a woman. Stephen Rea is that man, and Jaye Davidson is that woman. Or, rather, Jaye Davidson is *not* that woman. Jaye Davidson, after all, is a man. Now you know. Davidson plays a transvestite named Dil, who spends his/her days cutting hair and his/her nights in a bar called the Metro, pining over margaritas and lip synching to the odd pop tune. Rea plays a freedom fighter named Fergus, who abandons his country, his cause and his IRA sweetheart, played by Miranda Richardson. Fergus and Dil meet up in London. Fergus doesn't know that his exotic little flower is a man—and neither does the audience—until the truth is staring him in the face.

When *The Crying Game* was released, the film's distributor, Miramax, asked movie review-ers to keep Jaye Davidson's gender a secret, and they did. And did. And did. The movie, which was made for less than $5 million, became the proverbial hot ticket, as well as the subject of a bizarre publicity melee in which journalists vied to see who could write the longest article with-out actually saying anything. Jordan, Rea and Richardson all walked off with awards. David-son, however, was largely passed over because some critics nominated him as an actor, others nominated him as an actress, and still others didn't know *what* the hell to think. Then Oscar weighed in. *The Crying Game* snagged six Acad-emy Award nominations, including one with Davidson's name on it: Best Supporting Actor.

Jaye Davidson came from out of nowhere and, as you'll see, would not mind going back. (He returned in the sci-fi hit *Stargate*.) Neil Jor-dan cast the twenty-five-year-old Londoner after auditioning a slew of unknowns, many of whom were transvestites and did campy, but not terri-bly feminine, variations on the Bette Midler–Zsa Zsa Gabor theme. "I knew Jaye could sail through it if he was just to be beautiful and aloof," Jordan says, "but I worried about whether he could allow himself to move you as an audience. Then we did the scene where he gets his hair cut for the first time, and he suddenly began to act with this *pain* in his voice. It was extraordinary. Acting is a mysterious thing—you don't know where it comes from." But you do know when it works. Stephen Rea says: "If Jaye hadn't been a completely convincing woman, my character would have looked stupid. Everyone would have said, 'That's one *sick* Paddy.' "

There are people who have seen *The Crying Game*—seen Dil open his robe and twist in the wind, as it were—and yet persist in thinking that Davidson is a woman and that the penis in question is some sort of special effect. (Claymation perhaps?) Davidson has heard of such people, and he has an answer for them: "How mad! I mean, *as if!*" Of course, there are also people who insist that they *knew* Davidson was a man from the get-go. Charles Busch, the peerless New York–based writer and drag actor behind *Vampire Lesbians of Sodom,* says: "I knew in the first scene, but I couldn't believe that that was the big surprise everybody was talking about. It's no surprise to *me* that a girl has a dick. So I kept waiting for the big twist. I thought Miranda Richardson was going to reveal that she had a dick, too. I mean, *there's* a surprise for you."

Last December, Jaye Davidson came to America to shoot a Gap ad with Annie Leibovitz. While he was here, he granted two interviews, one as a woman and one as a man. The former interview was published in the *New York Times,* and though it did not make a single reference to Davidson's gender, it was accompanied by a photograph of the actor in a necklace and hoop earrings, his springy black hair swept up in a bun. The latter interview is now in your possession. It was conducted between nine at night and one in the morning in a clangorous Mexican restaurant in mid-Manhattan in the middle of a rainstorm. Davidson wore a bulky gray sweater, black jeans and Harley boots. He struck one as preternaturally poised, utterly sure of who and what he was.

Not long ago, Davidson went for a shiatsu massage, during which he was told, "Your heart is empty, and your liver is full." He took that to mean that he was guarded and that he drank too much. You be the judge.

This is the first time you've seen yourself in a movie.

Oh, it's scary. Very scary. I saw the final edit about six months ago. I'll never see it again.

Why?

Because I don't want to look at myself. I know what I look like.

When you saw the movie, what was your first reaction?

"Oh, shit." I'm not a performer, do you know what I mean? I don't leave messages on answer phones, in case of the hideous possibility that I will hear my own voice.

How do your friends know that you've called?

Well, they don't. I try and call back later, and eventually I get them.

So the idea of being in a movie must have been terrifying.

It was. It was repellent. In fact, I nearly backed out of it twice. When I first went out for the part, I didn't think in a million years I would get it. I just thought: "Yeah, I'll go have a look at this, why not? It's no skin off my nose." And when I got it, I just laughed my head off. I was at home. I got a phone call from the casting director, and I didn't know what to say. I just said, "Oh, thank you very much." And then I put the phone down and just had hysterical, nervous laughter. It wasn't joyous laughter. It was a nervous reaction. People close to me said, "Don't do this film—you won't be able to handle what happens afterwards." They said:

"You'll be reviewed. Your name will be in the papers. People will recognize you." So I had it written into my contract that I didn't have to do any publicity whatsoever.

But here you are.

Unless I agree on doing it.

It's not often that a newcomer refuses interviews.

No, it isn't. People who are usually in films are very hungry for it. It's their life and their passion. This is not my main passion.

We'll get to that. How were you "discovered"?

Do you know who the director Derek Jarman is? I was at the wrap party for *Edward II,* and I was very drunk. Someone said, "Oh, are you an actor?" I said no. They said, "Would you like to go out for a film?" And I said no and staggered off drunk. I was so drunk that I didn't remember it happening. But the person I was with gave them my number, and then I got a phone call.

Had you done any acting?

I'd been Spear Carrier on the Right—yeah. We've all done school plays when we're very young.

How did you approach the auditions?

What makes a good actor? It's not a question of being theatrical, is it? It's a question of being real. When I went into the screen test or whatever, I just thought, "I'm going to do what I think is right and wait to be told if it's wrong." And that's what I did. It seems like a blur now. A lot of it had to do with Dutch courage.

You drank before the audition?

Yeah. Apparently, I hold my drink very well.

What was your first impression of the script?

I thought: "This isn't going to work. We're not going to get away with this film." I thought everyone would hate the subject—the IRA, the racism, the relationships. I thought people would be very turned off by it. Then I heard who else was in it. I just thought, "My God, I

can't be in a film with these people—they're all *actors!*"

In the film you have a relationship with Stephen Rea. Were you comfortable with him?

I would imagine that Stephen would have been more uncomfortable with me than I would have been with him. See, I'm from another world from Stephen's life. Stephen is an actor—a Belfast actor, married with children. And he ends up working with someone like me. I felt sorry for Stephen. I can't speak for him, of course, but I just thought, "This poor man has to kiss me." That's what I thought: "The poor sod."

For "The Crying Game" to work, the audience has to believe that you're a woman. What made the casting director think you could pass for one?

I haven't got a clue.

What were you wearing at the party when you were discovered?

A pair of jeans and a T-shirt.

Do you enjoy wearing dresses?

Do I enjoy wearing dresses? I never, ever did drag. Never.

Were you shocked when they asked you to do drag?

No. I'm unshockable, fortunately—or unfortunately. I mean, when I went up for the part, I knew they wouldn't want me to play a gunslinging truck driver.

How did you know you could pass for a woman?

I've been mistaken for a woman in the street, so I thought, "Yes, I could get away with this." Maybe I should be locked away for a year and have all the psychoanalysts in the world pick my brain apart. Maybe I'm coming from somewhere completely new. But I keep telling people that I thought I could do it because of other people's reaction to me when I've been completely normal and I've walked across the road to get a pint of milk. I've worn a vest and a T-shirt, and I've said, "I'll have a pint of milk and twenty cigarettes, please." And they've said, "Yes, thank you, luv." Maybe I'm fooling myself, maybe it's some sort of defense mechanism, but it's always *other people.* What other people see, they are welcome to have.

When drag queens see "The Crying Game," they know that you're a man instantly, don't they?

Yeah. And so would I. I can read a pass queen and a drag queen and a sex change like *that.* It's like when you know someone is gay. They will say, "No, no." And their wife and children will say, "No, no, blah-blah-blah." Then, ten years later, you hear tricky little stories, and you just think, "Get over it, you're gay!"

Are you surprised that audiences believe Dil is a woman?

Yeah. Constantly. I don't have a brilliant body at all. I've got very broad shoulders. I've got very big feet. I've also got a very muscular neck. It's disgusting—it's just like a big, thick cord of muscle. But again, I know people take me for a woman. It happens all the time.

I must say that having seen your performance as Dil, I find it hard to believe that you've never done drag.

Before I did the film, I did have *one* night out in drag. I wore a white, silk-crepe, baby-doll dress. I had my hair up, and I had lilies in my hair. It was a fierce look and all that, but it was too much hard work.

How did it feel? Was it like Halloween or something?

No, it was kinky in London. It was during a Trinidadian carnival—in 1989, I think. It was the middle of summer, and it was a really hot English summer, which is rare. Three of us got up in drag, and it was just gorgeous. Just hysterical.

Let's back up for a minute. Where were you born?

I was born in California. I'm an American citizen, but I grew up in England.

What do your folks do?

My mother's a businesswoman. My father's dead.

Were both your parents black?

No, my mother's white.

How did your parents meet?

My father came to London, my mother was in London, and they met.

Can I ask how your father died?

No. We shall skip all that. We shan't even mention him. My mother would be very annoyed.

Are you close to your mother?

We've always had a fabulous relationship. We're very, very similar. We've both got a great sense of self-worth. And when we find something that we want to do, we do it hammer-on. We really *do* it. My mother's very correct and very beautiful. She's to be admired. She brought three children up and worked full-time and ran a house—all on her own.

You grew up in the country. What's to do?

What *does* one do in the country? I dunno. I had a great time. Well, I used to smoke a hell of a lot of pot and still do.

Where did you go after high school?

I started working for Walt Disney in their office in London. It was like earning pocket money. It was mad. You know how you have people who are inside the costumes? I was like that.

What costume were you inside of?

Pluto. It was hysterical.

What did you want out of life then?

I wanted to work in the arts. My dream come true would be to be an architectural historian and work with the royal palaces and all the fabulous art collections. But I'm not committed enough. I'm too trashy. I like to go out and get drunk.

What were you doing before you got the "Crying Game" role?

I was a fashion assistant. I bought the fabric. I made sure that everything was smooth in the workroom. And I scrambled all over London on the Tube, looking for buttons. It was great.

So why do a movie? Don't you have to want to be a movie star to do a movie?

No, you have to want the money. I earned almost half my yearly salary in seven weeks.

Your identity was such a well-kept secret that movie reviewers seemed afraid to mention you at all. Was that frustrating?

No, that was brilliant. The less said, the better. So far in this interview I've probably come across as very arrogant, which I wouldn't like to. When I compared my personal performance to Miranda Richardson's performance, to Jim Broadbent's performance, to Stephen Rea's performance, to Forest Whitaker's performance, I just thought, "This is *very* amateur." At any moment, I quite expected to be fired. I thought Neil had just settled for what he could get. It was a hard part to cast. He managed to find me, and he thought that I could possibly do it, so he settled for that.

Are you any better off financially than when you started the movie?

No. I'm in hideous amounts of debt. I'm overextended everywhere: banks, credit cards, everything. I am the original prodigal. I have to have the best of everything, yet I am incredibly poor. I'm on the dole, and they give me forty-three pounds a week. On that I have to feed and clothe myself and pay gas and electric bills.

You said that acting isn't your passion. But you don't want to spend an entire lifetime as a fashion assistant, do you?

Yes. I can see myself doing that job for a lifetime. I enjoy doing it. I don't want the responsibility of making a picture of a bloody dress. I want to make their vision real. I'm creative in my own life. I'm creative when I step out the door. I'm creative when I pick up a glass. Do you know what I mean? I'm one of those dreadful people who probably should have been born at the end of the nineteenth century and been in cafe society and just sat there chatting about absolute bollocks. That would have suited me fine.

Your agent's phone must be ringing now.

Well, I don't have an agent, because I don't want anyone to offer me another part. I don't want to be tempted out into crap films just for the money. And of course I'm tempted by money. I mean, we all want loads of money, don't we?

Someone must have approached you.

One person has, actually. You'll know about it when it happens. Oh, now I owe our producer, Stephen Woolley, fifty quid. He bet me fifty quid that I would act by the end of the year, and I'm going to do it. I've just decided, actually. This is the first time I've said I'm going to do it.

Would you like "The Crying Game" even if you weren't in it?

Yeah, I would, actually. I would like the subject matter, which hasn't been explored. The movie is about how you just *never know.* You never know what you will be attracted to—or who you will love—till it happens to you. I've only been in love once in my whole life, and I never thought I'd fall in love at all.

Why not?

I thought I was a bit hard-boiled. I couldn't really see it happening to me. I thought, "Who would be stupid enough to get involved with tricky Jaye?" I'm not really a shy person, but no one wants to be rejected, do they? Also, my looks are not attractive to the gay community. To be homosexual is to like the ideal of the sex. Homosexual men love very masculine men. And

I'm not a very masculine person. I'm reasonably thin. I have long hair, which isn't very popular with gay men. My behavior is often appalling. And I have a terrible reputation in London for being one of the unapproachables.

In the movie, Stephen Rea has no idea that your character is a man until he's confronted with irrefutable evidence. Is it possible to have a relationship with someone and not know?

Apparently so. Two of the people who were up for the part were in those relationships, and I just thought: "You're playing very tricky games. It's not going to come out well for you at all!" I mean, how *mad*, don't you think? I would never let anything go that far. Not in a million years. When I met my last lover, I said, "You know I'm a man, don't you?" And he said, "Yeah, I do." And I said, "Well, all right then."

There must be some people who can't deal with you.

Some people can't deal with me at all. At least once a month I'll be walking down the street and a bloke will look at me and then look at me again. The first time they looked they thought it was a woman, and the second time they look they see it's a man. And then a look of hatred comes on their face. And when I see that, I just think: "Fuck you, you're scared! You're scared of me, and you've got *every right* to be scared of me." What happens in the film is most men's worst nightmare come true. It's very scary to them, and it should be.

What are they scared of?

They're scared of their reaction. I feel very sorry for them, but it's their problem, and I shall let them deal with it. It doesn't wash on me at all. I don't have a problem with people hating me.

In the last few years, there's been some controversy about the way gays are portrayed in movies. Was that a concern of yours?

Some people are so precious—all this hoo-ha about bad role models and positive images! Of *course* gay people are murderers, bigamists, drug addicts and nasty people—just as much as heterosexual people are all of these things. You may be homosexual. You may be heterosexual. You may be black, white, European, Afro-Caribbean, whatever. What it all boils down to is, we are all people, and we all have the same human desires. It just happens that some desires go *this* way and some desires go *that* way. Some people desire men. Some people desire women. Some people desire drugs, and some people desire to be very nasty. It's sad when people are oppressed. But it's a question of rising above it. Personally, mentally and, if you have to, physically.

Have you?

I have been involved in physical violence. Absolutely. I don't take any shit from anyone. I am an incredibly strong person and an incredibly fast person. And once I do start bashing you about, you will not get up off the floor. It's as simple as that.

If you go back to the fashion world permanently, you'll be remembered as someone who came out of the woodwork, played a few roles, won some awards and . . .

And went back into the woodwork.

How does that feel?

It feels absolutely fine. It's other people that have a problem with it.

Won't it be hard to go back to being a fashion assistant?

No, all that was normal. This is bizarre. This is another world. Last night I met this girl who's a producer, and we went over to the Village in a massive black limousine. And I just sat in the back snickering away, thinking, "What's going on?!" At home I would be in a cab. Do you know what I mean? I'd be in a cab with some

Cockney driver bending my ear. I *shall* look back on all this. And everything will go into the box that I keep under my bed. Annie Leibovitz gave me her book, and she signed it: "To Jaye, blah-blah-blah." These are all wonderful memories. I have photocopies of all the reviews from America and England. They're all in the box, and I shall treasure them forever.

What's most important in your life?

My life.

That's not an answer.

It is the ultimate answer. The most important thing in my life is to live my life and to enjoy it—to do what I think is right and what I think is good.

What else is important?

Self. Self-worth. Self-evaluation. Self-respect.

What about leaving something behind?

Well, I've left this film behind, haven't I? There'll always be a copy of this film somewhere. I don't want to make an impression on the world. I don't want to make an impression on society. That's not important to me at all. The people I know and love can say, "Oh, do you remember Jaye, blah-blah-blah?" And someone else can say, "Oh, yeah, great, blah-blah-blah." And that's more than enough for me.

Brad Pitt

By Chris Mundy

DECEMBER 1, 1994

Behold Brad Pitt. Everyone else seems to be. On the way to this particular London pub, no less than three young ladies have come skulking out of the shadows to solicit a favor from said heartthrob. Each case is the same: A woman approaches demurely, flashes a smile in desperate need of quality dentistry and utters the question "Excuse me, are you Brad Pitt?" The answer quite obviously being yes, the script continues: "Do you think I could get a kiss?" Then, being a polite Springfield, Missouri, boy at heart, our hero complies.

The significance of these events is not the actual fusion of lips and cheeks. It is that Pitt has been unearthed at all. You see, Brad Pitt is a cagey bastard—a good ol' boy with brains. He is slippery, smart and extremely likable. These are qualities he uses to great effect. Just finding him is the hard part.

Our exhaustive investigation first brought us to New Orleans, home to the beginning stages of filming *Interview With the Vampire,* the film that—along with *Legends of the Fall*—is supposed to cement Pitt's star status. Problem is, from the beginning, production of *Interview* was, how shall we say, a world of shit. Anne Rice, the author whose novel was being adapted, was busy

shouting from the rooftops that *anyone* was a better selection than Tom Cruise to play Lestat, the vampire who recruits Pitt's character, Louis, into the undead. Cruise, meanwhile, was demanding complete control, a closed set and a veil of silence from anyone who dared get within spitting distance. And River Phoenix, who was slated to play the small but pivotal role of interviewer, had just died of a drug overdose. When our trail led to New Orleans, Pitt, as he often does, disappeared.

"You gotta understand," Pitt explains later in his soft-spoken Ozarks drawl, "my character wants to kill himself for the whole movie. I've never thought about killing myself. It was a sick thing. I don't like when a movie messes with your day." He smiles slyly and cocks his head. "Right now, I'd like to play a guy who just wants to fuck everybody so I can have a damn good time."

The fact that Pitt has just run the street-long gauntlet of British lust and finally been cornered—here in a quiet North London pub, pint of beer and cigarette in hand—is quite the coup. *Interview* is in the home stretch of filming in Paris, and Pitt, in turn, is at his breaking point. With five days off, it's time for a vacation. Except for all these annoying questions. When asked to describe the experience of doing *Interview*, Pitt says simply, "You know, *Legends of the Fall* was great." Queried about working with Cruise, Pitt gives an earnest look and talks of another *Vampire* actor, "I'm tellin' ya, Antonio Banderas is the greatest guy."

Okay, next topic. Better yet, more beer. A round is ordered. And another. Then, somewhere between the first and fiftieth beer, an epiphany. "The truth is, I don't want people to know me," Pitt says flatly. "I don't know a thing about my favorite actors. I don't think you should. Then they become personalities."

Which is a better way of saying that actor boy doesn't feel like spilling the beans just yet. Or ever, really. Pitt grabs his pint and leans back with the contented, chaw-in-the-mouth smile of a man who has just sold five cases of snake oil.

"I love to be able to do this—to run around and have adventures," Pitt says. "Why do an interview? Why can't you just write about our adventures?"

So begins our saga. Our adventure, if you will.

One certainly can't be expected to start an adequate adventure without clean underwear. Which explains why our cab is currently hurtling toward a department store instead of the station where our train is due to leave at any moment. Mr. Pitt needs some underpants. Mr. Pitt needs some socks. We procure the necessities, sprint ahead to the station and settle into the first-class compartment with seconds to spare. Next stop: Scotland.

The British countryside flashes by—a slide show of browns and off-browns—and Pitt settles in for the three-hour tour. His long hair is pulled into a loose ponytail, a small knapsack rests at his side, and he continually sketches in a journal that he carries with him at all times to help indulge his architecture addiction. From a distance he looks like just another student traveling through Europe: a wiry frame covered by baggy Indian-style pants, a loose-fitting shirt and a weathered leather jacket. Up close, however, he appears less boyish and more like the thirty-year-old man that he is. This is due in large part to the smattering of scars that are mapped across his face. A tour is requested.

"This one is from baseball," says Pitt, pointing to his cheekbone, "a pop fly that I lost in the sun. I still threw the guy out on second after it dropped on my face." He smiles and turns the other cheek. "This one was just one of those nights, one of those drunken nights." He stops suddenly. "I don't know if I want to say 'drunken night.' I mean, my parents are going to read this."

Pitt refers to his parents as "the biggest guides in my life." His mother, he says, was the first person to ever think he was talented. "She just thought it from Day 1," he says.

"Brad looks like his father, and he has the personality of his mother," says Chris Schudy, one of Pitt's best friends from college. "His mother is so down-to-earth, just a super woman. His dad is a great guy but more reserved. *A River Runs Through It* is almost a mirror image of Brad's family. When I saw the movie, I called him and said, 'You're not even acting. It's just your home unit.'"

Pitt's father, a manager for a trucking company, was frequently on the road but regularly took the kids on his trips. He also offered his son advice that still resonates. Once when Brad was playing in a tennis tournament and screaming and throwing his racket, his father walked on the court between games. "He just said, 'Are you having fun?'" says Pitt. "I got all huffy and said no. He looked at me and said, 'Then don't do it,' and then walked away. Boy, that put me in my place. I should have gotten my ass kicked, but he was so above that."

Little could Papa Pitt have known how seriously his son was to heed this lesson. Fast-forward a decade or so to the University of Missouri, in Columbia, where Pitt is happily biding his time as a member of the Sigma Chi fraternity. It's two weeks before graduation, and our star is just two credits shy of getting his degree in journalism with a focus on advertising. Rather than completing the necessary assignments, however, Pitt—in a manner not dissimilar to the Baltimore Colts sneaking out of town in the middle of the night to move to Indianapolis—loaded up his car, a Nissan named Runaround Sue, and drove to Los Angeles.

"It was such a relief," says Pitt. "I was coming to the end of my college and the end of my degree and the beginning of my chosen occupation. I knew I didn't want to do it. I remember being so excited as I passed each state line. I drove in through Burbank and the smog was so thick that it seemed like fog. I pulled in and went to McDonald's, and that was it. I just thought, 'Shouldn't there be a little more?'"

At the time, Pitt had $325 in his pocket and no acting experience whatsoever. To alleviate his parents' fears, he told them he was attending the Art Center College of Design, in Pasadena. He wasn't. In reality he was shuttling strippers to and from appointments, delivering refrigerators to college students and dressing up as a chicken outside a fast-food joint called El Pollo Loco. Anything to pay the rent. When he finally landed an acting job nine months later, Pitt came clean to his parents. His dad just said, "Yeah, I thought so."

"I always knew I'd leave Missouri," says Pitt. "But it's like that Tom Waits song: 'I never saw the morning until I stayed up all night / I never saw my hometown until I stayed away too long.' I love my hometown. I just wanted to see more. You'd come across a book or something on TV, and you'd see all these other worlds. It blew me away."

Of all the gin joints in Scotland, she had to end up here. Or something like that. It's midafternoon, and Pitt is seated in a Glasgow pub, trying to sand the edges off a post-Edinburgh hangover and attempting to put *Interview With the Vampire* into perspective. But there she is— the kind of naturally radiant barmaid who only saunters into film scenes. Or, as it turns out, into stories about film stars.

And lest anyone think that our young conquistador is only frequenting drinking establishments, it must be noted that the morning was spent conducting Pitt's primary objective for this city: a tour of all the buildings designed by architect Charles Rennie Mackintosh, one of Pitt's heroes. It's just that a quick lunch and a beer beckon. After that, the plan is to hop another train, head to the Scottish Highlands and try our hand at tracking the Loch Ness monster. Seriously. Problem is, each beer keeps getting better. And the barmaid . . . well, she keeps staying the same. We focus on *Interview*.

"Movies have always been cowboys and Indians for me," says Pitt, trying to explain the ordeal of filming. "But when they had offered the part to Daniel Day-Lewis, I heard his response was that he didn't like what it would do to him. Look, he's one of my favorites, but I thought, 'Jesus Christ, more actor bullshit.' Now I'd say I understand a little bit of what he was talking about. When I read the book, I thought it was great, and I think the movie is great. I'm really proud of it. It's just that for me, making the movie wasn't so great."

Nothing about *Interview* was easy. For anyone. When big budgets and Hollywood egos hang in the balance, however, things have a habit of working out in the end. At least on paper. In the days since filming completed, the dark, moody world of *Interview With the Vampire* has gotten unseasonably sunny. Anne Rice even reversed her position and purchased two entire pages in *Daily Variety* to accurately capture the awe she felt while watching Cruise inhabit the character of Lestat. Ah. Come on, everyone, group hug.

In truth, *Interview With the Vampire* remains remarkably true to the novel's narrative and its intensely brooding nature. Directed by Neil Jordan *(The Crying Game)*, *Interview* doesn't shy away from the ugly or grotesque aspects that make the story so compelling. Maybe the months of night shooting and tabloid rumors about on-set turmoil were worth it.

"I didn't realize there were any rumors about Brad and Tom not getting along," says Jordan. "They're two very different actors. And their characters were very different. Tom's character loves control and loves inflicting pain on Brad's character. Brad's character just wants to escape. In many ways they related to each other the way their characters did. Brad really suffered this role. He came into it totally exhausted from doing *Legends*. He did agonize."

Pitt shrugs off talk about animosity between himself and Cruise by continually pointing out that he was extremely impressed by Cruise's performance. There was no tension, insists Pitt, only slightly different lifestyles. Cruise is in complete control at all times. Pitt is continually berated by friends because, as they tell him, he's "always drifting." Pitt even maintains a practice of buying a bike in every film location so he can slip away quietly. When production is complete, he locks the bike up and moves on to wherever the spirit moves him. If he ever passes that way again, he immediately checks in to see if his mode of transportation is still available.

"I tell you, the machine Tom runs is quite impressive," Pitt will say a few months later when *Interview* has been completed. "I wouldn't want to live like that but still. . . . Listen, if you want to stay on top, you've gotta stay on top. A lot of times, Sean Penn's movies don't make money. And in my opinion, Sean Penn is the best we have in that age group. So you can't sit and make Tom out to be the bad guy. Tom Cruise is good in this film."

Pitt pauses.

"I like the guy, I honestly like the guy," Pitt says. "But at a point I started really resenting him. In retrospect I realize that it was completely because of who our characters were. I realize that it was my problem." He laughs. "People take everything so seriously. It's a movie, and it's done."

At this moment, however, as a crowd of Glaswegians begin to swell at this neighborhood watering hole, production of *Interview* is not yet finished. Someone has sent over a round of shots. And the barmaid? She's extremely smart, personable and funny. She's also currently seated at our table. So before things get out of hand—a point that will soon be marked by the arrival of a complimentary bottle of champagne—talk turns serious. The last stage of filming—in just a few short weeks—will be the interview portion of *Interview With the Vampire*. It is this segment of the film that was supposed to include River Phoenix. Pitt's voice, which is normally quiet but infused with Southern hospitality, grows even more hushed, and an earnestness replaces his usual folksy inflection.

"I knew River a little, but I wanted to know him more," says Pitt. "His death affected everyone on the movie, but at the same time it was real personal. You gotta realize, River did a role in *My Own Private Idaho* that took it to a level that none of these other young guys have gotten to yet. I was really looking forward to him being on the set. It just seems like when we lost him, we all lost something special."

And with that, the stillness of the afternoon air is broken by the minor explosion of the champagne cork. Glasses are filled, laughter ensues, and the barmaid is off duty and devoid of any plans for the rest of the evening. The night lies before us like a road twisting and turning into a question mark.

"By the way," says Pitt, leaning in close. "You realize that we're not leaving Glasgow, don't you?"

Brad Pitt has never been a student of film. He has always been a movie fan. Case in point: It seems that Pitt, given any topic in the world, can bring it back to *Planet of the Apes* ("You gotta get out and see things; that's what bugs me the most about religion, because it tells you not to," says Pitt. "That's why I love *Planet of the Apes*. At the end, when Charlton Heston sees the Statue of Liberty . . . *man*").

Pitt is also a self-taught bohemian. He is endowed with a Zen-like ability to wander. "I just like going for a little road trip," he says. "I'm not leaving anywhere. I'm going somewhere." But he also possesses the overwhelming self-confidence to know he'll always land on his feet. Taken to a Pavement concert in London, Pitt dove into the mosh pit alone, despite having never heard the band. He believes he will be a great father. Asked whether he would rather be a movie star or rock star, he says: "Are you kidding? A rock star. I want to do a male version of Marianne Faithfull's 'Why'd Ya Do It?' I'd tell her exactly why." He enchants those around him indiscriminately—male, female, young, old—but to such an extent that you question

his sincerity. Although he points out that "I don't go around robbing people, and I wouldn't say I'm that great in bed," he realizes that his role in *Thelma and Louise* (as the lovable, ne'er-do-well who literally charms the pants off Geena Davis) is the closest he's gotten to playing himself.

"Brad has kind of come into acting by being himself, hasn't he?" says Jordan. "He's come into it by being this incredibly charismatic character. But I think he's far better than he pretends he thinks he is. I think he's great, and I think he actually knows he's great. People are either stars, or they're not. They either project it, or they don't. The minute Brad walked into *Thelma and Louise* he did that. He was a star from then on."

Certainly *Thelma and Louise,* which also led to a romance between the then-unknown actor and megastar Davis, was the first domino to topple in Pitt's career. Unless, of course, anyone happened to catch *Glory Days,* a *90210*-style drama for Fox that mercifully expired after a handful of episodes. "It was terrible," says Pitt. "Man, I'd rather do nothin'." So despite having had a number of roles before it, *Thelma and Louise* will always be the foundation upon which Pitt's career rests.

A diverse slate of films found Pitt on a killing spree *(Kalifornia),* patrolling a cartoon universe *(Cool World)* and becoming a pathetic, pompadour-coiffed rockabilly idol *(Johnny Suede).* None of the three will ever inspire a stampede on a video store. They did, however, broaden Pitt's horizons—ultimately stretching all the way to Montana where he went to work on *A River Runs Through It,* the first quality film that Pitt was called upon to carry on his back.

"I felt a bit of pressure on *A River Runs Through It,*" says Pitt. "And I thought that it was one of my weakest performances. It's so weird that it ended up being the one that I got the most attention for."

This is Pitt's standard practice—to downplay his craft. Complimented for the innate understanding and dead-on realism hinted at by his perpetually stoned slacker in *True Romance*, Pitt simply says: "That was fun. But I was only there for a couple days." Asked about his greatest passions, acting fails to get a mention. Instead, Pitt babbles excitedly about music. He owns three guitars but swears his main connection is purely as a listener. His love of architecture and drawing is so consuming that he sketches and studies continually in his spare time. He also hunts down antiques and professes a fervent respect for anyone who creates beautiful hand-crafted furniture. And then, of course, he loves to wander aimlessly.

"I break everything into stages," Brad Pitt is saying. "There've been some good healthy stages and some that are really unhealthy. The unhealthy ones are sure more fun. And I'd say, right now, I'm just getting out of the moron stage. It's a shame we can't cover them all. They're very interesting, but I'd like this article to have a PG-13 rating."

Okay, Pitt has some control issues to work out, but one thing is certain. This is one great location to start a new life stage. It's late summer, and Pitt has just purchased a stunning new home in the Hollywood Hills. Typically, he immediately asks: "Can you please not write about this place? It's kind of special to me, really sacred." Suffice it to say that it is a home that stands as a monument to Pitt's obsessions. Gorgeous antique tables, chairs and Tiffany lamps litter the inside of a fortress that itself is nestled neatly into a perfectly sculpted compound. Not to cheat his musical fixation, the house was once owned by Jimi Hendrix's manager. And in case

you forgot his roots, the first shotgun Pitt's father gave him rests alongside another twelve-gauge and Pitt's handgun. Pitt might be Mr. Live and Let Live, but you're not going to get his gun unless you pry it out of his cold, dead fingers.

"It's a big deal in Missouri—the way I grew up—to have a gun," says Pitt. "And damn right. If someone comes into my house in the middle of the night, I'm going to shoot their ass. I tell all my buddies. You know, they'll be drunk and come sneak into the house to crash. I tell 'em, 'Don't be pulling that without letting me know you're there.'"

Pitt is seated by his swimming pool, and his every gesture seems remarkably relaxed and content. He is at his base camp. At one time in his life, Pitt set up house with ex-girlfriend actress Juliette Lewis—whom he met while filming the TV movie *Too Young to Die?* and whom he dated for three years—but that was a different feeling from the one invoked by this place. "That wasn't the same," says Pitt. "We were trying to be Sid and Nancy or something. We were idiots. We were just having a great time."

When Pitt is home in L.A., he doesn't venture out often. "I save wild nights for the road," says Pitt. "Or I have wild nights at home. All I know is that I'm not doing whatever Charlie Sheen did, because that boy's in the paper every other night."

So as Mr. Wandering Spirit lounges around the homestead these days, thoughts are filled with what comes next. His going rate per movie has leapt into the realm of the ridiculous (more than $3 million per movie), and he confesses that he is fighting to come to terms with just what the obligation of stardom entails. *Interview* promises to be a blockbuster, and *Legends of the Fall*, despite lapsing a tad into the domain of a TV miniseries, is utterly dominated by Pitt.

"There is a responsibility there," says Pitt. "I just haven't figured out what it is yet." In the interim, such complex and heady dilemmas are being bypassed for crappy late-night cable. "Outstanding," says Pitt when asked about his penchant for such cheese. "I spend all my time, until like four in the morning, watching bad movies. Richard Grieco did this one that is just the best. It's called *Tomcat: Dangerous Desires*. That's Tomcat, colon, Dangerous Desires. Wow." He laughs. "I was in one myself, and by all means, please seek it out. It's called *Cutting Class*. Butt awful."

But for all his nonchalance, it is clear what Brad Pitt wants most is to begin a career of some longevity and significance. He agonizes over roles more than ever. At the same time, almost every penny he has ever made has been sunk into the estate sprawling around him. So what's a young, free and easy neohippie to do? Pitt's plan is to search out the best and brightest of his generation. A moment is at hand in Hollywood, Pitt is sure, and he wants to be part of it. Problem is, young Hollywood is also full of a lot of assholes. That's not exactly a news flash. It is, however, a quandary.

"When I got back from *Vampire*, I wanted to meet some of the young contemporaries," says Pitt when talk turns to the Stephen Dorffs of the world. "I met a bunch of people, and it was that whole competitive, look-over, high-school-cafeteria thing. It was a shame. What's with that? That's why I was so impressed with Christian Slater. It was a tough spot to walk into, the end of the film, everyone's just looking to get done, River's gone. He came in and was just a real person. He walked in like a pro, no ego or anything."

Pitt grabs his can of cream soda and saunters down the stone steps toward his living room.

For a moment he pauses and looks across his backyard. "I mean, some things get harder, but then again, look at this place," he says. "Things get much easier, too. I'd love to have a Wilford Brimley career—Wilford it straight down the pipe. That would be ideal. But who knows, it could all go away. I could pull a Mark Hamill." He pauses weightily. "You come here with this impression that just isn't true. Being in the movies doesn't make you laugh any harder and doesn't make you any less sad."

Pitt walks inside to the stereo, replaces a Gipsy Kings CD with a Stone Temple Pilots one and settles into one of his antique chairs. He fields questions and fidgets in his chair. For all his elusiveness, Pitt gives the impression that he wants desperately to be understood. Not necessarily known, but most definitely understood. He pulls his knees up toward his chin.

"I have to use a cheesy word, but I'd say I try to guide my life by honesty," says Pitt. "And that's a hard thing. I haven't mastered it by any means. I can be a lying shit sometimes."

The question is asked: if it ever worries him that the job of acting is inherently dishonest. Pitt wriggles in his chair and indulges in a long, uncomfortable pause.

"I'm not worried because I'll never be too good an actor," says Pitt, his voice becoming exaggeratedly down-home. "I'm a good actor, I'm consistent, but I'll never be a great actor. Every now and then I'll be great. Every now and then I'll be lousy." He smiles contentedly, confident that he has made his point but still kept his cards close to his chest. As the night winds down, Pitt decides against heading out into the dark for a nightcap. He walks his guest to the driveway and watches the taillights fade down the street, content to stay safe on his side of the compound line.

River Phoenix (Farewell)

By Peter Travers

FEBRUARY 24, 1994

Enough with the rehashing of how River Phoenix, twenty-three, overdosed on cocaine and heroin, in 1993, outside the Viper Room, in L.A. Either Phoenix is reduced to another drug casualty for the just-say-no crowd to cluck over, or he's romanticized into pinup martyrdom—a James Dean for the nineties. Phoenix's talent and memory deserve better. He was an actor, an uncommonly gifted one.

Evidence of that can be found in *Silent Tongue*, a tale of love, death and shame in the Old West. It is Phoenix's penultimate performance: The last film he completed, Peter Bogdanovich's sweet but silly *Thing Called Love*, went swiftly to video. *Silent Tongue*, written and directed by Sam Shepard, is a more apt swan song. It shows Phoenix at his ambitious best.

Phoenix stood apart from his peers. When they acted in Westerns, the movies were mostly *Young Guns* vanity productions. Leave it to Phoenix to choose *Silent Tongue*, a demanding chunk of Shepard frontier poetry that shuns pretty-boy posturing. The first sight of Phoenix comes as a shock. In filthy clothes, with cracked lips and a crazed stare, he sits under a tree with a rifle, keeping guard by a fire. You can hear the flames crackle against the cold air. Seeing a bird in flight, he shoots it, rips off its feathers and climbs the tree where he places the prize plumage on the rotting corpse of an Indian woman tied to the branches. He then bends tenderly to kiss her, his eyes burning with grief.

It's an astounding opening scene, mysterious and rending. Shepard films the scene without words, but it's doubtful he could have done it as tellingly without Phoenix, who infuses the role with a unique intensity. Gradually, the film fills in more details about this obsessed character. His name is Talbot Roe, the backward son of Prescott Roe (Richard Harris), an earnest plainsman who will do anything for his only child. Last spring, the elder Roe bought his son a wife, the half-breed Awbonnie (Sheila Tousey), in exchange for three horses. The seller was Awbonnie's Irish father, Eamon McCree (Alan Bates), the perpetually soused proprietor of the Kickapoo Traveling Medicine Show. A few weeks earlier, Awbonnie died in childbirth (the baby with her), leaving Talbot dazed from sorrow and his father determined to buy him a replacement wife, Awbonnie's sister, Velada (Jeri Arredondo). "He's fallen even deeper inside himself," Prescott tells McCree. "He refuses to eat or speak. He just stands over her corpse like a lost soul."

As Talbot keeps watch, the ghost of Awbonnie—a streak of white paint running down her angry face—appears to rebuke him: "You're a dog, a low dog, to tie me here out of your selfish fear of loneliness." Awbonnie wants Talbot to throw her body in the fire so her spirit can be free. But even when this ghost knocks him down, chokes him, puts a curse on his father and cajoles him to kill himself, Talbot clings tenaciously to what is now only a mound of decomposing flesh.

During rehearsals, Shepard tied Phoenix to Tousey with twine to reinforce the bond he wanted Phoenix to feel. Phoenix rewards him with a performance of almost unbearable poignancy. As Talbot keeps his lonely vigil, Shepard gets close to the mythical transcendence he seeks. Talbot, his mind in a fever, finds reality and fantasy sliding into each other until he achieves a kind of peace. It's a perilous journey into letting go, and Phoenix never falters.

Letting go may prove tougher for the actor's admirers; *Dark Blood,* the movie Phoenix was making when he died, will never be finished. And the role Phoenix was set to play opposite Tom Cruise and Brad Pitt in *Interview With the Vampire* went to Christian Slater. So the film legacy of River Phoenix ends with *Silent Tongue.* It's a fitting capper to an extraordinary career.

My first and only meeting with River Phoenix took place in 1991 in tandem with the release of *My Own Private Idaho,* the Gus Van Sant film about male hustlers that contains his most memorable and revelatory performance. Phoenix had been trapped all day in a Manhattan hotel doing interviews about the breakthrough role, which had just won him the Best Actor prize at the Venice Film Festival. He was elated. Squinting out the window at a glimmer of sunshine peeping through the clouds, he suggested a walk instead of a restaurant sit-down. It was a chance to inhale the last of a rain-washed September afternoon and, he whispered conspiratorially, "to sneak a smoke."

Phoenix laughed at his own schoolyard jargon. Here he was—twenty-one, turning tricks onscreen and riding high as the flanneled, sneakered paragon of grunge cool. Why worry about a cigarette? He had an explanation: His mother hated his smoking, and he didn't want to be caught in the act in a hotel restaurant crammed with media types who might publicize his nicotine habit (he called it a phase) to young fans. You could see the conflicting emotions on his face: boyish mischief duking it out with the precocious maturity that came with being the son of missionary parents. Phoenix bristled at the notion. "I do what I want," he said, flashing a gaze of laser intensity. He used that gaze sparingly, in life and in the movies. His eyes— mostly darting or downcast—hid secrets. That's what drew audiences to him. Now, after his death, it's what draws us back to the twelve movies he made in three years.

The lure isn't morbid curiosity. His films are a legacy of achievement, not just of promise. A lot of bull has been disseminated about Phoenix since his death. He's either reviled as a Hollywood junkie or romanticized as the rebel angel. What this rare actor really was presumably doesn't cut it as hot copy—a smart, decent kid who made mistakes.

Phoenix played the role often; he knew its subtleties. He also knew that he screwed up in some films *(Little Nikita, A Night in the Life of Jimmy Reardon)* and merely showed up in others *(I Love You to Death, Sneakers).* But when he was on a roll, he could fill even a small part—say, young Indy in *Indiana Jones and the Last Crusade*—with vigorous intelligence.

In one year, 1986, he talked trash in Rob

Reiner's *Stand by Me* and found the fragility in the brutalized boy in Peter Weir's *The Mosquito Coast*. In Sidney Lumet's *Running on Empty* (1988), he won an Oscar nomination as the son of fugitive sixties radicals whose nomadic life mirrored his own. His farewell to his girl (Martha Plimpton) in that film exudes a raw tenderness most of his peers wouldn't risk. And yet in Nancy Savoca's *Dogfight*, Phoenix could transform himself into a burly, bullet-headed, misogynistic Marine, with utter conviction.

Phoenix could do anything, it seemed, except reconcile his idea of himself with the ideas of others. The struggle gives his work a special poignancy for those legions who know the feeling.

Phoenix captured youthful yearning and confusion better than any other actor of his generation. Catch him in *My Own Private Idaho* as he confesses his love to Keanu Reeves ("I really want to kiss you, man") with a grave honesty that will pierce your heart. It's almost too painful to watch those *Idaho* scenes in which the Phoenix character, who suffers from narcolepsy, convulses and collapses in the streets—it's a wincing reminder of his last moments on the sidewalk in front of the Viper Room. But it would be wrong to reduce the memory of this young actor to an antidrug campaign. His mistakes didn't make River Phoenix unique, his talent did. And through his films, that talent endures.

Drew Barrymore

By Chris Mundy

JUNE 15, 1995

Drew Barrymore is knocking back a beer. Not a beer, mind you, but a good old-fashioned Pilsener. Hops and barley. The kind of libation that would impair her ability to operate heavy machinery if, for some odd reason, there happened to be any heavy machinery in sight. It is a celebratory beverage, and Barrymore is in the mood for a little revelry. For one thing, she is flush with the afterglow of having flashed David Letterman.

Two nights ago, while demonstrating a striptease-style bump and grind on his desk, Barrymore lifted her T-shirt to present Dave with compelling evidence that she is not a little girl anymore. This afternoon, as she's walked the streets of New York, lascivious men of all ages have raised their thumbs in appreciation. Couple that with the fact that today is her ten-month anniversary with her boyfriend, Hole guitarist Eric Erlandson, and this would already be a banner day. But that's just the beginning. The true reason to rejoice is that Drew Barrymore has been liberated. Today, after almost eleven months of legal wrangling, she is officially divorced from Jeremy Thomas, thirty-two, the Welsh-born bar owner who shared with her six weeks of holy matrimony. Barrymore is

giddy. At one point she begins a sentence with the words "My ex-husband . . ." She stops. "Excuse me," she says. "The devil . . ." And then she promptly giggles. Not the worldly, knowing laugh she sometimes expels to let you know she's been around the block a few thousand times, but the girlish, almost childlike chortle she uses when trying to elicit a response from your inner baby-sitter. It is a hollow sound of adolescent embarrassment—perhaps to let you know she's done something naughty—but you both know she has never actually been an adolescent.

Barrymore raises her bottle, takes a slug and pauses for a moment as if to ponder whether anything has been left out. Being off the wagon, stripping, dating, divorce. Nope. If that doesn't cover people's most pressing questions for the time being, nothing will.

She takes another swig.

"I just want to be free," Barrymore says. "That's the whole point I've been trying to make since I was a child, and I'm still making it."

True enough. At the age of twenty, Drew Barrymore has lived her share of lives. These are not Shirley MacLaine–style lives, spread out

313

over centuries and existing in the deep recesses of her own mind, but rather the kinds of existences shared by aging country stars who sing about boozing, sparring and small-town jails with the accuracy of seasoned newspaper reporters. Drew Barrymore has done her living with a capital *L*. Maybe even all caps. Check the life ledger: child abuse, a year in an institution to rehab from alcoholism and drug addiction at the age of thirteen, attempted suicide, legal emancipation from her parents at fifteen, marriage, divorce, stardom, career extinction and, finally, stardom again.

Barrymore is less an actress than an icon, a living embodiment of tragedy and survival. At one point it seemed like campy fun for the world to laugh at her. When that clamor began to subside, she found these same forces beginning to laugh with her. Today, after the success of *Boys on the Side*—a just-released romantic turn—and a role in the upcoming *Batman Forever,* it is Barrymore who laughs loudest of all. The only adjective that adequately captures the Drew Barrymore oeuvre is *Melrosian*. But this we will attempt to reveal episodically.

Barrymore rests her drink on a table, hurls a dart toward the board and performs a three-second victory shimmy. At the moment she is her child self, dancing gleefully on the playground and hoping for approval. Within two minutes, however, she will speak about a morning meeting with a powerful producer like a jaded actress in the old Hollywood sense. Then, just as abruptly, the little girl will return.

"I'm an adult, and I'm a child," Barrymore says when the fluctuation becomes unnerving. "They go in and out. I get to be a kid now because I wasn't a kid when I was supposed to be one. But in some ways, I'm an old woman— lived it, seen it, done it, been there, have the T-shirt."

See if you can spot the telling symbolism in this picture.

It is midafternoon, and Barrymore is seated in the back booth of a dark bar in New York's East Village. In her left hand is a Budweiser. In her right is a grape-flavored Mickey Mouse lollipop. The topic of conversation is her mother. As is often the case, Barrymore's eyes are welling with tears.

"She just dedicated a book to me," Barrymore says. "My mom wrote a *Joy of Sex*–type book for the nineties. Very appropriate." She forces out a laugh and rolls the lollipop in her mouth. "Neither of us is ready to talk to the other one, but for her to dedicate that to me is her way of telling me that she loves me."

Mother and daughter have not spoken in almost four years. The silence, however, is no longer as eerily quiet. Two months ago, on Barrymore's twentieth birthday, Jaid Barrymore wrote her daughter a letter, and they have been corresponding by mail ever since.

Barrymore's emotions are mixed. On the one hand, this is a woman who instilled in her a piercing cynicism before Drew had reached preschool. "My mom always told me that I have to be totally accepting that the person I'm with is going to leave because we're all born alone on this earth, and we'll all die alone," says Barrymore. "Both my parents grooved on love, but both of them were not capable of having a relationship with another person. Not a lover, not a friend, not even their own family. It really fucked up my ideas of what love was supposed to be."

On the other hand, Jaid was fiercely protective. When Drew was six, a playground bully smashed her face-first into the pavement, cutting a swath across her chin that required fifteen stitches. The next day, when mother and mummy-wrapped daughter walked into the school, the six-year-old bully glared at them and laughed.

"I had asked her not to do anything because she's so fucking volatile that she'll do anything," says Barrymore. "But when he laughed, my mother grabbed him by the collar and said, 'If you ever fuck with my child again, I'll cut your fucking dick off.'" Barrymore roars with laughter. "Mom," she says to the thin air, "thank you for that."

Clearly, Barrymore believes some common ground must exist. Although she asked that her mom not be interviewed for this article, she predicts that sometime soon, she and her mother will be speaking again. Barrymore's father is a different story altogether. Although Barrymore doesn't know his precise location (she believes he might be down South), she does know this much: Her father has not owned a pair of shoes in forty years, does not believe in material possessions and lives the life of a vagabond—often muttering Scripture to unsuspecting passersby.

It wasn't always so. Born into one of Hollywood's most illustrious and entrenched acting dynasties, John Barrymore Jr. achieved modest success in the movies before drugs and alcohol proved to be his undoing. All that, unfortunately, was before his daughter knew him. Her first memory of her father was when she was three. He threw her into a wall.

"My father was a junkie and an alcoholic for thirty years," says Barrymore. "Nice combo, huh? So that breeds shitty behavior. It was hard for me to deal with [while] growing up. It was chaotic and violent and scary. When I was seven, I finally said, 'Look, Dad, see ya.' I wrote all over his cigarettes—'Fuck you, you're an asshole'—and I handed him the cigarettes and said, 'Smoke this, you motherfucker.' I threw a chair at him and told him to never touch me

again. I didn't speak to him again until I was fourteen."

By that time, Barrymore had grown-up problems of her own. Having achieved stardom in *E.T.* at the age of seven, she moved on to a series of successes in such movies as *Firestarter* and *Irreconcilable Differences*. She was a forty-year-old in a nine-year-old's body, and she played the role with precocious ease. Talk shows, drinks, movie offers, nightclubs, cocaine. All before the seventh grade. Then, at fourteen, it all seemed too much.

"I did attempt suicide, but I didn't really want to die," Barrymore says now. "At least I didn't want to disappear permanently. They rushed me to the hospital and saved me, and there I had to make a conscious decision. I made a conscious decision that I really wanted to live."

The hospital where she spent the next few months was a cross between a rehab center and a mental institution. On the inside she experienced characters like Lillian, the elderly woman in the adult ward who would suddenly slam down her lunch tray and in her best Mae West imitation scream, "You just paid a quarter for an orgasm!" On the outside, living on her own and trying to make ends meet, Barrymore filed the papers necessary to emancipate herself from her parents in order to legally work the same hours as eighteen-year-olds. Fifteen-year-old recovering substance abusers, she found, sometimes have a difficult time paying the rent.

"She's so appealing, and she's so bright, and she's such an essentially nice human being," says rock star David Crosby, who along with his wife, Jan, took in Barrymore for close to a year after her treatment. "We found it very easy to love her, and I still do. I knew her dad, and I know her mom. I've watched the four generations of major alcoholic destruction that she comes out of. So I feel very strongly about her.

She's an extremely talented kid who got dealt a very short hand. Her father was a disaster and never made any attempts to correct it—let's leave it at that. And to put it very mildly, as politely as I can, I disagree with her mother's approach to life rather much. I would really hope that Drew keep a distance from her. I will say this: I consider her mother one of the worst influences possible."

Luckily for Drew Barrymore, there were more parental substitutes—fantasy figures for most of the world but the only grounding forces in her existence. To this day, Steven Spielberg still tells Barrymore that she is his eldest child.

"If people like David and Jan and Steven weren't in my life, I'd probably be a lot more fucked up than I am," says Barrymore. "They made me believe that there actually were trustworthy people out there."

Barrymore fidgets and for a split second begins a microtirade about how Spielberg can only see her as his little girl. Then a moment later she smiles and admits that this is precisely the way she likes it.

This year on her birthday Spielberg sent a package to a restaurant where she and friends had gathered. In it was a blanket and a copy of the *Playboy* magazine in which Barrymore recently posed for a pictorial. The note said: "Here's my version of you in *Playboy* and a blanket to wrap yourself in." Inside the magazine Spielberg's art department had woven its own computer-generated wardrobe to cover her in every photo.

Drew Barrymore claims that no one who truly cares about her would dare call her Drew. It is a name she has heard and read so many times in so many contexts that she can barely stomach it. Some people call her D, but to most she is Daisy. Around her neck she wears a beaded, grade-school-style necklace that proudly spells out her flowery alias.

In person Barrymore is tiny, a miniature version of herself: ultrahip seventies leftovers tightly clinging to her matchstick limbs and a coquettish expression attached to a face that doesn't look a day removed from her role in *E.T.* Because of this she possesses the ability to charm those around her in two contradictory manners. One is overt: all over-the-top enchantment and a contagious overflow of positive energy. The other is passive: a thinly veiled sadness and a distinct awareness that she comes with her share of baggage and could certainly use a little help in carrying it. She uses both tactics equally, and each comes in handy. Her history, she knows, is one in which most of the world is well schooled.

"I think the day I read an article that doesn't talk about my past, I'll probably shit in my pants," says Barrymore out of the blue. "Just shit my pants. I've never shit my pants my whole life, but that will be the time."

A laundry problem is quickly averted. Talk turns to *Mad Love,* and Barrymore, without missing a beat, travels back in time to make a point.

"My character goes into an institution, and her brain starts to deteriorate," she says. "How many other fucking actresses can relate to that?" She stops, waves her arm in the air like a kid trying to get the teacher's attention and shouts at the top of her lungs, "I can!"

And so the question bubbles menacingly to the surface: Does she worry about drinking again after having lost a year of her life to institutionalized rehabilitation?

"Every time I take a sip of alcohol, I think, 'What will people think?'" Barrymore says. "That's strange. Try that on for fucking size, living your life in a fishbowl for everyone to judge you. How 'bout that?"

Instead of an answer, another question is asked. This time, it is whether—regardless of public opinion—she fears that drinking might shatter the fragile balance that she has achieved in her life and career. She is, after all, part of a family tree that has been tragically uprooted by its history of alcoholism. To this, she smiles sweetly.

"I'm fine," Barrymore says. "This is what kills me. Ask any person in this industry if I ever missed one fucking day of work or if I was ever unprofessional or threw a temper tantrum or walked onto the set drunk. It's never happened. Doesn't that stand for something?"

She pauses and affects the more dramatic tone of a veteran actress.

"The only reason anyone found out anything about me is because some guy broke into my hospital and reported it," she says. "I never asked him to exploit my story. Nobody ever would have known, because I never missed a day of work over it. This guy has some pretty gnarly karma coming. So to clear the record I had to tell people myself. I had to go, 'Okay, I'm getting my fucking life together.' And now I'm fine. I'm happy."

Barrymore dabs her hand at the tears that are beginning to chase each other down her cheeks and chooses her most childlike tone. "Can't I just be happy?"

It is not your typical uniform in which to commune with nature. We are seated in a park alongside New York's East River, and Drew Barrymore is extolling the virtues of the great outdoors. She is wearing a leopard-print coat and an intentionally loose, low-cut blouse circa *Charlie's Angels,* the Cheryl Ladd years. Her purple sunglasses are held together with a diaper pin, and her hair is in spiky disarray. It is a souvenir snapshot from the Sex Pistols' reunion picnic. If, of course, they ever decide to hold one.

More than any one thing, Barrymore seems defined by her inner battle between yearning for liberation and needing security and reassurance. She repeatedly and emphatically stresses that her friends are her family. Since the age of fifteen she has lived a life of utter independence. At the same time, she has almost never been without a boyfriend, and a large number of those relationships have been live-in. When she and Erlandson began dating last June, they set about cohabiting almost immediately.

It wasn't your typical beginning to a love story (unless your idea of romance involves vomiting, in which case your opportunities are probably rather limited). It was in Los Angeles, outside a rock club, and Barrymore had stepped outside to relieve herself of anything she had eaten in the last twenty-four hours. Suddenly a hand was placed on her shoulder. Noticing the tiny creature purging herself in the relatively seedy neighborhood, Erlandson had stopped to stand guard.

"I love him so much," says Barrymore at this moment, and countless others to come. "And I have a family now from Eric, too."

Of course, there is extended family as well. While Barrymore brings to the relationship her trailerful of issues, Erlandson enters the union with Courtney Love—his bandleader and a walking psychology experiment in her own right. It's enough to make you want to buy some popcorn, sit back and watch the carnage. During the rehearsal for Hole's *MTV Unplugged* taping, in fact, Love chastised Erlandson by saying, "You're the one with the girlfriend on the cover of *Playboy*."

Explaining her position, Barrymore flashes a

look of uneasy diplomacy. "We're not close at all," she says, "but that's fine. As democratically as possible, we don't feel the fucking need to be best friends. We respect each other's positions. No woman can suffer anything more torturous than losing the man she loves. In every way, that makes me totally accepting. I don't excuse actions, but it makes me totally accepting."

Quickly, another topic is suggested: a game of show and tell. Barrymore dumps out her backpack on request and begins reeling off the items: cigarettes, wallet, a photo of her kissing her boyfriend, Filofax, camera, pocket dictionary. She is asked to name the last word she looked up.

"I can't say," says Barrymore. "I actually looked it up and wrote it down, and it's really insane because it pertains a little too fucking closely to my life."

Barrymore is met with a slightly stunned silence.

"Okay, fuck it," she says. "But if you print it, you have to explain this. I looked up this word because I was obsessed with finding its purity. The last word I looked up was *nirvana.* The definition of *nirvana* is 'the final freeing of the soul from all that enslaves it.'"

For what seems like the hundredth time in the past few days, Barrymore begins to cry. "When I looked that up, it was just crushing to my soul."

"*Fuuuuck!*"

The person screaming is Drew Barrymore. The same Drew Barrymore who just recently said, "Please don't have a problem with me. Please do not judge me. Actually try, just for one second, to look at the good sides of my life. Look at what I'm going toward instead of what I've done before." But here she is, seated in a quiet but full hotel bar, screaming.

"*Fuuuuck!*"

She is not angry. On the contrary, these are *fuuuuck*s of joy—*baisers de joie,* if you will—it's just that they're a tad loud. She is attempting to explain how some days when you wake up in a surly mood, you just need to get it out of your system and then get on with your day.

It's an interesting point mostly because it illustrates something else altogether. While she often talks about her desire for anonymity, Barrymore continually does things to draw attention to herself. Lots and lots of attention. Tales of self-indulgent, look-at-me behavior stalk Barrymore and Erlandson like a bloodhound with a personal stake in the chase. She admits to the disturbingly contradictory behavior.

"It's weird, I know," Barrymore says. "My whole life has been this open book. I'm so used to it on one level, and I've learned to really cope with it because it's never going to be any other way. Everyone will always be curious about my life because it's been insane. All I have to say to those people is 'Fuck you,' and yet 'Take the ride.'"

Barrymore stops and fixes a serious expression on her face. "Do you think people are interested in me because of the tragedy or because of the survival?" she says.

The answer Barrymore receives is, both. The world is not littered with twenty-year-olds battling back from personal catastrophe to regain the form and stature they exhibited during kindergarten. It makes for an oddly compelling spectator sport. There's just no telling what aspect people are most drawn to. Some people attend hockey games for the fights, some for the precision skill of the athletes.

"I guess that makes sense," says Barrymore. "Sometimes it pisses me off, wondering which one people are interested in." She pauses. "I can't see myself the way other people see me. I'm not insecure. I've been through way too much fucking shit to be insecure. I've got huge balls. But I've been humbled. That makes you grateful for every day you have."

And so Barrymore exits, armed with the power of this new information. Two days later, interrogation complete, she sends flowers and a poem: "I watched you go down the sidewalk / Away went my being / Away went my friend / I will find you again."

It is a thoughtful offering that raises guilty questions. Is it a gesture of pureness, a response to human interaction and acceptance? Perhaps it is an attempt to control a situation—the act of someone with whom social engagement is less an art than a survival instinct. It doesn't really matter. Either way, it is sadly beautiful.

Jim Carrey

By Fred Schruers

JULY 13-27, 1995

O h, please, don't do that.
Jim Carrey puts his face just inches from a hole in a tall, wooden post and mutters into it. The live bat Carrey is trying to flush out pokes its hideous little snout out of an opening that looks too small for its busy, mottled-brown wings and stares back at the morphing human who now displays his own toothy grimace. Above and behind Carrey, fluttering shapes wheel and plummet.

"A bat colony right outside the place I'm staying—what are the chances of that?" asks Carrey. Indeed, he duels with the title character in the just-opened *Batman Forever,* playing the red-haired, green-suited Riddler, a human question mark who torments the brand-new Batman, Val Kilmer. Hollywood seems far away from this clearing out in the Texas hill country west of San Antonio, where Carrey is filming *Ace Ventura: When Nature Calls.* It's the sequel to the surprise comedy smash that turned him from the quite-impossible-to-miss white guy on TV's *In Living Color* to the star of three 1994 films *(Ace Ventura: Pet Detective, The Mask* and *Dumb and Dumber)* that spotlighted his sprawling demographic pull, raked in a combined $550 million in global box office and raised his salary to

a whopping $10 million a film. That was the sum the near-broke Carrey wrote on a 1990 check to himself "for acting services rendered" that he dated Thanksgiving, 1995. By the time of his father's death in 1994, he'd eclipsed that mark in yearly income, and he laid the check in his father's casket. "One thing I hope I'll never be is drunk with my own power," says Carrey with his practiced deadpan when talking about his fresh mushroom cloud of clout. "And anybody who says I am will never work in this town again."

The note of edginess in the joke is one the thirty-three-year-old Canadian clown sounds often. Insincere Guy is the man Carrey most dreads becoming. After a long day on the set of the *Ace* sequel, Carrey is standing outside his borrowed ranch house, drinking a fine red wine at sunset. His demons are at bay for the moment, although he's working on an untidy divorce and on the replacement of *Ace* director Tom DeCerchio with longtime pal Steve Oedekerk (author of the script, which features a missing . . . bat). Carrey's also awaiting reaction to his first megabudget epic—*Batman Forever* cost a reported $100 million. The movie audience is legendarily prone to the kind of spasms that vaulted Carrey to the top but is just as legendarily able to turn, as it did to comic phenom Eddie Murphy, and say, "What was your name again?"

Right now, Carrey is talking about the origins of his humor, obsessive energy and rage. The pain in Carrey's past leads his estranged wife, Melissa, to say: "I'm nervous for him. I think creative people need to be aware of the dark side that accompanies those gifts they have. I learned that the smile he wears is the biggest mask of all." Carrey's affection for his deceased parents alternates with unburied anger that comes out in virtual torrents, and his art (it *is* that, pratfalls, geek faces and all) proceeds from both wellsprings. "People think that I'm this weird guy," Carrey says. "But I'm up there spewing out all my crap, you know. I guess the audience does it through me—they get that kick, seeing somebody else do it. I've always thought it was a really healthy thing."

The Carrey who would spend eight hours before a set of mirrors perfecting faces, the Carrey who can't stop himself from working all day and well into the night for weeks on end, is no stranger to darkness and compulsion. The Riddler is "like any sycophant," says Carrey. "The type of guy who's basically saying he loves you more than life itself but deep down he hates you more than death—because he's grown to resent you." The object of much hero worship lately (fawned over by studio chiefs and schoolkids alike), Carrey walked on the star-laden *Batman* set as the guy who turned up when the first choice Robin Williams wouldn't. "I got in my innings," he says. "Don't worry about me."

Dinner is waiting inside as Carrey's little bat pal finally hops out of his hole, flares wings and membranes and darts into the darkening sky. But Carrey lingers, drinking a second glass of red in disciplined if savoring doses and sharing a reminiscence. He's talking about his need for concentrating on the task at hand, whether he's about to enter a frame, rewrite a joke or work at the drawings and sculptures he's done since childhood.

"I drew, and it's kind of still the same way—not quite as intense—but I used to draw in my room," Carrey says. "And when my mother asked me to take the garbage out, I would just go insane and break everything and knock shit off the shelves, just lose it. I was concentrating, I was so lost in it, it was like being in the womb, like meditation or something—you don't care about anything.

"I did pencil sketches and stuff like that," Carrey continues. "I won a couple of art exhibitions, actually. I was pretty good at it right from the start." The drawings were naturalistic, as opposed to his Daliesque later efforts. "I didn't get weird till I was older," he says. "My parents would come into the room and ask, 'What are you drawing?' It would be my dad looking at his watch with a gun in his hand. 'It's a portrait of you,' I said. 'It's called *Waiting to Die*.'" Although the pond in front of Carrey gathers enough light to show the odd ripple, his face can barely be seen now.

"I started making figurines, and I did a few of these paintings that just were really weird concepts—animals and stuff," Carrey says. "And I remember my sister coming down to visit me in L.A. and looking at the paintings on the wall and going, 'Are you okay?'"

Carrey leads the way up the grassy rise to the house, where, as we walk into a lamp-lit room, he acknowledges with a swirl of one hand the slightly disturbing wall decorations—about thirty stuffed and mounted animal heads, all tusk, tooth and fur. "And I'd say, 'Yeah, I'm okay—I have an outlet. What do you do?'"

This is the Carrey one gets used to over a couple of days—an unexpectedly studious sort with a sense of mission that never quite turns grandiose. He's very seldom "sssmokin'" like his masked creation but, rather, solicitous, unhurried (until he hits the dirt path leading to the film set) and often wistful as he reflects on his life. While Pauletta, his hair person since *In Living Color,* shellacs his topknot into its *Ace* wavy form, he listens to alternative rock—Live, Pearl Jam, Nirvana, Green Day—very loud, dutifully shouting answers over the blaster and the hair dryer. He makes eye contact, infallibly, and he regards people who come his way with an attentiveness some find almost daunting. "He's one of the few comedians who you can invite to a dinner with friends," says *Mask* director Chuck Russell, "who is just as interested in everyone at the table as they seem to be in him."

"My performing started out as a mixture of things," Carrey says. "It's really not all angst and I-gotta-go-onstage-or-I'm-gonna-kill-somebody kind of thing. Some of it is the anger, but it was born from really, truly just wanting to be special and to be noticed and wanting to make people laugh. It really was born from that, so it comes from a good place. It's just—the tools are your anger, the tools are your sadness, the tools are your joy, the tools are voices, faces—the tools are all those things."

"Jim finishes first and then disrupts the class" is one teacher's evaluation that sticks in Carrey's memory.

"I'd whip through my work and then go on a rampage," Carrey says. "But I had a great teacher in grade seven, and she was clued in." If he would leave the less extraterrestrial children in peace all day, the teacher promised, Carrey could have fifteen minutes in front of the class at day's end. So he would spend his spare moments making notes on that day's bits, from dinosaur imitations to an impression of a faculty member who he says would eye the boys in the locker room. "Even then I was ruffling feathers," he says.

For Carrey and his family in the Toronto suburb of Burlington, these were the relatively good times, but they were not to last. Carrey is the youngest of four children. After the birth of his sister Pat, his mother, Kathleen, suffered four miscarriages over several years before the arrival (in quick succession) of brother John, sister Rita and Jim. "Immediately from the time I hit earth [on January 17, 1962], I was weird as hell—this kid is *weird,*" Carrey says. "They tell me that to get out of eating, I would go into, like, a convulsive shake in my high chair, until it was impossible for them not to completely break down laughing." His father, Percy, was of French descent (the family name was originally spelled Carré), a frustrated sax and clarinet player who's scrapped his big-band dreams for the reality of an accounting job. Then, abruptly, he was laid off.

"It makes you mad at the world, you know?" says Carrey. "When you're a kid—'How can the world do this to my dad?'" Both parents had been subject to spates of depression—"Sometimes you could feel it in the air, just a sense of doom"—and his dad's mood darkened. "To first of all give up a dream, to settle for something safe, and then have that not pan out is a real double whammy," Carrey says. "My dad was a great guy, too—you'd meet him for five minutes and thought you knew him for fifty years."

In what Carrey calls the nothingland of Scarborough, Ontario, Percy Carrey found work in the massive Titan Wheels factory, where the Carrey kids reported after school to labor as janitors and security men, living feudal style in a big stone house next to the factory. Jim was fourteen and entered "a horrendous time in my life. I hated everything and everyone." He began tenth grade in "a new big-city school," and each night after classes, "we had to clean the whole, gigantic factory—huge. I can't tell you how many times I walked down to the plant and saw my brother beating the piss out of a sweeping machine, you know, with a fucking sledgehammer, just going, 'Fuck you and your mother's sister's cousin's friend.'"

Such outbursts recalled earlier days when Jim and his brother, John, would get hosed on beer and go on vandalism sprees. Soon, Jim went from straight-A grades to falling behind in class, exhausted from his nights of rage. "I was fifteen," he says, "pushing this sweeper down the damn hallway of executive offices of people I don't respect in any way because they're, you know, oppressing my father. I'd bury my arm in the wall, then I'd go through hours of elaborate conniving to come up with an alibi of how the sweeper went insane."

The family worked shifts amid Jamaican and Indian coworkers engaged in what Carrey saw as "a race war. I got totally caught up in the middle of it," he says. "We were all so angry, I lived my life just waiting for somebody to look at me the wrong way. I wanted it. I wanted to fucking do somebody in." His dad, once a model of color-blind piety, temporarily became a bigot—and the rest of the family along with him. Carrey, though he did chuck a bench at a coworker who braced him, avoided the bloodshed. Convinced that his only future would be in the factory ("maybe make foreman one day"), he quit school.

"I remember telling my father," Carrey says. "He was sitting in the security office pulling a shift—this brilliantly funny guy—and I tell him I'm quitting school. 'I'm going to quit school because I can't handle it anymore. I don't understand anything they're saying.' All I wanted was to sleep after pulling eight hours in the factory.

"He never showed a lot of emotion," Carrey says. "That wasn't Dad. There was just one tear. That was it. It was done. He said, 'You're a man. You're sixteen. You've had to be a man. You have to make your own decision at this point.'"

With its anger and self-loathing reaching a peak, the family quit the factory and set themselves adrift in a VW camper van. "It sounds sad," Carrey says. "We went to a couple of campgrounds, and we pitched a tent on my sister's lawn, and we lived like Gypsies, but we were so much happier than we'd been being those people we didn't like. We didn't have a place to live, but it was like somebody lifted a goddamned burden off our shoulders, and we became loving, happy, laughing people again, people that had food fights every Sunday." Carrey leans in, both sheepish and proud: "The first time my brother brought his fiancée to dinner, she got like a half a pound of butter stuffed down her bra."

Sitting by campfires with his future brother-in-law Al, Carrey took lessons in sexuality ("Al would say, 'First you massage the nipples . . .'"). "When I turned fifteen," Carrey says, "I said to myself, 'I'm not going to reach sixteen without losing my virginity.'" He went with his older brother and sister to a party where "we got totally fried, which is what you did up there," and was invited upstairs by a twenty-five-year-old. Using Al's techniques, Carrey came of age: "Me and this really skinny girl. And I remember Styx's 'Grand Illusion' was playing. Oh, it's pretty frightening, isn't it? And then, of course, I never saw her again."

Meanwhile, his father helped Jim find outlets for the comic antics that had outgrown the living room. "My dad used to say, 'He's not a ham, he's the whole pig,'" Carrey recalls. "He always pushed me, since I was a little kid, like a stage mother. I still have the disease—all I can think about is the frame and how to fill it."

Part of Carrey's success has been his grasp of what the media need. He knows how to feed the seals, from duck-walking through infotainment-show visits to much quieter reminiscences like this one. The stories are scarily true, the aspirations just a tad hyperbolic: "I just want [Ace II] to be killer funny, you know?" says Carrey. "Kick-ass, piss-your-pants, run-out-of-the-theater, rip-your-dick-off-and-throw-yourself-into-traffic funny."

At a club called Yuk Yuk's, in downtown Toronto, Carrey cajoled his muse. He had the stomped-down bitterness of all great comics; he had his comically limber body and frighteningly mobile face: He had a true gift for mimicry; he had nothing to lose. Getting over with the crowds but stymied by the limitations of being the funniest guy in Toronto, the kid who had sent his résumé to *The Carol Burnett Show* at age ten—and who is still an avid consumer of things Hollywood (first film seen: "Either *The Computer Wore Tennis Shoes* or *Blood Beast From Outer Space*")—headed to Los Angeles.

"I was seventeen, I'd saved my money, and I came down to get on at the Comedy Store," Carrey says. He ended up "looking like some choirboy—at Sunset and Vine." He was impressed by the palm trees, by the women in lipstick and pumps who approached him as if "it was Sadie Hawkins Day—'You wanna date?' I didn't know from a hooker. I had no idea what the hell that was about."

Carrey soon retreated to Toronto, not to return to Los Angeles for two years. At Yuk Yuk's the MCs would nail him with the typical provincial joke: "Our next act just got back from the Comedy Store, in L.A.—where he had great

seats." By 1981, Carrey had honed his stand-up act, building on such barbed impressions as a zealously smiling Michael Landon, Gandhi sneaking potato salad during a hunger strike and (more reverently) Jimmy Stewart displaying his relentless positiveness: "Well, I guess we're gonna have ourselves a nuclear holocaust." Tommy Davidson, who was later to work alongside Carrey on *In Living Color* (and the *Ace* sequel), remembers his fellow comic's arrival on the local stage when Carrey hit L.A. for good at age nineteen: "We were very critical, watched a lot of comics all the time, but he was just plain good. The first time we saw him, we were in awe of the things he could do."

Judd Apatow, then a stand-up and now a consultant to *The Larry Sanders Show*, instructed his manager, Jimmy Miller—brother of comic Dennis—to see Carrey ("He's freaking people out"). Carrey would do his "post-Armageddon Elvis," tucking in his arms and making little flippers of his hands. "Then," Apatow recalls, "he would sing an Elvis song, do all the Elvis karate moves but with these little arms. Sometimes the place would go nuts, and other times people were frightened."

What scared Carrey was the idea of opening for Vegas lounge acts ten years down the road. Even as new manager Miller was ready to book him in bigger venues, Carrey dug in his heels and scrapped his impressions. "I deleted that program," says Carrey. His good looks and comic zest got him a leading role on an NBC series called *The Duck Factory*, but the sitcom's stories of life in a cartoon shop didn't last. It was at this point that Carrey, perhaps too impulsively, addressed his old family obsessions. "From about age nineteen, I became the parent in my family," says Carrey. "When I got *Duck Factory*, I decided to be the hero son—'Okay, I've got a big show on NBC, I can move you down to live with me.' They lived with me for a while, until I ran out of money."

Carrey pauses. It's hard to know if his honesty is unwavering; it is often compulsive. He starts over: "I didn't run out of money—I ran out of patience, and I had to move them back to Canada. I was having bad dreams—I was strangling my mother in my sleep." Carrey the seasoned absurdist seems to be talking—but his expression shows he's now in touch not with his humor but with its dark roots. "I still supported them until I ran out of money. I went bankrupt."

Smoking, snorting and slacking off (until a pal told him he'd become a creep), Carrey marked time. He missed a few chances at solvency in those early eighties. Linda Ronstadt came to the Comedy Store in search of an opening act and ended up with a temporary boyfriend. Was this affair the end of Carrey's adventures with older women? "Well, you know, I felt I had things to teach her," he says. "And, no, there was the thing with Ruth Gordon."

Carrey would often chat with Melissa Womer as she waited tables at the Comedy Store. An aspiring actress who'd moved from Arizona to L.A. at seventeen, she saw his knack even in his offhanded repartee with fellow comics. "The dude is no flash in the pan," says Melissa Carrey in the California argot that pokes through her earnest philosophical bent. "He is what legends are made of." Sadly, she will be seeing the legend mostly on billboards once the dust from their contentious divorce case clears. Her spin on their early days is doomed to seem self-serving, but it's more out of sorrow than anger. "I miss him very much," she says. "I still love him with all my heart. I'd take him back in a second, because he's my friend and he just lost his way."

From the time of their first brief exchanges at the Comedy Store, it took almost two years for the romance to flower. Carrey had abandoned his successful onstage guise, watched his sitcom tank and was stewing over his direction, getting ready for his Dada stand-up phase. "He was in a deep depression," Melissa says, "in front of a TV, eating potato chips and Häagen-Dazs." Then-roommate Phil Roy, who has watched his "Heaven Down Here" songwriting collaboration with Jim become a hit for Tuck and Patti, recalls "chili and white bread every single night" as Jim's only choice for a hot meal in those days. Melissa recalls the wedding on March 28, 1987, as "an absolutely perfect day," ending with the couple sitting over untouched mahi-mahi at sunset in a hotel in Santa Monica, California, "bawling like idiots" at their happiness.

Finally stepping back onstage, Jim Carrey exorcised demons even as he did his comic stunt flying. Almost out of guilt over coming so close to becoming a Vegas type, Carrey, says Apatow, "changed with a vengeance. About '87, he had just returned to stand-up after taking a two-year break, and he was onstage completely improvising his act. He would go onstage and ramble like a madman. Some of it was hilarious, and other parts of it wouldn't work at all, but they would be so daring or so odd that I couldn't get enough of it. If it bombed, he would sit on the floor, and he would supposedly be talking to his wife: 'Yeah, honey, pretty soon we're going to be on easy street.' And then he would just start crying."

This is the Carrey who would crawl *into* the baby grand piano onstage and remain there, legs dangling, through the next comic's set, the Carrey who came out for a Comedy Store TV special wearing only a sock over his genitals, who would imitate fleeing cockroaches or do "worm boy" for extended periods. If he got heckled, Carrey says he would "put the audience through total living hell. I will either be the most entertaining person that you've ever seen or your worst enemy. I'm like a rat—when you back me into a corner, man, I fucking lunge."

The adventurous saw something in Carrey. Francis Ford Coppola talked to him for just five minutes about a part in *Peggy Sue Got Married* before saying, "Yeah, you're the guy," and cast him. He did *Earth Girls Are Easy* with Geena Davis and *Once Bitten*, in which Lauren Hutton's bloodsucker pulls the ultracherry Carrey off a Hollywood street ("I'm gonna be a vampire? I'm a day person"). He made the TV drama *Doing Time on Maple Drive* mostly as a calling card for the serious roles he eventually wants to do. Carrey was steady and affecting as the son who drinks, but he's not one to dwell on psychological prep work: "The superwhirliness of the underpresence of the character, you know, it's just bullshit. I was basically going moment to moment, trying to make it real. That's what it comes down to. You're playing house, and the one who does best wins. Like now, Tom Hanks plays house the best."

It's a simple compliment—if there's one career Carrey and his managers would love to emulate, it's that of King Tom—but that word *now* reverberates. Carrey does not lack confidence, but he does feel the stakes in acting are raised to a terrifying level when an actor portrays an unmasked, unpomaded, brain-empowered normal citizen: "I call it sea level—if they don't accept that, then it's really you they don't accept."

Alicia Silverstone

By Rich Cohen

SEPTEMBER 7, 1995

Alicia Silverstone is a kittenish eighteen-year-old movie star whom lots of men want to sleep with. "That part's not me," Silverstone says. "What people think about me, of doing with me—it can be gross." Along with many other celebrities, has-beens, will-be's and wanna-be's, Silverstone lives in the Hollywood Hills, in California, where she pads around the house in gym socks, doing nothing more exciting than her laundry. Meanwhile she tries to balance the inaudible pangs of adolescence (Let's get crazy) with the audible pangs of agents (You can't get crazy, you have a photo shoot) and saves her good looks and enthusiasm for a party that has never been thrown. Can you believe it? Alicia Silverstone, the prettiest girl in town, the next big thing, the star of nine movies in the past two years (including The Crush, in which she played a young woman who kisses and then tries to kill an older man, a movie that fixed her in the minds of many as a lustful, murderous, wildcat teen), an actress who with her appearance in Aerosmith's recent videos helped revive the band, the star of the smash Clueless, and she's stranded on a hill—a knocked-out, dreamy-eyed little Rapunzel waiting for some spectacle grand enough to allow her to let her

hair down. "If this is the life of a starlet," she says, sighing, "it's a yawn."

Silverstone grew up at the track. When she was in grade school, a book came out: Monty's Betting Tips. Monty is her father, and he was always taking her along on research outings, afternoons at the races where he led her, horse by horse, through the betting form, teaching her how to spot the sure thing. "Dad always did know horses," Silverstone says. There must be some connection between Monty's success with ponies and Monty's success with his daughter—something about conditions, breeding, handling and how they all amount to winning—but Silverstone has no idea what that connection is: "He was interested in encouraging me. That's all I know."

Monty Silverstone has a stable, conservative, full-time career (financial consulting, real estate), but he also had a more speculative venture: Alicia. By the time she could walk, he was running her as you would a fine horse. While she was in third grade, he took pictures of her, one of which she still keeps tucked behind a couch in her living room. "I look at it sometimes," Alicia Silverstone says, crossing the

327

room and pulling up a black-and-white poster-size photo: a six-year-old, bikini-clad Alicia on all fours on a white shag rug. "I look just the same as I do today," she says, gazing at a photo that brings to mind underground rings and police sting operations. "We went to a modeling agency with these photos, and they started sending me out on shoots. That's how I was introduced to the working world—as the flower girl in all these phony weddings."

Silverstone drops the photo behind the sofa and looks across the room. This is Silverstone's first home away from home. She grew up in suburban San Francisco, and the walls of her house are crammed with the kind of collages peculiar to freshman dorms: Silverstone and her big brother, David, as naked toddlers; Silverstone on Halloween (over the years, her costumes include ballerina, pumpkin, Playboy bunny, Debbie Gibson); the Silverstones on vacation looking determined to have fun; Silverstone and Sammy Nodowitz on a bright spring day. "When I was ten, Sammy and I were married in a mock ceremony at Sunday school," Silverstone says. Nodowitz wore a yarmulke and tails. A document was signed before the ceremony, so Silverstone fears that she and Sammy are legally married—that she is Mrs. Nodowitz! That one day there will be a knock, and it will be Sammy asking, "What's for dinner?" "He's the wild card," she says, falling onto the couch. "I'm always wondering, 'What's Sammy think of all this?'"

Silverstone is wearing jeans, a T-shirt, moccasins. Her jeans are unbuttoned. She's a pretty girl, but she's the kind of pretty girl who feels she must apologize for being pretty by calling herself short, fat, dumpy, homely, ugly, awkward, whatever. The kind of girl, that is, who tries to paint herself as a regular girl and in the process alienates a lot of girls who next to her

really do seem sort of regular. "If Alicia Silverstone is homely," they must wonder, "then what does that make me?" "I'm just some whacked-out, freaky little tomboy," she says. "There's half a million girls who could blow me away."

Silverstone has straight blond hair that falls around her shoulders, wide eyes and a mouth that people describe in ways that she finds inappropriate. They liken it to a slice of tangerine or call it wedge-shaped or say she has bee-stung lips. Well, if your lips were stung by a bee, do you have any idea how much that would hurt? "Like hell," she says. Silverstone's lips have not been stung by a bee. Nor does she have the vague, abstract, off-putting beauty of a super-model like Linda Evangelista or Stephanie Seymour. Silverstone is a girl you could conceivably date, a girl you did date, even, raised to the highest power. She has the brand-new look of a still-wet painting—touch her and she'll smudge.

As Silverstone talks, she bends to kiss her dog on the lips. "Are you the best-looking thing in the whole world?" she asks. "The most adorable? Yes, you are!" While she was filming *True Crime,* a dog limped onto the set, fresh from a car wreck. Silverstone took him in, patched him up and named him Samson. There's a reason for the name, but it's not that interesting. Samson has a dark face, tan eyebrows, a long dog nose and mournful dog eyes. "You just want to run, don't you?" she asks, flipping back his ear. "You're crazy happy!"

Samson is a big dog; Silverstone is a big-dog girl. There's a difference between girls who like big dogs and girls who like small dogs. While a girl who names her dog Snowball and says things like "Look, Snowball fits in my purse" is fragile, a girl who lets a rottweiler (Samson is part rottweiler) drag her all around town is a girl who seems ready for anything. "When I was a kid, all I wanted to do was work, have fun, talk, be noticed and talk, but even then I had too much personality to be good as a child model," she says, petting Samson. "When you're a kid model, they just want you to stand still and shut up. But it was a great way to make money, and even at eight I was a business lady and knew I needed money for the future."

As the assignments rolled in, and her picture appeared in ad campaigns, the young Silverstone was leading this other, very humdrum life. Her mother was a flight attendant with Pan Am, so every now and then the family flew off to London, where Silverstone's parents are from. Otherwise she was just another kid passing time in the playgrounds and backyards of suburbia, facing down the usual preteen dilemmas.

By the time she entered high school, though, Silverstone had begun to look enough like the girl in the Aerosmith video to realize things might be changing. "When I was a freshman, I was big into being a freshman," she says, folding her legs beneath her. "The first week of high school, these cool senior guys called me over. I was a little moron and had no idea what this was about. They invited me to this big senior party. I brought two friends, and we didn't drink, smoke, nothing. We were anti-everything. We lectured people. We were the only freshmen there, and when we came to school the next day, the rumor was 'Alicia got drunk and had sex with some of the guys.'"

While this experience taught Silverstone how the hint of sex spreads faster than the fact of respectability, it also taught her about image and how easily you can lose control of who people think you are. "So I decided to control just what I could, and that was my dream," she says. "I always wanted to be an actress. Look at Samson." She kisses him. "He's so cute. He looks just like a grandpa, a big, farty grandpa. So when I was in eighth grade, I started taking act-

ing classes with Judi O'Neill, a teacher who came up from L.A. to San Francisco once a month and held workshops."

After just a few classes, O'Neill took Silverstone to Los Angeles on a scouting trip, where she appeared, along with other young actors, in a series of showcases. "I attended one of those shows and saw Alicia do a scene," says Carolyn Kessler, Silverstone's agent, who speaks of that initial encounter as if it were a trip to the mountaintop. "She had this amazing energy that came right out at me—an energy full of truth and wisdom and honesty, a magnetic force that made me want to work with her."

Within a year of signing with Kessler, Silverstone was cast in *The Crush,* and her role would later win her MTV Movie Awards for Best Breakthrough Performance and Best Villain (Ralph Fiennes, nominated for *Schindler's List,* lost out). "I was looking for Gloria Swanson from *Sunset Boulevard* in a fourteen-year-old body mixed with Sue Lyon from *Lolita,*" says Alan Shapiro, who directed the film. "It was a lot to ask of someone who had never really done it before. Whereas some actors are concerned with looking cool, Alicia threw herself into it with abandon. She's completely willing to make an idiot out of herself, which any real artist has to be willing to do. She's a very intense girl."

Although Silverstone has an aversion to appearing naked onscreen ("I don't think it's necessary"), and a body double was used in those scenes in *The Crush* when her character does disrobe, the movie made her—like it or not—an object of sexual fantasy. "I can't speculate on how people see me," she says. "But I do wonder how they can see me as a sex symbol. I can't see anything about me that equals sex. It's strange to think of what other people might be thinking of me.

"And it's not nice to get written about," Silverstone says. "When you're written about, it's like being dragged out. All of a sudden, people are fixating on you. It's sad. Not long ago some person was going around the Internet claiming they were me, saying lewd things in my name. 'Come and get me' and other stuff I don't want to repeat. I don't want people to know who Alicia is. I want to be an actress. I want to create other people. I don't want other people to create me."

You sometimes hear former kid actors (Gary Coleman, Danny Bonaduce) bitch about having missed out on childhood. Well, Alicia Silverstone is not someone who missed out on childhood. She's missing out on it right now. When she was fifteen, in order to skirt child-labor laws, she was told by the producers of *The Crush* to go ahead and get emancipated—that is, made legally independent of her parents. "If you're emancipated, it means you're legally eighteen and can work crazy hours," Silverstone says, walking to the kitchen to microwave a quesadilla. (I am offered a bowl of bran.)

"It's too hard to get emancipated in L.A., so my dad tracked down a place in Oakland [California]," Silverstone says, returning with the quesadilla. "I had to stand before a judge and tell him I was living on my own, which was not true, and also tell him I was self-supporting, which was true. And then after sophomore year, I quit high school." Like many prison inmates, however, Silverstone went on to receive her GED.

To most middle-class parents, such an ordeal—in which the beloved daughter tells a robed official her parents are no longer needed—must seem an oddly public forum for what should be a family struggle, with the mood set by Freud and the resolution reached in therapy.

"I didn't want her to be emancipated," says Monty Silverstone. "But her agent kept telling me if she wasn't emancipated, she wouldn't get *The Crush.* So I weakened and sat Alicia down and said, 'Listen, you're emancipated, but you've got to promise you're always going to be my little girl. I don't want anything to change. It's got to be exactly as it is now.'"

"My parents were a bit concerned," says Silverstone, waving her quesadilla. (Sometimes a quesadilla is just a quesadilla.) "They were afraid I would hold it under their nose and say, 'You can't tell me what to do, I'm emancipated.' But nothing really changed."

In some ways, of course, everything changed: Never again would she be just the little girl at home. "I'll never forget the feeling the day she went off to do *The Crush,*" says mom Didi Silverstone. "This feeling of loss like I lost her. From that day on, it was never quite the same."

While other kids on her block were gearing up for the SAT, Alicia Silverstone was packing for Los Angeles. "I don't care that I've missed out on all that," she says, looking across the room. "That's not who I want to be. I went to Lutheran University, in Thousand Oaks [California], where my friend goes. I went up to the dorm, and there were like six guys there when I walked in. They had posters of naked girls on the walls, and they have that at every college I visit. Disgusting. It tells me, 'God, they have so many years to go.'

"Going back to college, I would have a hard time with the people," Silverstone says. "What I've learned in the past two years you can't learn from school, you can't learn from books. You only learn from experience: being alone, unsheltered, available to anyone who wants to bash you. I'm an open wound—anyone wants to take a shot, here I am."

Like many actors who strike while young, Silverstone is no longer subject to the forces and fears that are shaping her nonacting contemporaries. She is instead being raised by the moods and whims of Hollywood. As a result, she will bring to later life little of the experience that will create the personalities of her time—personalities she may be called on to play. At fifteen, Silverstone was snatched away from her suburban home and raised by wolves—the producers and directors of Hollywood. "I was never worried about Alicia," says her dad. "She's a Silverstone, and we're fighting sons of a gun. We've got a fighting-gut spirit and never let go."

Soon after the premiere of *The Crush,* Silverstone was spotted by Marty Callner, a director looking for a woman to costar with Stephen Dorff in "Cryin'," the new Aerosmith video. "He liked what he saw in the movie," says Silverstone. "And what he saw was a good actress, not a pretty girl. It's about what you have inside."

In the video, Silverstone feigns suicide by bungee-jumping off a bridge, teaching her boyfriend a valuable lesson. "After watching all these other videos, it's cool to see that one, to see a video with a real person," she says. "I'm never posing, never doing this supersexy stuff. I'm just being.

"Aerosmith made a hell of a lot of money off that video," Silverstone says, returning to her quesadilla. "Their sales tripled or something. They would have been crazy not to ask me back."

Aerosmith went on to cast Silverstone in two more videos, including "Crazy," in which she plays opposite Steven Tyler's daughter, Liv. For millions of MTV viewers, those videos have linked Silverstone with a certain style, a seventies sound and a summer mood that on the best evenings ends in the woods with grass stains, torn clothes and a brand-new girlfriend. "Alicia

has a seductive quality that goes way beyond her years," says Paul Rudd, her costar in *Clueless.* "Off-camera she's this silly eighteen-year-old, but that other thing is always there."

Silverstone fears her work with Aerosmith has been *too* successful. "I'd like to correct the idea that the videos came first," she says, folding her arms. "That's absurd. I'm not a video star turned actress. I'm a serious actress who spent a few days making videos. I've done a lot more than videos, you know."

In the last two years, in fact, Silverstone has been involved in so many projects that even she has trouble keeping track. Running through the titles, she sounds like someone ticking items off a grocery list: "I did *The Crush,*" she says, "then a movie called *Torch Song,* then *Shattered Dreams,* then my first Aerosmith video. Then a movie called *The Cool and the Crazy.* Another Aerosmith video. A movie called *The Babysitter.* Then *Hideaway,* with Jeff Goldblum. Another video. *True Crime. Le Nouveau Monde.* Then *Clueless.*"

With *Clueless,* Silverstone may have at last emerged from the tunnel of work—a tunnel composed of movies that came and went like road signs—onto a sunlit upland. For one thing, she got to work with director Amy Heckerling ("Amy just let me go," Silverstone says), who more than a decade ago launched about a dozen careers (Sean Penn, Jennifer Jason Leigh, Forest Whitaker, Judge Reinhold, Phoebe Cates, Eric Stoltz and Anthony Edwards) with *Fast Times at Ridgemont High.* "Here's how I found Alicia," says Heckerling. "I was minding my own business on my treadmill watching MTV when I saw 'Cryin'' and just went cuckoo bananas. She's funny and beautiful—anyone who shows even a glimmer of that mix becomes a major star. I'm thinking of people like Sally Field and Goldie Hawn."

In *Clueless,* which is based on Jane Austen's

Emma (a novel about a young control freak, 1816 style), Silverstone plays Cher Hamilton, a self-consumed, materialistic, thoughtless teen who with the help of plot twists and sight gags becomes a self-consumed, materialistic, thoughtful teen. "I'm not like Cher," Silverstone says. "I don't care about clothes, I don't dress up, I look like crap all the time. But the quality we do share is wanting to please everyone. I'm just now learning you have to separate your life from the life of your family, that your needs are different. Everyone goes through that." She signals Samson, who bounds across the room. "Some people just go through it later than others. Kids in college go through it, but slowly. They evolve. But since I'm out in the working world, I've had lessons most people don't get until their thirties. So I feel ready to confront the big things."

In the next few years such confrontations will likely be restricted to movie screens. Silverstone hopes to work with directors like Martin Scorsese and Bernardo Bertolucci and with such actors as Al Pacino and Christopher Walken. She spent June in Massachusetts at a Shakespeare camp where she did nothing but contemplate the Bard. "It was the most amazing experience of my life," says Silverstone, who recently auditioned for the lead in a film remake of *Romeo and Juliet*. "Nine movies in two years is a grind, but Shakespeare's lighting me up. Once again I know I love acting."

A film star in ascendancy gathers debris as does any celestial object—satellites and planets that remain fixed in orbit until the star implodes or is eaten away. As Silverstone is only now gaining the critical mass that equals gravity, she is being circled by only a few satellites. These include her publicist, Elizabeth Much. "Can you believe she's Jewish?" Much asks, looking approvingly at Silverstone. "Such shiksa beauty!"

For the most part, the people who surround Silverstone are a select few regulars who shuffle in and out of her life like characters on a sitcom. For the last several months, she had been sharing her house, in a chaste way, with Jennifer Rubin, who acted with Silverstone in *The Crush*. (Rubin's other titles include *A Nightmare on Elm Street 3* and *A Woman, Her Men and Her Futon*). And although Silverstone still keeps in touch with people from high school, she fears fame gets in the way. "I have no problem with it," she says, shrugging. "But it can get weird on the phone."

Boyfriends? "I had a boyfriend when I was in junior high," Silverstone says. "He was a Mexican named Willie. My next boyfriend was Chinese."

"She's always had unusual boyfriends," says Monty Silverstone. "Multinational fellows. To me, they're all nice fellows, but they couldn't make the films, any of them. She's a bit like Marilyn Monroe, I guess. She just likes the plainer type guy."

Until recently, that was the extent of Silverstone's romantic life. Just now, however, she is coming off her third relationship, a romance afflicted with Mission Creep—you go in wanting a little fun (movie, dinner) and wind up talking china patterns. "I used to have dreams that this guy would betray me," Silverstone says, frowning. "There was always a girl in these dreams, a waitress, and she would flirt with him and then hold his hand.

"A few nights ago, I dreamed I beat the crap out of another, completely different guy," Silverstone rambles on, eyes glazed. "I beat him badly. I'm no meany, but I dreamed I beat the shit out of him. His head became a punching bag, and my feet were up in the air like a cartoon. But I have no boyfriend now." She snaps out of her reverie. "I'm all alone and am fine with that."

Late in the afternoon, Silverstone follows a brick path that starts at her back door and climbs past the tree line and out onto a plateau from which she can look back at her house and across the hills to the valley below. The hills are studded with houses set at even higher elevations like a staircase leading nowhere. Silverstone rents the guesthouse of a Tudor mansion. Looking down through the trees she can see a basketball court, a tennis court and a man-made waterfall that empties into a pool, around which servants in tuxedos prepare for a party, their white gloves catching the sun. "Not invited," she says, folding her arms.

Silverstone follows the path up to a stone bench where she once came upon two groping teens. "I've lived up here a year, and that's the most exciting thing I've seen," she says. "They say there's a young Hollywood out there, but I'm not part of it. Guess I don't mix well."

Some people criticize Silverstone, saying she has done nothing worthy of fame—oddly, in long articles accompanied by glossy photos that only make her more famous—but they're wrong. She has done something worthy of fame: She has been in nine movies, and every time she has been hard not to watch. Just being appealing onscreen makes her of interest. It's not that people who are not in movies seem unreal; it's just that people who are in movies seem *more* real. People who are in movies, no one knows why, are touched with a heightened sense of reality, a presence that swirls around them like a fog.

"My interest is in becoming a good actress," Silverstone says. "I'm not interested in the celebrity of it all. Outsiders say, 'God, she's so successful!' And I'm like 'No, I'll tell you when I'm successful.'"

What most people think of as success (fan mail, box office) has a way of changing things. "My father used to say, 'Marry someone Jewish, and I'll buy you a house,'" Silverstone says, smiling. "Now I tell him, 'If I don't marry someone Jewish, I'll buy you a house.'"

Sean Penn

By Chris Mundy

APRIL 4, 1996

Sean Penn is famous for acting like an asshole. He has done it professionally, of course, in such movies as *Bad Boys, At Close Range, Carlito's Way* and now *Dead Man Walking,* his best performance—justly Oscar nominated—in an already inspired career. Yet he has also managed to retain his amateur status by having sucker punched photographers, failed Breathalyzers and logged his share of jail time, most notably the thirty-four days he served in 1987 after smacking a film extra—an activity frowned upon by those monitoring Penn's progress while he was on probation for clocking a guy who tried to kiss his then wife, Madonna.

It's now early afternoon, and Penn is contemplating his legend thus far while he stretches out on a bed in the hotel room he has rented for the day. He munches from a box of Cracker Jacks, sets the unopened prize on a desk and speaks in a low, steady murmur.

"It took me some time to learn how to smell a problem and get the hell out of Dodge," says Penn, thirty-five. "But now I've been doing that pretty successfully for a long time. And I get a fair amount of privacy beyond what I would get because of the way people perceive my image."

Penn mumbles a laugh and continues:

"When we were filming *Colors,* Bob Duvall said to me: 'I took this part because I get to kick your ass and throw you against a locker. Everybody in America wants to kick your ass and throw you against a locker. I'm gonna be a hero.'"

There is no delicate way to put this, so it's best just to come straight out with it: Penn is peeing in an empty wine bottle, a stone's throw away from a small table where a few of Hollywood's most upwardly mobile stars sit, watching intently.

Afternoon has given way to late night, the hotel bar is empty, Cracker Jacks have given way to vodka tonics, and Penn's cautious, resonant whisper has been replaced with a folksy, easygoing drawl. Penn's guests include the actors Ashley Judd, Josh Hamilton and Mira Sorvino. To hammer home the surreal nature of this gathering, both Judd and Sorvino, who have been shooting an HBO movie, are coiffed as Marilyn Monroe. Penn, being the most accomplished of the assembled mass, presides over the gathering with panache. He recites jokes, he tells stories, he finishes urinating. Almost.

"I need another bottle," says Penn.

He sets the brimming vessel in front of him, and the room erupts with laughter. He of the enormous bladder grins, and a second bottle is placed in his left hand before it quickly disappears under the tablecloth. . . . Relief.

There are many things that have brought us to this place, but the chief motivator—with all due respect to the vodka, which places a close second—is that Penn is an insomniac who lives in a 27^1/$_2$-foot trailer and, as such, spends a great deal of time away from his residence. Granted, this doesn't explain not making the hundred-yard trek to the bathroom, but it does speak to the deeper issue of why Penn has rented a hotel room less than twenty miles from his primary billing address.

"I don't consider that I have a home," says Penn. "I've got two kids, and if I don't have them with me, it doesn't feel like I have a home. At one time I lived with a woman and two children in a house, and that was a home. When my kids are with me, I rent a house. That was part of the deal for me getting as many days with them. They love the trailer, but she says it's better. She might be right, but the minute they walk out the door, I fall on my knees."

The woman in question is actress Robin Wright; the children are Dylan, four, and Hopper, two. The couple have recently tossed the flowers on a relationship that Penn says died a number of years ago, and Penn, as is his wont, has tortured himself with the questions of what went wrong, how to be a good part-time father and whether the pain of the breakup will inspire the kind of craft he most admires.

You see, Penn is one of those guys and then some. Not only did Penn go through a Charles Bukowski phase, he went through Charles Bukowski, spending virtually every Sunday with the barfly writer, telling stories and drinking. Penn chain-smokes; he wears a lot of black; he does all his writing on an electric typewriter, preferring old-school affectation to the efficiency of a word processor. His Hollywood friends are mostly older art-through-experience types like Marlon Brando, and his other friends are mostly older writers cut from the very same cloth, typified by David Rabe and Cormac McCarthy: real men doing manly things with men in a masculine way. And while Rabe and McCarthy are men of remarkable artistic ability, they also embody an aesthetic and a lifestyle that do not come naturally to a movie star of some stature.

Asked whether owning fifty acres of Malibu, California, property (the home he once shared with Madonna burned down in the area's fires in 1993) but choosing to dwell in a trailer isn't potentially offensive to people who have to live that way out of necessity, Penn initially explodes: "Anybody poor who thinks I'm condescending can kiss my ass. Anybody rich who thinks I'm jerking them can kiss my ass, too. I like the coziness of a small place. I'm not going to defend my lifestyle." But hours later, Penn brings up the topic again to amend his statement. "I'd never considered that that angle existed. I always figured you offended poor people if you drove a fucking Mercedes down Martin Luther King Boulevard. But it's not my obligation to deal with that. I think I've been through enough that I honestly don't give a fuck what anybody thinks about me except the people close to me. And the people close to me I probably give a shit too much."

To speak with Penn is to become versed in a language that is part self-analysis, part philosophy and part barroom poetry, all without the benefit of a translator. At first he is guarded, attempting a type of silent intimidation, and later he is cordial, sincere and likable, albeit in a way that occasionally makes you feel there should be other men in the room banging drums and weeping.

"I came to a very analytical point in my life toward the end of that family situation," says Penn. "And in order to look back on my life, I have to pass through the last seven years, and I'm not real happy about the past seven years of my life. I don't feel like looking back on that period right now. It'll have its day in court. I've been humbled plenty. My kids' mother humbled me."

Penn sips his drink quietly and pauses for a long time when asked why he refers to Madonna as "my ex-wife" and Robin Wright as "the mother of my kids."

"I suppose if I used my own terms . . ." Penn stops and indulges in another lengthy pause. "I'll leave it at that." He sips his drink and waits a moment. "But I will tell you that I wasn't going to a negative place."

And with that, Penn once again resumes his more genial posture—reciting a joke in the voice of Brando, suggesting a number of books, displaying the tattoo that reads NOLA DELIVER ME, which he got to commemorate a frighteningly wild night in New Orleans (hence the *Nola*)—but eventually he returns to a familiar theme.

"I'll tell ya probably the most naked thing I could say in an interview," says Penn, leaning forward in his chair. "I'm damaged. And I recognize that. But I have great faith in the resurrection of all beautiful things except innocence. Innocence is a constant, and damage to me is gauged by how far you've gotten away from innocence. I've learned in the last couple years about forgiving myself, but you might as well be speaking Greek if you tell me you have no regrets. I have very serious regrets. I've got regrets that don't have statutes of limitations on them."

The acreage that now houses Sean Penn's one-man trailer park is well protected. So well protected, in fact, that Penn says he has made seven citizen's arrests on the grounds during his tenure as tenant and sheriff.

"I near cut the ear off of one guy," says Penn, perhaps too giddily. "I had excessive-force charges against me. I cut his ear with a broken salad-dressing bottle. He was one of five guys who broke in that I arrested one night when I had a house up there." Penn laughs. "The property originally belonged to Olivia Newton-John, and I found one of her wackos looking for her—got him, put him in jail. He went crazy and beat up a guard. I get some wackos. I'm one canyon over from Topanga [Canyon], where the Manson family was. I'm a child of the sixties; I remember that shit."

Penn laughs again in a way that makes one wonder if at times his mental state might also be one canyon over from Topanga. While some people choose to pack heat, Penn chooses to stockpile for the apocalypse.

"Listen, we've got 382 functioning serial killers in the country who are at large," he says. "So I'm not going to be up there with my kids without a gun. Locked up? Yeah. There's combo boxes. I've gone through the Los Angeles Police Academy weapons training. I don't have one gun that I'm not expert in. I have very mixed feelings about guns, but I'm extremely careful about them. I don't have a love-hate relationship with guns. I have a caution-hate relationship."

Meanwhile, things are getting cozy. The hotel bar has long since closed shop, but the Penn group is busy chasing the sunrise. Ashley Judd sneaked off to her room only to return with more booze and chewing tobacco (everyone indulges in the former; only she partakes of the latter), and Penn has turned a nonbrooding cheek in order to charm the attentive round table. As testimony, Josh Hamilton politely waits his turn at storytelling, and Mira Sorvino takes off her shoes to rest her feet on Penn's chair.

It is a far cry from my first two meetings with Penn, during which he shifted uncomfortably in his seat, answered every query with suspicion and spoke in a self-consciously throaty mumble only a note or two above a yawn. At this point, when the conversation is diverted from him for a moment, Penn is happy to tackle the topic of whether it was a strange sensation to have introduced his ex-wife to her next beau, Warren Beatty. Penn laughs and leans forward. "I sent him a letter," says Penn. "It just said, 'Dear Warren: Yuck, yuck.'" And then, Penn laughs again.

"Sean and I are very good friends, but he also has a lot of friends," says David Morse, the star of *The Indian Runner* and *The Crossing Guard*, Penn's two forays into both writing and directing. "His life exists spread across the entire globe. My world has much smaller parameters."

In the beginning, Penn's world was as confined as yours or mine. Penn was raised in California's San Fernando Valley and Malibu; Penn's mother, Eileen Ryan, is an actress (she played a grieving mother in *The Indian Runner,* had her finger sucked by Jack Nicholson in *The Crossing Guard* and portrayed Penn's grandmother in *At Close Range*), and his father, Leo Penn, is a TV and movie director. Times, however, were sometimes difficult, because his father had been blacklisted as a Communist and had trouble getting work for years.

"Being blacklisted hit my father pretty hard in terms of momentum," says Penn. "And my parents had my brother Michael to support. Luckily my mother could get some TV gigs. My father didn't talk much about it, but I remember Elia Kazan was shooting a movie once on the beach at the bottom of our hill. I'd heard about Kazan because he had named names. And there he was at the bottom of our hill." Penn stops and his whisper gets even softer. "Very strange."

According to Penn, the greatest constant in his youth was the love and support of his parents, a fact that makes his breakup with Wright all the more poignant. "I've spent time with Sean and his family," says Timothy Hutton, whose friendship with Penn began when they filmed *Taps,* Penn's first movie, in 1981. "They're a very solid family, and they also know how to get under each other's skin. They're very real with each other. Nobody gets away with anything when they're around each other. It's great."

Which makes one wonder about the origins of Penn's occasionally violent temper. Asked about its genesis, Penn stays silent for a long while. "The only consistent area of violence in my life was surfing," he says finally. "I was a surfer on a beach that had a lot of heavy localism. If surfers from other areas came to our beach, it was not something that was allowed to happen; it's your beach, and the people around you back your action. It was built into the culture. At least there'd be a lot of vandalism to automobiles."

By high school, most of Penn's nonsurfing time was spent with his younger brother, Chris, and their friend Emilio Estevez, making Super 8 movies while brother Michael holed up in a room and played guitar. Which makes sense, considering that Chris now acts, and Michael is a recording artist. Estevez, of course, went on to divorce Paula Abdul.

"My brothers grew up in the same house as me, and we're all three extremely different," says Penn. "Chris hides his mind. He's a whip. And he's a bighearted guy, a gentle giant. Michael is really quiet and sensitive, but he has a pretty good sense of humor. I mean, he's not out telling jokes, but brother to brother, Michael rocks."

Still, in terms of established careers, it was the middle Penn who was the first out of the gate. With performances in *Taps, Fast Times at Ridgemont High* and *Bad Boys*, Sean Penn was an immediate presence in film, garnering a best-of-his-generation tag that he has not lost. He was also something of a serial fiancé, pledging allegiance first to Bruce Springsteen's sister, Pam ("Bruce was on the East Coast, so I hardly knew him," says Penn), then to *Racing With the Moon* costar Elizabeth McGovern before settling on Madonna and a tabloid existence that accelerated with his allegedly firing a gun at a hovering helicopter during his wedding and that ended three and a half years later, when a SWAT team interrupted his breakfast in order to let his wife retrieve a few material possessions. "I had made a threat that I would literally cut her hair off," says Penn. "She took it quite seriously. It was pretty dramatic."

These days, Penn and Madonna are on terms that do not require police assistance, and he recently surprised his ex by presenting her with a Most Fashionable Artist prize at the VH1 Fashion and Music Awards. "Any effortless thing that I could do to bring a smile to her face, I'd do—I'm crazy about her," says Penn, who refutes reports that Madonna was unhappy about her presenter by mentioning that the two went out for dinner with friends after the ceremony. Not that Penn has softened his view on the paparazzi that often got in the way of his flailing fists. The cameras stalk him still, on dates with singer Jewel Kilcher and, more recently, model Elle Macpherson. [*Ed. note: They stalked him, too, when he upped and married Robin Wright a few weeks after this story went to press.*]

"It's deceptive to judge people by what you've read so far in this decade," says Penn. "Things have changed. If I was twenty now, I'd be in jail for life. *Hard Copy* and *Inside Edition* didn't exist during my marriage. Imagine. I'd be in jail for murder one." Penn laughs. "This is your twenties—you're trying to figure out who the fuck you are. I'd take two years of state time beginning tomorrow rather than trade places with Leonardo DiCaprio. This guy's got the gift. And he's also got a wild spirit—no doubt about it. Great talent, a great face. He will not be presently lonely." Penn smirks. "I tell ya, if I do my state time, I'd do it with him." He snorts out another laugh. "I always joke with Brad Pitt that I'd rather it was him, but I'd have to make sure he had his long-haired look."

"I would be very very surprised if I win, because it has always seemed like a certain type of club that I never felt allowed to enter."

Penn stops pacing for a moment, perhaps searching for an answer. The question is whether he would accept the Oscar he deserves for his role in *Dead Man Walking*—the fact-based tale of a death-row inmate (Penn) and the nun (Susan Sarandon) who becomes his spiritual advisor—but Penn has been circling the question for the last few minutes.

"Which is not to say anything disparaging about it," he says. "It just seems really foreign to me, and if you're going to take people's positive judgments, you better be willing to validate their negative judgments. I think everybody knows that the Academy Awards are really just an advertising campaign for moviedom." (He lost to Nicolas Cage in *Leaving Las Vegas*.)

Penn sits down and lights what must be his seventy-seventh cigarette. Several years ago, when he wrote and directed *The Indian Runner*, Penn claimed that he had given up acting cold turkey. Then admitting that the responsibilities of having children and the desire to finance another movie made the payday his main motivation, he accepted a role in *Carlito's Way*. Now, with *Dead Man Walking*, Penn insists that the script was simply too good to pass up, a decision that sat well with his director.

"I wanted the best actor I could find to play opposite Susan, and Sean was my first choice," says Tim Robbins, who also adapted the screenplay from the book of the same name. "I think he's the best actor of our generation."

Casting was crucial because the success of *Dead Man Walking* hangs purely on the balance of its two lead actors. At times less a film than a two-person play, it is an emotionally draining study of these two primary characters, and both Penn and Sarandon, who was also nominated for an Oscar and won it, provide career performances. Penn's work, in fact, becomes all the more incredible when you realize that he spends almost the entire film in shackles.

What might surprise some is that Robbins—often as famous for the sheaf of colored ribbons attached to his public personae as he is for his acting and directing talents—has created a bleak but balanced look at capital punishment. Rather than being unjustly accused, Penn's character is simply a sociopath—"I could just imagine the conversation with some other actors," says Robbins. "'Don't you think this guy's unsympathetic?'"—and moviegoers on both sides of the death-penalty debate could easily walk out of the theater feeling vindicated in their beliefs.

"This movie provokes a lot of thought, but I don't think it surrenders to one side or the other," says Penn. "I remember there was a lot of complaining about the movie *Guilty by Suspicion*. My father and a lot of the people who were blacklisted were offended that although the movie was sympathetic to the Communists in America who lost the ability to work, the lead character stood up for people's freedom of belief but was not a Communist himself."

Nonetheless, in his new incarnation as nouveau writer-director Beat-type guy, acting is something that Penn would rather not process at all. Penn sees himself as a writer and director who occasionally acts to pay the bills. To that end, he is about to shoot a film—*The Bells of Hell*—in which he plays the Irish playwright, rogue and renowned boozer Brendan Behan. His carrying on tonight is pure Behan.

"The good news for the rest of us is that the types of films he wants to make are the kind that will find their way into smaller theaters," says Morse. "So in order to be able to do that, he will need to keep acting occasionally. He's such a courageous actor, and the chances and the choices he makes are incredible."

And, who knows, both fatherhood and directing might have softened Penn up a bit. At least to the extent that he now plays well with others.

"I didn't find him far removed from us at all," says Robbins. "From the first day he laughed, he joked. In between takes, he'd break character. I'd heard stories about him, but they were totally unfounded—that bullshit about having to refer to him as his character's name. That stuff usually comes from a source that has a personal vengeance involved. I asked him about it, and it came from a particular director or producer who he'd gotten into a difficult situation with. Total bullshit."

Penn freely admits that he is not a morning person. Therefore it's a pretty safe bet that this moment belongs not to the new day but to the previous night. It's 6 A.M., and despite the fact that the sun also rises, the evening lingers on. It might not be the freshest crowd—Judd and

Sorvino are beginning to look less like the Marilyn Monroe of *Some Like It Hot* and more like the Monroe of *The Misfits*—but all in all, it's a pretty strong performance by the new kids. Especially considering that Penn often seems intent on chasing a legacy that would make Hemingway feel like a pantywaist.

And thus it is part of the Sean Penn conundrum that his artistic sensibilities often overlap with a more basic boys-will-be-boys attitude. Penn clearly views himself as a kind of literary desperado—"There's just a pursuit of excellence that I respond to," he says—and he's comfortable knowing that outlaws such as himself might piss in a few wine bottles and toast a few sunrises. Then again, sometimes frat boys do the same damn things.

So, to understand Penn, it is important to grasp his contradictions. It's highly unlikely that the discrepancies escape him. Ask him what he romanticizes, and Penn grows flowery. "I romanticize love," he says. "I think everybody deserves adoration." Ask him if he doesn't also romanticize the rebel image typified by his stints in jail, and he grows defensive. "I've been in several jails here and there. When I spent the longest time, there was so much stress in my life at the time that if I was able to romanticize it somehow, it would be the relief I remember now. I sat in that cell day after day not knowing whether to laugh or cry. I just kept thinking, 'This is jail. Am I really a threat to society?'" But ask him to list both his best and worst character traits, and he shoots from the hip immediately with just one sentence: "I tell the truth."

So here sits Honest Sean, cigarette in hand, a bit liquored up, the morning breaking through the window. He has grown more comfortable as the interview has gone along, but he has also taken great pains to let you know that his cards are never far from his leather-jacketed chest.

"What is a pain in the ass is what you can't express because of the emotional politics of your personal life," says Penn. "All of the sudden you're offered this opportunity to express things in a way that will get to the people you want it to, and you know it's improper conduct." He pauses. "It also bothers me that every time you do an interview, you are propagating the notion that you are special. I'm always reluctant about that. It's the only thing that bothers me about being recognized."

That is what bothers Penn. Not his cowboy image, not the series of scars that hint at a less-than-perfect barroom-fighting record, not that he eats his home dinners outdoors because he happens to live in a trailer. No, what bothers Penn is that people will think—because he stars in movies—that he is a movie star. Penn scrunches his angular face to let you know he is about to express a pained, heartfelt thought.

"The way I've chosen to do things is almost because it's the only way I can have any confirmation that there's something important about this kind of work," he says. "This is the only way I can look in the mirror."

Penn sips his drink and smiles, content that in a short time he will walk one flight of stairs to his rented room, close the curtains on the impending day and face himself in the mirror, bleary-eyed but exactly the same.

THE WIZARDS
BEHIND THE
CURTAIN

E.T., ROLLING STONE, issue 374, July 22, 1982.
Photograph by Aaron Rapaport

Alfred Hitchcock

By Chris Hodenfield

JULY 29, 1976

He remembers going to the theater in 1905. The villain took the stage, bathed in green light, egged on by sinister music. The heroine was tickled by rose-colored lights, to flatter her face. And the villain—in 1905 the villain always had to kick the dog. "But I remember the green light," Alfred Hitchcock says, clapping his thighs with massive fleshy hands. He cocks his head: "You know, they were very clever at the turn of the century."

The great red face rarely breaks into a personal memory. He would rather talk of film technique, or perhaps some awful murder. He is the High Lama of Universal Studios, loved by all, as was proven recently with the release of his fifty-third film, *Family Plot,* a moderate stiff that enjoyed good reviews on the old man's reputation. At age seventy-six, his position secure, he should have no worries. The imposing snowman in the black suit, with the huge hands encircling his vast potbelly, he has eyes that even in an empty room seem to be addressing a small testimonial dinner. The deep, strangled voice fights its way from the fold of his jowls. He is telling a story from his collection, but he speaks in a somber, processional voice. Your own head bobs up and down as you follow him, and with

the end of every sentence you fall off the rim of Mount Rushmore.

Is this the price you pay for trying to make a dream look as if it really happened?

Several innocent people have gotten themselves mixed up in the company of Alfred Hitchcock. They have found themselves entangled in his stately rhythms, his parliamentary consideration, his dreamy underworld, trapped as if in a web of crime.

Normal people, just like yourself, begin to talk in that nasal foghorn voice, swollen tongues, dry-with-a-twist. Nobody can resist imitating the guy. Not even Alfred Hitchcock can resist imitating Hitchcock. Over and over again he tells the flat-footed reporters, "Self-plagiarism is style." It answers any question. The French, who have long idolized him, say that his style *is* the content. Boy, does he have a lot of style. Perhaps he is the only director who is a star to Middle America, thanks to his cameo movie appearances and the ten years of his television series, which he introduced and closed. So well had he cultivated the image of the mordacious undertaker *(Stories They Wouldn't Let Me Do on TV)* that after 1955 he couldn't walk the streets anymore. He actually directed nineteen of the shows, usually the season openers, including the infamous "Lamb to the Slaughter" episode in which Barbara Bel Geddes bludgeons her husband to death with a frozen leg of mutton, but the investigating police can't find the weapon because she serves it to them for dinner.

So he is a bankable director not only for his talents but for his face, which is featured prominently in the ads for *Family Plot*. In fact, it's about the film's only selling point. Ernest Lehman, an anxious yet genial man who wrote that script and *North by Northwest,* would say: "You realize very early when you're working with Hitch, that you're writing for a star, and that star is Alfred Hitchcock."

Hitchcock has had the same influence on movies that, say, Julius Caesar had on war-making. And not just the film critics who became directors, François Truffaut, Peter Bogdanovich, Eric Rohmer and Claude Chabrol, all of whom have written books on Hitchcock.

"Studying Hitchcock is better than most cinema courses: he is a classical filmmaker and he has certain classical rules," said Alan Pakula. Just before directing *The Parallax View,* Pakula screened *North by Northwest.* Previous to making *Klute,* he brushed up on the exhaustive Hitchcock-Truffaut interview book. He said you have to study these rules even if you want to break them.

Stanley Donen, whose *Charade* was a bald Hitchcock retread, even wanted to make a movie about a Hitchcock-type director and asked Ernie Lehman to write it. Then Donen wondered about landing Hitchcock for the lead role. (The movie never happened.)

Brian De Palma was still in short pants when he had his head twisted by *Vertigo.* Since then he has studied Hitchcock so well that his name is rarely mentioned without Hitchcock's right alongside. "Here's one of the few directors who advanced the form of cinema," said the director of *Obsession* and *Sisters.* "Anybody who knows anything about film grammar cannot help but be snowed under by Hitchcock. It's like studying Bach."

Once I walked out of a later-Hitchcock movie, *Marnie,* and ran into Martin Scorsese, director of *Mean Streets* and *Taxi Driver.* I felt thoroughly chumped and conned by the movie, which made Scorsese you-must-be-blind astonished. He quickly rattled off about fifty moments of genius—the way a camera moved down the stairwell, a kissing sequence, a perverse relationship.

These guys are usually the first to admit that there's no imitating the old man, that they have just learned some lessons, like the importance of good characters or timing or, as veteran composer John Williams found out on *Family Plot,* the use of silence.

It's amazing how many lessons have been lost on the makers of most of the recent large-scale grotesqueries that pass for fear movies. Hitchcock, with the exception of *The Birds,* has avoided the larger-than-life traumas and has never indulged in the cheapening cynicism of the modern disaster movie. In these, rather than feel any empathy with the characters in their plight, the audience can only feel contempt. The characters are given such a flimsy delineation, it seems these fools are supposed to *pay* for their silliness by falling out of airplanes, towering infernos, earthquakes. *Jaws* succeeded, for instance, because of three interesting characters and the fact that you never saw the mechanical shark until its presence was too sickeningly real. *. . . It was just like Hitchcock,* said the Hollywood insiders, for instance, where Roy Scheider is on the crowded beach looking for the shark and suddenly you hear the high-pitched scream and he bolts out of his chair, but it's only a woman playing, and by this time you feel as if you're holed up in a hotel room and the sirens are getting closer.

Well, the director of that one, Steven Spielberg, is in a flummox. He's twenty-eight years old, his flick has bagged $150 million for the company, and everybody calls him the New Hitchcock. All he wishes is that someday, people will refer to the beach sequence as "Spielbergian" rather than "Hitchcockian."

But what can he do? Back when he was eighteen years old, he sneaked into Universal Studios and onto the first soundstage with an open door. It was the *Torn Curtain* set, and Spielberg's eyes were immediately lifted across the huge mock opera house to Hitchcock, sitting on high, seemingly on a throne. Spielberg was grabbed from behind by an assistant director and tossed out on his ear.

The calendar pages fall from the wall. Boy Wonder, having directed, at age twenty-one, Joan Crawford in a *Night Gallery* episode, then *Duel* and *Sugarland Express,* now has his own clump of offices at Universal and he's got the devil himself on his payroll. But still he is haunted by the big man on campus. So last summer, as *Jaws* emptied the world's beaches, Spielberg got this itch. El Sahib was down on stage fifteen shooting *Family Plot.*

Spielberg crept onto the closed set, without appointment, to watch. He hadn't heard about the old man's Third Eye, supposedly in the back of his head. "His back was to me," Spielberg recalls, "sitting there in the chair, and he wasn't saying much of anything. He couldn't have had the peripheral vision, but something made him stand up, walk off the soundstage and into the alley."

Once more, an assistant director gave him the heave-ho. "So I left! It was *very* spooky."

Now as Steven Spielberg tunes in his car radio these days, he hears—all over Southern California—the advertisements for the Universal Studio Tour. It's Alfred Hitchcock, the studio frontpiece. Asking you to come out and see the *Jaws* exhibit, see the shark. Spielberg snaps off the radio, because this is all wrong. He feels it is beneath Hitchcock's dignity to do such a thing.

Spielberg should have known Hitchcock's motto: *We are all criminals, we who watch. We are all Peeping Toms. And we follow the Commandment, "Thou Shalt Not Be Found Out."*

A Hitchcock movie set has all the rhythm of a funeral parlor. The soundstage is dark, there is no shouting, the orders slip through the ranks by whisper. Hitchcock is personally a Mr. Anti-Frantic, and when he shuffles through the door, he is a stately locomotive, a short man on plodding legs. You can almost hear his theme music, Gounod's "Funeral March of a Marionette" . . . *the worms crawl in and the worms crawl out . . .* As he lumbers past to his seat, all hands immediately defer. It's what Karen Black calls his "omniscient shrewdness."

He takes his chair and settles deep and unmoving. It is clear that he has eliminated all unnecessary movement from his life. Each morning and afternoon, a chauffeur drives him over from his offices just a few buildings away. Hitch told Karen Black that he owes his longevity to a "placid metabolism." It was made even more regular last year by a heart pacemaker.

The actors and electricians all must realize that they are pieces of another man's puzzle. The top assistants dress as if they are bucking for a merit badge. The publicist got a haircut. This sure isn't what they call the New Hollywood. They all still talk about the extra in *North by Northwest* who, with one speaking line, showed up for work in a glaring print dress.

Hitchcock got a look and called the propman to put a canvas sack on her head. He called the painters to bring spray guns filled with gray paint. That's when the lady asked if she could change her clothes.

Hitchcock will only wear a dark suit. He owns a closetful, cut to his various weight stations. Cameraman Leonard South remembers that even in Marrakech, 124 degrees in the shade, Hitchcock would not loosen his collar. Once assistant director Howard Kazanjian stood there in some figure of a loud tie. Hitchcock paused, squinted, and asked, "Does your mother know what you're wearing?" And Kazanjian looked for a bottle cap to crawl under.

"It's like attending the Court of Saint James, isn't it?" asked William Devane, who played the villain-with-flawless-manners in *Family Plot*. He was in another man's world, and he knew it.

Hitchcock's set is not the place for the actor who likes to use the profession as a traveling psychology class. He needs "warm" actors, reasons Brian De Palma, who considers Hitch a "cold" director. De Palma considers himself a cold director as well. "If you tend to be cold—detached, intellectual, interested in form—then you should try to make the warmest people possible in those forms. It's important for a cold director to work with the warmest actors you can. Directors have to be aware of their blank areas. His best performances are when he used warm actors, like Ingrid Bergman or Jimmy Stewart. He isn't that emotional a director. His best pictures are like *Notorious*, when he's playing to a very emotional situation. And as he got older, he just didn't want anything to do with that."

Jimmy Stewart's four outings with Hitch include two of the master's more technically ambitious, *Rope* and *Rear Window*. (It has often been said that Hitchcock won't get steamed up for a picture unless he's got a technical impossibility to surmount. Like, how to shoot a movie entirely inside a lifeboat at sea. See *Lifeboat*.) When the sixty-eight-year-old actor recently met the Sherwood Oaks College in Los Angeles for a Hitchcock seminar, the young audience did everything but wash his feet. This was a man they could trust. The big shambling fella, he wants t'marry my dotter, that's okay with me . . .

"He, H-Hitchcock, actually has very little regard for the spoken word," Stewart said. "He actually doesn't like it very well. He thinks that the theater is the place for the words, and if we have to tolerate it in the movies, so-so be it. Just use it very sparingly and don't say anything, ah, unless it's absolutely necessary. He's an absolute villain to script girls and people that have to follow the lines. He pays no attention to the actual words—he's *done* all that, finished all that months before. He has all that in his mind, what he wants to get over in the scene. So when the script girl says to him, 'Mr. Hitchcock, Mr. Stewart didn't say anything *like* what's in the script,' he'd say, 'It sounded all right; *grammatically* it was all right.'"

This raised a big hoot.

"He's a visual man, just as John Ford is. He knows exactly what he wants as far as composition is concerned. I've never seen him look through the finder of a camera. First because I don't think that, uh, because of his tummy he could get near to the camera. . . . No, I-I'm sure he could if he wanted to. . . ."

Warm actor or not, working with Hitchcock is in itself a suspense-filled business. John Forsythe, remembering work on *Topaz* and *The Trouble With Harry*: "He's such a formidable person. He's a strong-minded little man, an austere figure, and actors are frightened of him."

The four actors chosen for *Family Plot* were all veterans, but are still thought of as New

School. Karen Black, in the end, seemed to find Hitchcock the man more fascinating than anything else about the project. Black, who is so sensitive that there almost seem to be eyes behind her eyes, tried to make her own part, a kidnapper, a little more sympathetic. Hitchcock couldn't understand this at all. Devane also had problems with the old man. Besides acting, Devane directs stage plays, and he had his own ideas. "He's not making the same movie I'm making, you know?" Devane said.

"I think they felt that in the process of work there would be more give-and-take as far as exchanging information goes," said Barbara Harris, who emerged from the movie as the strongest character. "If I had trouble, I would say, 'I don't know what I'm doing here.' And he would think. And all his suggestions would be very good and to the point and unconfusing. I call it Brechtian-type directing. Because he sees a scene, not so much for the subjective emotional intent that he's interested in, but what the scene is about. In the cab scene, I didn't know if I was supposed to be a sex-starved girl with my boyfriend, or what. He said it was a business scene. So then I became a businesswoman. Which is a Brechtian idea. Brecht would say, 'Well, what would Hamlet be like in the kitchen with the servants?'"

If anyone fell in love with Hitchcock, it was Bruce Dern. Face it, Dern is a ham. He stands there spouting like a lawn sprinkler; you need only look at that ferret face just once to guess his personality. The ideal Hitchcock character. No explanations needed. Likes a quick character sketch. Dern would see Hitchcock sitting in the gloom of the soundstage, alone and talking to no one, and Dern would see in the seventy-six-year-old man the lower-class Cockney kid, the fat boy who was never invited to play sports, product of a strict Jesuit upbringing, a boy who spent so much time by himself that he memorized the train and boat schedules of Europe. Well, Dern's eyes would mist and he'd go racing through the London newspapers to find a story that Hitchcock might find heartwarming. Tenderize him with possibly the details of a kitchen-sink murder in Northumberland. One of the other thespians accused him of kissing ass, but he didn't care. Hours the two spent together, Hitchcock telling him stories.

"Hitchcock says to me, 'I feel it in my knees today. I have arthritic knees. Wouldn't that be a name for a town? Arthritic Knees? "Where are you from?" "Well, I'm from Arthritic Knees, Nebraska."' And that's all, walks off. Of course, he expects you to fall on the floor. So I fell on the floor.

"I got to jack him up a little," Dern explained later, "get him ready for the day. He's bored with the whole fucking thing."

Still, Dern, like the others in *Family Plot,* was responsible for his own acting, and getting it down in the first couple takes. "It's frustrating sometimes because you say, 'Let me do another take on that, I didn't go deep enough.' And he says, 'Bruuuuce, they'll never know in Peoria.'"

That kind of operating philosophy demonstrates the director's splendid confidence in his movie construction, or else a contempt for Peoria.

We won't dwell too long on *Family Plot,* because Mr. Hitchcock would find himself at the wrong end of the finger of suspicion. He violated many of his own laws. While he has always been strong at setting a place for a movie, *Family Plot* took place in some limbo, half–L.A., half–San Francisco. The trick shots and screen magic that have in the past made his films dreams come to life, now look cheap. Even Brian De Palma was sardonic: "Hitchcock just got tired, he didn't want to do it anymore. That's sort of depressing, because here's a man who pioneered all these techniques and made them work. And now you're seeing his lack of interest."

While Hitchcock repeatedly claimed pride in this assemblage of characters, there was actually very little real character exposition. This bothered Lehman considerably: "Here and there he sort of dropped things in to pay lip service to who these people are, but he really didn't want them in the picture. I pleaded with him, so he put them back in the script and shot them, then edited them out of the picture.

The movie lacks the orgasm that goes hand in hand with Hitchcock suspense. It was all left up to his dry wit, which here was so dry it had dust on it. "It was English understatement," Hitch would say, "the basic style of all English crime literature, going back at least to Conan Doyle."

I began to think of him as a character out of a P.G. Wodehouse story: the man who suffers no greater agony than when he finds himself in his club one afternoon with mismatched socks. A schedule thrown into disorder puts Hitchcock into a fury, tightly held inside. If somehow he has to appear ten minutes late for an appointment, his secretaries will get out the word hours in advance. They keep files on every movie and moviemaker in the hemisphere. (Universal provides him with a staff, a driver, a screening room with projectionist always on call, his own editing room, art department and personalized parking spaces. It helps that he became one of the largest stockholders in MCA, after he traded his TV shows for stock.)

He is a maniac about clean offices, a straight desk, breaking at twelve-fifteen sharp for a daily lunch of ground top sirloin and black coffee. Before he leaves a bathroom, he polishes off the fixtures. While his On Campus reputation says

that he would think nothing of bricking up an insubordinate butler in the basement, it is soon apparent that he is a man of many fears. To portray fear, you have to know fear. The classic story, which he tells over and over again, happened at age five when his father sent him down to the local police station with a note. The desk sergeant read the note and locked him up for a few minutes, saying, "This is what we do to naughty boys."

He says it engrained in him a fear of the police so strong that he has long refused to drive a car. A traffic ticket would kill him. Once when his wife drove them out to their country home, he absently dropped a cigar butt out the window, then worked himself into a tremendous sweat, positive that he had just started a forest fire and that the Highway Patrol was gaining on him.

It would take such an anxious human to make common, everyday things objects of trembling and disgust. Gregory Peck, wrestling with his guilt in *Spellbound*, walks into the bathroom late one night. For some reason he wants to shave. He whips up the shaving mug. Sets it down. Queasy close-up of the lathered mug. The bathtub. The sink. All hideous and threatening.

"He's totally into looking at the pictures as they're coming, one after the other," said Brian De Palma. "Very few directors know how to do that. Or even *think* about it. It's important to know that Hitch started in the silent era. [Hitchcock and Luis Bunuel are the last from that era still working.] He knew how to tell a story purely through visuals, totally through putting the audience in the observer's eye. Young directors really don't understand it because they were brought up on sound. Photographing people yakking all the time."

The most memorable white-knuckle scenes

from Hitchcock movies are almost always silent. Gavin Lambert recently made a fine point: "Many scenes and details from his movies could be titled like surrealistic paintings: *Human Being Caged by Bird, Cigarette Extinguished in Fried Egg* [*To Catch a Thief*], and as a presentation of the extreme not even Dalí has gone further than *Young Man Dressed as His Dead Mother Knifing a Naked Girl Under a Shower.*"

The tilted nightmare patterns have led to chase scenes down Mount Rushmore or punch-outs on the Statue of Liberty. It was all too much for Raymond Chandler, who had a rough time writing *Strangers on a Train* with Hitchcock. He was baffled by all the dignified absurdity. "Every time you get set," he wrote to a friend, "he jabs you off balance by wanting to do a love scene on top of the Jefferson Memorial." Bad blood rose between the two, and Chandler's own perverse sense of logic couldn't take this "contest between a superficial reasonableness and a fundamental idiocy. . . . Is this the price you pay for trying to make a dream look as if it really happened?"

Shortly before our first meeting, I was plunged into a dream one night: when walking into a pawnshop, I found Alfred Hitchcock standing there with one elbow on the counter. He was smiling. A row of guitars hung above his head. I asked if I could see the red Gibson. Without taking his eyes off me, and grinning delightedly, he reached up and moved the guitar a few inches. The floor beneath me fell away. . . .

A week later I was ushered into Hitchcock's office. He was smiling. When I told him this, he grinned delightedly and said, "I do remember one dream. Once I was standing on Sunset Boulevard, where it starts to go green, top of Sierra. I was on my way to Romanoff's for lunch, and I was waiting for a Yellow Cab. And in the dream,

all the cars were period cars. And in the dream, I said to myself, 'It's no good waiting for a cab because this is a 1916 dream.'"

Hitchcock is a reluctant handshaker. His office is a large white room, spotless, wiped clean of all the fingerprints. Artificial flowers are thriving. A wall clock chimes every fifteen minutes, and a forty-five-minute interview lasts exactly that long because he will listen to the clock. "He's not a sponge," Karen Black had warned me. "He might not be that interested in *you.*"

In fact, only during the third interview did he begin to relax and dispense with the stories that date back to Harding's administration (during which he first directed a movie).

Hitchcock was on edge, however, even for the third visit, since his wife, Alma, was recovering from a stroke. Now he was hit by chest congestion. I thanked him for the time.

"Mmmmm, yes. The doctor says I should be in bed today, but I said, 'No, I have this interview to do, this . . . short interview. . . .'"

We got around to talking of his imitators. Because he is so visible, it is assumed he loves to act.

His face took on a bad taste. "I've been asked to be in several pictures. Charlie Laughton, God rest his soul, once said, you know, 'I'm going to direct a picture, can I come over to the house and spend an hour?'" Hitchcock paused, with a withering look. "I've been . . . forty years in directing pictures. An *hour.* It's like saying, I'm going to be a composer, can I come over to Leonard Bernstein's for an hour?

"In *The Lady Vanishes,* I had a lady disguised as a nun. And I suddenly cut to her foot, at the bottom of her robes, and she had on high-heeled shoes. Which gave the whole thing away. *Well.* I was asked to do a film for the United Nations, and they had a writer named something like Richard Condon, a good writer, and he knew he was writing it for me. And do you know he had four or five nuns turning into robbers? They can't help but put in things that I am quite content to do with once."

The nun in high heels reminded me of his Catholic background and the number of times he has gotten in sneaky digs at the Church. There is a kind of Catholic creative juice, I said, derived from a certain guilt and repression that make expression necessary.

"The Catholic *attitude*," he replied, nodding. (At that moment, I will swear on my catechism, the clock chimed.) "I was Jesuit educated. The only thing I learned was *fear*. To coin a phrase, they scared the bejesus out of me. And I was scared, as a boy, ages ten, eleven, twelve, and whether that's had any influence on the direction in which I go in picture making . . . *maybe*, I don't know.

"I was always interested in the ceremonial. I once *bribed* a master of ceremonies at a High Mass to let me be an acolyte. Which he did. But what I found out as soon as the Mass started was that I hadn't learned, or attempted to learn, the responses to the priest. It was only my childish anxiety to be a ceremonial figure."

Did you have an examination of conscience?

His deep upchuckle rolled around in the echo chamber of his jowls. "No, I was too young."

The French directors have repeatedly brought up the hoary Catholic bugaboo of original sin and Hitchcock, and he has always struck it down. I'd always thought renegade Catholics enjoy a love of blasphemy—tempered, usually, by a subconscious moral code.

"Well, there's a basic moral code. I don't like making films about criminals. I like making films about average people getting caught in bizarre situations." He began to cheer up. "One would be tempted to show a priest going to the beach, going into a cabana and coming out in just his shorts."

Wearing his clerical collar?

"Ah, hah! I would *like* to have him with a collar on, that would be quite nice. 'Father, you've got your collar on!' 'Don't worry, celluloid.'"

He is just enough of a rascal to get away with a bit like that. Sex-and-crime is, understandably, his favorite subject, and he can, at a drop, reel off the details of any wonderful murder that was shaded by sex.

"Oh, that's a very common thing, you know. If you take Christie . . . did you ever read the Christie case? Christie the murderer. I think he killed eight women." He shook the room with a massive clearing of throat. "He was a bald-headed, short, mild-mannered little man, very quiet. He could only get—he was impotent, you see—he could only get his sexual satisfaction by strangling a woman in the act. And then he hid the bodies, in cupboards, under the floorboards of the house. And went on living there with all these bodies . . ."

He could have been reciting a favorite recipe. He knew the entire trial transcript by heart, of course, and was not too visibly shaken when he revealed that the wrong man had been hanged. Since the subject of fear was up, I brought up his habit of arousing intense but subtle apprehensions around small objects, a key in the hand, a cigarette lighter, rather than a block-buster fear, like an earthquake.

"Well, they're objective films, that's another thing. They're films of danger. You see, the suspense element can be just as upsetting as the most horrific film. You arrive at suspense by letting the audience in. By not concealing things. That's why I never believe in mysteries. I call them 'mystifyings.' You see. A mystery, or a whodunit, is not an emotional expression on the part of the audience. It's more or less an intellectual one, like a crossword puzzle.

"In order to have suspense, you've got to give an audience all the information you can. I've simplified it for years: that you and I are talking here for five minutes and suddenly a bomb goes off under that table. Which would give the audience about ten seconds of shock." He was assuming a professorial tone.

"But go back and tell the audience that there's a bomb under there that's going off in five minutes . . . now think of the audience's emotions as we're talking. They'll say, 'Oh, my God, look, look, look!' And they'll be going to the clock. *But.* The difference is that if you put somebody through the wringer like this, somebody's foot has to touch it and say, 'What's this? Oh, my God, it's a bomb, throw it out the window!' And it goes out the window and then blows up. And in that way you've relieved the audience. If you don't relieve them, then they're very angry at you for putting them through that.

"I made a film years ago called *A Woman Alone* [*Sabotage*], a Joseph Conrad story. And I had a little boy carry a bomb—a package, he didn't know it was a bomb, the audience did— all the way across London. It's set to go off at one o'clock. He's held up by every possible means, even the Lord Mayor's procession. Finally he gets on a bus and it's moving very slowly. And I show every clock in the street, keep cutting to this package, and I go past one o'clock. One minute. Two minutes. And at *four* minutes past, the whole thing goes up." After all these years, he was still pleased.

"I remember at a press show, a woman on the London *Observer* runs up to me with both fists raised. She says, 'How *dare* you do a thing like that!' This is an intellectual presswoman, the equivalent of the *Sunday Times.* She says,

'I've got a five-year-old boy at home.' Oh, was she mad."

The theatrical side of him comes out in this kind of story, and he takes on the clever look of a homicidal choirboy.

"People say, 'What do you prefer to do? What type of subject?' And I think I must have said this around the twenties, the late twenties. I said, 'I like muuuurder. By the babbling brook.' Which is: You can have the most idyllic scene, and you can have the tiny little waterfalls over the stones, and there's a victim lying with the head in the water. No blood, because the blood has all been washed away.

"And incidentally, while we're on the subject of blood, I am not a devotee of blood in films. To such a degree that I made the film *Psycho* in black and white. I could have made it in color, but I didn't want to show that blood in the bathtub, because it would have alienated a lot of people and upset them. As it would have done me.

"Truffaut said one of the things he learned from me was the use of the camera as a subjective thing. Being sub-*jec*-tive means that the camera is able to envision—and this is where it becomes pure cinema—it visualizes something and *reacts* on an individual.

Yes, and puts the onus of guilt, or danger, on the person in the audience.

"Well, I suppose the most subjective film I've made is *Rear Window.*" (A classic with James Stewart as a photographer confined to his apartment with a broken leg. Snooping with a telephoto lens, he comes to suspect murder in a nearby building. Most of the film is shot from his vantage point.)

"But they don't *do* that enough," he said, returning to the moviemakers who never learned his lessons. "They don't put the camera in the *mind* of the person. They shoot things like in the theater, purely objective. I don't care what you say, when you see these cars crashing in the street, or *The French Connection,* this is all seen from the sidewalk." His eyes rolled with displeasure. "You put the audience on the sidewalk! So they're never involved with the actual crashes.

"Look at the cliché, which I think is the biggest of all clichés: Two people are in a train. In a compartment. And now and again they'll take the audience out of the dining car, or whatever it is, and put them all in a field. And watch the train go by. You see it in every picture with a train. The whole audience, transported to a field, and they look up and there it comes along and goes by."

When I asked him if he was a people watcher, he quickly denied any possibility with a clip of the head.

"People watcher? No. Well, it depends on what you mean by people watching. You mean, do I observe people and then reserve my opinion about them? Uhm, I don't think so, no." He fidgeted a moment. "The only people watching I've ever done was when I went to art school and, in one of the courses, they sent you to a railway terminal with a sketch pad and you would sketch people in their different attitudes. That's the only people watching I've ever done.

"In other words, people have always said to me, and I apply that here, 'Why do you always use cool blondes?' Leading ladies who are cold. Because I don't like the obvious sex object, like Marilyn Monroe, which tells you everything in one look. I think one should discover, in the course of the story, what sort of person the person is. Getting acquainted with them. So it takes time, as you call it, to become a people watcher." An imperceptible sniff. "If you're inclined that way.

"You take a woman like Ingrid Bergman. She was what we called an apple-cheeked peasant girl. When she first came here. *But* she's a Swede . . ." A catty insinuation curled his voice, and his eyebrows lifted. "And she's a nooorthern European."

With such emphasis, she now sounded completely wanton.

"You can get these Englishwomen who look like schoolteachers with beaky noses. And they're the sexiest of all."

I mentioned that *The Birds,* on recent examination, was all character study up until the last quarter.

"Right!" For the first time, he lit up. He extended an arm over his chair to the shelf at his side. This was an expansive gesture. "Well, you see, the structure there . . . the event overpowers the story. In other words, the birds had to come into what we call a very average normality: a spoiled girl who went to cocktail parties . . . well-to-do parents, San Franciscan, fond of jokes and so forth. . . . Now the setup there was something of such a very maudlin-nothing nature . . ." His soiled look broke slowly into a sly glint. "The birds *have* to come in . . . and de-*stroy* her."

He knew it would milk a laugh. I laughed.

"If you look back to the famous stories of H.G. Wells, *The War of the Worlds, The War in the Air,* he did many, many of this type, what I call catastrophe stories. But the people in them were never of much consequence. *The Time Machine:* the concentration was on the menacing events, rather than on the people.

"Now, even if you look at the basis of 'The Birds,' by Daphne du Maurier, you'll find that the people in the short story were of no consequence. I suppose when people say to me, 'What's your favorite film?' I say *Shadow of a Doubt.* There you've good people, written by Thornton Wilder, and the catastrophe that comes into that family, through the young girl—you've seen it?—is not physical, an earth-quake, the birds or towering inferno. The trag-edy, the thing that upset this whole family, was that you've got a mass murderer in the midst [Joseph Cotten]. A murderer of rich widows. So I made the theme 'The Merry Widow Waltz,' you see?" The smile came out of its cage.

"When I first came to America, I was sup-posed to work on *The Titanic*. [He instead switched to make a movie of *Rebecca*.] And I researched it, and I've seen a lot of films of the *Titanic* and, ah, they're like that other thing, *Ship of Fools*, you know, lots of little characters all over the ship, from the captain down to low-est person in steerage. But I began thinking about that in personal terms. How do I show a sinking ship?"

Animated like this, he is a sight to behold.

"I wanted to go to a card table, where four men were playing poker: go close to the whiskey and soda . . . the level is changing in the glass, tilting, you see? Same effect! Mind you, we've already told the audience that the ship has been struck. Then you go and say, 'Here are the in-nocent people, they don't know what's going on.' We might go down to the kitchen and I'd see a chef is putting the final touches to a beau-tiful cake with a pastry bag."

He delicately demonstrated a smudge. "And the audience would say, 'Don't bother! Don't bother! It's never going to be eaten! The ship's going down!'"

The walls shook with this.

"So that's how you apply the personal story to the catastrophe. So one is, I would say, a peo-ple *incident* watcher, rather than just a people watcher."

That settled, I asked if it was true that, for *The Birds*, the trainers had to stitch together a thousand pairs of tiny boots to get a thousand strawberry finches to hold still. He shook his head gravely and listed to one side, resting his weight on an elbow.

"We rented those finches, and the trouble we had with them was in the room. They were all wired in, the set was like a cage. But we had to put air pipes all around the bottom, because the finch, being a domestic bird, tended to perch. He always went for a perch. So we had to keep blowing them with a gentle breeze into the air."

I asked after his villains, who are very often smooth characters with one giveaway, like two-tone shoes, or picking the teeth with a diamond tiepin or a missing finger.

"Well," he grunted, "that's a class thing, you see. In England, that would be a class thing. More than the sinister. But after all, you used to have a smiling Nixon, didn't you? You couldn't stick a label on him and say 'villain,' could you? It's their *acts* that do it, their be-havior.

"Now, years ago, twenty . . . thirty . . . oh, no . . ." His eyes pulled up short. His mind seemed to be leafing through a very long book. "What am I talking about? I'm too young to know about these things. In the turn of the cen-tury, let me put it that way. I can remember as a child going to the theater, and when the villain entered, they put a green light on him. And the villain, in the very early days, *must* kick the dog . . ."

We were sitting in a clean white office in Uni-versal City. His huge hands encircled his vast potbelly. A nasal tuba harrumphed a funeral march, and somewhere a nice old lady in white gloves was taking apart the vicar with her prun-ing shears. Won't the police ever arrive? Mr. Hitchcock remembered going to the theater in 1905.

Steven Spielberg

By Michael Sragow

J U L Y   2 2 ,   1 9 8 2

Steven Spielberg is, in any conventional sense, the most successful movie director in Hollywood, America, the Occident, the planet Earth, the solar system and the galaxy. Three of his movies—*Jaws, Close Encounters of the Third Kind* and *Raiders of the Lost Ark*—are action-fantasy classics that rank among the biggest money-makers of all time. They are surpassed by *E.T. the Extra-Terrestrial*, a lyrical piece of sci-fi about the human, and alien, condition (conceived, coproduced and directed by Spielberg).

Spielberg is the scion of a suburban upbringing and a public-school education. His mother was a concert pianist and his father a computer scientist who moved his family of four children "from Ohio to New Jersey, Arizona, Saratoga and Los Angeles." From age twelve on, Spielberg knew he did one thing best: make movies. When college time came, he enrolled in film school at Cal State Long Beach. In 1969, on the basis of a twenty-four-minute short called "Amblin'," Spielberg was able to sign with Universal, where he directed episodes of "Night Gallery," "Marcus Welby" and "Columbo"; the terrifying TV-movie *Duel;* his first feature, *The Sugarland Express;* and his breakthrough, "primal scream" thriller, *Jaws.*

E.T. the Extra-Terrestrial is another breakthrough for Spielberg. His previous movies have all been spectacles of some species, even the out-of-control slapstick epic *1941.* Their escapism grew out of Spielberg's childhood fantasy life: "When I didn't want to face the real world," he says, "I just stuck a camera up to my face. And it worked." Making *E.T.,* however, compelled Spielberg to face the reality of his childhood pain and left him feeling "cleansed." Now, he says, "I'm trying to make movies by shooting more from the hip and using my eyes to see the real world."

The day after a triumphant out-of-competition screening of *E.T.* at Cannes in May, I spoke to Spielberg in his New York City hotel suite. He exuded casualness, from his NASA cap to his stockinged feet, as well as confidence that his most intimate movie might also prove to be his best loved. Talking about *E.T.,* his favorite contemporary directors and the troubled state of the motion-picture business, Spielberg seemed itching to take on the world.

Everything seems to have come together for you with "E.T." Certainly few filmmakers have had such a good shot at being both profoundly personal and phenomenally popular.

You know the saying, the book wrote itself. This movie didn't make itself, but things began to happen from its inception in 1980 that told me this was a movie I was ready to make. I'm not into psychoanalysis, but *E.T.* is a film that was inside of me for many years and could only come out after a lot of suburban psychodrama.

What do you mean by suburban psychodrama?

Growing up in a house with three screaming younger sisters and a mother who played concert piano with seven other women—I was raised in a world of women.

In a lot of your movies, the women or the girls are the more elastic characters, emotionally.

That's right, they are. I like women, I like working with women. *E.T.* had a plethora of them. A woman coproducer, a woman writer, a woman film editor, a woman assistant director, woman costumer, woman script person, women in construction, women in set design, a woman set dresser. I am less guarded about my feelings around women. I call it the shoulder-pad syndrome; you can't cry on a shoulder that's wearing a shoulder pad. This is something from my school days of being a wimp in a world of jocks.

How much of a wimp were you?

The height of my wimpery came when we had to run a mile for a grade in elementary school. The whole class of fifty finished, except for two people left on the track—me and a mentally retarded boy. Of course *he* ran awkwardly, but I was just never able to run. I was maybe forty yards ahead of him, and I was only one hundred yards away from the finish line. The whole class turned and began rooting for the young retarded boy—cheering him on, saying, "C'mon, c'mon, beat Spielberg! Run, run!" It was like he came to life for the first time, and he began to pour it on but still not fast enough

to beat me. And I remember thinking, "Okay, now how am I gonna fall and make it look like I really fell?" And I remember actually stepping on my toe and going face hard into the red clay of the track and actually scraping my nose. Everybody cheered when I fell, and then they began to really scream for this guy: "C'mon, John, c'mon, run, run!" I got up just as John came up behind me, and I began running as if to beat him but not really to win, running to let *him* win. We were nose to nose, and suddenly I laid back a step, then a half-step. Suddenly he was ahead, then he was a chest ahead, then a length, and then he crossed the finish line ahead of me. Everybody grabbed this guy, and they threw him up on their shoulders and carried him into the locker room, into the showers, and I stood there on the track field and cried my eyes out for five minutes. I'd never felt better and I'd never felt worse in my entire life.

You once said you managed to win over some of the jocks by starring them in a film called "Battle Squad." By making films like "Jaws," were you still trying to ingratiate yourself with hard guys?

Yeah, hard-liners. Hard, cynical liners. But not just three or four jocks in my elementary or junior high school. I'm talking about millions of people.

Do you mean that making movies is a way of showing off?

With the exception of *Close Encounters,* in all my movies before *E.T.,* I was giving *out,* giving *off* things before I would bring something *in.* There were feelings I developed in my personal life . . . that I had no place to put. Then, while working on *Raiders,* I had the germ of an idea. I was very lonely, and I remember thinking I had nobody to talk to. My girlfriend was in California, so was George Lucas. Harrison Ford had a bad case of the turistas. I remember wishing one night that I had a friend. It was like, when you were a kid and had grown out of dolls or teddy bears or Winnie the Pooh, you just wanted a little voice in your mind to talk to. I began concocting this imaginary creature, partially from the guys who stepped out of the mother ship for ninety seconds in *Close Encounters* and then went back in, never to be seen again.

Then I thought, what if I were ten years old again—where I've sort of been for thirty-four years, anyway—and what if he needed me as much as I needed him? Wouldn't that be a great love story? So I put together this story of boy meets creature, boy loses creature, creature saves boy, boy saves creature—with the hope that they will somehow always be together, that their friendship isn't limited by nautical miles. And I asked Melissa Mathison, who is Harrison Ford's girlfriend and a wonderful writer, to turn it into a screenplay.

Did you hire her because you admired her work on "The Black Stallion?"

I did admire *The Black Stallion,* but it was more because Melissa was one of the few people on the *Raiders* location I could talk to. I was pouring my heart out to Melissa all the time.

In "E.T.," the view of growing up is both uplifting and painful. If Elliott hadn't befriended E.T., he'd still be one lonely kid.

To me, Elliott was always the Nowhere Man from the Beatles song. I was drawing from my own feelings when I was a little kid and I didn't have that many friends and had to resort to making movies to become quasi-popular and to find a reason for living after school hours. Most of my friends were playing football or basketball or baseball and going out with girls. I didn't do those things until very late.

Is "E.T." your imaginary revenge—turning the Nowhere Man into a hero?

Oh, yeah, absolutely. When I began making *E.T.,* I thought that maybe the thing to do was

go back and make life the way it should have been. How many kids, in their Walter Mitty imaginations, would love to save the frogs or kiss the prettiest girl in class? That's every boy's childhood fantasy.

Have you been able to fulfill your own childhood fantasies?

I guess I still haven't been able to shake off the anesthetic of suburbia.

The anesthetic of suburbia—that implies that it protects you from pain and from any kind of raw feeling.

And real life. Because the anesthetic of suburbia also involves having three parents—a mother, a father and a TV set. Two of them are equilibriums, but one of them is more powerful, because it's always new and fresh and entertaining. It doesn't reach out and tell you what to do.

To me, the key suburban feeling is claustrophobia.

There was no privacy in suburbia because my mom's friends would come in the morning, drink coffee and gossip. And it *was* claustrophobic. It's a reality to kids; in suburbia you have to create a kids' world apart from an adult world—and the two will never eclipse. In an urban world, the adult world and the child world are inseparable. Everybody gets the same dose of reality every day. In suburbia, kids have secrets. And that's why I wanted *E.T.* to take place in suburbia. What better place to keep a creature from outer space a secret from the grown-ups?

How heavily did you base the movie on contemporary suburban experience, as opposed to your own memories?

In today's world, a twelve-year old is what we were at sixteen and a half. So a transformation happened once I cast the film with real kids. Not stage Hollywood actors, you know—kids who've never been in a casting director's office or an art director's room. Real people, just real people—that's who we cast.

Dialogue changed considerably. I never would have called my brother, if I'd had one, "penis breath" in front of my mother. It's not the most popular word in the Pac-Man generation's vernacular, but it's a word that's used every once in a while, and it conjures up quite gross and hilarious images. I wanted the kids to say something that would shake up the mother, 'cause I wanted her to laugh first, then reprimand, instead of just saying, "How dare you say that in my house!" *That's* the fifties mother, the one who got attacked by the Martians who ate the dog. *Today's* parent, being my age, would burst out laughing and then suddenly realize, "Omigosh, I'm the father, I can't laugh at that. Sit down, son, and never say that word again, or I'll pretend I'm *my* mom and dad back in the fifties, and you'll have to learn from them."

I think kids tend to look at adults as just melodramatic excuses for people. A lot of kids look up to look down. And I found, even when I was giving Henry Thomas [Elliott] direction, that if I was out of touch with his reality, he would give me a look that seemed to say, "Oh, brother, he's old." I could always tell when I was reaching Henry. He would smile and laugh, or he'd say, "Yeah, yeah, right." I was constantly being rewarded or corrected by people three times less my age. I was moving *faster* than the kids. So I slowed myself down and began to metabolize according to them instead of Steven Spielberg.

Did that scare you?

The thing that I'm just scared to death of is that someday I'm gonna wake up and bore somebody with a film. That's kept me making movies that have tried to outspectacle each other. I got into the situation where my movies were real big, and I had a special-effects depart-ment and I was the boss of that and that was a lot of fun. Then I'd get a kick out of the production meetings—not with three or four people, but with fifty, sometimes nearer to a hundred when we got close to production—because I was able to lead troops into Movie Wars. The power became a narcotic, but it wasn't power for power's sake. I really am attracted to stories that you can't see on television and stories that you can't get every day. So that attraction leads me to the Impossible Dream, and that Impossible Dream usually costs around $20 million.

François Truffaut helped inspire me to make *E.T.* simply by saying to me, on the *Close Encounters* set, "I like you with *keeds,* you are wonder with *keeds,* you must do a movie just with *keeds*. . . ." And I said, "Well, I've always wanted to do a film about kids, but I've got to finish this, then I'm doing *1941,* about the Japanese attacking Los Angeles." And Truffaut told me I was making a big mistake. He kept saying, "You are the child."

To me, your biggest visual accomplishment is the contrast between suburbia in the harsh, daytime light, when everything looks the same, to the mysterious way it looks at night. By the end, you get a mothering feeling from the night.

Yeah, it *is* Mother Night. Remember, in *Fantasia,* Mother Night flying over with her cape, covering a daylight sky? I used to think, when I was a kid, that that's what night really looked like. The Disney Mother Night was a beautiful woman with flowing, blue-black hair, and arms extended outward, twenty miles in either direction. And behind her was a very inviting cloak. She came from the horizon in an arc and swept over you until everything was a blue-black dome. And then there was an explosion, and the stars were suddenly made in this kind of animated sky. I wanted the opening of *E.T.* to be that kind of Mother Night. You know, you come down over the trees, you see the stars, and suddenly you think you're in space—wow, you're not, you're in a forest somewhere. You're not quite sure where; you might be in a forest on some distant planet. It was Melissa's idea to use the forest; at first, I thought of having the ship land in a vacant lot. But she said, "A forest is magical . . . there are elves in forests."

You've coproduced both "E.T." and "Poltergeist." "E.T." seems to have gone very well, "Poltergeist" seems to have had trouble. How did you react to facing turmoil as a producer?

Well, the turmoil is essentially created by wanting to do it your own way and having to go through procedure. That is why I will never again *not* direct a film I write. It was frustrating for Tobe Hooper [the director], and it was frustrating for the actors, who were pretty torn between my presence and his on the set every day. But rather than Tobe's saying, "I can't stand it. Go to Hawaii, get off the set," he'd laugh and I'd laugh. If he'd said, "I've got some ideas that you're not really letting into this movie, I would love you to see dailies, consult, but don't be on the set," I probably would have left.

Has a producer ever held you in line and helped you in the way, say, Darryl Zanuck is supposed to have helped John Ford?

George Lucas, on *Raiders*. He didn't come in and cut my movie or dictate policy or style or substance. But he was always available to talk, and he was never lacking in ideas.

I don't know of more than four executives in this town who know how to cut a movie and how to execute one. The people who are in charge today wouldn't know how to save a *Heaven's Gate* if indeed it needed saving. I think that the overall attack that was launched on the director, Michael Cimino, is more interesting and worthy of analysis than the *Heaven's Gate* cataclysm. Everybody destroyed Cimino because his movie cost

$30 million. Way down deep, I think the outcry was a primal scream from movie lovers, saying "Please bring the budgets down, please give us better ideas and more entertainment, and give us more intellectual stimulation as well as the pleasure of butter on the popcorn. Don't crush yourselves under the weight." I wish Cimino had been left alone, because, of all the new guys coming up, Michael's got a chance to be David Lean [*Lawrence of Arabia*]. Michael is maybe as technically skilled as Billy Friedkin, Francis Ford Coppola, Brian De Palma and Martin Scorsese. I like this guy Michael Mann [*Thief*], and Alan Parker [*Shoot the Moon*]. But they are more of the Scorsese-Coppola school than . . . our group.

You say that with a twinkle in your eye. You don't mind there being . . .

I don't mind having two groups. I think the business is one big melting pot anyway. I'm just saying that there are different sensibilities. I think George Lucas and I and some of the others—the Chicago to California group as opposed to the Chicago to New York group—are more frivolous with the imagination. The West Coast has different sensibilities than the East Coast.

I think the other group—Francis and Marty and some of the European filmmakers—bring a lot of their urban development into their movies and take their films very seriously. They internalize who they are and express that on film. I think if you put everybody together and rated them, Marty would have to be the best *filmmaker* of our generation. George Lucas is the best *moviemaker*. You see, George and I have fun with our films. We don't take them as seriously. And I think that our movies are about things that we think will appeal to other people, not just to ourselves. We think of ourselves first, but in the next breath we're talking about the audience and what works and what doesn't.

How do you respond to the idea that what Scorsese does is more adult than what you guys are doing?

Well, it *is* more adult, because it appeals to our anxiety-riddled, darker side. It appeals to the unknown persona. My movies and George's appeal to things that are lighter in nature. I think the difference is terrific. Can you imagine if everybody made *Raiders of the Lost Ark* last year? I think studios were spoiled the first day *Gone With the Wind* made more money than any movie ever. I think from that moment on, decision-makers wanted movies that would be hugely successful. So every time I see a small picture take off, whether it's *Animal House* or *Diner,* I cheer. I think it's bullshit when people

say the success of *Raiders* precludes the success of *Diner.* I think a success like *Raiders* feeds the pocketbook that's gonna finance *Diner.* You can't have a *Diner* without *Raiders.* But you can't have good movies without *Diner.*

You talked about your group deferring to the audience occasionally. But in the case of "E.T.," it seems you didn't have to do that.

Well, when I started *E.T.,* I was fat and happy and satisfied with having the films I had on my list. And I just didn't feel I had anything to lose. I actually had *nothing* to lose. I had nothing to prove to anybody except myself—and any people who might have wondered if I ever had a heart beating beneath the one they assume that Industrial Light and Magic [the Lucasfilm special-effects company] built for me. *E.T.* is my personal resurrection.

Jean-Luc Godard

By Jonathan Cott

JUNE 14, 1969

From the opening moments of his first feature film, *Breathless* (1959), to the apocalyptic climax of *Weekend* (1967), his fifteenth feature, Jean-Luc Godard revealed himself as the most innovative filmmaker of the sixties. During this extraordinary fertile period, Godard combined a romantic inventiveness and an intellectual urgency to create works that often used the conventions of Hollywood action films to explore the nature of the medium itself.

After 1968, Godard, much to the disappointment of many of his admirers, turned his back on his films and began collaborating on a series of experimental, analytical and politically militant video works *(Wind From the East, Letter to Jane, Number Two)* that reexamined almost every element of traditional moviemaking and often criticized not only the work of other directors but also Godard's own methods.

"I know nothing of life except through the cinema," Godard said in 1962. "I didn't see things in relation to the world, to life or to history, but in relation to cinema. Now I am growing away from all that . . . I thought *Breathless* was a realistic film, but now it seems like *Alice in Wonderland,* a completely unreal, surrealistic world." As Susan Sontag has written: "Life—

the world; death—being completely inside one's own head."

In Godard's second feature film, *Le Petit Soldat,* the O.A.S. gunman protagonist quotes Lenin's dictum: "Ethics is the esthetics of the future." Looking back now, we see that this exile and deserter, in search of his self, not knowing "where to give his heart," ironically was pointing to Godard's recent unswerving and uncompromising concern with using film as a way to "change the world."

There is no more joking self-consciously about the image of films—no more references to *Johnny Guitar.* Godard's new films are not about politics in the way that *Le Petit Soldat* or Alain Resnais' *The War Is Over* are. Rather they present a political consciousness in the guise of quasi-documentary footage and thus attempt to make you watch and listen and think. "To look around one's self, that is to be free," Godard said.

Godard's new questioning of the relationship between art and politics reveals itself in recent personal confrontations such as when he asked the audience at the 1968 London Film Festival to watch the uncut version of *One Plus One* outside the theater on a makeshift screen and re-

360

turn their tickets and send the refund to the Eldridge Cleaver Defense Fund. Put to a vote, only twenty persons decided to walk out. Godard said: "You're content to sit here like cretins in a church." During the shouting that followed, he hit producer Ian Quarrier, who later explained why he added to the end of Godard's film a complete recorded version of the Rolling Stones' "Sympathy for the Devil" ("ten million teenyboppers in America alone.")

One Plus One intersperses shots of the Stones creating "Sympathy for the Devil" (from a slow ballad to the final rhythmic holocaust) with scenes of Black Power militants in a Battersea automobile junkyard reciting texts by LeRoi Jones and Cleaver, shooting white nightgowned girls; an interview in lush green woods with Eve Democracy (Anne Wiazemski), who replies yes or no to questions defining the liberal temperament; a pornographic bookstore where Mr. Quarrier reads out from *Mein Kampf* while customers give the Nazi salute then slap two bandaged young men who chant, "Peace in Vietnam."

This interview was recorded in English driving out to the airport and during an airport dinner.

Why *is it that in the last few films, your portrayal of the hippie revolutionaries, in "Weekend," let's say, and in "One Plus One" . . .*

They were not hippies. Their long hair isn't necessarily related to hippieness. They were more Yippies than hippies because they didn't hesitate to take up guns. I remember a discussion in Berkeley this year. I had an interview with Eldridge Cleaver, and he was reproaching people like Jerry Rubin and Abbie Hoffman. He said: "Those Yippie people like toy guns. We Black Power people like real guns."

The idea of an action film, which you are obviously

influenced by in your early films, usually leads to a kind of right-wing philosophy, whereas you've gotten rid of the action sequences now in "One Plus One."

I don't know what action is. I'm trying to demystify the movies at the same time as making them. I'm always amazed that so many of the militants are so fond of Westerns, which I hate. They are not bothered by the fact that it's a fascist form. They don't care. They enjoy it. But a lot of people who lack their intelligence or their militancy are poisoned by that. The militants aren't, but the other people, the so-called ordinary people, are. That's why the scientists of the movie or of the theater or of literature have to work on theory, to try to indicate how to found new bases, a new grammar, a new philosophy, a new mathematics out of it. And you discover how to do that by being linked to the militant people, by being yourself as militant as you can be.

But I had a sense of the impotency of the whole revolutionary movement because everyone was quoting something or someone else. There are all these microphones and cameras. Eve Democracy can only say yes or no.

Because she is democracy. What else can democracy say?

But Frankie Dymon, too?

Yes, but this is the way it is. And it has to be shown and told frankly, so that we can analyze it better and know how to do it. There is no meaning in the movie. The meaning comes before and after. The screen is nothing.

I just had a feeling of futility about everything that happened.

Yes, more or less. But the only ones to escape from that were the blacks.

John Lennon recently replied to your comments about the Beatles' not doing anything politically . . .

I'd like to see John Lennon play Trotsky in a film.

What did you mean when you were supposed to have said: The Jefferson Airplane is me?

I didn't say that.

How do you feel about the Stones and the Jefferson Airplane? They're two such different groups.

Well, the Rolling Stones are much more accomplished than Jefferson Airplane, who are more like tribal people. That is, they present something which exists: the music and the hippie. There is some invention, but it should be politicized. The Stones are more political then Jefferson Airplane, but they should be more and more so every day. The new music could be the beginning of a revolution, but it isn't. It seems more like a palliating to life.

In "One Plus One" you show some interviews. There's one with Eve Democracy. And there's Frankie Dymon, the Black Power advocate in the film, being prompted and having statements fed to him.

I wouldn't say fed. They were rehearsing, trying to learn from their comrades in the U.S. who are engaged in a more dangerous fight than their own in England.

What did you want to do with the Rolling Stones in "One Plus One" when they constructed "Sympathy for the Devil"?

I just wanted to show something in construction. To show that democracy was nowhere, not even constructive. Not destructive, of course, just saying, "We are against war," but doing nothing for peace, not having the strength to follow the black man who is going to be a revolutionary.

One of the points, too, was that Eve Democracy was walking in a lush green field and the black people were in a junkyard.

That's true.

And do you think of using colors conceptually in your films? In "Made in U.S.A.," the color seems much more aesthetically beautiful than what happens in the film itself.

I think the ideology of beauty should be very well analyzed, first destroyed and then analyzed. Because we are completely mystified by beauty. So maybe we have to make horrible songs first in offer to destroy and then to learn what beauty is. We have been taught what beauty is, but we don't really know.

You don't feel a sense of loss at all? Are you happier with yourself?

Yes, much.

You're making a lot of film critics and audiences unhappy.

I just forget about that. My idea of film hasn't changed. It's just gone further in its own direction and needs to find the right allies. I would have arrived at the same position I'm at now, but in five years. But because of the May-June events, it came in two months. And I was late, and I'm still late compared to other comrades who have simpler ideas about these things.

It was exactly the opposite with Bob Dylan. Maybe he was too early. Maybe he was going in the right direction but too early for him. And he couldn't stand it, really, even if it was successful. He didn't have the political mind and thought. And now he's kind of broken, and he has to protect himself and then go into the woods again.

The door-to-door theater in "La Chinoise"; is that what you think you're doing in films now?

Yes. I just think I have fewer ideas, and other less analytical people have better ideas, more militant ideas, in other words.

How do you feel now about your "war" film, "Les Carabiniers"?

I don't feel. I don't think you should feel about a movie. You should feel about a woman, but not about a movie. You can't kiss a movie. Let's have a look and talk about it, but certainly not feel about it. That's what the Church says, feel about God.

You're attacking culture now the way people used to attack religion.

Yes, it's the same thing.

What do you think now about the disagreement you had with Ian Quarrier at the Film Festival, your punching him and the people heckling you.

I'll protect myself better next time, that's all. I was very disappointed with the Rolling Stones. They didn't even say it was the wrong idea to add the completed version of their song on to the end of the film. I wrote to them and they didn't say anything. It was very unfair for them to accept their being emphasized over all the others in the film. Each group of people is equal to the other, and one shouldn't overemphasize the playing of the Stones by repeating them. If the film is distributed, it will have a new title, the title of their song—"Sympathy for the Devil"—a producer's idea. It's unfair not from a personal point of view, but from a political point of view, unfair to the black people.

Let's say someone goes to "One Plus One" and comes out saying the whole revolutionary movement is useless.

This is because he doesn't know how to look at pictures, because he thinks he has to say something afterwards. When you open a book of mathematics, if you've never studied mathematics, you can't say anything. And here just because you have shadows which resemble reality, you think you're the authority about that and that and that. No, obviously, there's nothing to say. You can say something tomorrow or two days afterwards. You can talk to other people. But you have to say: I have seen that and that. I've seen a girl in the woods. She was named Democracy. I've seen black people reading that and that. And then maybe you ask questions about it. Why was it that way? And then you try to see what it means.

The film might not convince you that the revolutionary movement was correct.

The film doesn't have to convince. You shouldn't speak like that. It has to convince that there are better people than others. It's as if in one or two hours of a picture or twenty pages of a book—you want the whole truth about the whole society, about everything, and it has to be right. It's absolutely wrong. It's impossible. It took Mao fifty years to write his little red book. Fifty years of fighting. And then it was very natural. It came from everything he had learned.

But the Rolling Stones' song covers a lot of ground, it contains a lot of material.

No, that's wrong. It has very little. That's why I was so angry with that ending. We should know only a little bit of it. We don't know what kind of song it is. It's just words, the beginning of words. It never goes to the end. Because the Rolling Stones are still at the very beginning.

But you hear what they're singing about at the very beginning, about Satan, about the Kennedys, the czar, about hippies getting killed before reaching Bombay. There's a lot of content in that one song.

No, there's very little. It's just that you hear it twenty times.

You seem to have such a clear idea of what you're doing, yet there are so many contradictions in the film.

Not in the film, but in the way you look at it. My films are much clearer than they were two or three years ago. They still might be very neophytic, because they're very simple. When you go out of *One Plus One*—ordinary people I mean, people who like James Bond—you might say: This is very complicated, I don't understand anything. But if you go out of the last James Bond film and I ask you, can you tell me what you've seen, you can't. No. There were twenty thousand things in James Bond. The movie showed for two hours. I ask, was he in a car? Yes. What color was it? Do you remember the color? He was with a girl. What was he saying to her? And just after he left the girl, what was he doing? He can't remember. Maybe he could remember one or two moments. But he couldn't remember or describe to me the sequence of the story. It's like a mixed salad. You can't describe a mixed salad. There are too many things in it.

And then I ask him, you have just seen *One Plus One.* Do you think it's complicated? Well, let's see if it's complicated. Let's remember what you've seen. People playing music. Yes, you remember that. What else? Well, there were black people in a junkyard throwing guns and reading things. And there was a girl in the woods. And in four minutes he can remember everything there was in the movie. And there is no more. Yes, but why? he says. I didn't understand why that girl was in the woods just before the sequence of the black people. And I ask him, what do you think? What's she saying? She was only answering yes and no. Well, what kind of questions was she being asked? Do you remember any? And on and on like that. It's a very simple thing, really very simple. . . . These people have been taught that a James Bond film is a simple movie, while in fact it's really complicated and complicated in a dreadful, in a silly way, because there was no need for complication.

I think you're cheating now because a James Bond film is much simpler emotionally and intellectually than "One Plus One."

Yes, maybe, in its reality. The world is more complicated, but not *One Plus One.*

What if a James Bond fan comes out of the movie and says, "One Plus One" bored me. You couldn't really disagree with him if that was how he felt. "One Plus One" is a very intellectual film; it makes you think.

That's because it's the only film like that. If there were a hundred more, made by a hundred different people, it wouldn't be like that. Forget about the film, just think about the black people, think about the music people.

In the film you say that for an intellectual to be revolutionary, he has to give up his intellectuality; but in order to see the film you have to use your intellect.

You have to give it up at a certain time, but in order to use it again. It's important to give up being an intellectual in the way that the bourgeois conceives of an intellectual. We have to give up being that kind of an intellectual.

Will you be working with more groups like the Jefferson Airplane or Rolling Stones in the future?

No, I don't think so.

What about your idea of using television as much as possible now?

Oh, you can't do that. You get more mystified than ever.

So where is there to go now?

You make very small movies to show to fewer people more often. More movies to fewer people but much more often. So you can survive.

You have a lot of courage.

No, it's very natural. I couldn't do anything else. You have to know how to survive. You have to be optimistic, because the world situation is so bad. Marx said that. I'm an optimist because things are so bad they must get better because they can't be worse than they are. It's the same today.

A lot of what you're saying sounds to me extremely suicidal.

Not at all. Maybe when I was doing *Weekend* I was that way, but not any longer.

I just hate to give up the idea of your old films.

They are what they are, what I was at that time.

Do you feel more like a medium now, someone whom ideas go through?

No, more like a worker, a student, or a worker concerned with student power. When you do something bad, you're not ashamed, you're sorry for it. Okay, it's bad, I must do it better, but you sleep very well. It doesn't matter. And if a very good friend of mine says, I hate your picture, I'm no failure at all. I say, tell me why you think it's bad. But five years ago, that response from a friend made me very sad. Which was crazy. I don't understand how I could have felt that.

John Cassavetes

By Grover Lewis

MARCH 30, 1972

Los Angeles—The rascular density—the number of bona fide sonsofbitches per cubic foot—normally runs high in Musso & Frank's Grill, an enclave of truly civil service located in the heart of the feverish overboogie of beautiful downtown Hollywood. Since 1919, the posh, softly lit bistro on Hollywood Boulevard has been a favorite watering hole for the monied riffraff of the Dream Dump—a sequestered place for agents and producers and other such swinish orders to wine and dine, wheel and deal and, hopefully, shove it up somebody's heart.

Slumped in a corner booth of the restaurant, looking as if he doesn't belong there at all, dressed in faded corduroys and a dark V-necked sweater and chain-smoking Winstons, John Cassavetes, the film actor and director, is trying to explain all about himself to a luncheon guest, who also looks as if he doesn't belong there. The same holds true for the third man in the booth, Seymour Cassel, the star of Cassavetes' films *Faces* (an Oscar nomination for that) and *Minnie and Moskowitz;* wearing baggy jeans and a frayed jacket, Cassel looks, in fact, just like your typical aging Queens street freak.

"I tell you the kind of thing I like to do,"

Cassavetes drawls, hunching his shoulders forward and reaching for his second Bloody Mary. "Like this—I ran into Irene Papas not long ago in London—you familiar with that crumby Greek actress? Okay, so she puts on this phony imperious air she has and says to me, 'Jawn, I don't vant to tawk to you anymore. You haff belief in fascistic Amerika.' So I say to her, 'Listen, Irene, I don't want to hear any more of your silly bullshit, either. Your head is full of trash and I think you're a phony cunt.' Then I sit down beside her, see, and just start talking normally, as if nothing had happened. Ha! I *love* to pull that kind of shit on people who deserve it!"

"There's a bunch of 'em around," Cassel says, grinning and waggling a finger in a circle at his temple, "just haywired."

"This here guy," Cassel says, indicating Cassavetes to the luncheon guest and enunciating each syllable distinctly, "is the most individual guy I've ever worked with. If I had a choice, he'd be first every time. Also, he's my friend, and his wife"—Cassel is referring to the actress Gena Rowlands—"she's my friend, too, and a great lady like my wife, and Gena and John fight like dogs and cats all the fuckin' time—it's fuckin' hilarious—"

Cassavetes nods fondly: "Yeah, well, we fight and argue and kill each other off every single day, Gena and me. But that's only surface, because we both have the understanding that when we don't do that, it's all over—"

"—and the only goddamn thing that could ever ruin John's and my friendship," Cassel goes on, thumping the table for emphasis, "is that John's got this story that he wants to do with Lee Marvin and me and George Scott. And I want him to do it with Lee Marvin and me and *him*. If he doesn't act with me in that goddamn picture, I swear it's gonna be head and head soon."

"Maybe it'll happen," Cassavetes murmurs, swirling the pale pink liquid in his glass, "maybe it'll happen, who knows? The thing about acting is . . . Well, I like to do it—this September, I'll be making an Elaine May picture with Peter Falk called *Mikey and Nicky,* and I look forward to that—but I'm a Greek and a New Yorker, see, I always want to have the edge. Okay, so I've got Seymour, and he's an edge to me because he's a thinking, feeling person. Same for Gena, same for just about everybody I've used in my pictures. But they're not 'good actors'— that's a lotta bullshit. There's no such thing as a 'good actor.' What it is, you know, is an extension of life. How you're capable of performing in your life, that's how you're capable of performing on the screen. Everything else is just a failure to accomplish that."

"Yeah," Cassel puts in, "that's true. Personally, I don't really look for anything in a part as much as I look for the beginning of a whole concept. I don't care how big the part is, or how small, or how great it is. With John here—well, hell, I would merely walk across the screen for him if he asked me to. And I'd find a way to do it and enjoy it and make it enjoyable. My ambition isn't all that great. I've been an actor twelve,

almost thirteen years, and there's two things I'm really proud of—*Faces* and *Minne and Moskowitz.* I could be working all the time, particularly now, but I'd rather not have to look back later and say, 'Oh, Christ, I did that, I did that once.' Nah, not for me. I'd rather just go along for months enjoying my wife and children and friends, going into bars, talking to people. That's all I understand of life. And every two years, I get to do something I love. With John, though, it's different. He drives, he works all the time. Besides acting, he's been responsible for, he's *created* six pictures—uh, *Shadows, Too Late Blues*—let's see—*A Child Is Waiting, Faces, Husbands, Minnie*—"

"Continuity is a problem," Cassavetes says with a frown, lighting one Winston from the butt of another and cocking his head to avoid the smoke. "You know—getting the financing to go from this one to the next one. I'm not terribly fond of too many people in the film business, and they're not too fond of me. But I have to approach them. I consider them to be like a bank. I try to eliminate my personal view of their loneliness, their emptiness, when I talk to them. I try not to judge them too harshly by my own standard, which is never, never to lie and to stand up for what you believe at *certain times,* not at all times.

"Take Stanley Kramer. He was the producer of *A Child Is Waiting.* We had a different feeling toward life, he and I. There is *no* way we could have gotten along together under any circumstances. I *hate* the son of a bitch—I wouldn't glorify him with five seconds of my time. And every time I say anything derogatory about him, which is very rarely, I can just envision the son of a bitch, tears welling up in his eyes, asking: "What did I do to deserve this?' "

"*Take* Stanley Kramer," Cassel guffaws. The dining area is rapidly filling up now with the kind of people who look like they belong there. Cassavetes watches the gaudy ebb-and-flow of the room for a minute, then leans forward, hugging his arms to his chest:

"Mankind has finally found the lowest common denominator, you know it? Which is money. It's the lowest, most base, silly excursion into loneliness I've ever seen. Seven, eight years ago, the kids of America started rebelling against that. Then, somehow, that was taken over and commercialized and used as a way to make money, too. The Youth Market. Ha! Reporters would ask me, 'Who're you directing to—the Youth Market?' Well, sure, why not? You make pictures for the young because they're the people who can still feel. You have to be part of youth, and you make pictures to be part of youth. But I don't think of youth being the *market*—I think of youth being life.

"And life is men and women. Life isn't, say, politics—politicians are only bad actors grubbing around for power. Listen, after a screening of *Minnie* the other night, some guy asked me why I didn't make an antiwar movie. Why did I want to make a movie about people getting married and being happy and in love with one another and all that? Well, why the fuck should I want to make a movie about a war? Pro or con? I'd rather deal with the longings of the mind, the heart. There's nothing else to say, and I'm never going to make any other pictures except about men and women.

"Right now I think my films are the best films made, but that's only because I'm lucky. I'm lucky in that the age is so fucked-up that almost everybody else has lost all feeling toward individual people. I'm very proud and very fortunate that I haven't done that. Thirty years ago, a lot of people—Capra, John Ford, talents like that—were doing what I'm doing today. Back then, I'd probably have been ranked ten-thousandth down the line, would probably never have had the opportunity to make two films, much less six or seven. But right now, I've got the market.

"And it's because I care about men and women. And people respond to that. *Husbands,* for example. I think *Husbands* is one of the best pictures ever made. Okay? Okay, so some strange woman walked up to me on the street in New York and said, 'I've seen you. Who are you?' I said, 'I'm John Cassavetes.' She said, 'No, I don't know you, never heard of you.' I asked her where she'd seen me and she said, 'I saw you in a picture with three people.' I asked her if Ben Gazarra was one of them. No, she said, she didn't know him, either. So I said, 'Peter Falk? You must know Peter Falk.' Nah, she also never heard of him. Then she said, 'Just three guys, that's all. I hated the picture, and I saw it twice.'"

When the laughter dies away, Cassel expels a long breath and waggles a thumb in Cassavetes' direction. "Jeez, this guy," he wheezes fondly, "this outrageous, outrageous guy."

Stanley Kubrick

By Tim Cahill

AUGUST 27, 1987

He didn't bustle into the room, and he didn't wander in. Truth, as he would reiterate several times, is multifaceted, and it would be fair to say that Stanley Kubrick entered the executive suite at Pinewood Studios, outside London, in a multifaceted manner. He was at once happy to have found the place after a twenty-minute search, apologetic about being late and apprehensive about the torture he might be about to endure. Stanley Kubrick, I had been told, hates interviews.

It's hard to know what to expect of the man if you've only seen his films. One senses in those films painstaking craftsmanship, a furious intellect at work, a single-minded devotion. His movies don't lend themselves to easy analysis; this may account for the turgid nature of some of the books that have been written about his art. Take this example: "And while Kubrick feels strongly that the visual powers of film make ambiguity an inevitability as well as a virtue, he would not share Bazin's mystical belief that the better filmmakers are those who sacrifice their personal perspectives to a 'fleeting crystallization of a reality [of] whose environing presence one is ceaselessly aware.'"

One feels that an interview conducted on this level would be pretentious bullshit. Kubrick, however, seemed entirely unpretentious. He was wearing running shoes and an old corduroy jacket. There was an ink stain just below the pocket where some ballpoint pen had bled to death.

"What is this place?" Kubrick asked.

"It's called the executive suite," I said. "I think they put big shots up here."

Kubrick looked around at the dark wood-paneled walls, the chandeliers, the leather couches and chairs. "Is there a bathroom?" he asked with some urgency.

"Across the hall," I said.

The director excused himself and went looking for the facility. I reviewed my notes. Kubrick was born in the Bronx in 1928. He was an undistinguished student whose passions were tournament-level chess and photography. After graduation from Taft High School at the age of seventeen, he landed a prestigious job as a photographer for *Look* magazine, which he quit after four years in order to make his first film. *Day of the Fight* (1950) was a documentary about the middleweight boxer Walter Cartier. After a second documentary, *Flying Padre* (1951), Kubrick borrowed $10,000 from relatives to make

Fear and Desire (1953), his first feature, an arty film that he now finds "embarrassing." Kubrick, his first wife and two friends were the entire crew for the film. By necessity, Kubrick was director, cameraman, lighting engineer, makeup man, administrator, propman and unit chauffeur. Later in his career, he would take on some of these duties again, for reasons other than necessity.

Kubrick's breakthrough film was *Paths of Glory* (1957). During the filming, he met an actress, Christiane Harlan, whom he eventually married. Christiane sings a song at the end of the film in a scene that, on four separate viewings, has brought tears to my eyes.

Kubrick's next film was *Spartacus* (1960), a work he finds disappointing. He was brought in to direct after the star, Kirk Douglas, had a falling-out with the original director, Anthony Mann. Kubrick was not given control of the script, which he felt was full of easy moralizing. He was used to making his own films his own way, and the experience chafed. He has never again relinquished control over any aspect of his films.

And he has taken some extraordinary and audacious chances with those works. The mere decision to film Vladimir Nabokov's *Lolita* (1962) was enough to send some censorious sorts into a spittle-spewing rage. *Dr. Strangelove* (1964), based on the novel *Red Alert,* was conceived as a tense thriller about the possibility of accidental nuclear war. As Kubrick worked on the script, however, he kept bumping up against the realization that the scenes he was writing were funny in the darkest possible way. It was a matter of slipping on a banana peel and annihilating the human race. Stanley Kubrick went with his gut feeling: he directed *Dr. Strangelove* as a black comedy. The film is routinely described as a masterpiece.

Most critics also use that word to describe the two features that followed, *2001: A Space Odyssey* (1968) and *A Clockwork Orange* (1971). Some reviewers see a subtle falling off of quality in his *Barry Lyndon* (1975) and *The Shining* (1980), though there is a critical reevaluation of the two films in process. This seems to be typical of his critical reception.

Kubrick moved to England in 1968. He lives outside of London with Christiane (now a successful painter), three golden retrievers and a mutt he found wandering forlornly along the road. He has three grown daughters. Some who know him say he can be "difficult" and "exacting."

He had agreed to meet and talk about his latest movie, *Full Metal Jacket,* a film about the Vietnam War that he produced and directed. He also cowrote the screenplay with Michael Herr, the author of *Dispatches,* and Gustav Hasford, who wrote *The Short-Timers,* the novel on which the film is based. *Full Metal Jacket* is Kubrick's first feature in seven years.

The difficult and exacting director returned from the bathroom looking a little perplexed. "I think you're right," he said. "I think this is a place where people stay. I looked around a little, opened a door, and there was this guy sitting on the edge of a bed."

"Who was he?" I asked.

"I don't know."

"What did he say?"

"Nothing. He just looked at me, and I left."

There was a long silence while we pondered the inevitable ambiguity of reality, specifically in relation to some guy sitting on a bed across the hall. Then Stanley Kubrick began the interview.

I'm not going to be asked any conceptualizing questions, right?

All the books, most of the articles I read about you—it's all conceptualizing.

Yeah, but not by me.

I thought I had to ask those kinds of questions.

No. Hell, no. That's my . . . [*He shudders.*] It's the thing I hate the worst.

Really? I've got all these questions written down in a form I thought you might require. They all sound like essay questions for the finals in a graduate philosophy seminar.

The truth is that I've always felt trapped and pinned down and harried by those questions.

Questions like [reading from notes] "Your first feature, 'Fear and Desire,' in 1953, concerned a group of soldiers lost behind enemy lines in an unnamed war; 'Spartacus' contained some battle scenes; 'Paths of Glory' was an indictment of war and, more specifically, of the generals who wage it; and 'Dr. Strangelove' was the blackest of comedies about accidental nuclear war. How does 'Full Metal Jacket' complete your examination of the subject of war? Or does it?"

Those kinds of questions.

You feel the real question lurking behind all the verbiage is "What does this new movie mean?"

Exactly. And that's almost impossible to answer, especially when you've been so deeply inside the film for so long. Some people demand a five-line capsule summary. Something you'd read in a magazine. They want you to say, "This is the story of the duality of man and the duplicity of governments." [A pretty good description of the subtext that informs *Full Metal Jacket*, actually.] I hear people try to do it—give the five-line summary—but if a film has any substance or subtlety, whatever you say is never complete, it's usually wrong, and it's necessarily simplistic: truth is too multifaceted to be contained in a five-line summary. If the work is good, what you say about it is usually irrelevant.

So let's talk about the music in "Full Metal Jacket." I was surprised by some of the choices, stuff

like *"These Boots Are Made for Walkin',"" by Nancy Sinatra. What does that song mean?*

It was the music of the period. The Tet offensive was in '68. Unless we were careless, none of the music is post-'68.

I'm not saying it's anachronistic. It's just that the music that occurs to me in that context is more, oh, Jimi Hendrix, Jim Morrison.

The music really depended on the scene. We checked through *Billboard*'s list of Top 100 hits for each year from 1962 to 1968. We were looking for interesting material that played well with a scene. We tried a lot of songs. Sometimes the dynamic range of the music was too great, and we couldn't work in dialogue. The music has to come up under speech at some point, and if all you hear is the bass, it's not going to work in the context of the movie.

Why? Don't you like "These Boots Are Made for Walkin' "?

Of the music in the film, I'd have to say I'm more partial to Sam the Sham's "Wooly Bully," which is one of the great party records of all time. And "Surfin' Bird."

An amazing piece, isn't it?

"Surfin' Bird" comes in during the aftermath of a battle, as the marines are passing a medevac helicopter. The scene reminded me of "Dr. Strangelove," where the plane is being refueled in midair with that long, suggestive tube, and the music in the background is "Try a Little Tenderness." Or the cosmic waltz in "2001," where the spacecraft is slowly cartwheeling through space in time to "The Blue Danube." And now you have the chopper and the "Bird."

What I love about the music in that scene is that is suggests postcombat euphoria—which you see in the marine's face when he fires at the men running out of the building: He misses the first four, waits a beat, then hits the next two. And that great look on his face, that look of euphoric pleasure, the pleasure one has read described in so many accounts of combat. So he's got this look on his face, and suddenly the music starts and the tanks are rolling and the marines are mopping up. The choices weren't arbitrary.

You seem to have skirted the issue of drugs in "Full Metal Jacket."

It didn't seem relevant. Undoubtedly, marines took drugs in Vietnam. But this drug thing, it seems to suggest that all marines were out of control, when in fact they weren't. It's a little thing, but check out the pictures taken during the battle of Hue: You see marines in fully fastened flak jackets. Well, people hated wearing them. They were heavy and hot, and sometimes people wore them but didn't fasten them. Disciplined troops wore them, and they wore them fastened.

People always look at directors, and you in particular, in the context of a body of work. I couldn't help but notice some resonance with "Paths of Glory" at the end of "Full Metal Jacket": a woman surrounded by enemy soldiers, the odd, ambiguous gesture that ties these people together.

That resonance is an accident. The scene comes straight out of Gustav Hasford's book.

So your purpose wasn't to poke the viewer in the ribs, point out certain similarities . . .

Oh, God, no. I'm trying to be true to the material. You know, there's another extraordinary accident. Cowboy is dying, and in the background there's something that looks very much like the monolith in *2001*. And it just happened to be there.

You don't think you're going to get away with that, do you?

[*Laughs*] I know it's an amazing coincidence.

Where were those scenes filmed?

We worked from still photographs of Hue in 1968. And we found an area that had the same 1930s functionalist architecture. Now, not every bit of it was right, but some of the buildings were absolute carbon copies of the outer industrial areas of Hue.

Where was it?

Here. Near London. It had been owned by British Gas, and it was scheduled to be demolished. So they allowed us to blow up the buildings. We had demolition guys in there for a week, laying charges. One Sunday, all the executives from British Gas brought their families down to watch us blow the place up. It was spectacular. Then we had a wrecking ball there for two months, with the art director telling the operator which hole to knock in which building.

Art direction with a wrecking ball.

I don't think anybody's ever had a set like that. It's beyond any kind of economic possibility. To make that kind of three-dimensional rubble, you'd have to have everything done by plasterers, modeled, and you couldn't build that if you spent $80 million and had five years to do it. You couldn't duplicate, oh, all those twisted bits of reinforcement. And to make rubble, you'd have to go find some real rubble and copy it. It's the only way. If you're going to make a tree, for instance, you have to copy a real tree. No one can "make up" a tree, because every tree has an inherent logic in the way it branches. And I've discovered that no one can make up a rock. I found that out in *Paths of Glory*. We had to copy rocks, but every rock also has an inherent logic you're not aware of until you see a fake rock. Every detail looks right, but something's wrong.

So we had real rubble. We brought in palm trees from Spain and a hundred thousand plastic tropical plants from Hong Kong. We did little things, details people don't notice right away, that add to the illusion. All in all, a tremendous set dressing and rubble job.

How do you choose your material?

I read. I order books from the States. I literally go into bookstores, close my eyes and take things off the shelf. If I don't like the book after a bit, I don't finish it. But I like to be surprised.

"Full Metal Jacket" is based on Gustav Hasford's book "The Short-Timers."

It's a very short, very beautifully and economically written book, which, like the film, leaves out all the mandatory scenes of character development: the scene where the guy talks about his father, who's an alcoholic, his girlfriend—all that stuff that bogs down and seems so arbitrarily inserted into every war story.

What I like about not writing original material—which I'm not even certain I could do—is that you have this tremendous advantage of reading something for the first time. You never have this experience again with the story. You have a reaction to it; it's a kind of fallin'-in-love reaction.

That's the first thing. Then it becomes almost a matter of code-breaking, of breaking the work down into a structure that is truthful, that doesn't lose the ideas or the content or the feeling of the book. And fitting it all into the much more limited time frame of a movie.

And as long as you possibly can, you retain your emotional attitude, whatever it was that made you fall in love in the first place. You judge a scene by asking yourself, "Am I still responding to what's there?" The process is both analytical and emotional. You're trying to balance calculating analysis against feeling. And it's almost never a question of "What does this scene mean?" It's "Is this truthful, or does something about it feel false?" It's "Is this scene interesting? Will it make me feel the way I felt when I first fell in love with the material?" It's an intuitive process, the way I imagine writing music is intuitive. It's not a matter of structuring an argument.

You said something almost exactly the opposite once.

Did I?

Someone had asked you if there was any analogy between chess and filmmaking. You said that the process of making decisions was very analytical in both cases. You said that depending on intuition was a losing proposition.

I suspect I might have said that in another context. The part of the film that involves telling the story works pretty much the way I said. In the actual making of the movie, the chess analogy becomes more valid. It has to do with tournament chess, where you have a clock and you have to make a certain number of moves in a certain time. If you don't, you forfeit, even if you're a queen ahead. You'll see a grandmaster, the guy has three minutes on the clock and ten moves left. And he'll spend two minutes on one move, because he knows that if he doesn't get that one right, the game will be lost. And then he makes the last nine moves in a minute. And he may have done the right thing.

Well, in filmmaking, you always have decisions like that. You are always pitting time and resources against quality and ideas.

You have a reputation for having your finger on every aspect of each film you make, from inception right on down to the premiere and beyond. How is it that you're allowed such an extraordinary amount of control over your films?

I'd like to think it's because my films have a quality that holds up on second, third and fourth viewing. Realistically, it's because my budgets are within reasonable limits and the films do well. The only one that did poorly from the studio's point of view was *Barry Lyndon*. So, since my films don't cost that much, I find a way to spend a little extra time in order to get the quality on the screen.

"Full Metal Jacket" seemed a long time in the making.

Well, we had a couple of severe accidents. The guy who plays the drill instructor, Lee Ermey, had an auto accident in the middle of shooting. It was about one in the morning, and his car skidded off the road. He broke all his ribs on one side, just tremendous injuries, and he probably would have died, except he was conscious and kept flashing his lights. A motorist stopped. It was in a place called Epping Forest, where the police are always finding bodies. Not the sort of place you get out of your car at one-thirty in the morning and go see why someone's flashing their lights. Anyway, Lee was out for four and a half months.

He had actually been a marine drill instructor?

Parris Island.

How much of his part comes out of that experience?

I'd say 50 percent of Lee's dialogue, specifically the insult stuff, came from Lee. You see, in the course of hiring the marine recruits, we interviewed hundreds of guys. We lined them all up and did an improvisation of the first meeting with the drill instructor. They didn't know what he was going to say, and we could see how they reacted. Lee came up with, I don't know, 150 pages of insults. Off the wall stuff: "I don't like the name Lawrence. Lawrence is for faggots and sailors."

Aside from the insults, though, virtually every serious thing he says is basically true. When he says, "A rifle is only a tool, it's a hard heart that kills," you know it's true. Unless you're living in a world that doesn't need fighting men, you can't fault him. Except maybe for a certain lack of subtlety in his behavior. And I don't think the United States Marine Corps is in the market for subtle drill instructors.

This is a different drill instructor than the one Lou Gosset played in "An Officer and a Gentleman."

I think Lou Gosset's performance was wonderful, but he had to do what he was given in the story. The film clearly wants to ingratiate itself with the audience. So many films do that. You show the drill instructor really has a heart of gold—the mandatory scene where he sits in his office, eyes swimming with pride about the boys and so forth. I suppose he actually is proud, but there's a danger of falling into what amounts to so much sentimental bullshit.

So you distrust sentimentality.

I don't mistrust sentiment and emotion, no. The question becomes, are you giving them something to make them a little happier, or are you putting in something that is inherently true to the material? Are people behaving the way we all really behave, or are they behaving the way we would like them to behave? I mean, the world is not as it's presented in Frank Capra films. People love those films—which are beautifully made—but I wouldn't describe them as a true picture of life.

The questions are always, is it true? Is it interesting? To worry about those mandatory scenes that some people think make a picture is often just pandering to some conception of an audience. Some films try to outguess an audience. They try to ingratiate themselves, and it's not something you really have to do. Certainly audiences have flocked to see films that are not essentially true, but I don't think this prevents them from responding to the truth.

Books I've read on you seem to suggest that you consider editing the most important aspect of the filmmaker's art.

There are three equal things: the writing, slogging through the actual shooting and the editing.

You've quoted Pudovkin to the effect that editing is the only original and unique art form in film.

I think so. Everything else comes from something else. Writing, of course, is writing, acting comes from the theater, and cinematography comes from photography. Editing is unique to film. You can see something from different points of view almost simultaneously, and it creates a new experience.

TV commercials have figured that out. Leave content out of it, and some of the most spectacular examples of film art are in the best TV commercials.

Give me an example.

The Michelob commercials. I'm a pro-football fan, and I have videotapes of the games sent over to me, commercials and all. Last year Michelob did a series, just impressions of people having a good time—

The big city at night—

And the editing, the photography, was some of the most brilliant work I've ever seen. Forget what they're doing—selling beer—and it's visual poetry. Incredible eight-frame cuts. And you realize that in thirty seconds they've created an impression of something rather complex. If you could ever tell a story, something with some content, using that kind of visual poetry, you could handle vastly more complex and subtle material.

People spend millions of dollars and months' worth of work on those thirty seconds.

So it's a bit impractical. And I suppose there's really nothing that would substitute for the great dramatic moment, fully played out. Still, the stories we do on film are basically rooted in the theater. Even Woody Allen's movies, which are wonderful, are very traditional in their structure. Did I get the year right on those Michelob ads?

I think so.

Because occasionally I'll find myself watching a game from 1984.

It amazes me that you're a pro-football fan.

Why?

It doesn't fit my image of you.

Which is . . .

Stanley Kubrick is a monk, a man who lives for his work and virtually nothing else, certainly not pro football. And then there are those rumors—

I know what's coming.

You want both barrels?

Fire.

Stanley Kubrick is a perfectionist. He is consumed by mindless anxiety over every aspect of every film he makes. Kubrick is a hermit, an expatriate, a neurotic who is terrified of automobiles and who won't let his chauffeur drive more than thirty miles an hour.

Part of my problem is that I cannot dispel the myths that have somehow accumulated over the years. Somebody writes something, it's completely off-the-wall, but it gets filed and repeated until everyone believes it. For instance, I've read that I wear a football helmet in the car.

You won't let your driver go more than thirty miles an hour, and you wear a football helmet, just in case.

In fact, I don't have a chauffeur. I drive a Porsche 928 S, and I sometimes drive it at eighty or ninety miles an hour on the motorway.

Your film editor says you still work on your old films. Isn't that neurotic perfectionism?

I'll tell you what he means. We discovered that the studio had lost the picture negative of *Dr. Strangelove.* And they also lost the magnetic master soundtrack. All the printing negatives were badly ripped dupes. The search went on for a year and a half. Finally, I had to try to reconstruct the picture from two not-too-good fine-grain positives, both of which were damaged already. If those fine-grains were ever torn, you could never make any more negatives.

Do you consider yourself an expatriate?

Because I direct films, I have to live in a major English-speaking production center. That narrows it down to three places: Los Angeles, New York and London. I like New York, but it's inferior to London as a production center. Hollywood is best, but I don't like living there.

You read books or see films that depict people being corrupted by Hollywood, but it isn't that. It's this tremendous sense of insecurity. A lot of destructive competitiveness. In comparison, England seems very remote. I try to keep up, read the trade papers, but it's good to get it on paper and not have to hear it everyplace you go. I think it's good to just do the work and insulate yourself from that undercurrent of low-level malevolence.

I've heard rumors that you'll do a hundred takes for one scene.

It happens when actors are unprepared. You cannot act without knowing dialogue. If actors have to think about the words, they can't work on the emotion. So you end up doing thirty takes of something. And still you can see the concentration in their eyes; they don't know their lines. So you just shoot it and shoot it and hope you can get something out of it in pieces.

Now, if the actor is a nice guy, he goes home, he says, "Stanley's such a perfectionist, he does a hundred takes on every scene." So my thirty takes become a hundred. And I get this reputation.

Initial reviews of most of your films are sometimes inexplicably hostile. Then there's a reevaluation. Critics seem to like you better in retrospect.

That's true. The first reviews of *2001* were insulting, let alone bad. An important Los Angeles critic faulted *Paths of Glory* because the actors didn't speak with French accents. When *Dr. Strangelove* came out, a New York paper ran a review under the head MOSCOW COULD NOT BUY MORE HARM TO AMERICA. Something like that. But critical opinion on my films has always been salvaged by what I would call subsequent critical opinion. Which is why I think audiences are more reliable than critics, at least initially. Audiences tend not to bring all that critical baggage with them to each film.

And I really think that a few critics come to my films expecting to see the last film. They're waiting to see something that never happens. I imagine it must be something like standing in the batter's box waiting for a fastball, and the pitcher throws a change-up. The batter swings and misses. He thinks, "Shit, he threw me the wrong pitch." I think this accounts for some of the initial hostility.

Well, you don't make it easy on viewers or critics. You've said you want an audience to react emotionally. You create strong feelings, but you won't give us any easy answers.

That's because I don't have any easy answers.

Francis Ford Coppola

By David Breskin

FEBRUARY 7, 1991

In the last decade of disappointment and disaster, Francis Ford Coppola lost his studio and his audience and his fortune; lost his artistic instincts and his confidence; and lost, above all, a son. What he never lost was his desire to make art.

But given his position as a rusted boy wonder, he'd have to make more than art: He'd have to make commerce. Enter *Godfather, Part III,* his bid for both financial and artistic redemption, his ticket to the third act of his own life. With the film released to a riotous orgy of opinion, Coppola found himself with a sharp stone in his shoe: The casting and performance of his nineteen-year-old daughter, Sofia, in one of the film's key roles, provoked a barrage of criticism. (In the reviews, his daughter was killed, but the bullets were meant for him.) That Coppola would risk so much on family—for family— says everything about a man for whom the border between life and art long ago collapsed. Coppola talked about such matters early last November in the penthouse office-bedroom of the building he owns in San Francisco.

In "Godfather, Part II," consigliere Tom Hagen, upon finding the dead prostitute, says: "The girl has
no family. It's as if she didn't exist." And he repeats it, like a mantra. It's another sign of the centrality of the family in your work—that family is how you do exist—so I'd like you to start by talking about yours.

Well, I was born in 1939 and raised in a second-generation Italian-American family, so my infant memories of World War II and that era were the first things to consider. Also, because my father was a musician, we traveled a lot. It was in my father's gypsy nature not to stay in any one place too long.

I thought that our moving every year, and the many schools I went to because of it, tended to let me encapsulate *time* differently. In some way it allowed me to remember things in a much more vivid way than kids who are just raised in one neighborhood. I went to twenty-five different schools before college. Each one was a little episode of my life—ages four and five and six and seven—like a separate movie with a separate cast of characters. My childhood, and my memories of my childhood, have always remained very vital to me and very *accessible*. I may have only been in a particular neighborhood for six months, but I still remember what the pretty girl's name was and what the bad boy's name was.

Francis Ford Coppola and Al Pacino converse on the set of *The Godfather*.
Copyright © 1996 by Paramount Pictures. All rights reserved.

We were a family of five. A brother five years older [Augie] and a sister six years younger [Talia Shire]. My mother [Italia] was an extremely good-looking woman, and my father [Carmine] was very handsome and in a glamorous profession—I saw him dress in a tuxedo. My initial memories of them were very idealized and very full of love. My brother was very nice to me, and we had all sorts of uncles and aunts in that sort of second-generation Italian family.

My first impression of family was that it was very much like a fairy tale. We were taught that Italians had great culture. And my father was the solo flute player for Toscanini. So there was always an element of glamour and romance to my family, and to this day, if I do gravitate to them or they are the wellspring of my fondness, it's because from when I was a little kid, they were.

Yet there was a lot of tension there as well. Your father dominated the scene, and there was always the risk that he was failing or would fail. He was dissatisfied as an artist, even if he was at a fairly high level.

He was at a high level as an instrumentalist, but in those days it wasn't like today—where a virtuoso flute player is on records and is a celebrity. He always had ambitions to write music, to do Broadway, to conduct opera. He longed for recognition in areas other than playing the flute. So he weaned himself off at that nice, comfortable career as a symphonic instrumentalist and started to branch off into other areas. One was movies. In fact, when I was born, he had just gotten back from Hollywood. He'd been there a couple of years and had tried to get started as a film scorer, making connections.

Was his level of frustration, what he perceived as his failure, painful for you?

Oh, yeah. Yeah. Literally, when we said our prayers, in the end we said, ". . . and give Daddy his break." Even before I knew what "his break"

was. I thought it was the brake of the car! The way they saw things, getting your break was political—it was who you knew. Even to this day, I take great exception to this attitude. I always felt it was your talent and your willingness to keep working; if no one will hire you to do a play, then to go do the play anyway. A glancing difference between my father and I is that I feel talent can be realized by hard work and imaginative application. It's not politics, it's not who you know.

It's ironic that he got his big break scoring your movies—he did know you.

[Laughs] I know. We were very involved in my father's talent. That was the focus of our family. If I went to school and said my father was a soloist for Toscanini, people thought I was special—even though I was new in the neighborhood.

You idolized your older brother, Augie [Nicolas Cage's father]—he was older than you, better looking, smarter, more successful socially—but wasn't it hard not to resent him for that?

But he was always so *kind* to me. And so affectionate. And so generous. He didn't have to take me to the movies and introduce me to his friends. Rather than be competitive with him, I just wanted to be like him.

Wasn't there anger under the surface? That your dad and his "talent" was always the focus of attention and that you were not considered as talented as he or Augie?

I never had a big competitive thing. I just wanted to be accepted by them. I never had those kind of needs to be a famous person. I don't think there was any anger connected to it, because for me, my ambition was more to have a year's subscription to *Popular Mechanics*.

We're going to cut to the record, Francis. When you were nine, you wrote your mother a note that said:

"Dear Mommy, I want to be rich and famous. I'm so discouraged. I don't think it will come true."

She *has* that note. I think I was older and already pursuing the drama and show-business world. I always felt I had a lot of gifts but that my gifts were somehow not easily showable. I was not good at anything, except science.

You had polio and were paralyzed for a year when you were ten and described yourself as "a lonely ugly duckling, sad and sick and thinking." How much of that kid do you still carry around or did you carry in your formative artistic years?

Well, I would say that my childhood years are very vividly what I'm like now. And what happened after that didn't make much of a difference. Polio, and the fact that I was the new kid in school every year, and that my name was Francis, which was a girl's name. And I was very skinny and looked like Ichabod—gangly. And I had a very big lower lip—which was the bane of my life, my lower lip. Of everything, the thing most profound to me is the shape of my lower lip. Everything that happened came from this condition.

And in 1949 I was struck with polio, taken out of school and didn't see another kid except my sister. Sitting in that room, paralyzed, watching television, listening to the radio, playing with my puppets, cultivated a kind of make-believe private life, augmented by technology. I became obsessed with remote control. Obviously, if you're paralyzed, how to turn the channel of the TV is very important.

Do you ever think now, sitting off the set in the Silverfish [Coppola's Airstream trailer, from which he monitors the shooting], that the idea of "remote" and the idea of "control" have been realized in a quite substantial, quite personal way?

There's no doubt that it goes back to that year I spent in bed—looking at a monitor, listening to radio. I spent a lot of time with my puppets; I became quite a puppeteer. I'm sure that my taste for directing—being this person doing it all by remote control—probably comes from something I was comfortable with as a kid.

So I lived a tremendous fantasy life, all my life. And I still do. I spend most of my time by myself. And I do the same kinds of things I used to do: I play with the technology, I edit, I make-believe. The same things I did in the garage.

Was there a Rosebud in your youth—something unrecoverable?

I would say that the five-year-old Francis, who was the *best* Francis that there ever was, is still here, intact, whenever I choose to be comfortable with that. I do still approach things with that enthusiasm. And in a man, the line between enthusiasm and megalomania is very blurry.

Early in your career, you were a very ambitious, driven man—you felt like the greatest thing around if people liked a picture and an abject failure if they didn't.

Very much so. And now, at age fifty-one, in terms of my ego, I really have taken myself off the market in terms of ever really being gratified. Gratified in the way I saw, let's say, Peter Bogdanovich gratified once when I saw the screening of *The Last Picture Show*. I remember that very vividly. Boy, that audience saw that picture, and that audience was *with* that picture in such a fabulous way that when it was over, everybody in that theater, including myself, stood up and gave him a standing ovation. It was thrilling to be there. But I've never experienced anything like that. Except once, when I did a college play, the cast gave me an ovation like that. But never again since. And I sort have reconciled myself that that will never happen to me, except maybe when I'm eighty years old and they trudge me out to give me some humanitarian award. In other words, I have taken myself "off the hook" on a number of issues that young people fantasize about. And that's one of them.

Was your son Gio's death [in a boating accident in 1986] a part of taking yourself off the hook, in a way?

Well, sure, but I'm not sure I even totally understand that event, because I've never been able to look at it in front of my eyes. I always look at it this way. [*He looks out of the corners of his eyes.*] And as the years go by, I realize I don't want to look at it.

After that, I realized that no matter what happened, I had *lost*. That no matter what happened, it would always be incomplete. The next day, I could have all my fondest dreams come true: Someone could give me Paramount Pictures to organize the way I would do it and develop talent and technology. And even if I did get it, I lost already. There's no way I could ever have a complete experience, because there will always be that part of me missing. It makes you react to things with more of a shrug. If you told me that people saw my *Godfather* film and thought it was the greatest thing since chopped liver and for the first time in ten years I can go out and buy a car without figuring how I'm going to pay for it, I would be happy, but in the end it would make me sad.

If "Godfather III" is a success, it would make you sad?

No. It's just that anything that makes me happy is always followed by a footnote of being sad. Because what I really wish could happen is already gone. You can see a picture of my two kids, Roman and Sofia, taken after that accident happened, and it's a picture of *three* kids. Because you can see on their faces the one that's missing. I try to understand. That's what makes us human beings. Would you rather be a rock? Would you rather not have those feelings? That's why tragedy is such an exalted art form.

Once the trauma wears off, you never experience the world again in quite the same way.

Aeschylus said something really beautiful, something like "This thing pours on your heart, drop by drop, until in awful grace of God comes wisdom." In a way, you *can't* experience things in a bigger, deeper way, until you understand or have some tragedy.

I was always a magical kid. All I had to do was say a Hail Mary, and it would come true. That story Fredo tells in *Godfather II*—every time you say a Hail Mary you catch a fish—that was me! I once caught twenty-two fish because I said twenty-two Hail Marys. And then all of a sudden, you say the Hail Mary and it doesn't work, in the most profound sense you could imagine. It just makes you realize that being a human being is not to have everything go the way a child wants it to go.

In a sense, losing a kid like that, that particular kid, the relationship we had, it will just be my story. [*Pauses, teary*] I always was shocked that Odysseus comes back and his son, Telemachus, rejoins him, and I didn't know that in the next chapters Telemachus is killed. Oh! You never told me that! It gives it another slant. It's your stripes for being a human being. You have to understand it in the bigger sense of things. And of course, I have two great kids, and we all share the vitality of that boy, and in some funny way he still figures into things; he's still around in a magical way. He was a magical kid. We got him for so many years. And for the twenty-two years he lived, he had a complete life; someone could live eighty years and not do what he did. It's not like I'm a *broken* guy. But in a way, there's always going to be that arm missing. It'll never come back, I guess.

If it takes the edge off the successes, perhaps it also might take the edge off the failures you'll no doubt encounter—they might not be as devastating from now on.

I'm less interested in successes or failures, quite frankly, at all. The thing about the failures: I still have that new-kid-in-school thing, I hate to be *embarrassed*. It's very embarrassing to be taken to task all the time in the newspapers, and all your neighbors see it and they don't want to bring it up. I never have been such a megalomaniac that it is not very easy to hurt my feelings.

Is that one of the reasons you're threatened to leave Hollywood filmmaking? From your second feature on, in 1967, you've been threatening to go make cheap, little "amateur" movies on your own.

My happiest thing is to be *cozy*. Just to have a little place, my own thing, a little shop. It could be opulent, but it would always be cozy. And I would like my career to be cozy. I envy people like Woody Allen, who has found a way to function: He writes a script every year, he makes a movie every year, and people find it interesting.

Weren't there times, at the height of your success, where you wondered, "Is this me?" It happened in such a hurry.

I was the first one! It wasn't like Hollywood was filled with young people. There had been Orson Welles, the boy wonder, who was an example for everyone. But generally, the motion-picture industry was closed—men in their fifties who had worked in the studio system. So for me, not only was I one of the first young people in a generation that had fallen in love with film, but I was also one of the first young people to become rich overnight. I was interested in the communications age. What was my dream here twenty years ago? I bought a radio station, a theater, a magazine, a film company. I was already thinking about the kind of communications company that these guys are supposedly

thinking about now, except I was doing it. And I was greeted with general resistance: Who is this megalomaniac and what is he doing? God, how many of all the filmmakers who have made money have put any of that money into their love? George Lucas, that's it. And why George Lucas? Because he is my younger brother in a way, and so George did a lot of things that we cooked up together. I don't see any of these other fortunes going into anything other than hard securities. Now it's people saying: Let's make movies that have incredible chase scenes, that have violence, let's make *Die Hard*. That's not coming out of young men and women involved in something *alive*. That's not alive.

To be really respected in this culture is not about being courageous and having imaginative ideas, it's about being financially successful. The real decision on how good *Godfather III* really is will be made not on the basis of whether it has an independent life as a work of art but on the basis of how much money it makes. It's sad.

I was very crestfallen during *Apocalypse Now* that America didn't see me there in the Philippines with an American flag, saying, "I claim this for the American film industry!" I wanted to be thought of as American and that America would be proud that if I had $30 million of my own money that I would fearlessly invest it in a movie that had serious themes. I was crushed that they ridiculed *Apocalypse* because it seemed to be such an out-of-control financial boondoggle, and yet for *Superman*, which cost so much and was about nothing, there was respect.

Why were people rooting for you to fail?

Because I had had a big success with *The Godfather*, and then I tempted fate and had another success with *Godfather II*. That's enough. That's *enough*.

In "Godfather III," some of your associates were

upset that you cast your own daughter, Sofia, as Michael Corleone's.

Look, we make decisions every day that my associates banter and argue about. What went on in this movie is no different. A lot of times I put people in movies that I have a gut reaction about that other people don't see. Al Pacino in the first *Godfather* is the biggest example. There wasn't a chorus of approval.

I knew you had to fight hard for him. You had to fight even harder for Marlon Brando!

I could give you fifteen examples. All these Paramount guys were hovering around. It was bullshit. They wanted to have a famous chick in there with Andy Garcia! It got very weird. I said: "Look, guys, get off my set. Get out of here. You had nothing to do with the first two *Godfather* pictures. Don't *bug* me now."

What you must have figured out by now is that I made a casting choice. Sofia was right for the part, and no one else on the horizon was. That character has to do something very specific. I was thrilled to have gotten Winona Ryder [the original choice for the role]. I went way out of my way to accommodate her, 'cause she was coming late to the picture. And so when she couldn't do it, I had nowhere else to turn, and I reached out for my daughter, more as I always do with members of my family, because I knew I could count on her. The thing about Sofia is she's real, she's authentic.

Paramount was ready to just fly Madonna in there. It's got to be Diane Keaton's daughter! It's got to look like Al! If you've seen the stills, Sofia looks like their daughter. It was *casting.* If she had not been my daughter but had been the baby-sitter that I had seen on the set, I might have done the same thing. If I had felt that the girl had enough stuff to come across.

There was a lot of commotion on the set. And Sofia cried. And I talked to her that night and said, "What do you think, Sofie? Do you have the guts to try this, 'cause I think you're right for the part, and if I don't cast you, I don't know who I'm going to cast. I'd rather cast you—and we'll do it together and nurse our way through it—than have them send some thirty-five-year-old actress because they want to put her on the cover of a movie with Andy Garcia." And she said she'd do it. She had the guts to do it.

If Sofia was a kid when "Godfather III" started, she's certainly not anymore.

No, she's retained it. She had a big finger pointed at her, and she was tough enough. I wouldn't have subjected her to it otherwise.

At the end of 1987, you were still saying you had no interest in gangsters—

I don't!

—and you would not do "Godfather III" because you'd just have to tell the story again, which you were loath to do. By the end of 1988, you were in. What changed your mind?

I really felt that if they gave me carte blanche to do *Godfather III,* I might have an opportunity to do something artistic. All I needed was a concept to be interested in, so I wouldn't think it was just drivel. And then I started to think about all that had happened to me—now that I'm older—all those thoughts that a man has: God, I've made mistakes, will my children love me, am I leaving anything, really? And I realized I could approach Michael more as that kind of man. That he could be older, that he could be a kind of King Lear.

I thought I had one last card to play, which is Michael's dialogue with himself about his morality. Was he a good man or a bad man? If he was a good man, how does he feel about how he stained himself? If he was a bad man, how does he feel about his hypocrisy in relation to his children? With younger people, you want to portray yourself as a good person because you want them to believe in good. So, just in itself, that was interesting to me. And then I began to think I could do it in a Shakespearean play. So I thought if I work on it, if I stay up enough nights on it, maybe I'll be able to get a handle on it. And that's why I attempted to do it. And if I am able to bring Michael Corleone to life and he's a man in the third act of his life, then it will have been a success.

Let's go back to your period as a director for hire: "The Cotton Club," "Peggy Sue Got Married," "Gardens of Stone." Was that a dark period for you?

Well, I knew that I was in trouble. And a lot of things in my life were falling apart. I was fighting to keep my home. And my response to trouble is to work hard. That's my conditioned response. I was digging myself out of a hole. I enjoyed making *Rumble Fish* very much, making a stylistic flight of fancy. *Tucker* was pleasant being with George Lucas again. I didn't like the script for *Peggy Sue Got Married;* but it's like with a girl and she isn't really "the one"—after you get to know her, you find something about her that you like. I can't say I dislike any of my films. Every one of them has something endearing, or interesting, or that I was able to enjoy.

Did you ever feel in those years like Natalie in "The Rain People," who says to her husband, "I used to wake up and it was my day . . . and now it belongs to you"? Did you feel then that your day belonged to the studios and the lawyers?

I've felt that throughout my career. I felt that on *Godfather III.* I thought there were unreasonable demands being made on me, as far as time. I thought if I could have made it over a slightly longer period of time that I could have finished the script before we were cast. I feel like that little bit of rush turned a difficult job into an even more difficult job. Every day I have to be worried about something? Would it really have

been a less good work if it came out six months later? What's the difference? Paramount waited for sixteen years—they couldn't get it together—why do I gotta do it in sixteen months?

At the same time, I also know that pressure can bring out good things that wouldn't come if you didn't have your back up against the wall.

Do you see your life as a tragedy?

No, not at all. I have a great family. I have a wonderful career. Even if I was to be, with *Godfather III,* disgraced as I was in the past, I'm a very flexible kind of artist. There are a million options. I could direct a soap opera and probably enjoy it. I could write. I could do something technical. I love comedy. There's no project I couldn't direct. But everybody's life is tragic. That's why we read the Greeks. Human life is tragic. Everybody's life. And in that sense my life is a tragedy, but only in that sense.

For a time, you said you wanted to leave the ending of "Apocalypse Now" vague, because you wanted your own life to answer the question of whether Willard stays at the Kurtz compound, in the heart of madness, or comes back down the river. Do you feel you've come back down the river?

I feel I have really. I still get . . . I, I'm a depressive person. A manic-depressive person.

Have you been diagnosed as such by doctors?

Yeah.

Have you ever tried to take medications?

I did for a while, a few years. But I didn't like it, it made me nauseous all the time, and I felt I ought to be able to arrive at some sort of stability more through my mind. Although they say it's chemical. But I didn't like the thought that I was going to be on this medication, and I just stopped. They said, "You'll be depressed," so I said, "Well, I'll be depressed." They said, "Just don't shoot yourself."

My wife just gave me this William Styron book on depression. She said I should read it because I sound like him. I can get depressed. I can get sad. I wonder: "What am I doing? Am I doing what I want to be doing? Everything is so hard. Nobody likes me. I've done so much good, and yet I'm fifty-one years old and I'm in exactly the same situation as when I was twenty-five. I've got this little company that's always on the verge of bankruptcy." I can get pretty depressed.

Are you ever afraid that medication would take the edge off the creativity?

Although they say that it doesn't, you wonder about that. I'm such a person of such enthusiastic fits, I may stay up all night to do something. When I was taking it . . .

How long ago was that?

I haven't taken it for about maybe three years. But I took it after *Apocalypse* for about four years. This was lithium. I always maintained that if I could get the elements of my life into a little more reasonable harmony . . . I wouldn't have so many depressed times if I didn't have so many problems. But then my wife says that's not true.

That you would create them.

Yeah. So I'm hoping now if I get a breather—I'm in pretty good shape physically. I'm very strong. I've never, ever been sick. Even in *Apocalypse,* the so-called nervous-breakdown phase was more, I think, related to the fact that I was doing all these things that I hadn't done before. I was smoking cigarettes. I never smoked cigarettes. I was smoking grass. I had never smoked grass.

There was talk you had a bad cocaine habit.

Never. I never was a cocaine type. The only drug I really experienced was grass. I had cocaine three times in my life, and it wasn't good for me. I don't understand its appeal. I'd tell you if I did. The only drug I ever used was grass. And all of it recently, during [and since] *Apocalypse.*

And I was in, you know, like love triangles, and I was tired, and Marty [Sheen] had just had a heart attack, and it was my own money, and I didn't feel good about my relationship with my wife. I didn't feel my wife understood me. She was always very conventional in her thinking, like everybody else. A lot of things I do at first are not popular, and I am hungry for some approval or encouragement. I felt she was meddling and lining up with the people that I . . .

What I learned was that when you are really overwhelmed with problems, it's easy to faint on the floor or have an epileptic fit.

You used to have convulsive fits in front of people to get what you wanted, didn't you? Back at UCLA film school, or trying to get Brando cast in "The Godfather"?

I am an epileptic, and these fits are real. I never did it to get something. But at a moment of weakness, it's always a voluntary option. I think even to a real epileptic. But the difference is it's an easy step to do it but a very hard step to get back. That was an interesting thing I learned.

I was exhausted. The cigarettes, more than anything else, were making me weird. The personal relationships were changing—up until the *Apocalypse* period, I'd been pretty innocent: The romances I'd had were pretty conventional, schoolboy kind of romances.

Male artists often use the power or presence of a female to get them going to help them create.

There is something to be said—whether it's real or just conditioning—for the idea that a girl can be a muse. Especially a girl who has confidence in you. See, I never felt that my wife had any confidence in me. And her confidence in me made me feel confident. And then when all that got disrupted, I was floating around. Now I attach more importance to how my kids are. It's more like an older person's point of view.

Values shift as you age.

You're not as *hungry* for stuff as you were. I'm not as hungry for that kind of woman—that kind of succubus. They're just real creatures. But as a younger man I always idealized them so much.

What saved your marriage?

I think the bottom line is that a man like me operates with a kind of lodestone of loyalty and commitment to his family that in the end is not easily disrupted. In the end, you do what you feel is right, and what you feel is right comes from your upbringing, your family. In the end, I realized you could change wives every ten years and be in the same situation. And that it's better to just have one wife. That marriage is best in the long term.

It could all work out really nicely. I still have my company, and I like the company now more than I have. It seems to run more evenly, logically. I like this role of the gray eminence. People *want* to come see me, talk to me. The young director working on something wants my opinion. I like that. The grandfather.

Well, when you become a grandfather . . . you see what my granddaughter looks like? [*He walks across the room to show a photo of Gio's daughter, born after his death.*] This is Gia. [*He then points to a photo of Sofia, removes it from the wall and holds it in his hand.*] That's what I wanted for Michael's daughter. I wanted her to represent the part of Michael that was still pure. Any person, no matter who—Saddam Hussein, whoever the villain of the day is—there is a part of him that is sweet and kind, and it's when they lose that that they lose all. [*He looks down at the photo of Sofia.*] The real truth was the girl was like this.

Tim Burton

By David Edelstein

MAY 2, 1988

It's hard to imagine someone being instantly in sync with Pee-wee Herman, but in 1984, when twenty-six-year-old Tim Burton was asked to direct his first feature, *Pee-wee's Big Adventure,* he brought something special to the party: a passion for wacko individualists. "I believed Pee-wee," Burton says without a trace of irony. "So I thought, 'Let's just go through the movie and believe him, whatever he does.' I love extreme characters who totally believe themselves. That's why I had fun with Betelgeuse."

Betelgeuse, played by Michael Keaton, is the anarchic superspook of *Beetlejuice,* which Burton has directed like a cheerfully indulgent parent—he lets his little monsters run wild, to the exclusion of pace, point and structure. This isn't your standard, slick ghost comedy—the plot chases its own tail, and the jokes are a blend of the brainy and the infantile. The picture, a whatzit, has provoked its share of bewildered reviews. The fat guy and the other one didn't like it, and the *New York Times* said it was for people who think a shrunken head is funny.

Luckily for Burton, *millions* of people think a shrunken head is funny, especially when it sits on top of a full-size body and stares out of bulging, doleful eyes. *Beetlejuice* grossed about $32 million in its first two weeks, and Burton has relaxed and made the most of his movie's addled reception.

"I've been enjoying the bad reviews," he says ebulliently. "These bland newscasters, they have to say the word *Beetlejuice,* and they have to show a clip—and I don't care what anybody says, it makes me wanna see the movie. It's really funny. It's like you're watching some hallucination, like somebody's putting something else behind them that they don't know about. It was like the feeling I got when I saw Andy Warhol on *The Love Boat.*"

Burton, a former animator, thrives on weird juxtapositions—they're the key to his genius. His style is dork chic: He wears shapeless, oversize jackets, and his hair is shoulder length. Under heavy lids, he has sad, spacey eyes. He's the sort of guy who uses words like "nutty" without ironic emphasis, who pronounces something "great, great, great—like, so *cool*" and then, to illustrate a point, casually sketches a bizarre creature with a second head coming out of its mouth.

Amiable and unpretentious, he has a whiff of stoned melancholy about him, like someone who thinks too much and makes sense of too little. And that's where he nestles his movies, in that twilight zone between the humdrum and the flabbergasting. If the two don't quite gel, so much the better—and funnier.

"The things that interest me the most are the things that potentially won't work," Burton says. "On *Beetlejuice,* I could tell every day what was gonna work and what wasn't. And that was very invigorating. Especially when you're doing something this extreme. A lot of people have ragged on the story of *Beetlejuice,* but when I read it, I thought, 'Wow! This is sort of interesting. It's very random. It doesn't follow what I would consider the Spielberg story structure.' I guess I have to watch it more, because I'm intrigued by things that are perverse. Like, I was intrigued that there was *no story.*"

Beetlejuice is a haunted-house comedy turned inside out: Its heroes are a pair of attractive, lovable ghosts driven bats by ghoulish people. When they can't take any more, they call in the title character, a "bio-exorcist." As played by Michael Keaton, with frazzled hair, rotted teeth and fungoid cheeks, the scuzzy con man blasts the movie into slapstick heaven—he's a sleaze-ball wizard.

When Burton first read Michael McDowell's script, he thought he could have written it himself—it carried his trademark blend of the outlandish and the matter-of-fact. In *Pee-wee's Big Adventure,* for instance, the trucker Large Marge turns toward the camera and her eyes balloon out of her skull; then they retract and she goes on talking, as if nothing unusual had happened. And in *Beetlejuice,* Keaton's head spontaneously gyrates on its shoulders; when it stops, he asks, slightly peeved, "Don't ya hate it when that happens?"

The deadpan style resembles the great Warner Bros. cartoons, and the best gags are like jack-in-the-boxes—they zoom out of the screen

and then snap back in. The disorientation is exhilarating. In *Beetlejuice,* Burton deftly blurs the line between a large model of the New England town (in which Betelgeuse, bug size, makes his home), "real life" and the afterlife. Bo Welch, who designed the sets, describes it as "a hierarchy of reality that leads you into unreality. Tim would encourage me to push that border. I'd go a certain distance, and he'd say, 'Let's go further,' and I'd go, 'Arrghhh!' and then be thrilled when we did it."

Burton lets his actors push that border, too. Take, for instance, Burton's collaboration with Michael Keaton. "I turned down the role because I didn't quite get it, and I wasn't looking to work," says Keaton. In the original script, Betelgeuse was underwritten, vaguely Middle Eastern and more evil. But Burton wanted to change the tone and invited Keaton to come up with his own shtick. "It turns out the character creates his own reality," he says. "I gave myself some sort of voice, some sort of look based on the words. Then I started thinkin' about my hair: I wanted my hair to stand out like I was wired and plugged in, and once I started gettin' that, I actually made myself laugh. And once I got the basic attitude, it really started to roll."

And what was the attitude?

"The attitude is 'You write your own reality, you write your own ticket. There are no bars, I can do anything I want and under any rationality I want . . .'"

He stops himself from analyzing it too much. "At some point," he says, "you show up on the set and just go *fuckin' nuts.* It was *rave* acting. You rage for twelve or fourteen hours; then you go home tired and beat and exhausted. It was pretty damned cathartic. It was rave and *purge* acting."

"The thing I love about Michael is that he *gets into it,*" says Burton. "He'd say some funny thing that wasn't in the script, and we'd get ideas from that. I enjoyed working that way. My animation background—you sit around with a bunch of guys and talk about what would be a good idea to do. The whole cast was like that. It was this hallucination we were all involved in. We knew what we were doing, but we didn't know what we were doing."

Like Keaton, defenders of *Beetlejuice* are the first to admit its flaws. But since when do great comedies have to be seamless? As its biggest champion, Pauline Kael, wrote in *The New Yorker*, "The best of W.C. Fields was often half gummed up, and that doesn't seem to matter fifty-five years later. With crazy comedy, you settle for the spurts of inspiration, and *Beetlejuice* has them . . . enough . . . to make this spotty, dissonant movie a comedy classic."

The comedy classicist has an unlikely hometown—Burbank, or "the pit of hell," as Burton calls it. "Probably his out-of-place-ness comes from growing up there," says Bo Welch. "It's in the middle of the movie business, but it's so mundane that it forces your imagination to work overtime." As a kid, Burton loved to draw, put on shows and play pranks—like the time he covered his brother in fake gore and pretended to hack him up with a knife. (A neighbor phoned the police; Burton still shivers when he talks about it.)

From college at Cal Arts he landed a plum job with Walt Disney Studios. "They were trying to train new animators," he says. "All the old guys had retired, so what was left in charge was these second-stringers. They were older; they were bitter that they weren't the ones that were in the limelight. So a lot of things besides creativity leaked in. What drove me nuts is, here you are at Disney—'Best animation in the world,' they say. 'A dream come true.' And on the other hand, they say, 'Remove part of your brain and become a zombie factory worker.' The split that it created drove people nuts. So you either succumb to it or you leave.

"Classic example: I was at Disney, I was in animation for a year, I was totally freaked, I was so bored. They liked my designs, so they said, 'Why don't you do some for *The Black Cauldron*? Great, great, go wild.' So I spent months, I came up with everything under the sun. One thing I thought was really creepy: It had these birds and their heads would be like hands with eyes; instead of beaks there'd be hands grabbing you.

"Finally, they brought in this other guy, Andreas, that you would consider classic Disney—cutesy little animals and stuff. And it was, 'Your stuff's a little, kinda out there, Tim, but we want to get you together with this guy—maybe the two of you can come up with, like, Disney but, like, a little different.' By the end of two weeks, we didn't get along—he was doing his thing and I was doing mine. He'd take my drawings and try to translate 'em. So finally the producer comes in and says, 'Tim, here's a graph. This is Andreas and this is you. We wanna go somewhere right about here in terms of the style.'

"From that I moved into live action," Burton says.

In 1984, Burton directed a live short for Disney called *Frankenweenie*, the story of a boy who brings his dog back to life. The movie was meant to accompany *Pinocchio*, but the ratings board found it disturbing and slapped it with a PG rating; when Disney was shaken up in 1984, the film got lost in the shuffle.

Frustrated by Disney's inaction, Burton was liberated by a friend at Warners, who screened *Frankenweenie* for Pee-wee Herman and his producers. "It was the easiest job I ever got," says Burton of *Pee-wee's Big Adventure*. "I had a much more difficult time getting that busboy job six months earlier." In spite of horrible reviews, the daft little sleeper grossed $45 million domestically.

In August, Burton will begin shooting in London his most expensive picture: *Batman*, a $20-million action comedy starring Keaton that promises to go way beyond the comic books and TV show. In keeping with his taste for incongruity, Burton wants "to get a little more real with it" than you'd expect. "There's tension and insanity," he says. "We're trying to say this guy is obviously nuts, but in the most appealing way possible. I go back to what I thought comic books gave people. People love the idea that once they dress up, they can become somebody else. And here you have a human being in what I would consider the most absurd costume ever created.

"The villain is the Joker [Jack Nicholson], the coolest of all. And also the flip side of Batman. Here you got a guy [Batman] who is rich, and something bad happened to him, and instead of getting therapy, he fights crime. But it's still kinda schizophrenic—it's something he questions in his own mind. And the Joker, something happened to him, too, but he'll do or say *anything*, which is another fantasy that all of us have—it's total freedom. So you've got two freaks. It's so great."

The split is pure Burton: One unhappy character dresses up to express something but still feels hopelessly out of place in the real world; another, an extremist, creates his or her own demented reality. Burton clearly identifies with the former, but the latter—Pee-wee, Betelgeuse, the Joker—charges him up, inspires him to dazzling heights.

Both types have attempted to impose their personalities on a void—which is sort of how Burton grew up, as an awkward, artistic kid in Burbank. Maybe that's why he's drawn to any organic expression of character, no matter how clumsy. As a child he was moved by bad movies (notably those by Ed Wood), the kind it's trendy to laugh at. "There's a lot of weird stuff in them—somebody had an *idea*. It went really wrong, and yet you can see somebody's strange mind. I love that."

Hollywood tends to quash such self-expression—it lives by formulas. But Burton slipped through the net, and he's hopping with joy. "If *Beetlejuice* turns out to be successful, I will be so happy," he says, "and so *perversely* happy. I'm for anything that subverts what the studio thinks you have to do."

Jonathan Demme

By Anthony DeCurtis

MARCH 24, 1994

It really shouldn't surprise anyone that Jonathan Demme would defy Hollywood taboos to direct a movie about AIDS, homophobia and social justice or that the movie *Philadelphia* would earn over $40 million in its first two months and nab five Academy Award nominations. *Philadelphia* was fueled by three of the director's staunchest convictions: that helping out people who are having a hard time is less a duty than a pleasure; that bigotry is more the result of ignorance than evil; and that for all the country's political outrages, goodness is deep in the American grain. Despite his impeccable downtown–New York credentials, Demme, who just turned fifty, is less a card-carrying member of the cultural elite than a suburban product who, however astonishingly, believes what he was taught in civics—and is determined to act on it.

Certainly little about Demme's early history, first on Long Island, where he was born, and later in Florida, would indicate either his idealism or his eventual success. His ambition to be a veterinarian evaporated when chemistry class at the University of Florida proved insurmountable. He was writing about movies for local papers when his father, then head of publicity at the Fontainebleau Hotel, in Miami Beach, introduced him to studio mogul—for once, the term can be used unironically—Joseph E. Levine. Levine glanced at some of Demme's reviews—a rave over *Zulu,* one of Levine's movies, natch—proved especially persuasive, and Demme was offered a job as a press agent in New York.

A few years later, while working in Ireland as a publicist on the set of a film by B-movie titan Roger Corman, Demme was invited to write a screenplay for Corman's new company, New World Pictures. The result, *Angels Hard As They Come* (1971), a motorcycle movie based (*very* loosely) on *Rashomon,* began Demme's film career in not exactly earnest. He continued working for Corman, making his debut as a director in 1974 with *Caged Heat,* a quite literally revealing look at women behind bars, and following it up with *Crazy Mama* (1975) and *Fighting Mad* (1976).

Demme's uniquely sweet American vision began to manifest itself after he split from Corman. He directed *Citizens Band* (1977, retitled *Handle With Care*), an eccentric, bighearted exploration of CB-radio culture, and later, *Melvin and Howard* (1980), about Melvin Dummar, the working-class Nevadan who claimed that Howard Hughes had named him the heir to his fortune.

Demme's baptism by fire came with *Swing Shift* (1984), which he conceived of as an exploration of the lives of working women in factories during World War II but which Goldie Hawn, the film's executive producer and female lead, saw as a star vehicle for herself. Hawn played the heavy, and faced with adding thirty minutes of scenes he couldn't stand, Demme walked.

Following that debacle, Demme delivered a run of films that established him as a significant new directorial voice. *Stop Making Sense* (1984), a splendid rendering of Talking Heads' exultant 1983 tour, won a National Society of Film Critics Award for Best Documentary. Then *Something Wild* (1986), a comedy of urban manners that veers into a violent suspense plot, managed to capture every nuance of life in New York in the mid-1980s, from bohemianism to stockbroker paranoia—all set to a fun and friendly, if dauntingly in the know, soundtrack.

Swimming to Cambodia (1987), a documentary of performing artist Spalding Gray's riveting monologue about his experiences in Southeast Asia on the set of *The Killing Fields,* seems indistinguishable from Gray onstage. All of Gray's intelligence, neurosis, humor and sheer humanity are palpably, and somewhat eerily, present. *Married to the Mob* (1988) features Michelle Pfeiffer as a mob wife looking to go straight: In its affectionate send-up of gangster movies, the film, like *Something Wild,* demonstrated Demme's ability to be simultaneously parodic and unapologetically emotional. Even when his characters are cartoons, he seems to love them.

Demme became an industry powerhouse himself—Goldie Hawn, beware!—with *The Silence of the Lambs* (1991), based on the terrifying serial-killer saga by Thomas Harris. The film racked up five Academy Awards (including Best

Director for Demme, Best Actress for Jodie Foster and Best Actor for Anthony Hopkins); particularly estimable was Hopkins' gripping portrayal of Dr. Hannibal "the Cannibal" Lecter, which lifted the grisly character into the pantheon of American film roles. Despite criticism from gay activists over the depiction of gender-bending murderer Jame Gumb, *Silence* earned more than $130 million.

With *Philadelphia,* Demme took on the story of a gay lawyer with AIDS (Tom Hanks has been nominated for an Academy Award for the role) who is fired by his firm and wins a wrongful-termination suit with the help of an initially homophobic lawyer (Denzel Washington). The film has realized Demme's hope of bringing a gay-oriented AIDS drama into the heartland, though again, not without generating fierce controversy.

Some gay activists—most notably Larry Kramer, author of *The Normal Heart*—have attacked what they consider to be *Philadelphia*'s avoidance of gay sexuality (between Hanks and his lover, played by Antonio Banderas) and its too rose-colored view of Hanks' extended and supportive family. Few people with AIDS are quite so fortunate, they say.

Both as a director and a producer (through his company Clinica Estetico, which roughly translates into Portuguese as "beauty parlor"), Demme has had a hand in a number of small-budget documentaries focused on social issues, including the ongoing series *Haiti Dreams of Democracy; Cousin Bobby* (about the director's cousin Robert Castle, a radical clergyman in Harlem); and *One Foot on a Banana Peel, the Other Foot in the Grave,* an AIDS film directed by Demme's late friend the artist Juan Botas.

Demme has been busy for a man who now says that he hopes to cut back his activities in order to better enjoy life with his wife, Joanne

Howard, an artist, and their two children in Nyack, New York, where the two interviews for this story took place. His unstoppable enthusiasm, torrent of words, quick, explosive laughter and energetic engagement of any idea put in front of him suggest that any slowing down of his pace might prove undetectable to the rest of us.

Why did you want to make an AIDS movie?

My friend Juan Botas became sick. Juan was my wife Joanne's soul mate. They had the kind of friendship that was completely without restraint. Juan and I also became good friends— you can see him in his documentary, *One Foot on a Banana Peel.* So when Juan said that he was HIV-positive, I reacted in the only positive way I could, which was to try to work somehow.

I talked to my partner Ed Saxon, who was very keen on the idea, and also to Ron Nyswaner, who had done the shooting script for *Swing Shift*—a wonderful writer. That Ron was gay didn't hurt. Anyway, the desire to do a film on AIDS was born of Juan's sickness.

We looked for a story for a long time, and we decided it would be pointless to make a film for people with AIDS. Or for their loved ones. They don't need no movie about AIDS. They live the truth. We wanted to reach people who *don't* know people with AIDS, who look down on people with AIDS.

You made a conscious decision about that?

When I read in the papers that *Philadelphia* was "targeted for the malls," part of me goes, "Oh, my God, that sounds so calculated." But we *were* calculated about it. We calculated what audience we aspired to.

How exactly did you do that?

We started off with angrier scripts, very politicized. Scripts that were informed with the rage I felt when confronted with society's not only

indifference but hostility to my sick, courageous friend. Ron and I were pissed, and we were not only aggressive, we were *assaultive.* There was a desire to just, like, stick AIDS in your face and say, "Look at it, you scumbags."

Tom Hanks' character displays conviction and intelligence but very little anger. Where did that aspect of the story go?

If your immune system is imperiled, the best way to stay alive is to strive for as much serenity as possible—stress is debilitating and will hasten the onslaught of the illness. We made a choice to get spiritual. We had scenes of Tom meditating to tapes, things like that. We felt this guy is so committed to staying alive, at least long enough to see his name vindicated, he is going to identify rage as a wasted emotion. Maybe we went a little too far on that side.

I find it admirable that he isn't more actively angry. The whole time we're talking, though, I keep picturing ACT-UP demonstrations—and I admire that, too. People who are afflicted with this disease are entitled to all the anger they feel like venting. Our choice for this particular guy was he was going to avoid rage.

What about the charge that the gay couple in the movie doesn't get a bed scene?

We had one scene showing the guys preparing to go to sleep. It was like "We've *done* it! They're in *bed* together! And, sure enough, one of them wears pj's, the other doesn't. And, gosh, they're a lot like you and me." But then you're back in court, and all this other shit's happening. So we made a choice: The film was edited, finally, to tell its strongest story in the best possible way. And that was the story about the fight for vindication.

I feel the film is richly permeated by feelings of love and attachment between Tom and many people in his life, including Antonio. Their scene together toward the end of the picture in the hospital is one of the most intimate, beautiful scenes between two people I've seen in a long, long time. I think it's stunning.

But didn't Denzel Washington reportedly tell Will Smith that whether you play a gay character or not, you never kiss another man onscreen?

I wouldn't fault Denzel for telling Will Smith that. That's Denzel responding to the same concern that Ron, Tom, Antonio and I had. It's a real concern. When we see two men kissing, we're the products of our brainwashing—it knocks us back twenty feet. And with *Philadelphia*—I'm sorry, Larry Kramer—I didn't want to risk knocking our audience back twenty feet with images they're not prepared to see. It's just shocking imagery, and I didn't want to shoehorn it in.

Denzel ain't a homophobic guy—he had difficulty understanding some parts of his character's extremes. I think he was saying: "You'd better watch out, with the kind of climate that exists, you don't want to be identified as the guy who makes out with other guys. It could work to your detriment in seeking other roles."

It also becomes the only issue that gets discussed. The movie is two hours, but it becomes the movie in which two guys kiss.

Well, in *Prelude to a Kiss*, which I didn't see, Alec Baldwin kissed an old man—wasn't that considered the coup de grâce of that movie? I think we found that there was no way people were going to pay to see that.

There was also a lot of speculation that you made "Philadelphia" to atone for offending the gay community, which perceived "The Silence of the Lambs" as homophobic. Did that whole flap have much of an impact on you?

I hadn't been paying attention to the absence of positive gay characters all that much, so I came away from the protests enlightened—and it made me happy that I was already working on *Philadelphia* before *Lambs* came out.

By the way, maybe you can explain something. Who on earth would get the shit kicked out of them and then turn around and do something nice for the people who kicked the shit out of them? I don't get that.

Well, the reasoning runs, "Jonathan so much wants to do the right thing, to advance the cause of people he sees as oppressed, that it would sting him to get criticism from them."

Right.

"So whether he believed it was justified or not, he would in some way try to make up for it."

Well, I try to be nice—but not *that* nice [*laughs*].

The thing about *Philadelphia*, targeting the malls and everything: I didn't have some *better* version—some deeper, more complicated version—of this movie that we turned away from. We set out to make a movie dealing with AIDS discrimination, and there it is. And I've got to tell you: When I sit in a theater, and Denzel says, "Let's talk about it, our fear, our hatred, our *loathing* of homosexuals," I'm like "*What?* An American movie is saying *that*? Holy shit! I *love* that."

You started out making films with Roger Corman. What are some of the things you learned from him?

Roger used to refer to himself—and we heard this *endlessly*—as being 40 percent artist and 60 percent businessman. That was *soooo* Roger—to have a formula, even for that. But I'll be damned, 20-some-odd years later, boy, he's right. You'd *better* be 60 percent businessman, because if you don't have an eye, a *passionate* eye, on getting the picture done at the right cost, you just ain't going to get to make a whole lot more of them. So, the terror of going over budget remains happily with me to this day. It's a healthy aesthetic.

Corman also stressed that movies should contain an element of social critique, something that's obviously stayed with you. Even in a jail-girl titillation like "Caged Heat," you had a plot about the medical exploitation of prisoners.

This is before *Cuckoo's Nest* came out. I thought [*laughs*], "It may only be showing in drive-ins, but it shows what's going on in prisons: We are lobotomizing patients to make them nonviolent." It's true, that's Roger's formula: Your picture must have action, nudity, humor—and a *little bit* of social statement, preferably from a liberal perspective. I'd love to get in deeper with Roger, as to "Is the social statement there because audiences like it? Or, *finally*, is that a little bit of *you* getting in there?" [*Laughs.*].

Another way that has played out for you is that you've always created strong roles for women.

I just admire that extra something that women bring to getting through the day, faced with all of the hassles that we males put in their face. I'm appreciative of that, and I'm glad my movies reflect that.

I root for the underdog. One of the things that made us think *Philadelphia* might have a chance of succeeding was that we came up with the David and Goliath one-liner: It's the little guy going up against the big guys. I'm much more interested in that than the eminently capable guys vanquishing their lessers. I mean, my Stallone movie would be *Rocky*, not *Rambo*. Rambo's better armed, he's smarter—superior firepower doesn't interest me.

Also, as someone who's been force-fed things European and male, I long for more variety—in my own life and in what I see onscreen. I'm not interested in boy movies, and I'm not interested in white-people movies. I want to see movies that reflect the country I live in.

People have found fault with *Philadelphia:*

"Oh, look at this. You got the noble gay guy who goes to the black lawyer and who lives with a Latin. How PC." *Excuse* me—that's America. We got black attorneys now. We got tons of Latins. The ongoing melting pot has a lot of appeal to me.

You've been inventive in your use of music. What do you see as the role of music in films?

I love manipulating the viewers' emotions through music—and I think it's fair. Music is such an inescapable part of reality—our lives are infused with it. We go to the cleaners, and there's a certain aural mood there as a result of whatever's on the radio. You go home, there'll be a different mood. You've got to honor that dynamic. It's just another tool to try to suck people into the experience.

Like you're watching the scene between Denzel and Tom in the library. One guy is poised to extend himself, overcoming certain hurdles to do so. The other guy is daring to think that maybe someone who had rejected him is reaching out to him. I think it's okay for a movie to now send you some musical signals to reaffirm that this is a significant moment.

Of course, there's also the now-famous opera scene in "Philadelphia," where Tom Hanks uses an aria that's playing as a way of confronting his impending death. It's very long, and it's one of the most controversial scenes in the movie. Did you foresee that response?

No. It wasn't until I watched the first cut of it after the picture was finished that I . . . You know, there's two schools of thought on this. There are those who can't believe this overly theatrical, ludicrous sequence and are completely untouched by it. There are also those, myself included, who have a big emotional epiphany through that scene. I mean, I was *devastated* the first time I saw it cut together—tears coming down my face. I was so moved, I couldn't believe it.

But back in the script, I never knew. I knew nothing about opera. I wasn't sure how it should be played. But I always trust great actors. Truthful actors will discover the truth of the scene. Tom and I never discussed how it should be played. Denzel—we didn't talk, either. That's Take One in the movie.

Was the scene in which Hanks and Banderas wear sailors' uniforms a joke about gays in the military?

No. That was just for elegance. Having a party hosted by gays, now you're in a minefield. Are you going to have drag or not? Then I realized, they're an elegant couple, they would throw a swellegant, Cole Porter–type party. So the idea of the guys in dress naval—they'll look so handsome, they'll look so elegant. The gays-in-the-military thing came after that, and we were chortling.

It had a timely resonance.

When we showed the picture at the White House, shortly after the shot of the guys dancing in uniform, President Clinton left the room—he had to relieve himself. But I thought that was kind of . . . interesting timing.

What was it like to screen the movie at the White House?

I'm greedy. It wasn't enough that the movie was seen at the White House—I hoped that with the fifty or so guests, there would have been ten minutes devoted to a discussion about AIDS in our country. But instead, President Clinton took the guests on a guided tour of the White House. I was disappointed by that.

The enormous success of "Silence of the Lambs" really put you on the map as a major director. You probably couldn't have made "Philadelphia" without it. Has that success affected you in more personal ways?

At certain points, I was afraid there was something—a missing chink of skill—that was going to prevent me from having a movie that was financially successful. That frightened me. So when *Silence of the Lambs* became an unqualified success, I took a huge sigh of relief. I mean, I can't tell you how wonderful that felt.

How do you account for the fear?

I didn't go to film school; I didn't work toward being a filmmaker. I stumbled into writing movie reviews so I could get into the movies for free. Then my father introduces me to Joseph E. Levine, and Levine offers me a job in the movie business. "A huge stroke of luck" doesn't catch it.

Maybe that's one of the reasons I work so hard, I'm still trying to justify that luck. It's also why I'm amazed when I get to actually finish a picture, because I'm still afraid of being found out: *"He* can't direct! *Look!* What? Look! He's . . . he's a *phony!"* So there's that still, but I try to use it healthfully—"But, wait, I've made several pictures, now surely I'm entitled to . . ."

Actually, as we sit here discussing these things, I get very terrified of the whole bizarre process [*laughs*].

Speaking of good fortune, how did you get Bruce Springsteen and Neil Young to write original songs for "Philadelphia"? [Each song has been nominated for an Academy Award.] Did you expect them both to write such introspective ballads?

I thought: "Let's reassure people. Let's get these guys who, if anything, are identified with a testosterone, machismo kind of thing." Like "Hey, if Bruce and Neil are part of this party, it's going to be something for the unconverted."

I thought: "What we need is the most up-to-the-minute, guitar-dominated American-rock anthem about injustice to start this movie off. Who can do that? Neil Young can do that." So we edited a title sequence to "Southern Man" to help him see how his music could power the images we were working with. He said, "I'll try." Six weeks later, "Hi, it's Neil, I'm sending a tape." So in comes this song. We were crying the first time we heard it. I went: "Oh, my God, Neil Young trusts this movie more than I do. Isn't that pathetic?"

But now we're back to square one. Even as I'm going, "He trusts the movie more than I," I *still* don't trust it, because now I'm going to call Bruce Springsteen! The same exact dialogue goes on—"So we still need to kick ass at the beginning." Then, one day, this tape shows up. Again, it was not the guitar anthem I had appealed for. Springsteen, like Neil Young, trusted the idea of the movie much more than I was trusting it.

So, after "Philadelphia," what's ahead?

Well, the great thing about documentaries is that if you're interested in social issues, you don't need a $20-million budget to put them onscreen. We made *One Foot on a Banana Peel*

for less than $30,000. It's wonderful. It sheds light on the experience of having AIDS in a very different way than *Philadelphia* does.

That's taken away my fervor to do big-budget versions of social issues—unless they offer the possibility of making some wild megillah of an entertainment, like the project we're working on based on Taylor Branch's biography of Dr. Martin Luther King, *Parting the Waters.*

What do you have in mind for that?

I'm picturing a cross between *Nashville* and *Battle of Algiers*! But I couldn't be more excited by anything than making the next Tom Harris book.

I'm probably not as open to full-tilt entertainments, "Never mind the message, let's just have a ball" kind of films, as I might have been five, certainly ten years ago. I'd rather read books and be a lazy person than just make a movie anymore.

Quentin Tarantino

By David Wild

NOVEMBER 3, 1994

Quentin Tarantino, madman of movie mayhem, has a mother. How's that for a shocker? She has seen *Reservoir Dogs,* the 1992 heist film that made a cult sensation of her writer-director-actor son and raised the stakes on movie gore with a ten-minute torture scene featuring the severing of an ear. "That happens to be my mother's favorite scene," says Tarantino, thirty-one a high school dropout who has gone from video-store clerk to genius auteur du jour in just a few feverishly busy years. Mom has just checked out *Pulp Fiction,* a wildly ambitious and darkly comic crime anthology about Los Angeles lowlife that won the Palme d'Or at Cannes, opened the prestigious New York Film Festival and put her son in the hot-contender line at the Oscars. Although the film includes shootings, stabbings, S&M, homosexual rape and a drug-overdose sequence that leaves audiences reeling, Mom doesn't flinch. Tarantino's West Hollywood, California, bachelor apartment is another matter. "That's not particularly my decorating style," she says with a laugh.

Chez Tarantino is hardly the sort of glitzy home in the Hills one might imagine to house a ballsy, Generation X–rated triple threat on the verge of becoming his own one-man genre.

Rather the homey—okay, messy—pad looks like a kitschy pop-culture Valhalla. Movie posters, videos, laser discs, albums, fanzines, books and assorted film artifacts fill every available inch. Along with memorabilia from his own movies—including that razor used in the infamous ear-slicing scene—there's a frighteningly lifelike head of B-movie diva Barbara Steele, a pack of genuine *Texas Chainsaw* chili, a *Zorro* knife given to him by Jennifer Beals, a Robert Vaughn doll and what is undoubtedly one of the world's most impressive collections of film- and TV-related board games.

"I've been collecting all this shit for years," says Tarantino, who is wearing a RACER X T-shirt today. "Then I finally decided I wanted to start collecting something new. At first I chose lunch boxes, but they really rape you on lunch boxes. They're just too fucking expensive. And as for dolls, well, you can't have much fun with them! You have to keep them in the box. So, I started with board games." Proudly, he shows off his collection, which he has broken down by genre. *The Dukes of Hazzard,* he reports, is a particularly fine game. The bedroom is dominated by a personal collection of tapes large enough to open a video store of one's own. The fare here

Director Quentin Tarantino encourages his hero of *Pulp Fiction*, John Travolta. *Copyright © 1994 Miramax Films*

ranges from art-house classics to *Ma Barker's Killer Brood* and a healthy number of vintage blaxploitation flicks.

You also can't help noticing the shrine to John Travolta above the ledge of Tarantino's fireplace. Certainly part of the satisfaction for Tarantino of making *Pulp Fiction* came from the opportunity to work with Travolta, a.k.a. Vinnie Barbarino, head sweathog on one of Tarantino's TV faves from the seventies, *Welcome Back, Kotter.* The movie helps restore the forty-year-old actor's stardom to its prior luster after a string of less than challenging roles. In a film of standout performances from Bruce Willis, Samuel L. Jackson, Uma Thurman, Tim Roth, Amanda Plummer, Christopher Walken, Harvey Keitel and Tarantino himself, Travolta scores a stunning comeback as the henchman, hot dancer and heroin junkie Vincent Vega. Tarantino will happily expound for hours on the "total brilliance" of the actor's work thirteen years ago in Brian De Palma's *Blow Out.* "John's a real sweetheart, and we became friends," he says. "I just gave John a role like the ones he used to do, and I took him seriously. But getting to know John, I can sort of see why he did all those *Look Who's Talking* baby movies, because the character is kind of similar to who he is in real life—he's this kind of goofy, charming kind of guy."

Travolta was similarly charmed. "I've been doing this for twenty years now, and I've never seen anyone have more fun on a movie set than Quentin," he says. "And it's contagious. You think, 'If this guy can get off as much as he does, then I *definitely* want to get on board this boat.' His knowledge of film is acute. His joy of film is acute. Just the pure wattage of Quentin as a human being is extraordinary. And his willingness to accept criticism as well as admiration and not get introverted by it just floors me. I'm so envious of it. I can't find his fear."

All this mutual admiration begs a question: When Tarantino first met with Travolta before casting him, did he mention that he had a shrine to the actor above his fireplace? "No, I didn't tell John about the shrine," Tarantino says. "But I *did* bring along my Vinnie Barbarino doll so he could sign it for me."

The success of *Pulp Fiction* tastes sweet to Tarantino. Not so long ago, the most high-profile credit this engagingly intense wanna-be could boast was playing one of three Elvis imitators on an episode of *Golden Girls.* He made his first splash with *Reservoir Dogs,* an existential heist film with an unseen heist, and returned a year later as the writer of Tony Scott's underrated *True Romance.* More recently, Tarantino was in the public eye for writing the story that, shall we say, *evolved* into Oliver Stone's controversy-raising *Natural Born Killers.* Somehow he even found the time to briefly help out pal Julia Sweeney (who has a cameo in *Pulp Fiction*) with the now-you-see-it-now-you-don't movie *It's Pat.*

But for all this activity, Tarantino is definitely *not* your average Hollywood careerist. Extremely confident yet decidedly unpretentious, he remains very much a fan—one with strong and exceedingly far-flung tastes. Talking with a ROLLING STONE writer, the tall, lantern-jawed Tarantino makes a point of addressing the non-burning issue of how *Perfect,* a movie that starred Travolta as a ROLLING STONE writer, was woefully underappreciated. He's the guy who loved Kevin Costner's megaflop *Wyatt Earp.* An avowed *Baywatch* watcher, Tarantino is happy to ponder the frankly frightening issue of David Hasselhoff's big-screen potential. He's also the rare and brave aesthete able to make the qualitative judgment that *Look Who's Talking Too* represents the creative apex of that cinematic Travolta trilogy.

Tarantino's pop-culture-freak status has even

informed his own performances. In *Reservoir Dogs* he made a memorable appearance as Mr. Brown, arguing passionately with Mr. Pink (Steve Buscemi) over the true meaning of Madonna's "Like a Virgin." Mr. Brown insists that the lyric is "a metaphor for a big dick," while Mr. Pink rather more romantically suggests that the song is about love. For the record, Her Blondness eventually settled the matter. "Madonna liked the movie a lot, but she said I'm not right," says Tarantino. "She signed my *Erotica* album, 'Dear Quentin, It's about love, it's not about dick. Madonna.'" In *Sleep With Me,* Tarantino nearly steals the show with a cameo as a partygoer lecturing passionately on the homosexual subtext of *Top Gun.*

Even the Tarantino kitchen—with its apparent lifetime supply of Yoo-Hoo prominently displayed next to a big box of Captain Crunch—suggests a sort of gleefully arrested development. But after some years where he had trouble getting arrested in Hollywood, Tarantino has established himself as a mature and much in demand talent. Still, it wasn't long ago that Tarantino was just a clerk toiling at Video Archives, a cinéaste-run video store in Manhattan Beach, California. "People ask me if I went to film school," he says. "And I tell them, 'No, I went to *films.*'"

The clerk Christian Slater played in *True Romance* was based on Tarantino's younger days living near the Los Angeles airport. "All day long he just sees people taking off and leaving," says Tarantino. "And he's going nowhere. I'm not that guy anymore. That guy is someone who's never had a girlfriend, he's very inexperienced and naive. He's only had failure in his life." In the hands of director Tony Scott (who also happened to direct *Top Gun*), the film became a hyperviolent but highly romantic theme-park ride. "Tony did a great job," Tarantino says

admiringly. "The movie was really cool. Of course, the whole thing was bizarre for me to see—like watching a big-budget feature of your home movies."

Admiring would *not* be the word to describe Tarantino's feelings regarding what became of his *Natural Born Killers* screenplay, which Oliver Stone ultimately chose to substantially rework with his collaborators. Tarantino declined script credit, taking responsibility only inasmuch as the movie was based on a story by him. In fact, bringing up *Natural Born Killers* is the single easiest way to quiet this otherwise affable chatterbox. Asked if he has seen the film, Tarantino turns strangely silent.

"No," he says finally. "It's just kind of out there, and it doesn't have *anything* to do with me," he says after being coaxed to elaborate. "I think people pretty much know that I have distanced myself from the film. If you like it, then that's Oliver. If you *don't* like it, that's Oliver, too."

In fact, the release date of *Pulp Fiction*—a film substantially closer to his heart—was pushed back by Tarantino, producer Lawrence Bender and Miramax Films partly to distance it from *Killers*. "I don't want that association," he says. "I could just see all those double reviews in ROLLING STONE, *Time* and *Newsweek.* You know, a photo from it next to a photo from *Pulp.* We'd be forever linked."

Pulp Fiction began with a five-hundred-page first draft. For Tarantino, "the only strange thing about writing *Pulp* was that for once, I knew what I was writing was going to get made," he says. "It's not so ethereal anymore. And if it's going to be made, it ought to be worth making. That's a harsh magnifying glass." Certainly, Tarantino bit off a lot with the intricately plotted *Pulp,* a film he early on described as "an anthology about a community of crooks." In writing *Pulp Fiction*, he says he was influenced by the writings of J.D. Salinger: "When you read his Glass-family stories, they all eventually add up to one big story. That was the biggest example for me." Some writer pals advised Tarantino that he might have difficulty following up his *Dogs* debut. "Callie Khouri, who wrote *Thelma and Louise*, and Richard LaGravenese, who wrote *Fisher King*, both told me I was going to have trouble writing the next one," he recalls. "Fortunately, it really wasn't *that* difficult."

Even having the *Pulp* script put in turnaround by TriStar ended up helping Tarantino to make the film for a lean $8 million at Miramax—part of the reason the movie's already out of the red. "I enjoyed making *Pulp* even more than *Dogs* because this time I sort of knew what I was doing," Tarantino says. "Back when we were making *Dogs*, Lawrence and I used to joke that we were the least experienced guys on the set. Because we *were*. This time around, we'd been there and done that, which made the whole thing a lot more fun." Tarantino has nothing but raves for all the cast, including Keitel, who makes a dramatic appearance—alongside Tarantino—as the Wolf, a resourceful Mr. Fix-It. This seems to be typecasting, since Keitel proved a savior when he helped kick-start Tarantino's career by signing up to be a reservoir dog.

To hear Tarantino tell it, the hardest part since *Pulp* is getting down to work with all the Hollywood distractions. "A lot of young directors get a little success and turn into phone junkies," he says with a slight tone of disgust. "All they do is *talk*. My attitude is, *fuck* all these phone calls, forget all these meetings, you have work to do! Eighty percent of the people calling you in this business, their *job* is to make phone calls all day. But that's not *our* job."

On a sunny Hollywood afternoon, Quentin

Tarantino is in his natural habitat: the movies. Lately, making movies can get in the way of watching them, but this isn't one of those days. This afternoon he's one of the few nonsenior citizens attending a lunchtime screening of *Mad Love* at the Los Angeles County Art Museum. "I think most of the people here must have seen it when it came out in 1935," he says, checking out the crowd.

Mad Love—later adapted as *The Hands of Orlac*—is a nicely twisted Karl Freund film starring Peter Lorre as a crazed physician who's driven by love to undertake some rather misguided surgery. Tarantino is psyched to finally see it. Somehow he has always missed the film, but he's already well versed in its lore. "The director was the cinematographer of *Metropolis*," he explains excitedly. "And in Pauline Kael's famous essay 'Raising Kane,' she claims that this was the movie cinematographer Gregg Toland did before *Citizen Kane* to try things out for *Kane* later." With that, he sits back and smiles as the theater darkens.

After the movie lets out, Tarantino walks out into a blindingly sunny L.A. day. Over lunch at nearby Johnnie's, a no-frills diner that served as a *Reservoir Dogs* location, he's asked if it's unusual for him to be coming out of a film in the middle of a beautiful day. "Not at all," he says. "I go to movies *whenever* I can. I mean, I've done a few interviews where people have said they want to hang out with me on an average day and do what I do. And I always think they're waiting for me to take them horseback riding or something. They've definitely got the wrong guy. I go to movies, sometimes more than once a day, and I watch TV with friends. Occasionally, I go to coffee shops. That and I work. *That's* what I do."

This state of affairs is not a recent development. It has pretty much been the same routine since Tarantino grew up in L.A.'s South Bay in the shadow of the Los Angeles International Airport. His parents had already split when a two-year-old Quentin and his mother, Connie, moved west from Knoxville, Tennessee, where she had been a student. According to Connie, who later remarried, Quentin was already demonstrating an insatiable appetite for movies. "Some people describe me as a permissive mother," she says. "I took Quentin to every movie I saw. I didn't censor his material." Soon, the young auteur's bedroom was beginning to resemble his current apartment. "I kept a pretty tight rein on Quentin in the rest of the house," she says, laughing.

"My mother worked very hard to supply me with a nice house to live in," Tarantino recalls. "We lived in Harbor City, which is middle class but a little rough." Connie describes the area as upper-middle class—"even if that doesn't fit in with the rags-to-riches story some people want to tell about him." But she adds that "even early on, Quentin was drawn to some rough neighborhoods." The attraction, it goes without saying, was the movies.

Young Quentin—who both mother and son agree hated school—had found his refuge. "See, Harbor City's positioned between Torrance, which is an okay neighborhood, and Carson, which is rougher," he explains. "I spent a lot of my time in Carson because that's where the Carson Twin Cinema was. That was the theater that showed all the kung fu movies and the Allied International movies like *The Van*. The first time I met Danny De Vito, I said, 'Oh, yeah, Danny, you were in *The Van* and *Pom-Pom Girls*.' There was also the Del Amo Mall theater, where all the real Hollywood stuff played, and I went there, too. Basically, I spent my life at the movies.

"I grew up going to the grind houses and to the art houses and loving them both equally," Tarantino adds. "That sort of defines my aesthetic. I mean, it's not like I'm some arty guy just getting off on myself. I think studios are afraid of one thing, and that is someone's going to make a boring movie. My stuff may not be obvious, but it's not esoteric, either. I'll never write a movie about sheepherders contemplating God and life."

Tarantino broke into movies professionally as a teenager by ushering porn watchers at the Pussycat Theater in Torrance. He'd already tried his hand at writing his first screenplay, penning something called *Captain Peachfuzz and the Anchovy Bandit*. At twenty-two—around the time he started shooting a never-completed 16mm film called *My Best Friend's Birthday*—he got a much more satisfying and educational job working at Video Archives, a relatively small operation that Tarantino proudly calls "the best video store in the Los Angeles area." It was there that he met up with like-minded movie freaks such as fellow clerk Roger Avary, for whose directorial debut, *Killing Zoe*, Tarantino served as an executive producer. "Now Video Archives is like L.A.'s answer to the *Cahiers du Cinéma*," Tarantino says with a laugh. "At William Morris they'll be telling agents, 'You've gotta check out the scene at that video store.'

"I basically lived there for years," he continues. "We'd get off work, close up the store, then sit around and watch movies all night. Other times Roger, our friend Scott and I would take a Friday and plot things out so we could see all four new movies we were interested in. We always took whatever we got paid and put it right back into the industry."

A few nay-saying critics have called Tarantino's work derivative. Some saw *Reservoir Dogs* as borrowing heavily from earlier movies, including Kubrick's *The Killing*. "Generally, I've been treated really well by the press," says

Tarantino, who still regrets that Pauline Kael—"one of my biggest influences, my Kingsfield," he calls her—retired before *Reservoir Dogs* came out. "But a few critics have said, ironically enough, that *Dogs* felt like a film-school movie—that it's a film more about movies than about life experiences. I don't agree. I think one of the strengths of the film is that it *is* realistic: It does give you a glimpse into the criminal life. But I also like the idea of my films commenting on film itself. A lot of directors I love have done that." Suddenly, Tarantino grins wildly. "And the fact of the matter is, the shots I actually *did* rip off no one has caught yet.

"Part of the fun of making movies is that you're on ground that's been covered before," he says, "and you can use that as a jumping-off point for all the weird places you want to go. I'm trying to make a combination of a movie movie and a real movie. I want to make movie movies with *real* consequences."

One real consequence of the artful brutality that has marked the movies Tarantino has made thus far is the reputation it has earned him—like Peckinpah before him—as the thinking man's poet of violence. Some audiences still may be having flashbacks to the ear-amputation scene in *Reservoir Dogs,* which Tarantino—a pop-music lover of extremely catholic tastes—played out to the cheerful strains of Stealers Wheel's seventies classic "Stuck in the Middle With You."

"It never bothered me when people walked out," Tarantino says. "It just meant that scene *worked.* Go to a video store and nine out of ten films in the action-adventure section are more graphic than mine. But I'm not interested in making a cartoon. I'm interested in making the violence *real.*"

Pulp Fiction offers no shortage of scenes for its exhausted but exhilarated audience to talk about on the way out, including that memorable male-on-male S&M rape scene. "Well, *Deliverance* did it," he says. "*American Me* did it, too. There's like *three* butt-fucking scenes in *American Me.* That's definitely the one to beat in that particular category!"

As it turned out, nobody beat *Pulp Fiction* at Cannes. The win of the Palme d'Or surprised many observers but not Tarantino himself. "I thought it was in the realm of possibility," he says, smiling. "Basically, it was like no one knew about our movie, then it was like *boom!* It's like people who really shouldn't know what the Palme d'Or is, they all of a sudden knew what I won. I guess it's sort of like *sex, lies, and videotape* just coming out of nowhere. After Cannes was over, I went to Paris to chill out. Let me tell you, when you win the Palme d'Or, *don't* go to Paris to chill out. Cannes is their Oscars, so everyone was coming up saying, 'You're the American who won the big award.' "

Today, Tarantino—who doesn't have a girlfriend at the moment and who has apparently failed to develop the habit of having torrid affairs with his actresses—says that he wants to take a break. "I've got to take some time to have a life," he says.

Tarantino, who was thanked by Kurt Cobain in the liner notes for *In Utero,* seems to be on the verge of turning into a cinematic slacker icon. But his mother—who is boycotting *Natural Born Killers* out of respect for her son—says success hasn't spoiled him yet: "No, I haven't seen any change in Quentin. He's just as self-confident as he's always been."

In terms of the long run, Tarantino explains that he simply wants to stay on the treacherous career path that he has set for himself. "When you look at a career in Hollywood, it seems like there's two roads," he says as he sits back happily among the meaningful clutter of his home. "There's the studio-hack career or the art-film career. They're *both* dangerous roads. Nobody wants to turn into a hack. But the art-film trip is just as bad because you get lost and start disappearing up your own ass. But there *is* another road, I think, where the budgets of your film depend on what type of movie you're making, where you're making a movie you really want to make and that someone might really want to see.

"All I have to do is stay on that road."

THE REVIEWS

SM14170   JUNE 30th, 1977 • ISSUE NO. 242   85¢UK50p

ROLLING STONE

Diane Keaton, the Next Hepburn

'Really? Do You Think So? Really? Well, La-De-Dah.'
By Ben Fong-Torres

States in Siege

Rhodesia
By Jan Morris

The Beatles Live

at the
Hollywood Bowl

Last Notes from Home

A Work in Progress
By Frederick Exley

Diane Keaton, ROLLING STONE, issue 242, June 30, 1977.

The Fifty Essential Maverick Movies of the ROLLING STONE Era

By Peter Travers

(The date given is the film's U.S. release.)

1. *Bonnie and Clyde* (Directed by Arthur Penn/ Starring Warren Beatty, Faye Dunaway, Gene Hackman and Estelle Parsons, 1967): Beatty was barely thirty when he produced and starred in this gangster classic using the Depression-era story of Clyde Barrow (Beatty) and Bonnie Parker (Dunaway, before self-parody soured her talent)—bank-robbing lovers on the run—to reflect the youth rebellion of the sixties. Those who only know Beatty as the aging stud of *Dick Tracy* and *Love Affair* will marvel at his wit and passion. The no-gloss violence, especially the climax, retains its power to floor you.

2. *The Graduate* (Directed by Mike Nichols/ Starring Dustin Hoffman, Anne Bancroft and Katharine Ross, 1967): Hoffman became the symbol of college-age sixties youth, conflicted about career (plastic!) and sex (he loves the daughter of the married woman he's fucking) as his character fights a losing battle with conformity to a soundtrack by Simon and Garfunkel. Nichols' high-style direction, the pungent script by Buck Henry and Calder Willingham and the erotically funny sparring of Hoffman and Bancroft—coo-coo cachoo, Mrs. Robinson— haven't lost their bouyancy or rueful grace.

3. *2001: A Space Odyssey* (Directed by Stanley Kubrick/Starring Keir Dullea and Gary Lockwood, 1968): On its initial release, Kubrick's visionary masterpiece about the dawn of man and technology and the death of language and imagination hit home mostly with intellectuals (Deconstruct that monolith) and acid trippers (Dig that time warp). These days the daring of Kubrick and screenwriter Arthur C. Clarke is justly celebrated as a landmark of cinematic ambition and reach.

4. *Faces* (Directed by John Cassavetes/Starring Gena Rowlands, Seymour Cassel and Lynn Carlin, 1968): Cassavetes is widely hailed as the father of American film mavericks. To get at raw truths, he encouraged actors to go for broke, often testing audience endurance. *Faces,* an agonizing study of infidelity, is brilliant and exasperating. But you won't forget these searching performances, especially Cassel's, or Cassavetes' improvisatory style and dark humor, which shame the formula pap dished out by the major studios. In the year of *Faces* and *2001,* the Brit musical *Oliver!* took the Best Picture Oscar.

5. *The Night of the Living Dead* (Directed by George A. Romero/Starring Duane Jones and

Judith O'Dea, 1968): Nobody expected much from this now immortal horror film about flesh-eating zombies shot on the cheap ($114,000) in Pittsburgh by first-time director Romero, but it remains the rogue model of ghoulish terror that imitators working with megabudgets, including Romero himself, can't begin to match. From that opening cemetery scene to the sight of children devouring their parents and a climax that offers no comfort to the tormented audience, it's the stuff that bad dreams are made of.

6. *Weekend* (Directed by Jean-Luc Godard/Starring Mireille Darc and Jean Yanne, 1968): France's gonzo genius takes his artful scalpel to materialism in a surreal satire that puts humanity on trial. The scene is a highway, the drivers are armed and a traffic jam—the most vivid in film history—results in explosive emotions and massive carnage. It's not a pretty picture, just a coldly funny and devastating one from a master muckraker.

7. *Easy Rider* (Directed by Dennis Hopper/Starring Hopper, Peter Fonda, Jack Nicholson, Karen Black and Phil Spector, 1969): Released at the end of the sixties, this low-budget road movie summed up the rebel spirit of the decade as tokeheads Hopper and Fonda hopped on their hogs to look for America with a young and never-better Nicholson along as a repressed lawyer out for a chance to howl. Though the film's psychedelic imagery seems a bit dated now, its mythic status has grown with the years. This is the surprise success that made sex, drugs, and rock & roll money words in Hollywood and put youth culture in the driver's seat. For an exhilarating period, until spectacle and sequelitis restored formula to the throne, experimentation became big box-office. There were side-effects—self-indulgence, excess and shame-

less pretension (notably Hopper's directorial followup, *The Last Movie*). There was also fierce creativity and an audience eager to respond to the challenge.

8. *The Wild Bunch* (Directed by Sam Peckinpah/Starring William Holden, Robert Ryan, Warren Oates and Ernest Borgnine, 1969): Peckinpah's aging outlaws hightail it to Mexico to lick their wounds and go out in a bloody burst of glory. The film drew fire for scenes of slo-mo brutality that wouldn't raise an eyebrow in the current era of natural born killers. What really counts is the poetic way Peckinpah reinvents the Western to find the terror and the beauty in violence.

9. *Medium Cool* (Directed by Haskell Wexler/Starring Robert Forster and Verna Bloom, 1969): Gifted cinematographer and civil-rights activist Wexler turned director and produced a wrenching and influential document about a TV cameraman (Forster) who can't stay detached when riots break out during the 1968 Democratic convention in Chicago.

10. *Five Easy Pieces* (Directed by Bob Rafelson/Starring Jack Nicholson, Karen Black and Susan Anspach, 1970): Everybody remembers the hilarious scene in the diner when Nicholson brings a bullying waitress to her knees. But Rafelson's grieving comedy of manners—Nicholson is a classical pianist who flees his elitist family to work as an oil rigger—registers even more strongly in the fierce moments that pit the individualist against his own desire to conform.

11. *Woodstock* (Directed by Michael Wadleigh, 1970): From Joan Baez to the Who, from Joe Cocker to Jimi Hendrix, the film presents the

outdoor rock concert as love-in. It's all here: the sex, the drugs, the rain, the mud, the Portosans and the music that came down in torrents— sometimes magic (Hendrix), sometimes just noise (Sha Na Na). Martin Scorsese helped edit a weekend in upstate New York into three hours of split-screen utopia for the time capsule.

12. *Gimme Shelter* (Directed by David and Albert Maysles and Charlotte Zwerin, 1970): A pulverizing Rolling Stones concert held at California's Altamont Speedway becomes the dark side of the Woodstock dream as a member of the crowd is stabbed by a Hell's Angels security guard while Mick Jagger wails "Under My Thumb."

13. *A Clockwork Orange* (Directed by Stanley Kubrick/Starring Malcolm McDowell, 1971): Kubrick stirred controversy and created a wickedly funny version of hell with this futuristic gang banger from the bitingly satiric novel by Anthony Burgess. McDowell gives a career performance as Alex, a raping, murdering thug who endures an aversion-therapy program from the state that robs him of his moral right to be bad.

14. *The Last Picture Show* (Directed by Peter Bogdanovich/Starring Timothy Bottoms, Jeff Bridges, Cybill Shepherd, Ben Johnson, Cloris Leachman and Ellen Burstyn, 1971): This sharply observed and beautifully acted film of Larry McMurtry's novel of restless youth in small-town Texas during the 1950s is Bogdanovich's finest two hours onscreen. He hasn't since recaptured the knack of blending emotional generosity with rigorous daring.

15. *The Conformist* (Directed by Bernardo Bertolucci/Starring Jean-Louis Trintignant and Dominique Sanda, 1970): Bertolucci floods the screen with imagery in showing how the Trintignant character detaches himself from feeling to fit in as a member of the Fascist secret service in Italy during the 1930s. Despite the notoriety for *Last Tango in Paris* and the Oscars for *The Last Emperor*, *The Conformist* is the film that marks Bertolucci most clearly as a master.

16. *The Godfather* (Directed by Francis Ford Coppola/Starring Marlon Brando, Al Pacino, James Caan and Robert Duvall, 1972): Simply the greatest gangster epic ever produced in America—that includes *Part II* in 1974 but not the misguided *Part III* in 1990—and proof positive that popular entertainment can rise to the level of art.

17. *Superfly* (Directed by Gordon Parks Jr./Starring Ron O'Neal and Sheila Frazier, 1972): In the best of the blaxploitation flicks, O'Neal plays Priest—a pusher who hides his cocaine in a crucifix and sets up one last big score before going straight. Parks, accused at the time of glorifying drugs, was actually skewering white-racist notions of what makes a hero.

18. *Pink Flamingos* (Directed by John Waters/Starring Divine, David Lochary, Edith Massey and Mink Stole, 1972): Bad taste at its comic peak as Waters, on a $10,000 budget, sticks it to the censors with the help of star Divine, a three-hundred-pound cross-dresser named Harris Glenn Milstead. The characters vie for the title of "filthiest person alive," and Divine adds the coup de grâce by munching on dog shit. Waters tamed his style in later films, but his subversive spirit remains intact.

19. *Mean Streets* (Directed by Martin Scorsese/Starring Robert De Niro and Harvey Keitel, 1973): In this electrifying tale of gangsters in

New York's Little Italy—bolstered by a superb rock soundtrack—Scorsese marked his territory and became America's poet of violence and challenged Catholicism. De Niro, as the psychotic Johnny Boy, also launched his career rocket.

20. *American Graffiti* (Directed by George Lucas/Starring Richard Dreyfuss, Ron Howard, Cindy Williams, Paul LeMat and Candy Clark, 1973): Growing up in 1962 after high-school graduation gave Lucas the chance to blend music, action, a young cast and the romance and terror of adolescence into one of the best and least sentimental coming-of-age movies ever.

21. *Badlands* (Directed by Terrence Malick/ Starring Martin Sheen and Sissy Spacek, 1973): A neglected American masterpiece with Sheen and Spacek giving career performances as a couple on a killing spree (the story was loosely based on the fifties true-crime story of Charlie Starkweather and Carol Fugate). Malick followed his stunning debut with *Days of Heaven* in 1978, then disappeared.

22. *Chinatown* (Directed by Roman Polanski/ Starring Jack Nicholson, Faye Dunaway and John Huston, 1974): In 1930s Los Angeles, Dunaway hires detective Jake Gittes (Nicholson) to find her missing husband. Robert Towne's tale of corruption and political cover-ups is the definitive script of the Watergate era, and Polanski and the never-better cast catch every moral nuance. The last scene and last line ("Forget it, Jake, it's Chinatown") is a chilling image of desolation.

23. *Nashville* (Directed by Robert Altman/Starring Keith Carradine, Lily Tomlin, Ronee Blakley and Michael Murphy, 1975): Altman uses a political rally held in the capital of country music to create a brilliant mosaic of American life that grows more rewarding with each viewing. Here's a film for the time capsule that ranks with *M*A*S*H*, *McCabe and Mrs. Miller* and *Short Cuts* as Altman peaks.

24. *Monty Python and the Holy Grail* (Directed by Terry Gilliam and Terry Jones/Starring John Cleese, Graham Chapman, Eric Idle and Michael Palin, 1975): The peerless Python troupe delivers inspired and often scatological lunacy to send up Camelot, crusades and every stupid myth about knights. Don't argue or I'll blow my nose at you and fart in your general direction.

25. *Taxi Driver* (Directed by Martin Scorsese/ Starring Robert De Niro, Jodie Foster, Harvey Keitel and Cybill Shepherd, 1976): Another Scorsese gem with De Niro as a Vietnam vet and New York cabbie who snaps violently when a teen hooker, indelibly played by Foster, drops him too deep into moral chaos. "Are you talkin' to me?" De Niro asks his mirror. This visionary film talks to all of us.

26. *Annie Hall* (Directed by Woody Allen/Starring Woody Allen and Diane Keaton, 1977): No movie romance catches the funny confusion and piercing sadness of love better than the Woodman's treatise on what makes opposites attract. Keaton's la-di-da WASP princess—"You're what Grammy Hall would call a real Jew," she tells Allen on their first date—is a classic creation.

27. *Saturday Night Fever* (Directed by John Badham/Starring John Travolta, 1977): Its influence extends further than turning disco and white suits into a fever. Travolta's striking rendering of a Brooklyn dancer has toughness and

extraordinary physical grace that time hasn't dimmed.

28. *The Chant of Jimmie Blacksmith* (Directed by Fred Schepisi/Starring Tommy Lewis and Jack Thompson, 1978): This Australian film is based on a novel by Thomas Keneally *(Schindler's List)* about a half-caste aborigine, beautifully played by Lewis, who explodes in violence when two cultures tear him apart. Schepisi crafts a precise and devastating picture of racism.

29. *Apocalypse Now* (Directed by Francis Ford Coppola/Starring Marlon Brando, Robert Duvall and Martin Sheen, 1979): Coppola looks at Vietnam through the prism of Joseph Conrad's *Heart of Darkness* and scores a visual knockout in this surreal epic of war ("the horror, the horror") as soldier Sheen heads upriver to Cambodia to assassinate Brando's rogue colonel.

30. *The Brood* (Directed by David Cronenberg/Starring Samantha Eggar and Oliver Reed, 1979): Cronenberg reacts to the pieties of the Oscar-winning *Kramer vs. Kramer* with a horror film about children and divorce (he was going through his own at the time) that turns sexual anxiety and marital rage into monstrous flesh. Still as daring as the day it was hatched.

31. *Raging Bull* (Directed by Martin Scorsese/Starring Robert De Niro, Joe Pesci and Cathy Moriarty, 1980): In Scorsese's hands, the life of boxer Jake LaMotta—De Niro in the performance of his life as the trim rebel and the fat mess he became—becomes a searing study of macho ritual with fight scenes that heighten the spectacle of the ring into a thing of beauty and terror.

32. *Return of the Secaucus Seven* (Directed by John Sayles/Starring Jean Passanante, Gordon Clapp, David Strathairn and Karen Trott, 1980): College friends from the sixties share a weekend in New Hampshire that opens old wounds about misplaced ideals and mismatched love affairs. Sayles' low-budget debut film distills a generation without an ounce of the gloss that infected *The Big Chill.*

33. *Blow Out* (Directed by Brian De Palma/Starring John Travolta, Nancy Allen and Dennis Franz, 1981): De Palma's twisted take on Antonioni's *Blow-Up* features Travolta as a soundman who uses his technical skills to uncover a political assassination and learns instead to find his heart. In the guise of a conspiracy thriller, De Palma grapples movingly with his personal obsessions.

34. *The Terminator* (Directed by James Cameron/Starring Arnold Schwarzenegger, Linda Hamilton and Michael Biehn, 1984): Cameron cast Ah-nuld as a killer robot and created a new mold for action pictures that is still being imitated. *T2* in 1991 was bigger, but the original is still the best.

35. *Stranger Than Paradise* (Directed by Jim Jarmusch/Starring John Lurie, Eszter Balint and Richard Edson, 1984): Lurie, Edson and Balint—Lurie's cousin from Hungary—leave New York to look for America and find it in cool, funny and desolate images that mark Jarmusch as an original.

36. *Brazil* (Directed by Terry Gilliam/Starring Jonathan Pryce, Kim Greist and Robert De Niro, 1985): The corporate culture of the future tries to crush the dreams out of Pryce's little clerk, giving the great Gilliam a chance to use his considerable gifts for satire and production design to create a nightmare vision of dehuman-

ization that has been widely imitated but never equaled.

37. *Blue Velvet* (Directed by David Lynch/Starring Kyle MacLachlan, Isabella Rossellini, Laura Dern and Dennis Hopper, 1986): MacLachlan's innocent falls through the rabbit hole of Norman Rockwell America to find the chaos world underneath. Lynch's perverse masterwork, highlighted by Hopper's violently mad hatter, is the most exhilarating and disturbing movie of the eighties.

38. *Platoon* (Directed by Oliver Stone/Starring Charlie Sheen, Willem Dafoe and Tom Berenger, 1986): Sheen stands in for writer-director Stone as the young soldier making a pilgrim's progress through the horrors of Vietnam in a war film of startling feeling and searing realism.

39. *Sid & Nancy* (Directed by Alex Cox/Starring Gary Oldman and Chloe Webb, 1986): Cox brings the punk-rock era to unnerving life in this drug-dipped love-and-death story between Sex Pistol Sid Vicious (a never-better Oldman) and groupie Nancy Spungen (a funny and touching Webb).

40. *Do the Right Thing* (Directed by Spike Lee/Starring Danny Aiello, Ossie Davis, Ruby Dee, John Turturro, Richard Edson, Bill Nunn and Rosie Perez, 1989): Lee writes, directs and stars as Mookie, the delivery boy for a white-owned pizza parlor in a black Brooklyn neighborhood, in this passionate and incendiary film that ended the eighties on a high note of revolutionary film fervor.

41. *Drugstore Cowboy* (Directed by Gus Van Sant/Starring Matt Dillon, Kelly Lynch, James Le Gros and Heather Graham, 1989): Dillon, wife Lynch and their pals rob pharmacies for prescription drugs in this seminal road movie. With precision, humor and none of the usual moralizing, Van Sant locates the seductiveness and the dead-endedness of the junkie life.

42. *sex, lies, and videotape* (Directed by Steven Soderbergh/Starring James Spader, Andie MacDowell, Peter Gallagher and Laura San Giacomo, 1989): Three topical obsessions get an invigorating going over from writer-director Soderbergh in his impressive debut film, featuring an outstanding performance from Spader as the liar with the videotape who can't have sex.

43. *Heathers* (Directed by Michael Lehmann/Starring Winona Ryder and Christian Slater, 1989): A dark comic classic that owes much to the acid-dipped script by Daniel Waters. Ryder is superb as a high-school student who hates herself for joining forces with the school queen bees—they're all named Heather—until killer Slater turns up to put Ryder and the Heathers out of their misery.

44. *The Killer* (Directed by John Woo/Starring Chow Yun-Fat, Sally Yeh and Danny Lee, 1989): Woo is the Hong Kong director who rewrote the book on violent action as a pop-culture morality fable. This story of an assassin (Yun-Fat) who falls for the girl singer (Yeh) he has blinded in a gunfight is Woo the master at his most extravagant and moving.

45. *Batman* (Directed by Tim Burton/Starring Michael Keaton and Jack Nicholson, 1989): Burton's dark poetic vision of the comic-strip crusader redefined the notion of a superhero. Audiences had a better time with Nicholson's villainous Joker. Ditto Michelle Pfeiffer's whip-

smart Catwoman in *Batman Returns* and Jim Carrey's manic Riddler in *Batman Forever*. But it's Burton's subversive conception of the haunted hero in the original that broke new ground and promises to stand the test of time.

46. *Thelma & Louise* (Directed by Ridley Scott/ Starring Susan Sarandon and Geena Davis, 1991): The two stars put flesh, blood and spirit into screenwriter Callie Khouri's feminist road movie—it's a spitfire of a script—and director Scott *(Alien, Blade Runner)* shows he has a heart as well as a gift for art direction as the film's two feisty heroines drive off a cliff into screen legend.

47. *Unforgiven* (Directed by Clint Eastwood/ Starring Eastwood, Gene Hackman, Morgan Freeman and Richard Harris, 1992): Eastwood deconstructs the Western and his entire career in a film that challenges the audience to examine its own attitude toward violence in movies and in life. It's a high-wire act for Eastwood. In four decades in the saddle, he's never ridden this tall.

48. *The Crying Game* (Directed by Neil Jordan/ Starring Stephen Rea, Miranda Richardson, Forest Whitaker and Jaye Davidson, 1992): Au-diences were taken by surprise by writer-director Jordan's revolutionary foray into sexual and po-litical role-playing. When the shock wears off, Jordan's compassion and the heartfelt perfor-mances of Rea and Davidson linger in the memory.

49. *The Piano* (Directed by Jane Campion/Star-ring Holly Hunter, Harvey Keitel, Sam Neill and Anna Paquin, 1993): Campion emerges as a world-class filmmaker with this stirring and sexually explosive love story about a mute mail-order bride (Hunter), who arrives in New Zealand with her daughter (Paquin) to live with farmer Neill and finds herself in an erotic bar-gain with neighbor Keitel.

50. *Pulp Fiction* (Directed by Quentin Taran-tino/Starring John Travolta, Samuel L. Jackson, Uma Thurman and Bruce Willis, 1994): Taran-tino's *tour de force* isn't just the best and most innovative crime film made in America since *Mean Streets,* it's the movie that galvanized audi-ences and other filmmakers to shake things up again. Like *Easy Rider* in the sixties, *Pulp Fiction* leaves you with the exhilarating impression that a new rebel storm is brewing and anything is possible.

Fifty More Rebel Movies of the ROLLING STONE Era to Get You Thinking

By Peter Travers

1. *Blow-Up* (Directed by Michelangelo Antonioni/Starring David Hemmings and Vanessa Redgrave, 1966): Photographer Hemmings uncovers the dark side of swinging London.

2. *In Cold Blood* (Directed by Richard Brooks/Starring Robert Blake and Scott Wilson, 1967): Truman Capote's true-crime story is scaldingly delivered.

3. *Greetings* (Directed by Brian De Palma/Starring Robert De Niro and Allen Garfield, 1968): De Palma's counterculture send-up of everything from draft dodging to JFK conspiracy theorists.

4. *Belle de Jour* (Directed by Luis Bunuel/Starring Catherine Deneuve and Michel Piccoli, 1966): Deneuve is a housewife who moonlights as a hooker in Bunuel's masterful social satire.

5. *Once Upon a Time in the West* (Directed by Sergio Leone/Starring Charles Bronson and Henry Fonda, 1968): The ultimate Leone spaghetti Western—riveting and revolutionary.

6. *Midnight Cowboy* (Directed by John Schlesinger/Starring Dustin Hoffman and Jon Voight, 1969): Voight's stud and Hoffman's pimp defy convention and help movies grow up.

7. *Z* (Directed by Costa-Gavras/Starring Yves Montand and Jean-Louis Trintignant, 1969): A fact-based French political thriller that shamed Hollywood with its fire and intelligence.

8. *Alice's Restaurant* (Directed by Arthur Penn/Starring Arlo Guthrie and Pat Quinn, 1969): Guthrie's funny and touching song for aging children is a movie that deftly captures an era of hippie promise.

9. *M*A*S*H* (Directed by Robert Altman/Starring Elliott Gould and Donald Sutherland, 1970): Altman's slashing comedy of medics in war broke every rule and made up a few of its own.

10. *Dirty Harry* (Directed by Don Siegel/Starring Clint Eastwood, 1971): Eastwood's fascist cop tore into liberal values and provoked argument. Got a problem with that? Well, do ya, punk?

11. *Aguirre: The Wrath of God* (Directed by Werner Herzog/Starring Klaus Kinski, 1972): The

brilliant Herzog probes the roots of greed as cuckoo Kinski raids the Amazon for gold in 1560.

12. *Don't Look Now* (Directed by Nicolas Roeg/ Starring Julie Christie and Donald Sutherland, 1973): Venice, sex, horror and the death of feeling masterfully explored by Roeg in an underrated beauty.

13. *Enter the Dragon* (Directed by Robert Clouse/Starring Bruce Lee, 1973): Lee at his kung fu fighting best is poetry in motion. Lots of imitators since his death; no real contenders.

14. *The Conversation* (Directed by Francis Ford Coppola/Starring Gene Hackman, 1974): Hackman's professional wiretapper finds his own privacy invaded in Coppola's stinging indictment.

15. *Going Places* (Directed by Bertrand Blier/ Starring Gerard Depardieu and Patrick Dewaere, 1974): Two horny French punks stomp on women and the law in Blier's strong black comedy of alienation.

16. *One Flew Over the Cuckoo's Nest* (Directed by Milos Forman/Starring Jack Nicholson and Louise Fletcher, 1975): Ken Kesey's book about an attempt to kill the rebel spirit keeps its power onscreen.

17. *All the President's Men* (Directed by Alan Pakula/Starring Robert Redford and Dustin Hoffman, 1976): The reporters who blew the whistle on Watergate in a film that still makes you want to cheer.

18. *Star Wars* (Directed by George Lucas/Starring Mark Hamill, Carrie Fisher and Harrison Ford, 1977): For good or ill, still the most influential and pervasive sci-fi epic in screen history.

19. *The Last Waltz* (Directed by Martin Scorsese/Starring the Band, 1978): The Band's farewell concert—guests include Bob Dylan, Eric Clapton and the Staples—is a thing of lasting beauty.

20. *Eraserhead* (Directed by David Lynch/Starring Jack Nance, 1978): Lynch's mysterious and mind-bending picture of urban desolation is impossible to shake.

21. *Being There* (Directed by Hal Ashby/Starring Peter Sellers, 1979): The image of Sellers as a simple, TV-addicted gardener ("I watch") who is misinterpreted as a genius remains a haunting rebuke.

22. *Fast Times at Ridgemont High* (Directed by Amy Heckerling/Starring Sean Penn and Jennifer Jason Leigh, 1982): Cameron Crowe's book of high school and the mall is a movie of perfect satirical pitch.

23. *Blade Runner* (Directed by Ridley Scott/ Starring Harrison Ford and Sean Young, 1982): Scott's much-imitated futuristic thriller gets the look right and the deadening soul sickness as well.

24. *Diner* (Directed by Barry Levinson/Starring Mickey Rourke, Kevin Bacon and Paul Reiser, 1982): Friends in need in Baltimore in the 1950s—beautifully done and still Levinson's best film.

25. *Stop Making Sense* (Directed by Jonathan Demme/Starring Talking Heads, 1984): A

Heads concert that catches the peculiar and undeniable genius of rock rebel David Byrne.

26. *Choose Me* (Directed by Alan Rudolph/ Starring Genevieve Bujold and Keith Carradine, 1984): A radio talk show about sex makes for a haunting film about love from the underappreciated Rudolph.

27. *Blood Simple* (Directed by Joel Coen/Starring Frances McDormand and John Getz, 1985): The debut of the Coen brothers—director Joel and producer Ethan—is a film noir of distinctive style and wit.

28. *Lost in America* (Directed by Albert Brooks/ Starring Brooks and Julie Hagerty, 1985): A couple trade their yuppie prison for the open road and find moral chaos in Brooks' sharp-witted farce.

29. *Something Wild* (Directed by Jonathan Demme/Starring Jeff Daniels, Melanie Griffith and Ray Liotta, 1986): Demme's violent comedy of broken relationships is a shocking, superbly acted original.

30. *The Fly* (Directed by David Cronenberg/ Starring Jeff Goldblum and Geena Davis, 1986): Seen as a horror film or an AIDS parable, Cronenberg's remake of the 1958 *Fly* provokes and frightens.

31. *She's Gotta Have It* (Directed by Spike Lee/ Starring Tracy Camilla Johns, 1986): Lee's invigorating debut is a brash and sexy comedy that does the right thing by its black female protagonist.

32. *Near Dark* (Directed by Kathryn Bigelow/ Starring Adrian Pasdar, Jenny Wright and Bill

Paxton, 1987): Bigelow's gorgeous vampire road movie is like nothing you have ever seen.

33. *Women on the Verge of a Nervous Breakdown* (Directed by Pedro Almodovar/Starring Carmen Maura and Antonio Banderas, 1988): Almodovar lights a flame under Spanish cinema with this comic fireball.

34. *The Thin Blue Line* (Directed by Errol Morris, 1988): Morris' documentary helped get convicted killer Randall Adams out of prison and stands on its own as a piece of freaky Americana.

35. *Wings of Desire* (Directed by Wim Wenders/Starring Bruno Ganz and Peter Falk, 1988): Wenders turns Berlin into a literal city of angels and crafts a tone poem unparalleled in the cinema.

36. *Crimes and Misdemeanors* (Directed by Woody Allen/Starring Allen, Mia Farrow, Martin Landau and Alan Alda, 1989): A startling comedy-drama that probes Allen's views on sin and responsibility.

37. *Roger & Me* (Directed by Michael Moore, 1989): Moore took heat for his methods in blasting General Motors honcho Roger Smith for job layoffs, but his mocking style reinvented documentary.

38. *Longtime Companion* (Directed by Norman René/Starring Bruce Davison and Campbell Scott, 1990): Still the most devastating and feeling American film yet made on the subject of AIDS.

39. *The Grifters* (Directed by Stephen Frears/ Starring Anjelica Huston, John Cusack and An-

nette Bening, 1990): Straight-up film noir if that's your poison with Huston in the performance of her life.

40. *Raise the Red Lantern* (Directed by Zhang Yimou/Starring Gong Li, 1991): Zhang leads China's new rebel filmmakers with this study of female servitude, graced by the luminous Gong Li.

41. *Bad Lieutenant* (Directed by Abel Ferrara/Starring Harvey Keitel, 1992): Call it Ferrara unplugged as the great Keitel busts enough sex, violence and religion barriers to earn the film's NC-17 rating.

42. *The Player* (Directed by Robert Altman/Starring Tim Robbins, 1992): Altman packs a sting in every joke as he sticks it to Hollywood for turning out formula pap and to audiences for lapping it up.

43. *Reservoir Dogs* (Directed by Quentin Tarantino/Starring Harvey Keitel, Tim Roth and Steve Buscemi, 1992): Tarantino's heist-film debut shows a fully formed talent to astonish.

44. *Naked* (Directed by Mike Leigh/Starring David Thewlis, 1993): Thewlis' London cynic rages hilariously at a soulless world in a stick of cinema dynamite from writer-director Leigh, whose 1996 release, *Secrets and Lies,* is another peak.

45. *Quiz Show* (Directed by Robert Redford/Starring Ralph Fiennes and John Turturro, 1994): A 1950s TV scandal sparks Redford to

make an angry comedy about the slow death of American values.

46. *Hoop Dreams* (Directed by Steve James, 1994): A landmark basketball documentary about two inner-city students that says more about family values than you'll hear from Congress or a pulpit.

47. *Crumb* (Directed by Terry Zwigoff, 1995): A documentary about the hilarious and harrowing life and times of cartoonist R. Crumb shows what a dysfunctional family can do to art and vice versa.

48. *Leaving Las Vegas* (Directed by Mike Figgis, 1995): Career performances from Oscar winner Nicolas Cage as a drunk on a death trip and Elisabeth Shue as the hooker who loves him but doesn't save him caress and clarify every haunting note in Figgis' jazzy, jolting fugue.

49. *Dead Man Walking* (Directed by Tim Robbins, 1995): Sean Penn as a bastard on death row and Susan Sarandon as the nun who counsels him bring brilliance and rare grace to Robbins' compassionate and even-handed take on capital punishment.

50. *Fargo* (Directed by Joel Coen, 1996): Kidnap, murder, Minnesota, snow, strange accents and a pregnant sheriff named Marge (Frances McDormand in an unforgettable performance) figure in this black-comic classic from the Coen brothers, who wouldn't know how to make a dull movie or an obvious move. Long may they reign.

ABOUT THE CONTRIBUTORS

David Breskin is a ROLLING STONE contributing editor. He has produced albums for Vernon Reid, Bill Frisell, Ronald Shannon Jackson and John Zorn, and he is the author of a novel, *The Real Life Diary of a Boomtown Girl,* and *Inner Views,* a compilation of his ROLLING STONE interviews with film directors.

Tim Cahill cowrote the Academy Award–nominated documentary *The Living Sea,* and is the author of five books, including *Jaguars Ripped My Flesh* and *Pecked to Death by Ducks.*

Rich Cohen is a ROLLING STONE contributing editor.

Nancy Collins is a special correspondent for *PrimeTime Live* and a contributing editor to *Vanity Fair.*

Christopher Connelly is a former ROLLING STONE editor and former executive editor of *Premiere* magazine.

Jonathan Cott has been a ROLLING STONE contributing editor since the first issue in 1967. He is the author of twelve books, including two books of conversations: *Forever Young* and *Visions and Voices.*

Cameron Crowe, a former ROLLING STONE contributing editor, is a filmmaker. His films include *Say Anything* and *Singles.*

Anthony DeCurtis is a ROLLING STONE contributing editor and a former editorial director at VH1. He is the editor of *Present Tense: Rock & Roll and Culture* and coeditor of *The* ROLLING STONE *Album Guide* and *The* ROLLING STONE *Illustrated History of Rock & Roll.* He is currently at work on a book about R.E.M.

Hillary de Vries writes for the *Los Angeles Times.*

David Edelstein has contributed to ROLLING STONE, *New York* and *Vanity Fair,* among other publications.

David Felton is formerly the ROLLING STONE faith and morals editor. He now works at MTV, where he is officially the "oldest" staff member.

Tim Findley is a writer based in Fallon, Nevada, where he also produces a daily radio program as the media consultant to the Truckee-Carson Irrigation District. A former ROLLING STONE associate editor and contributing editor, Findley also put in two decades as a newspaper and television reporter in San Francisco before becoming a principal assistant to California Assembly Speaker Willie L. Brown Jr. In addition, he served for an interim period as bureau manager for the United Press International in San Francisco. He is the coauthor of *The Life and Death of the SLA.*

Ben Fong-Torres began writing for ROLLING STONE in 1968 and served as senior editor until 1981. He has written for numerous magazines, and his books include *The Motown Album, Hickory Wind* and his memoirs, *The Rice Room.*

Jeff Giles is a senior writer at *Newsweek* and has written ROLLING STONE coverage of Winona Ryder, R.E.M. and Robin Williams.

Robert Greenfield is an award-winning novelist, journalist, screenwriter and playwright. He now also works as a producer and an adjunct professor of writing at the college level.

David Handelman, after winning the 1982 ROLLING STONE College Journalism Award, was a senior writer for the magazine from 1987 to 1991. He has also written for *Esquire, Premiere, GQ, US* and the *New York Times Magazine.* He is currently a contributing editor at *Vogue.*

Lynn Hirschberg has written for ROLLING STONE, *Vanity Fair* and *New York,* among other publications.

Gerri Hirshey is a ROLLING STONE contributing editor. She also writes for *GQ* and *Vanity Fair* and is the author of *Nowhere to Run: The Story of Soul Music.*

Chris Hodenfield, after fifteen years at ROLLING STONE, went on to edit *American Film* magazine. He is now senior editor at *Golf Digest.*

Elizabeth Kaye is a former ROLLING STONE contributing editor and a contributing editor at *Esquire.* She is also the author of the book *Mid-life: Notes from the Halfway Mark.*

Grover Lewis (1935–1995) was a ROLLING STONE writer and associate editor from 1971 to 1973. His specialty was traveling to movie locations with such rugged characters as Sam Peckinpah, Robert Aldrich, Lee Marvin and Robert Mitchum. His work has appeared in the *Village Voice, Playboy, New West/ California* magazine, the *St. Petersberg Times,* the *Washington Post* and the *Los Angeles Times.* His books include *Academy All the Way,* a collection of music and film reportage, and *I'll Be There in the Morning If I Live,* a volume of poetry. At the time of his death, Lewis was working on his autobiography for HarperCollins.

Chris Mundy is a ROLLING STONE contributing editor. He is originally from Omaha and now lives in New York City.

Steve Pond has been a contributor to ROLLING STONE since 1979. His work also appears in *Premiere, Movieline, US* and the *New York Times.*

Richard Price is a novelist and screenwriter.

Alan Rinzler was ROLLING STONE associate publisher and vice-president from 1970 to 1974, during which time he was also president of the then–book division, Straight Arrow Books. He is now director of La Cheim Children and Family Services, a victims of crime clinic in Oakland, California, a practicing psychotherapist and also senior editor for psychology books at Jossey-Bass, a division of Simon & Schuster.

David Rosenthal is a former ROLLING STONE managing editor. He is currently executive editor of Random House and publisher of Villard Books.

Paul Scanlon is a former managing editor of ROLLING STONE and the former editor of *GQ.*

Fred Schruers is a ROLLING STONE contributing editor.

Michael Sragow was a film critic and an associate editor of ROLLING STONE from 1981 to 1983. He now writes capsule movie reviews for the *New Yorker* and essays for the *Atlantic Monthly,* the *Modern Review* and other publications. He edited *Produced and Abandoned: The National Society of Film Critics Write on the Best Films You've Never Seen.*

Peter Travers has been the film critic and senior features editor for film at ROLLING STONE since 1989.

Philip Weiss is a novelist and has contributed to ROLLING STONE, *New York,* the *New York Observer* and other publications.

David Wild is a ROLLING STONE senior writer.

Joe Wood is a *Village Voice* senior editor. He writes essays and fiction, and is the editor of *Malcolm X: In Our Own Image.*

Bill Zehme was a ROLLING STONE senior writer until 1994 and currently maintains that position at *Esquire.* He is the author of *The* ROLLING STONE *Book of Comedy* and is at work on a biography of comedian Andy Kaufman.

INDEX